ATLAS *of the* WORLD'S RELIGIONS

ATLAS *of the* WORLD'S RELIGIONS

Second Edition

Edited by

Ninian Smart
and
Frederick W. Denny

OXFORD
UNIVERSITY PRESS

OXFORD
UNIVERSITY PRESS

Oxford University Press, Inc., publishes works that further
Oxford University's objective of excellence
in research, scholarship, and education.

Oxford New York
Auckland   Cape Town   Dar es Salaam   Hong Kong   Karachi
Kuala Lumpur   Madrid   Melbourne   Mexico City   Nairobi
New Delhi   Shanghai   Taipei   Toronto

With offices in
Argentina   Austria   Brazil   Chile   Czech Republic   France   Greece
Guatemala   Hungary   Italy   Japan Poland   Portugal   Singapore
South Korea   Switzerland   Thailand   Turkey   Ukraine   Vietnam

Copyright © 2007 Laurence King Publishing Ltd

This book was designed and produced by
Laurence King Publishing Ltd, London

Published by Oxford University Press, Inc.
198 Madison Avenue, New York, NY 10016
www.oup.com

Library of Congress Cataloguing in Publication Data are available

ISBN 978-0-19533-401-2

1 3 5 7 9 8 6 4 2

Cartographic Editor: Ailsa Heritage
Second Edition prepared by: Heritage Editorial and bounford.com
Cartography: Advanced Illustration Ltd, Congleton, Cheshire, UK
Design: PJL Design
Copyeditor: Liz Wyse
Picture Research: Mary Jane Gibson and Louise Thomas
Place Name Consultant: Pat Geelan
Index: Margaret Binns

Printed in Singapore

ABOUT THE AUTHORS

THE EDITOR
Ninian Smart was founder of Britain's first department of Religious Studies at Lancaster in 1967. He had previously taught at Aberystwyth, London and Birmingham. In 1977 he went to the University of California for half of the year, spending the other half at Lancaster, and in 1988 he retired from Lancaster. He held the posts of Professor Emeritus and J. F. Rowny Professor at UC Santa Barbara but retired finally in 1999. Among other books, he wrote *Reason and Faiths* (1958; rev. ed., 2000), *Doctrine and Argument in Indian Philosophy* (1964; rev. ed., 1984) and *Dimensions of the Sacred* (1996). He was elected President of the American Academy of Religion for 2000. He died in 2001.

THE EDITOR: SECOND EDITION
Frederick Mathewson Denny is Professor Emeritus of Religious Studies at the University of Colorado at Boulder. A University of Chicago PhD (1974), he has held previous academic appointments at Yale University and the University of Virginia. His research and writing have focused mostly on Islam and Muslim peoples, with particular interest in their ritual practices, devotional piety, ecological awareness, naming practices, human rights discourses, and wide range of social and cultural diversity from Egypt to Indonesia and across North America. He edits a scholarly book series, 'Studies in Comparative Religion', at the University of South Carolina Press and has written the widely-used college textbook *An Introduction to Islam* (3rd ed., 2006). He served on the Board of Directors of the American Academy of Religion for eleven years.

RELIGION TODAY
THE HISTORICAL GEOGRAPHY OF RELIGION
Frank Whaling was Professor of the Study of Religion at Edinburgh University until his retirement. He has written or edited thirteen books and seventy papers in the fields of comparative religion, Indian religion, the methodology of religious studies, theology of religion and the history of religion. He has been Visiting Professor at Dartmouth College, Indiana University, Witwatersrand University, Calcutta University and the Chinese Academy of Social Sciences in Beijing.

Gordon D. Newby since 1992 has been the Chair of the Department of Middle Eastern and South Asian Studies and a Professor in the Graduate Program of West and South Asian Religions at Emory University. He received his PhD in Mediterranean Studies at Brandeis University. He has taught at Washington State University, Brandeis University and North Carolina State University. His research specialities include early Islam, Muslim relations with Jews and Christians, and comparative sacred texts. Among his scholarly works are *A History of the Jews of Arabia* (1989), *The Making of the Last Prophet* (University of South Carolina, 1989), and contributions to *A Concise Encyclopedia of Islam* (2002).

Martin Ramstedt received his PhD in anthropology from Munich University, Germany. From 1997–2001, he was a European Science Foundation research fellow at the International Institute for Asian Studies in Leiden, The Netherlands, working on Hinduism in modern Indonesia. He conducted a five-year research project on alternative spiritualities in the Netherlands at the Meertens Institute in Amsterdam. He is currently senior researcher at the Max Planck Institute for Social Anthropology in Halle/Saale, Germany, investigating the role of religion in Indian-Indonesian commercial relations.

THE HINDU WORLD
Daud Ali (PhD, University of Chicago) is Senior Lecturer in early and medieval Indian History at the School of Oriental and African Studies (SOAS), University of London. His area of specialization is early medieval Indian history (c̣.300–1200 CE). He is author of *Courtly Culture and Political Life in Early Medieval India* (Cambridge, 2004). He has also co-authored, with Ronald Inden and Jonathan Walters, *Querying the Medieval: Texts and the History of Practice in South Asia* (Oxford, 2000), and edited *Invoking the Past: the Uses of History in South Asia* (Oxford, 1999).

BUDDHISM
Stephen Hodge graduated from the School of Oriental and African Studies (SOAS), University of London, before becoming the first Westerner to be fully ordained and initiated as a monk in the Shingon tantric tradition. He remained a monk for several years in Japan and is now one of the UK's foremost experts on Tibetan Buddhism and early tantric materials. He has edited and translated several early tantric texts and also taught Buddhism at Birkbeck College, University of London before his retirement.

EAST ASIAN TRADITIONS
Wendy Dossett is Lecturer in Religious Studies, University of Wales, Lampeter. She has written widely on Buddhism, Japanese Religions, and Jodo Shinshu, including chapters on 'Japanese Religions' in *Human Nature and Destiny and Picturing God* in the 'Themes in World Religions' series, edited by Jean Holm and John Bowker, 1994.

THE PACIFIC
Niel Gunson, a Pacific historian, has spent most of his working life at the Australian National University, with periodic visits to the Pacific, studying missionary contact, the European background, and traditional religion and authority. He is a long-time editor of *The Journal of Pacific History* and a founder of *Aboriginal History*. He is best known for his seminal study, *Messengers of Grace* (1978).

ANCIENT NEAR EAST AND ANCIENT EUROPE
Thomas O'Loughlin is Professor in the Department of Theology and Religious Studies, University of Wales, Lampeter. His main interest lies in the phenomenon of historical re-interpretation by which religions recycle their own and others' sacred narratives. He has also written on the relationship between perceptions of place and religious self-understanding.

JUDAISM
Dan Cohn-Sherbok is Professor of Judaism at the University of Wales, Lampeter. He is the author of over forty books, including *God and the Holocaust* (1989), *Modern Judaism* (1996) and *Understanding the Holocaust* (1999). **Lavinia Cohn-Sherbok** was a Consultant Editor for the *Oxford Dictionary of World Religions* (1997) and is the author of *A History of Jewish Civilization* (1997) and *Who's Who in Christianity* (1998).

CHRISTIANITY
Michael Walsh studied at Oxford with the intention of becoming a historian of the Christian Church, particularly of its first centuries. Later his interests moved to the contemporary Church: he has written on the controversial Catholic organization Opus Dei and has published a critical biography of Pope John Paul II, as well as a number of other studies of the papacy in general. A secondary interest is the role of saints in Christian history. From 1972 he was Librarian of Heythrop College, University of London, and has also been Visiting Professor at Liverpool Hope University.

Richard H. Jackson is Professor of Geography at Brigham Young University. He received his PhD at Clark University. He and his wife, Mary, are the parents of four children and are descendants of ancestors who were part of the overland journey of the Mormon pioneers of the mid-nineteenth century. He has written extensively about the Mormons, including editing *The Mormon Role in the Settlement of the West* (paperback 1978), and as co-editor of the *Atlas of Mormon History* (1995).

Robin M. Wright completed his undergraduate degree in Sociology and Anthropology at Bates College in 1972, and his Master's (1974) and Doctorate (1981) in Anthropology at Stanford University. He is an anthropologist, scholar of religions and specialist in indigenous religions. He has published widely on shamanism, mythology and the history of indigenous peoples of South America, including: *Transformando os Deuses* (editor: vol. 1, 1999, UNICAMP; vol. II, UNICAMP, 2004; vol. III, Ashgate, 2007); *Cosmos, Self and History in Baniwa Religion* (University of Texas, Austin, 1998); *Historia Indígena e do Indigenismo no Alto Rio Negro* (Mercado de Letras, 2005); *In Darkness and Secrecy: The Anthropology of Assault Sorcery in Amazonia* (co-editor with Neil Whitehead, Duke, 2004); and *Waferinaipe Ianheke. A Sabedoria dos Nossos Antepassados* (organizador, ACIRA/FOIRN, São Gabriel da Cachoeira, 1999). One of its founding members, for eight years he was the coordinator of the Center for Research in Indigenous Ethnology at UNICAMP, where he is a Full Professor in Ethnology, having recently retired for medical reasons; he continues to do research on indigenous religions at the Center for Latin American Studies in Gainesville, Florida (EUA).

ISLAM
Simonetta Calderini is Lecturer in Islamic Studies and World Religions at the Department of Theology and Religious Studies, Roehampton Institute, London. She was awarded a PhD in Islamic Studies from the School of Oriental and African Studies (SOAS), University of London, and holds degrees and diplomas from the Oriental Institute, University of Naples, the American University in Cairo and Bourguiba Institute, Tunis. She is the author of *Mauritania* (1992), *Intifada* (1993) and *Women and the Fatimids in the World of Islam* (2006).

AFRICA
Louis Brenner is Professor of the History of Religion in Africa at the School of Oriental and African Studies, University of London. His research has focused primarily on the history of Islam and of Muslim societies in Africa. He is author of *West African Sufi: The Religious Heritage and Spiritual Search of Ceerno Bokar Saalif Taal* (1984) and *Réflexions sur le Savoir Islamique en Afrique de l'Ouest* (1985). **Jason R. Peirce** graduated from the School of Oriental and African Studies (SOAS), University of London, in 1995 and obtained a maîtrise in Medical Anthropology from the University of Paris X – Nanterre in 1997.

INDIGENOUS RELIGIONS
Paul Heelas is Professor in Religion and Modernity at the Department of Religious Studies, Lancaster University. His publications include *The New Age Movement* (1996) and, together with Linda Woodhead, *Religion in Modern Times* (1999).

Michael J. Zogry is an Assistant Professor in the Department of Religious Studies at the University of Kansas. An affiliated faculty member in the Center for Indigenous Nations Studies, his research focuses on First Nations religions and the study of ritual.

CONTENTS

NOTE ON SPELLINGS AND PLACE NAMES

The names of all countries, major physical features and regions, and cities (modern or historical) are spelled in accordance with English conventional usage, e.g. India, Nile, Anatolia, Carthage.

For all other names the general practice is to show them in terms of the contemporary forms that fit the time-scale of the maps concerned. Thus Latin names in the classical world, Sanskrit or Prakrit names in the early dynastic states of India, e.g. Nicaea (modern Iznik), Pataliputra (modern Patna). All Chinese names, whether ancient or modern, are spelled in accordance with the now widely accepted Pinyin system. For the early modern period contemporary names may reflect a political administrative situation rather different from today's, e.g. Königsberg (now Kaliningrad), Breslau (now Wrocław), Pozsony (now Bratislava).

All names in languages using Roman alphabet are spelled with all the diacritics appropriate to those languages, e.g. Białystok, Göteborg, Poznań. But names derived from transliteration or transcription from non-Roman alphabet languages, e.g. Arabic, Hebrew, Japanese, Korean, Persian, Sanskrit, are spelled without the often unfamiliar diacritics used in the scholarly romanization of these languages, e.g. Mansuriyah (not Manṣūrīyah), Sravasti (not Śrāvastī).

Introduction to the First Edition

ON THE VERGE OF A NEW CENTURY it is a good time to launch an atlas of the world's religions for several reasons. First, we have an excellent knowledge of the history and spread of religions in the aftermath of the collapse of the Cold War. Second, new maps can help to show how the major religions have developed. Third, they can illustrate ways in which, in an important sense, religions are now globalized. This means that all worldviews in the world are in interaction with the others. No worldview is isolated. Even the Inuit in northern Canada are getting knowledgeable about the Dalai Lama; and the inhabitants of Papua New Guinea are influenced by Muslims from Indonesia to West Africa. The main religions, such as Sikhism and Buddhism and Christianity, are in frequent cultural and spiritual contact. Those who are experiencing all this pluralism can benefit from a geographical display of this complex and fascinating world of religions.

On the whole, we have traced the changes in the world since early times by reference to broader traditions: such as Buddhism, Hinduism, Islam, Judaism and so on. Sometimes this can be a bit entangled, as in South Asia, which was long shared between the Hindu and Buddhist (and Jain etc) traditions. This way of doing it enables us to give continuous and coherent accounts of the teachings and practice of Buddhism, for instance, and of other important religions.

We can also illustrate developments in the world by seeing the trade routes and lines of communication. We can often see how sea and river routes, until the nineteenth century, were the fastest and most convenient means of going from one area to another. Admiral Mahan's famous and influential book, *The Influence of Sea Power on History* could be echoed by *River and Sea Influence in the Spread of Religions*, if anyone were to write it. We can observe it in the expansion of the Theravada in Southeast Asia; the permeation of Islam to the far reaches of Indonesia and to the southern Philippines; the effects of Iberia into Latin America; the reach of Christianity into the Mediterranean and round the Irish Sea; the voyages of the Vikings down the rivers of Russia; and the reach of African ideas into Brazil, the Caribbean and North America. On the other hand, there were longer and slower adventures over land routes: the grinding Russian conquest of Siberia; the plantation of Buddhism, Nestorian Christianity and Islam along the Silk Route; and the Mongolian invasions of Europe and the Middle East.

There are various geographical aspects to the division of religions. For example, the drifting apart of Eastern Orthodoxy and the Latin Catholic traditions; and the division between Protestant and Roman Catholic countries in the areas of the West, and how that (rough) division between North and South has been reproduced in the New World. Or again the more elaborate Mahayana and the more austere Theravada were divided overseas between China and other countries on the one hand and Southeast Asia on the other.

Again, a view of the geography can cause you to see how the national boundaries in Africa do not correspond to the cultural and linguistic divisions of the continent. And then again, the pockets of indigenous religions in Russia, Scandinavia, India and so forth show something of the underlying types of religions before the larger traditions take over.

In some ways the geographical mode of looking at cultures may lead us to see things differently. Greater India, including Southeast Asia, and Greater Africa, taking in both mainland Africa and Africa beyond the Atlantic, might make a lot more sense than our modern division of continents and regions.

These are all examples from (relatively) the modern world, when continents at least were in touch with one another, here and there (and often we underestimate the contact between them - for instance between China and India in early days; and between Rome and South India and Sri Lanka). But in more ancient times, civilizations grew up in relative isolation from one another. Even so, it is interesting to observe how not dissimilar patterns emerged. I am not arguing that all religions somehow testify to the same truth. There are differences, which are important. But at the same time, sacrificial methods, for instance, were found in widely differing civilizations; and very often they had similar views about the gods.

We can also note here and there how modern religions are historically less important than they once were, but even so live on – for instance Zoroastrianism. Other faiths have died out. But they were once vital: for instance, Roman religion. And other worldviews, such as Neoplatonism, have been embraced by Christianity and had enormous influence upon it. So the Atlas contains spreads on both ancient and modern changes in religion.

Another advantage of the present volume is that it provides a general history of religion. It does not necessarily compete with other histories, but it does give the general reader and seer of the maps an account of the development of religion. Not only that, but the volume furnishes a glossary of key terms used in varying worldviews, and a bibliography if our readers wish to explore further. The geographical index supplies them too with a ready reference to the places which have been important in the evolution of religions.

The general aim of our project in providing this Atlas is to open people's ideas to the creation of religions. You can see that they are not just products of spirituality (which they are) but also of geography: consequently questions of power and politics enter in. But still they have important origins in experience and ideas. This should not be forgotten in a period when a more down to earth appraisal of religions and ideologies is fashionable.

Maybe people can also, through an Atlas such as this, be aroused by the future. We can perhaps see that the indigenous religions of the world may come together in an alliance to protect their interests. We can note how the massive growth of independent Christian churches in Africa will begin to shift some of the influence of Christianity in the world. The emigrations and diasporas since the advent and demise of colonialism means that no longer are religions confined to their countries of origin. They can see how secular worldviews, such as scientific humanism and Marxism, have caused the balance between traditional religions and atheism to be shifted in a number of areas.

Religions today are often bound up with nationalism. The countries of the world have often been politically decisive in this. Towards the end of the twentieth century, the Soviet Union split up into varying cultural areas. Religion was not the only factor in the formation of the new nations: but it was indeed a factor in many cases. The Atlas can also illustrate how often the warfare in the world is often a product of religious divides. While we have been keen to reflect the spiritual forces between faiths, we have not been unmindful of the negative impact of religious divisions.

This was true of the past as well as the modern world. Our main task, however, has been to help enlighten people in the facts of the world. It is vital to understand others, and this will be a tool towards this goal. The comprehension of history is vital in preparing us for the future. Too often our decisions and judgements about the world have not been taken in the light of the configurations of religion. And a major factor in all this is how they have come to exist in their geographical reality.

NINIAN SMART
Santa Barbara 1999

Introduction to the Second Edition

The First Edition of this Atlas appeared just before the twenty-first century opened up a whole new millennium. Although at the time the Atlas broke new ground in the comparative study of religions by using cartography in cooperation with historical, cultural and geopolitical discourses, it now needs extending and not just updating in our fast-moving global era. So, just as we who were involved in developing the Second Edition have been standing on the shoulders of the leading scholars who conceived and created this absorbing and timely reference work, under the masterful eye of its distinguished lead editor, the late Ninian Smart, so also do the ten additional two-page cartographic spreads stand on the foundations of a long-established tradition.

Over the last decade or so, four striking dynamics have emerged which have changed our view of the world irrevocably. They dominate our headlines, radio and television broadcasts, and our computer screens. All were perceptible in varying degrees when the First Edition was being prepared, but few could have predicted the enormous impact they would have, globally, in such a short space of time. And all four are intrinsically linked and inseparable.

Firstly, a broad consensus has developed that environmental change and ecological damage to all species is a process which is not only part of our collective responsibility, but a process which might just be manageable within sustainable parameters with a concerted, international collaborative effort.

Secondly, the escalating power of modern computerized communications has become inescapable – among them, signally, the dynamism which is provided for the exchange and dissemination of ideas and information by the Internet. In fact, this new edition of the Atlas would simply have not been possible without this amazing innovation, with contributors old and new scattered across the globe.

Thirdly, there has been the recognition of the process of globalization – for some a threat to local cultures and economies, a kind of new and invidious industrial/economic imperialism, but for others an opportunity for transnational outreach, understanding and homogeneity.

Lastly, there has been the recognition of the void between the developed and the developing worlds. This was crystallized for everybody by the events of 9/11. Few had suspected the profound disparities, the gulf of mutual misunderstanding and the sheer level of resentment which was rapidly thrown into stark relief that day. Terms like 'axis of evil', 'infidels', 'crusades' and '*jihad*', redolent of medieval religious conflicts most thought long-buried, suddenly became the stuff of international political rhetoric and, indeed, everyday conversation.

However, it is not the task of a book of reference such as this to analyse the present or prognosticate on the future, but rather to observe and record what has happened as dispassionately as possible. So, although the above dynamics are implicit in the innumerable detailed updates throughout the Atlas, the substantial new materials have been selected to reflect those historical processes which have emerged as significant factors since the First Edition was published.

One new spread deals with Christian Renewalism, represented by a considerable range of Pentecostal and Charismatic expressions of evangelical piety and practice reflecting experiences of the Holy Spirit. A widely-agreed current estimate of the number of Renewalist Christians in the world today is around 500 million out of a total global Christian population of two billion. Another new spread concerns the Church of Jesus Christ of Latter-Day Saints (LDS), also known as Mormons, who are spreading their American-born faith community across similarly wide regions of the world. Both the Renewalists and the LDS have seen their principal growth areas in the developing world. By contrast, the previous section on Indigenous Religions has been expanded, acknowledging the continuing importance and promise for peoples' pride of heritage and continuation of core values in many regions of the world.

Although religions have long undergone changes and developments over time by migrations of their adherents to different regions, today's world is witnessing unprecedented levels of large-scale movement of peoples from their places of origin or long-term residence to entirely new cultures and societies with often markedly different belief-systems, values and customs. Thus, new material has been added on contemporary religious diasporas, which exist not only in the West but also in other global regions. Religious diasporas give rise to self-aware sub-communities that help adherents who migrate away from their native abodes – for a number of reasons ranging from oppression to economic necessity – maintain their beliefs, moral values, social customs and cultures, while also participating in and contributing to new host countries and cultures. Another form of demographic shift, made increasingly possible by modern mass transport, is pilgrimage – surely the original manifestation of the world's largest current industry, tourism. How many travellers today, listed as tourists, are in fact engaged in a pilgrimage of one kind or another? New material has been added which examines this extraordinary and largely voluntary phenomenon.

New ways of thinking about religious and cultural geography have been addressed. Now included is an evaluation of the role of religious place names and sacred sites in the toponymy of the world's map; there is also now an examination of the languages and scripts of religion – where they originated, how they figure in religious beliefs and practices, and their movements and dispersions. Indeed, languages of long-established religious traditions such as Judaism, Islam, Hinduism, Buddhism, Christianity and Confucianism have exerted considerable influence, and are integral to the ways in which diasporic sub-communities sustain themselves as much in devotional life as in everyday conversation. For example, substantial numbers of Muslims in North American cities such as Montreal, Houston, Los Angeles and New York speak Farsi, Arabic, Urdu and Swahili, representing their religio-cultural backgrounds of Iran, the Arab world, southern Asia and eastern Africa, respectively. Equally large numbers of Confucianists, Buddhists and Shintoists from eastern Asia in cities like Vancouver, San Francisco, Toronto and Chicago speak Korean, Chinese and Japanese in everyday life. Of course, the languages listed here are by no means spoken only by religiously active citizens!

Other new topics include Christianity with its multifarious forms and challenges in South America, a vital continent which straddles the developing/developed world nexus; and an appraisal of religion and ecology, with a particular focus on water management and deforestation in Africa and Asia, which also looks at ways in which religious bodies and initiatives are increasingly addressing those as well as other urgent matters crucial to securing a sustainable environment and a more equitable distribution of resources among the world's population.

Today's global citizens urgently need to have access to clear information that helps them to develop a reliable public understanding of religion, including its historical, socio-cultural, ethical, spiritual, political, ecological and geographical dimensions, as well as its manifold, complex and sometimes ominous contemporary agendas and trajectories. An obvious example of this is the proliferation of global Islamic *jihadist* terrorist movements that in various ways are threatening Muslims fully as much as other peoples in our post-9/11 world. What is motivating them, and how can they be understood and addressed in informed and effective ways? The Second Edition of the *Atlas of the World's Religions* is designed to contribute to this undertaking. As my predecessor, Ninian Smart, wrote in his Introduction to the First Edition: 'It is vital to understand others, and this will be a tool towards this goal. The comprehension of history is vital in preparing us for the future.'

And I can do no better than to echo his words and intentions.It is my hope, therefore, that in updating and expanding this classic publication, it will continue to contribute to our understanding of the complexities of today's world for the foreseeable future.

FREDERICK MATHEWSON DENNY
Boulder, Colorado, 2007

RELIGION TODAY

RELIGION IN THE WORLD TODAY

THE WORLD, with the exception of Antarctica, has only been divided into defined nation-states comparatively recently. Sometimes nations are defined by religion, but relations between religion and state vary greatly. The arrangement and complement of the world's nations has altered during the twentieth century, due primarily to the demise of empires, culminating in the collapse of the Soviet Union. The only extensive empire left is the People's Republic of China.

This process has affected religion profoundly. The disappearance of enforced Marxist ideology allowed older religious forces to re-emerge, from Orthodoxy in Russia, Islam in Central Asia and Lutheranism in the

Baltics, to Buddhism in Cambodia. By the early 1990s, only North Korea, China, Vietnam, and Cuba still embraced Marxism, while other states, such as Iraq, Syria, Algeria, Tunisia and, to some degree, Turkey, were run in theory on secularist principles. But most nations either tolerated or encouraged pluralism, although modern political Islam, notably in Iran, Libya, Saudi Arabia, and Sudan, has been less tolerant (*map 1*).

Religion and Conflict

While nation-states predominate, they may include ethnic and religious areas seeking autonomy or independence. Moreover, ethnic and religious mixing has

Members of the Findhorn ▶
Community in Scotland share in group meditation. Such private group prayer or meditation sessions are more common in the West, often meeting in halls or home. They are sometimes part of a New Age religion engaged in private fulfilment.

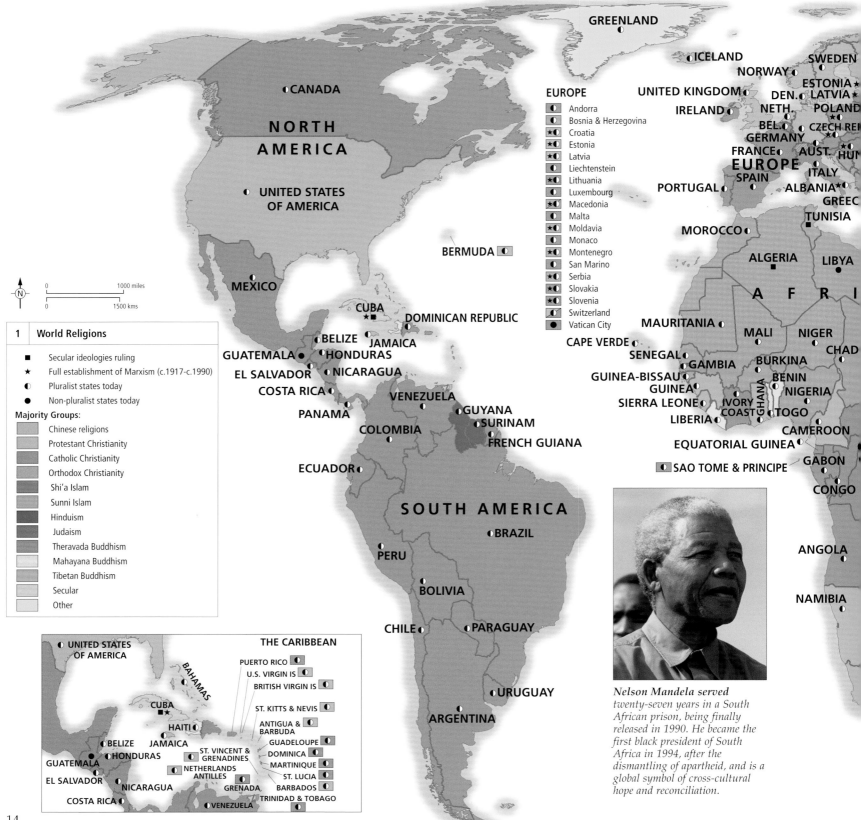

1	World Religions
■	Secular ideologies ruling
★	Full establishment of Marxism (c.1917-c.1990)
◑	Pluralist states today
●	Non-pluralist states today

Majority Groups:
- Chinese religions
- Protestant Christianity
- Catholic Christianity
- Orthodox Christianity
- Shi'a Islam
- Sunni Islam
- Hinduism
- Judaism
- Theravada Buddhism
- Mahayana Buddhism
- Tibetan Buddhism
- Secular
- Other

GREENLAND

ICELAND
SWEDEN
NORWAY
ESTONIA
UNITED KINGDOM
DEN. LATVIA
IRELAND
NETH. POLAND
BEL.
CZECH REP
GERMANY
FRANCE
AUST. HUN
EUROPE
SPAIN
ITALY
PORTUGAL
ALBANIA
GREECE
TUNISIA

CANADA

NORTH AMERICA

UNITED STATES OF AMERICA

BERMUDA

EUROPE
- ◑ Andorra
- ◑ Bosnia & Herzegovina
- ★◑ Croatia
- ★◑ Estonia
- ★◑ Latvia
- ◑ Liechtenstein
- ★◑ Lithuania
- ◑ Luxembourg
- ★◑ Macedonia
- ◑ Malta
- ★◑ Moldavia
- ◑ Monaco
- ★◑ Montenegro
- ◑ San Marino
- ★◑ Serbia
- ★◑ Slovakia
- ★◑ Slovenia
- ◑ Switzerland
- ● Vatican City

MEXICO

CUBA
DOMINICAN REPUBLIC
BELIZE JAMAICA
GUATEMALA HONDURAS
EL SALVADOR NICARAGUA
COSTA RICA
VENEZUELA
PANAMA
GUYANA
COLOMBIA SURINAM
FRENCH GUIANA
ECUADOR

SOUTH AMERICA
BRAZIL
PERU

BOLIVIA

CHILE PARAGUAY

URUGUAY
ARGENTINA

MOROCCO
ALGERIA LIBYA
MAURITANIA
MALI NIGER
CAPE VERDE CHAD
SENEGAL
GAMBIA BURKINA
GUINEA-BISSAU BENIN
GUINEA NIGERIA
SIERRA LEONE IVORY COAST TOGO
LIBERIA GHANA
CAMEROON
EQUATORIAL GUINEA
SAO TOME & PRINCIPE GABON
CONGO

A F R I

ANGOLA

NAMIBIA

0   1000 miles
0   1500 kms

THE CARIBBEAN

◑ UNITED STATES OF AMERICA

BAHAMAS

PUERTO RICO ◑
U.S. VIRGIN IS ◑
BRITISH VIRGIN IS ◑

CUBA ■★
HAITI ◑
ST. KITTS & NEVIS ◑
ANTIGUA & BARBUDA ◑
BELIZE JAMAICA
HONDURAS
ST. VINCENT & GRENADINES
GUADELOUPE ◑
DOMINICA ◑
MARTINIQUE ◑
NETHERLANDS ANTILLES
ST. LUCIA ◑
GUATEMALA
EL SALVADOR
NICARAGUA GRENADA BARBADOS ◑
TRINIDAD & TOBAGO ◑
COSTA RICA
VENEZUELA ◑

Nelson Mandela served twenty-seven years in a South African prison, being finally released in 1990. He became the first black president of South Africa in 1994, after the dismantling of apartheid, and is a global symbol of cross-cultural hope and reconciliation.

increased around the world because of refugee movements and greater ease of transport and migration. Another factor is the growth of new religious movements, especially in the West, Japan, Russia, sub-Saharan Africa and the South Pacific; vigorous forms of Protestant evangelism are particularly prevalent in Central and South America.

In the new millennium several nations have been involved in a variety of civil wars or regional struggles incorporating a religious or ideological element: these include Bosnia, Iraq, Sri Lanka, Algeria, Israel and Palestine, Shan and Karen parts of Burma, Kashmir, the Philippines, East Timor, Chechnya, Abkhazia, Afghanistan and southern Sudan. Less overt struggles are continuing to occur in various parts of the world. Ethnic conflicts with a less pronounced religious element have taken place in Rwanda, Angola, Liberia and Somalia.

The Globalization of Religion

Although loyalties remain between traditional religions and nationalism, itself almost a religion in its various dimensions, a wider global vision is beginning to emerge. Blocs of nations are forming in Europe, the Americas, the Middle East, the Confucian Far East, the Pacific Rim and Southeast Asia which, while not abandoning nationalism or a background in the Christian, Muslim, Confucian, Buddhist, Hindu, or Jewish traditions, take global needs more seriously. While internal divisions remain within, and between, religions involving traditional, modernist and radical groups, ecumenism is growing through internal discussion and inter-faith dialogue. At the start of a new millennium, the united forces involved in tackling global dilemmas concerning ecology, human rights, and spiritual transcendence can be seen as not merely particular nation-states or religious traditions, but as the human beings who together inhabit planet Earth.

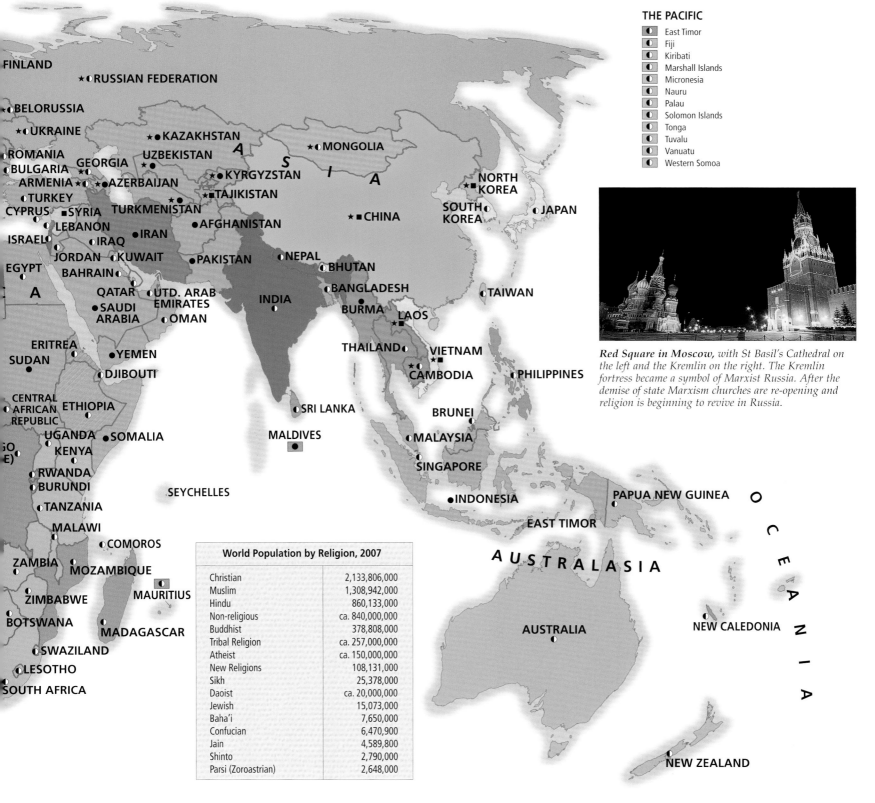

THE PACIFIC

- East Timor
- Fiji
- Kiribati
- Marshall Islands
- Micronesia
- Nauru
- Palau
- Solomon Islands
- Tonga
- Tuvalu
- Vanuatu
- Western Somoa

Red Square in Moscow, with St Basil's Cathedral on the left and the Kremlin on the right. *The Kremlin fortress became a symbol of Marxist Russia. After the demise of state Marxism churches are re-opening and religion is beginning to revive in Russia.*

World Population by Religion, 2007	
Christian	2,133,806,000
Muslim	1,308,942,000
Hindu	860,133,000
Non-religious	ca. 840,000,000
Buddhist	378,808,000
Tribal Religion	ca. 257,000,000
Atheist	ca. 150,000,000
New Religions	108,131,000
Sikh	25,378,000
Daoist	ca. 20,000,000
Jewish	15,073,000
Baha'i	7,650,000
Confucian	6,470,900
Jain	4,589,800
Shinto	2,790,000
Parsi (Zoroastrian)	2,648,000

TRADITIONAL PRIMAL RELIGIONS AND MINORITY WORLD RELIGIONS TODAY

THE MAJOR world religious traditions, such as Christianity, Buddhism and Islam, and major worldviews of Marxism and nationalism (*see* pp. 20-21) are powerful and important forces within today's world. But traditional primal religions, and minority world religious groups, such as the Sikhs, Jains, Parsis (Zoroastrians), Shintoists and Jews, are nevertheless significant, especially as they frequently overlap with other religious forces. African indigenous churches, for example, often combine features from Christianity, African primal religion, and new religious movements.

Primal Religions

The word 'primal', although sometimes challenged, is a convenient way of bringing together the traditional and tribal religions of various peoples of Africa, inner Asia, Southeast Asia, the Indian subcontinent, North and South America, Australia and the Pacific (*map 1*). Some of these peoples are hunter-gatherers by background, such as the

Australian Aborigines, the Congo Pygmies, the Kalahari Bushmen, the Arctic Inuit, and some Amazonian tribesmen. Others, particularly in parts of Africa, are pastoral nomads, while others, as in parts of the Americas, are settled agriculturalists. All have felt the impact of the twentieth-century world: population growth, increasing pressure on the land, development and modernization, processes of industrialization, the spread of cities, and the variety, depth and all-pervading nature of contemporary change and global culture.

While the challenge to traditional beliefs has been overwhelming, the response has taken varied forms. In some cases, there has been absorption, whether shallow or deep, into a major tradition, often Christianity but also Islam, Hinduism and Buddhism. In other instances, the primal tradition has been reduced by contact with the modern world. By contrast, some traditional beliefs are restated in response to the modernist challenge, which can even stimulate new creative activity, as in the case of

Iavalapiti men wearing ritual costumes blow sacred flutes in the Amazon, Brazil, where rituals, myths and symbols have remained all-important.

P89876

A view of the ghats at Varanasi (Benares) from Talasayin Ghat, the main burning Ghat, used for cremations. The 84 ghats encompass the whole of life: worship, festival, cremation, philosophy, folk religion

1	Traditional Religions and Primal Minority World Religions

- widely diffused traditional, tribal beliefs
- diffused traditional, tribal beliefs
- Chinese indigenous religion: primal, popular taoist, popular Buddhist
- Shintoism
- ✸ Jewish populations of over 50,000
- ■ Jains
- ◆ Zoroastrians/Parsis
- ■ Sikhs

the Umbanda of Brazil, or revitalize existing traditions – a process seen amongst the Native Americans and Australian Aboriginies. Some groups adjust their beliefs to accommodate the new cultures – an adaptation exemplified by the cargo cults of Melanesia. The survival and re-emergence of Chinese primal religion after the Marxist attempt to extirpate 'superstition' is a symbol of its resilience under pressure. Today, all of China's religious communities – Buddhist, Daoist, Confucian, Muslim, Catholic, Protestant and primal – are growing in one of the few remaining communist states.

Minority World Religions

The Jews have a homeland in Israel and most Jews live there or in the United States. Although still viewed as a major religious tradition, the Jewish population is now less than it was before the Holocaust, and the countries with more than 50,000 Jews do not include Poland which, before World War Two, had 4 million Jews. The Parsis, descendants of the Zoroastrians, are mainly resident around Bombay in India and are small in numbers. The Jains too live mainly in India, with pockets elsewhere, and their numbers are slowly growing. The Sikhs remain strong in their heartlands of the Punjab in India. The search of some of them for their own state of Khalistan occasionally finds support abroad, and there are sizeable Sikh communities in the United States, Britain, Canada, Malaysia and France. Shinto in Japan has recovered from the collapse of the Shinto state at the end of World War Two in 1945 and is forming new religious movements and inter-religious contacts in various parts of Japan.

Plural religious contacts are becoming increasingly common. The Hindu holy city of Varanasi (Benares) which has a headquarters or branch ashram of virtually every significant Hindu group in India, and which views its boundaries between the three rivers of the Ganges, Varuna and Asi as sacred, also contains groups of Sikhs, Jains, Muslims and Christians, as well as Buddhists who live at Sarnath where the Buddha preached his first sermon (*map 2*). Folk deities are present too as well as secular elements and some new religious movements. This mix of major, minor, secular, traditional, and new is more pronounced in cosmopolitan cities in the West and less so in some traditional Muslim cities. In more traditional areas, the spread of urbanization and impact of deforestation and desertification are likely to increase this trend towards religious pluralism and interplay.

2	Varanasi - Mixed Religions in the Hindu Sacred City

Hindu temples:
- □ Bhairava
- □ Siva
- ■ Devi
- ■ Visnu
- ■ Ganesa
- ◪ ghat (stone steps to river)
- ■ Buddhist
- □ Christian
- ■ Muslim
- ■ Sikh
- ■ Jain
- ■ folk deities
- ⊗ tents of holy men
- ～ sacred river

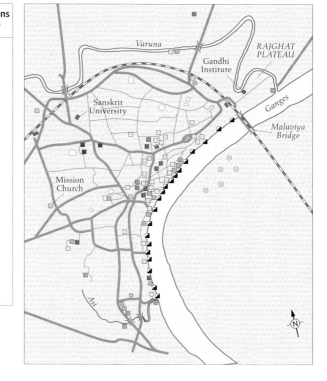

DIASPORIC RELIGIONS TODAY

ALTHOUGH THE TERM 'diaspora' is most closely associated with the demographic dispersals of the Jews at various points over the last two millennia (*see* pp. 132–135), in the last two centuries the occurrence of religious diasporas arising from colonization and decolonization, asymmetrical processes of democratization and globalization, and violent conflicts across the globe, has proliferated.

The Modern Diasporic Condition

The conditions leading to the dispersion as well as the relationships with the host societies might vary. The Hindu Sindhis, for example, lost their former homeland (Sindh) in present-day Pakistan after the partition of India in 1947. They entertain a tightly-knit transnational network which in many respects rivals that of the classically diasporic Jews or overseas Chinese. Many Muslims from Kosovo and Bosnia on the other hand, who fled their homelands in the Balkan Wars in the 1990s, have blended into Europe's heterogeneous Muslim diaspora, hitherto motivated by colonial legacy (in France and the UK) or by economic migration. Large numbers of Turkish Alevis, who entered Germany as guest workers (*gastarbeiter*) from 1962 onwards, have increasingly secularized the performance of their communal ritual *cem* – the focus of their heterodox Islamic religiosity repressed in their home country – a result of their exposure to a secular host culture.

Members of diasporic groups retain a real or imaginary connection with their homeland and are committed to the continuation of their respective traditions. They usually harbour doubts as to their full acceptance in the host society, even though globalization has made multiple identities and loyalties generally more acceptable. Some diasporic communities have tried to resist covert 'assimilation' by insisting on their uniqueness, and have sometimes stirred the imagination of members of their host societies too, such as the number of native English Sufis who have converted to Islam, or the American converts to Chinese Chan Buddhism.

The term 'diaspora' has meanwhile become an evocative metaphor for discomfort, alienation and transcendence by a whole variety of traffickers of transnational spaces with a longing for a spiritual home. They need not be disenfranchised or legally disadvantaged, and their anterior homeland might be purely fictional. Some metaphorically 'diasporic' Dutch members of the Western neo-pagan community, for instance, have adopted a spurious Celticity as their spiritual identity, longing for a mythic 'homeland' modelled on Arthurian Avalon.

There are also diasporic religious communities, like the Wahhabi Muslims of various ethnic origins in Europe, who are engaged in a transnational propagation of an alternative Islamic modernity with regard to the secular culture of the urbanized West. As this modernist Islamic

The Tibetan Monastic Institute at Rikon in Switzerland constitutes a spiritual home for all Tibetan Buddhist exiles. Its functional modernist architecture echoes the sweeping vertical palisades of the Potala Palace in Lhasa, as does its setting near the Alps.

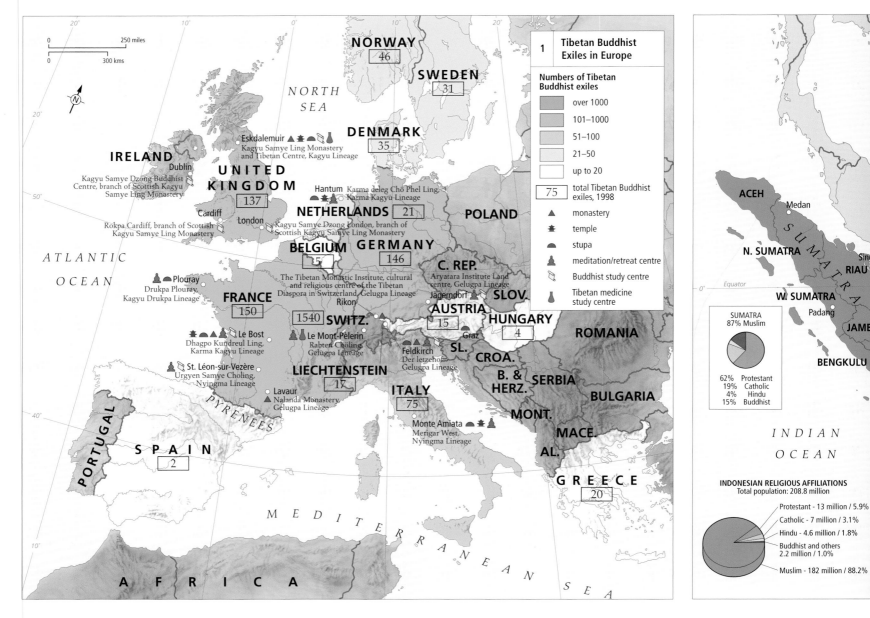

utopia has no historical precedent, the spiritual home of the movement lies, presumably, somewhere in the future.

The degree of preservation and change of a diasporic religious tradition as well as the degree of integration into a host culture is contingent upon the attitude of the community as well as on their socio-cultural, legal and political environment. Indicators often include attitudes towards women's empowerment, familial and cultural traditions, and inter-generational relations, while for the host culture multi-culturalism and religious pluralism frequently become politically-charged issues.

Tibetan Buddhism in Europe

Following the futile 1959 revolt against the Chinese annexation of their homeland, scores of Tibetans fled their homeland (map 1). In the early 1960s, Switzerland offered asylum to some 2000 Tibetan refugees. They found a congenial environment in the Swiss Alps and a growing interest in their religion and culture from Swiss (and Western) society at large. In 1968, the Monastic Tibet Institute was founded in Rikon, near Zurich, catering to refugees and interested Westerners alike. In 1985, it hosted a Kalachakra initiation performed by the Dalai Lama, which was attended by 6000 people comprising both Westerners and Tibetans. In 2002, the Dalai Lama gave the same initiation in the Austrian town of Graz, and in 2003, the first Buddhist cemetery in Europe was inaugurated by Tibetan lamas in Vienna. Tibetan medicine too has attracted widespread interest. While the number of diasporic Tibetan priests remains relatively small, their impact in Europe and North America has been considerable, attracting many thousands of local adherents.

The Hindu Diaspora in Indonesia

The Hindus in Indonesia represent one of the more interesting minority religions in the world's largest modern Muslim state (map 2). Hindus enjoy a secure minority status along with Protestants, Catholics and Buddhists. The largest Hindu ethnic group are the Balinese Hindus, although there are around 50,000 Indonesian Hindus of Indian descent living throughout the country, the vast majority being Tamil in North Sumatra, or Punjabi who live mainly in the cities of Java.

In the early 1950s, some Hindu Sindhi merchant families migrated to Medan in Sumatra. There, they formed a separate Indian community alongside the local Tamils, descendants of bonded labourers who had been shipped from India to the Sumatran plantations in the nineteenth century. From the 1980s, most Sindhis relocated to the capital, Jakarta, forming a local community of some 1500 people. They became important sponsors of the modernist Indonesian Hindu movement that developed after the Muslim-dominated Indonesian Ministry of Religion assessed Balinese Hinduism as not being in accord with constitutional monotheism. As Sindhis identify with a more universalist and modernist Indian culture and spirituality, they introduced some modern global monotheist Hindu movements to Indonesia, such as the Hare Krishna or Satya Sai Baba movement. While, in terms of religious practice, Indonesian Hindus (who comprise members of different Indonesian ethnic groups) and Indonesian Sindhis are still two separate communities, both groups congregate when philosophical or financial matters pertaining to the development of Indonesian Hinduism need to be discussed.

Balinese Hindus at the Melasti ceremony held at Nyepi, the Balinese New Year which occurs in the spring. Each community carries its deity statues to the sea or a sacred stream for purification.

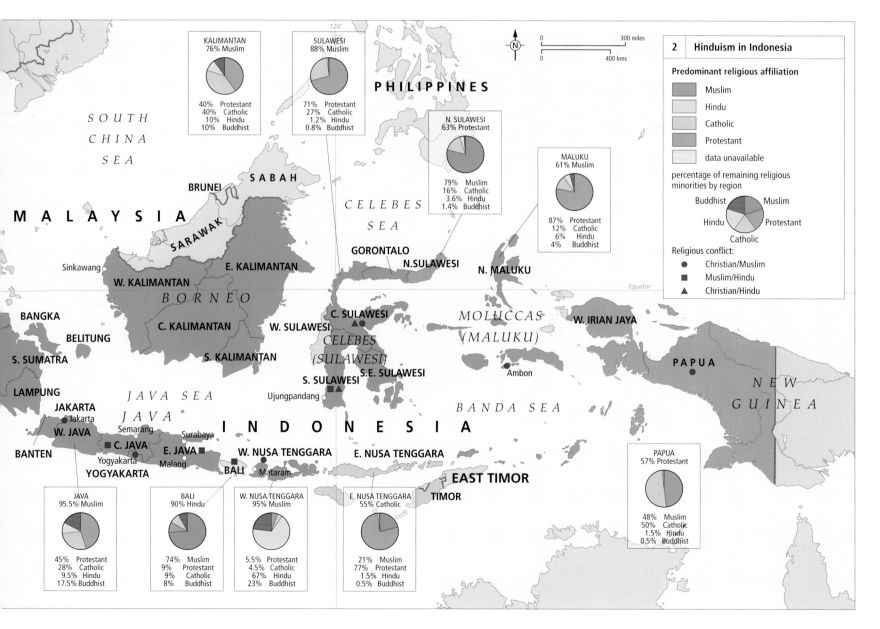

NEW RELIGIONS IN THE MODERN WORLD

A SUMMARY of the religious situation in the modern world cannot be complete without an examination of contemporary phenomena such as Marxism, New Age philosophies and New Religious Movements.

Secular Alternatives

Official Marxism arose in Russia in 1917, and spread rapidly after 1945, becoming, at the height of its advance, the creed of thirty-five nations (*map 1*). Officially atheist, it could evoke faith and fervour, as in the case of Chairman Mao. It could also be seen to contain most of the elements (community, rituals, festivals, ethics, social involvement, scripture, concepts, aesthetics and even spirituality) associated with religion. Marxism is a more strident version of other secular alternatives, such as secular humanism and nationalism; by its fruits it has, in many places, been betrayed.

The New Age movement is characterized by extensive networks which connect disparate peoples in different places. It stresses both meditation and holistic medicine, and focuses on both women's and global issues. It is distinguished by its feel for the new science, and its lack of organization. It appeals to a number of Westerners because of its sense of vagueness and freedom from organizational constraints, and its stress on individuality.

New Religious Movements

There are thought to be over 40,000 New Religious Movements in the world today (*map 2*). Most New Religious Movements have strong leaders, firm messages and clear principles. Some are small, some have memberships of well over a million. Some are part of a major tradition (for example, the African Independent

A dance in honour of Chairman Mao who, after the Marxist takeover of China in 1949, became a revered figure. Marxism has since lost political control in many places, and in Marxist China all religions are reviving.

Churches), others have broken away from a major tradition (for example, the Baha'is from Islam, and the Brahma Kumaris from Hinduism). Some are Western by background, many are non-Western. New Religious Movements represent an important innovation in modern religion. Although comparatively small, many of them have a global outlook: the Baha'is claim to have a presence in virtually every nation of the world, and the Brahma Kumaris (with only 600,000 people) are found in over eighty nations. They offer variety, novelty, change and heterodoxy. They are popular at a time of rapid change, especially in the new millennium.

- Healthy, Happy, Holy Org., 1969
- Church of Scientology, 1950
- Erhard Seminar Training
- Human Potential Movement
- Children of God, 1968, 25,000
- Jehovah's Witnesses, 1884, 16m
- Church of Jesus Christ of Latter Day Saints, 1830, 13m
- Christian Science, 1879, 2m
- Theosophical Society, 1875
- Spiritualism, 500,000
- Pentecostalism, 1906

PACIFIC

OCEAN

0 — 2400 miles
0 — 3600 kms

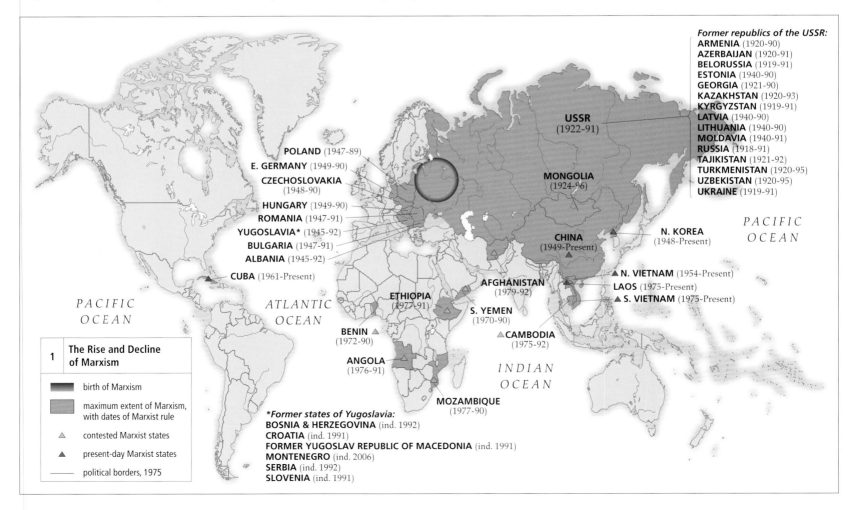

1 The Rise and Decline of Marxism

- birth of Marxism
- maximum extent of Marxism, with dates of Marxist rule
- △ contested Marxist states
- ▲ present-day Marxist states
- — political borders, 1975

POLAND (1947-89)
E. GERMANY (1949-90)
CZECHOSLOVAKIA (1948-90)
HUNGARY (1949-90)
ROMANIA (1947-91)
YUGOSLAVIA* (1945-92)
BULGARIA (1947-91)
ALBANIA (1945-92)
CUBA (1961-Present)

USSR (1922-91)
MONGOLIA (1924-96)
CHINA (1949-Present)
N. KOREA (1948-Present)

AFGHANISTAN (1979-92)
ETHIOPIA (1977-91)
S. YEMEN (1970-90)
BENIN △ (1972-90)
△ CAMBODIA (1975-92)
ANGOLA (1976-91)
▲ N. VIETNAM (1954-Present)
LAOS (1975-Present)
▲ S. VIETNAM (1975-Present)
MOZAMBIQUE (1977-90)

PACIFIC OCEAN
ATLANTIC OCEAN
INDIAN OCEAN
PACIFIC OCEAN

Former republics of the USSR:
ARMENIA (1920-90)
AZERBAIJAN (1920-91)
BELORUSSIA (1919-91)
ESTONIA (1940-90)
GEORGIA (1921-90)
KAZAKHSTAN (1920-93)
KYRGYZSTAN (1919-91)
LATVIA (1940-90)
LITHUANIA (1940-90)
MOLDAVIA (1940-91)
RUSSIA (1918-91)
TAJIKISTAN (1921-92)
TURKMENISTAN (1920-95)
UZBEKISTAN (1920-95)
UKRAINE (1919-91)

Former states of Yugoslavia:
BOSNIA & HERZEGOVINA (ind. 1992)
CROATIA (ind. 1991)
FORMER YUGOSLAV REPUBLIC OF MACEDONIA (ind. 1991)
MONTENEGRO (ind. 2006)
SERBIA (ind. 1992)
SLOVENIA (ind. 1991)

Findhorn, 1965
Neo-Paganism
Church of New Jerusalem (Swedenborg), 1783, 50,000

Baha'is, 1863, 10m

Ahmadiyah, 1889, 7m
Brahma Kumaris, 1937, 600,00

many large local movements eg
Unification Church, 1954, 2m
Chondogyo, 1860

Anthroposophical Society, 1912

Rissho-Kosei-Kai, 1938, 5m
Reiyu-Kai, 1925, 2m
Soka-gakkai, Nichiren Shoshu 1935, 20m
Konkokyo, 1859, 500,000
Seich No Ie, 1930, 3m
Tenrikyo, 1837, 3.5m
Mahikari, 1959, 150,000

Rastafarians, 1936, 500,000

Voudoun, Santeria

various movements

many large local movements eg
Subud, 1933

Cargo movements, 1920

Aladura Churches, 10m

Kimbangu Church, 1921, 6m

Kenya Independent Churches, 10m

Afro-American Spiritism, 50m

Zionist Churches, 18m

Int. Soc. for Krishna Consciousness, 1965, 300,000
Transcendental Meditation, 1958, 3m
Sathya Sai Baba, 1940, 3m
Swami Narayans, 6m
Ananda Marg, 1955

2	New Religious Movements		
country of origin	centre	source	
◆	●		Buddhism
◇	○		Hinduism
◆	●		Christianity
◆	●		Islam
◆	●		Daoism
◆	●		Shintoism
◆	●		Sikkhism
◆	●		Human Potential
◇	○		non-aligned

(date of formation and numbers of adherents shown where known)

Religious Rejuvenation

With the coming of independence to many new nations there has been a renaissance in their religions. Islam, Hinduism and Buddhism have new vitality, Christianity is growing quickly in many parts of the Third World, and the Jews now have a homeland in Israel. European Christendom has disappeared for ever and there is a new sense of secular and religious pluralism.

For some of these religions, ethnic and societal questions and matters of traditional practice are of crucial importance: for example, the status of the caste system in Hinduism, the definition of a Jew as one born of a Jewish mother, and the role of traditional Shinto religion in modern Japan. Both nationalism and secular humanism remain strong forces: primal religions are expanding slightly after a seemingly rapid decline; the minor traditions of the Sikhs, Jains, Parsis remain small; Chinese religions are growing.

The New Globalization

Seeing the Earth from space has given a new perspective to humans, as has the advent of the millennium. There is an increasing sense that particular national and religious concerns, while not unimportant, point beyond themselves to a global context. The great cultures and religions of the world are open to each other in a new way and they meet, not on the recent premise of the supremacy of the West, but on the basis of global dialogue. Global challenges, and inherited problems, are pressing: the environment is over-exploited and humanity is over-concerned with the partial and the external and is in retreat from sources of inwardness and transcendence. But global resources – ecological, physical, human, social, moral and spiritual – are extensive.

The New Millennium

Divisions remain within and among religions, between traditionalists and radicals and between liberals and fundamentalists. Within religions issues such as homosexuality, birth control, and female leadership are contentious. Religious flashpoints include Chechinia, Sri Lanka, Sudan, Palestine, Kaskmir, the Balkans and various ramifications of 9/11. However, ecumenical movements, interfaith dialogue and global interplay across religions all have an important role in the modern world. All religious movements share in the quest for a global ethic, without the need to abandon particularity. There is, for the first time, a sense that all of humanity must face and meet the problems and challenges of the new millennium.

The Earth can now be seen *as a revolving globe from space. This new perspective provides a stimulus to global thinking across religions and across the nations of the world.*

MODERN PILGRIMAGES

TRADITIONAL PILGRIMAGE destinations are covered in entries on specific traditions in this atlas. Many of these are still active in the modern world, sometimes in unprecedented ways due to the relative ease of long-distance travel, and can thus today involve massive movements of people across the face of the planet. Disentangling those travellers who are pilgrims from the total numbers quoted for mass tourism can be difficult. The annual Muslim *hajj* to Mecca now numbers nearly 3 million pilgrims, and Roman Catholic Rome and even the healing shrine at Lourdes in France attract numbers of this order, too. There are many new pilgrimages, as well as revivals of long defunct ones. A modern phenomenon is the close association between pilgrimage in the traditional religious sense, and modern sightseeing tourism to religious sites, to appreciate their art, architecture and culture. However, religious pilgrimages often have similar general purposes, the most common being providing opportunity for a rite of passage from one state of spiritual awareness to another, usually involving 'communitas', a shared experience. However, a humanist may argue that the sheer aesthetic experience of seeing St Peter's basilica in Rome or Angkor Wat in Cambodia has a similar psychological effect.

Pilgrimages Old and New

One of the most popular modern Catholic pilgrimage sites is Knock, Ireland's revered Marian shrine in County Mayo, which started with an apparition of the Virgin Mary, St Joseph and St John in 1879. Since then, Knock has attracted increasing numbers of pilgrims (today around 1.25 million per annum), so a purpose-built airport was constructed, and Pope John Paul II visited in 1979 on the occasion of its centennial.

Another modern Christian pilgrimage centre, of Anglican orientation but also revered by Roman Catholics, is the restored medieval shrine of Our Lady of Walsingham, known as 'England's Nazareth', in Norfolk. The shrine, established in 1061, fell into neglect after the Reformation, but was reinvigorated in 1897 when public devotion was renewed by a procession of pilgrims from King's Lynn. In the 1920s, the Anglican vicar of Walsingham led a vigorous restoration effort including new buildings for worship, lodging and meals. Today, thousands of pilgrims, mostly from English parishes, make pilgrimage to Walsingham each year.

Although the Muslim *hajj* (pilgrimage) to Mecca is required once in every Muslim's life by Islamic law (provided health and means suffice), Muslims also like to visit shrines and cemeteries where *walis* (saints) repose. Such a 'visit' is known in Arabic as *ziyara*. Shi'ite and Sunni Muslims make *ziyaras* to Medina, where the Prophet and many other early Muslim saints are buried. Shi'ites also visit Karbala', in Iraq, where Husayn, the Prophet Muhammad's grandson was martyred; and to nearby Najaf, where the fourth Imam Ali is buried, and to shrines in Iran.

Sunni Muslims also make *ziyaras* to saint shrines throughout the Islamic world. Indonesians honour nine saints, known as Wali Songa who, according to tradition, brought Islam to Java in the fifteenth century. Shrine-tombs in many archipelago cities are visited, particularly when the saints' birthdays or other special dates are being honoured. Egyptian Muslims venerate many saints in small village tombs as well as major cities. The shrine-tomb of Sidi Ahmed al-Badawi in the delta city of Tanta draws millions of Egyptian pilgrims to the saint's annual, week-long *mawlid* (birthday celebration). Although spiritual rewards are sought, the Tanta *mawlid* is also a major agricultural and commercial fair, with street

entertainment, food, a parade with decorated floats, Sufi orders marching with flags and drums, and a certain street emphasis on sexual fertility as in ancient times.

Across South, Southeast and East Asia today, vast numbers of Hindus, Buddhists, Shintoists, Confucians,Taoists and other religious followers continue to fulfil diverse and complex varieties of pilgrimages, among the most impressive being the Hindu gathering of Kumbh Mela, attracting some 70 million at its major festival every twelve years, and the annual Chinese Spring Festival which sees an average 32 million travelling across the country annually to celebrate the New Year at their family homes.

New Pilgrimage Forms

Near the end of summer thousands of people from around the world descend on the Black Rock Desert in Nevada to participate in a celebration known as the Burning Man Festival. The festival has no specific

The traditional overland journey to Santiago de Compostela attracts over one million people each year. It is one of the few remaining examples of a pilgrimage in which the journey, usually on foot, is almost as important as the destination for those involved.

The Burning Man Festival: annual New Age gathering in September in Black Rock Desert, Nevada (since 1990), where for two weeks a temporary commerce-free city is created devoted to community, free expression and 'radical self-reliance' culminating in the immolation of a giant male structure and the clearing of the site

CANADA

UNITED STATES OF AMERICA

Boys Town

Chimayo

Guadalupe

Wixárika

MEXICO

Ste. Anne de Beaupré

ATLANTIC OCEAN

Vietnam War Memorial, Washington DC The Run for the Wall annual motorcycle pilgrimage of Vietnam veterans from California ends with a visit to the Vietnam memorial on Memorial Day at the end of May. A citizen's pilgrimage, for many it has deep religious significance

Site is a holy place of tobacco and peyote for Huichol people and their visions

Canindé

BRAZIL

Rio de Janeiro

The Burning Man *festival in Nevada, USA, is the most striking example of a number of New Age festivals combining a variety of belief-systems with arts and liberal expression in a sense of temporary community and release from everyday constraints.*

religious orientation; it was started in 1986 on a San Francisco beach, when a human effigy was burned on the summer solstice, attracting great attention and celebration with spontaneous music-making, dancing, and strong community feeling. The well-organized event moved to Black Rock in 1990, and is held annually with careful planning, ticket sales, workable layout and appealing creative events. One of the main attractions for participants is the demanding travel required to reach the site in northwest Nevada. The hot desert environment requires fortitude and dedication. Burning Man is a new kind of secular, pilgrimage-passage rite, combining spirituality, tourism, risk, separation, 'communitas', artistic expression, entertainment and renewal that appeal to many today. In Europe, many annual music festivals, notably at Glastonbury, have similar characteristics.

Another new secular pilgrimage, 'Run for the Wall', each May has Vietnam veterans riding motorcycles across the USA from California to the Vietnam War

Memorial in Washington DC. These pilgrims are provided with food and encouragement in towns where they stop en route, arriving by Memorial Day to visit the simple black stone wall inscribed with names of the thousands of deceased veterans in order to honour them as well as to seek healing of their own continuing emotional and physical wounds.

The Kumbh Mela occurs *every twelve years on the* sangam *or confluence of the Ganges, Yamuna and Saraswati rivers at Allahabad in northern India. Principally a bathing ritual, led by Hindu* sadhus, *the event can attract over 70 million participants over its three-week festival.*

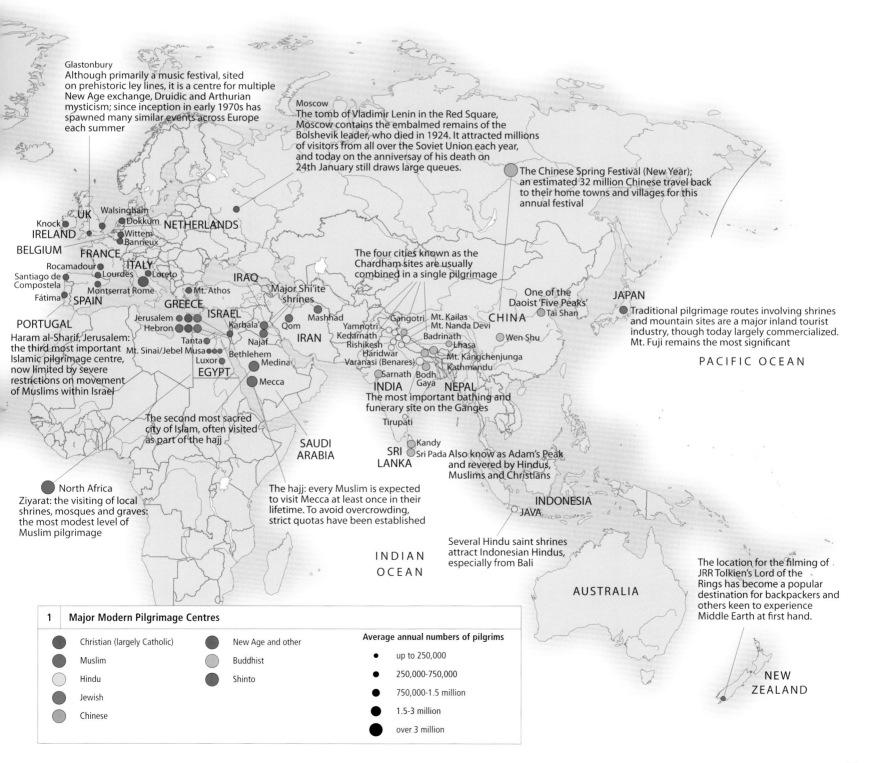

Glastonbury
Although primarily a music festival, sited on prehistoric ley lines, it is a centre for multiple New Age exchange, Druidic and Arthurian mysticism; since inception in early 1970s has spawned many similar events across Europe each summer

Moscow
The tomb of Vladimir Lenin in the Red Square, Moscow contains the embalmed remains of the Bolshevik leader, who died in 1924. It attracted millions of visitors from all over the Soviet Union each year, and today on the anniversary of his death on 24th January still draws large queues.

The Chinese Spring Festival (New Year); an estimated 32 million Chinese travel back to their home towns and villages for this annual festival

The four cities known as the Chardham sites are usually combined in a single pilgrimage

One of the Daoist 'Five Peaks'

JAPAN
Traditional pilgrimage routes involving shrines and mountain sites are a major inland tourist industry, though today largely commercialized. Mt. Fuji remains the most significant

PACIFIC OCEAN

Knock
Walsingham
UK
IRELAND
Dokkum
Wittem
BELGIUM
NETHERLANDS
Banneux
FRANCE
Rocamadour
Santiago de
Compostela
Lourdes
ITALY
Loreto
Fátima
Montserrat Rome
SPAIN
GREECE
Mt. Athos
IRAQ
Major Shi'ite
shrines
Tai Shan
CHINA
Wen Shu

PORTUGAL
Jerusalem
Hebron
ISRAEL
Karbala
Qom
Mashhad
Gangotri
Mt. Kailas
Mt. Nanda Devi
Haram al-Sharif, Jerusalem: the third most important Islamic pilgrimage centre, now limited by severe restrictions on movement of Muslims within Israel
Tanta
Najaf
IRAN
Yamnotri
Kedarnath
Badrinath
Lhasa
Mt. Sinai/Jebel Musa
Bethlehem
Luxor
EGYPT
Medina
Rishikesh
Haridwar
Varanasi (Benares)
Mt. Kangchenjunga
Kathmandu
Mecca
Sarnath Bodh
Gaya
INDIA
NEPAL
The most important bathing and funerary site on the Ganges

The second most sacred city of Islam, often visited as part of the hajj
SAUDI
ARABIA
Tirupati

SRI
LANKA
Kandy
Sri Pada
Also know as Adam's Peak and revered by Hindus, Muslims and Christians

North Africa
Ziyarat: the visiting of local shrines, mosques and graves; the most modest level of Muslim pilgrimage

The hajj: every Muslim is expected to visit Mecca at least once in their lifetime. To avoid overcrowding, strict quotas have been established

INDONESIA
JAVA

Several Hindu saint shrines attract Indonesian Hindus, especially from Bali

INDIAN
OCEAN

The location for the filming of JRR Tolkien's Lord of the Rings has become a popular destination for backpackers and others keen to experience Middle Earth at first hand.

AUSTRALIA

NEW
ZEALAND

1	Major Modern Pilgrimage Centres	
● Christian (largely Catholic)	● New Age and other	**Average annual numbers of pilgrims**
● Muslim	○ Buddhist	• up to 250,000
○ Hindu	● Shinto	• 250,000-750,000
● Jewish		● 750,000-1.5 million
○ Chinese		● 1.5-3 million
		● over 3 million

RELIGION AND ECOLOGY

THE MODERN WORLD has produced unprecedented rates of population growth, industrial expansion, natural resource extraction, land cultivation, animal species endangerment and outright extinctions, deforestation, water use, large-scale migrations into previously unpopulated regions, and degradation of the earth's atmosphere (*maps 2 and 3*).

Many religions have a fundamental relationship with the natural world – Buddhism, Islam, Sikhism and Shinto, in addition to many indigenous traditions – in contrast to most other organized religions whose focus has been the human condition. Further, new quasi-spiritual movements such as the Norwegian-based Deep Ecology have emerged with a specific environmental agenda. However, most major organized religions have been slow to respond to a widely-acknowledged modern crisis. While the British charities Oxfam and Christian Aid had their roots in famine-ridden Second World War Europe, in subsequent decades both have developed an increasing array of projects overseas, addressing poverty, health and refugee issues without regard to location or religion; population, health and population control issues were also targeted by Médecins Sans Frontières (MSF, established 1971), but these and many more organizations were largely voluntary in nature, albeit receiving financial and logistical support from various religious organizations. Strangely, popular support for such projects found its greatest focus from fund- and awareness-raising popular music events such as Live Aid (1985), and from the emergence of 'green' politics, notably in Germany, Scandinavia and the Netherlands in the same decade. Meanwhile, the Catholic Church's refusal to condone birth control did little to ease population pressure or the spread of AIDS in the developing world.

Many major religious organizations are, however, today increasingly engaging in ecological activism for sustainable environments (*map 1*). In 2007, the Vatican hosted a conference on climate change and development, addressing both scientific evidence and theological-ethical concerns. One bishop stated: 'Climate change is one of the signs of the times affecting the Catholic Church as a global organization. The Catholic Church must take a stand on this present-day and urgent question.' The bishop called for a papal encyclical addressing the 'future of creation' in order to 'energize'

2 | Fresh Water Availability

Availability of fresh water (cubic metres per capita per annum)

- over 50,000
- 15,000–50,000
- 5000–15,000
- 1700–5000
- 1000–1700
- below 1000

3 | Desertification and Deforestation

- hot arid desert
- semi-arid/Sahel
- cold polar desert
- forest areas under threat

1 | Environmental Projects

- principal environmental crisis points

Specific environmental initiatives sponsored by faiths:

- drinking water
- training/management
- Muslim
- Hindu
- Buddhist
- Shinto
- Daoist/Confucian
- Christian

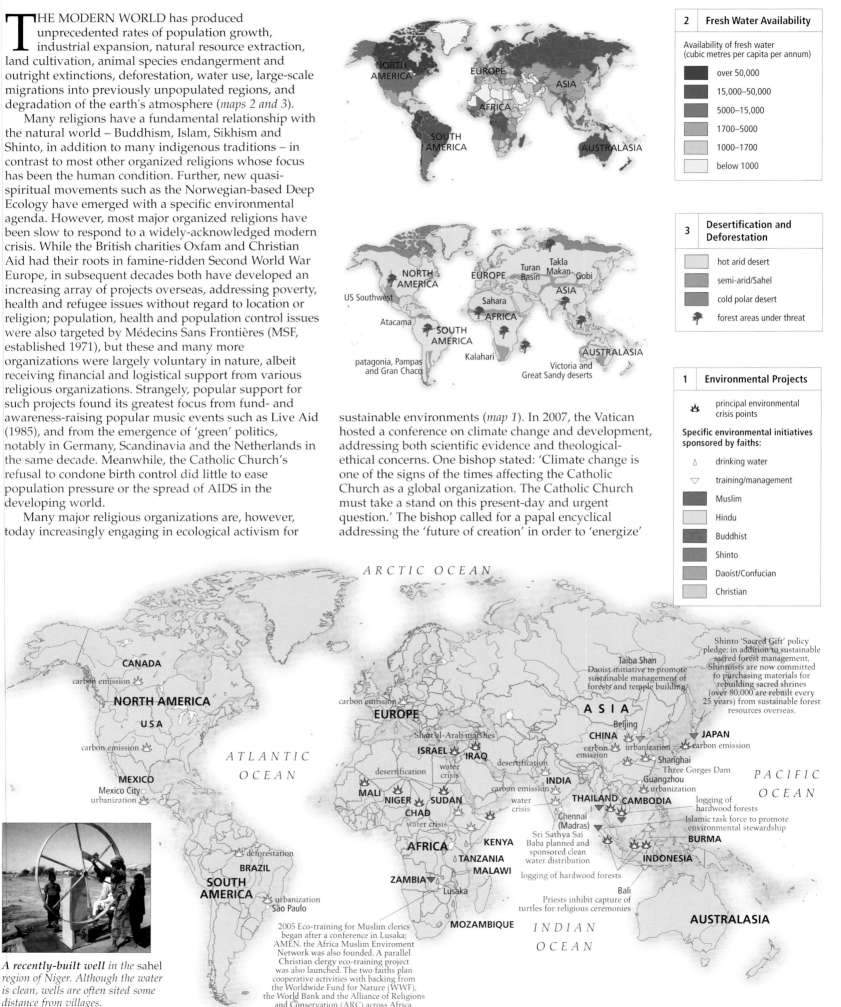

A recently-built well in the sahel region of Niger. Although the water is clean, wells are often sited some distance from villages.

Catholics, people of other religions and world opinion generally on climate change and the global environment.

Other religious communities are also beginning to address the challenges of climate change to ensure a sustainable environment for generations to come. There is a new Islamic environmentalism developing in Indonesia, which has the world's largest Muslim population and is the fourth most populous country in the world. One Indonesian Muslim environmental activist – Damayanti Buchori – has asserted that Islam is like Christianity in affirming that humans are the stewards of the Earth, acting as agents of God the Creator. 'We are the ones who take care of Earth because we have brains and are able to think.' She translates a verse from the Qur'an: 'Do not follow the greed that will damage the Earth, the greed that will bring extinction' (Sura 26:151-152). Another Indonesian Muslim environmentalist, Ridha Saleh, Deputy Director of Walhi, his country's largest grass-roots environmental organization, has stated: 'Saving the environment is service to God! It's the same as praying to God. We should see all dimensions of religion.' His organization is not limited to working with Muslims, but also with a prominent Catholic group in Indonesia as well as other groups. He asserts: 'The environment doesn't have an ideology. When disaster comes, child and adult, Muslim and Christian, everybody is afflicted.' Indonesia has influence on Muslims worldwide through its work as a member nation of the global Organization of the Islamic Conference, and signs of a developing 'green' global Islamic environmentalism are becoming stronger each year.

Safe Drinking Water

Many people in the developing world today do not have access to potable water. When water is available, it is often at a considerable distance from where people live. Women and girls in many traditional societies in Africa and Asia often spend much of their day walking long distances to get water from wells, followed by an exhausting return home with full containers. Millions of children in underdeveloped countries die each year from waterborne diseases due to lack of drinkable water.

Religious organizations, often combinations of Christians and Muslims working together, are improving water access, especially in the critical regions of the desertifying sub-Saharan Sahel. In southeast India's Andhra Pradesh province, the Sri Sathya Sai Baba organization, an energetic service-oriented Hindu community, in the 1990s funded, designed and built major supply and distribution projects that provide safe drinking water to more than two million rural people. In addition, the organization took the lead in completely rebuilding a decrepit, dry canal to provide clean water from the Krishna River to the huge city of Chennai (Madras).

In Israel and the Palestinian territories, however, political control of land areas is underpinned by access to and control of scarce and precious water supply. Here it has become a hot political issue, among so many others. Palestinians are in effect (and by law) dependent upon Israel for their supplies of drinking water (*map 4*).

Palestinians in Gaza queuing for water. Mains supplies from Israel are frequently disrupted, and limited quantities are then brought in by lorry.

Deforestation: A Buddhist Response

Tropical forests have been drastically reduced in many regions of the world due to improper land use, unemployment, shortage of fuel, shifting cultivation, cattle grazing and cash-cropping for sawn wood. In addition to South America's enormous Amazon rainforest – where there has been little resistance to powerful commercial interests – Southeast Asia too is being severely deforested. A Buddhist ecology movement in Thailand features 'ecology monks' taking action against the destruction of forests and pollution of air and water by economic and consumer interests. In 1991, over 50 Thai monks conducted a tree ordination ceremony by wrapping all the large trees with monks' robes in a national park threatened by dam construction. Buddhist tree ordinations are steadily increasing in number and effect, now also in Cambodia, promising spiritual merit for people who preserve trees and demerit for those who gratuitously destroy them. It is clear that Thai and Cambodian Buddhism, along with other major organized religions, have acquired an active environmental role, with a political edge, which shows no signs of diminishing.

A Buddhist tree-ordaining ceremony. By wrapping the trees in priestly robes, the plant effectively becomes a sacred site. This form of peaceful activism is proving successful in preserving some of the forests of Thailand and Burma from unfettered destruction .

LEBANON
SYRIA
Tyre
Litani
Al Qunaytirah
Safad
GOLAN
HIGHTS
Haifa
LAKE TIBERIAS
(SEA OF GALILEE)
Raqqad
Nazareth
Yarmuk
Irbid
Arab
Jenin
Northeast Aquifer
c.150 million cubic metres annually
Hadera
SAMARIAN
HILLS
Nablus
Faria
Jordan
Zarqa
Az Zarqa'
WEST
BANK
Eastern Aquifer
c.130 million cubic metres annually
Tel Aviv
Holon
Ramallah
Amman
Western Aquifer
c.350 million cubic metres annually
Jericho
Ashdod
Soreq
Jerusalem
areas under
Palestinian
administration
Bethlehem
Lakhish
JUDAEAN
HILLS
DEAD SEA
Gaza
Shiqma
Heidan
Hebron
Mujib
GAZA STRIP
Beersheba
Habesor
areas under
Palestinian
administration
ISRAEL
el Hasa
JORDAN
Araba
NEGEV
DESERT
MEDITERRANEAN SEA
0   30 miles
N
0   45 kms

4 | The Jordan River System
Israel
Israeli-occupied territories since 1967 war
disputed border
x-x-x-x ceasefire line
watershed
water flow

EGYPT
SINAI
Eilat Aqaba
GULF OF AQABA

THE HISTORICAL GEOGRAPHY OF RELIGION

THE HISTORY OF RELIGION has been long and varied. In the pre-history of Palaeolithic times, humans chipped stone tools, developed the bow, domesticated dogs, and lived by hunting. A religious dimension to human life began to emerge with the ritual treatment of skulls from c.500,000 BCE onwards, as indicated by 'Beijing man', an early discovery of *Homo erectus* from China. From 75,000 BCE, there is evidence of deliberate burial. The striking cave art of western Europe, from about 30,000 BCE, may well have had its roots in a sense of religion and mystery. Today, hunter-gatherers such as the Pygmies, Bushmen, Aborigines and Inuit, are a distant reminder of those Palaeolithic beginnings.

The Urban Revolution

The rise of agriculture and animal-husbandry in c.8000 BCE led to the development of settled village life. The rituals, myths and symbols of the early farmers evolved from their close relationship with nature, and centred upon the rhythm of the crops and the seasons. They sensed a close relationship between themselves, the Mother Earth they were cultivating and the gods they felt to be close, and religion was part of their total communal life. There were no separate practitioners or buildings to mediate the sacred.

This began to change in about 3,500 BCE with the rise of cities in the Tigris-Euphrates valley of Mesopotamia, the Nile valley of Egypt, the Indus valley of the Indian sub-continent, and separately around Anyang in China. The invention of the plough, rise of irrigation, appearance of sea-travel, use of metallurgy and, above all, the emergence of writing were all factors in the rise of cities. As farmers were able to grow enough crops to feed the entire urban population, city-dwellers built up wider contacts and engaged in specialized activities, such as crafts, trade and religion. Separate temples, priests, myths, rituals and festivals developed, along with the possibility of written scriptures and theologies that could be transmitted by non-oral means. Sacred kings appeared and personal religious questions concerning suffering, meaning, death and the afterlife became more central.

The Axial Age

During the sixth to fifth centuries BCE, great religious leaders emerged in four areas of the world whose work was to lead to the rise of some of the classical world religions. In Greece the Ionian philosophers prefigured the glory of Graeco-Roman thought, the rise of reason, and the role of philosophy within religion. In the Middle East, Zarathustra in Persia and Hebrew prophets such as Amos, Isaiah and Jeremiah, opened up the prophetic strand within religion, with its stress upon ethical monotheism. In India the Buddha and the Jain Mahavira were alive in the fifth century, not long after the Hindu Upanisads emerged, with their view of salvation as rooted in a round of rebirths rather than a single life. In China, the philosopher Confucius and the beginnings of the Daoist religious tradition developed an ethical humanism.

WORLD RELIGIONS

Beijing Man, China, c.500,000	Neolithic Revolution, c.8000	End of Indus Valley civilization, India, c.1500	Confucius, c.551-479		**CE**	Rise of Mahayana Buddhism, c.50	Mani, 216-c.275	Shotoku, 593-621		East and West Christian churches separate, 1054	Ramanuja, d. 1137	Guru Nanak, 1469-1539		Bahaullah, 1817-94	Russian Revolution, 1917	First landing on the moon, 1969

► to 10,000 ► 10,000 ► 1000 ► 500 ► 250 ► 200 ► 400 ► 600 ► 800 ► 1000 ► 1200 ► 1400 ► 1600 ► 1800 ► 1900 ► 2000 ►

Lascaux Caves, France, c.15,000	Early cities, Sumer, c.3000	Gautama Siddhartha, c.563-483	Alexander the Great, 356-323	Jesus, c.6 BCE-26/36 CE	Jerusalem falls to Rome, 70	Christianity tolerated in Roman Empire, 313	Muhammad, 570-632	al-Ghazali, d. 1111	Martin Luther, 1483-1546	World Parliament of Religions, Chicago, 1893	State of Israel, 1948

The seeds of the Zoroastrian, Hindu, Buddhist, Jain, Hellenistic and Chinese religious traditions had been sown. The Jews meanwhile, in virtual exile from their homeland from 587 BCE to 1948 CE, helped to pave the way for the Christian and Muslim traditions, whose rise was triggered by the life of Jesus of Nazareth and, in the seventh century CE, of Muhammad.

Religions were now more universal in outlook, especially the three great missionary traditions – Buddhist, Christian and Muslim. Their ultimate aims lay beyond this world in heaven, *nirvana*, or *moksa*. Paradoxically, their other-worldly gaze brought this-worldly success. Great religious civilizations arose. In Europe, the Christian faith prevailed. Islam spread across North Africa into Spain and, eventually, eastwards into India. The Hindu tradition in India thrived in a multi-religious culture including Buddhists, Jains, Christians, Jews, Parsis (and later Sikhs and Muslims). In China the *Sao Chiao* ('the three ways'), produced a fusion of the Confucian, Daoist and Mahayana Buddhist traditions.

Elsewhere, primal traditional religions spread in the Americas, Australasia, Oceania, southern Africa and the Arctic regions. Eurasian barbarian tribes became absorbed into the great religious traditions as they came to dominate the four areas of Europe, the Middle East, India and China. Some older religions, such as the Graeco-Roman, Ancient Near Eastern, Egyptian, Hellenistic and Zoroastrian traditions, waned or disappeared, while Shinto emerged in Japan.

The remaining major and minor religions developed their own religious communities, rituals, ethical systems, scriptures, doctrines, aesthetic treasures and spirituality. All five great traditions focused on transcendence, although by different means: God in Christ, Allah through the Qur'an, Yahweh through the Torah, Brahman through a Hindu deity or the *atman*, and Nirvana through the Buddha or the Dharma. The four great areas and their religions were roughly parallel, equal and separate.

Western Dominance

This changed in around 1500 CE when Europe and Christianity broke out of their medieval isolation. Great navigators reached the Americas and Asia and later Oceania and Australasia. The rise of the West coincided with a time of relative weakness elsewhere. Christianity spread into the new areas that were opened up and partly absorbed some of their primal religions. At the same time, the West forced the rest of the world to engage with Western science, languages, education, democracy and secularization, stimulating other religions to engage in reform. The rise of vernacular devotion and a stress upon the laity in the Protestant Reformation, Shi'ite Islam, *bhakti* Hinduism and the new Sikh tradition turned attention back in the direction of this world and activism within it. The world began to become smaller as civilizations and religions came closer together.

Since 1945 this process has accelerated. The end of the old European empires has been followed by the rise and decline of Marxism and the emergence of new nation-states, heralding the resurgence of their religions. With the growth in communications and world population, all religions have become universal. Primal religions have weakened but not collapsed and thousands of New Religious Movements have arisen. Secular humanism has increased, stressing the relevance of religion for this world.

Religions, as well as stressing their particular views, have now set up an evolving inter-faith dialogue at global and local levels as they seek together for global solutions to global problems. The quest has started for a new dialogue and a new global vision.

EARLY HUMANS

E VIDENCE FOUND by Mary Leakey at Laetolil in Tanzania reveals that hominids walked there with an upright gait 3,600,000 years ago, giving tangible proof to the belief that 'humanity began in Africa'. These oldest hominids, the Australopithecines, disappeared between 2 and 1.5 million years ago, leaving the Earth to a new hominid species, Homo, which was eventually to evolve into *Homo sapiens*, our own species.

The Religion of the Hunter-Gatherers

Palaeolithic religion refers to the beliefs of the early human beings who lived up to the Neolithic period, which began about 8000 BCE. The focus of palaeolithic civilization was hunting and gathering, whereas the Neolithic revolution was characterized by advances in agriculture and the growth of settled communities.

Four different types of artefacts can yield clues about the nature of Palaeoloithic religion (*map 1*): human skull finds, burial sites, cave paintings and female figurines. Early skull remains, such as those of Peking Man found at Zhoukoudian in China dating back about 500,000 years, show evidence of ritual treatment.

Early remains of intentional burials, such as those at Teshik-Tash in Uzbekistan, La Ferrassie in France and Monto Circeo in Italy, dating from 70,000 BCE onwards, reveal bodies lying on the right side, with heads sometimes facing east and legs in a flexed or crouching position. Animal bones and tools were placed nearby, possibly as burial gifts. Why should Palaeolithic humans bury their dead? There appears to have been some comprehension of death and a desire to give this rite of passage some ritual expression.

These early ivory carvings may have been fertility symbols and were found in Siberia, which still remains an influential area for wider religion.

1	The Spread of Early Humans and Rise of Palaeolithic Religions

→ spread of humans before 100,000 years ago

→ spread of humans 100,000-30,000 years ago

→ more recent spread of humans

— limits of Lower Palaeolithic up to 100,000 years ago

■ present-day hunters

◆ sites with date in years before present (BP)

0   1200 miles
0   1800 kms

SIBERIA
Homo sapiens
30,000 BP

SCANDINAVIA
Homo sapiens
15,000 BP

CZECH REPUBLIC
Mladeč Homo sapiens
33,000 BP

EUROPE
GERMANY
Bilzingsleben Homo erectus
400,000 BP

FRANCE
Lascaux Caves
c.15,000 BP
La Ferrassie

AUSTRIA
Willendorf
Venus figurine
c.30,000 BP

SPAIN
Altamira Caves
c.14,000 BP
Monte Circeo

ASIA

RUSSIA
Diuktai Cave Homo sapiens
14,000 BP

Zhoukoudian Homo erectus
c.500,000 BP

CENTRAL ASIA
Teshik-Tash
c.70,000 BP

ISRAEL
Qafzeh Homo sapiens
92,000 BP

JAPAN
Homo sapiens
30,000 BP

CHINA
Liujiang Homo sapiens
15,000 BP

PACIFIC
OCEAN

HAWAII
c.1,600 BP

PHILIPPINES
Tabon Cave Homo sapiens
30,000 BP

MICRONESIA

AFRICA

PYGMIES

KENYA L.
Baringo hominid
4,500,000 BP

TANZANIA
Laetolil upright hominid
3,600,000 BP

ATLANTIC
OCEAN

BUSHMEN

MADAGASCAR
peopled
c.1,500 BP

INDONESIA
Sangiran Homo erectus
c.1 million BP

MELANESIA

PAPUA NEW GUINEA
Huon Peninsula 40,000 BP

ABORIGINES

AUSTRALIA

POLYNESIA

INDIAN
OCEAN

AUSTRALIA
Upper Swan
38,000 BP

SOUTH AFRICA
Klasies River Homo sapiens 100,000 BP

NEW ZEALAND
from Polynesia
c.1000 BP

A famous Palaeolithic figurine found at Willendorf near Krems in Austria. The female characteristics are exaggerated and it may have been linked to a maternity or fertility cult.

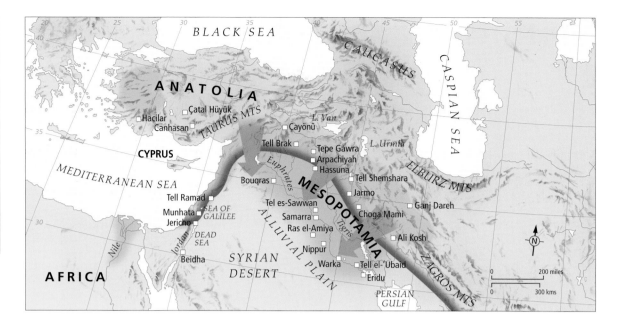

2	Neolithic Religion in the Ancient Near East c.8000 BCE

area of wild cereals — movement into the alluvial plain

limit of rain-fed agriculture — Neolithic sites

Cave paintings, such as the outstanding examples at Altamira in Spain, with its ceiling of bisons, and Lascaux in France, with its hall of bulls, were clearly not art for art's sake, and had religious implications. They portray various animals but also humans with animal attributes that seem to be masked dancers, sorcerers, or human-animal figures. They have been variously interpreted as shamans or deities, and the paintings are seen as part of sympathetic magic or hunting rituals.

Palaeolithic figurines, such as the Venus of Willendorf, have exaggerated female characteristics that seem to imply pregnancy, birth and nurture. They appear to be associated with fertility and possibly with mother goddesses. The evidence is inexact but religious interpretations are not inappropriate.

The Neolithic Revolution

Religious ideas and practices were also connected with the Neolithic civilizations that flourished from 8000 BCE onwards. Features of the neolithic revolution included the rise of agriculture, the domestication of plants and animals, the invention of pottery and the growth of settled villages. There was also a focus on the sanctity of nature, the cycle of the seasons, and mother goddesses. Nine Neolithic civilizations have been investigated archaeologically – in the Near East, southeastern Europe, northwestern Europe, Malaysia, northern China, Japan, northern Africa, the Nile Valley and middle America. In some of these regions, there is evidence of ancestor cults, fertility rites, household gods, pottery and rock art, megalithic monuments and burial rituals. The earliest, and best known, neolithic civilizations are in the Near East (*map 2*), with its religious centres such as Çatal Hüyük in Anatolia (6300–5400 BCE).

It seems likely that in the Neolithic era there arose an increasingly close relationship between human beings, the earth they were learning to cultivate, and the transcendant power, or powers, they believed to reside in both. Villages, with their myths, rituals and symbols embracing the whole community, had arrived. As yet there were no separate priests, temples, or writing – they were all aspects of urban civilization. Although religious sophistication has since evolved, the pattern of village religion and settled agricultural communities has remained an important cultural force, persisting from Neolithic times until the present.

THE FIRST ORGANIZED RELIGIONS

THE RISE of city civilizations brought profound religious developments in their wake. Cities developed in around 3500 BCE in Mesopotamia and slightly later in Egypt. Urban civilization diffused into the Indus Valley, and arose spontaneously in China.

The invention of the plough and use of irrigation radically improved agricultural productivity, while the development of sea travel, the rise of metallurgy and the appearance of writing all opened up for city-dwellers interests beyond farming. Extensive land and sea transport communications with other areas enabled concepts, knowledge and trade to be shared with other societies (*map 1*). Specialists who were not involved in agriculture, such as the Sumerian temple communities, began to appear. The division of labour had emerged on the world scene.

Religious specialization also came into play in the form of separate priesthoods, temples, festivals, theologies and eventually scriptures. Religious authority of another sort arose in the form of sacred kingship, seen

especially in the pharaohs of Egypt. Although the neolithic inter-relationship between human beings, nature and the gods remained, a gradual distancing of cities from the natural world occurred. More personal religious questions, concerning suffering, meaning and life after death, became more pressing. Religion was becoming a separate and personal concern as well as a group matter.

The Nature of Urban Religion

The form of religious life in the cities differed between Mesopotamia, Egypt, the Indus Valley and China. The relative isolation of ancient Egypt in the unique Nile valley gave her stability. Religion was characterized by the worship of, and sacrifice to, local and state gods in sometimes elaborate temples. The pharaoh was seen as an incarnation of the god Horus and was responsible for the cult of all the gods. Egyptian optimism about the after-life was symbolized in mummies and pyramids. A vague premonition of monotheism can be seen in the

Writing arose in the early cities from the fourth millennium BCE. This early Chinese script written on animal bone may have been used in messages to ancestors. The symbols represent objects not sounds as elsewhere.

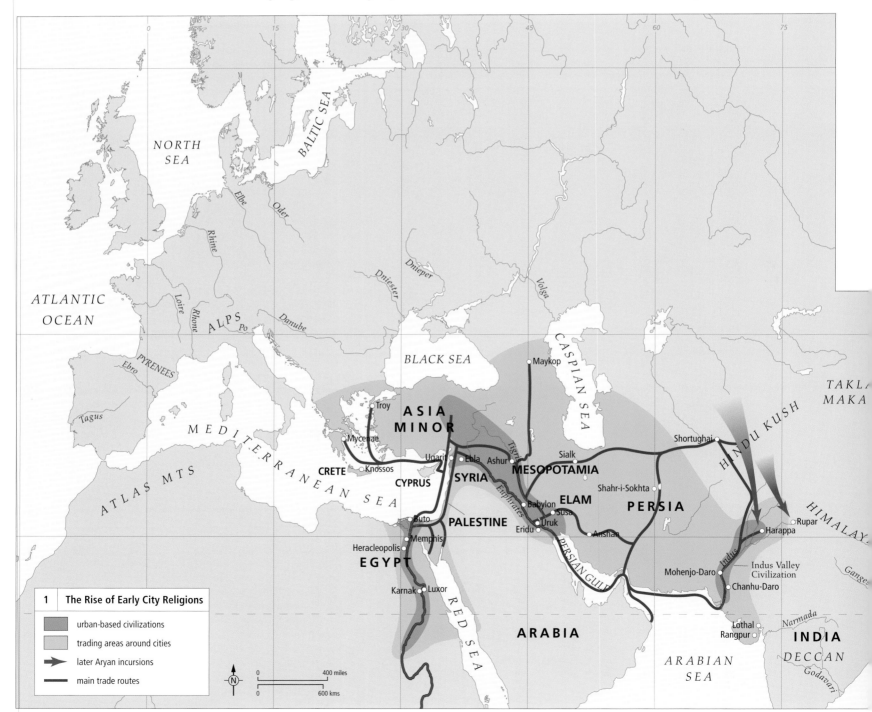

1	The Rise of Early City Religions
	urban-based civilizations
	trading areas around cities
➤	later Aryan incursions
—	main trade routes

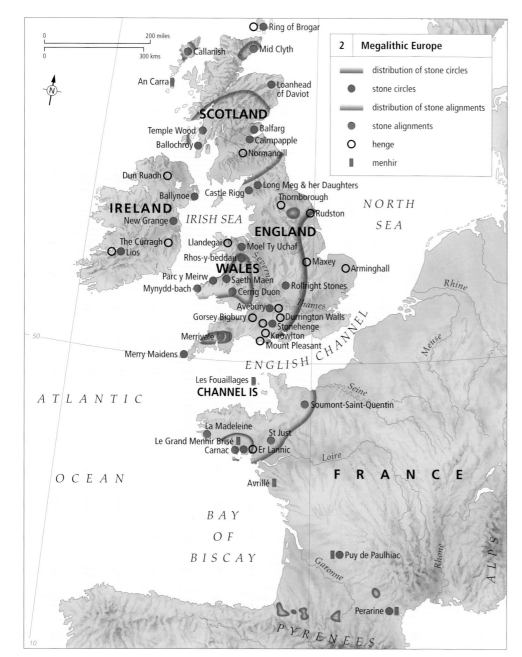

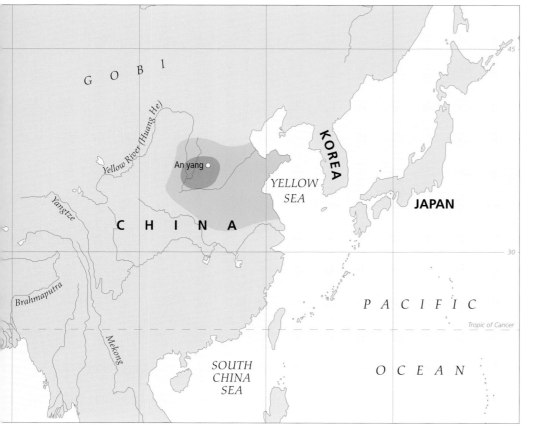

unsuccessful attempt by the pharaoh Akhenaten to establish Aten as the sole national deity in the 14th century BCE.

Mesopotamia saw a succession of peoples and religions ranging from the Sumerians, Babylonians, Assyrians, Hurrians and Hittites to the West Semitic groups. State religions, with their temples, kings and annual festivals, were characterized by their mythologies: epic creation stories, tales of the ritual victories of god-kings such as Marduk and of myth-ritual state ceremonies. It was out of this Egyptian and Middle Eastern milieu that the Jewish concern for the land and ethical monotheism were to emerge.

The script of the Indus valley civilization has not yet been deciphered. While there is no evidence of great temples, excavations reveal structured streets and great baths. Worship appeared to focus on mother–goddesses, a yogic god who seems to prefigure the Hindu deity Siva, phallic symbols, and possibly sacred trees. There also appears to have been a stress upon domestic religion - all of which find echoes in later Hinduism.

Chinese civilization arose spontaneously around Anyang in isolation from the other three centres. The earliest known Chinese script was used for messages to ancestors, and there also seems to have been a veneration for the deified powers of nature. In Chinese writing each symbol stood for an object, whereas elsewhere symbols began representing the sounds of human speech. In either case, the possibility arose of retaining knowledge in writing, of more sustained theologies, and of written scriptures – which began to emerge at this time.

The early cities used priesthoods and temple-centres, with their literate elites, to control local production and organize long-distance trade, which led to the gradual spread of urbanization. Although temples, priests, worship, sacrifices, myths, rituals, festivals, theologies, epics and scriptures were all becoming separate from the rest of life, their central importance was transmitted through state rituals, domestic religion, writing and through the significant figures of sacred kings, such as the Egyptian pharaohs, the Babylonian kings, and the emperors of China.

The Megalith Builders

From about 6000 years ago in western Europe mysterious stone circles, stone alignments, henges, menhirs and thousands of great standing stones called megaliths appeared (*map 2*). Found as far apart as the Orkneys and Malta, they seem to have served various purposes: as burial chambers, as possible fertility cult centres, as astronomical observatories to mark seasonal changes (as possibly at Stonehenge). The megalithic civilization turned out to be fleeting whereas the contribution of the early cities to the history of world civilization has been both major and long-lasting.

The entrance to the Luxor temple in Egypt *is flanked by statues of Ramses II (1299-1232 BCE). He was seen as a 'pharaoh-god', alongside the main Egyptian gods Re-Harakhti, Ptah and Amun, and thus as a sacred king.*

THE AXIAL AGE AND THE FIRST WORLD RELIGIONS

THE EMERGENCE in the sixth century BCE, in various parts of the world, of key religious thinkers and leaders was to bring into being the first great religious traditions of the world and, indirectly, the four great civilizations of Europe, the Middle East, India and China. It was once thought that the Ionian philosophers of Greece, the great Jewish prophets, Zoroaster, the Buddha, the Jain Mahavira, the Hindu Upanisads, Confucius and Laozi all emerged in the sixth century. Doubt has now been cast upon the historicity of Laozi, Zoroaster's dates have been pushed back before 1000 BCE, and it is suggested that the dates for the Buddha and the Mahavira should be brought forward into the fifth century. Nevertheless the wider impact of Zoroaster's work and the beginnings of the Daoist tradition date back to this sixth–fifth century BCE (*map 2*).

The First Monotheists

In Ionia, the early Greek philosophers uncovered the gift of reason, and the possibility of faith in reason, that was to be applied to religion and to life in general by Plato, Aristotle and others. Humane philosophy and the philosophy of religion were born. In the Middle East, in sixth-century Persia and later in Parthia, Zoroaster's prophetic worldview, with his sense of the cosmic conflict

between good and evil and the need to choose between what became known as God and the Devil through the agency of a righteous community, was given pragmatic effect. The Hebrew prophets Isaiah and Jeremiah pursued the prophetic note of ethical monotheism, and this worldview of right and wrong, God and the Devil, and ethical choice of the ultimately One God was later passed down into the Christian and Muslim traditions.

Eastern Traditions

In India the Hindu Upanisads, the Sanskrit sacred books, appeared in the sixth century BCE and the Hindu tradition began its march to dominance in India. Shortly afterwards two great figures, the Buddha and the Mahavira, were born in the same area. The Jain tradition with its stress upon non-violence and relativism has remained small but influential (as in Gandhi's case). The ongoing effect of the Buddha's work, first in India where the Mauryan emperor Asoka became a Buddhist and then in Sri Lanka and further Asia, has been immense. Meanwhile, in China, Confucius was alive in the sixth century BCE and the beginnings of the Daoist worldview were also emerging. The Confucian and Daoist worldviews, although opposite as in the Yin and Yang theory, complemented each other and would soon be

Confucius, one of the constellation of world cultural and religious leaders who arose around the sixth century BCE. His moral, social and political precepts helped to form China.

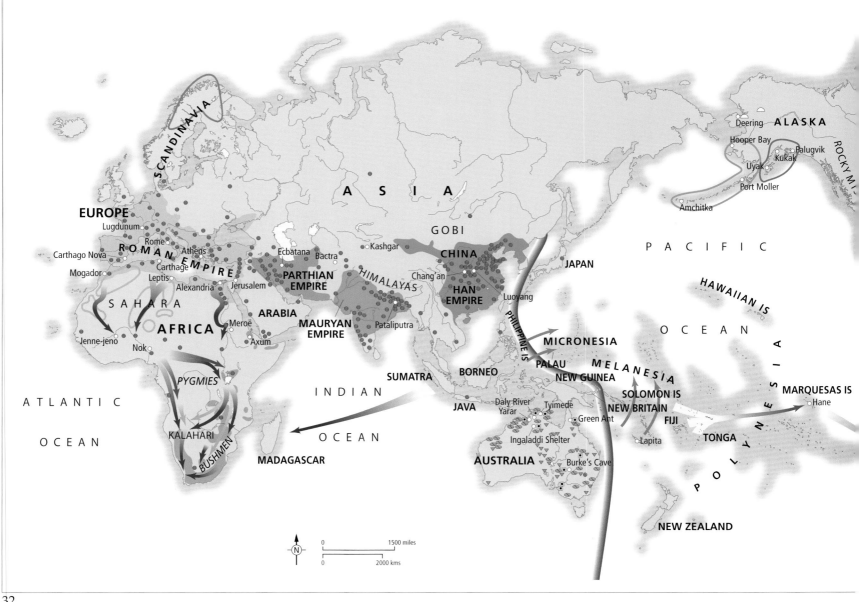

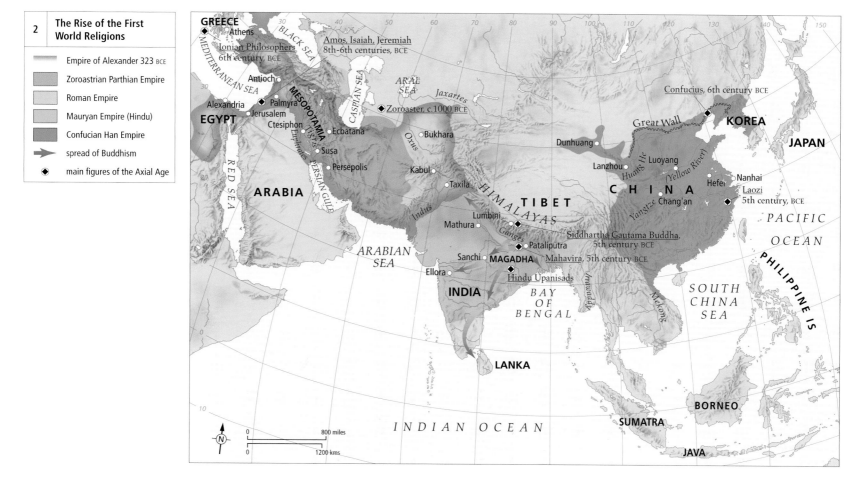

2 The Rise of the First World Religions

- Empire of Alexander 323 BCE
- Zoroastrian Parthian Empire
- Roman Empire
- Mauryan Empire (Hindu)
- Confucian Han Empire
- → spread of Buddhism
- ◆ main figures of the Axial Age

1 The Cultural Margins of the Ancient World

Africa:
- • equal to 1 million people
- → spread of iron-working
- — chariot carvings
- → spread of Bantu to 1 CE
- → spread of Bantu after 1 CE
- areas of African rock art
- → Indonesian migration to Madagascar

Australia:
- ▣ point finds
- ▽ panaramittee engravings
- ◉ figurative art styles

The Americas:
- — Adena, 1000-300 BCE
- — Hopewell, from 300 BCE
- — Basketmaker I, up to 1 CE
- — Chavín, 1200-200 BCE
- — Olmec homeland, c.1200-300 BCE
- — pre-Classic Maya, c.300 BCE-300 CE

The Arctic:
- ⌒ Arctic Small Tool tradition, c.2000 BCE
- — Pacific Inuit
- — Aleuts
- — Saami

The Pacific:
- eastern limits of human settlement at 30,000 years before present
- → spread of Melanesians to 1 CE
- → spread of Polynesians to 1 CE

joined by the Mahayana Buddhist worldview in the *San Chiao* ('the three ways') of China. The Han empire (206 BCE-220 CE) was officially Confucian, and civil service exams in the Confucian Classics began at this time and lasted until this century.

By the third century BCE, the beginnings of the Zoroastrian, Hindu, Buddhist, Jain, Confucian and Daoist traditions were already in evidence. In 334-323 BCE, the epic march of Alexander the Great to India's northwestern borders introduced Greek Hellenistic religion into the Middle East. As a consequence, four different religious outlooks can be discerned in Greek philosophy, Middle Eastern prophecy, Indian notions of rebirth and metaphysical introspection and Chinese ethical humaneness.

The Cultural Margins

On the periphery of the ancient world, traditional and primal cultures continued to expand (*map 1*). From c.500 BCE, the Bantu tribes began their move into southern Africa bypassing the Pygmies and Bushmen on the way. In North America the Adena, Basketmaker and Hopewell cultures emerged (1000 BCE to 700 CE); in central America the Olmec culture was important (1200–300 BCE); the pre-classic culture of the Mayas dominated the Yucatán peninsula from c.300 BCE. In Australia, Aboriginal point finds, paranamittee engravings, and figurative artstyles have been uncovered, dating back to 5000 BCE. The Indonesians migrated to Madagascar, and Polynesians colonized Easter Island, one of the last places to be settled by humans, about 1500 years ago. They erected hundreds of carved statues there, reaching over 12 metres in height and 85 tonnes in weight – they were found abandoned in the seventeenth century. In the Arctic, Inuit settlements were expanding from c.2000 BCE.

Though bereft of writing, these cultures on the margins had access to spiritual transcendance through their own myths, ritual and symbols. Nevertheless, although expanding physically, they were falling behind Han China, Mauryan India, Parthian Persia and the emerging Roman empire in cultural and religious sophistication.

THE SPREAD OF RELIGION IN THE CLASSICAL WORLD

FROM THE first century CE, the major religious traditions expanded and set up, with the exception of the later rise of Islam, a religious picture that is recognizable today (*map 1*).

The Rise of Christianity

The Christian tradition arose in Israel through the phenomenon of Jesus of Nazareth. It spread westward into Europe, combining the prophecy of the Hebrews and the philosophy of the Greeks. After early persecutions by Rome it was recognized by Constantine in 313 through the Edict of Milan, and the martyr church became the imperial church under emperors such as Justinian. The barbarians, who threatened the Roman empire from the north and east, were later absorbed into Christianity as it became established in Rome. The Christian tradition spread across southern Europe and North Africa and Christian influence reached as far as Persia and India. New religions which had arisen in the the Middle East and the Mediterranean, such as Mithraism and Graeco-Roman mystery cults, declined as the churches grew.

After Jerusalem fell to the Romans in 70 CE, the Jews distanced themselves from the Christians. Having lost their temple, they used their rabbis and synagogues around the Gentile world to develop their oral law in a new form of Rabbinic Judaism.

Eastern Traditions

The Zoroastrian Sasanid empire of Persia remained a threat to Christian Europe until it was later overrun by the rise of Islam. Within Persia Mani, born about 216 CE, founded Manichaeism, which became a missionary religion to both east and west. Manichaeism, borrowing from Gnostic and Zoroastrian beliefs, saw the world in dualistic terms – as an opposition between body and soul, matter and spirit, Satan and God.

Further east, the Hindu tradition consolidated its hegemony within India itself and continued to spread, along trade routes, from India into Southeast Asia – to this day, the Thai monarch has the name of a Hindu deity, Rama. From the first century CE, Buddhism made spectacular advances from India into China, where society, language and beliefs were different. A new form of devotional Buddhism, called Mahayana, slowly emerged in China, greatly aided by translators such as Kumarajiva, who translated into Chinese the difficult Sanskrit of the Mahayana Sutras. Chinese forms, such as Pure Land and Ch'an, emerged within the Mahayana tradition. In Japan Ch'an became Zen. The Buddhist mission from India into China was much helped by the opening of the Silk Road (*map 2; see also* pp. 72-75, 86-77).

Within China Mahayana Buddhism developed a complementary relationship with the indigenous

The Buddhist grottoes at Datong, Shanxi province, China were hewn out and decorated under the northern Wei dynasty (386–534 CE). Buddhist art reached China via the Silk Road and was a visual education in Buddhism for ordinary people.

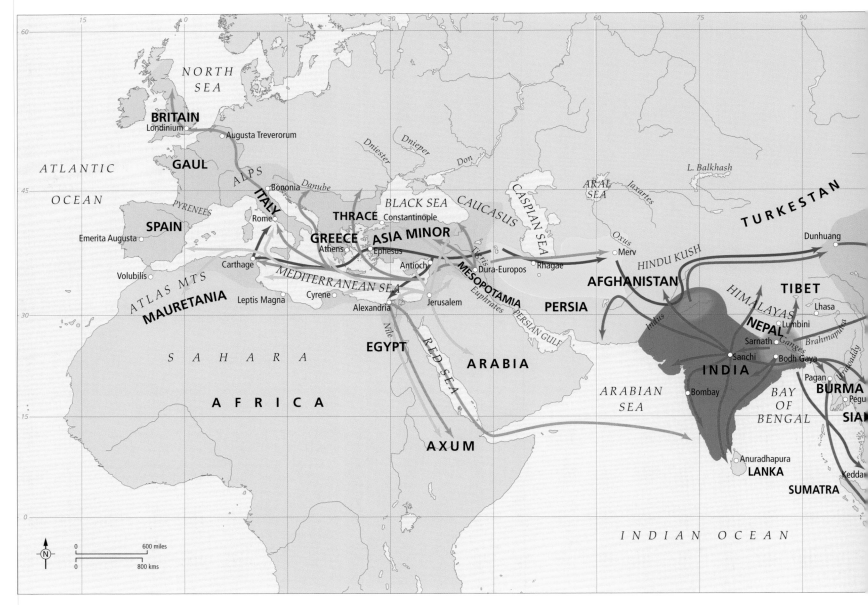

Confucian and Daoist traditions. Japan also began to emerge as a cultural offshoot of China with its own Shinto tradition aided by Confucian, Daoist and Mahayana Buddhist elements.

The Rise of Devotional Religion

In all of these emerging great traditions, a warm sense of personal faith was a common theme: Christians were devoted to Christ, Hindus to Siva, Visnu and the Goddess, and Mahayana Buddhists were devoted to Bodhisattvas such as Amitabha.

Paradoxically, although the aim of life came to lie beyond this world in heaven, (or *nirvana*, or *moksa*), religious traditions were becoming truly embedded in this world, with their own buildings, ethical systems, beliefs, scriptures, spirituality, worship and sacraments (often centred upon birth, initiation, marriage, and death). As St Augustine put it, in response to the trauma of the sack of Rome, this world too could become in some sense the city of God. Institutionally organized religious communities had come to stay, whether arranged socially, as among the Jews and Hindus, or through the *Sangha* of the Buddhists, or the Christian Church.

Barbarian Incursions

The four civilizations that were developing in Europe, the Middle East, India and China were all threatened by incursions from the steppe region of central Asia. The Aryans, who formed the early core of the Hindu tradition, had themselves been invaders. Northern China was taken over by barbarian rulers, who promoted superb Buddhist cave paintings and sculptures at places such as Dunhuang and Lungmen. The northern

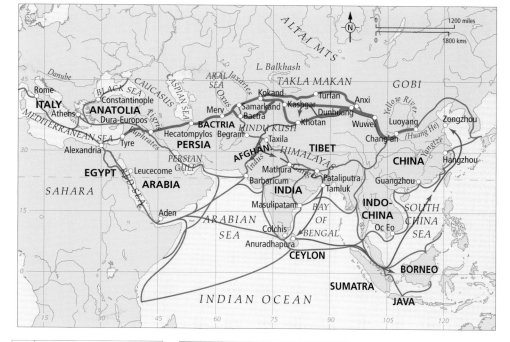

2	The Silk Road
——	Silk Road
——	other trade routes
——	travels of Fa Xian, 399–414

A mosaic panel from S Vitale, Ravenna (547 CE), depicting the Emperor Justinian in a procession bringing gifts to be offered at mass. It symbolizes the close relationship between church and state after the Emperor Constantine, which encouraged the rise of Christendom.

European tribes who invaded and sacked the Roman empire eventually became Christianized.

Towards the end of this period the crisis of barbarian invasions further affected the four emerging civilizations and their religions. Pastoral nomads irrupted into the crescent of classical civilizations ranging from the Mediterranean to China with disastrous impact: the Roman empire collapsed, China north of the Yangtze was partly devastated, Sasanid Persia was weakened, and the Hindu Gupta rule in India was ended. The Silk Road was closed again and the four areas became partly cut off from one another.

In Europe, the Middle East, India and China religions began to develop in isolation. In western Europe, Latin theology developed alongside the Roman administration. Eastern Christianity, centred upon Constantinople, moved in a more Greek Orthodox direction. The mystery religions of Greece, Rome, Mesopotamia and Egypt retreated or disappeared. Jewish synagogues spread around the Middle East. Theravada Buddhism in Sri Lanka and India began to separate from Mahayana in China and its environs. Chinese Buddhism co-existed with neo-Daoism and Confucianism. In India, the Hindu tradition became much stronger, both through the development of the caste system and the rise of more popular devotional religion stimulated by the great epics, the *Ramayana* and *Mahabharata*.

After the earlier missionary spread, the internal consolidation of ideas, scriptures, buildings and institutions ensued. The four civilizations and their religions were becoming roughly equal, parallel and separate. But all four regions were destined for further disruption when the Mongols again erupted out of Central Asia in the thirteenth century.

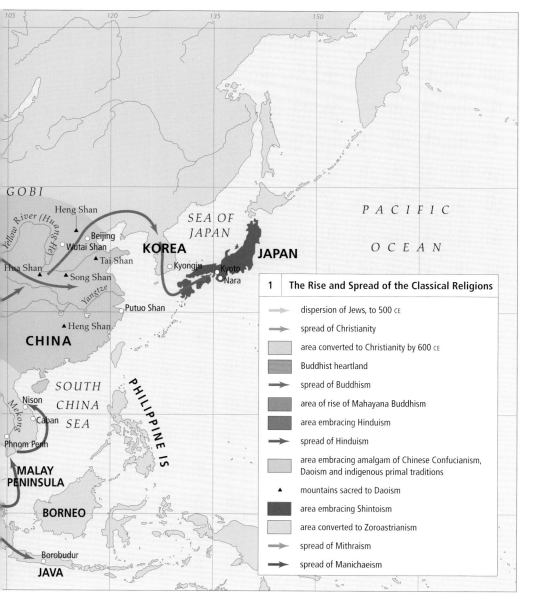

1	The Rise and Spread of the Classical Religions
→	dispersion of Jews, to 500 CE
→	spread of Christianity
	area converted to Christianity by 600 CE
	Buddhist heartland
→	spread of Buddhism
	area of rise of Mahayana Buddhism
	area embracing Hinduism
→	spread of Hinduism
	area embracing amalgam of Chinese Confucianism, Daoism and indigenous primal traditions
▲	mountains sacred to Daoism
	area embracing Shintoism
	area converted to Zoroastrianism
→	spread of Mithraism
→	spread of Manichaeism

THE RISE OF ISLAM AND THE MAJOR WORLD RELIGIONS TO 1500 CE

THE LAST major religious tradition to arise was that of Islam. After the migration (Hejira) of Muhammad from Mecca to Medina in 622 CE, he became the overall leader of the whole city of Medina, and Islam began a dramatic expansion. By 661 CE, during the golden age of Muhammad and the four early caliphs, Islam had spread through much of North Africa and the Middle East (*map 1*), the Qur'an had been finalized, the Arabic language had begun to permeate what became the Arab world, and Islam was poised to expand still further. By 1258 Islam had penetrated into Spain in the west and India in the east and was at least equal in strength to Europe, India and China.

The Great Religious Traditions

During the medieval period Europe was dominated by Christianity, India – although multi-religious – was becoming more Hindu, and China had a combined Confucian, Daoist and Mahayana Buddhist culture. Islam prevailed in the Middle East, and the four regions became roughly equal, roughly parallel and roughly separate (*map 2*). Christianity spread within Europe, absorbing the various northern tribes, including the marauding Vikings; and with the rise of Russia its Orthodox branch began to venture east into the steppes. Islam ventured into Europe, reaching Spain in the west and, eventually, Turkey in the east. In early Spain creative contacts developed between the Christian, Muslim and Jewish communities. Elsewhere, on the other hand, the Crusades exacerbated the sense of hostility between Christians and Muslims.

Islam became established in India through the medium of the Mughal empire, which had also received Syrian Christians, some Jews, some Parsis (who settled in Bombay after fleeing from the Muslim invasion of Persia) and later the Sikhs. All these groups co-existed with India's majority Hindus, Jains and Buddhists (who virtually died out in later medieval India). In China the neo-Confucian revival, centred on Chu Hsi (1130–1200), incorporated elements of Daoism and Buddhism, and in Southeast Asia Buddhism grew in strength. European Christendom became the most beleaguered of the four major religions, beset by Islam to the south and Tartar and Mongol hordes to the east. Within Europe, except for early Spain, the Jews were spasmodically persecuted.

Parallel Religions

Although the four major religions were radically different some linking patterns can be discerned. Transcendence, and the means by which it was achieved, mattered; whether it was seen in terms of reaching God through Christ, Allah through the Qur'an, a Hindu personal deity through the mediation of a Brahmin, or the enlightened state of Nirvana through the Buddha or the Dharma (the Buddha's transcendent teaching). The monastic or mystical communities of each tradition encouraged the development of inward spirituality. In all four religions, the future life, whether in heaven or beyond the round of rebirths, mattered as much as, if not more, than this life. In the Christian world, theological and philosophical syntheses of faith emerged in the work of Aquinas and Bonaventura in around the twelfth and thirteenth centuries. These syntheses were echoed by Maimonides in the Jewish world, al-Ghazali in the Muslim world, Chu Hsi in China, and Ramanuja in India.

Each tradition saw the development of different branches of the faith; Catholic and Orthodox Christianity, Sunni and Shi'ite Islam, Theravada, Mahayana and

Tibetan Buddhism, and Hindu communities centred specifically upon Siva, Visnu and the Goddess. All of the traditions were distinguished by elaborate rituals, festivals and sacraments, great ethical systems, and beautiful buildings, sculpture and literature.

In the wider world the American Indians, the Inca and Aztec cultures, the peoples of southern Africa, the Aborigines of Australia, the Maoris of New Zealand, and the peoples of Oceania were cut off mainly by sea from the classical traditions, as were the peoples of Siberia and the Arctic, through the exploits of Mongol invaders.

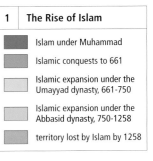

1	The Rise of Islam
	Islam under Muhammad
	Islamic conquests to 661
	Islamic expansion under the Umayyad dynasty, 661-750
	Islamic expansion under the Abbasid dynasty, 750-1258
	territory lost by Islam by 1258

2	World Religions, c.1500 CE
	Theravada Buddhism
	Tibetan Buddhism
	Hinduism
	Hindu-Buddhism
	Mahayana Buddhism mixed with Confucianism and Daoism
	Mahayana Buddhism mixed with Confucianism, Daoism and Shinto
	Islam
	Catholic Christianity
	Russian Orthodoxy
——	African states
- - - -	Ghana, c.700-110
- - - -	Mali, c.110-1400
	Aztec Empire
	Inca Empire

North American cultural areas:

	Arctic
	Sub-Arctic
	Northwest coast
	Plateau
	California
	Southwest
	Great Plains
	Northeast
	Southeast

SIOUX indigenous groups

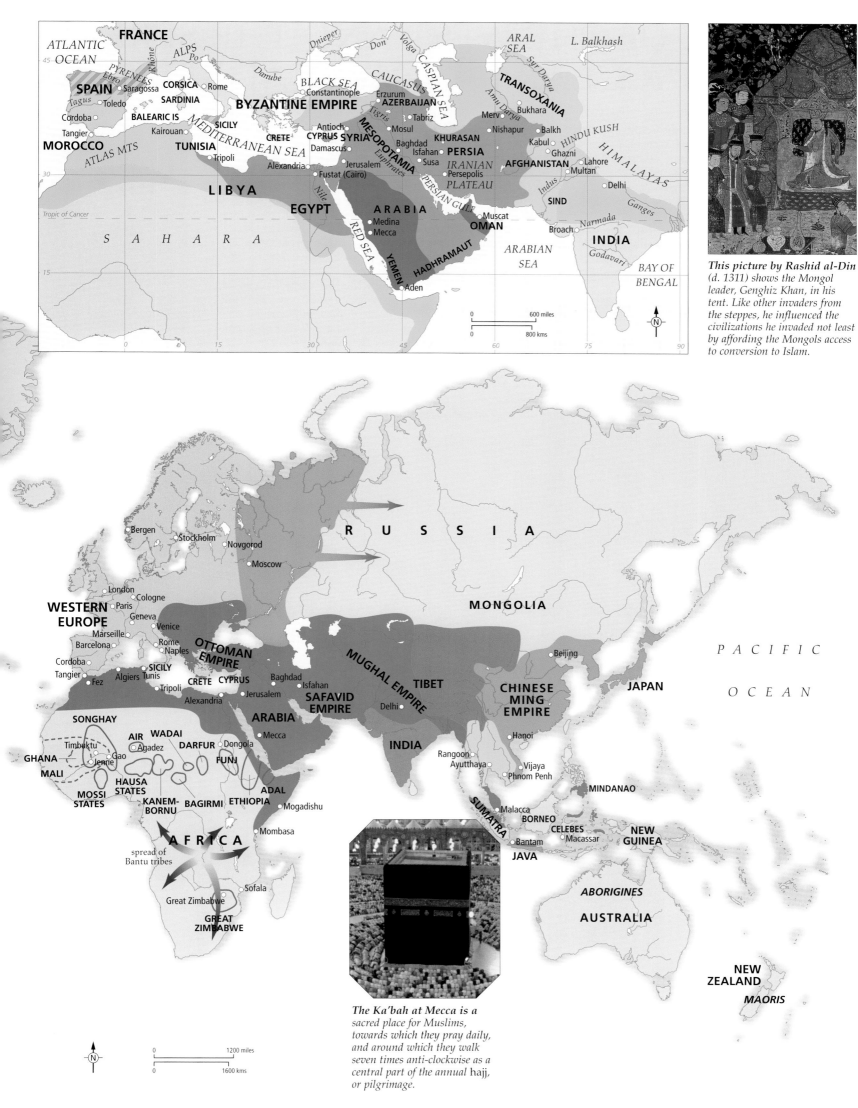

FRANCE

ATLANTIC OCEAN

Dnieper

ARAL SEA

L. Balkhash

ALPS

Rhône

Po

Don

Volga

CASPIAN SEA

SPAIN
Saragossa
CORSICA
◦ Rome

Ebro

Tagus

Toledo

Cordoba ◦

Tangier ◦

BALEARIC IS

SARDINIA

PYRENEES

Danube

BLACK SEA

◦ Constantinople

CAUCASUS

Erzurum ◦

AZERBAIJAN

Tabriz ◦

TRANSOXANIA

Amu Darya

Sur Darya

Merv ◦

Bukhara ◦

SICILY

CRETE

CYPRUS

Antioch ◦

SYRIA

MESOPOTAMIA

Mosul ◦

Tigris

Nishapur ◦

Balkh ◦

KHURASAN

HINDU KUSH

MOROCCO

ATLAS MTS

TUNISIA

MEDITERRANEAN SEA

Kairouan ◦

◦ Tripoli

Damascus ◦

Baghdad ◦

Euphrates

Isfahan ◦

PERSIA

Kabul ◦

Ghazni ◦

Lahore ◦

HIMALAYAS

Alexandria ◦

Jerusalem ◦

Fustat (Cairo) ◦

Susa ◦

IRANIAN PLATEAU

Persepolis ◦

AFGHANISTAN

Multan ◦

Delhi ◦

LIBYA

EGYPT

Nile

ARABIA

PERSIAN GULF

SIND

Indus

Ganges

Tropic of Cancer

S A H A R A

RED SEA

Medina ◦
Mecca ◦

Muscat ◦

OMAN

Broach ◦

Narmada

INDIA

Godavari

ARABIAN SEA

YEMEN

HADHRAMAUT

Aden ◦

BAY OF BENGAL

0 ___ 600 miles
0 ___ 800 kms

N

This picture by Rashid al-Din (d. 1311) shows the Mongol leader, Genghiz Khan, in his tent. Like other invaders from the steppes, he influenced the civilizations he invaded not least by affording the Mongols access to conversion to Islam.

Bergen ◦

Stockholm ◦

Novgorod ◦

R U S S I A

Moscow ◦

London ◦

Cologne ◦

WESTERN EUROPE

Paris ◦

Geneva ◦

Venice ◦

Marseille ◦

Rome ◦

MONGOLIA

Barcelona ◦

Naples ◦

OTTOMAN EMPIRE

CRETE

CYPRUS

Baghdad ◦

Isfahan ◦

MUGHAL EMPIRE

TIBET

Beijing ◦

PACIFIC OCEAN

Cordoba ◦

Tangier ◦

Fez ◦

SICILY

Algiers Tunis

Tripoli ◦

Alexandria ◦

Jerusalem ◦

SAFAVID EMPIRE

Delhi ◦

CHINESE MING EMPIRE

JAPAN

SONGHAY

ARABIA

INDIA

AIR

WADAI

Timbuktu ◦

Agadez ◦

DARFUR

Dongola ◦

Mecca ◦

Rangoon ◦

Hanoi ◦

GHANA

Jenne ◦ Gao ◦

FUNJ

Vijaya ◦

Ayutthaya ◦

MALI

HAUSA STATES

Phnom Penh ◦

MINDANAO

MOSSI STATES

KANEM-BORNU

BAGIRMI

ADAL

ETHIOPIA

Mogadishu ◦

SUMATRA

Malacca ◦

BORNEO

CELEBES

Macassar ◦

NEW GUINEA

AFRICA

Mombasa ◦

Bantam ◦

JAVA

spread of Bantu tribes

Sofala ◦

Great Zimbabwe ◦

GREAT ZIMBABWE

ABORIGINES

AUSTRALIA

NEW ZEALAND

MAORIS

The Ka'bah at Mecca is a sacred place for Muslims, towards which they pray daily, and around which they walk seven times anti-clockwise as a central part of the annual hajj, *or pilgrimage.*

0 ___ 1200 miles
0 ___ 1600 kms

N

THE RISE OF THE WEST AND THE SPREAD OF VERNACULAR DEVOTIONAL RELIGION

I N ABOUT 1500 CE two significant developments occurred; the rise of vernacular devotion across all major religions and the aggressive rise and spread of the West and western Christian tradition (*map 1*).

In the Far East devotional religion had already been introduced by Mahayana Buddhism, especially Pure Land Buddhism, the Buddhism of faith, in vernacular languages such as Chinese, Japanese and Tibetan. In the West, the Protestant Reformation in Europe saw the rise of Protestant churches separate from Rome and the translation of the Bible into German, English and other European languages, on the principle that all could have access to it devotionally through the priesthood of all believers. After the Council of Trent the Roman Catholic Church responded to the Protestant stress on justification by faith by evolving its own form of semi-vernacular devotion through people such as St John of the Cross, El Greco and Loyola in Spain (*map 2*).

Just as Latin was replaced by local languages in northern Europe, in India Sanskrit was replaced by vernacular tongues. This process is apparent in the work of Tulsidas, who wrote about the Hindu deity Rama in Hindi, by Chaitanya who extolled Krsna in Bengali, and by Guru Nanak who used Punjabi to interpret the new Sikh religious tradition in the Punjab. In Persia the new Shi'ite Safavid dynasty used Persian rather than Arabic to express a fervent Islamic devotion (*map 3*).

In about 1500 CE Europe began to escape from its medieval isolation through sea travel; Columbus found America, Cabot explored Canada, Vasco da Gama sailed round the Cape of Good Hope to India, Cabral reached America and India, and Magellan and del Cano

A stylized portrait of Guru Nanak (1469–1504) who came to be seen as the first Guru of the Sikh tradition. He used the Punjabi language to express fervent universal devotionalism.

El Greco's picture of the Burial of Count Orgaz, *Toledo, Spain, 1586. The Counter-Reformation responded to the Spanish Reformation through people like St John of the Cross, as well as through the devotional aestheticism of artists such as El Greco.*

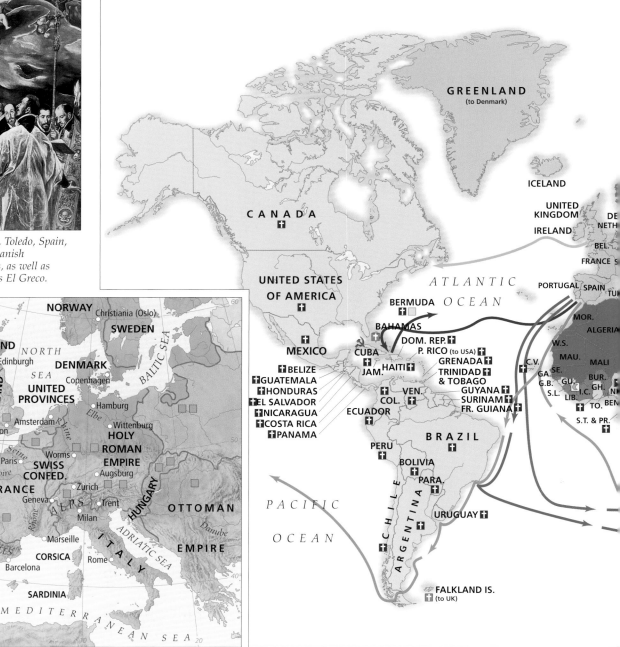

The Rise of Vernacular Devotional Religion in 16th-century Europe

Roman Catholic
Lutheran
Calvinist
Anglican
minority church

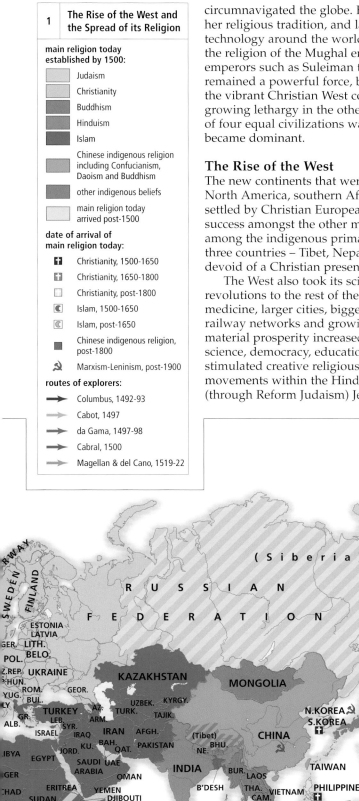

1	The Rise of the West and the Spread of its Religion

main religion today established by 1500:

- Judaism
- Christianity
- Buddhism
- Hinduism
- Islam
- Chinese indigenous religion including Confucianism, Daoism and Buddhism
- other indigenous beliefs
- main religion today arrived post-1500

date of arrival of main religion today:

- Christianity, 1500-1650
- Christianity, 1650-1800
- Christianity, post-1800
- Islam, 1500-1650
- Islam, post-1650
- Chinese indigenous religion, post-1800
- Marxism-Leninism, post-1900

routes of explorers:

- Columbus, 1492-93
- Cabot, 1497
- da Gama, 1497-98
- Cabral, 1500
- Magellan & del Cano, 1519-22

circumnavigated the globe. Europe could take her trade, her religious tradition, and later her science and technology around the world into new continents. Islam, the religion of the Mughal emperors and Ottoman emperors such as Suleiman the Magnificent (1520–66), remained a powerful force, but the rapid expansion of the vibrant Christian West coincided with a period of growing lethargy in the other great civilizations. The era of four equal civilizations was now over. The West became dominant.

The Rise of the West

The new continents that were uncovered, South America, North America, southern Africa and Australasia, were settled by Christian Europeans. Missionaries had less success amongst the other major religious traditions than among the indigenous primal traditions. Yet by 1945 only three countries – Tibet, Nepal and Afghanistan –were devoid of a Christian presence.

The West also took its scientific and industrial revolutions to the rest of the world, introducing better medicine, larger cities, bigger factories, expanding railway networks and growing trade. Longevity and material prosperity increased. In addition, Western science, democracy, education, and social reform stimulated creative religious, and other, reform movements within the Hindu, Muslim, Buddhist and (through Reform Judaism) Jewish traditions.

The Impact of the West

Primal religions which had existed in relative isolation in Siberia, the South Sea islands and parts of the Americas, Asia, Africa and Australasia were subject to severe change. Lay involvement in all religions became more pervasive and more attention was paid to this-worldly matters such as social reform and material advances. The West was admired for its progress but criticized for its intolerance. As greater knowledge emerged about other religions, a dialogue slowly began. Renewal movements developed in various religions which aimed either to borrow from the West and Christianity, like Ram Mohan Roy (1772–1833) in India, or to react against them. The agenda had been set by the West. Her trade, empires, administrators, merchants held sway. The world was becoming one through the process of westernization, which in turn stimulated the desire for reform and independence. The rise of comparative religion and incipient inter-faith dialogue provoked deeper discussion on all these matters.

Eventually, two world wars fomented by Western nations, the growth of nationalism, rising expectations, the desire for the autonomy of Christians in other lands and the cascading momentum of change in the world would close the chapter on the rise of the West.

Religious Reforms

While a debate was opening up in Europe and America between the Christian tradition, already fragmented by the Reformation, and a culture increasingly influenced by humanistic, nationalistic and scientific values, significant reform movements began in other traditions. Moses Mendelssohn (1729–86) developed Reform Judaism. In India, Neo-Hinduism was promulgated by Roy, the Tagores, Ramakrishna, Vivekenanda, Gandhi, Aurobindo and Radakrishnan. Reform Islam movements were led by al-Afghani, Muhammad Abduh and Muhammad Iqbal (1873–1938). Anagarika Dharmapala and others brought about innovations in Buddhism. All pursued reform through re-interpretation. Other traditions, such as Tibetan Buddhism, remained staunchly traditionalist. The Hindu Arya Samaj in India, the purist al-Wahab (1703–92) in Arabia, and Orthodox Judaism sought conservative reformation. Others, such as the Baha'is in Islam and the Mormons in Christianity, formed new religious movements in search of radical reform.

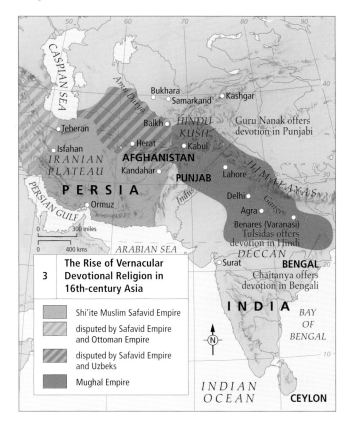

3	The Rise of Vernacular Devotional Religion in 16th-century Asia

- Shi'ite Muslim Safavid Empire
- disputed by Safavid Empire and Ottoman Empire
- disputed by Safavid Empire and Uzbeks
- Mughal Empire

LANGUAGE, SCRIPT AND RELIGION

T HE CONFLUENCE OF languages, scripts and religious beliefs is a complex story that reaches back to the beginnings of our recorded history and remains a major issue of religious identity in many areas today. Some of the complexities of the map of languages, religions and scripts become clearer through an examination of examples drawn from various countries, regions and periods of history.

The Power of Alphabets

Alphabetic writing is fast becoming the dominant mode of writing among all nations and cultures, and a major factor in its spread has been its use as a vehicle for religious writing. Alphabetic writing first appears in the mid-second millennium BCE at Ugarit, on the Mediterranean coast of modern Syria. The inhabitants of Ugarit were seafaring traders living between the two super-powers of the time, the Hittites in the north and the Egyptians in the south. They wrote on clay tablets like the Akkadians to their east, a writing system classified as cuneiform. Unlike Akkadian, however, the people of Ugarit developed an alphabetic cuneiform system, possibly under Egyptian influence. Egyptian Hieroglyphics had alphabetic, syllabic and logographic features and never fully separated the alphabetic system from the rest of their writing system because of its close association with the gods and the divine realm. The Ugaritic alphabet contained thirty characters, most of which represented separate sounds, but it appears that extra letters were added to make the number thirty, corresponding to the number of days in the lunar month. This number-letter association imbued the alphabet with powerful religious as well as practical powers, and the number-letter association remained in all the subsequent alphabets derived from this region. Phoenician, Greek, Hebrew, Syriac, Latin and the Arabic alphabets all exhibit a number-letter association, and the letters are used for counting as well as spelling words.

Alphabets became closely associated with both magic and religion. From many places in the ancient Near East, we find amulets written with alphabetic acrostics that have numerical values as well as word meanings. Deities in the ancient Near East had numerical as well as name designations, and texts would often indicate the number of the deity or demon, in the case of magic, as well as the name. In Judaism, the practice of translating words into numerical values and numbers into words was common. Known as Gematria, it was used as a system of biblical interpretation and mystical speculation. Since each word had a numerical value derived from adding the number values of each letter, it was often felt that every word with the same numerical value could be substituted for the original word. This form of textual exegesis gained strength when Neoplatonism was adopted by various religious traditions as a basis for their theologies. Gematria is also found in Greek, Latin and some early Arabic texts.

Language and Script

The appearance of Judaism, Christianity and Islam at various periods forged a strong identity between each language, script and religion. In each of the traditions, it came to be believed that God spoke to humans and listened to prayers in a particular language. Hebrew became identified as God's language for Jews, for example, and Arabic as God's language for Muslims. These languages became the liturgical languages for the groups, the languages in which worship was conducted, whether or not the majority population spoke that language as a native tongue or not. Today, one finds Jews around the world praying in Hebrew while speaking a number of the world's languages, and Muslims likewise pray in Arabic when their native languages might be Bahasa Melayu or English.

Many early Christians, when Christianity separated from Judaism, adopted Greek as the liturgical language and argued for religious as well as political reasons that all who were 'orthodox' needed to use Greek. When the various church councils met to decide matters of doctrine, creed and dogma, the language of liturgy was a major topic of discussion, and the Syriac and Coptic churches broke from Greek-speaking Constantinople over language and script as well as other political and theological issues.

Script often more than language became a marker of identity. Judeo-Arabic, Judeo-Spanish (Ladino), Judeo-Persian, and Judeo-German (Yiddish) all use the Hebrew script as indicators of the Jewish nature of the language and the speakers. Likewise, Persian, Urdu, pre-modern Turkish, and other Islamic languages use versions of the Arabic script. In the case of Urdu, the Arabic script as well as some religious vocabulary derived from Arabic and Persian separate the Urdu from

Islamic art is iconoclastic, and thus is characterized by complex geometric forms and elaborate calligraphy, often in combination.

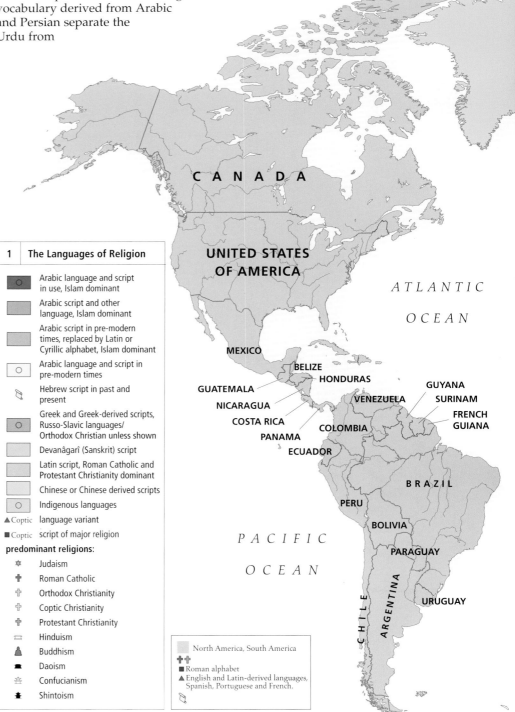

1	The Languages of Religion
○	Arabic language and script in use, Islam dominant
	Arabic script and other language, Islam dominant
	Arabic script in pre-modern times, replaced by Latin or Cyrillic alphabet, Islam dominant
○	Arabic language and script in pre-modern times
	Hebrew script in past and present
○	Greek and Greek-derived scripts, Russo-Slavic languages/ Orthodox Christian unless shown
	Devanâgarî (Sanskrit) script
	Latin script, Roman Catholic and Protestant Christianity dominant
	Chinese or Chinese derived scripts
○	Indigenous languages
▲ Coptic	language variant
■ Coptic	script of major religion

predominant religions:

✿	Judaism
✝	Roman Catholic
☦	Orthodox Christianity
☥	Coptic Christianity
✚	Protestant Christianity
☯	Hinduism
▲	Buddhism
■	Daoism
龠	Confucianism
✸	Shintoism

North America, South America
✝✝ Roman alphabet
▲ English and Latin-derived languages, Spanish, Portuguese and French.

Hindi, which uses the Devanâgrî script identified with Hindu Sanskrit, although they are both the same language at base. On Malta, the Roman Catholic population speaks a dialect of Arabic, but use the Latin alphabet, and Poland, also Roman Catholic, uses the Latin alphabet for its Slavic language, while Russia uses the Cyrillic alphabet because the population was missionized by the Orthodox St. Cyril, who is credited with inventing the Russian alphabet from Greek. The Coptic alphabet is another example of an alphabet modified from the Greek alphabet for religious purposes, in this case for writing Egyptian without using the more cumbersome hieroglyphics, which were associated with non-Christian religious practices.

Modern Christian missionaries have developed alphabets for languages without writing systems in order to promote Bible translation and written creeds. Organizations like the American Bible Society, the International Bible Society and others have translated at least one book of the Bible into 2,400 of the world's languages.

Syllabic and logographic scripts are still used for religious writings, even when modern alphabets are used for secular purposes. The Indian Devanâgrî script's name itself means 'divine city', and is associated with both the writing of Hindu sacred texts and also the sacred sounds. The sound 'Ôm' that has become so popular a meditative mantra is said to be formed by making all the sounds from the opening of the mouth to its closing, thus replicating the creative speech-sounds of the deity Vac at the beginning of creation. The Chinese writing system is similarly held to have been taken from the gods by a vision of a deity whose features resembled what were to become the Chinese characters.

Even in the face of political attempts to unify populations with modern, alphabetic scripts, traditional religious feelings resist these changes. This can be seen in the unsuccessful attempts in Lebanon to adopt the Latin alphabet and in Turkey, where modernist reforms in the late 1920s changed the Turkish writing system to a Latin-based script, but some religious voices are calling for a return to the script of the Qur'an. Religious belief and strong senses of tradition combine to preserve the strong linkages between religion, language and script in the major world religions.

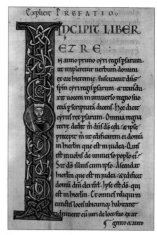

For western Christianity, Latin was the language of the Church and of the Bible. Before the invention of printing, Bibles and psalters were elaborately copied by hand, often incorporating vivid decoration. However the translation of the Bible into English, became a key text in the English Reformation. Latin remained the language of Catholic liturgy and the Mass until, despite some strong objections, it was suppressed in the 1980s in favour of vernacular languages.

Daoist 'grass' script is a highly stylized representation of Chinese characters; the action of painting these is regarded as a spiritual and magical act.

RELIGIOUS NAMES AND PLACES

THE MAP OF THE WORLD today bears innumerable traces and patterns of religious observance, movements and diasporas embedded within a wealth of place names and toponyms, while many societies around the world bear witness to their religious roots in the choice of personal or given names.

Personal Names

Religious identities have been universally expressed and embodied by means of personal and place names. The Jewish and Christian sacred scriptures contain names that are foundational in various ways. For Jews and Christians alike the names Abraham, Sarah, Jacob, Rachel, Deborah, Moses, Miriam, Joshua, David and Daniel are still used.

Jews have traditionally used scriptural names, whereas Christian naming practices – in the Roman period using chiefly Apostles' names such as John, Peter, Paul, James – developed over a millennium, reaching a peak in the central period of medieval western Europe when saint veneration flourished and added to the Christian name repertory (e.g. Francis, Claire, Margaret, Bernard). Christian naming, at least in the European West and later the Western Hemisphere, has remained fairly stable from medieval times.

Muslim naming practices have been similar with respect to favouring the names of founding figures, e.g. the Prophet Muhammad, his Companions, his family, and many early adherents. Even so, Muslims also use names from their particular cultures and regions, often alongside universally approved names such as Muhammad; the first four caliphs Abu Bakr, Umar, Uthman, and 'Ali; Khadija (Muhammad's first wife), Fatima (Muhammad's daughter and 'Ali's wife), Aisha, Zayd, and others. Muslim names usually have at least three different parts: the *ism* is the personal name (e.g. Umar, Zaynab); the *nisba* indicates relation to a

birthplace, tribe, or school of thought, e.g. *Qudsi* ('from Jerusalem'), *Khariji* ('from the Kharijite tribe'); the *kunyah* indicates the relation of a parent to a firstborn child, either *Abu* ('father of') or *Umm* ('mother of'), e.g. *Abu Dawud*, ('Father of David'), *Umm Kulthum* ('Mother of Kulthum'). Muslims also use nicknames (*laqab*), indicating honour, e.g. *Sayf al-Dawlah* ('Sword of the State'), physical disability, like *Timur-i lang*, 'Limping Timur' ('Tamerlane'), and other attributes.

Place Names

Biblical place names have been influential in how people have remembered the rise of monotheism. Ancient Israelites named certain places but also kept the names of previously existing Canaanite sites (Jerusalem, Megiddo). Biblical place names do not necessarily have religious meanings, as some are natural/biological (En-Gedi, 'Spring of the Goat') or topographical (Gibeon, 'hill'). Heirs of the Bible may, however, tend to regard scriptural place names in more spiritual ways. Biblical names were rarely bestowed on sites in Europe or the Western Hemisphere except where Puritan Protestants settled, notably in Colonial America. There are about 803 biblical place namings in the United States using 101 different names, according to one study. The top twelve in frequency, with a total of 466 uses, are, in descending order of occurrence: Salem 95, Eden 61, Bethel 47, Lebanon 39, Sharon 28, Goshen 33, Jordan 27, Hebron 26, Zion 24, Antioch, Paradise, and Shiloh 19 each. Other names occurring more than ten times include Beulah, Bethlehem, Canaan, Mount of Olives, Bethany and Carmel.

Saints' names have also been widely used for Christian place

Beyond the Catholic heartland of Europe, frequent instances of Christian place names may be found as here, at Broadstairs in the Isle of Thanet, Kent, the first area of Britain to be converted to Christianity by the missionary, St Augustine.

3 — The Catholic Imprint in California

— northern limit of Spanish settlement

● Spanish missions

For both natives and mestizos, the dramatic mountains and lakes of the Andes are inhabited by spirits, both good and evil.

names – extensively in European countries such as France, Italy and Spain – but rarely in northern Europe. Where Roman Catholics have settled in the Americas, saints' names have also been widely adopted for towns, cities and other sites. California has almost 100 places with saints' names and Quebec nearly 400.

Muslim place names often express meanings connected with the spread and defense of Muslim power from the Atlantic to Southeast Asia. We do not find the sacred place name Mecca used, rarely Medina ('city') or Jerusalem in places where Muslims conquered and settled (although there is Kudus in northern Java, from Al-Quds, 'The Holy', which is the Arabic name for Jerusalem). We find names such as Dar esSalaam ('the Household of Peace'), Rabat ('secure hospice'), and the Arabic definite article al- is often encountered in Spanish place names and other words and very frequently in place names in Arabic-speaking lands (e.g. al-Qahira, 'the Victorious,' Cairo, Egypt.) Arabic geographical and astronomical names and terms are numerous.

Beyond religious city and town names, adherents of diverse traditions have also venerated rivers and mountains, the names often reflecting this. Mt Kailas, in southwestern Tibet, is perhaps the ultimate sacred mountain for Hindus and Buddhists; Nanda Devi, 'Mountain of Bliss', in India near Nepal, is also important. In Japan Fuji-san is regarded as sacred. In ancient Europe and the Middle East sacred mountains included Olympus and Parnassus, as well as Mt Athos of Greek Orthodox

monastic tradition, while Biblical events were often associated with mountains (Mt Zion in Jerusalem, Mt Sinai where Moses received the divine commandments) In Latin America, especially the Andes, most mountains are regarded as the domain of the spirits.

Although not as numerous as sacred mountains, sacred rivers are prominent in some regions, particularly South Asia. The Ganges, originating in the western Himalayas, is the holiest river in India and passes by many sacred sites (e.g. Varanasi) on its way to the sea. Other holy rivers in South Asia include the Brahmaputra, sacred to Buddhists and Hindus, and the Yamuna, sometimes called the 'Southern Ganges'. The appeasing of river and lake deities occurred in prehistoric Europe, sub-Saharan Africa and South America, while for the Ancient Egyptians the life-giving Nile assumed a sacred nature.

2 | Biblical Place Names in Ohio

Bethesda Biblical place name

1 | Sacred Place Names
▲ sacred mountains
● other sacred natural sites
□ other names of religious derivation

THE WORLD'S RELIGIONS

THE HINDU WORLD

HINDUISM, the dominant faith of India today, remains one of the most difficult religions to define. It does not consist of a core set of doctrines or a single system of behavioural norms. From its origins at the dawn of civilization in the Ganges plain in the first millennium BCE up to the present, Hinduism has changed with the tides of history. Modern Hinduism includes beliefs as diverse as pantheism, monotheism, and even atheism. Its prescriptive injunctions on diet, dress, marriage and liturgical procedure remain bewilderingly diverse, varying not only across regions but through a caste-divided social order. Since the end of the nineteenth century, the study of Hinduism has become inextricably tied to the question of the historical origins of India as a nation. This re-interpretation of beliefs and practices has led to an overly unified understanding of Hinduism, stressing continuity over disjuncture, unity over diversity.

HINDUISM is not a term which ancient Indians would recognize. First coined by Turkic Muslim elites, the term 'Hindu' simply referred to all those who lived on the other side of the Sindhu river. From this perspective, Hindu included the entire gamut of beliefs and practices existing in pre-Islamic India, some of which have subsequently been differentiated, like Buddhism and Jainism. The best way to approach Hinduism is to connect particular beliefs and practices with political and socio-economic developments. Judging from the early 'Hindu' texts themselves, there seems to be no reason to limit the scope of inquiry to spirituality alone; for classical Hinduism has no single term which may be easily translated by the word 'religion'. Instead, Hindu texts organized human life into four 'goals' – rectitude (*dharma*), acquisition (*artha*), pleasure (*kama*) and liberation (*moksa*). The first three of these were understood as worldly pursuits and defined in complementary opposition (and inferiority) to the last, liberation from the world. While it might be tempting to designate the activity associated with the goal of liberation as religion proper, in fact many of the rules associated with the more 'worldly' goals bear strong religious assumptions. In fact, these 'goals of man' are an integration of human life into a single encompassing and only partially divisible hierarchy.

THE HINDU WORLD

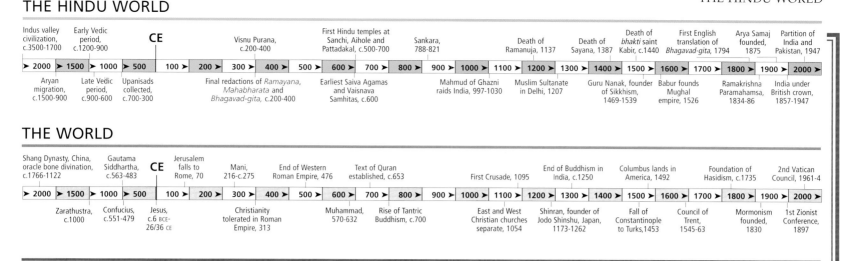

THE HINDU WORLD

Indus valley civilization, c.3500-1700 | Early Vedic period, c.1200-900 | CE | Visnu Purana, c.200-400 | First Hindu temples at Sanchi, Aihole and Pattadakal, c.500-700 | Sankara, 788-821 | Death of Ramanuja, 1137 | Death of Sayana, 1387 | Death of *bhakti* saint Kabir, c.1440 | First English translation of *Bhagavad-gita*, 1794 | Arya Samaj founded, 1875 | Partition of India and Pakistan, 1947

➤ 2000 ➤ 1500 ➤ 1000 ➤ 500 | 100 ➤ 200 ➤ 300 ➤ 400 ➤ 500 ➤ 600 ➤ 700 ➤ 800 ➤ 900 ➤ 1000 ➤ 1100 ➤ 1200 ➤ 1300 ➤ 1400 ➤ 1500 ➤ 1600 ➤ 1700 ➤ 1800 ➤ 1900 ➤ 2000

Aryan migration, c.1500-900 | Late Vedic period, c.900-600 | Upanisads collected, c.700-300 | Final redactions of *Ramayana*, *Mahabharata* and *Bhagavad-gita*, c.200-400 | Earliest Saiva Agamas and Vaisnava Samhitas, c.600 | Mahmud of Ghazni raids India, 997-1030 | Muslim Sultanate in Delhi, 1207 | Guru Nanak, founder of Sikkhism, 1469-1539 | Babur founds Mughal empire, 1526 | Ramakrishna Paramahamsa, 1834-86 | India under British crown, 1857-1947

THE WORLD

Shang Dynasty, China, oracle bone divination, c.1766-1122 | Gautama Siddhartha, c.563-483 | CE | Jerusalem falls to Rome, 70 | Mani, 216-c.275 | End of Western Roman Empire, 476 | Text of Quran established, c.653 | First Crusade, 1095 | End of Buddhism in India, c.1250 | Columbus lands in America, 1492 | Foundation of Hasidism, c.1735 | 2nd Vatican Council, 1961-4

➤ 2000 ➤ 1500 ➤ 1000 ➤ 500 | 100 ➤ 200 ➤ 300 ➤ 400 ➤ 500 ➤ 600 ➤ 700 ➤ 800 ➤ 900 ➤ 1000 ➤ 1100 ➤ 1200 ➤ 1300 ➤ 1400 ➤ 1500 ➤ 1600 ➤ 1700 ➤ 1800 ➤ 1900 ➤ 2000

Zarathustra, c.1000 | Confucius, c.551-479 | Jesus, c.6 BCE-26/36 CE | Christianity tolerated in Roman Empire, 313 | Muhammad, 570-632 | Rise of Tantric Buddhism, c.700 | East and West Christian churches separate, 1054 | Shinran, founder of Jodo Shinshu, Japan, 1173-1262 | Fall of Constantinople to Turks, 1453 | Council of Trent, 1545-63 | Mormonism founded, 1830 | 1st Zionist Conference, 1897

The Vedas

Perhaps one of the most useful understandings of Hinduism has been to designate those religious orders who recognize the Vedas, ancient texts composed in Sanskrit between 1500 and 500 BCE, as a supreme scriptural authority. What these various orders have understood as the meaning of the Vedas, however, has differed greatly. In fact, one of the most important themes in the history of Hinduism is the way in which various religious orders have departed from and tried to reconstitute the Vedic tradition from which they arose. The original Vedic religion, centred not around the Veda as a revelatory book, but instead around the institution of the sacrifice, developed into a number of distinct religious orders and philosophical movements which radically and irrevocably transformed Vedism at the same time as they claimed to represent the original meaning of the Vedas. These post-Vedic developments, which begin with the revolution in

religious values in the Indo-Gangetic plains approximately 600 BCE, have broadly been termed as 'Hinduism' by modern scholars. So in a way it would be accurate to say that what unifies Hinduism in this more limited sense is both on the one hand an acknowledgement of the sanctity of the Vedas as revealed scriptures, and on the other a departure from the core doctrines and practices enshrined therein. In an important sense, the Vedas remain an 'empty signifier' in later Indian history.

Later Vedic Traditions

The world of the Vedas was transformed by a number of developments. A movement of religious specialists arose who renounced domestic life in pursuit of new spiritual ideals. Their congregations became arenas of intense philosophical debate. This revolution in values gave rise not only to movements against the Vedic sacrificial religion, like Buddhism and Jainism, but also to new speculations within the fold of Vedic knowledge. The Upanisads, the later texts of the Vedas, were collections of enigmatic mystical reflections on the sacrifice that marked a gradual transformation of the Vedic religion. This movement set the stage for yet more radical reforms of Vedism.

By the third century BCE there was a growing movement which broke with Vedic polytheism and celebrated a particular god above others as the ontological ground of the universe. These theistic movements, drawing on both Vedic and non-Vedic mythology, elevated either the deities Visnu or Siva to this exalted status of lord of the universe, and came to be known as Vaisnavas and Saivas, respectively. Their doctrines were contained in the 'epics' of the *Mahabharata* and *Ramayana*, theocentric histories called *Puranas*, and liturgical manuals known as *Agamas* and *Samhitas*. Saivism and Vaisnavism gradually gained the patronage of Indian kings from the Gupta period (c.320-550 CE), who built elaborate temples in honour of Visnu and Siva.

Medieval and Later Hinduism

Theistic Hinduism was more inclusive than the sacrificial cult, and gave rise to a number of populist movements in medieval India that challenged the dominant socio-religious order. These popular movements also formed a crucial conduit for the exchange of religious ideas between religious communities after the coming of Islam. The responses of the Hindu religious elite to the displacement of Hindu kingship tended to be more conservative, however, as Hinduism witnessed new forms of idealistic philosophy, including a revival of Vedic interpretation and a hardening of the caste system. The colonial era witnessed a further transformation of Hinduism as its philosophies and religious practices were newly assessed by the British ruling elite, who tended to favour the philosophical ideas of Buddhism and the Upanisads over the supposedly 'debased' forms of theistic devotionalism common during their time. Such judgements affected contemporary Indian reformers who created a new history of Hinduism as the ethos or spirit of the Indian nation through its history. The nationalistic moorings of these reforms, apart from their consequences for the practice of everyday Hindu life, have raised yet other questions as to the role of religion in the modern Indian state today.

THE ORIGINS OF EARLY INDIA

THERE HAVE BEEN two major theories as to the origins of Indian civilization, one dominant throughout most of the nineteenth century, and the other, which modified it significantly, since the 1920s. Both were occasioned by two great discoveries; Sir William Jones's revelation in 1786 that Sanskrit and Greek must have derived from a common linguistic heritage, and John Marshall's excavations in the 1920s of the archaeological remains of a vast and complex civilization in the northwest of India. The link between Sanskrit and Greek suggested to scholars that a group of 'Indo-European' speaking peoples migrated from their home in Central Asia southward and westward to Asia and Europe. One branch of these people, who called themselves noble or 'Aryan' and spoke an early form of Sanskrit, arrived in northern India in approximately 1500 BCE, conquering and colonizing the land and its inhabitants. The discovery of a civilization around the Indus valley which was older and more technologically sophisticated than Aryan society posed new questions in Indian history, some of which remain unanswered even today. Most importantly, our understanding of the advent of the Aryans must be re-evalued in the light of our growing knowledge of early Indian society.

The Earliest Indian Civilization

The origins of the Indus civilization date to the fourth millennium BCE, and by about 2800 BCE the Indus valley had emerged as the most advanced region of the subcontinent. The civilization was originally a loose confederation of cities, with agricultural hinterlands, nested around the river system of the Indus and its tributaries (*map 1*). Amongst the most important early Indus cities were Kalibangan, Harappa, and Mohenjo-daro; the latter two seem to have gained dominance in internecine wars and established India's first empire sometime about 2200 BCE. From this time the major settlements show a similar pattern – a large lower city divided into rectangular sectors, dominated by an acropolis which contained substantial assembly halls, public baths and granaries. The common layout of these cities suggests not only the political integration of empire, but an internally stratified society.

Thousands of intricately made steatite seals and clay and bronze figurines have been recovered from Indus sites. Indus artefacts have also been found as far afield as Mesopotamia (*map 2*), indicating trade, probably the export of timber, gold, copper and ivory, with the ancient civilization of Sumer. Mesopotamian sources refer to the Indus civilization as 'Meluhha'. From the Indus side, trade was most likely carried out from Lothal, in modern Gujarat, and other ports now lost to modern knowledge.

The Indus Civilization: Art and Ritual

It is certain that the people of the Indus possessed some religious beliefs – the public baths and assembly halls suggest ritual functions, and many of the figurines and seals depict imagery that may be of a religious nature. One seal, for example, shows a figure seated in yogic posture, which suggests some connection to later ascetic practices or perhaps to the early iconography of Siva. Other artefacts suggest links with later motifs in Indian art. While this connection is certainly more than plausible, at present the lines of descent are broken and

One of over 2000 steatite seals recovered from Harappan sites in northwest India. This seal represents a typical scene of a horned animal standing before a stand, what some scholars have called a 'trough', but more likely an implement connected with some sort of religious or ritual activity. Above the animal are ideograms of the still undeciphered Indus script.

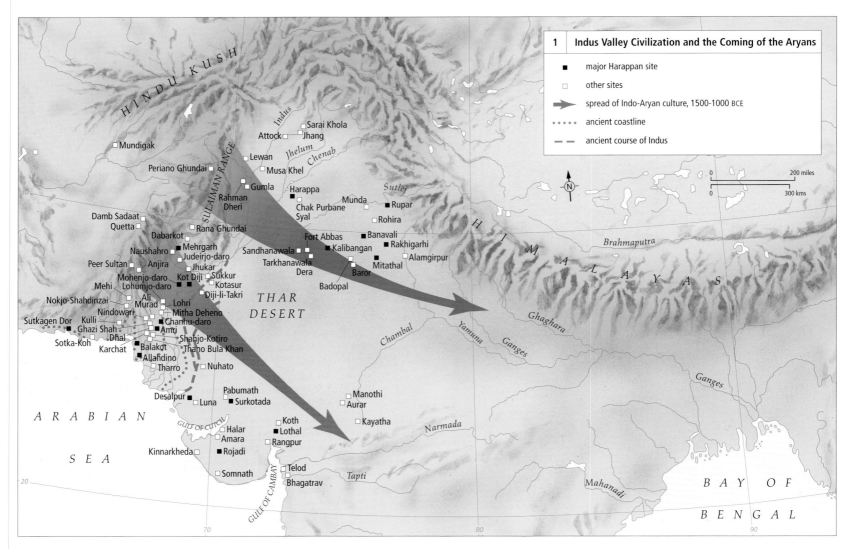

1	Indus Valley Civilization and the Coming of the Aryans
■	major Harappan site
□	other sites
→	spread of Indo-Aryan culture, 1500-1000 BCE
.....	ancient coastline
– –	ancient course of Indus

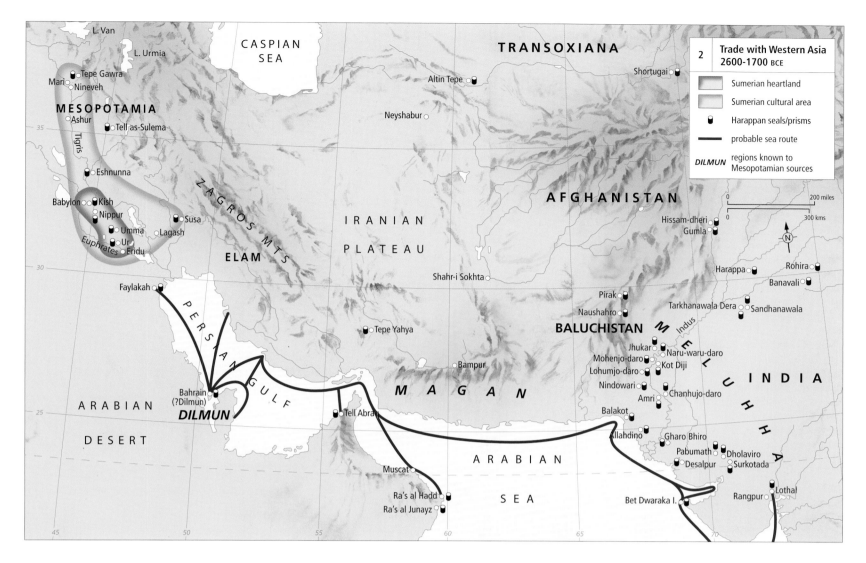

A Brahmin, wearing a sacred thread which indicates his membership in the three upper classes (dvija) eligible for the sacrifice, takes part in a modern performance of a Vedic sacrifice. Visible is the fire (agni), central to the Vedic sacrifice. The more elaborate public sacrifices mentioned in the Vedic texts are performed quite rarely in modern times.

unclear, and we can only speculate as to the meaning and uses of these objects. The key to unlocking these mysteries may lie in a still undeciphered script on the Indus seals. The script has been interpreted variously – as non-phonetic trading symbols, as the earliest representation of the Dravidian family of languages spoken in south India today, and recently in Hindu nationalist circles, as Vedic Sanskrit itself – but no theory has been accepted unanimously by scholars.

The Advent of the Aryans

By 1700 BCE the Indus valley settlements were deserted, and within 200 years northwest India witnessed the fateful arrival of the peoples known as 'Aryans', who brought a new way of life to the subcontinent which is, in some ways, still evident today. The Indus settlements were probably depopulated as a result of climatic alterations that changed the courses of key rivers, disturbing irrigation networks. The technology

and perhaps the culture of the civilization was carried to other regions of India, and may have set the stage for later urban development in the Gangetic plain.

Recent research has suggested that the nomadic Aryans, once thought to be invaders of the Indus region, might be more accurately described as migrants, who arrived from the northwest in a gradual and uneven set of movements which spanned half a millennium. The archaeological evidence for the forcible conquest of the subcontinent by an ethnically homogeneous group is meagre, leading to speculation that the theory of Aryan incursion has been misplaced from the start. It is certain that, by the middle of the first millennium BCE, Aryan culture – not necessarily the migrants themselves – had spread through the Indo-Gangetic plain to cover most of northern, central, and perhaps even southern India. The advent of the Aryans should be seen as the spread of a new way of life rather than the movement of a single group of people.

Early Aryan Beliefs

What were the beliefs of the Aryans? It is difficult to reconstruct their original beliefs since the earliest evidence, the Sanskrit hymns of the Vedas which were brought together around 1000 BCE in a collection called the *Rk Samhita* (or *Rg Veda*), already shows signs of an established Indian context. It is clear, therefore, that the Vedas, the earliest available Sanskrit texts, in fact evolved within the subcontinent and thus represent an amalgamation of two cultures, not the possession of one. The *Rg Veda* portrays a world of many gods, which were propitiated with elaborate public sacrifices. The sacrifices, which evolved into increasingly elaborate rituals, often involved the immolation of an animal (or even human) victim as a food offering to the gods, a practice some scholars have speculated had its origin in the violent agonistic contests of the nomadic Aryan clans.

RELIGIOUS AND SOCIETAL CHANGE IN THE GANGETIC VALLEY

THE FIRST HALF OF the first millennium BCE saw the consolidation of the Vedic way of life in the Indo-Gangetic plain. One of the chief technological developments of this time was the production of iron, at first used mainly for weapons and then increasingly for farming tools. Archaeologists have identified pottery styles associated with this society, the 'Painted Grey-ware' (c.1000-500 BCE) of the Gangetic plain and the related 'Northern Black Polished Ware' (c.500-100 BCE) (*map 1*). The latter, found over a wider geographical area, represented the expanding material networks of early Gangetic culture. The spread of advanced iron-based agriculture provided the food surpluses necessary for the emergence of a class-stratified society, leading to the growth of cities and the development of small polities (*janapadas*) across northern and central India. It is possible that, during this time, Gangetic culture spread beyond its home, perhaps as far as the southern peninsula, where a distinct group of languages called 'Dravidian' still exists today (*map 2*). The first historical sources which emerge from the south, in approximately 200 BCE, show clear evidence of Aryan influence.

Vedic Sacrifice

During this period the rites of Vedic sacrifice grew into an elaborate public cult. The corpus of literature associated with sacrifice was divided into three, and later four, branches, individually and collectively known as the Vedas: the *Rk*, *Yajus*, *Sama* and *Atharva*. The *Rk* and the *Sama* were hymns and melodies sung to the gods during the sacrifice; the *Yajus* consisted of directions for the manual manipulations at the ceremony; and the *Atharva*, somewhat later, was concerned with

This sculptural relief from the Bactro-Gandharan region of modern Pakistan depicts the death (parinirvana) *of the Buddha. According to Buddhist texts, his body was cremated and his remains taken as relics by the kings of India, who built stupas over them. The relics, conceived of as the material body of the Buddha, were honoured* (puja) *with flowers, silks and ornaments by monks and laity alike.*

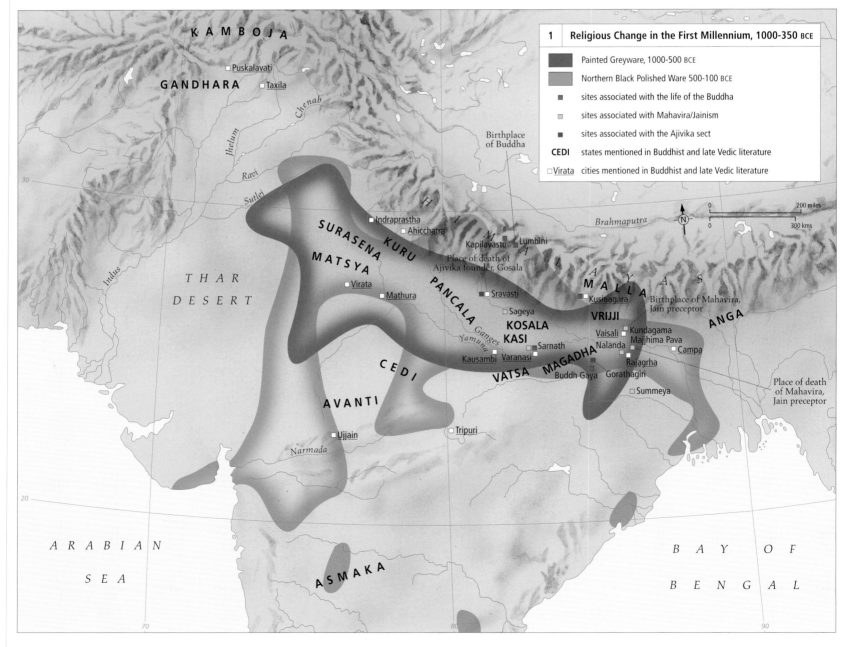

1	Religious Change in the First Millennium, 1000-350 BCE

Painted Greyware, 1000-500 BCE

Northern Black Polished Ware 500-100 BCE

■ sites associated with the life of the Buddha

□ sites associated with Mahavira/Jainism

■ sites associated with the Ajivika sect

CEDI states mentioned in Buddhist and late Vedic literature

□Virata cities mentioned in Buddhist and late Vedic literature

A portable image of Mahavira, the founder of Jainism, dating from the ninth century CE. Though similar to the Buddha in his iconography, Mahavira often appears naked, and one of the orders that evolved from the early Jain monastic order called itself sky-clad (digambara), wearing no clothes. The other major order was known as 'white clad' (svetambara) and allowed women to enter the monastic fold. Today most Svetambaras are in the north and most Digambaras are in the south.

imprecatory and injurious rites. Each Veda in turn contained different types of material: *Samhitas* or 'collections' (sometimes also called *Vedas*); *Brahmanas* and *Aranyaka*s, rules and explanatory texts; and finally *Upanisads*, later and more speculative treatises. The sacrifice was conceived of as a reciprocal exchange between men and the gods. Offerings, vegetal or animal, were burnt in the fire (*agni*) as food for the gods, who in return bestowed prosperity in the form of rain and sons. The gods consumed part of the offering and the remainder was eaten by sacrificer and officiants. The pastoral roots of the sacrifice were evident in the centrality of the cow, which was the preferred sacrificial food for both gods and men.

The Vedic sources speak of four estates or *varnas* (often translated with the Portuguese word 'caste'): the priests (*Brahmins*); the nobility (*Ksatriyas*); agriculturalists and merchants (*Vaisyas*); and the servile classes (*Sudras*). The sacrifice was open only to the three upper *varnas* and power remained concentrated in the hands of the priests and nobility, who together performed the most elaborate sacrifices. One of the most famous of thesewas the *asvamedha*, or 'horse sacrifice', in which a horse was let loose to roam the countryside, followed by the king's retinue who challenged the monarchs of the lands into which it wandered. After a year, the horse was directed back to the sacrificial enclosure where, along with other domestic animals, it was strangled as an assurance of royal prosperity.

Renunciatory Movements

The sacrifice, with its agonistic moorings in the tribal life of the Aryan clans, became increasingly unviable in urbanized society. Instead, a new religious practice emerged, both within the Vedic priesthoods and beyond them. This was renunciation – the abandonment of worldly life for the pursuit of spiritual enlightenment. The sixth to fourth centuries BCE saw the emergence of three great

renunciatory movements, Buddhism, Jainism and Ajivikism, founded by Gautama Siddhartha, Mahavira and Makkhali Gosala respectively.

While the quest for 'enlightenment' seems quintessentially Indian, it had little or no place in the older Vedic religion, and nearly all of the renunciatory movements were critical of the sacrifice. Buddhists and Jains rejected it as violent and destructive. *Upanisadic* philosophy, although rooted in the Vedas, 'internalized' the sacrifice and elevated it to a metaphysical level, implicitly distancing itself from the older ritualism. The new concern was the 'individual self' (*atman*), which formed the point of departure for Jains, Ajivikas and Upanisadic thinkers, who tended to see it as eternal, and the Buddhists, who rejected its existence altogether.

Religious change went hand in hand with other developments in society. The ideology of renunciation presupposed the affluence of possessions, as renouncers were dependent on those who lived the worldly life. The birth of philosophies which centred on the self paralleled the growth of individualized forms of property typical of stratified societies.

The transmigration of souls was an important new doctrine. Each soul was thought to be born again and again in an endless cycle of rebirths, both on earth and in heaven, on the merit of its actions (*karma*). This cycle of rebirth (*samsara*), deemed to be a condition of suffering – 'the human plight', was counterposed to freedom from rebirth known as enlightenment (*moksa* or *nirvana*). This dichotomy, held by the majority of the post-Vedic religions, whether, Buddhist, Hindu or Jain, underpinned the division of religious practices into those which conferred worldly gains (but ultimately only perpetuated rebirth), and those which led to liberation. The sacrifice came to be placed in the former category and was forever altered in the process.

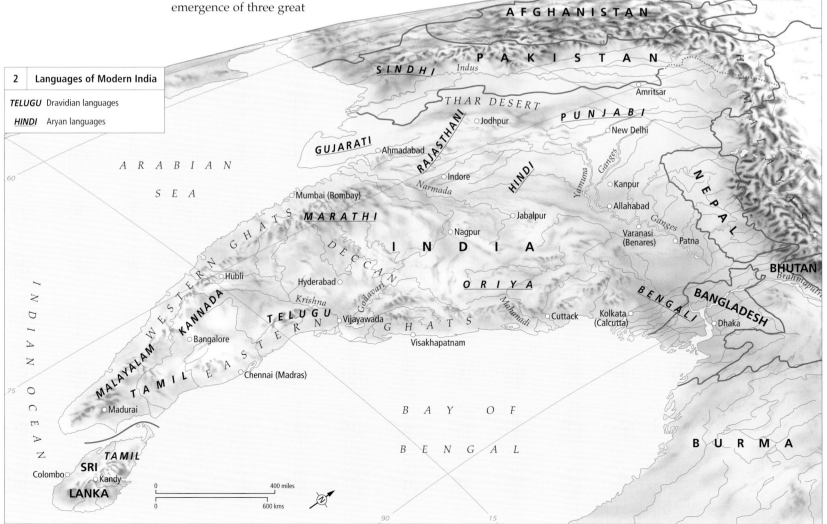

THE TRIUMPH OF BUDDHISM AND THE EMERGENCE OF EMPIRE

BY THE FOURTH CENTURY BCE the kingdom of Magadha, in modern Bihar, emerged as the most powerful polity among the *janapadas* of northern and central India. Shortly after Alexander the Great's incursion into India in 327 BCE, Chandragupta Maurya established himself as king at the Magadhan capital of Pataliputra (modern Patna), initiating India's first historic empire. Under his grandson, Asoka (268–232 BCE), who established his rule over most of the subcontinent, the empire reached its zenith. The extent of Asoka's empire is often charted with reference to inscribed pillars and rock-faces throughout the subcontinent which contain his imperial edicts in a language known as Magadhi (*map 1*). During the Mauryan era, town planning, sanitation,

1	Asokan India, 269-232 BCE
■	Asokan monastery
▢	Asokan inscription
■	Asokan stupa
YONAS	political area

An inscription on this pillar at Vidisa, *near Sanchi, says that it was erected in 113* BCE *by one Heliodorus, an Indo-Greek native of Taxila 'in honour of Vasudeva', an early name of Visnu. Although modelled on the Asokan prototype, this pillar is topped with an image of the Garuda bird, later considered to be the mount of the god Visnu. It represents one of the first archaeological evidences we have of an early form of Vaisnavism in India.*

writing, and monumental architecture appeared all over the subcontinent. Perhaps the most important legacy of the Mauryan empire was its alignment of the entire subcontinent within a single historic trajectory which long outlived the Mauryan state itself, and the Ganges valley culture from which it had developed (*see also* pp. 68-69).

Mauryan Religion

The non-Vedic religious orders flourished under the Mauryans. Chandragupta Maurya is said to have retired to a Jain monastery in southern India at Sravana Belgola. Asoka's edicts described his conversion to Buddhism and his commitment to spreading this faith. They proclaimed that 'no living being should be slaughtered' and 'no festive gatherings should be held' – clearly a prohibition of the Vedic sacrifice. He built Buddhist monasteries and reliquary mounds (*stupas*) throughout the subcontinent, and also gave generously to Jain and Ajivika monks, fulfilling the ethic of giving (*dana*) which is crucial to both of these religions. The non-Vedic religious orders spread to the south as well, and at first were firmly linked with trading activities. During the Mauryan period Buddhism was established in Sri Lanka, while Jain centres in Ujjain and Sravana Belgola formed the springboards for 'missions' to the south (*map 2*). The earliest inscriptions in Tamil, a southern Dravidian language, date to the century after Asoka, and are found in cave-residences around the city of Madurai. They record gifts to either Buddhist, Jain or Ajivika monks who were in contact with centres in the north.

The Vedic Canon

The Buddhist triumph in courtly circles signalled a further decline in the rites of public sacrifice. The response of the Vedic priesthoods was to elevate the Vedic texts to the status of inviolable and authoritative words on the one hand, and to open up their meaning to formal interpretation on the other. The primary method of achieving this had been to create a Vedic canon, called *sruti*, or 'that which was heard', distinguished from another class of explanatory, interpretative writing called *smrti*, meaning 'that which is remembered'. Detached from the sacrifice, the Vedas became the empty signifiers of orthodoxy. The sacrifice was now merely one possible religious ritual which could be derived from the transcendent Vedas.

Simultaneously, the sacrifice was reworked into a domestic cult which centred on the hearth of the upper-caste householder. *Smrti* texts called the *Grhya Sutras* described detailed rituals marking the life-events of the twice-born male. These rituals were far less elaborate than the older public ceremonies and were uniformly vegetarian. These life-cycle rituals, still practised today, are among the last remnants of the Vedic sacrifice in modern Hinduism.

Later *smrti* manuals organized human life into four 'stations' (*asramas*): studenthood; householdership; forest-life; and complete renunciation. Four 'goals' (*purusarthas*) were also identified: pleasure (*kama*); acquisition (*artha*); righteousness (*dharma*); and liberation (*moksa*). These schemes clearly show the influence of renunciatory movements on Vedic religion, although the renunciation of worldly life was not expected of every householder. Some scholars have seen these schemes as an appropriation or containment of renunciation by the Vedic priesthoods rather than an acceptance of it.

A Defensive Orthodoxy

The Vedic priesthoods began to conceive of their own era as one of moral and cosmic decay. Drawing on dice-throws mentioned in Vedic rituals, they held that the world evolved through four eras, or *yugas*, of decreasing moral value: the Winning Age (*krta yuga*); the Age of the Trey (*treta yuga*); the age of the Deuce (*dvapara yuga*); and finally, the Losing Age (*kali yuga*). According to one text, the meaning and injunctions of the eternal Vedas themselves changed through the ages. Asceticism was appropriate for *Krta*, knowledge for the *Treta*, sacrifice for the *Dvapara*, and donation to Brahmins for the dissolute Losing Age. While sacrifice and renunciation are elevated to the status of higher forms of religion, they are simultaneously deferred from the present as being inappropriate for times of moral decay. This rather defensive remaking of the Vedic religion, which may be designated as 'smarta' (from *smrti*), however, would soon be overtaken and supplemented by new religious movements that were to fuse many of the insights of Buddhism with the conservatism of orthodoxy.

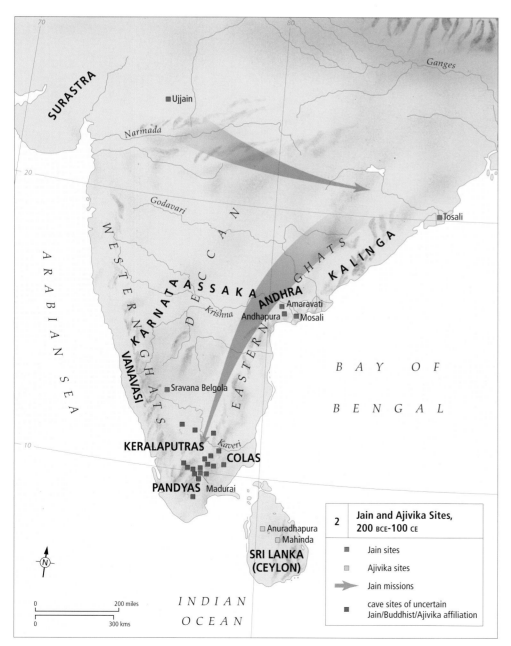

Jain and Ajivika Sites, 200 BCE-100 CE

2
- Jain sites
- Ajivika sites
- Jain missions
- cave sites of uncertain Jain/Buddhist/Ajivika affiliation

This capital from an Asokan pillar depicts four royal lions facing in each of the cardinal directions. Balanced on their heads would originally be the wheel, associated with the Buddhist idea of universal kingship. The pillar, upon which the capital sat, included edicts of the king and its placement near a Buddhist stupa at Sarnath underscores king Asoka's commitment to that religion.

CITY LIFE AND THE NEW RELIGIOUS ORDERS 100 BCE TO 350 CE

T HE MAURYAN EMPIRE left a network of widely spread pockets of civilization throughout the subcontinent which shared a more or less uniform material and religious culture. These cultural areas continued to grow, despite the disintegration of the Mauryan state after Asoka's death. In the second century BCE the northwest of India was repeatedly invaded, first by Greeks from Bactria and Parthia, and then by nomadic peoples who had been displaced from their homes in Central Asia. First among these were the Sakas, who settled in western India in the first century BCE. They were followed by a more powerful clan known as the Kusanas, who established themselves in Purusapura,

near modern Peshawar, and gradually extended their rule inland over most of northern India in the first century CE. The Deccan region was dominated by the Satavahanas, who ruled from Paithan, and the far south saw the emergence of three smaller dynasties – the Colas, Ceras and Pandyas (map 1).

Trade and Exports

Western and southern India enjoyed a vigorous sea-trade with the Roman Mediterranean, while the northwest linked up with overland routes between China and the West (map 2). Exports included turquoise, diamonds, indigo and tortoiseshell, which brought in return copper,

A relief from the south Indian stupa of Amaravati (first century BCE) depicting veneration of the bodhi tree and the seat of enlightenment (vajrasana) at Buddh Gaya. On a footstool beneath the seat appear a pair of feet, marked with spoked wheels, a sign of the Buddha. Above the seat are three umbrellas, a sign of eminence, and silk strips decorate the Bodhi tree.

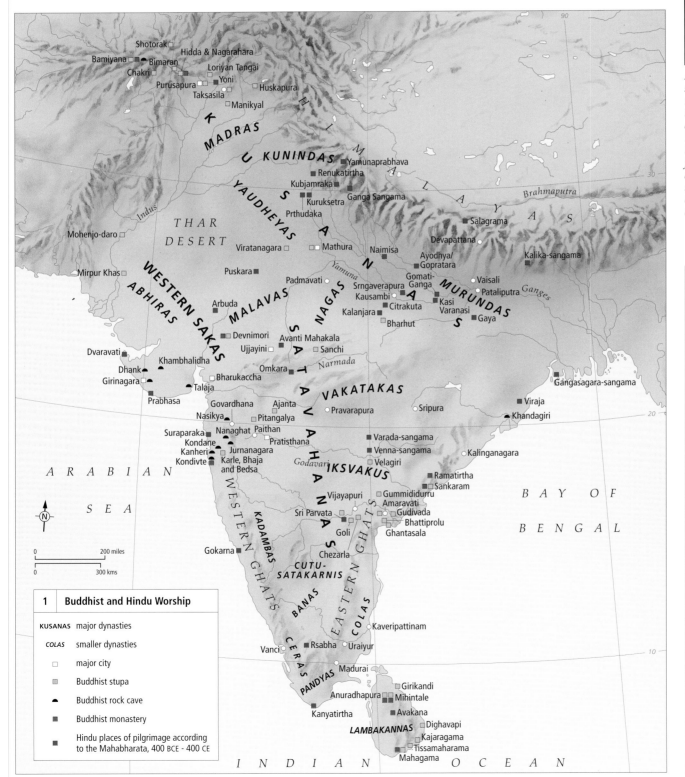

1	Buddhist and Hindu Worship
KUSANAS	major dynasties
COLAS	smaller dynasties
▫	major city
▪	Buddhist stupa
◣	Buddhist rock cave
■	Buddhist monastery
◉	Hindu places of pilgrimage according to the Mahabharata, 400 BCE - 400 CE

2	Eurasian Trade Routes
—	land trade routes
—	sea trade routes
◉	Roman coin hoards

gold and slaves from the West and silk from China. Exotic commodities played important social roles in Indian society. Silk, for example, was used extensively in Buddhist stupa-ritual. The inflow of commodities also accelerated urbanization, which reached its high-water mark. A class of urban elite, their wealth accumulated from agriculture and domestic and foreign trade, led lavish courtly lifestyles where they 'refined' themselves through the new aesthetic genres of drama (*natya*) and ornate poetry (*kavya*). The dynasties of the far south, which also enjoyed trade with the Mediterranean (as evidenced by the discovery of Roman coin hoards) saw the emergence of a vibrant poetic tradition in Tamil.

Religious Development

The major dynasties of the period held eclectic beliefs, but, judging from the remaining monuments, Buddhism remained the central public religion. Stupas, rock-cut reliquaries and monasteries appeared throughout the subcontinent (*map 1*). Buddhist institutions, like the Satavahana-sponsored cave-monasteries near modern Bombay, appeared increasingly along coastal and inland trade routes. Stupas, which housed the relics of the Buddha, were considered sites of the Buddha's ongoing corporeal presence in the world and were honoured (*puja*) with flowers, dance, song and precious substances. A new, ecumenical movement, arose in Buddhist circles which called itself 'the Great Way' (*mahayana*).

A noticeable change in both the political and religious spheres was the increasing use of classical Sanskrit. The language of the anti-Vedic religions as well as of the Mauryan court had been Pali or Prakrit. New forms of Buddhism, especially Mahayana, used Sanskrit, and the Sakas and Kusanas adopted Sanskrit at their courts. The first courtly poem in Sanskrit, a biography of the Buddha, the *Buddhacartia*, was composed in Kusana domains and the first Sanskrit inscription was issued in 150 CE by a Saka king in western India.

Saivas and Vaisnavas

Other religious changes were afoot. While ascetic figures like Buddha and Mahavira had represented a revolution in values in eastern India, western India had seen a different, but no less influential, transformation. New religious movements, arising within and beyond the reforming Vedic priesthoods, had placed a single god above all others as divine lord of the cosmos. These new movements, which can be designated collectively as 'theist', spread rapidly throughout the subcontinent, and were dominated by two orders – Pasupatas, the ascetics who held that Pasupati, a form of Siva, was the lord of all things, and those that held that Bhagavata, or Visnu, was the sovereign of the cosmos. These orders were later to evolve into various branches followed by large contingents of supporters. They were known collectively as Saivas (followers of Siva) and Vaisnavas (followers of Visnu).

While Visnu and Siva had been members of the Vedic pantheon, they hardly possessed the powerful profiles in the Vedic religion that they were later accorded by theists. Compared to the distant Vedic gods, fed in an almost contractual manner through the sacrifice, Siva and Visnu had more immanent and dynamic roles to play in the lives of men. Accounts of the dramatic intervention of Visnu in the political history of the subcontinent are recounted in the Vaisnava epics of the *Mahabharata* and *Ramayana*. Pilgrimage to places where Siva or Visnu crossed down into this world (*tirthas; map 1*) emerged as an important new religious practice and underscores the transformed relation between gods and men in the theist movement. In fact, Siva and Visnu came to be revered in ways much closer to the the propitiation of the Buddha as a corporeal entity than the older sacrificial 'feeding'. It could even be argued that despite their nominal assent to Vedic authority, Vaisnavas and Saivas were often in unacknowledged dialogue with Buddhism.

Inset against the symbol of the phallus (linga) *the god Siva stands atop a demon-like figure associated with ignorance. Dating from the first century* BCE, *this is the earliest representation of the god available to us and anticipates later iconography, of both the* linga *and free-standing forms of Siva found in temples throughout medieval India.*

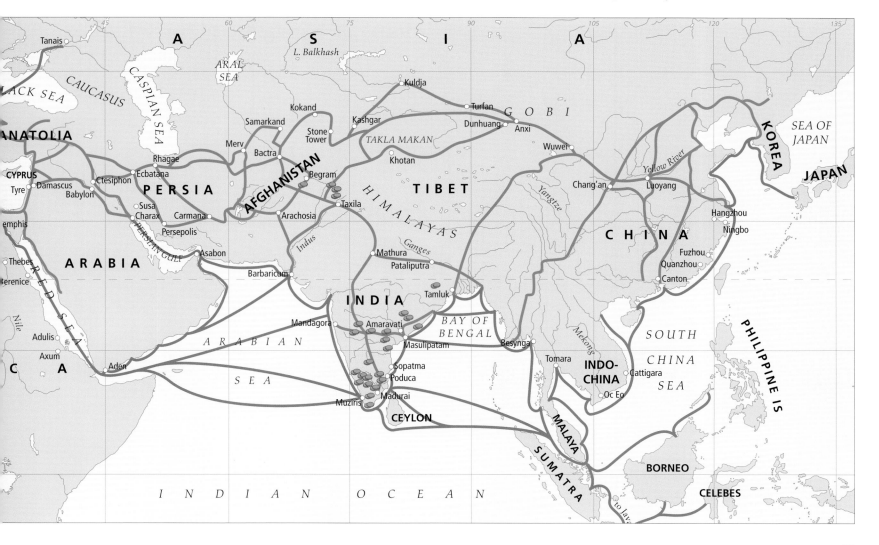

GUPTA INDIA

THE GUPTA PERIOD (c.320-550 CE) has been hailed by many as India's 'classical' age, when literature, art and polity attained a balanced perfection. The Guptas arose from obscurity in the fourth century CE and through military conquests and marriage alliances with the Vakatakas of the Deccan gradually extended their influence over much of north and central India. The most powerful Gupta sovereigns were Chandragupta (320-335) and his son Samudragupta (335-375). The latter performed a famous 'conquest of the quarters' immortalized in a eulogy inscribed onto an Asokan pillar inscription found at Allahabad. The juxtaposition of these two inscriptions, separated by over 500 years, conveys the sense of history and ambition of the Gupta emperors. While the extent of their empire is often exaggerated, there is little denying the importance of their rhetoric for the development of the Indian polity.

Gupta Religion

Religiously, the Guptas were eclectic. They made gifts to the stupa at Sarnath and may have founded the famous Buddhist university at Nalanda. They also patronized Jain institutions at Mathura and Udayagiri (*map 1*). They also, however, consistently identified themselves, in both sculptural motifs and in their courtly eulogies, with Vaisnavism, and theistic cults made tremendous progress during Gupta times. Gupta kings were well known for their patronage of literature and art, and the classical Gupta age of Indian culture nurtured famous poets like Kalidasa, author of a number of Sanskrit dramas and poems.

From Gupta times, the reforming Vedic priesthoods, whether *Smartas* (exegetes of the reformed sacrificial cult) or theists, tended to associate together as 'brahmin communities', known as *agraharams* or

A copper-plate inscription (tamrasasana) recording the donation of land to a community of Smarta brahmin liturgical specialists known as a caturvedimangalam. Such 'gifts', which entailed the redirection of revenues enjoyed by the king to the donors, have been found in staggering numbers throughout the subcontinent. Because they contain genealogical accounts of their donors (usually kings) and details regarding land tenures and social hierarchies, these inscriptions have been valuable sources for the reconstruction of medieval Indian history.

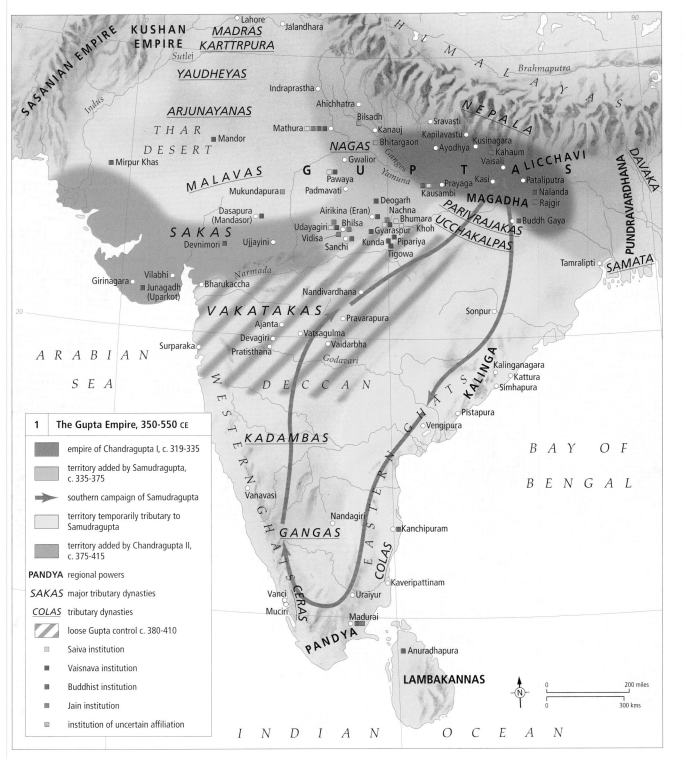

1	The Gupta Empire, 350-550 CE
▬	empire of Chandragupta I, c. 319-335
▬	territory added by Samudragupta, c. 335-375
→	southern campaign of Samudragupta
▬	territory temporarily tributary to Samudragupta
▬	territory added by Chandragupta II, c. 375-415
PANDYA	regional powers
SAKAS	major tributary dynasties
<u>COLAS</u>	tributary dynasties
▨	loose Gupta control c. 380-410
▫	Saiva institution
▪	Vaisnava institution
▪	Buddhist institution
▪	Jain institution
▫	institution of uncertain affiliation

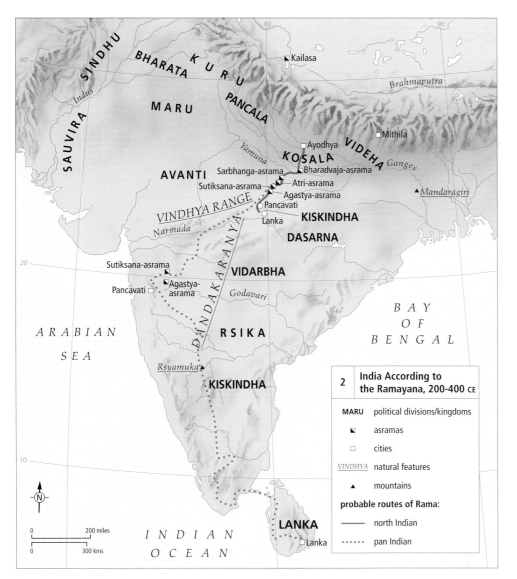

This sculptural relief, in a cave at Udayagiri in modern-day Madhya Pradesh depicts an incarnation (avatara) of the god Visnu, Varaha (or the Boar) rescuing the goddess of the Earth from her submersion under the sea. The garland around his body and the lotus above his head indicate his divine status. This work, along with others in surrounding caves, was no doubt commissioned during the Gupta period (c.400 CE) and together they represent one of our earliest sets of positively identifiable Hindu art.

caturvedimangalams. Here they carried on their religious activities, supported by the donations of kings and lords. These priestly stipends, which redirected the tax revenue of villages, are inscribed on documents called copper-plates, or *tamrasasana (see fig. opposite).*

Myths and Histories

From Gupta times, Saivas and Vaisnavas composed texts called *Puranas*. These theocentric world-histories tell of the creation, geographical parameters and inhabitants of the universe as well as discussing its purpose and evolution. The notion of god in the *Puranas* is 'aspectual' or 'emanationist'. The *Puranas* posit a single cosmic overlord who 'emits' from his own being not only the physical material of the cosmos, but various creative, preservative and destructive agencies in the form of lesser gods who act on his behalf in the cosmos. Important among these were the incarnations, or *avataras*, of Visnu, when Visnu entered the world to save the cosmos from destruction.

The stories of Visnu's most prominent incarnations were recounted in the *Ramayana* and *Mahabharata*. In the *Ramayana*, the young prince Rama is exiled with his wife Sita from his father's kingdom and forced to live in *asramas*, or ascetic hermitages. After Sita is captured and taken to the island of Lanka by the demon Ravana, Rama, with the aid of Hanuman, lord of the monkeys, rescues his wife, rids the world of Ravana and wins back his kingdom. While the *Ramayana* is closer to myth than actual history, its landmarks do have resonances with regions known from historical times and it served as a myth of origin for some later dynasties of the south. Two possible routes for the exploits of Rama are shown on *map 2*, one confined to north India, the other pan-Indian.

In the *Mahabharata*, Visnu as Krsna was the helper of the Pandava brothers in their struggle for succession to the overlordship of Bharata, or India, the subject of the *Mahabharata*. Such actively powerful incarnations were appropriate for Visnu, whose particular role in both Vaisnava and Saiva cosmology was to preserve the universe. Many kings in medieval India believed themselves to be possessed of a small particle of his being.

Vedic Reforms

Theists extended and transformed Vedic religion. The *Bhagavad-gita*, a dialogue in the *Mahabharata* between Arjuna and Krsna about the duties of life from a theist perspective, declares that those who follow the three Vedas without realizing that their author and essence was none other than Visnu himself, would gain merit, but eventually fall back into the world of *samsara*. These remarks were directed against the Smartas, who held that the Vedas were authorless and eternal. Vaisnavas and Saivas, on the other hand, held that the Vedas were identical to, or created by, Visnu or Siva. The antagonism between the theists and Smartas is often incorrectly understood as the tension between popular and elite dimensions of a single religion. It would be more accurate to describe them as two different responses to the eclipse of the Vedic sacrificial religion, one basing itself on a transcendant Veda and a domestic cult which centred on the hearth of the upper-caste householder, and the other elevating a single divine being above both the Veda and the sacrifice.

In the sphere of religion, Gupta India, when compared to the periods that preceded and followed it, appears to have been a time of flux and transition. While Buddhism remained important in urban and courtly circles, alongside it, vying for power, were the reformed Vedic sacrificialists and the theistic cults. Jainism, for its part, declined in its eastern homeland, surviving tenaciously in pockets in western and southern India, where it remains an important minority religion even today.

THE TRIUMPH OF TEMPLE-HINDUISM

EARLY MEDIEVAL India witnessed the emergence of many new kingdoms, richly documented by thousands of stone and copper-plate inscriptions. Despite their increasing regional diversity, they still convey the sense of a common political and religious culture. The political history of this period may be divided into a succession of three imperial formations, each composed of hierarchies of kings struggling for hegemony. The first of these emerged not long after the fall of the Guptas to Huns from Central Asia, and consisted of three major dynasties – the Pushyabhutis of northern India, the Calukyas of the Deccan, and the Pallavas in the south – and lasted for nearly 150 years (c.600-750). A new rivalry emerged in the period from c. 750-950 between the Pratiharas of northwestern India,

the Palas of eastern India and the Rastrakutas of the Deccan (*map 1*). By the close of the tenth century the ancient Cola lineage rose to dominate a 250-year (c.950-1200) struggle for empire that involved the revived Calukya lineages of the Deccan and the less powerful successor states of the Pratiharas in northern India, which would later be known as the Rajputs.

Contacts with Southeast Asia

Throughout this period, political power gradually shifted to the south, particularly with the rise of the Rastrakutas, who were deemed by the Arab traveller Masudi to be the most powerful dynasty in India in his time. Since Gupta times southern and eastern India had maintained contacts, through trade and the emigration of Hindu and

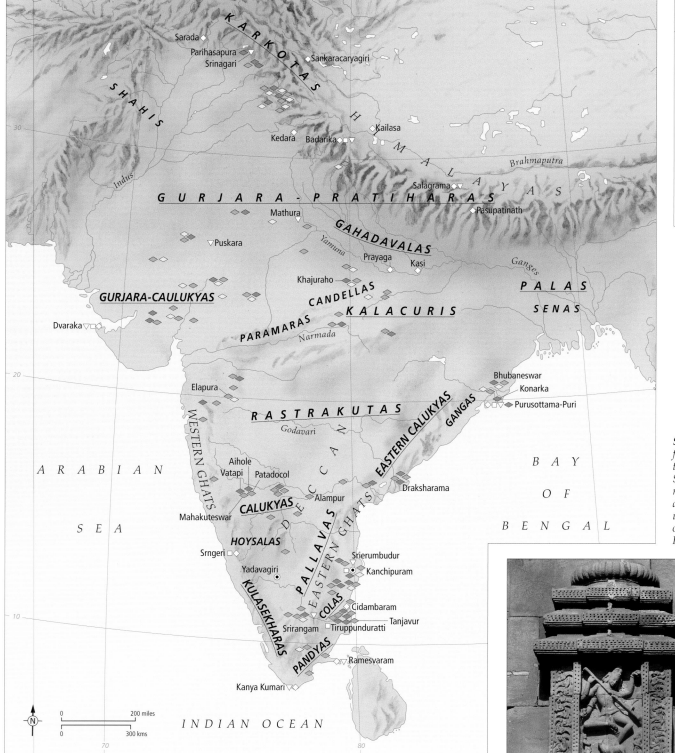

1	**Dynastic Politics and Hindu Temples**
PALAS	major dynasty
SENAS	other dynasty
◇	sites associated with Sankara
□	principal religious centres associated with Sankara
▽	sites associated with Ramanuja
⊙	principal religious centres associated with Ramanuja
◆	selected major Vaisnava temple
◆	selected major Saiva temple
◇	selected major Sakta temple

Sculptures adorned the outer facades of Hindu temples like this one at the Brahmeshwar Siva temple at Bhubaneswar in modern day Orissa. The facade depicts small stylized pavilions, underscoring the importance of ornamental architecture in Hindu public worship.

On festival days, *this image of Siva as 'Lord of the Dance' (nataraja) was carried through the streets surrounding the temple on procession (note the hole at the base of the image for attaching it to a carriage). This image, a bronze from southern India dating to the Cola period, was no doubt the mobile counterpart to the stationary cylindrical aniconic form of Siva, known as a 'linga', housed in most Siva temples of the period.*

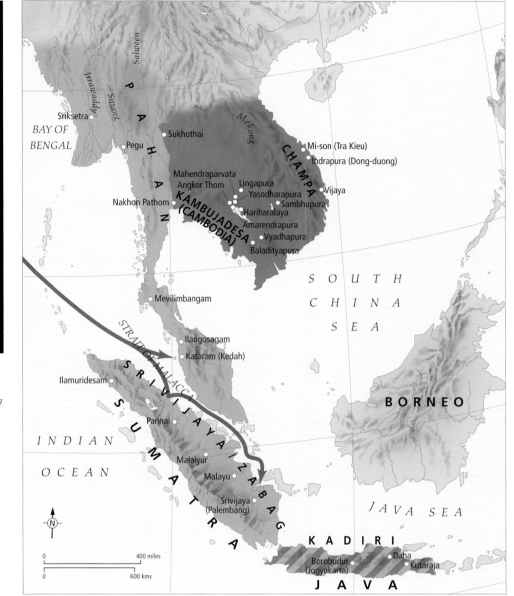

2	The Spread of Indian Culture to SE Asia

- area of Buddhist cultural influence
- area of Hindu cultural influence
- Cola raids, 11th century

Buddhist savants, with the the courts of Southeast Asian kingdoms, where a hybrid religious and courtly culture developed, heavily influenced by Indian traditions. There was regular contact between Buddhist monks in the kingdom of Srivijaya and Buddhist centres in India, especially Nalanda, where a Srivijaya king established a monastery for students of his own realm. The same kingdom established a diplomatic enclave and Buddhist monastery in Nagapattinam in southeast India during Cola times. During disputes between the two dynasties a land grant at the monastery was revoked, and the Colas sent a naval expedition to Srivijaya, but it was resumed after relations had normalized (*map 2*).

Indian Temple-Cults
The post-Vedic orders flourished in early medieval India. The Smarta philosopher Sankara (d. 841) systematized a monistic (*advaita*) philosophy as the essence of the Vedas, and was matched in his endeavour by the famous Vaisnava philosopher Ramanuja, who championed a quasi-dualist (*visistadvaita*) theistic alternative. Of all developments, by far the most important was the triumph of Vaisnavism and Saivism, which dislodged Buddhism from courtly circles and promoted temple-cults which became widespread throughout the subcontinent. These temples were usually dedicated to some form of Visnu or Siva, but from medieval times many temples were devoted exclusively to goddesses, known as Sakta temples. The sacred geography that these temples created, dotting the countryside, remains the defining and distinctive feature of Hinduism even today.

In the sanctum of the temple was a consecrated icon conceived of as a partial embodiment of God. Unlike the mobile altar of the Vedic sacrifice, the temple was a permanent structure, reminiscent of the Buddhist stupa. Ritual manuals known as *Agamas, Tantras* and *Samhitas* outlined the procedures of temple worship. In temple worship known as *puja*, (also with Buddhist parallels), the deity was awakened, dressed, bathed, fed and entertained on a daily basis as if he were a king. Most stationary images, hidden in the sanctums of temples, had mobile counterparts which were taken on processions through the village or city on festival days.

The Political Impact
The relationship between devotee and God was known as *bhakti*, often translated as 'devotion'. Dating back to early texts such as the *Bhagavad-gita*, the word *bhakti*, derived from the root *bhanj*, meaning to share, implied that human action was subsumed into God's agency, thus requiring the surrender of its fruits. This theology had obvious political implications. The religious devotion between lord and devotee obtained equally between king and underlord. In fact, the vocabulary of devotion and submission in temple worship first occurred in early Gupta manuals on statecraft and polity. The Hindu temple, with its subsidiary pavilions and plethora of attendant deities, mirrored the royal court. Not surprisingly, temples became beneficiaries of huge gifts from the court and its functionaries, usually in redirected revenue from agricultural land, making them a powerful presence in the agrarian landscape, where they spread the culture of Bhakti.

ISLAM AND HINDUISM IN SOUTH ASIA

THE ISLAMIC PRESENCE in South Asia can be divided into two broad periods. Although Afghani rulers like Mahmud of Ghazni and Muhammad Ghur raided northwestern India for the gold hoarded in Hindu temples in the eleventh and twelfth centuries, the first Islamic polity was not established in India until the thirteenth century, when Qutb ud-Din Aibak established a Sultanate at Delhi. Muslim influence continued to spread more widely throughout the fourteenth century.

Muhammad bin Tughluq extended Sultanate power to the south, leaving a weak successor state which broke up into five smaller sultanates by the end of the fifteenth century. But the Sultanate's push southward was met by stiff opposition from a Hindu empire centred in Vijayanagara (or 'City of Victory', map 3), which proved to be the greatest of the southern kingdoms, bringing nearly all of the south under its umbrella before its demise in wars against the Deccani sultanates in the sixteenth century.

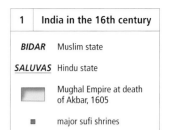

1	India in the 16th century
BIDAR	Muslim state
SALUVAS	Hindu state
	Mughal Empire at death of Akbar, 1605
■	major sufi shrines

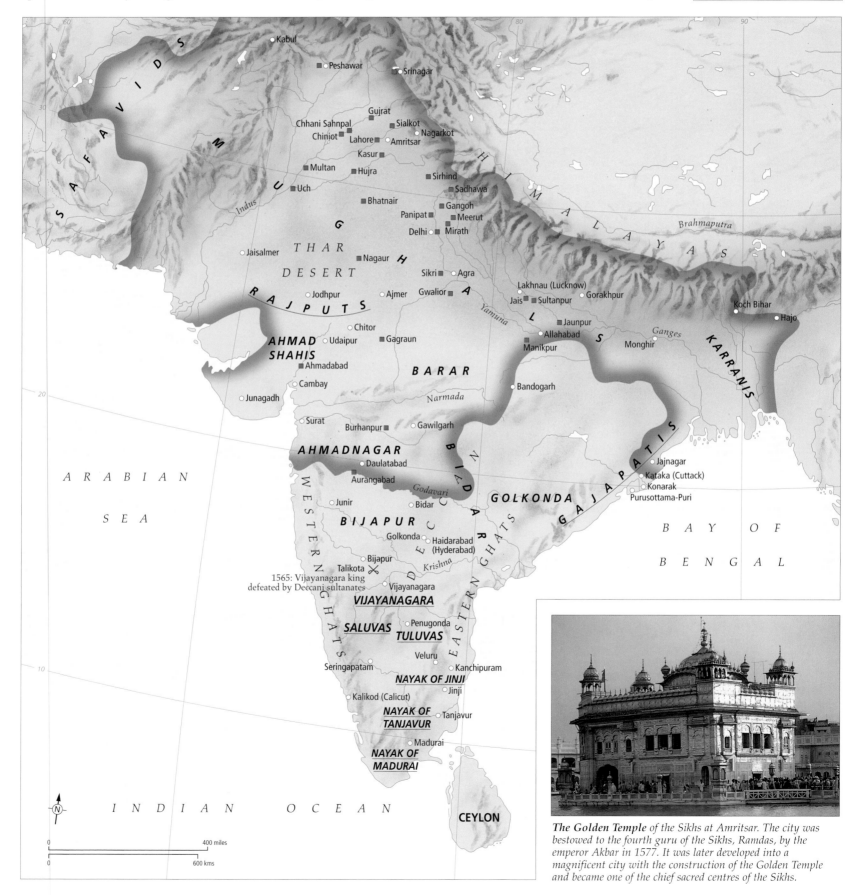

The Golden Temple of the Sikhs at Amritsar. The city was bestowed to the fourth guru of the Sikhs, Ramdas, by the emperor Akbar in 1577. It was later developed into a magnificent city with the construction of the Golden Temple and became one of the chief sacred centres of the Sikhs.

The Rise of the Mughals

By the end of the fifteenth century the power of the Sultanate was considerably weakened, and in 1526 Babur, descendant of the Mongol Timur, defeated Ibrahim Lodi, the last sultan of Delhi, to establish a new Muslim imperium in north India, known as the Mughal empire (*map 1*). The Mughals consolidated their power in a society where many Hindu groups accepted the legitimacy of Muslim rule. They established an empire of complex and shifting alliances (the most famous of which were those sealed through marriage with the Hindu Rajput kings of Rajasthan) that produced one of the most splendid cultural legacies India has ever known. Among the more famous Mughal emperors were Akbar (1542-1605) and Aurangzeb (1658-1707).

The rise of Islamic polities inevitably led to religious change in the subcontinent. In the course of wars, Hindu temples were destroyed and mosques erected in their place, but conversions, though popular among the lower orders who sought escape from the caste system, were not widespread. Muslims constituted one-fifth of the population in the areas of their heaviest concentration and Muslim rulers had to come to terms with the fact that their subjects were largely Hindu. Some Muslim emperors, like Akbar, fused the religions into an imperial cult, while others, like Aurangzeb, honoured their distinctiveness while giving clear but hardly unprecedented favour to Islam.

At one level, the new situation led to a hardening of orthodoxy. The conservative factions of the Muslim religious leadership were a force to be reckoned with for their rulers. Hinduism, meanwhile, saw a hardening of of its own law-codes and a renaissance of Vedic scholarship under the brothers Sayana and Madhava at

Vijayanagara. But there was also both accommodation and mutual influence between the religions. The bridge for such links was Sufism and *bhakti*.

Mystics and Poets

Sufism, or Islamic mysticism, came to prominence in tenth-century Persia. Its search for ecstatic union with God drew suspicion and sometimes persecution from the Muslim orthodoxy, which only furthered Sufi esotericism. India, with its traditions of asceticism, provided a sympathetic atmosphere for Sufis. They formed orders under *pirs*, or teachers, and resided in hospices called *khanqahs*. Sufis provided a crucial conduit for religious exchange at the grassroots level, and were revered by Hindus and Muslims alike.

In north India Muslim rule unwittingly freed *bhakti*, conceived of as an absolute relation between God and devotee, from its earlier function as a theology of feudal relations, allowing its liberating potential to be tapped by new reformers. North India now became the ground for religious change. The *bhakti* tradition developed around particular saints (*sants*) who composed poetry in the languages of the people, and vibrant vernacular traditions developed during this period. The southern Indian, Ramananda (1400-70), preached devotion to Rama in Varanasi. In Rajasthan, Mirabai (1503-73) rejected her mortal husband in favour of a life-long commitment to Krsna. After an epiphany, Caitanya (1486-1533) of Bengal preached absolute devotion to Krsna. The blind poet Surdas (1483-1563), who lived in Agra, was also devoted to Krsna (*map 2*).

New Religious Orders

While Sufism and *bhakti* shared similar ideas, *bhakti* tended to be less esoteric. The Islamic influence on the *bhakti* movement was indirect, as the *sants* used a Hindu vocabulary to express their devotion. But two thinkers stand out as having founded new religious orders which drew equally on both religions. The poet Kabir (1398-1448), born a lowly Muslim weaver, ridiculed orthodoxy and asceticism and argued that Hindu and Muslim beliefs were both inadequate apprehensions of a single God. Guru Nanak (1469-1539), born in rural Punjab, joined a Sufi order but left to travel and preach a devotion to God that was neither Hindu nor Muslim. Both leaders founded new religions expressing the aspirations of the common man against orthodoxy, inevitably in the hands of the elite. They gained large followings amongst farmers and artisans. In time, the followers of Kabir (Kabirpanthis) came to be regarded as a Hindu sect, while the followers of Nanak, the Sikhs, maintained their autonomy, and developed their own orthodoxy, hierarchy and identity.

2	Bhakti Poet-Saints, 13th to 18th centuries
•	Poet-Saints and regions of activity

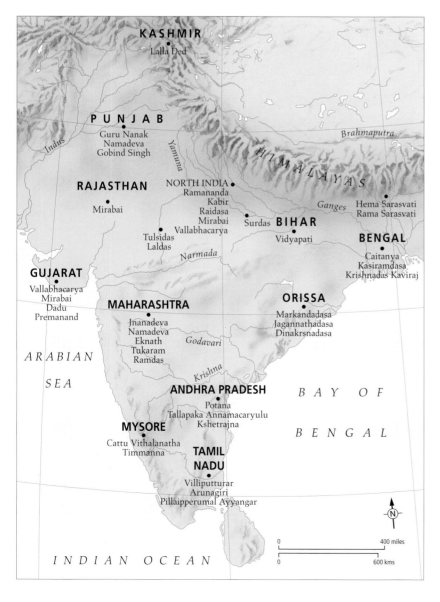

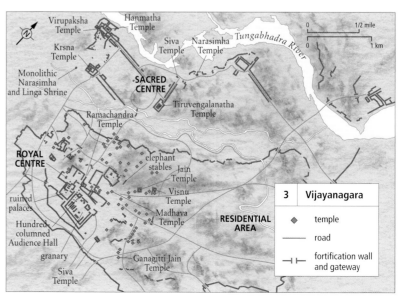

BRITISH INDIA

THOUGH EUROPE had known of India in medieval times, significant contact between the two regions emerged only in the sixteenth century, when the Portuguese established trading enclaves in western ports such as Goa, Diu and Bombay. They were followed in the seventeenth century by the Dutch, French, Danes and English, who set up East India Companies to enable their merchants to profit from the lucrative Asian trade in spices and textiles. At first, the Western presence was limited to the coast, with trading rights obtained from local rulers. But the quest for competitive advantage over both indigenous and rival European interests led to a growing involvement in Indian affairs. The eighteenth century saw the decline of the Mughal empire, and the gradual triumph of British interests over those of other European nations. The British East India Company gradually developed from a trading company, operating from Calcutta, Madras and Bombay, to a revenue-collecting government, with widespread powers. In 1858, the company was dissolved and India was ruled directly by the British Crown until independence in 1947.

The British Orientalists

Portuguese missionaries had established footholds in the coastal trading enclaves in the sixteenth century, but they added little to the tiny Christian community in India

This engraving, depicting the offering of human heads to a Hindu idol, appeared in the Jesuit polymath Athanasius Kircher's encyclopedic work China Illustrata (1667). Despite an implicit condemnation, for Kircher the study of pagan religions was important because the idea of God was thought to be immanent in all ancient religions, albeit in different degrees. Some have argued that this attitude was the beginning of modern ethnography.

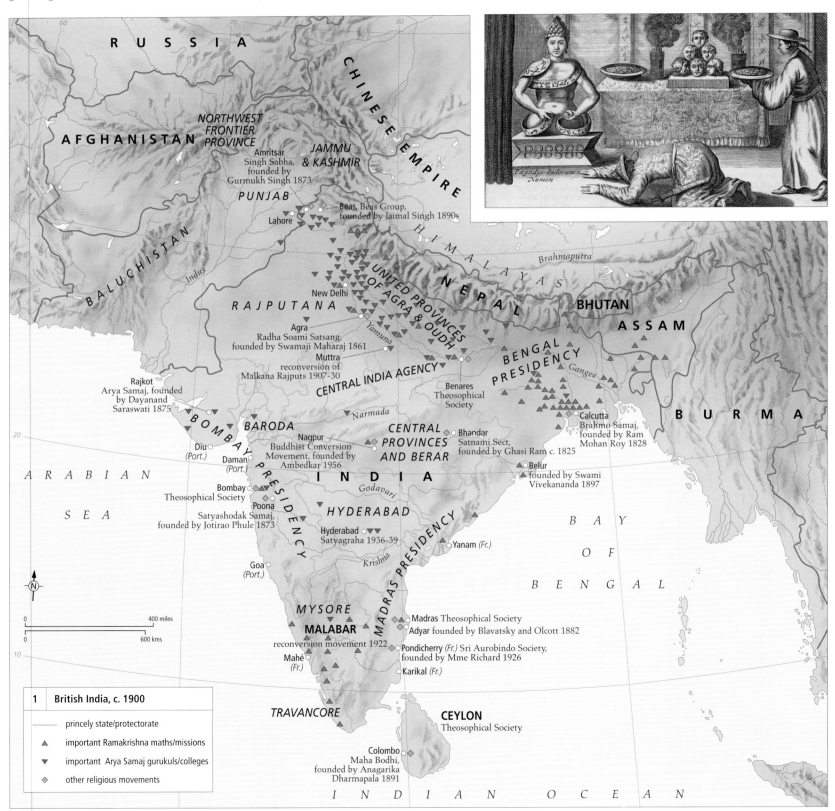

1 British India, c. 1900

— princely state/protectorate

▲ important Ramakrishna maths/missions

▼ important Arya Samaj gurukuls/colleges

◆ other religious movements

which dated from the fourth century. The British, with their mainly economic interests, did not encourage a missionary presence. Their goal became to 'civilize' rather than convert, though civilization often possessed a Christian aura, especially in its criticism of Hinduism.

Nevertheless, the British felt that familiarity with Indian beliefs would help them rule more effectively, a policy that led to the translation of the numerous Sanskrit works, perhaps most notably the *Bhagavad-gita* in 1785. In 1786 William Jones, a Calcutta judge, suggested that Sanskrit and Greek had descended from a single ancestor, initiating one of the most important intellectual pursuits of the nineteenth century – comparative philology. Jones and scholars like him were dubbed Orientalists because of their generally sympathetic attitude to India, which they saw as the repository of great idealistic stirrings. They championed the Upanisads and the monistic philosophy of Sankara (*advaita*) as the epitome and pinnacle of Indian thought. Their perception of the rest of Hinduism, however, was less flattering. The golden age of philosophy had long passed as the detritus of popular, Dravidian and magical beliefs slowly choked the Aryan genius. Their task was to return the pristine knowledge of ancient India to its debased heirs.

The Hindu Response

The British Orientalists met with a mixed response (*map 1*). Ram Mohan Roy (1772-1833) of Bengal shared their revulsion towards superstition and idolatry and campaigned for the abolition of degenerate customs like *sati* (widow immolation). In 1828 Roy founded the Brahmo Samaj, or 'Society of God', which followed a rational and monistically-oriented monotheism. The Theosophical Society, founded abroad by Colonel Olcott and Madame Blavatsky in 1875 (and resettled in India at Adyar), on the other hand, celebrated Indian religion as part of a universal mystic faith. Two critics of the posture of Brahmo Samaj, Ramakrishna Paramahansa (1836-86) and his disciple Vivekananda (1863-1902) of Bengal, sought to regenerate Hindu self-confidence.

Vivekananda acted as spokesman for Hinduism at the Parliament of World Religions at Chicago in 1893, and founded the Ramakrishna Mission in 1897, preaching an ethical Vedanta both in India and abroad (*map 2*).

The Gujarati Dayanand Saraswati (1824-83) founded the Arya Samaj in 1875, championing the Vedas as the root of all human knowledge and civilization. He argued that the Vedas were monotheistic, rational, and even scientific, and were opposed to Puranic polytheism, Vedantic escapism, and caste hierarchy. Dayanand's Hinduism also took on an assertive character, leading to reconversions in India, and missions abroad. The connection between religion and national regeneration was perhaps most clearly exemplified by the life of English-educated Bengali Aurobindo Ghose (1872-1950), whose nationalist political activities led to imprisonment before he escaped to Pondicherry (a French possession) in 1910 where he dedicated his life to meditation. A small circle of students around him developed an ashram in Pondicherry and centres elsewhere.

The Neo-Hindus

Most of these movements, sometimes called 'neo-Hindu', advocated a return to a pristine Hinduism along with a reform of its current condition. They were paralleled by similar trends amongst the Sikhs. Despite their high profile, they attracted small numbers – the Arya Samaj, claiming the largest following, numbered only 500,000 in 1921. Their social bases were generally upper-caste, often with merchant and middle-class followings. Their real importance lay in their connection with the wider realm of society and politics. The Arya Samaj and movements like it reflected a general trend in Indian society in the late nineteenth century, which, following the Orientalists, viewed Hinduism as India's unique cultural heritage and contribution to the world. While this assertion no doubt was forged as a response to the domination of the material and economic worlds of most Indians by the colonial state, its fateful equation of Hindu spirituality with national identity was to have profound consequences.

The goddess Kali dancing on her prostate spouse Siva. An example of a distinctive school of painting which grew up near the Kalighat temple in Calcutta during the nineteenth century. Combining the minimalist style of Western natural history painting with bold and colourful folk motifs to depict religious and secular themes, the Kalighat school flourished until the 1930s.

2	Indian Migrations and Hinduism abroad
■	Arya Samaj
◈	Sri Aurobindo Society
◇	Maha Bodhi Society
◉	Radha Soami Satsang (Agra)
◎	Radha Soami Satsang (Beas)
▲	Ramakrishna centres
◆	Theosophical Society
→	colonial migrations, 19th to early 20th century
➜	post-colonial migrations

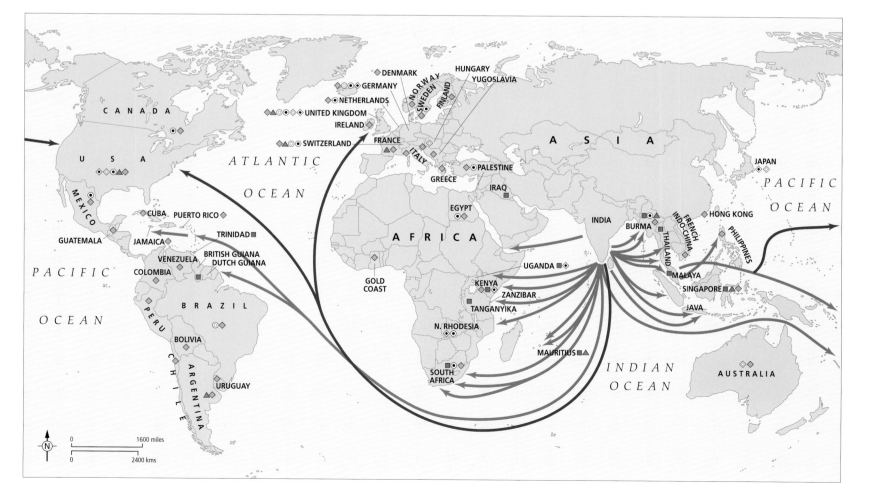

INDEPENDENT INDIA

AT ONE LEVEL, Hinduism has continued as it always was. Saiva, Vaisnava and Sakta, or Mother Goddess, temples all over India still attract millions of devotees, who come to make offerings (*puja*) and gain visions (*darsana*) of their gods. Hindus continue to take vows, celebrate religious festivals, and make pilgrimages to bathing sites and other locales of significance, like the twelve *Jyotirlingas*, the places where Siva's aniconic form, the *linga*, is said to have appeared (*map 1*). However, some doctrines have gained a much higher profile over the last century. Sankara's philosophical monism (*advaita vedanta*), for example, has come to be seen as the philosophical 'essence' of Hinduism, and its ashrams, founded by Sankaracharya, enjoy tremendous prestige. Since the early twentieth century, India has also produced a number of religious movements which have gained adherents from the West. Some of these, such as the Hare Krishnas, who follow the Bengali Vaisnava saint Caitanya, are orthodox. Others, like the teachings of Rajneesh, who blended various types of mystical and tantric teachings, are syncretic. Many of these spiritual leaders have set up ashrams, or communes, where Europeans and Indians alike have taken refuge from the bustle of the modern world. India continues to attract a steady stream of Western 'seekers' who arrive in India hoping to find themselves.

A New Cultural Identity

Saivas, Vaisnavas and Saktas did not see themselves as sects of a single overarching religion called Hinduism in pre-Islamic India, but as competing doctrines. This situation gradually changed. With the establishment of Islamic polities, the major theistic orders lost the key structures of state patronage which had sustained them as public cults and ruling ideologies. This situation was transformed further under the Raj. The British understood the Persian usage of 'Hindu' as a specifically religious term. Eventually, Saivas, Vaisnavas, Saktas and Smartas all came to be perceived as 'sects' of a single religion. 'Hinduism' was then projected back onto the ancient past as India's unifying cultural identity.

While this view may have been inaccurate historically, when it was taken up by key spokesmen and reformers it had extremely important effects. Firstly, it united a growing English-educated upper-caste, middle-class together under a single religious aegis. Secondly, it associated Hinduism with the Indian 'nation'. Thirdly, it posed Islam as an alien faith and medieval India as a dark period of national history. At first, these spokesmen

and the middle-classes to which they addressed themselves constituted a tiny minority, but they formed the backbone of the nationalist movement, and it is their vision which, more than any other, shaped the politics of independent India.

They were not without opposition. Low-caste movements in Tamil Nadu and Maharashtra opposed and even rejected Hinduism, which they claimed had always worked in the interests of the upper castes and persecuted the lower. In 1927 B. R. Ambedkar, an untouchable, later to become an author of the Indian Constitution, publicly burnt the Laws of Manu, a Brahmanical legal textbook which advocated the pouring of molten lead into the ears of untouchables if they heard the Vedas. He later converted, along with nearly two million untouchables, to Buddhism.

Religious Tensions

Linking Hinduism with national identity further polarized the tensions between Hindus and Muslims. Many Muslim organizations responded by taking up minority or separatist positions, fearing for their fate in an independent India. The separatist line overtook the Muslim League in the 1930s, and was a key factor in the partition of India in 1947. Both before and after independence, violence between Hindus and Muslims, known as communalism, became a permanent feature of Indian life.

Under the leadership of Jawaharlal Nehru, the Indian nationalist movement eventually consolidated a secular consensus. However, Hinduism remained an available political language, whether for Gandhi in his attempts to secure communal harmony, or for those with less secular goals who sought to threaten India's minorities. One such organization was the Hindu Mahasabha, later Rashtriya Swayamsevak Sangh (RSS), founded in 1926, which agitated for a 'Hindu Rashtra'. One of its adherents murdered Gandhi for his vision of communal harmony.

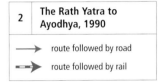

2	The Rath Yatra to Ayodhya, 1990
→	route followed by road
⇒	route followed by rail

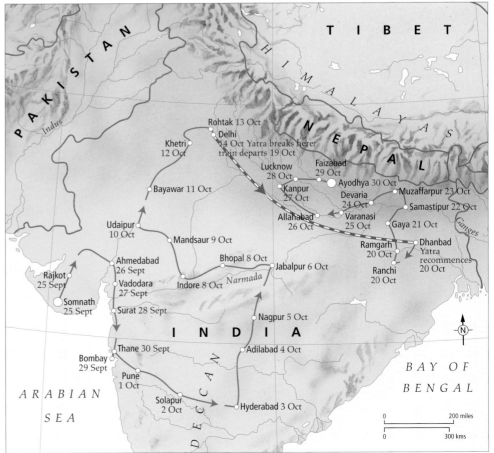

Here devotees perform worship (puja) to Ganesa, offering him lights (arati) and sweets, his favourite food, during Ganesa Chathurti, a popular festival in many Indian cities, especially Bombay. They are worshipping a festival image (utsavamurti) which, after the concluding procession, is immersed in the sea.

More recently, this group, in conjunction with derivative organizations, including the Bharatiya Janta Party (BJP), conducted a campaign for the destruction of a sixteenth-century mosque which they claimed had been built atop a Hindu temple at the site of the God Rama's birthplace in Ayodhya. The BJP led a procession (*Rath Yatra*) from Somnath in Gujarat, where the ruler Mahmud of Ghazni had repeatedly sacked a temple in the twelfth century, to Ayodhya (*map 2*). The agitation culminated in the destruction of the mosque, and rioting which racked the country for several weeks. A BJP government came to power in India in 1998, and ruled until 2004.

A colourful image of Siva, his wife Parvati, and their elephant-headed son, Ganesa. Mass-produced images like these, with their realist style and gaudy colours, form an important part of Hindu domestic worship, and can be seen framed in houses and shops, where they are often honoured with incense and flowers.

1	Modern India

Hindu holy places:

- ⊡ places consecrated to Visnu
- ☐ places consecrated to Siva
- ✛ places consecrated to Sakta, the Mother Goddess
- 〰 sacred bathing sites
- ▲ twelve *Jyotirlingas* of Siva
- △ five *pithas* of Sankara
- ● Gurus, Rishis and Holy Men
- ◆ Jain holy places
- ◆ Sikh holy places

BUDDHISM

BUDDHISM came into being some two thousand five hundred years ago, during a time of great intellectual and religious upheaval in northeastern India. Its founder was Gautama Siddhartha (c.563-483 BCE or later), the son of the ruler of a small principality, who later became known as the Buddha, the Enlightened One. Yet, unlike the founders of other world religions, he did not claim to be the channel of a divine message. Instead, he claimed to have discovered certain universal spiritual facts, and the teachings he based on these became the starting point for one of the great religions of the world. From India, Buddhism spread throughout many areas of East Asia and in this century it has attracted numerous followers in both Europe and the USA.

BY THE fifth century BCE, before the birth of the future Buddha, many intellectuals and spiritual seekers were challenging the supremacy of the Vedic teachings and attempting to find their own answers to the human predicament. Northeastern India was undergoing considerable political and social turmoil through the breakdown of the older clan-based principalities and the introduction of a money economy. Gautama himself was born into an aristocratic family which ruled the small country of the Sakyas in the Himalayan foothills. Later legend describes his father, Shuddhodana, as being a king, but his family were not so much hereditary kings as elected rulers. At his birth, a sage predicted that he would become either a great emperor or an enlightened being.

The Buddha's Enlightenment
At the age of thirty, disillusioned with his life of luxury, Gautama left the palace at Kapilavastu and became a mendicant seeker of truth. After six years of travels and instruction, he went to the banks of the River Nairanjana and plunged himself into intensive meditation. There he gained the profound insight into the nature of human existence that earned him the title of Enlightened One (Buddha). Although he gave token recognition to the traditional gods, the religion he founded does not depend on a personal creator god. Instead, like many other heterodox seekers of his time, the Buddha accepted the concept of reincarnation, the apparently unending cycle of births and deaths experienced by all living beings, as the reason

BUDDHISM

600	500	400	300	200	100	CE	100	200	300	400	500	600	700	800	900	1000	1100	1200	1300	1400	1500	1600	1700	1800	1900	2000

Above the line: Gautama Siddhartha, c.563-483 · 2nd Council, Vaisali, c.373 · King Asoka, 268-32 · Early Mahayana, c.100 · Buddhism in China, c.40 · Xuan-Zang in India, 630-46 · Rise of Tantric Buddhism, c.700 · Mahayana is state religion of Vietnam, 939 · Nalanda destroyed, 1199 · Buddhism to Mongolia, 1300s · First Buddhist studies in Europe, c.1820 · Great Council of Buddhism, Burma, 1956

Below the line: 1st Council, Rajagrha, c.482 · Buddhism in Sri Lanka, c.250 · King Kaniska, 78-102 · 3rd Council, Kashmir, c.100 · Asanga active, c.400 · Buddhism in Tibet, c.640 · Borobudur completed, c.800 · Theravada adopted in Burma, 1057 · End of Buddhism in India, c.1250 · 1st Dalai Lama in Tibet, 1391-1475 · First Buddhist groups in the West, 1890s

THE WORLD

600	500	400	300	200	100	CE	100	200	300	400	500	600	700	800	900	1000	1100	1200	1300	1400	1500	1600	1700	1800	1900	2000

Above the line: Confucius, c.551-479 · Plato, 429-347 · Aristotle, 384-323 · Jerusalem falls to Rome, 70 · Mani, 216-c.275 · End of Western Roman Empire, 476 · Text of Qu'ran established, c.653 · First Crusade, 1095 · Columbus lands in America, 1492 · Council of Trent, 1545-63 · Foundation of Hasidism, c.1735 · 2nd Vatican Council, 1961-4

Below the line: Torah given scriptural status, c.450 · Mencius, c.371-289 · Jesus, c.6-26/36 · Christianity tolerated in Roman Empire, 313 · Muhammad, 570-632 · Christian iconoclasm, 726-842 · East and West Christian churches separate, 1054 · Shinran, founder of Jodo Shinshu, Japan, 1173-1262 · Fall of Constantinople, to Turks,1453 · Amritsar founded, 1577 · Mormonism founded, 1830 · 1st Zionist Conference, 1897

for the world's existence. Through meditation, he saw that overall the lives of beings are characterized by unhappiness and frustration as a result of a misplaced attachment to their self-identity and material possessions. This causes beings to engage in various forms of behaviour and actions that drive rebirth, through the process known as *karma*. The Buddha saw that unless beings radically reorientate their lives, they have no escape from this otherwise endless cycle. Furthermore, he understood that if one were to break the sequence of events involved in *karma* through insight into its dynamics, it would be possible to bring rebirth to an end. This cessation of rebirth is known as *nirvana*, a state characterized by peace and spiritual insight.

The Buddha's Teachings

According to the Buddha this spiritual sickness is permanently curable by following the course of treatment he prescribes. Central

to this are the Four Noble Truths (*arya-chatvari-satya*), which state that life is characterized by all-pervasive unhappiness and frustration, that the source of this misery is attachment and ignorance, that this situation can be overcome, and that the way to do this is to follow the Eightfold Path (*ashta-anga-marga*). This is a set of eight therapeutic elements covering all aspects of social and personal life, and is to be applied simultaneously rather than sequentially: right view and intention, right speech, conduct and livelihood, and right effort, mindfulness and meditation. All Buddhist teachings can be related to these eight aspects of the path, even those that evolved in later centuries.

The other innovative element of the Buddha's teaching was his understanding of the mechanics of existence. The Buddha taught that what we are and what we become is a result of a chain of events known as the twelve links of interdependent arising (*pratitya-samutpada*). According to this, spiritual ignorance sets off a chain reaction which leads to a series of continual rebirths with their concomitant suffering. People are unwilling to accept the fact of change and impermanence (*anitya*) because of their attachment to the temporary happiness they find in their lives and possessions. In particular, they posit an unchanging core to their existence: their self-identity or soul (*atman*). In order to protect this illusory self, people behave in ways that are generally unwholesome (*akushala*) in nature, leading to more suffering despite any apparent short-term benefits.

An understanding of this process determines the moral quality of one's actions: ultimately a person is responsible for their own spiritual fate, whether pleasant or unpleasant. It is this combination of morality and meditational insight that makes Buddhism unique.

The Later Development of Buddhism

The centuries following the Buddha's death saw many developments in India and beyond. Buddhist monks not only transmitted his teachings throughout India, but missionaries were sent to establish thriving Buddhist communities in most Asian countries, from Afghanistan to Japan. They also introduced Indian concepts of art, literature, science and medicine that were to have a profound influence on the local cultures. Large Buddhist monasteries were founded throughout India, China, Tibet and the countries of Southeast Asia, often with royal patronage. At the same time, many foreign monks came from China, Tibet and Indonesia to study in India at the great Buddhist universities such as that at Nalanda. The presence of Buddhist monks in Alexandria around the second century CE is noted by early Christian writers and it is possible that Neo-platonists such as Plotinus were influenced by Buddhist teachings.

The teachings also evolved over time, with the rise of the scholastic Eighteen Schools and the development of the Great Way (Mahayana) around the first century BCE, which emphasized self-sacrifice and compassion. Later there emerged Tantric Buddhism, which made extensive use of complex rituals and iconography.

Although Buddhism continued to flourish in Southeast and East Asia, it was largely destroyed in India and Western Asia by the twelfth century CE at the hands of Muslim invaders and by the revival of Hinduism. In this century, Buddhism has been re-established in parts of India, especially among the 'untouchable' castes, and has also attracted many followers in the USA and Europe.

EARLY BUDDHISM

Marked by the sacred ▶
*Bodhi tree, the site of the
Buddha's Enlightenment near
the River Nairanjana is now the
focal point of the Mahabodhi
Temple in Buddh Gaya.
The original tree itself does
not survive, although the
present one is said to be a
cutting from it.*

AT THE TIME of the Buddha's birth, northern India was dominated by the two large kingdoms of Kosala and Magadha, with a number of small principalities and republican confederacies along the Himalayan foothills. Known as Gautama, he was born c.563 BCE at Lumbini, a small settlement in the Sakyan principality. His father, Shuddhodana, tried to prevent Gautama from entering the religious life, but after a series of chance encounters in his late twenties he became profoundly disillusioned with his situation. Leaving home and family, he took up the life of a mendicant and after six years of fruitless searching, he achieved enlightenment at a place by the River Nairanjana later known as Buddh Gaya. He then went to Sarnath where he gave his first sermon and gained his first followers, thus founding the Buddhist monastic community, the Sangha. Buddhist missionary activities started very soon after: having gathered some sixty disciples the Buddha sent them out across India to spread his message.

The Later Life of the Buddha

Three places were of special importance to the Buddha in his lifetime. One was Rajagrha, the capital of Magadha, ruled by King Bimbisara and later by his son Ajatashatru, both important patrons of the Buddha and his growing community. Many of the Buddha's sermons were delivered on the nearby Vulture's Peak (Gridhrakuta). Most of the Buddha's later life was spent in Sravasti, the capital of Kosala ruled by King Prasenajit. Because of its prime location on the main trade routes, Sravasti was an ideal location for the spread of his teachings. The Buddha also had great affection for the town of Vaisali, the capital of the Vrjji republican confederacy. Despite his own aristocratic background, the Buddha esteemed such republics and modelled the Sangha on similar democratic lines. When he was eighty, he began his final journey, travelling north from Rajagrha. After passing through Vaisali, he dined at the house of Cunda in Papa. Falling ill, he eventually reached Kusinagara where he passed away into *nirvana*. He was cremated here and his ashes were divided into eight portions, which were given to the main kingdoms of northern India.

The First Buddhist Councils

Soon after the Buddha's death, the first council was held in Rajagrha (c.482 BCE) to compile and authenticate the oral teachings given to his followers. In the following decades, the Sangha grew in importance, attracting many lay supporters from all walks of life. The places connected with the Buddha's life became thriving monastic and pilgrimage centres, often with royal support. By this time, the kingdom of Magadha had become a large empire that incorporated all the surrounding kingdoms. One

*As a unique experiment to
implement Buddhist teachings
throughout his empire, King Asoka
(268-232 BCE) had a large number of
multi-lingual pillars and rock
surfaces carved with his
humanitarian edicts to promote
justice and tolerance. Some have
even been found in northwestern
India bearing inscriptions in Greek
and Aramaic.*

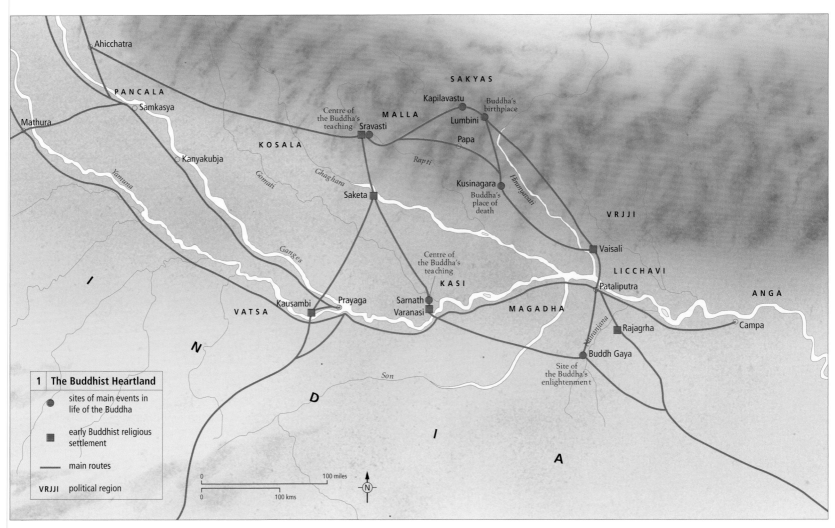

1 **The Buddhist Heartland**

● sites of main events in life of the Buddha

■ early Buddhist religious settlement

— main routes

VRJJI political region

hundred and ten years after the Buddha's death, a second council was held in Vaisali (c.373 BCE), not to deal with doctrinal disputes but to settle some trivial questions that had arisen concerning the Vinaya, the monastic code of conduct. As there was no final agreement over these matters, a split occurred in the Sangha with the minority Sthaviras breaking away from the more liberal Mahasanghikas.

The Early Diffusion of Buddhism

In 327 BCE, the armies of Alexander the Great invaded northwestern India. After Alexander's death, a Hellenistic kingdom was established in the area around Gandhara, Purusapura and Taxila. Buddhist missionaries were soon active in this area, eventually gaining the support of local rulers such as Menander (c.155-130 BCE). Greek influences were strongly felt for several centuries, especially with the introduction into India of religious

statuary depicting the Buddha and events from his life. Taxila became the location of the first great Buddhist university and was the starting point for missionaries journeying into Central Asia.

In the third century BCE, the Mauryan Empire under King Asoka (268-232 BCE), with its capital in Pataliputra, reached its greatest extent at the cost of many lives. King Asoka is said to have been so shocked by the loss of life that he converted to Buddhism, becoming one of its most significant figures. Under his patronage, all the main Buddhist centres were greatly expanded with new monasteries and stupas to enshrine the holy relics. More important was his implementation of Buddhist concepts of social welfare and tolerance, promulgated by the multi-lingual edicts located throughout India on stone pillars and cliff sides. Asoka also sent Buddhist missionaries to Sri Lanka, Bactria, Syria and Alexandria using the many overland and sea trade routes (*see also* pp. 54-55).

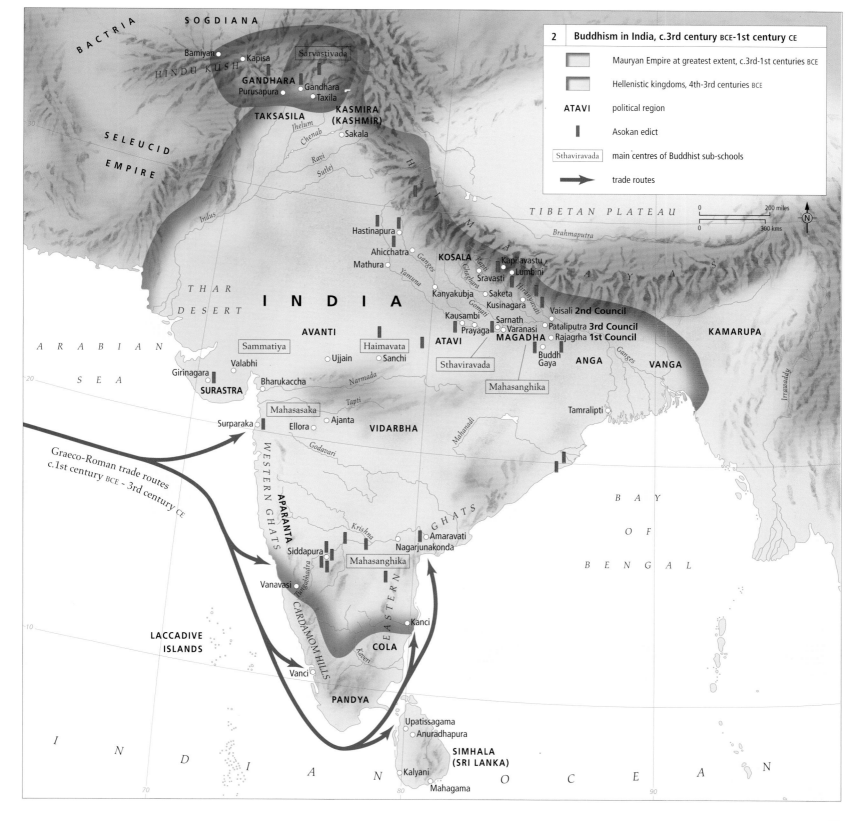

LATER BUDDHISM IN SOUTH ASIA

AFTER ASOKA, Buddhism underwent doctrinal diversification with the emergence of the Eighteen Schools, such as the Sarvastivadins, the Sammatiyas, the Mahishasakas and others in particular areas of India. But although disagreements were fairly passionate, these groups often lived in monastic harmony. After a period of unrest following the fall of the Mauryan Empire, India was invaded by Scythians from Central Asia who, under the rule of King Kaniska (78-102 CE), established the prosperous and peaceful Kusana Empire over most of northern and central India. King Kaniska called Buddhists together in Kashmir for the Fourth Council (c.100 CE) in an attempt to resolve the differences between the Eighteen Schools. He and his successors were also responsible for building many monasteries and monuments, including the great stupa at Sanchi. Southern India was ruled by the Satavahana kings who also supported Buddhism.

Mahayana Buddhism

With the emergence of Mahayana at this time, a revolution occurred in Buddhism. It stressed the importance of compassion and social responsibility through the actions of the *bodhisattva*, a person who dedicates his life to saving others. The spread of literacy enabled the new scriptures associated with Mahayana

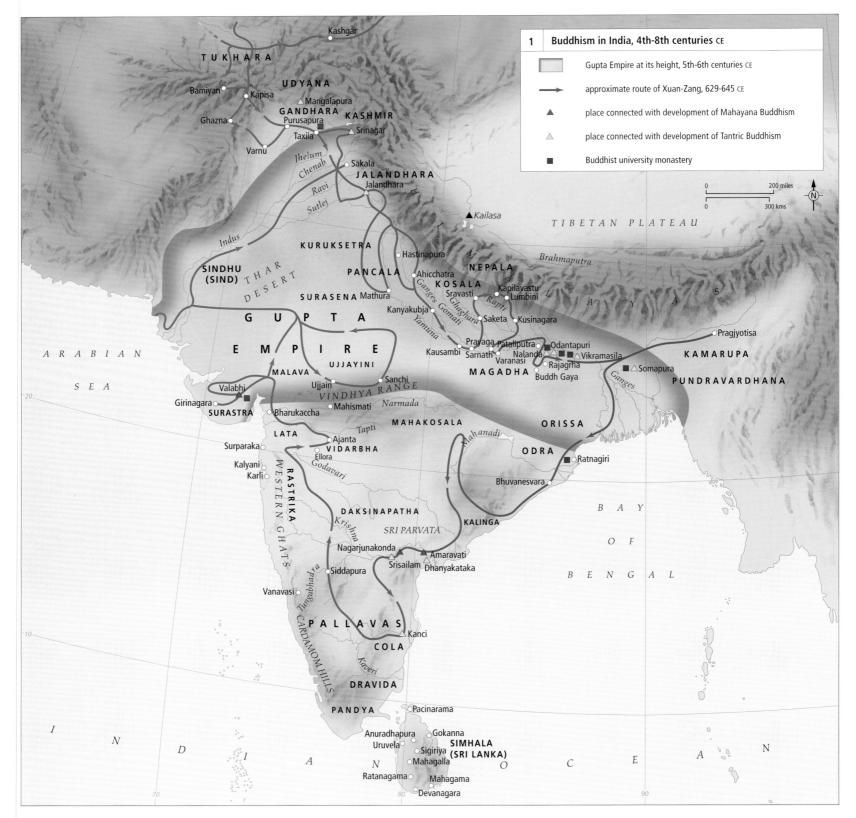

1 | **Buddhism in India, 4th-8th centuries CE**

Gupta Empire at its height, 5th-6th centuries CE

→ approximate route of Xuan-Zang, 629-645 CE

▲ place connected with development of Mahayana Buddhism

△ place connected with development of Tantric Buddhism

■ Buddhist university monastery

So profound was the impact of Nagarjuna's revolutionary teachings that he was later regarded as virtually a second Buddha. He is usually depicted encircled by the sacred serpents, guardians of the hidden texts he discovered and later popularized.

such as the *Lotus Sutra* to reach a wide audience among lay people. Nagarjuna (c. second century CE) was the founder of the Madhyamika school of Mahayana, teaching that all conceptual systems are unreliable mental constructs that lead to contradictory conclusions. His teachings were further systematized by his follower Aryadeva.

The Gupta Empire

With the decline of the Kusana Empire, Chandragupta I (319-335 CE) established the Gupta Empire, based in Orissa and Magadha. This period was a glorious era in Indian history, a time of great cultural, artistic and religious activity, with considerable royal support being given to Buddhism. Great Buddhist universities were established or enlarged at Nalanda, Valabhi, Ratnagiri and Vikramasila, attracting students from all over India and the rest of Asia. Based at Nalanda university, the brothers Asanga and Vasubandhu, dissatisfied with the strictures of Madhyamika, developed the psychologically sophisticated Yogachara school. Many scriptures were produced to provide authority for new teachings, such as those concerning rebirth in the Pure Lands in other universes, guaranteeing enlightenment. Renowned teachers in the late Gupta period include Dignaga and Dharmakirti who perfected the Buddhist system of logic.

Bamiyan in Afghanistan was a thriving *early monastic centre founded during the Hellenistic period. It was famous for its cave dwellings and the giant standing Buddha, a brilliantly painted and gilt figure carved into the cliff face. Contemporary Chinese pilgrims tell us that it was visible from a great distance, though even by the seventh century this area was already in decline. The shrine was destroyed by the Taliban in 2001.*

The Decline of Buddhism in India

The fifth century saw the destruction of Buddhist centres in north west India, such as Taxila, by the Huns who were extremely hostile to Buddhism. Under their onslaught, the Gupta Empire faltered and then fell. Once again centralized government in India disappeared, until the reign of King Harsavardhana (606-47) of the short-lived Pusyabhuti dynasty. His reign was one of great international contact, especially with China when numerous Chinese monks visited India for study. The famous Xuan-Zang spent sixteen years at this time studying Buddhism and travelling around India, leaving us a detailed record of his travels (*see also* pp. 86-87).

During this period, southern India was divided into three kingdoms: the Calukyas in the south west, the Pandyas in the south and the Pallavas in the south east. Dravidinian cultural influences were still strong at this time and though generally not hostile to Buddhism, the patronage given to Buddhism by the rulers of these kingdoms did not match that given in the north.

The final period of Buddhist prosperity began with the founding of the Pala dynasty in 750 CE based in Magadha and Orissa. The universities of Somapura and Odantapuri became particularly associated with Tantric Buddhism. Developed late in Buddhist history, this offered a swift path to enlightenment by using visualization, ritual and sexual yoga. This form of Buddhism was to become prominent in Tibet.

With the erosion of Indian influence in the northwest, Buddhist monks retreated back into central India. But it was the series of devastating Muslim invasions from Afghanistan that ended seventeen centuries of Buddhism in India, culminating in the destruction of the great university of Nalanda in 1199 CE with the burning of its library and the slaughter of all the monks.

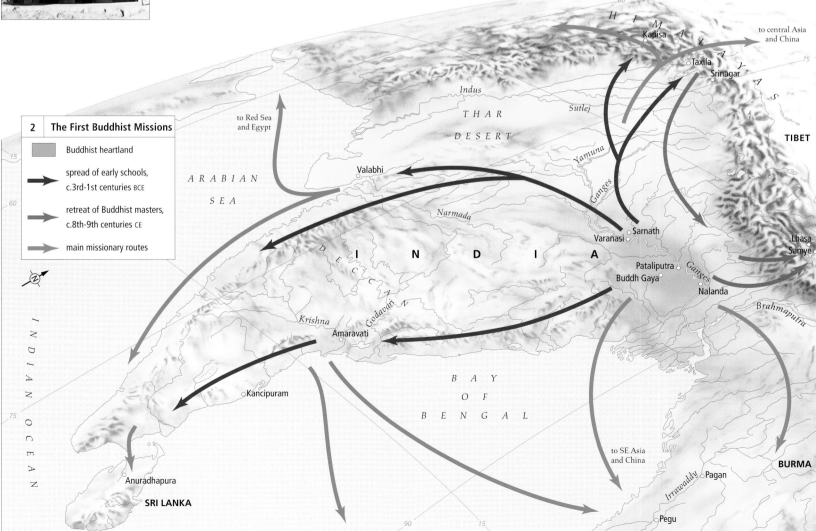

2	The First Buddhist Missions

Buddhist heartland

spread of early schools, c.3rd-1st centuries BCE

retreat of Buddhist masters, c.8th-9th centuries CE

main missionary routes

THE SPREAD OF BUDDHISM INTO SOUTHEAST ASIA

F ROM ITS earliest days Buddhists engaged in missionary activities throughout Asia but great impetus was given to this by Asoka. His son Mahinda is said to have brought (c.250 BCE) monks and scriptures to Sri Lanka, leading to the founding of the influential Mahavihara monastery in the capital Anuradhapura (*map 1*). This was followed by the Abhayagiri monastery that was to become the rival of the Mahavihara monastery. Until this time, the chief form of Buddhism in Sri Lanka was Theravadin, related to the conservative Sthaviras from the time of the Second Council (c.373 BCE).

The arrival of Mahayana in the third century CE attracted the support of monks at the Abhayagiri monastery and the hostility of those at the Mahavihara monastery. The situation was resolved during the reign of King Voharika Tissa, who built a new monastery, the Jetavana, for the Mahayana sympathizers. Buddhism continued to flourish in Sri Lanka thereafter, even being visited by monks from China, such as Fa Xian (412-13; *see also* pp. 86-87). From the seventh to the twelfth centuries there were repeated invasions by the powerful south Indian kingdoms of the Pallavas, the Pandyas and the Colas, who each sacked Anuradhapura, bringing its influence to an end (c.993). Sri Lanka was finally liberated by Vijayabahu (1055-1110), and with the reunification of the country, Mahayana Buddhism was expelled and the Theravadin Mahavihara monastery was granted supremacy in 1160.

The Spread of Buddhism to Burma

Apart from early legendary contacts, Indian culture including Buddhism began to make an impact in Burma during the culturally sophisticated Mon period (the fifth to the tenth centuries) especially at Suddhammavati (Thaton) and at Pegu. The earliest Buddhist images that have been found indicate a strong southern Indian influence. The modern Burmese nation begins with the rise to power of the Myamma people who founded their capital at Pagan (841). During the early Pagan Kingdom, Mahayana and Tantric Buddhism was predominant but Theravada was adopted by King Anuruddha (1044-77) after his conquest of Mon in 1057. Magnificent Burmese temples were constructed in Pagan during this period, which lasted until the city was sacked by the Mongols under Kublai Khan in 1287.

The Spread of Buddhism to Indonesia

The Srivijayan kingdom, established in Sumatra c.600 CE, played an influential role in the region until the end of the thirteenth century, with vassal states in Malaysia, Java and Borneo. Hinayana communities from India are known to have been established in Srivijaya by the seventh century with Mahayana arriving shortly afterwards. Due to strong diplomatic ties with China, it was a regular port of call for Chinese pilgrims, such as Fa Xian, on their way to India. Similarly, the great Indian teacher Atisha, who taught in Tibet, studied in Srivijaya around 1110 CE. The Shailendra kings (750-930) in central

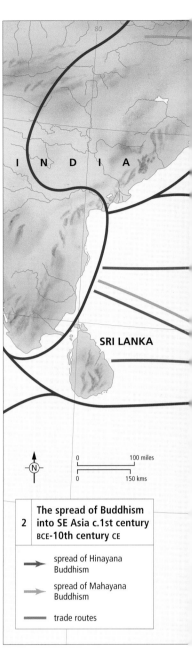

INDIA

SRI LANKA

| 0 | 100 miles |
| 0 | 150 kms |

2 The spread of Buddhism into SE Asia c.1st century BCE-10th century CE

→ spread of Hinayana Buddhism

→ spread of Mahayana Buddhism

── trade routes

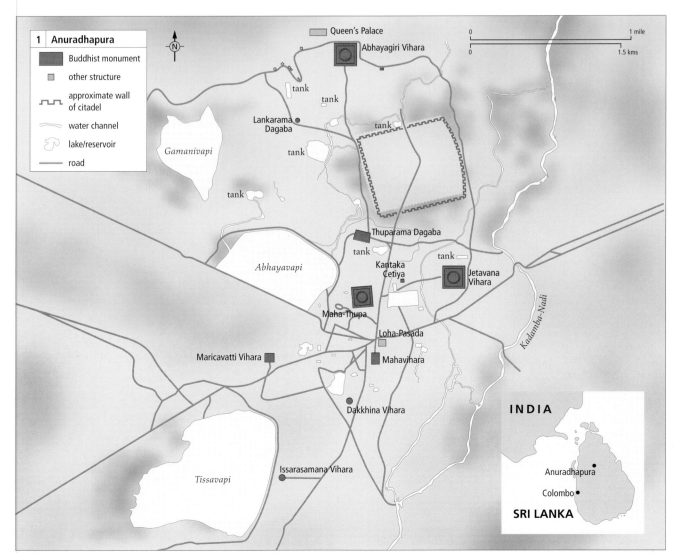

1 **Anuradhapura**

■ Buddhist monument

▪ other structure

⊓⊔ approximate wall of citadel

〜 water channel

☙ lake/reservoir

── road

Queen's Palace

Abhayagiri Vihara

tank

tank

Lankarama Dagaba

Gamanivapi

tank

tank

tank

tank

Thuparama Dagaba

tank

tank

Abhayavapi

Kantaka Cetiya

Jetavana Vihara

Maha-Thupa

Loha-Pasada

Maricavatti Vihara

Mahavihara

Kadamba-Nadi

Dakkhina Vihara

INDIA

Anuradhapura

Colombo

SRI LANKA

Tissavapi

Issarasamana Vihara

0   1 mile

0   1.5 kms

***Colossal statues of the Buddha** are found in many parts of Asia. The early medieval figures at Polonnaruwa (Sri Lanka) at the Gal Vihara depict a reclining Buddha (14m long) with attendant disciples (7m high).*

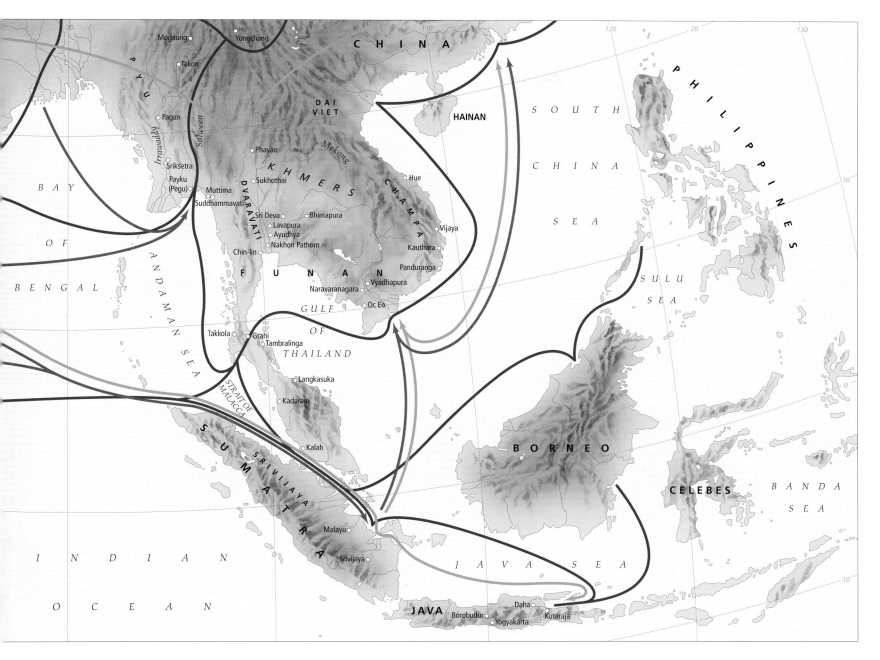

Java were devoted patrons of Mahayana Buddhism and it was c.800 that they sponsored the building of the Mahayana-Tantric temple of Borobudur. Thereafter religious life in Indonesia was strongly syncretic with a blend of Hindu Saivite and Mahayana practices that still survives in some parts of Java and Bali amidst the predominantly Indonesian Muslim cultures of the present.

Buddhism in Vietnam, Cambodia, Thailand and Laos
Buddhist Hinayana missionaries from India had arrived in Champa (southern Vietnam) by the second century CE, but following the activities of Vinitaruci (c.580) Mahayana made gradual headway. The Dai Viet in the north were more strongly influenced by Chinese culture and when they unified the country in 939, Mahayana Buddhism was adopted as the state religion. Later, Vietnamese Buddhism was dominated by an eclectic mixture of forms of Thien (Zen) and Pure Lands practices.

Buddhism came late to Cambodia, Laos and Thailand. Though the Khmers had strong cultural links with both India and China, their rulers favoured various forms of brahmanical and Saivite Hinduism, with Mahayana Buddhism making only a late impression on the culture. After the founding of Angkor, strong support was given to Mahayana by King Jayavarman VII, but thereafter the rulers had a preference for a Saivite and Mahayana syncretic form of religion. Throughout this period, Laos was in turn under Khmer, Thai, Vietnamese and Burmese control. Independence was only achieved in 1350, at which time both Khmer and Sinhalese monks were invited to teach by the king.

Though there was some Buddhist presence when Thailand was under Khmer rule, even the independent kingdom of Sukhothai in the north showed only lukewarm interest in Buddhism. It was not until the founding of the kingdom of Ayutthaya in the south that Buddhism became predominant through the activities of Theravadin Burmese monks around 1350 onwards. Thereafter Buddhism was adopted as the Thai state religion.

The great stupa at Borobudur in Java is a three-dimensional mandala, depicting an idealized realm of the Buddhas with its inhabitants. The lower portions are covered with intricate bas-reliefs illustrating the previous lives of the Buddha Sakyamuni.

BUDDHISM IN CENTRAL ASIA

The Silk Road meandered *across the barren, inhospitable wastes of the Central Asian deserts, linking China with the West and with India and encouraging the growth of the oasis city states.*

THE IMPORTANCE of the so-called Silk Road for cultural exchange between China and India perhaps outweighs its role as a trade route (*map 1*). Throughout the Buddhist period, the multi-cultural oasis city states and kingdoms along the route of the Silk Road were inhabited by many different races. While bringing their own genius into play, they were also influenced by their powerful neighbours: China, India, Tibet and Iran. Buddhist influences were first felt around the time of Asoka via the Hellenistic kingdoms of Bactria and Gandhara. According to legend, he sent missionaries as far as Khotan on the southern branch of the Silk Road. By 100 CE, Buddhism was well established in Afghanistan and Gandhara under the auspices of the strongly Buddhist Kusana empire, as shown by the cave temples and the giant Buddhas at Bamiyan (c.250 CE). After a period of destruction by the Huns in the early fifth century, the Western Turks founded a loosely governed empire (c.550-800) that controlled most of the Silk Road and the oases at its western end. The rulers of this empire were early converts and became staunch patrons of

Buddhism. The society they ruled consisted of many racial groups, but strong artistic influences were felt from India and Iran. However, from the early ninth century, Buddhism began to succumb to Islam in the Afghan region.

Chinese and Other Influences

Meanwhile, the Chinese had extended their influence throughout the Takla Makan region by the late Han dynasty (c.200 CE) to control the nomadic tribes in the area. Early paintings (c.200-300 CE) found at locations such as Miran show distinctly Chinese influences. It was at this time that Dunhuang began to flourish as a frontier town (*map 2*). However, a weak and divided China (fifth to sixth centuries) lost control of this area, allowing the emergence of thriving independent city states in the oases along the Silk Road. Though the Western Turks were powerful at this time, the individual areas of the Silk Road were occupied by a very mixed population. The settlements on the northern branch around Kucha and Turfan were occupied by the

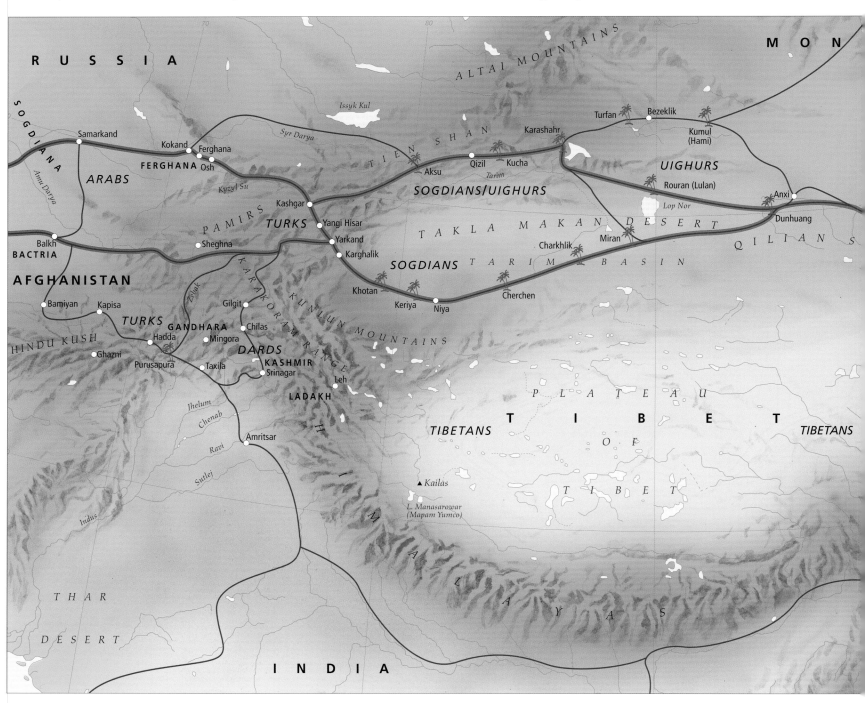

mysterious Indo-European Tokharian people who favoured both Buddhism and Manichaeism, as did many of their neighbours. Another group who lived throughout the region, especially to the west, were the Sogdians, an Iranian people originally from the Samarkand area. The Sogdians were mainly active as merchants and scribes but also as Buddhist missionaries. It was they who introduced the Aramaic-based script which was later used by the Uighurs, Mongols and Manchus. Strongly Mahayana in belief, it was through their efforts that Buddhist practices and literature were spread amongst the Turks and the Uighurs in the region.

Political Change after 700 CE

The eighth and ninth centuries saw much conflict in Central Asia, triggered by the sudden Tibetan rise to regional domination. Not only did the Tibetans humiliate the Chinese by occupying their capital Chang'an in 763, but they also settled in Dunhuang and made it an important Tibetan cultural outpost. At this time, most Central Asian oases were under nominal Tibetan control, as can be seen by the strong Tibetan influence in their artistic achievements. As Tibetan political influence weakened in the east, their place was taken for a while by the Uighurs who had established an empire in eastern Turkestan (755-840). These people were well disposed towards Buddhism, although officially their state religion was Manichaean. The ending of Tibetan control of Dunhuang marks the return to strongly Chinese styles of painting and sculpture in the Caves of the Thousand Buddhas, as well as at Turfan and Bezeklik.

The weakness of the Chinese in the area during the Song period allowed the Tangut people (Xi-xia) to control the Gansu corridor including Dunhuang. They set up a multi-racial Buddhist state (990-1227) which occupied most of the former Uighur lands. They were especially interested in the then new technology of printing, devising a unique script, still not fully understood by scholars, to translate and then print the Buddhist canon. It was during a period of civil unrest in the eleventh century that an enormous cache of Buddhist texts in Tibetan, Chinese, Uighur and other languages was sealed into one cave at Dunhuang, remaining forgotten until rediscovered by the French scholar Paul Pelliot.

Dunhuang flourished as a cosmopolitan frontier town between the sixth and twelfth centuries. The wealth its trade generated was used to excavate the cave temples and decorate them with murals and statues. It was here that the French scholar Paul Pelliot discovered a priceless hoard of ancient Buddhist manuscripts in Tibetan, Chinese and other Central Asian languages.

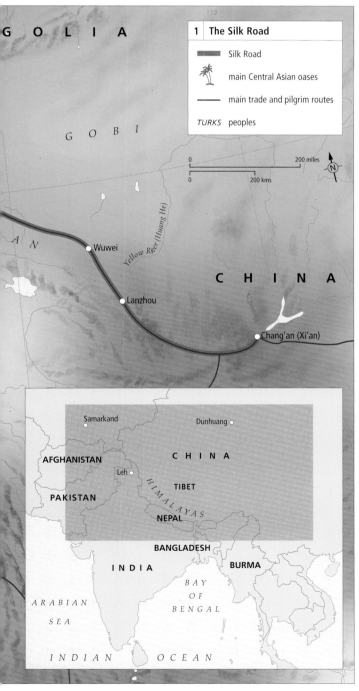

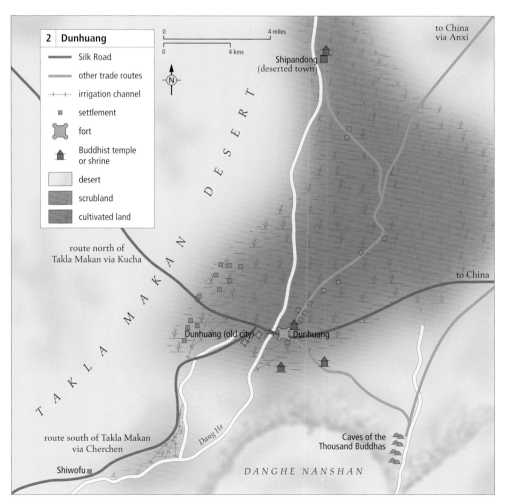

TIBETAN BUDDHISM

THE ORIGINS of the Tibetan state can be traced back to the early, legendary kings who occupied the Yarlung Valley area in Central Tibet, and whose large tumuli graves can be found at Chongye. Contact with India and China under the thirty-third king, Srong-tsen Gam-po (c.569-650), marked the earliest encounters with Buddhism. During his reign a writing system for Tibetan was developed. One of the holiest Buddhist shrines, the Jo-khang in Lhasa, was also built at this time.

The rapid expansion of the Tibetan empire during the reign of Tri-song De-tsen (756-813) generated huge riches which were partly dedicated to the introduction of Buddhism. The first monastery was built at Samye, based on that at Odantapuri in India, under the guidance of the scholar-monk Shantarakshita and the tantric master Padmasambhava, who was invited from India for this purpose. There the first Tibetan monks began the enormous task of translating the Buddhist scriptures. Samye was also the location of the great debate (c.792) between rival representatives of Indian and Chinese Buddhism. At its conclusion, the Indian party was deemed to have won and the Chinese were ordered to leave Tibet. With the assassination of King Ral-pa-chen in 836 CE, his brother Lang Darma reverted to the pre-Buddhist Bon religion and severely persecuted Buddhism. After his death in 842, the Tibetan empire collapsed and for a while the country broke up into a number of small kingdoms. The most important of these

was Guge in the far west, with its capital at Tsaparang, which helped preserve Buddhist learning during the centuries of turmoil that affected Tibet. Famous scholar-monks, such as the great translator Rin-chen Zang-po (958-1055), lived in this area and sponsored visits by outstanding Indian monks such as Atisa who arrived in Tibet in 1042. The Muslim invasion of India with its destruction of all major Buddhist monastic centres began soon after, and many Indian Buddhist monks from Kashmir and northwestern India also took refuge in this area of Tibet.

Religious Renaissance

The decline of Buddhism in northern India coincided with a cultural and religious renaissance in Tibet. Cut off from their Indian mentors, Buddhism in Tibet began to diversify and flourish with the emergence of the four main lineages during the early medieval period. Initially based at Samye and other monasteries in central Tibet, the Nyingmapas traced their descent from the very introduction of Buddhism by Shantarakshita and Padmasambhava but underwent further doctrinal developments during the twelfth and thirteenth centuries. Shortly after the death of Atisa in 1054, his followers established the Kadampa lineage at Ratreng in 1057. Though often overshadowed by his famous disciple Milarepa, the lay yogin Marpa (1012-98) is viewed as the founder of the Kagyupa lineage which flourished in

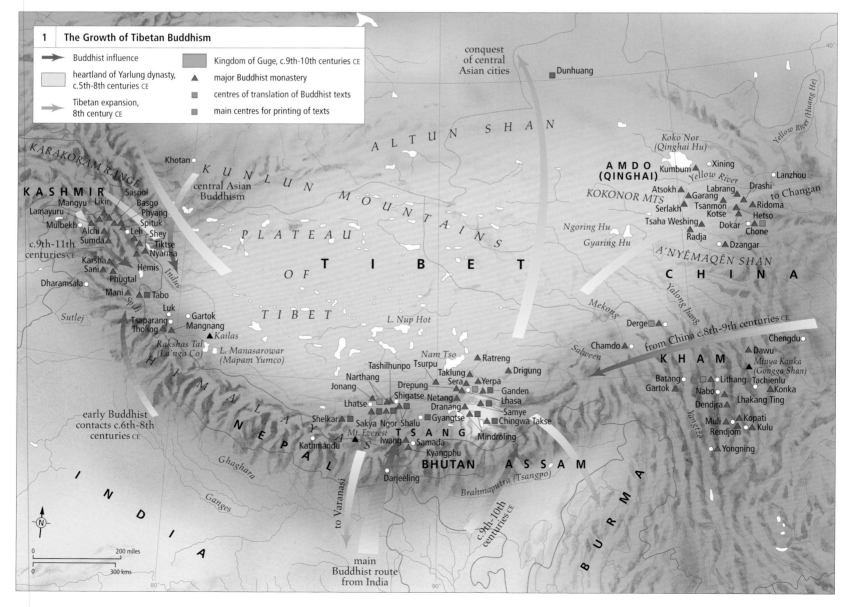

1 | **The Growth of Tibetan Buddhism**

→ Buddhist influence

▢ heartland of Yarlung dynasty, c.5th-8th centuries CE

➜ Tibetan expansion, 8th century CE

▢ Kingdom of Guge, c.9th-10th centuries CE

▲ major Buddhist monastery

▪ centres of translation of Buddhist texts

▪ main centres for printing of texts

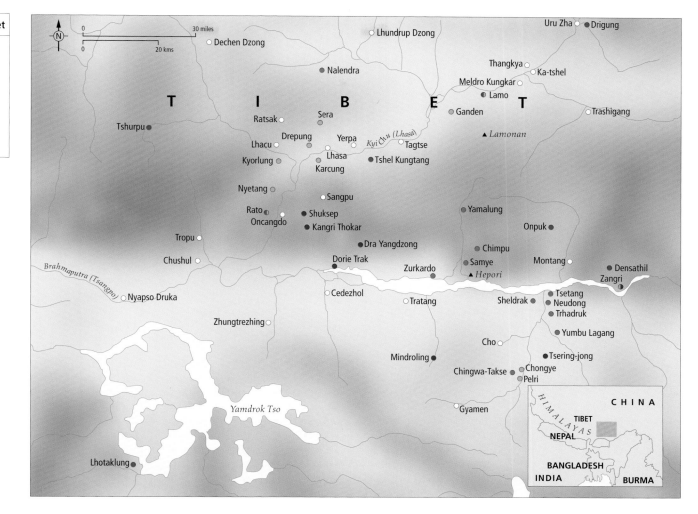

2	Buddhism in central Tibet

location of major temples and monasteries:
- early temple/monastery
- Nyingmapa
- Kagyupa
- Sakyapa
- Gelukpa

Built in the late eighth century, Samye was the first Buddhist temple in Tibet. It had three contrasting storeys, using Indian, Chinese and Tibetan architectural styles, and adorned internally with murals and statues.

Originally an early medieval fortress, the massive multi-storeyed building of the Potala has the typical Tibetan high sloping external walls. The Fifth Dalai Lama (1617-82) was responsible for its later enlargement and embellishment as an official residence for the Dalai Lamas, who used it until 1959.

central and later eastern Tibet. The Sakyapa lineage which was politically dominant in the thirteenth century was founded at Sakya in 1073 by Konchok Gyelpo (1034-1102). In 1409 the reformer Tsongkhapa (1357-1419) founded the monastery of Ganden, which led to the transformation of the old Kadampa lineage into the Gelukpas.

During the thirteenth century, the Sakyapas won the backing of the Mongols who had made themselves overlords of Tibet. The influential monk Phakpa (1235-80) acted as a cultural and spiritual advisor to the Mongols and was appointed their vice-regent in Tibet. However, Tibet regained full independence soon after the fall of the Mongol dynasty in China (1368) and at the same time the Sakyapa rule was overthrown by the monk Changchub Gyaltsen, who established the Phagmo-trupa hegemony, which favoured the Kagyupas. After this collapsed in 1434, a period of instability followed which ended with the political ascendancy of the Gelukpas over all Tibet under the great Fifth Dalai Lama (1617-82). Though they had some contact with Buddhism previously, the mass

conversion of the Mongols, especially to the Gelukpa lineage, dates from this time. Jesuit missionaries arrived in Tibet in 1661, but Christianity failed to make any headway due to cultural and linguistic difficulties. Though the Tibetans treated the Christians with tolerance and curiosity, initially regarding Christianity as a bizarre form of Buddhism, the missions were ended in the 1740s, when it was felt that the missionaries had abused the hospitality of the Tibetans and were asked to leave.

Later Developments and the Chinese Invasion

Though interrupted by brief periods of unrest, such as that instigated by Lha-zang with the support of the Qing rulers of China in 1706, Tibet generally enjoyed several centuries of peace until the Chinese communist invasion of 1950. The various lineages continued to establish monastic centres throughout Tibet but also tended to stagnate along rigid sectarian divisions. A final flowering of Tibetan religious culture began in eastern Tibet in the eighteenth century with the emergence of the Eclectic Movement (*ri-me*), inspired by the Nyingma scholar Jik-me Ling-pa (1730-98) and the Kagyupa polymath Kong-trul (1811-99).

One of the greatest achievements of Tibetan Buddhism is the translation and preservation of the Indian Buddhist scriptures. The texts were placed in two major groups: the words of the Buddha in the Kanjur, and treatises and commentary literature in the Tenjur, totalling some 360 large volumes. Initially this collection of texts was handed down through manuscript copies, but with the development of large-scale woodblock printing in China, a number of printed editions of the scriptures were produced. The earliest of these was produced in 1410 in Beijing, followed by several others there. The Tibetans also produced editions at Lithang (1621), Chone (1731) and Derge (1733) in eastern Tibet, as well as at Narthang (1732) in central Tibet. Several other editions were also produced during the following centuries, the latest during the 1920s.

BUDDHISM TODAY

Buddhism still flourishes in ▶
Southeast Asian countries, where
it is common for young boys to
spend some time as monks as part
of their upbringing. Recently, a
revival of interest has also led to a
number of young women
becoming nuns.

BUDDHISM in Asia has survived the impact of
European colonization and the upheavals of the
twentieth century with varying degrees of success,
and it has also begun to attract serious followers in the
West. Buddhism had disappeared from most of India by
the thirteenth century after the Muslim invasions of that
time, although it lingered on in parts of Bengal and
southern India, while the holy places associated with the
Buddha continued to be visited by pilgrims from Sri
Lanka and Tibet. It was not until the 1950s that Buddhism
began to return to India. Dr Bhimrao Ambedkar (1891-
1956) saw the caste system as an evil preventing the
creation of a just society and he came to see Buddhism as
a solution to the question of 'untouchability'. Ambedkar
and many of his followers converted to the Theravada
form of Buddhism in 1956. Subsequently, there have been
mass conversions in Maharashtra, Madhya Pradesh,
Karnataka and elsewhere in India.

Despite some early European oppression, Buddhism
remains dominant in Sri Lanka, as well as the other
countries of Southeast Asia, though the tragic events of
the Pol Pot era led to the murder of the entire monastic
population of Cambodia. Recent years have also seen a
resurgence of Theravada Buddhism in Indonesia,
especially through the efforts of the Dutch-educated
Jinarakkhita Thera in the 1950s and 1960s, as well as of
Mahayana Buddhism supported by Chinese immigrants.

The fate of Buddhism in the countries with
communist regimes has varied. The beginnings of a
Buddhist revival were cut short in China after 1947 and
since then official policy has fluctuated between hostility,
indifference and the more recent tolerance. On the other
hand, the Chinese communist presence in Tibet has been
an unmitigated disaster with the total destruction of
thousands of temples and monasteries by the 1960s. As
Buddhism is a focal point for Tibetan national sentiments,
it continues to be regarded with suspicion by the
authorities. Likewise, organized Buddhism was virtually
eliminated in Mongolia in the period from the 1930s to
the 1950s, though it is now undergoing a revival.

Buddhism in the West

The modern era has seen the growth of Western contact
with Buddhism, with a bi-directional flow of visitors to

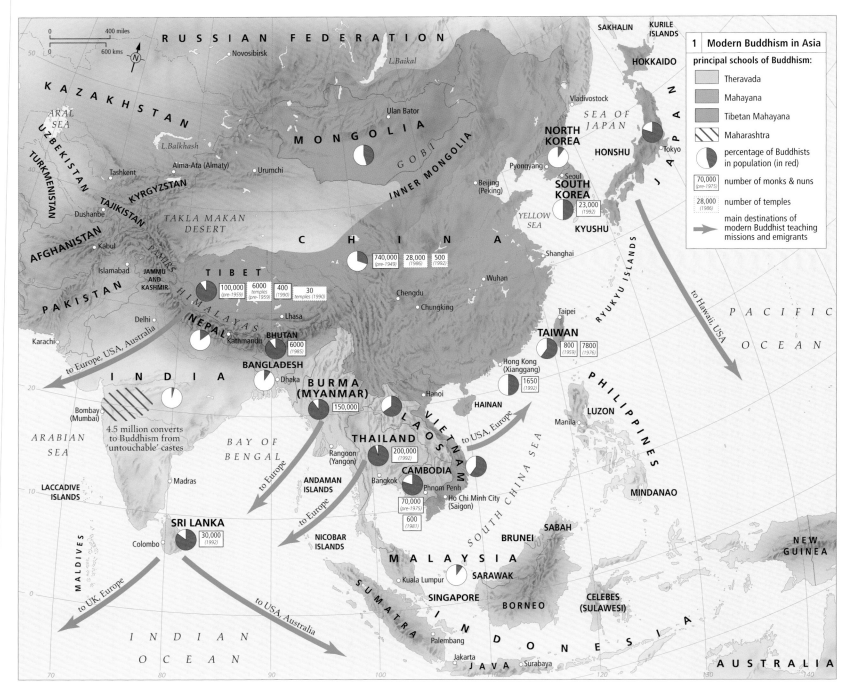

and from the East. Apart from a few scholars working in the mid-nineteenth century, general interest in Buddhism dates from the founding of Theosophy in 1875 by Olcott and Blavatsky who greatly valued Buddhism. Though not Buddhist itself, Theosophy was a vehicle for the introduction of Buddhist ideas into the West. Such Western converts to Buddhism as Ananda Metteyya (Allan Bennett, 1873-1923) and Nyanatiloka (Anton Gueth, 1878-1957) soon followed. The Sri Lankan layman Anagarika Dharmapala (1874-1933) founded the first Western Buddhist organization in the USA (1897), while the first Buddhist organization in Britain was founded in 1907. Though often small in size,

similar groups were established in other European countries during the pre-war years.

With the decline of Christianity in the post-war era, Buddhism has begun to attract greater numbers of followers in the West. Before the 1950s, Theravada was almost the only form of Buddhism known, but subsequently other schools have also become popular. Zen Buddhism from Japan became better known in the immediate post-war years, especially through the writings of Daisetsu Suzuki. As a side effect of the Chinese invasion of Tibet, many monks fled from there as refugees and eventually set up communities both in India and in most Western countries. Exact figures are not available, but perhaps more than half of Western Buddhist devotees now follow some form of Tibetan Buddhism. Apart from these three main forms of Buddhism found in the West, there are also smaller groups following various forms of Chinese Mahayana, Vietnamese Zen, Japanese Pure Land and Shingon. The modern Japanese Nichiren Shoshu movement, though regarded with suspicion by other Buddhists, has also attracted large numbers of followers internationally.

Buddhist Centres in the West

Many Western countries, especially those having the longest contact with Buddhism, now have monastic centres organized by Western monks and nuns, while there are often small groups and centres active within reach of most people (*see also* pp. 18-19). The numbers of these groups have mushroomed in recent years. For example, in the early 1950s there were only about a half dozen such groups in Britain whereas now there are several hundreds, including the monastic centres at Amaravati (Theravada), Throssle Hole (Zen) and Samye Ling (Tibetan). In the wake of recent political changes, Buddhism is also becoming popular in the former East European countries, including Russia.

Inspired by the teachings of the Lotus Sutra, a modern Japanese Buddhist movement has endeavoured to build pagodas in many cities throughout the world, such as this one in London, to foster world peace and understanding.

EAST ASIAN TRADITIONS

EAST ASIA is ethnically, culturally and religiously diverse. It has seen major empires rise and decline as well as cultures that have persisted for centuries in isolation. Major trade routes have been as vigorous in their trafficking of ideas as in their trade in silks and spices. Indeed, even before the beginning of the first millennium there was significant trade between the Han Empire in China and the Romans, providing an early link between the West and the Far East.

IN MODERN East Asia economic and cultural diversity is plain to see. The contrast is striking between the towering, sprawling, cosmopolitan cities, such as Singapore or Manila, powerhouses of technological and economic activity, and the rural backwaters of regions such as the Toraja heartland of Sulawesi, or the mountain homes of the hilltribes of Thailand and Laos. However, communities all over East Asia, whether urban or rural, literate or illiterate, static or nomadic, share many of the same basic beliefs and practices, which are grounded in the notion of the immanence of the ancestors.

The Shang oracle-bone inscriptions, from around 5,000 years ago, point to an ancient civilization in China characterized by a cult to the ancestors and a belief in divination and shamanism. In Japan, the eighth-century records, the *Kojiki* and the *Nihongi*, recount the stories of the mythic ancestors of the nation and of the imperial family. In Indonesia the religious practice of *aluk todol*, honouring the ancestors, is widespread. The belief, not only in the identity-providing, totemic, power of the ancestors, but also in their intervention for good or ill, in the daily lives of ordinary people is not confined to rural tribespeople, but thrives alongside the hedonism and consumer-capitalism which characterizes the cities. Moreover, it is a belief so fundamental to East Asian peoples that even the foreign empires, and the sweeping missions of Islam and Christianity could do nothing to dislodge it.

EAST ASIA

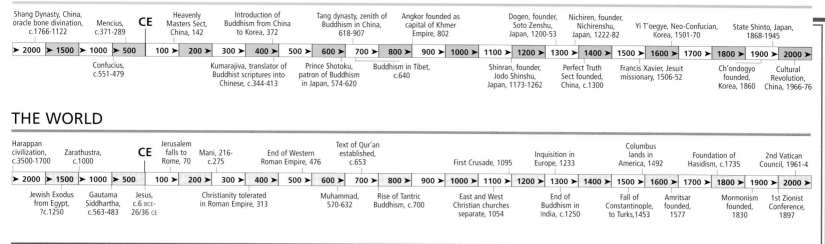

Shang Dynasty, China, oracle bone divination, c.1766-1122 — Mencius, c.371-289 — **CE** — Heavenly Masters Sect, China, 142 — Introduction of Buddhism from China to Korea, 372 — Tang dynasty, zenith of Buddhism in China, 618-907 — Angkor founded as capital of Khmer Empire, 802 — Dogen, founder, Soto Zenshu, Japan, 1200-53 — Nichiren, founder, Nichirenshu, Japan, 1222-82 — Yi T'oegye, Neo-Confucian, Korea, 1501-70 — State Shinto, Japan, 1868-1945

➤ 2000 ➤ 1500 ➤ 1000 ➤ 500 | 100 ➤ 200 ➤ 300 ➤ 400 ➤ 500 ➤ 600 ➤ 700 ➤ 800 ➤ 900 ➤ 1000 ➤ 1100 ➤ 1200 ➤ 1300 ➤ 1400 ➤ 1500 ➤ 1600 ➤ 1700 ➤ 1800 ➤ 1900 ➤ 2000 ➤

Confucius, c.551-479 — Kumarajiva, translator of Buddhist scriptures into Chinese, c.344-413 — Prince Shotoku, patron of Buddhism in Japan, 574-620 — Buddhism in Tibet, c.640 — Shinran, founder, Jodo Shinshu, Japan, 1173-1262 — Perfect Truth Sect founded, China, c.1300 — Francis Xavier, Jesuit missionary, 1506-52 — Ch'ondogyo founded, Korea, 1860 — Cultural Revolution, China, 1966-76

THE WORLD

Harappan civilization, c.3500-1700 — Zarathustra, c.1000 — **CE** — Jerusalem falls to Rome, 70 — Mani, 216-c.275 — End of Western Roman Empire, 476 — Text of Qur'an established, c.653 — First Crusade, 1095 — Inquisition in Europe, 1233 — Columbus lands in America, 1492 — Foundation of Hasidism, c.1735 — 2nd Vatican Council, 1961-4

➤ 2000 ➤ 1500 ➤ 1000 ➤ 500 | 100 ➤ 200 ➤ 300 ➤ 400 ➤ 500 ➤ 600 ➤ 700 ➤ 800 ➤ 900 ➤ 1000 ➤ 1100 ➤ 1200 ➤ 1300 ➤ 1400 ➤ 1500 ➤ 1600 ➤ 1700 ➤ 1800 ➤ 1900 ➤ 2000 ➤

Jewish Exodus from Egypt, ?c.1250 — Gautama Siddhartha, c.563-483 — Jesus, c.6 BCE-26/36 CE — Christianity tolerated in Roman Empire, 313 — Muhammad, 570-632 — Rise of Tantric Buddhism, c.700 — East and West Christian churches separate, 1054 — End of Buddhism in India, c.1250 — Fall of Constantinople, to Turks, 1453 — Amritsar founded, 1577 — Mormonism founded, 1830 — 1st Zionist Conference, 1897

Writing and Thinking

As well as practices associated with the ancestors, another unifying feature of East Asian culture was the early development of the ideographic script, shared for much of the region's history by China, Korea, Japan and much of Southeast Asia. While in the Western mind Islam and Christianity, as religions 'of the Book', may be associated with bringing literacy to the benighted East, in fact Confucian culture, education and government was established on the basis of written sources centuries before the Christian era. Different scripts have since developed, but scholars link the pictorial style of the ideograph which was fundamental to the written form of most East Asian languages, with what is sometimes described as a distinctive East Asian way of thinking. In contrast to the apparently logical and philosophical thought forms which spring from Indo-European languages, the East Asian mind is often described as more aesthetic and intuitive. This view, however, may be one of the many symptoms of an orientalist outlook, which sees the East as 'other'. Both Indian and Western logic and philosophy have played parts in the cultural history of East Asia, and not only as part of the baggage of European and Indian empires, but also as part of indigenous ways of thinking. In Japan, for instance, the distinctively Japanese Kyoto school of philosophy has contributed world class philosophers, in the Western sense of the term, to the international scene.

Religious Commitment

The comfortable co-existence of a number of religions in the life of communities is a striking feature of East Asian culture. Not only are most East Asian countries pluralist in terms of the diversity of religions which are represented in them, but people will happily participate in a number of them during their lives. Thus in the Philippines, for example, devotion to the Virgin Mary and visits to the *baylan* or spirit medium would both be appropriate religious activities for an individual. In Japan, a Shinto wedding would be celebrated for a couple who at the end of their lives would have Buddhist funerals. In pre-Communist China four religions worked more or less in harmony in people's lives; Confucianism, Daoism, Buddhism and Shamanism. This feature of East Asian religious life sometimes strikes Westerners as in conflict with the logical need to either commit to or reject different religions on the basis of the truth claims they make. It is often, and correctly, pointed out that the Western notion of exclusive commitment is a relatively new one which has grown only in the context of pluralism and secularization, and to evaluate the East on its basis is to fail to recognize the composite nature of all religious traditions. It might also be argued that the reason East Asians appear to participate in a number of religions at once is because Western scholars have created artificial boundaries between religions on the basis of their own essentialist viewpoints.

Colonialism and Communism

In order to understand the religious traditions of East Asia it is important to recognize the role of the various empires in changing the religious contours of the region. Not all empires were European. Many Chinese dynasties had expansionist policies, as did some Japanese, and these had an impact on the religious beliefs of East Asia. The Khmer Empire (ninth-thirteenth centuries), the remnants of which can be seen at Angkor, introduced a syncretic Hindu-Buddhism mixed with notions of divine kingship to most of Southeast Asia. The Majapahit Empire brought Hinduism to Indonesia, and the Indian-Javanese traditions of the fourteenth century are still preserved, more or less intact, on Bali. The foreign empires of Islam and Christianity were also to have enormous impact on the region. Islam flourishes in much of East Asia, and whilst Christianity has fared generally less well, it is still powerfully represented in many parts, for instance in South Korea.

As well as having experienced the transformative effects of empires, many parts of the region have, in the latter half of the twentieth century, undergone the ordeal of Communist revolution. As is clear from research undertaken in the twenty-first century, such revolutions have, however, failed to eradicate religion. Moreover, though as yet small-scale, there are religious rebuilding and rehabilitation programmes in many East Asian countries.

CONFUCIANISM

CONFUCIUS is the latinized rendering of Kongfuzi (K'ung fu-tzu), who lived 551?–479 BCE in Qufu, Shandong (*map 2*). Little is known about his life, but his thought is recorded in the *Analects*, a collection of discourses with his disciples. The 'Five Classics' are also attributed to Confucius, although these developed over a long period, with much later additions.

Confucianism is a moral philosophy, the central teaching of which is *ren (jen)*, the virtue of humaneness, which is associated with benevolence, loyalty, respect and reciprocity. Confucius described five relationships: between ruler and minister; father and son; husband and wife; elder and younger brother, and friend and friend. In each relationship the superior has a duty of care and the inferior has a duty of loyalty and respect. All people are ultimately subject to the will of Heaven (*tiamchi; t'ien-chih*), which is the primary reality, the ultimate source of morality and order. It is not the subject of speculation, but is related to through ritual. In some texts it is synonymous with Shangdi (Shang-ti), the Lord-on-high. The Emperor was thought to rule with the mandate of Heaven.

According to Confucius, rituals and regular sacrifice are required as well as *ren* and proper relationships. The Cult of Heaven required the Emperor, as Son of Heaven, to perform an annual animal sacrifice at the Temple of Heaven in Beijing (*map 3*). Other sacrifices were offered to the earth, sun, moon, and to the imperial ancestors. After his death Confucius himself became the focus of a cult.

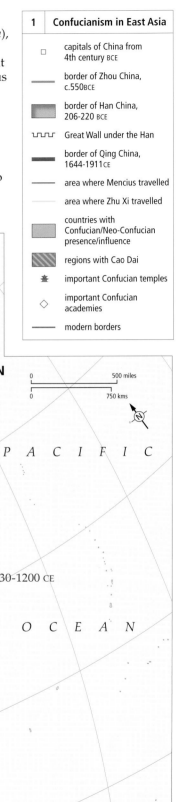

1	**Confucianism in East Asia**
□	capitals of China from 4th century BCE
	border of Zhou China, c.550 BCE
	border of Han China, 206-220 BCE
⊔⊔⊔	Great Wall under the Han
	border of Qing China, 1644-1911 CE
	area where Mencius travelled
	area where Zhu Xi travelled
	countries with Confucian/Neo-Confucian presence/influence
	regions with Cao Dai
⛩	important Confucian temples
◇	important Confucian academies
	modern borders

birthplace of Confucius, 551 BCE
birthplace of Mencius, c.371 BCE
birthplace of Zhu Xi, 1130-1200 CE

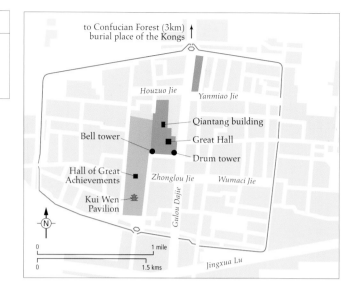

to Confucian Forest (3km)
burial place of the Kongs ↑

Houzuo Jie — Yanmiao Jie

Qiantang building
Bell tower — Great Hall
Drum tower
Hall of Great Achievements — Zhonglou Jie — Wumaci Jie
Kui Wen Pavilion

0 — 1 mile
0 — 1.5 kms
Jingxua Lu

Confucianism was later developed by Mencius (Mengzi/Meng-tzu; c.371–289 BCE) who, like Confucius, was an itinerant advisor to rulers. The *Book of Mencius* describes Heaven as immanent; to be found in the human heart. Xunzi (Hsün-tzu, 312–238 BCE) reformed Confucianism by purging it of apotropaic practices, thus driving a wedge between the Confucianism of the elite and the folk religion of the people.

Mozi (Mo-tzu, c.470–391 BCE) was originally a Confucian who developed his own school of thought, emphasizing extreme virtue and universal love. This went against the grain of mainstream Confucianism, which emphasized filial love. Ultimately, traditional Confucianism was to prevail, though Mohism has been in vogue for short periods.

Neo-Confucianism

During the Han era, Confucianism became the state orthodoxy, though with additional subsidiary elements, such as divination. Later, in the Song dynasty, a group of philosophers, the most important of whom was probably Zhu Xi (Chu Hsi, 1130–1200 CE), reformulated Confucian doctrine. Zhu Xi distinguished Confucian realism from Buddhist idealism, but retained Buddhist influence in that he tackled metaphysical questions and advocated meditation. Zhu Xi's influence was to be felt for the next

six centuries, since his commentaries on the classics became part of the core curriculum for the civil service examinations.

Neo-Confucianism (*Songni-hak*) was the state ideology of Korea during the Yi dynasty (1392–1910), and though no longer espoused by the state it remains an important feature of Korean culture. In Japan, Confucianism, as part of the culture of the continent, was adopted in the sixth and seventh centuries and perpetuated by the Taika reforms (645–6). Confucianism provided the foundation for Japanese feudalism, and remains the ethical basis of society, despite its removal from the education system by the occupying powers at the end of World War II.

Confucianism Today

Confucianism lost its state support at the close of the Qing dynasty, and all public ritual practice drew to an abrupt end with the Cultural Revolution (1966–76). However, scholarship of Confucian thought remains a tradition, and in overseas Chinese communities there has recently been a resurgence of both popular and scholarly interest in Confucianism (*map 1*). In China itself, despite Mao Zedong's criticism of Confucianism, contemporary Communist officials have observed the birthday of Confucius, which reflects changing attitudes. At a popular level, the social structures and ethics of Confucianism remain in place. Filial piety is still the foundation of Chinese society.

In East Asian countries with large Chinese populations, the practice of Confucian rituals, including ancestor veneration and the cult of Confucius, is observed alongside the beliefs and practices of other religions, Chinese or otherwise. As in China, a number of religions are practised as complementary, and syncretism is part of the religious lives of Malaysia, Indonesia, Indochina, Korea and Japan. It is sometimes more helpful to see Chinese religion as a seamless whole rather than to split it into its constituents: Buddhism, Confucianism, Daoism and Shamanism.

Cao Dai is a syncretist Vietnamese sect that combines elements of Confucianism, Daoism, Buddhism and Christianity. Revelations are made from the Supreme Being, Cao Dai, and other 'spirits' such as Confucius, the Buddha, Jesus, Muhammad, Sun Yat-sen, Victor Hugo and Joan of Arc, to young spirit mediums who teach that God will protect humanity from materialism. As a politically motivated grass-roots movement, Cao Dai is anti-Communist, and it contributed a great deal to the fall of the Diem regime in 1963. Membership remains strong.

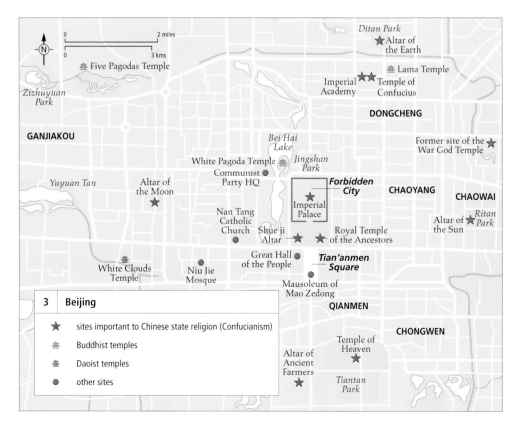

Ditan Park
Altar of the Earth
Five Pagodas Temple — Lama Temple
Imperial Academy — Temple of Confucius
DONGCHENG
Zizhuyuan Park
GANJIAKOU
Bei Hai Lake — Jingshan Park
White Pagoda Temple — Former site of the War God Temple
Communist Party HQ — Forbidden City — CHAOYANG — CHAOWAI
Yuyuan Tan — Altar of the Moon
Nan Tang Catholic Church — Imperial Palace — Ritan Park
Shue ji Altar — Royal Temple of the Ancestors — Altar of the Sun
Great Hall of the People — Tian'anmen Square
White Clouds Temple — Niu Jie Mosque — Mausoleum of Mao Zedong
QIANMEN

3	Beijing

★ sites important to Chinese state religion (Confucianism)

Buddhist temples

Daoist temples

● other sites

CHONGWEN
Altar of Ancient Farmers — Temple of Heaven — Tiantan Park

The Gate to the Temple of Confucius in Qufu, Shandong. Over a kilometre long and laid out like an imperial palace, the Temple of Confucius does not reflect the humble origins of the sage. It was added to by successive emperors over a number of centuries and now ranks with the Forbidden City as one of the great architectural achievements of China.

DAOISM

THE TERM 'DAOISM' (Taoism) is used to refer both to Daoist philosophy, *Daojia (Tao-chia)*, and religion. Daoist philosophy, which survives in two Schools, the Heavenly Masters Sect and the Perfect Truth Sect, has, perhaps more than any other school of thought, given form to Chinese and East Asian culture, notably in the fields of traditional medicine and science.

Scholars argue that it is artificial to separate the religions of China: Daoism, Confucianism, Buddhism and Shamanism. The notion of exclusive commitment is Western, and Chinese religion is comprised of all four strands. Each of the religions, however, has had periods of ascendancy and each has, at one time or another, been adopted by the state. Daoism was, for example, adopted by Tang dynasty rulers. Occasionally, persecution has been a feature of the relationship between some of these religions, but the general trend has been towards syncretism. Daoism, which developed from traditions of divination, ancestor worship and shamanism, was also an important influence on the development of Chan (Ch'an) Buddhism from the sixth century onwards.

There are two classical texts for philosophical Daoism: the *Laozi (Lao-tzu* or the *Daodejing, Tao-te Ching)* and the *Zhuangzi (Chuang-tzu)*. The authorship of both texts is uncertain. The first is attributed to Laozi (Lao-tzu), the legendary founding patriarch of Daoism, traditionally a contemporary of Confucius (sixth century BCE), and the second to Zhuangzi (Chuang-tzu), a contemporary of Mencius (fourth century BCE). Religious Daoism, however, has a huge canon, many texts of which date from the fifth century CE and are sectarian in nature.

The Dao

The central notion of philosophical Daoism is that of the Dao. The *Daodejing* warns 'The Dao that can be spoken of is not the eternal Dao', so definitions such as 'the way', 'nature', or 'unchanging principle of the universe', should be recognized as provisional. The practitioner of Daoism tries to live in harmony with the Dao, which may involve world-denying practices, the rejection of rules and rationalism, and the practice of *wu wei (wu-wei)*, or 'non-action'. Allied to living in harmony with the Dao is the quest for balance between *yin* (the feminine) and *yang* (the masculine) and between the Five Elements. As well as being a manual for right living, the *Laozi* is also a political treatise open to a range of interpretations.

The Quest for Immortality

The quest for physical immortality has long been associated with Daoism, and, in conjunction with the science of alchemy, was a staple of Chinese culture from

Laozi riding his Ox, *Ming Dynasty (ink and watercolour on silk) National Palace Museum, Taipei, Taiwan. It was on Laozi's mythical journey to the West that he was asked by the Keeper of the Pass to write the* Daodejing.

Nun in a Daoist Temple, Heng Shan, Shanxi. Monks and nuns live in separate temples but follow similar traditions. Fasting and physical exercise are central to practice. Some temples grow grain and tea, others provide medical assistance to the general public. There are some monks and nuns who are not affiliated to any temple and live as hermits in the mountains.

around the seventh century BCE to the thirteenth century CE. The human body was perceived as mortal only insofar as it deviated from the Dao. Practices such as cultivating and preserving *qi (chi)* energy or life force through exercise (such as *taijiquan, t'ai-chi-ch'üan*), breathing exercises, and other techniques, were designed to bring the body of the Daoist into harmony with the Dao and thus achieve immortality. Other practices included the swallowing of mercury or jade in the belief that these substances would immortalize the body alchemically. Under the later influence of Buddhism the practice of good deeds was believed to lead to immortality.

China has a number of sacred mountains, many of which are associated with Daoist practice. Heng Shan in Shanxi, for example, boasts the sixth-century Hanging Temple (*see fig. opposite*), and a pilgrims' staircase, which rises to the summit about 2,000 metres above sea level. Mountains have traditionally been the retreat of the Daoist sage, far away from civilization in places where nature is expressed fully and powerfully.

Religious Daoism

The quest for immortality, along with many other teachings which now appear in religious Daoism, is first attributed to the Yellow Emperor, Huang ti, believed to have reigned from 2696 to 2598 BCE, and was popularized in the tales of the Eight Immortals (some of them historical figures) of the Tang, Song and Yuan dynasties.

By c.100 BCE Laozi and the Yellow Emperor were being worshipped as deities and by the third century CE Laozi was seen as the primal man who gave life to the planet. At some time in the first or second century CE a healer and exorcist from Jiming in Sichuan, Zhang Ling (Chang Ling), claimed a special revelation from Laozi and declared himself 'Heavenly Master' – a ruler over all the spirits and forces of heaven. This marked the founding of a patrilineal school of Religious Daoism which flourished in China until the Communist period, when its headquarters moved to Taiwan (*map 1*).

Numerous other schools of religious Daoism also developed, including some with political and millenarian interests, but the only other one to survive the political upheavals of the twentieth century was the Perfect Truth Sect, a monastic school dating to the Yuan dynasty.

Both religious and philosophical Daoism have influenced the cultures of the Chinese diaspora, and have also been integral to the religious landscape of

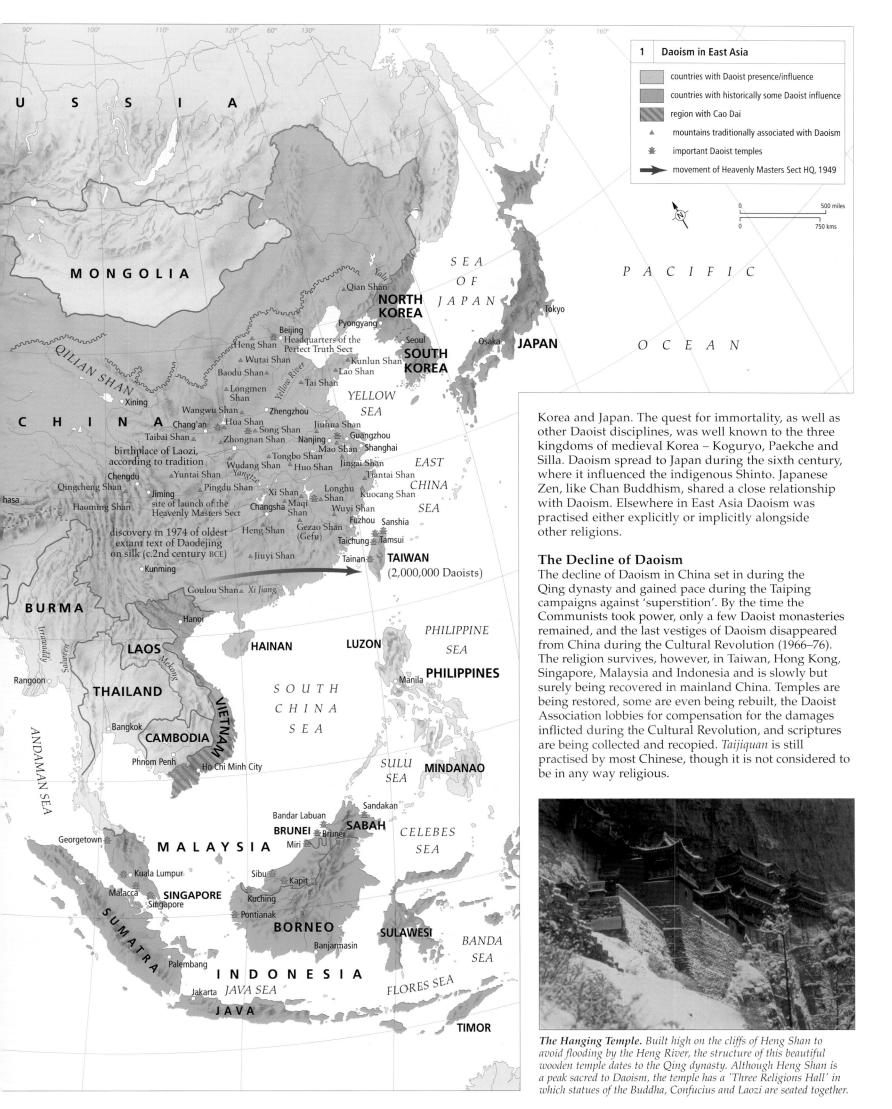

1 **Daoism in East Asia**

countries with Daoist presence/influence

countries with historically some Daoist influence

region with Cao Dai

▲ mountains traditionally associated with Daoism

⚟ important Daoist temples

➡ movement of Heavenly Masters Sect HQ, 1949

Korea and Japan. The quest for immortality, as well as other Daoist disciplines, was well known to the three kingdoms of medieval Korea – Koguryo, Paekche and Silla. Daoism spread to Japan during the sixth century, where it influenced the indigenous Shinto. Japanese Zen, like Chan Buddhism, shared a close relationship with Daoism. Elsewhere in East Asia Daoism was practised either explicitly or implicitly alongside other religions.

The Decline of Daoism

The decline of Daoism in China set in during the Qing dynasty and gained pace during the Taiping campaigns against 'superstition'. By the time the Communists took power, only a few Daoist monasteries remained, and the last vestiges of Daoism disappeared from China during the Cultural Revolution (1966–76). The religion survives, however, in Taiwan, Hong Kong, Singapore, Malaysia and Indonesia and is slowly but surely being recovered in mainland China. Temples are being restored, some are even being rebuilt, the Daoist Association lobbies for compensation for the damages inflicted during the Cultural Revolution, and scriptures are being collected and recopied. *Taijiquan* is still practised by most Chinese, though it is not considered to be in any way religious.

The Hanging Temple. Built high on the cliffs of Heng Shan to avoid flooding by the Heng River, the structure of this beautiful wooden temple dates to the Qing dynasty. Although Heng Shan is a peak sacred to Daoism, the temple has a 'Three Religions Hall' in which statues of the Buddha, Confucius and Laozi are seated together.

CHINESE BUDDHISM

BUDDHISM ENTERED China around the first century CE. The Silk Road provided one route through which Buddhist ideas entered the country. The Chinese also sent pilgrim monks through Central Asia to India to add to the growing corpus of scriptures for translation. Fa Xian (Fa Hsien, 338–422) went to India in search of the Vinaya Pitaka. Much later, another monk, Xuan-Zang (Hsuan-tsang, 596–664), immortalized in the great Chinese classic *Journey to the West*, brought back much of the Mahayana Canon *(map 1)*. The translation of the first phase of scriptures to arrive in China was largely done by the Central Asian monk, Kumarajiva (344–c.413).

As a foreign religion, Buddhism had to adapt itself to Chinese culture. The Chinese were at first resistant to a religion which taught transmigration and celibacy – both concepts were at odds with their age-old traditions of ancestor veneration and filial piety. Buddhism gradually assimilated these native traditions. The break-up of the Han dynasty and the ensuing political and spiritual chaos in China led to disillusionment with Confucianism and widespread popular interest in the foreign religion, which seemed to have much in common with Daoism.

Chinese Buddhist Schools

A number of significant philosophical schools of Buddhism emerged during the fifth and sixth centuries, most of Mahayana character. Two schools were especially important. San-lun ('Three treatise school') was the Chinese form of Madhyamika, Faxiang (Fa-hsiang) was the Chinese form of Yogachara. Though neither survived as intact sects, they influenced the more distinctively Chinese Tiantai (T'ien t'ai), Huayan (Hua-yen), Chan (Ch'an) and Qingdu (Ch'ing-t'u). Some temples in contemporary China still have historical links with these two schools, such as the Jiaxiang Temple in Shaoxing, which belongs to San-lun.

Tiantai Buddhism was founded by Zhiyi (Chih-i, 538–97). It synthesized the diversity of Buddhist doctrines into a system which assigned them different levels of truth, and claimed the *Lotus Sutra* as the culmination of the Buddha's teaching. The Huayan school of Buddhism developed an epistemology based on the *Avatamsaka Sutra*.

Chan Buddhism traces its lineage to Kasyapa, a disciple of the historical Buddha who received a special, intuitive, transmission of the teachings. This typified the later Chan notion of the direct transmission of enlightenment from

The Longmen caves, Luoyang, Shanxi, contain 97,306 statues carved out of a sheer limestone cliff by the Yi River. Dating to the early sixth century, they were commissioned by the imperial family and other wealthy families, but many have been vandalized since.

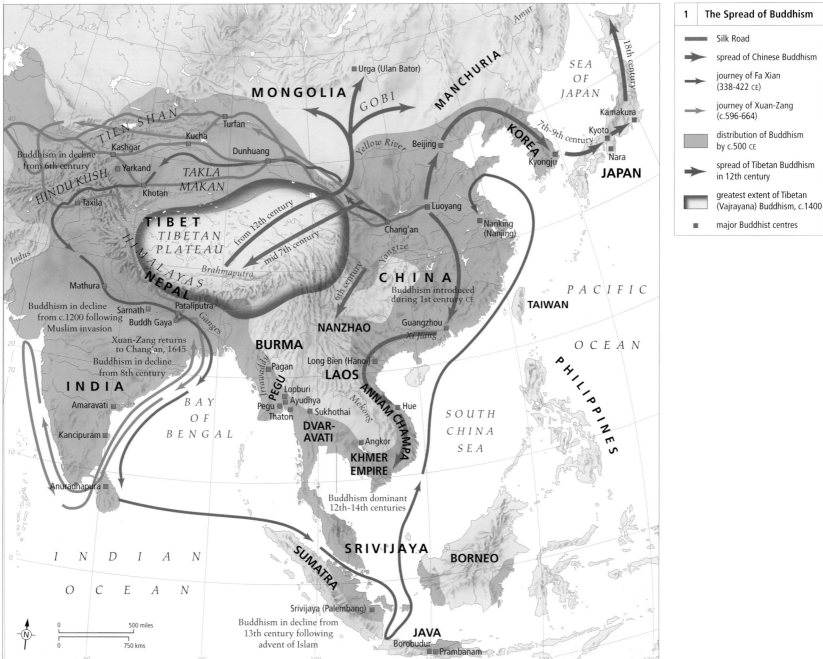

1	The Spread of Buddhism
▬▬▬	Silk Road
➤	spread of Chinese Buddhism
→	journey of Fa Xian (338-422 CE)
→	journey of Xuan-Zang (c.596-664)
▨	distribution of Buddhism by c.500 CE
➤	spread of Tibetan Buddhism in 12th century
▨	greatest extent of Tibetan (Vajrayana) Buddhism, c.1400
■	major Buddhist centres

Map labels: Amur · Urga (Ulan Bator) · MONGOLIA · GOBI · MANCHURIA · SEA OF JAPAN · 18th century · TIEN SHAN · Turfan · Kucha · Dunhuang · Kashgar · Yellow River · Beijing · KOREA · 7th-9th century · Kamakura · Kyoto · Buddhism in decline from 6th century · Yarkand · TAKLA MAKAN · Khotan · Kyongju · Nara · JAPAN · HINDU KUSH · Taxila · TIBET · TIBETAN PLATEAU · from 12th century · Luoyang · Nanking (Nanjing) · Indus · mid 7th century · Chang'an · Yongtze · Brahmaputra · 7th century · CHINA · Buddhism introduced during 1st century CE · PACIFIC · Mathura · HIMALAYAS · NEPAL · 6th century · TAIWAN · Buddhism in decline from c.1200 following Muslim invasion · Sarnath · Pataliputra · Buddh Gaya · Ganges · NANZHAO · Guangzhou · Xi Jiang · OCEAN · Xuan-Zang returns to Chang'an, 1645 · BURMA · Long Bien (Hanoi) · Buddhism in decline from 8th century · Irrawaddy · Pagan · LAOS · PHILIPPINES · INDIA · Amaravati · Lopburi · Ayudhya · Pegu · Sukhothai · Hue · PEGU · Thaton · ANNAM CHAMPA · BAY OF BENGAL · DVAR-AVATI · Mekong · SOUTH CHINA SEA · Kancipuram · Angkor · KHMER EMPIRE · Buddhism dominant 12th-14th centuries · Anuradhapura · INDIAN OCEAN · SUMATRA · SRIVIJAYA · BORNEO · Srivijaya (Palembang) · Buddhism in decline from 13th century following advent of Islam · JAVA · Borobudur · Prambanam

0   500 miles
0   750 kms

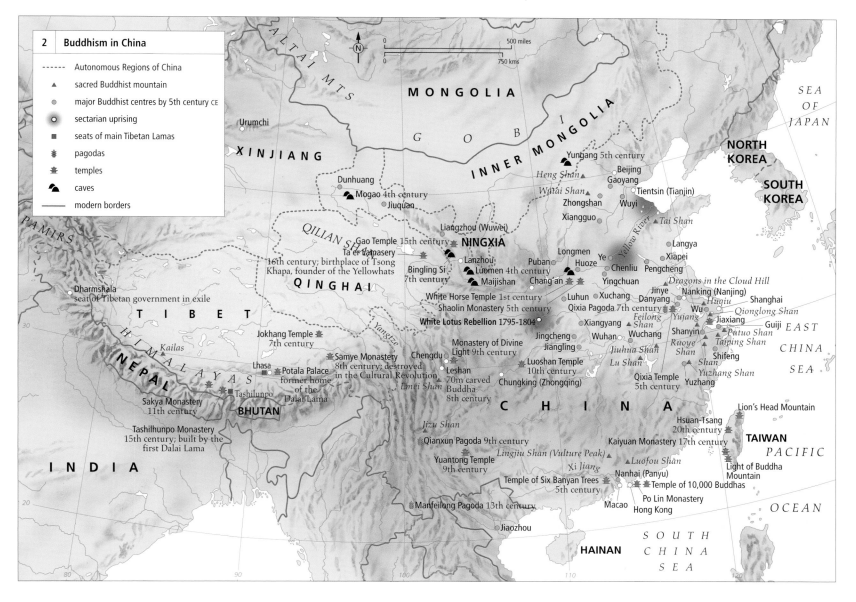

2 Buddhism in China

- - - - - Autonomous Regions of China
▲ sacred Buddhist mountain
● major Buddhist centres by 5th century CE
◎ sectarian uprising
■ seats of main Tibetan Lamas
⚘ pagodas
🏯 temples
⛰ caves
——— modern borders

master to disciple, removed from scriptures, doctrines and practices. The semi-legendary monk Bodhidharma is credited with bringing the tradition to China during the early sixth century, where it became sinicized, especially through contact with Daoism. Of the many schools that developed, two emerged as significant: Linji (Lin-chi) and Caodong (Tsao-tung). Chan became enormously popular during the Sung dynasty (960–1269). One of the greatest Chan temples is Shaolin on Songshan mountain.

The most popular form of Buddhism, Pure Land (Qingdu, Ch'ing-t'u), is centred on devotion to the Buddha Amitabha. It appealed to the laity since it made rebirth in Amitabha's Pure Land or western paradise, in which enlightenment was assured, available to all who called on the name of the Buddha; a practice called *nien-fo*. The notion of an afterlife was particularly compatible with folk beliefs about the immanence of the ancestors.

Tibetan Buddhism
When Buddhism penetrated the isolated Himalayan kingdom of Tibet in the seventh century, it took on distinctive characteristics through interaction with the

indigenous Bon religion. There are a number of schools of Tibetan Buddhism, one of which, the Gelugpa, is the school to which the Dalai Lama belongs.

For most of their history, Tibet and China have had diplomatic relations. During the Yuan dynasty the two were unified, though Tibet was to become autonomous again a number of times. In 1950 Chinese troops entered Tibet. In 1959 the Fourteenth Dalai Lama and his supporters fled to Dharmshala in northern India, from where he has protested about the the ongoing Chinese occupation of Tibet and the worst excesses of the Cultural Revolution (1966–76), a period which was to see the partial destruction of some of Tibet's great monasteries such as Samye (*map 2; see also* pp. 74-75).

Buddhism in Contemporary China
Buddhism has been largely in decline in China since the thirteenth century, when it lost ground to Neo-Confucianism. Later sectarian Buddhist uprisings such as those (1795–1804) by the millenarian White Lotus sect were suppressed by the Emperor. The importance of Chinese Buddhism may be best measured in terms of its influence on the religions of South and East Asia, particularly Japan. However, its role in the interplay between the great religions of China, and its effect especially on the development of Daoism, should not be underestimated.

Buddhism survived the Cultural Revolution to some degree and in 1953 the Chinese Buddhist Association was formed, both as an umbrella organization and as a way for the government to monitor Buddhist activities. The Association has secured funding for numerous rebuilding and renovation projects. Recent research suggests that as many as forty percent of the twenty-first century Chinese population consider the Buddha worthy of veneration.

Yungang Caves, Shanxi.
The caves took forty thousand workmen nearly a century to carve. Construction began in 453 CE when nearby Datong was capital of the Wei Dynasty. In addition to the sharp, almost Caucasian noses of many of the Buddhas, there is much foreign influence in the carvings, including Indian deities and Persian and Greek symbols.

RELIGIONS OF KOREA

KOREAN RELIGION has much in common with Chinese religion. Confucianism, Neo-Confucianism, Daoism, Buddhism and native Shamanism have been practised together more or less harmoniously for a long period of Korea's history. In contrast to China, however, Christianity became a numerically significant religion in Korea after its introduction towards the end of the Choson dynasty (1392–1910). At the same time, Korea saw the formation of a number of new religious movements which were to play an important role, both religiously and politically, in the lives of many ordinary Koreans during the Japanese annexation and occupation, which began in 1910. Some of these new religions continue to be significant.

Korea is separated into North and South along the 38th parallel, and in North Korea, the communist regime officially discourages freedom of religious practice. Since the late 1980s, however, some official recognition of religions has been achieved.

The Shamanic Tradition

The earliest Korean historical records, the *Samguk sagi* (Records of the Three Kingdoms) and the *Samguk yusa* (Stories of the Three Kingdoms), which date from the twelfth century, mention shamanic practices and shamanic foundation stories relating to Korea as a whole and to the three ancient kingdoms of Koguryo, Paekche and Silla. The legendary founder of Korea was a shaman-king called Tangun, the Sandalwood Prince, who was the son of a bear-woman and descended from the god of heaven. In modern times the shaman, or *mudang*, is a ritual specialist who becomes possessed by spirits so that these can be propitiated or petitioned by the community.

Confucianism, Daoism and Buddhism

In Korea (*map 1*), Confucianism is the strongest of the three religions which came from China. By the beginning of the Silla dynasty (618–935) its influence was widespread and filial piety was the ethical norm. Filial piety developed into patriotic loyalty to the state, and these two combined have been the mainstay of Korean society ever since. Neo-Confucianism was popularized in Korea by Yi T'oegye (1501–70), a strict follower of Chu Hsi. Daoism, which is related to the indigenous shamanic folk religion, has been practised in Korea since the seventh century. Korean Daoism follows the Heavenly Masters Sect model.

Buddhism was most influential in Korea during the Silla period when the major schools of scholastic Buddhism were introduced from China. In the former Silla capital of Kyongju (*map 2*) many sites and remains can be

Worshippers at Pulguk-sa Buddhist Temple. Situated near the ancient Silla capital of Kyongju, Pulguk-sa is Korea's most famous Buddhist temple. It was first constructed in 535 CE, when Buddhism was given royal sanction, and remains one of the oldest monasteries in Korea.

Map

CHINA

Paektu-san

HAMGYONG-SANMAEK

Kimch'aek

Kanggye

Hamhung   Hungnam

Tongjoson-man

Ch'ongch'on

Mt Kumgangsan
sacred to Shamans   Sorak-san   Kangnung

NORTH KOREA   Wonsan   T'AEBAEK-SANMAEK   Wolchong-sa 645CE

Odae-san   Pusok-sa 676CE

Ch'unch'on   T'aebaek-san
sacred to Shamans

Taedong   Nam-gong

Kwangnung
15th century   Ch'ongmyo   **SOUTH**   Andong   P'ohang   Pulguk-sa 561CE
Honinnung   Songgyun'gwan   **KOREA**   Sokkuram Grotto   Sillan tombs

Sinuiju   Pyongyang   Chogye-sa   Ch'ungju   Kyongju   3rd century
Namp'o   Kaesong   Yongju-sa 9th century   Paekche Tombs
Seoul   Chikchi-sa   Sogni-san   Taegu   5th century
5th century   Kumi
Inch'on   Ch'ongju   Haein-sa   Tonghae
Ch'onan   13th century   Pusan

Haeju   Popju-sa   Taejon   *SOBAEK-*   Kaya-san   T'ongdo-sa
SANMAEK   17th century;
Magok-sa   largest Korean
7th century   Buddhist temple
complex

Mani-san   Chiri-san

KOREA BAY

Kyonggi-man   Heartland of
Won Buddhism   Yosu
Sunch'on

Kwangju

SEA OF JAPAN

KOREA STRAIT

YELLOW SEA

EAST CHINA SEA

CHEJU STRAIT   **CHEJU-DO**
Halla-san
sacred to Shamans
Sanbanggulsa
sacred to goddess Sanbang-bok

Legend

1	Religion in Korea
▲	sacred mountains
☗	Buddhist temples
▦	Confucian shrines
⬚	tombs
◣	cave
—	modern borders

0   100 miles
0   150 kms

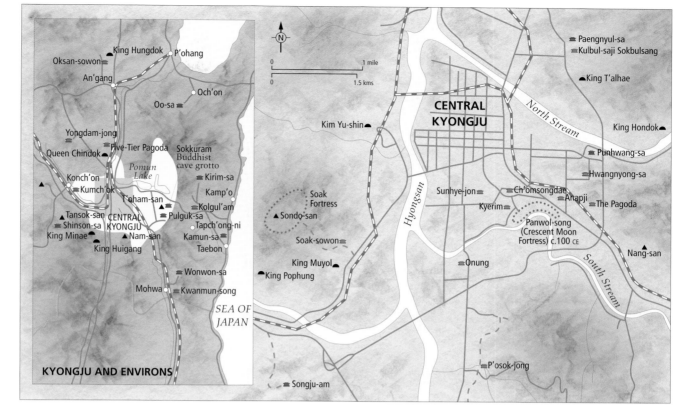

| 2 | Central Kyongju |

2 Central Kyongju

- 🏯 Buddhist temples
- ▲ sacred mountains
- ⛩ Korean shrines
- ⬥ tombs
- ⋯⋯ ancient sites

King Hungdok • P'ohang
Oksan-sowon
An'gang
Och'on
Oo-sa
Yongdam-jong
Queen Chindok • Five-Tier Pagoda
Sokkuram Buddhist cave grotto
Pomun Lake
Kirim-sa
Konch'on
Kumch'ok
Kamp'o
T'oham-san
Kolgul'am
Tansok-san
Pulguk-sa
Shinson-sa
Tapch'ong-ni
King Minae
Nam-san
Kamun-sa
King Huigang
Taebon
Wonwon-sa
Mohwa
Kwanmun-song

SEA OF JAPAN

Paengnyul-sa
Kulbul-saji Sokbulsang
King T'alhae
Kim Yu-shin
CENTRAL KYONGJU
King Hondok
Punhwang-sa
Hwangnyong-sa
Sunhye-jon
Ch'omsongdae
Anapji
The Pagoda
Kyerim
Panwol-song (Crescent Moon Fortress) c.100 CE
Soak Fortress
Sondo-san
Soak-sowon
Onung
Nang-san
King Muyol
King Pophung
P'osok-jong
Songju-am

KYONGJU AND ENVIRONS

found from this period and earlier. Son (Ch'an) Buddhism was the most important form of Korean Buddhism until the monk Chinul (1158–1210) founded the Chogye sect, which unified the various schools with Son. Buddhism was restricted and sometimes oppressed by Confucian policy, especially in the fifteenth century, when different schools, of which Chogye was only one, were forcibly merged. Today Chogye Buddhism is considered the dominant form.

Christian Converts
About a quarter of Koreans are Christians, making the religious constitution of Korea markedly different from its East Asian neighbours (*map 3*). There are various theories to explain the popularity of Christianity in Korea; the sympathy between Christianity and shamanistic practices, the role of Christian missionaries in resistance to Japanese colonial rule and the breakdown of traditional culture as a result of industrialization and urbanization are all seen as important factors in the growth of the new religion. The pace of development, from the arrival of the first Jesuit missionaries in the seventeenth century to the construction of Pastor David Yonggi Cho's 10,000-seater auditorium at Prayer Mountain outside Seoul, has been considerable.

New Religious Movements
During the Japanese colonial period, the desire for independence expressed itself in part in the formation or reinvigoration of new movements, known collectively as

Tonghak (Eastern learning), some of which expressed nationalist tendencies. The largest of these is the still influential Ch'ondogyo, the 'Religion of the Heavenly Way', which sees God (Ch'onju) in human beings. Won Buddhism, founded in 1916, draws on Buddhism, Confucianism, Christianity and Ch'ondogyo, but doctrinally focuses on the notion of *dharmakaya*. Unlike many other forms of Buddhism, Won is committed to serving society, especially through education.

Perhaps the most high-profile of all Korea's modern movements is that of the Unification Church, or 'Moonies'. Founded by Rev Sun Myung Moon in 1954, the movement believes that Moon himself, as the Messiah, will establish the Kingdom of God on earth. The Kingdom will be brought about, according to the Church, through perfect families – mass weddings are a striking feature of the movement. Though high-profile, the Moonies are not numerically strong in Korea.

Moonie Wedding, Seoul, February 1999. Some of the more than 25,000 couples from around the world raise their arms and shout 'for ten thousand years!' during a mass wedding at the Unification Church Blessing '99 at the Chamsil Olympic Stadium in Seoul, presided over by Rev and Mrs Sun Myung Moon.

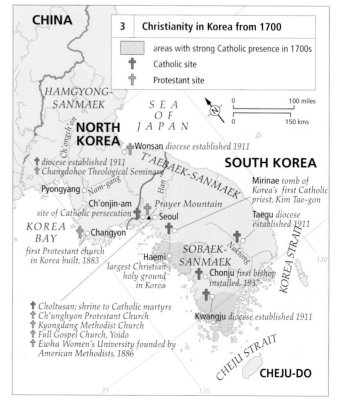

3 Christianity in Korea from 1700

CHINA

- areas with strong Catholic presence in 1700s
- ✝ Catholic site
- ✝ Protestant site

HAMGYONG-SANMAEK
SEA OF JAPAN
NORTH KOREA
Wonsan *diocese established 1911*
diocese established 1911
Changdohoe Theological Seminary
Pyongyang
Ch'onjin-am *site of Catholic persecution*
Prayer Mountain
Seoul
KOREA BAY
Changyon
first Protestant church in Korea built, 1883
Haemi
largest Christian holy ground in Korea
SOBAEK-SANMAEK
Chonju *first bishop installed, 1937*
T'AEBAEK-SANMAEK
SOUTH KOREA
Mirinae *tomb of Korea's first Catholic priest, Kim Tae-gon*
Taegu *diocese established 1911*
Kwangju *diocese established 1911*
KOREA STRAIT

- ✝ Choltusan; shrine to Catholic martyrs
- ✝ Ch'unghyon Protestant Church
- ✝ Kyongdang Methodist Church
- ✝ Full Gospel Church, Yoido
- ✝ Ewha Women's University founded by American Methodists, 1886

CHEJU STRAIT
CHEJU-DO

RELIGIONS OF JAPAN

AS AN ISLAND archipelago, Japan has experienced long periods of cultural isolation, some of which have been politically enforced. This, coupled with the relative homogeneity of the population, has led to the development of a highly distinctive, and possibly unique, religious tradition. The two dominant traditions of Shinto and Buddhism have interacted at all levels, from the doctrinal to the popular.

Shinto – the 'Way of the Gods'

Shinto is the indigenous religion of Japan which emerged from the shamanistic practices of antiquity. The *Kojiki* (Record of Ancient Matters) and *Nihongi* (History of Japan) were composed in the early eighth century. They tell the stories of the ancestral *kami* (gods), Izanami and Izanagi, who were the creators of Japan, as well as the Japanese and the other *kami*. They also tell of Amaterasu Omikami, the sun goddess and progenitrix of the Japanese imperial family.

As a life-affirming religion, Shinto presides over rites of passage relating to birth, marriage and procreation, and avoids those relating to death, which is seen as polluting. However, the deceased, especially the ancestors and the war dead, are considered to be *kami*. The *kami* are also immanent in mountains (for instance Mt Fuji), rivers, wild animals, even stones. Shinto is primarily a religion of ritual purity, but at a popular level it involves the propitiation of *kami*, who are either benign or malevolent, and the belief in luck, auspicious and inauspicious times and places and various magico-religious practices.

As a religion which legitimates the divine origins of Japan and her imperial household, Shinto was adopted by the Meiji government (1868–1912) and persisted as the state religion (to the exclusion of Buddhism) until the end of World War II, when constitutional separation of state and religion was enforced by the occupying powers. Shinto survived in the form of Shrine (as opposed to State) Shinto, which is free from governmental control.

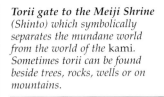

Torii gate to the Meiji Shrine (Shinto) which symbolically separates the mundane world from the world of the kami. Sometimes torii can be found beside trees, rocks, wells or on mountains.

Early Japanese Buddhism

Buddhism was introduced to Japan from Korea in the sixth century as part of the perceived superior culture of the continent, and remained largely a foreign religion in which only aristocrats were interested. Devotion to the Yakushi, the medicine Buddha, was particularly popular, and consistent with the Japanese interest in this-worldly benefits. The regency of Prince Shotoku (573–622), credited with being the first to perceive Buddhism as an ethical religion, is marked by temple-building. The Horyu-ji is particularly associated with him. During the Heian period (794–1185) two forms of Buddhism were ascendant. Tendai was the Japanese form of the Chinese Mahayana tradition, T'ien t'ai. Shingon, a form of esoteric Buddhism founded by Kukai (774–835), is based on Koya-san.

Buddhist Dissenters and Reformers

The Kamakura period (1185–1333) was to see Buddhism become Japanized, and repackaged to suit the masses. The great Tendai training temple, the Enryakuji, on Hiei-san

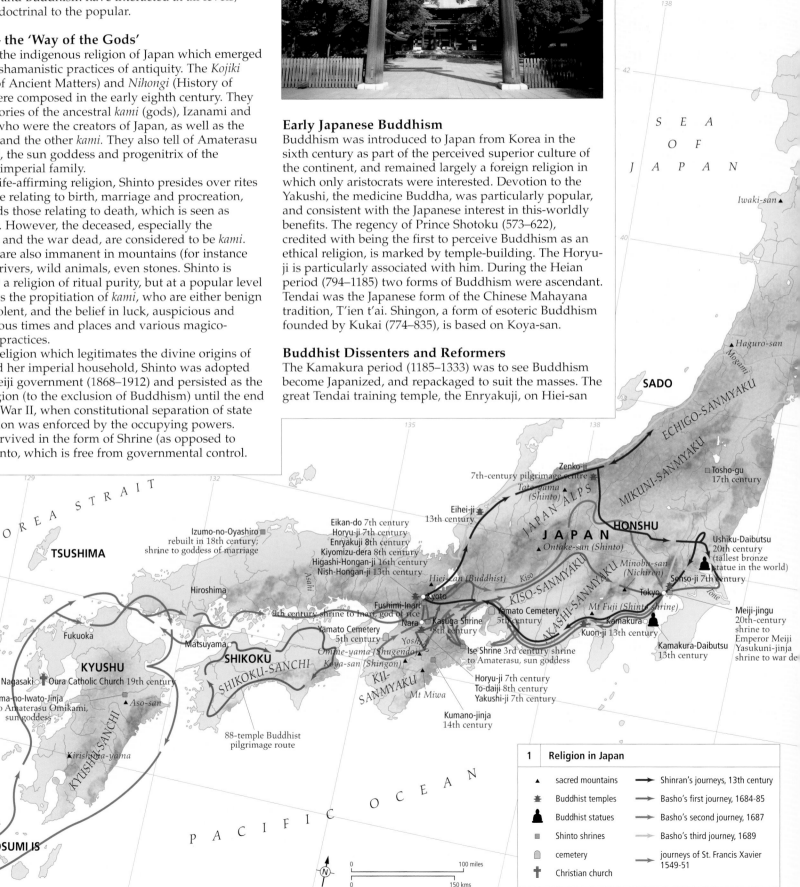

1 Religion in Japan

▲ sacred mountains	→ Shinran's journeys, 13th century
✸ Buddhist temples	→ Basho's first journey, 1684-85
▲ Buddhist statues	→ Basho's second journey, 1687
▪ Shinto shrines	→ Basho's third journey, 1689
▢ cemetery	→ journeys of St. Francis Xavier 1549-51
✝ Christian church	

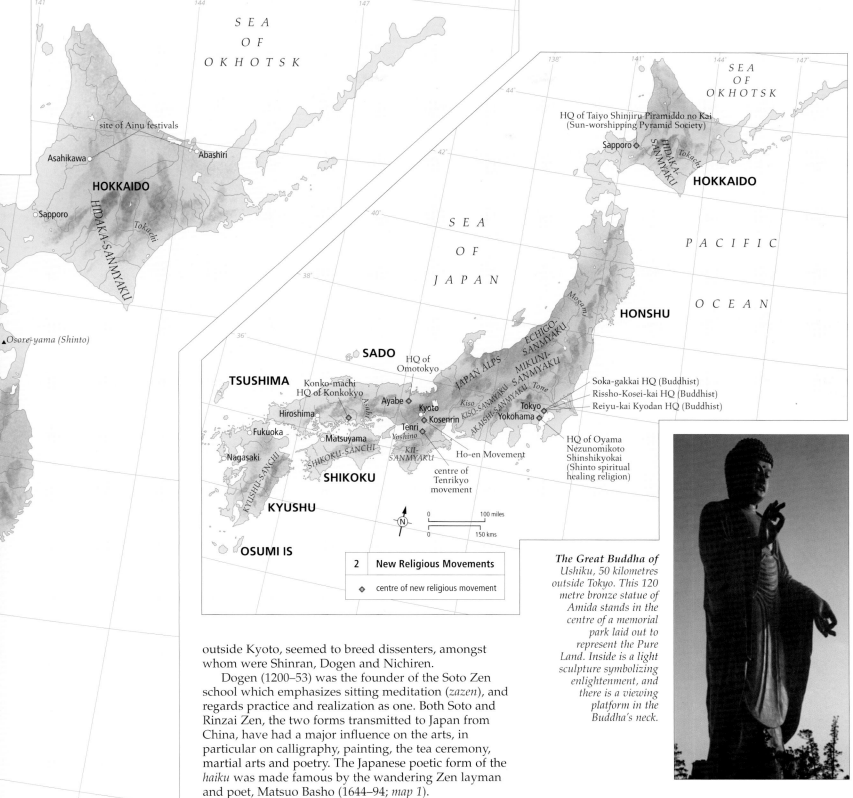

The map and surrounding labels:

S E A   O F   O K H O T S K

site of Ainu festivals

Asahikawa   Abashiri

HOKKAIDO

HIDAKA-SANMYAKU

Sapporo   Tokachi

▲ Osore-yama (Shinto)

SEA OF JAPAN

SADO

TSUSHIMA   HQ of Omotokyo

Konko-machi HQ of Konkokyo

Ayabe   Kyoto

Hiroshima   Asahi   Kosenrin

Tenri   JAPAN ALPS

Fukuoka   Yoshino   Ho-en Movement

Matsuyama   KII-SANMYAKU

Nagasaki   SHIKOKU-SANCHI

SHIKOKU   centre of Tenrikyo movement

KYUSHU-SANCHI

KYUSHU

OSUMI IS

ECHIGO-SANMYAKU   MIKUNI-SANMYAKU   KISO-SANMYAKU   AKAISHI-SANMYAKU   Tone   Mogami

HONSHU

HQ of Taiyo Shinjiru Piramiddo no Kai (Sun-worshipping Pyramid Society)

Sapporo

HOKKAIDO

HIDAKA-SANMYAKU   Tokachi

P A C I F I C   O C E A N

S E A   O F   O K H O T S K

Soka-gakkai HQ (Buddhist)
Rissho-Kosei-kai HQ (Buddhist)
Reiyu-kai Kyodan HQ (Buddhist)

Tokyo   Yokohama

HQ of Oyama Nezunomikoto Shinshikyokai (Shinto spiritual healing religion)

N

0   100 miles
0   150 kms

2	New Religious Movements
◆	centre of new religious movement

The Great Buddha of Ushiku, 50 kilometres outside Tokyo. This 120 metre bronze statue of Amida stands in the centre of a memorial park laid out to represent the Pure Land. Inside is a light sculpture symbolizing enlightenment, and there is a viewing platform in the Buddha's neck.

outside Kyoto, seemed to breed dissenters, amongst whom were Shinran, Dogen and Nichiren.

Dogen (1200–53) was the founder of the Soto Zen school which emphasizes sitting meditation (*zazen*), and regards practice and realization as one. Both Soto and Rinzai Zen, the two forms transmitted to Japan from China, have had a major influence on the arts, in particular on calligraphy, painting, the tea ceremony, martial arts and poetry. The Japanese poetic form of the *haiku* was made famous by the wandering Zen layman and poet, Matsuo Basho (1644–94; *map 1*).

Shinran (1173–1262) founded Jodo Shinshu, the 'True Pure Land School', which remains Japan's single largest denomination of Buddhism. Drawing on the Chinese Pure Land tradition when all else seemed to have failed to bring him to enlightenment, Shinran relied totally on the 'Other Power' of *Amida*, relinquishing all 'self-effort' practices which he claimed lead to pride and egoism.

Shinran wrote in the vernacular, and his teachings were further simplified by one in his line of successors, Rennyo (1415–49). Like Shinran himself, Jodo Shinshu priests marry, since celibacy is a 'self-effort' practice liable to result in egoism, and Temple-mastership is patrilineal. Since Jodo Shinshu is orientated towards the afterlife, much of its ritual function in Japan relates to funerals and memorial services.

Nichiren (1222–82) rejected less of his Tendai heritage than Shinran, though he simplified it to focus on the *Lotus Sutra*. In fact, for Nichiren the *Lotus* so distilled Buddhist teaching that simply uttering its name purified the mind. Coupled with this notion was a nationalistic

fervour and a belief that the salvation of Japan from impending disaster lay in the acceptance of the *daimoku*, the name of the *Lotus Sutra*. Nichiren's remains are enshrined on Minobu-san (*map 1*).

Christianity and New Religious Movements

Francis Xavier's journeys of 1549–51 had some success in bringing Christianity to Japan, but missionaries were banned in 1650. Around 2% of the population is now Christian (*see also* pp. 94-95).

After the separation of state and religion was declared in 1945 there was a considerable growth in the number of new religious movements, many of which drew on ancient traditions but repackaged them to suit the new post-war culture of Japan (*map 2*). Tenrikyo, for example, draws on Shinto and ancient shamanism, and claims that the land on which it has built its own city, Tenri, is where humanity was created and the universe originated. In 2000, the cult of Aum Shinrikyo, infamous for its sarin gas attacks on the Tokyo subway in 1995, changed its name to 'Aleph'.

MAINLAND SOUTHEAST ASIA

STRIKING FOR both its diversity of languages and ethnic groups, this region of the world is rich in religious belief and practice. Here, ancient tribal traditions fuse with the great religions of Buddhism and Hinduism, which have held out, in large part, against many threats: periods of communism; materialism driven by drugs; prostitution and tourism; military dictatorships and political unrest (*see also* pp. 58-59, 72-73).

The earliest religious practices in the region were based on the recognition of rice as fundamental to life. Neolithic sites link rice with fertility. Such sites also demonstrate well-formed beliefs in an afterlife. The Plain of Jars in central Laos, perhaps now better known as the most bombed region during the Vietnam War, is scattered with immense 2000-year-old stone urns, possibly used as funeral encasements for nobility. Another feature of ancient Southeast Asian religious life is the Dong-son drum, cast in bronze and dating to the first millennium BCE, and found at sites all over the region. These drums suggest widespread shamanic practices, although it is likely that they were put to different sorts of ritual use by different peoples. Among the most ancient of beliefs in the region is belief in spirits, called *nats* by Tibeto-Burman peoples, *phi* by the Thai, *hon* by the Vietnamese and *pralu'n* by the Khmer. This belief persists and has been assimilated into the non-indigenous religions.

The native religions of the region were eventually enveloped by the foreign traditions which swept through Asia. Hinduism and Theravada Buddhism were both introduced from India. Theravada, with its Pali scriptures and monastic practices, also arrived in the region from Sri Lanka. Mahayana Buddhism, Daoism and Confucianism all came from China. The Chinese, who ruled Vietnam from the Han to the Tang dynasties, played a significant role in the religious history of Vietnam for over ten centuries.

Indigenous and Imported Religions

Theravada Buddhism has provided the dominant theme in the religious history of both Burma and Thailand. It is the state religion in Thailand and defended by the king.

In Burma, Buddhism was disestablished by the military regime in 1962, and the Buddhist *sangha* (community) continue to provide a focus for opposition to the government. The contemporary situation contrasts strikingly with the glories of Burma's Buddhist past, which are reflected in the monuments of Pagan, the ancient capital, and the Shwedagon Pagoda of Rangoon (*map 2*). The Golden Age of the Pagan Dynasty, during which some 5000 temples and monuments were built, began in the eleventh century, when Anawrahta (1044–77), a convert to Theravada from Tantra, ascended the throne. It ended some two centuries later when Kublai Khan marched on Pagan.

The richness of Thailand's Buddhist past compares to that of Burma. The ancient capitals of Sukothai and Ayuthaya were centres of Buddhist culture and architecture, though Ayuthaya eventually fell to the Burmese in 1763. The Thai Royal family have had a long association with Buddhism, and some kings, for example Rama V, spent years as a monk before ascending the throne. Recently Thai Buddhism has become more critical of the establishment, and radicals like Bhikkhu Buddhadasa and Sulak Sivaraksa gained a reputation for speaking out on issues of concern for Buddhists.

Before the foundation of Cambodia's most prestigious empire, the Khmer, religious practice was dominated by

Angkor Wat ('city temple') *is part of Angkor Thom, a great temple complex which was at the heart of the Khmer Empire. Discovered in 1858 by French naturalist Henri Mouhot, Angkor Wat was built by Suryavarman II (1112–52 CE) and dedicated to Visnu. The architecture is in the archetypal Cambodian religious style. The mandala-style layout of the temple combines with extraordinary sculptures and friezes of the* Ramayana *and a variety of Buddhas and bodhisattvas to secure the place of Angkor Wat amongst the world's greatest religious monuments.*

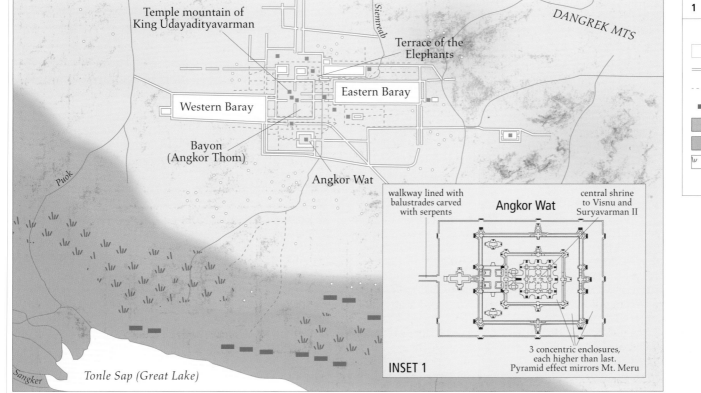

Temple mountain of King Udayadityavarman

Terrace of the Elephants

Siemreab

DANGREK MTS

Western Baray

Eastern Baray

Puok

Bayon (Angkor Thom)

Angkor Wat

Sangker

Tonle Sap (Great Lake)

1	Angkor
▪	Khmer temple
☐	water reservoir (baray)
═	dyke with causeway
-----	ancient canal
▬	earthworks for flood retention
▨	fertile alluvial plain
▨	seasonally flooded area
⸜ ⸝	rice cultivation
○	ponds

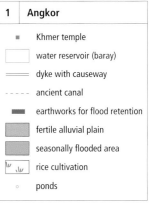

walkway lined with balustrades carved with serpents

Angkor Wat

central shrine to Visnu and Suryavarman II

3 concentric enclosures, each higher than last. Pyramid effect mirrors Mt. Meru

INSET 1

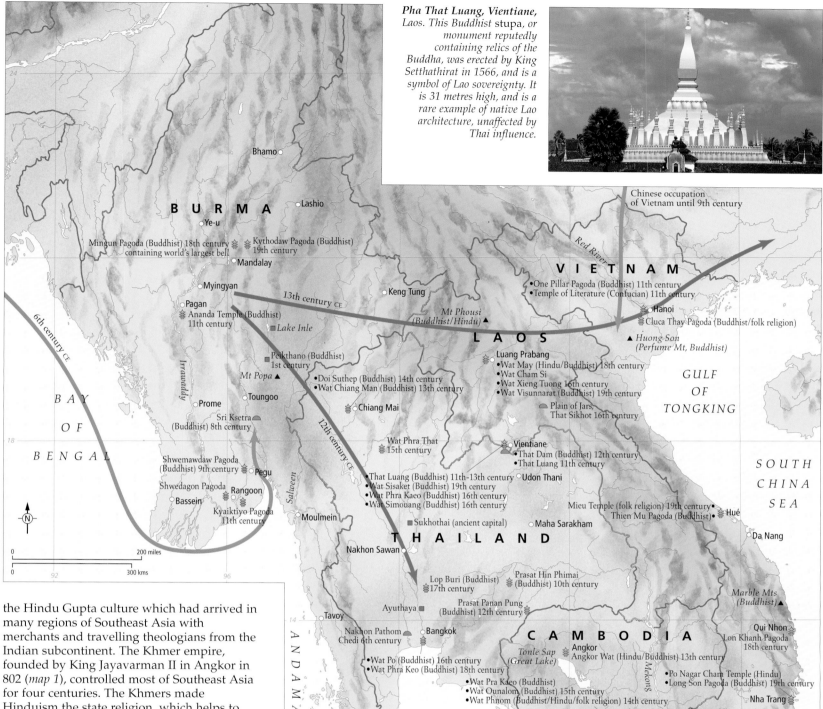

Pha That Luang, Vientiane, Laos. This Buddhist *stupa,* or *monument reputedly containing relics of the Buddha, was erected by King Setthathirat in 1566, and is a symbol of Lao sovereignty. It is 31 metres high, and is a rare example of native Lao architecture, unaffected by Thai influence.*

the Hindu Gupta culture which had arrived in many regions of Southeast Asia with merchants and travelling theologians from the Indian subcontinent. The Khmer empire, founded by King Jayavarman II in Angkor in 802 (*map 1*), controlled most of Southeast Asia for four centuries. The Khmers made Hinduism the state religion, which helps to account for the Buddhist-Hindu syncretism, evidence of which is to be found all over Southeast Asia. The kings of the Khmer empire were seen as manifestations both of Siva and, at times, of the Buddha. The Khmer empire went into decline in the thirteenth century, bankrupted by its ambitious programme of monument-building. The rise of Mahayana Buddhism led to higher expectations regarding the morality of the kings. Theravada Buddhism was to dominate Cambodia in later centuries, before it was violently excised by the Khmer Rouge, who promulgated a programme of revolutionary social reform which led to the deaths of over one million Cambodians and a violent civil war, 1975–9.

Lao religion followed the Cambodian pattern, with Theravada being the state religion until Laos fell to the communists in 1975. Ten years later Lao Buddhism began to recover, though it remains carefully monitored by the government.

Vietnamese religion remains largely sinicized, though it still retains traditional animism and ancestor cults. Chinese-style Mahayana Buddhism is widely practised and many Buddhists have become deeply involved in politics. In 1963 the monk Thich Quang Duc immolated

himself as a protest against the Diem regime, and the itinerant Thich Nhat Hanh is one of the most outspoken Buddhist political activists of the modern period.

The Buddhist Monuments of Southeast Asia

Monuments all over Southeast Asia approximate to some degree to the Indian *stupa. Stupas* were reliquaries for the historical Buddha, and became focal points for the *sangha.* Pagodas, *chedis,* and *thats* are all reminiscent of the *stupa.* Many in Southeast Asia do reputedly house relics, for example the Shwedagon Pagoda in Rangoon is supposed to hold some of the Buddha's hairs, but for the most part these monuments mark the tombs of important nobles, and reflect the Buddhist cosmos in their structures.

2	Mainland Southeast Asia
▲	sacred mountains
☗	wats/pagodas
⌂	stupas/chedis
■	other religious sites
→	spread of Mahayana Buddhism, with dates
→	spread of Theravada Buddhism, with dates

ISLAM AND CHRISTIANITY IN ASIA

BOTH CHRISTIANITY and Islam spread eastwards from their respective places of origin. Generally, with some striking exceptions, their rate of success diminished the further east they reached. Neither religion made significant inroads into eastern China, Japan or Southeast Asia (apart from French Indochina). Today, however, South Korea stands out as a predominantly Christian country, and Malaysia and Indonesia are strongly Muslim. The Philippines, too, provide a contrast to most of East Asia, with a strong Spanish Christian heritage and significant Muslim influence in the south.

Christian Missions to Asia

Christianity is traditionally thought to have reached India with the Apostle Thomas, who went by sea to Cochin and founded churches all over southern India. He died in Mylapore in 72 CE after twenty years of missionary work on the subcontinent. The early spread of Christianity in Asia (*map 1*) was facilitated by the proliferation of Christians in the Persian Empire and the movement of ideas along the Silk Road. Nestorian Christianity spread furthest; extensive missionary activity took it as far as China. The arrival of the Nestorian monk, Alopen, in China is recorded on the eighth-century stone 'Nestorian Monument', and Nestorian texts were found in the Buddhist caves of Dunhuang (*see also pp. 154-155*).

Later Christian missions to Asia were made by religious orders, such as the Dominicans, the

Augustinians, the Franciscans and later the Jesuits, amongst the most illustrious of whom were Matteo Ricci, Roberto de Nobili and their predecessor, the Spaniard, Francis Xavier (1506–52), who was canonized in 1622. Xavier was sent by Rome as a missionary to the colonies of Portugal, but pushed on beyond them into China and Japan. Xavier's commitment to the conversion of Japan had only limited success. Christians were persecuted and the religion was banished in 1650. When missionaries returned in 1859, however, they discovered that the church had to some degree survived underground.

The Dutch, Portuguese and British empires brought both Catholicism and Protestantism to large parts of Asia, but in many places, anti-colonial Islamic (and, in India, Hindu) movements limited the influence of Christianity. Interestingly, however, a semi-indigenous and syncretic form of peasant Christianity developed in China, and presented a significant challenge to the Qing dynasty in the form of the Taiping Rebellion of 1850–63.

In many Asian countries, Christianity suffers from its colonial associations, which have been used to justify its persecution, both by communist regimes and also by the nationalist movements instrumental in the independence of a number of countries from colonial powers.

The Spread of Islam

During the Umayyad Empire Islam spread rapidly eastwards, stretching as far as the borders of China and

Ubudiah Mosque, Kuala *Kangsar, Perak, Malaysia. Widely regarded as the most beautiful mosque in Malaysia, the Ubudiah was designed by an English engineer and built in 1913 on orders of Idris Murshidul, 28th Sultan of Perak.*

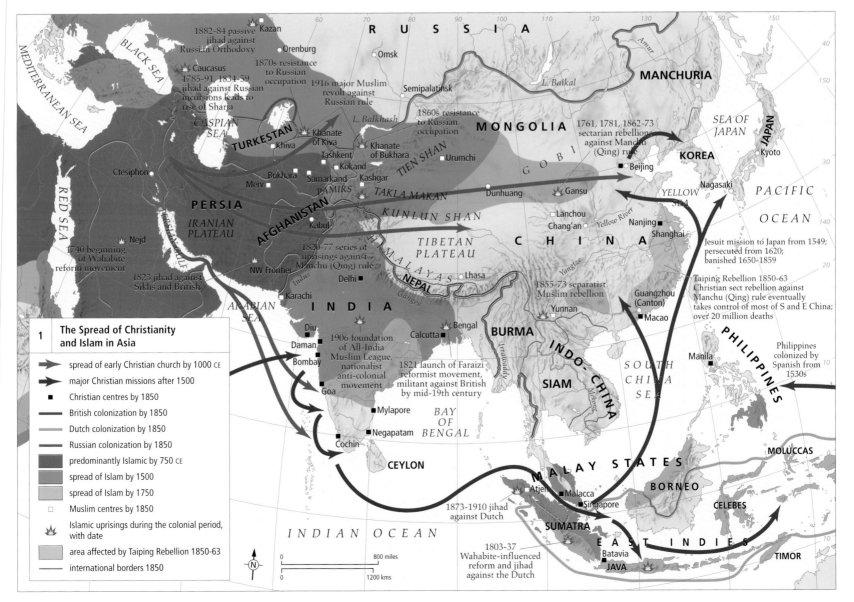

1 | The Spread of Christianity and Islam in Asia

- → spread of early Christian church by 1000 CE
- → major Christian missions after 1500
- ■ Christian centres by 1850
- — British colonization by 1850
- — Dutch colonization by 1850
- — Russian colonization by 1850
- predominantly Islamic by 750 CE
- spread of Islam by 1500
- spread of Islam by 1750
- □ Muslim centres by 1850
- ☙ Islamic uprisings during the colonial period, with date
- area affected by Taiping Rebellion 1850-63
- — international borders 1850

1882-84 passive jihad against Russian Orthodoxy
1870s resistance to Russian occupation
1785-91, 1834-59 jihad against Russian incursions leads to rise of Sharia
1916 major Muslim revolt against Russian rule
1860s resistance to Russian occupation
1761, 1781, 1862-73 sectarian rebellions against Manchu (Qing) rule
1740 beginning of Wahabite reform movement
1823 jihad against Sikhs and British
1820-77 series of uprisings against Manchu (Qing) rule
1855-73 separatist Muslim rebellion
1906 foundation of All-India Muslim League, nationalist anti-colonial movement
1821 launch of Faraizi reformist movement, militant against British by mid-19th century
Jesuit mission to Japan from 1549; persecuted from 1620; banished 1650-1859
Taiping Rebellion 1850-63 Christian sect rebellion against Manchu (Qing) rule eventually takes control of most of S and E China; over 20 million deaths
Philippines colonized by Spanish from 1530s
1873-1910 jihad against Dutch
1803-37 Wahabite-influenced reform and jihad against the Dutch

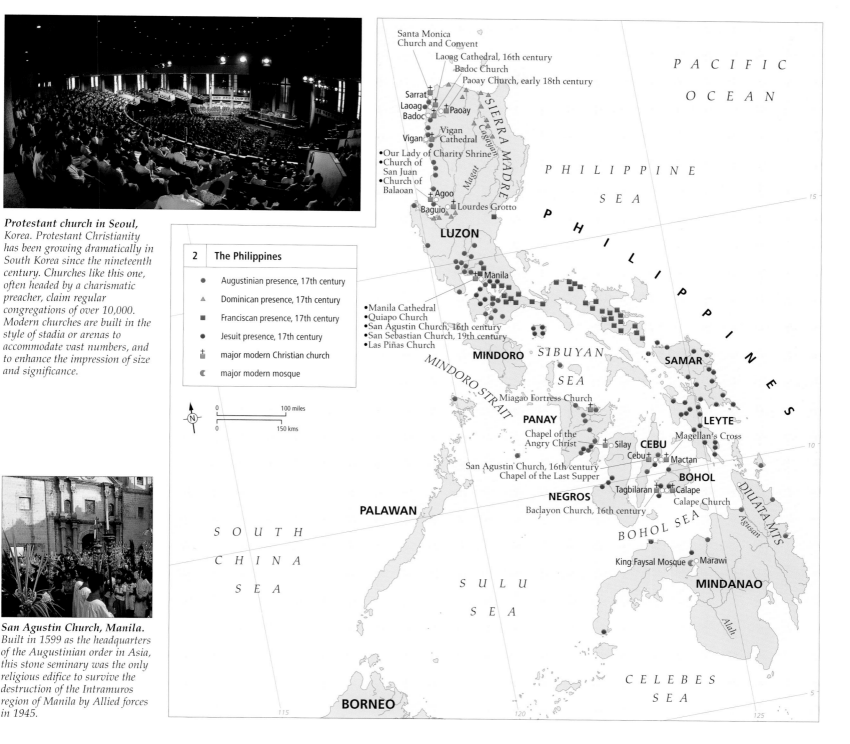

Protestant church in Seoul, Korea. Protestant Christianity has been growing dramatically in South Korea since the nineteenth century. Churches like this one, often headed by a charismatic preacher, claim regular congregations of over 10,000. Modern churches are built in the style of stadia or arenas to accommodate vast numbers, and to enhance the impression of size and significance.

San Agustin Church, Manila. Built in 1599 as the headquarters of the Augustinian order in Asia, this stone seminary was the only religious edifice to survive the destruction of the Intramuros region of Manila by Allied forces in 1945.

2	The Philippines
●	Augustinian presence, 17th century
▲	Dominican presence, 17th century
■	Franciscan presence, 17th century
●	Jesuit presence, 17th century
⊞	major modern Christian church
☪	major modern mosque

India by the mid-eighth century. This spread was effected by forcible conversion of polytheists, and by the protection of the Peoples of the Book, the Christians and Jews, as *dhimmis* (protected minorities) in return for taxes paid to fund Muslim expansion.

The expansion under the 'Abbasids, who succeeded the Umayyads, was temporarily halted in 1258 by the Mongols. This resulted in a cultural shift away from the erstwhile dominance of the Arabs and towards Persians and Turks. Arabic, however, remained the *lingua franca* and expansion continued, though at a less frantic pace, until the seventeenth century, when countries as far afield as Indonesia and Malaysia became largely Muslim. Most Muslim countries subsequently became subject to European rule. Their eventual independence from Europe owed much to Islamic resistance movements, such as the Wahabite-driven resistance to the Dutch in Indonesia, and the Faraizi resistance to the British in India. The history of Islam in India reached a turning point in 1947 when the partition of India, negotiated by Muhammad Ali Jinnah of the Muslim League, created the Islamic state of Pakistan.

In northern and western China and Central Asia Islam remains relatively strong. There are large numbers of Muslim Uighurs, Kazakhs, Kirghiz, Uzbeks and Tajiks, as well as the indigenous Chinese Hui. Islam suffered less than other religions during the Cultural Revolution, partly because its membership was largely from ethnic minorities and so was of little interest to the Red Guard.

Religion in the Philippines

The indigenous folk religion of the Philippines has not been completely obscured by the dominance of Roman Catholicism, and, as elsewhere in Asia, Christianity is characterized by a degree of inculturation. Catholicism was introduced to the Philippines through colonization by Spain. Philip II of Spain saw no distinction between colonization and evangelism. At the Synod of Manila in 1580 the Jesuits, Augustinians, Dominicans and Franciscans shared out the islands between themselves for proselytization (*map 2*). The Jesuits have continued to maintain their interest in the Philippines, developing Christian communities there and evolving a liberation theology in response to the corrupt regime of President Marcos, who was ejected in 1986. Independent churches, such as the Aglipayan Church, have large congregations, and Islam remains strong on Mindanao despite the ambivalent attitude to the religion on the part of the occupying Americans at the turn of the twentieth century.

95

INDONESIAN AND MALAYSIAN RELIGIONS

THE MALAY PENINSULA and the islands of Malaysia and Indonesia have been subject to a variety of religious influences, due both to cultural encounters through trade routes, and to the imposition of religious beliefs during colonial rule. There have been periods of both Buddhist and Hindu supremacy and some significant Christian influence (*map 1*), though the region is now dominated by Islam (*see also* pp. 18-19, 72-73, 198-199).

Discoveries of Hindu and Buddhist inscriptions in Indonesia suggest that Hinduism was practised prior to the fourth century CE and well established, through trade routes, by the fifth century. By the sixth century there is evidence of Buddhist influence on Sumatra and Java, and from the eighth century onwards a sophisticated relationship, involving some syncretism, developed between the two traditions. The zenith of Indian culture was the fourteenth-century Majapahit Empire, which unified Indonesia and imbued it with a distinctive culture and religion, recorded on monuments all over the region.

In Bali (*map 2*), the Indo-Javanese culture of the sixteenth century was preserved until the early twentieth century, when the island fell to the Dutch. Balinese religion is a mixture of Hinduism and traditional animism, with one supreme god who rules over numerous others, such as Visnu, Siva and Dewi Sri, the rice goddess. Life cycle rituals, including puberty rites, teeth-filing, marriages and funerals, are the staples of village life.

Religious and Cultural Diversity

The Chinese population of Indonesia, though small and persecuted in recent times, has always practised Chinese religions, and many towns and cities have a designated Chinese temple which may contain features of Confucianism, Daoism, Buddhism and folk religion.

Temple of Siva, late ninth century, Prambanam, Java. Before the arrival of Islam, the Hindu god Siva was worshipped widely on Java.

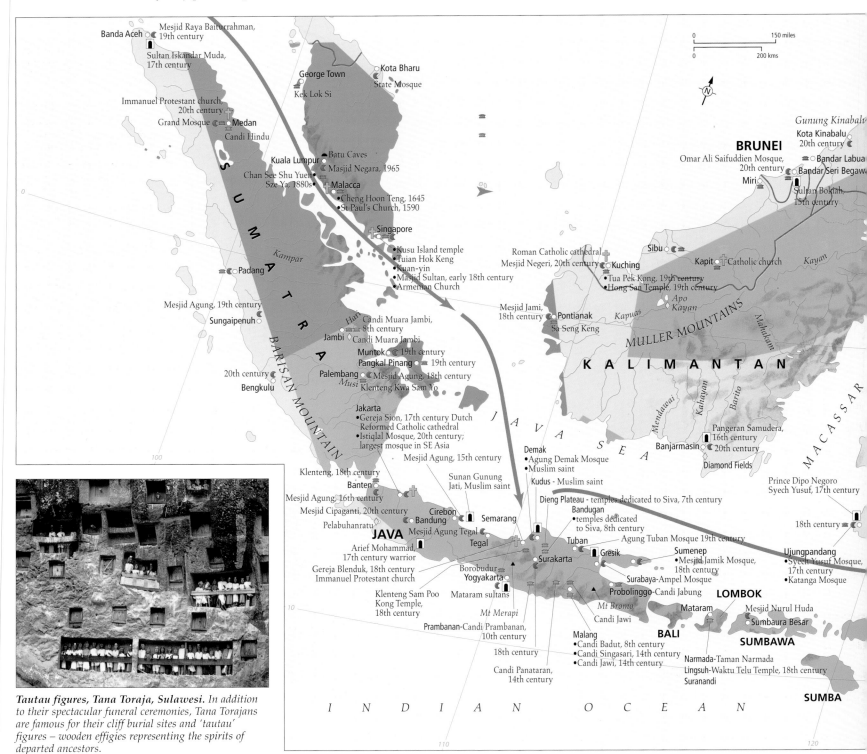

Tautau figures, Tana Toraja, Sulawesi. In addition to their spectacular funeral ceremonies, Tana Torajans are famous for their cliff burial sites and 'tautau' figures – wooden effigies representing the spirits of departed ancestors.

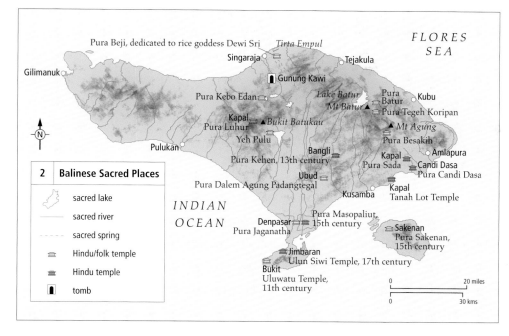

Pura Beji, dedicated to rice goddess Dewi Sri · *Tirta Empul* · *FLORES SEA*
Singaraja
Tejakula
Gilimanuk
■ Gunung Kawi
Pura Kebo Edan · *Lake Batur* · Pura Batur · Kubu
Mt Batur ▲ · Pura Tegeh Koripan
Kapal ▲ *Bukit Batukau*
Pura Luhur · ▲ Mt Agung
Yeh Pulu · Pura Besakih
Pulukan
Bangli · Amlapura
Pura Kehen, 13th century · Kapal · Candi Dasa
Pura Sada · Pura Candi Dasa
Ubud
Pura Dalem Agung Padangtegal · Kusamba · Kapal · Tanah Lot Temple

2 Balinese Sacred Places

⌁ sacred lake
― sacred river
--- sacred spring
⊟ Hindu/folk temple
⊟ Hindu temple
▮ tomb

INDIAN OCEAN

Pura Masopaliut · 15th century
Denpasar
Pura Jaganatha
Sakenan · Pura Sakenan, 15th century
Jimbaran
Ulun Siwi Temple, 17th century
Bukit
Uluwatu Temple, 11th century

0 ——— 20 miles
0 ——— 30 kms

By the thirteenth century, Islam was exerting a major influence in Indonesia and ultimately prevailed, despite the arrival of Catholicism with the Spanish and Portuguese in the fifteenth century, and of Protestantism with the Dutch and English in the sixteenth century Today, Islam claims around 90 per cent of the population. There are two main Islamic traditions in Indonesia, known in Javanese as *Agami Jawi* and *Agami Islam Santri*. The former is syncretistic and involves devotion to deities of Hindu origin, though the main emphasis is on key Islamic tenets. *Agami Islam Santri* is a more strict form of Islam, and is puritan in its adherence to the Qur'an and *shar'ia*. This striking diversity of religions and cultures have all contributed to the development of modern Indonesia. It is hardly surprising that the main source for ethics, other than *shar'ia*, is *adat*, or customary law, deriving from a diversity of religious sources.

The population of peninsular Malaysia and East Malaysia (Sabah and Sarawak) is predominantly Sunni Muslim. The spread of Sufism in the fourteenth century was a major factor in the Islamization of Malaysia, perhaps because it tolerated some assimilation of the indigenous culture. Islam was declared the official religion in 1957.

Traditional Religions

Governments throughout Malaysia and Indonesia do not recognize traditional religions, which are therefore under pressure to assimilate to state recognized religions. In isolated areas, however, pre-Hindu practices have been preserved, generally amongst tribal peoples; for example the wandering Kubu of the forests of Sumatra, the Punan and the Kayan of Kalimantan and the Toraja of Sulawesi.

Beliefs and practices vary from group to group, but common themes include a this world–other world dualism, and the immanence of a hierarchy of spirits including ancestors, all of which are potentially malevolent and require sacrifice. For some tribes the most worthy sacrificial animal is the water buffalo. Life cycle rituals, for example circumcision, tattooing and teeth filing, provide the means by which the individual relates to the wider cosmos. Divination and augury are also widely practised.

The Chinese make up the largest ethnic minority in Malaysia. Some are Muslims, but most follow traditional Chinese religions. In East Malaysia, however, Christianity provides the greatest challenge to Islam, with about 40 per cent adherence. Nonetheless, Christianity is kept in check in Malaysia by government policy, which is oppressive to the religion. The small Theravada Buddhist Sangha enjoys the protection of the state.

In Singapore 75 per cent of the population is Chinese. In the 1980s the government promoted Confucianism, though this was resisted by the non-Chinese, most of whom are either Sunni Muslim or Christian. Protestant evangelical sects have become more numerous recently.

Sam Sing Kung Temple, 19th century
Sandakan
• St Michael's, 19th century
• All Saints, 19th century

CELEBES SEA

Ban Hing Kiong Temple, 19th century · Manado
HALMAHERA
PACIFIC OCEAN

Tentena ⊹ 19th century Protestant church
RAIT
JLAWESI
Rantepao-Waktu Telu Temple, ancestor worship, 18th century

MOLUCCAS
BURU · CERAM

IRIAN
MAOKE MOUNTAINS
JAYA
Paluit

Baubau ○ 16th century
FLORES SEA
BANDA SEA

FLORES
"Chapel of Virgin Mary
nde Larantuka
Dili ⊹ Cathedral of the Immaculate Conception
EAST TIMOR

ARAFURA SEA

TIMOR · *TIMOR SEA*

140

97

THE PACIFIC

OCEANIA, embracing Australia, New Zealand, New Guinea and the numerous high islands and coral atolls of the Pacific, is a natural laboratory for the study of religion. The region contains the greatest number of distinct religions and cults for any land mass. There are over 1,435 language cultures. But survivals and evolving forms of the world's oldest religions also exist side by side with the world's most pervasive faiths and many newly evolved belief systems and cults.

THE INDIGENOUS RELIGIONS fall into several geographical categories each associated with thousands of years of distinct shamanic evolution. The *karadji*, as he was known in southeastern Australia, with his believed ability to travel in the spirit world, levitate, cross vast distances at will, manipulate quartz crystals and cure the physical body by treating the psychic body had much in common with the *taulaaitu* (spirit anchors) and other shamans of Polynesia and Micronesia. They also went into trances, healed the psychic body and claimed to change shape into birds, animals and fish and travel in the spirit world.

In New Guinea and parts of Melanesia, traditional shamanic practices were less recognizable largely through the phenomenal dominance of sorcery and fetish magic, though spirit possession, shape-changing and flying were not unknown and many of the rituals were based on shamanic transformation.

Apart from Australia, where human habitation goes back well over 40,000 years, it is difficult to 'age' the various indigenous religions. In most of Melanesia it can be assumed that religious beliefs connected with agriculture and fertility are thousands of years old. On the other hand, when hunter-gatherers became agriculturists in more recent periods and vice-versa there were bound to be new religious consequences, leading some observers to conclude the absence of religion.

In the more recently settled island world (from about 2,000 BCE to 1500 CE) it is difficult to know whether the shamanic subculture came with the immigrants or developed locally. Certainly the oldest shamanic figures of central and eastern Polynesia like Maui look as if they evolved in the Pacific, while some of the *aitu* of central Polynesia could be late introductions from the east. Some believe the shamanic hero Tiki to have been of South American origin.

Local cults, which might be regarded as separate religions, developed in many areas, usually around sacred sites or ancestors renowned for their shamanic or sacred powers. The so-called sky-god cults of southeastern Australia ritualized the memory of creator

| 50,000 | 25,000 | 5,000 | 1000 | 500 | 1000 | 1500 | 1600 | 1700 | 1800 | 1900 | 2000 |

Top: Evidence of human settlement, New Guinea and Australia, 43,000 · Beginning of Lapita Culture, 1600 · Settlement of Eastern Polynesia, 500-300 · CE · Settlement of New Zealand and Hawaii, 800-900 · Magellan crosses Pacific, 1521 · Cultural changes in Fiji and Tonga, 1570-1630 · First Protestant missionaries, Tonga, Tahiti and Marquesas, 1797 · Free Church of Tonga, 1885 · Pacific Conference of Churches formed, 1961

Bottom: Settlement of Island Melanesia begins, 28,000 · Settlement of Micronesia and Western Polynesia, 1300-1000 · Decline of Lapita Culture, 200 · Peak of high culture in Pohnpei and Kosrae, 1300 · Last Maori migration to New Zealand, 1530- · First Jesuit missionaries, Mariana I, 1668 · British settlement of Australia, 1788 · Mormon missionaries, 1844 · Uniting Church formed in Australia, 1977

THE WORLD

| 50,000 | 25,000 | 5,000 | 1000 | 500 | 1000 | 1500 | 1600 | 1700 | 1800 | 1900 | 2000 |

Top: Early Ice Age, c.40,000 · Lascaux Caves in France, c.15,000 · David, King of Israel, c.1000-960 · Gautama Siddhartha, c.563-483 · CE · Mani, 216-c.275 · First Crusade, 1095 · Fall of Constantinople, to Turks, 1453 · Amritsar founded, 1577 · Foundation of Hasidism, c.1735 · World Parliament of Religions, 1893 · 2nd Vatican Council, 1961-4

Bottom: Venus of Willendorf, c.25,000-30,000 · Indus valley civilization, c.3500-1700 · Zarathustra, c.1000 · Jesus, c.6 BCE-26/36 CE · Muhammad, 570-632 · East and West Christian churches separate, 1054 · Council of Trent, 1545-63 · Pilgrim Fathers to America, 1620 · Mormonism founded, 1830 · 1st Zionist Conference, 1897 · Great Council of Buddhism, Burma, 1956

---

ancestors, it being usual shamanic practice to attribute the physical landscape to ancestors with supposed paranormal powers. Influential cults developed throughout Polynesia and Micronesia, intimately connected with the leading sacred families. These cults were frequently at the heart of tribute systems. Clients brought offerings and 'first fruits' from outer or neighbouring islands in return for the gods' fructifying influence and protection.

The Arrival of Christianity

Catholic Christianity is the first of the universal faiths that can be documented in the Pacific, although Hindu, Buddhist, and Arab Muslim sailors may have reached some of the islands without leaving much trace. Indian scholars have described parallels between Hinduism and some Polynesian beliefs and practices. (For example, a god named Varuna was found in the Tuamotus.) The first Spaniards

crossed the Pacific in 1521. Thereafter the limited influence of European castaways was likely.

The first concerted missionary attempt was that of the Jesuit Fathers, under the patronage of Queen Mariana of Spain, who began the evangelization of the Mariana Islands in 1668. A Spanish expedition left two Franciscan missionaries on Tahiti in 1774 but they made no converts and were taken off in 1775. In this period the Dutch Protestants got no further east than Timor and nearby islands in the Arafura Sea, managing to convert several by 1770.

Missionary Activity

The major thrust of modern Christian missionary activity began in 1797 with the arrival of Protestant artisan missionaries sent by the London Missionary Society who were placed in the Society Islands, Tonga and the Marquesas. Despite little progress for almost two decades and complete failure in the Marquesas, the conversion of significant chiefs in the major Polynesian groups led to the rapid conversion of most of Polynesia during the second and third decades of the nineteenth century. Protestant missionary work began in Melanesia in the 1830s and was much slower, the conversion unit being the local village rather than a chiefly confederation. Catholic missions were also active in Polynesia and Melanesia in this period. Only in Mangareva, the Marquesas, Easter Island, Wallis, Futuna and New Caledonia did Catholicism become the dominant faith.

Australia was first settled by the British in 1788, largely as a convict colony. The first chaplains appointed through the influence of prominent Evangelicals made some attempts to convert Aborigines by adopting orphans and by religious instruction, but it was left to dedicated individuals to carry out mission work for the major British societies. The most successful missions were often carried out by non-British nationals. Most of the chaplains supported the governors in maintaining a virtual Anglican establishment. Roman Catholics in particular were severely penalized, especially after the Irish Rebellion of 1798, and even the first official Catholic chaplains who arrived in 1820 were subject to special conditions. Nevertheless, as a result of immigration and because of Protestant fragmentation Australia's Catholics have become the most institutionalised Christian group.

New Zealand early became a mission field for Evangelical Protestants. The influx of predominantly English and Scottish settlers, and predominantly Protestant Pacific Islanders from the 1960s, has resulted in a largely Protestant nation.

Later Developments

Reaction to Christianity has sometimes been extreme. Although various post-Christian cults and millenarian movements took place in Polynesia and Micronesia, Christianity is firmly wedded to traditional values and aspirations. In Melanesia there is a greater division between the mainline churches and the syncretist 'custom' churches and movements. After the Second World War, cargo cults and millenarian movements proliferated, especially in New Guinea, the Solomons and Vanuatu. In Australia and New Zealand there is a high degree of secularization and the Australian policy of multi-culturalism, implemented since the 1970s, has been matched by the growth of Buddhism, Islam, New Age beliefs and fundamentalist sects.

PRIMAL RELIGIONS OF OCEANIA

THE HUNTER-GATHERERS who settled in Australia and the agricultural people who settled in New Guinea at least 40,000 years ago lived in a spirit world dominated by the landscape. Time was cyclical and religious rituals were mainly used to invoke spirits or recycle the living. Hunter ancestor spirits were mostly male. Beneficent serpent goddesses and bisexual mythic beings originating in a planter culture linked northern Australia with New Guinea and the Solomons.

Colonists and Settlers

The arrival in Melanesia, during the second millennium BCE, of Austronesian-speaking pottery-making peoples from Southeast Asia led to a revival of an earlier obsidian trade and a thriving Lapita pottery culture embraced

New Caledonia, Vanuatu and western Polynesia (*map 1*).

Although the Polynesians and Micronesians were superb sailors they could only make their epic voyages eastwards into the Pacific under abnormally severe El Niño conditions, which reversed the normal wind patterns. Austronesian speakers penetrated Micronesia in the second millennium BCE, others reached Samoa and Tonga at about the same time, and had already reached Tahiti and the Marquesas early in the Christian era. Maui, the most pervasive culture hero of the Polynesians, had probably originated as a wind god. Like his Greek counterpart Hermes he was also a shamanic trickster with a magic phallus.

Other invaders from Southeast Asia, a seafaring aristocracy possibly connected with the Orissa-Bali

Wooden image of A'a atea (Avatea), the original eastern Polynesian god of the firmament studded with lesser gods, from Rurutu (Austral Islands), often identified with Ta'aroa.

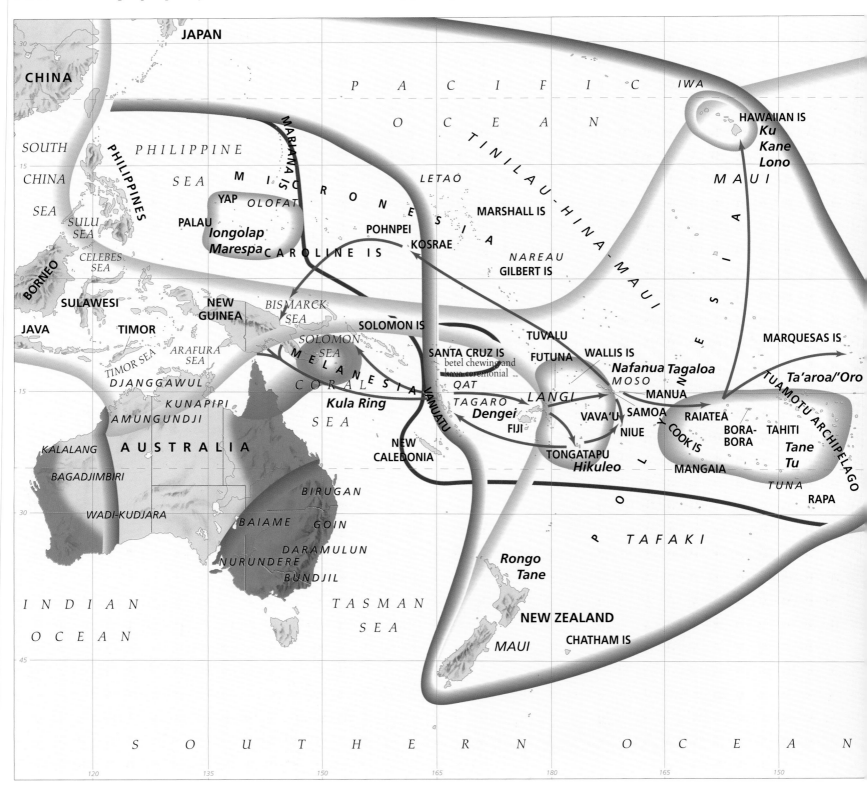

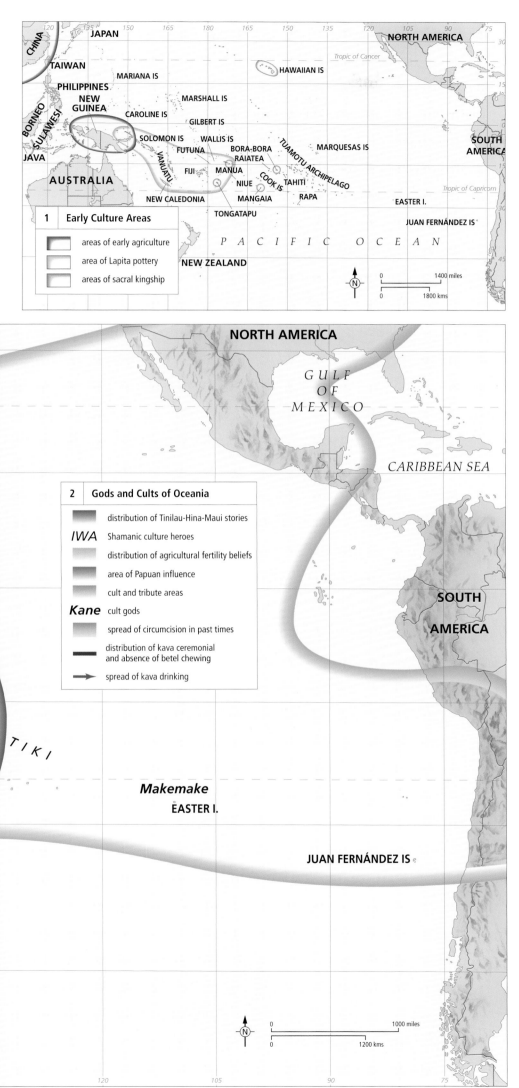

1 Early Culture Areas

- areas of early agriculture
- area of Lapita pottery
- areas of sacral kingship

2 Gods and Cults of Oceania

- distribution of Tinilau-Hina-Maui stories
- *IWA* Shamanic culture heroes
- distribution of agricultural fertility beliefs
- area of Papuan influence
- cult and tribute areas
- *Kane* cult gods
- spread of circumcision in past times
- distribution of kava ceremonial and absence of betel chewing
- spread of kava drinking

trading complex, arrived in Polynesia in about 200 BCE. Their introduction of earth ovens and wells reduced the need for pottery. The cult of their seagod Tangaloa (Ta'aroa) eventually reached the Leeward Society Islands where it replaced and at the same time absorbed the character of an earlier cult devoted to the primordial creators Atea (Vatea) and Papa. Followers of the Papa-atea cult eventually reached western Polynesia where they lived in uneasy truce with the Pulotu people.

The Pulotu people (named for their mirror-image afterworld), with their divine rulers the Tu'i Manu'a and the Tu'i Tonga, practised a Hindu-type fertility cult which developed into an extensive tribute system. The male fertility god was represented by the sacred king and the (frequently female) war god was represented by the war leader or secular king. The mother of the Tu'i Tonga was always a Samoan. First fruits were brought twice yearly to the Tu'i Tonga with elaborate ritual.

In the late sixteenth and seventeenth centuries severe El Niño conditions and volcanic activity apparently led to renewed population movements. Invaders established new patrilineal dynasties in Fiji. In Samoa and Tonga, political changes were accompanied by a religious revolution. The failure of the Tu'i Tonga dynasty to produce male heirs led to the sacred power or *mana* passing to the Tu'i Tonga Fefine (female) and her children by her Fijian husband. Hikuleo, hitherto a male fertility god, took on a female persona and the Tongan war god was replaced by the Fijian war god Taliai Tupou. The new dynasty revised the creation myth and probably introduced the mildly psychoactive *kava* drink as a drug of social control.

Sacred Cults and Libations

Kava-drinking spread from Vanuatu throughout the island world, although there was a marked social divide passing through the Carolines and Melanesia (*map 2*). East of this divide *kava* was used as a ceremonial or chiefly beverage, while to the west of the *kava* line betel chewing prevailed. In the Santa Cruz Islands betel co-existed with *kava* ceremonial. *Kava* was at the centre of most chiefly and religious rituals and used in household libations which were made to the gods.

Elaborate cults of sacred kingship, fertility and warfare also developed in the Society Islands and Hawaii. The Ta'aroa (Tangaloa) cult, later replaced by the war god 'Oro, spread from Raiatea throughout the Society, Cook and Tuamotu archipelagos with its sacred altar meeting place Taputapuatea, human sacrifice, dramatic performances and infanticide. The priests of these cults were highly skilled in esoteric lore, practising fire walking and sleight of hand in Raiatea and rivalling the chiefs in Hawaii.

The arrival of the Europeans destabilized the island societies, introducing disease and famine, and the power of the sacred kings waned. Shamans proliferated, and secular rulers emerged who looked to Christianity to legitimize their status.

Tasmanian Aborigines *performing a corroboree or nocturnal ritual dance in which the male dancers re-enact the transformations of spirit ancestors or invoke their support, as drawn by Joseph Lycett in 1830.*

101

TRADITIONAL RELIGION IN THE SOUTHWEST PACIFIC

WHILE MELANESIA was the first Oceanic region to be settled, New Zealand was the last. Traditional religion in Melanesia was so closely linked with the landscape and agricultural needs of the people that most village communities were participants rather than clients in religious ceremonies. In many places the ancestors were believed to return at annual New Year festivals or other ritual periods to praise or rebuke the people, bless the crops and preside at initiations. The ancestor spirits were represented by masked dancers usually wearing elaborate headdresses, the most famous being the Dukduk of the Tolai people of New Britain. Similar masked visitants were known in Irian Jaya, Mapoon in northern Australia and Vanuatu.

With the coming of Christianity, indigenous religions were frequently transformed. Most of the new religious movements which emerged, such as the Mamaia in Tahiti, Siovili in Samoa and most of the Maori movements, were primarily millenarian though they also had syncretic features. This was also true of Marching Rule, the John Frum Movement and other Melanesian movements which usually started within the mission churches (*map 2*). While some cargo cults contained syncretic elements, they were really responses of a traditional kind to newly introduced material culture and technology.

Christianity and Cargo Cults

The leaders of the cults attempted to explain the arrival of Europeans in terms of their own traditions. The myth of three brothers was widespread; one brother was the father of the grassland people, the second was the father of the bush people, while the third brother went away and never returned. The third brother learnt new magic which gave him access to the goods of the spirit world and his descendants returned with this property. The gods of the cargo cults were seen as either ancestors or the returning dead who would also make the goods available to their descendants. When God was invoked in

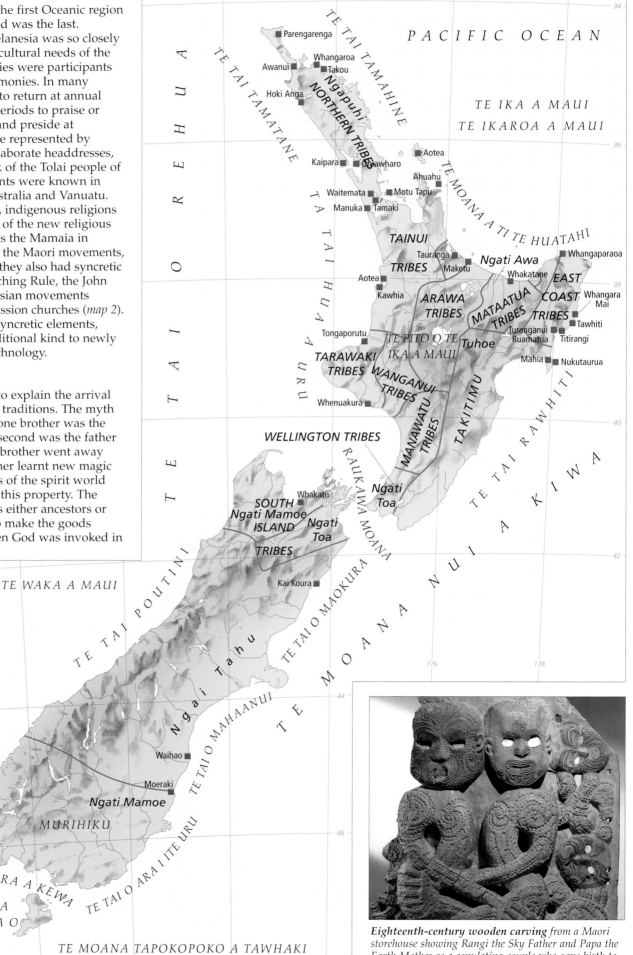

1 Maori Tribal Distribution

TAINUI group tribal name

Tuhoe tribal name

■ legendary canoe landing site

— tribal boundaries

0 —— 100 miles
0 —— 150 kms

Eighteenth-century wooden carving *from a Maori storehouse showing Rangi the Sky Father and Papa the Earth Mother as a copulating couple who gave birth to the gods of the Maori pantheon.*

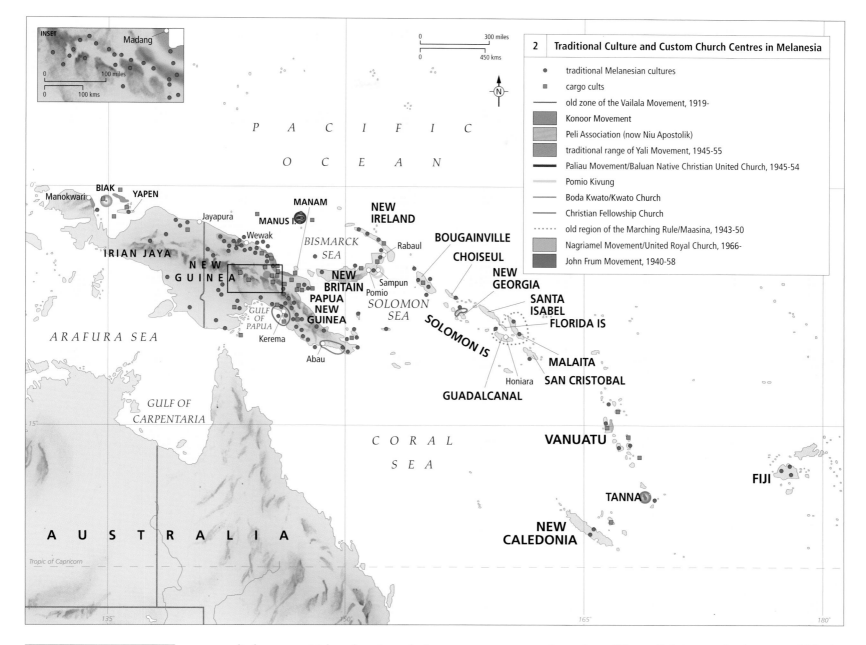

Map legend:

2 Traditional Culture and Custom Church Centres in Melanesia

- traditional Melanesian cultures
- cargo cults
- old zone of the Vailala Movement, 1919-
- Konoor Movement
- Peli Association (now Niu Apostolik)
- traditional range of Yali Movement, 1945-55
- Paliau Movement/Baluan Native Christian United Church, 1945-54
- Pomio Kivung
- Boda Kwato/Kwato Church
- Christian Fellowship Church
- old region of the Marching Rule/Maasina, 1943-50
- Nagriamel Movement/United Royal Church, 1966-
- John Frum Movement, 1940-58

Elaborate headdress and spirit mask of barkcloth on cane worn by male dancers initiating young men into the Hevehe cult of the Elema people of the Gulf of Papua.

some cults he was not Jehovah or Jesus but a transformed traditional god such as God-Kilibob of the Madang district, New Guinea.

While in Polynesia and Micronesia belief in spirits, herbal medicine and traditional prohibitions are usually accepted as being consistent with a Christian profession, the more usual traditional survivals in Melanesia, sorcery and magic, exist in opposition to Christianity.

Early Settlers in New Zealand
The first attested settlement of New Zealand was c.800 CE. Traditions and religious developments indicate that several Polynesian migrations to New Zealand took place between the ninth and sixteenth centuries. The idea of a large Maori fleet arriving about 1350 CE has been discredited, but canoe traditions are preserved in great detail. Some contain mythical elements, while others may refer to journeys within local waters (*map 1*).

The earliest traditions relate to canoes connected with Maui and possibly the *Takitimu* canoe with its complement of *tohunga* or priests. The Maori priesthood, with its schools of learning indicative of a hierarchical society such as Hawaii or Tonga, was highly developed, suggesting that the first arrivals may have been the victims of a religious revolution. This fits with traditions of eastern Polynesian refugees from the Tonga-Samoa area, the Papa-atea people who had adopted the Tongan high god Langi (Rangi) and were probably expelled from Tongatapu. The eastern Polynesians introduced the cult of Tane, the principal cult god of Tahiti and Huahine, and the sacred *patu* or ancestral club.

A number of Tonga Pulotu people, devotees of Maui, probably came with them or arrived separately, some moving to the South Island. They probably built the first *pa* or fortified hill sites. Rongo, a fertility or war god elsewhere in Polynesia, was probably introduced from the Cook Islands and associated with Tane. Later arrivals, probably Marquesans who had reached Rapa, brought priests skilled in tattooing and the esoteric lore of the master shaman Tawhaki (Tafaki) in the *Mowhao Matarua* canoe. Others who settled in the South Island may also have come via Rapa or Raivavae; their god Matemate was possibly brought from Easter Island.

The Diverse Traditions of New Zealand
The last canoes to arrive, the *Tainui* and perhaps the *Arawa*, made the difficult voyage direct from Raiatea probably as late as the early sixteenth century and possibly with the assistance of Spanish navigators. These late arrivals brought the sweet potato and superior skills in *pa* building and weaponry, but made no innovations in the local religion which was largely agricultural in character. Hawaiki, the old name for Raiatea, came to refer to other homelands and even took on some of the characteristics of the mirror image world of Pulotu. The blending of so many diverse traditions produced a rich oral literature comparable to that of the Celts. The prominence given in Maori society to prophets and holy persons claiming to have visions and work miracles has led to the widespread acceptance of the leaders of visionary, traditional, syncretist and millenarian cults.

CHRISTIANITY IN THE PACIFIC

APART FROM THE extension of Philippine-style Catholicism into the Marianas and the western Carolines, most of the Oceanic world was unaffected by Christianity until the beginning of the nineteenth century. The London Missionary Society (LMS), founded by British Calvinistic Methodists and Dissenters, only succeeded in converting the people of Tahiti after the battle of Feipi in 1815 when the victorious chief Pomare II, backed by the missionaries, imposed Christianity, threatening to remove the intestines of dissidents and dry them in the sun. Similar 'national conversions' took place in the Leeward Islands, resulting in four Christian kingdoms with separate judicial systems.

Other Protestant missionary societies also entered the field. The Church Missionary Society (CMS), comprising

Evangelical Anglicans, entered New Zealand in 1814. The American Board of Commissioners for Foreign Missions (ABCFM), an Evangelical Reformed society based in Boston, entered Hawaii in 1820, and the Wesleyan Methodist Missionary Society, an arm of the British Methodist Conference, took over the work in Tonga and Fiji, and sent missionaries to New Zealand and Samoa.

Christian Converts

Churches, mostly on the Congregational or Methodist model, were soon established throughout Polynesia. The LMS called for Islander church members to volunteer for missionary service as 'native teachers', spearheading the conversion process. All over Polynesia, the conversion of individual chiefs encouraged whole communities to

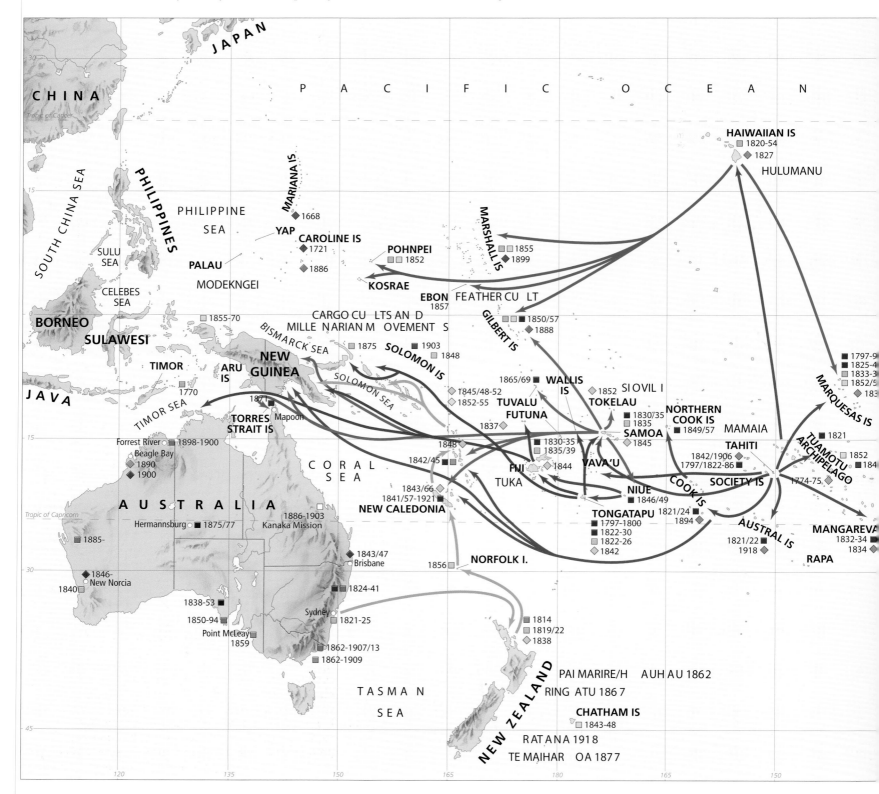

Island churches ranged from bizarre Gothic structures to simple coral lime chapels. The entrance to Piula (Beulah) Methodist Church in Samoa reflects the open elevated appearance of the Samoan *fale*.

adopt the new religion or *lotu*. Pioneer work was usually continued by resident European missionaries or Islander pastors trained at one of the mission institutions such as Malua in Samoa. Hawaiian pastors, belonging to the Hawaiian Evangelical Association, worked in the Marquesas and Micronesia. The success of the Protestant missionary enterprise owed much to the dedication of its island agents, many of whom died of illness, suffered privations and even martyrdom, especially in Melanesia.

Two new missionary orders formed to resuscitate Catholicism after the French Revolution, exercised great influence in the Pacific. They were the Society of the Sacred Hearts of Jesus and Mary (SSCC or Picpus Fathers) and the Society of Mary (SM or Marist Fathers). Using Valparaiso as their port of entry, the Picpus Fathers sought a foothold in Hawaii and the Society Islands, while the Marists looked to Wallis and Futuna. The Picpus Fathers achieved their goal after strenuous Protestant opposition and French naval intervention in

Oil painting known as 'The Cession of Matavai' by Robert Smirke, RA (based on a sketch by William Wilson) showing the reception of Captain James Wilson and the missionaries by the sacred chiefs and high priest of 'Oro in Tahiti in 1797.

Tahiti. Mormon missionaries were also opposed by the Protestants. In 1844, they started work in the Tuamotus and Tahiti before they were established in Salt Lake City.

The Ultimate Price

Over twenty indigenous Christians were martyred in Tahiti and Mangaia, and LMS missionaries were killed in Tonga (1799), but it was the death of the veteran LMS missionary, John Williams, attempting to introduce missionaries to Erromanga (Vanuatu) in 1839, and the death of Peter Chanel, afterwards canonized, leader of the first Marist mission to Futuna, in 1841, which had the most public impact. Other martyrdoms followed, of Presbyterian missionaries in the New Hebrides (Vanuatu), the Wesleyan Thomas Baker in Fiji (1867), the Anglican Bishop Patteson in the Solomons (1871) and the exploring LMS missionary James Chalmers in Papua (1901). Islander martyrs were honoured locally.

Early Protestant missionaries worked harmoniously except in Samoa where rivalry between the LMS and Methodists originated in local politics. The appointment of Bishop Selwyn to the New Zealand bishopric (1841), which included much of Melanesia, threatened stability. The LMS, anxious to transfer its stations in New Caledonia and Vanuatu to the CMS, refused to hand over to the direct control of a high church bishop. Anglicans confined themselves to northern Vanuatu and the Solomons. In more liberal times the LMS handed its Torres Strait mission to the diocese of Carpentaria.

Christianity Today

The most important comity agreement was between the LMS, Methodists and Anglicans in Papua with the tacit support of the administration. Though Catholic and Adventist missions were admitted under this scheme they refused to acknowledge it and by 1914 it was no longer workable. The Dutch government pursued a similar policy in Irian Jaya, dividing the country into Protestant and Catholic spheres. With the opening up of the New Guinea Highlands and advances in aviation, mainstream churches and Evangelical sects penetrated almost every valley.

Although Christianity is now the dominant religion of Oceania, the process of conversion was not easy. Throughout Polynesia the chiefly church was often repressive and quasi theocracies developed with rigid morality laws and harsh punishments. In Tonga King Tupou I and his missionary adviser Shirley Baker set up their own Free Church and persecuted the mission church, setting off a process of fragmentation and reunion. Syncretist churches, often millenarian in character, are strongest in Melanesia and New Zealand. Despite enlightened theological education, the combination of biblical literalism and visionary prophecy has not always been healthy, exemplified in the Tuamotus in 1987, when local charismatic Catholic cultists burnt six 'heretics' to death.

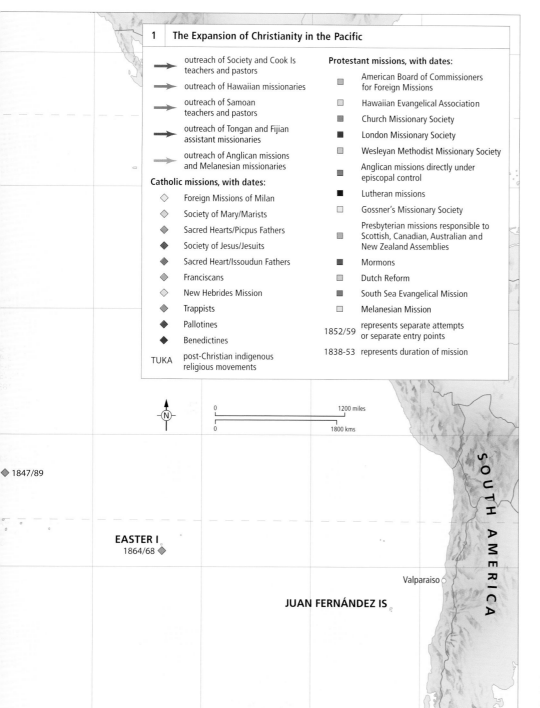

1 The Expansion of Christianity in the Pacific

→ outreach of Society and Cook Is teachers and pastors

→ outreach of Hawaiian missionaries

→ outreach of Samoan teachers and pastors

→ outreach of Tongan and Fijian assistant missionaries

→ outreach of Anglican missions and Melanesian missionaries

Catholic missions, with dates:

◇ Foreign Missions of Milan

◇ Society of Mary/Marists

◆ Sacred Hearts/Picpus Fathers

◆ Society of Jesus/Jesuits

◆ Sacred Heart/Issoudun Fathers

◇ Franciscans

◇ New Hebrides Mission

◆ Trappists

◆ Pallotines

◆ Benedictines

TUKA post-Christian indigenous religious movements

Protestant missions, with dates:

▫ American Board of Commissioners for Foreign Missions

▫ Hawaiian Evangelical Association

▪ Church Missionary Society

▪ London Missionary Society

▫ Wesleyan Methodist Missionary Society

▪ Anglican missions directly under episcopal control

▪ Lutheran missions

▫ Gossner's Missionary Society

▪ Presbyterian missions responsible to Scottish, Canadian, Australian and New Zealand Assemblies

▪ Mormons

▫ Dutch Reform

▪ South Sea Evangelical Mission

▫ Melanesian Mission

1852/59 represents separate attempts or separate entry points

1838-53 represents duration of mission

N

0 — 1200 miles
0 — 1800 kms

◆ 1847/89

EASTER I
1864/68 ◆

SOUTH AMERICA

Valparaiso

JUAN FERNÁNDEZ IS

120 105 90

RELIGION TODAY IN AUSTRALIA AND THE PACIFIC ISLANDS

IN 1788 CHRISTIANITY in the Pacific region was confined to a group of islands contiguous to the Philippines, some very small islands in the Arafura Sea evangelized by Portuguese Catholics and Dutch Protestants, and one Evangelical clergyman ministering to a small nominal Christian convict settlement at Port Jackson. Two hundred years later Christianity in its various denominations has become the dominant religion. Other world faiths can be found in all the major centres of population in Australia, Hawaii and Fiji.

The Missions of New Guinea

New Guinea, in particular, is a patchwork of differing Christian traditions reflecting the country's diverse colonial history (*map 1*). In 1855 missionaries from Gossner's Society began work in West Irian, eventually merging with the Utrecht Zendings Vereeniging in the north. Catholic missions were concentrated in the south. Since Indonesian independence there has been a proliferation of Baptist and other Australian or American based missions working in the north and in the hitherto unevangelized highlands.

Both Lutheranism and Catholicism were entrenched in the former German colony of New Guinea. In Papua, with its heritage of British and Australian administration, British and Australian missions predominated. The London Missionary Society was the first, entering via its Torres Strait mission in the 1870s and concentrating on the south coast. One of its stations, Kwato, became an industrial mission, and eventually left the LMS under the leadership of Charles Abel, whose family were responsible for training an elite corps of Papuan men and women who filled many public positions in independent Papua New Guinea. Australian Methodists worked in New Britain and the Papuan islands, sharing the northeast Papuan coast with the Australian Anglicans.

The major thrust of Catholic activity began in 1885 with the arrival of Fathers of the Sacred Heart of Jesus (MSC) at Yule Island. Although the old comity agreements broke down the mainstream churches combined in various government and church committees.

The Second World War, especially the Japanese invasion, ended the days of missionary paternalism. While many missionaries retreated to Australia, others stayed, and a number of Anglicans and Catholics were beheaded by the Japanese. Some Pacific Islander pastors shepherded their flocks through the crisis. The post-war ecumenical movement saw better relations between Catholics and Protestants. In 1961 the LMS churches formed the Papua Ekalesia which united with the Kwato Extension Association in 1964. In 1968 the Papua Ekalesia joined with the Methodist United Synod of Melanesia and the Port Moresby United Church to form the United Church of Papua New Guinea and the Solomon Islands.

The Conversion of Aboriginal Australia

The LMS, Wesleyan, Anglican and Gossner missions established before the 1840s to evangelize the Aborigines 'protected', translated, provided assistance and taught useful skills even if they did not make many converts, then the sole criterion of success. Population decline, settler opposition and lack of funds were the real reasons for terminating missions.

The second wave of missionary activity (*map 2*) was more successful because of the choice of isolated or inland stations and the 'closed community' nature of the German Lutheran, Moravian and Gossner missionaries, Spanish Benedictines, Italian Passionists and Austrian Jesuits. A few British Protestants worked in more settled areas but often took on the wrath of pastoralists.

The last phase of mission activity took place in the north, where Anglican, Presbyterian, Methodist and

Bahai house of worship,
Sydney, dedicated 1961. The first Bahai 'pioneers' entered the South Pacific in 1920. Although separate national bodies were established in Australia (1934) and New Zealand (1957) their numbers are greatest in Papua New Guinea, Kiribati and Tonga.

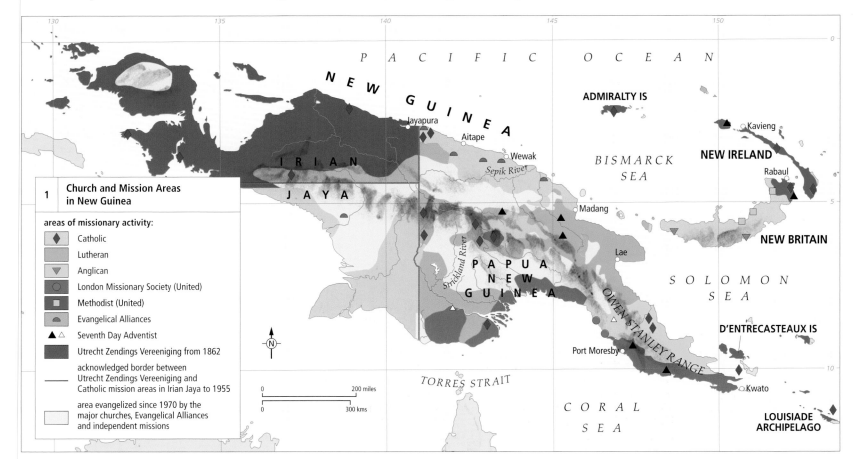

1 Church and Mission Areas in New Guinea

areas of missionary activity:

- ◆ Catholic
- ▉ Lutheran
- ▽ Anglican
- ◯ London Missionary Society (United)
- ▢ Methodist (United)
- ⬭ Evangelical Alliances
- ▲ △ Seventh Day Adventist
- Utrecht Zendings Vereeniging from 1862
- —— acknowledged border between Utrecht Zendings Vereeniging and Catholic mission areas in Irian Jaya to 1955
- area evangelized since 1970 by the major churches, Evangelical Alliances and independent missions

0   200 miles
0   300 kms

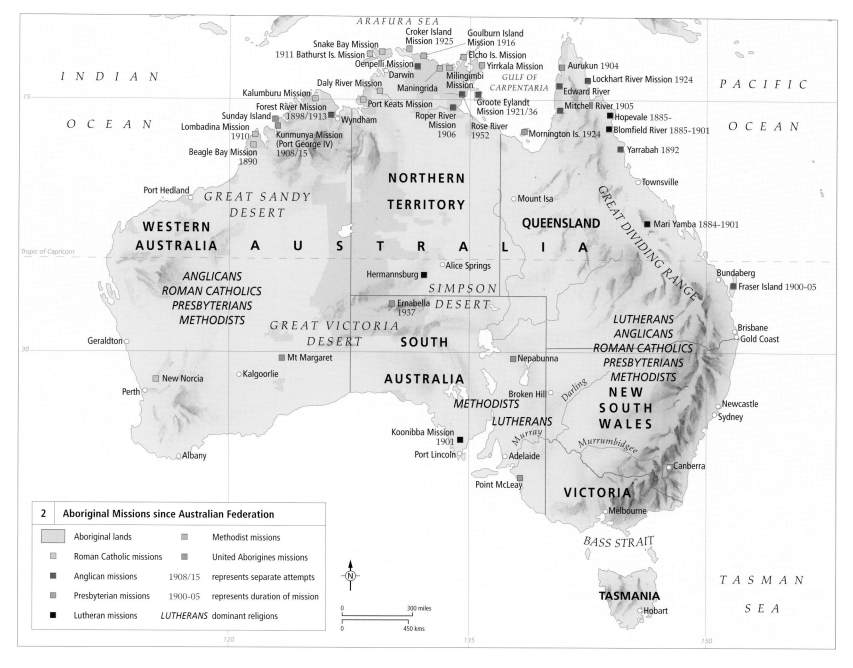

ARAFURA SEA

INDIAN

OCEAN

15

Snake Bay Mission
1911 Bathurst Is. Mission
Croker Island
Mission 1925
Goulburn Island
Mission 1916
Oenpelli Mission
Elcho Is. Mission
Yirrkala Mission
Aurukun 1904
PACIFIC
Kalumburu Mission
Darwin
Daly River Mission
Maningrida
Milingimbi
Mission
*GULF OF
CARPENTARIA*
Lockhart River Mission 1924
Edward River
OCEAN
Forest River Mission
1898/1913
Port Keats Mission
Groote Eylandt
Mission 1921/36
Mitchell River 1905
Sunday Island
Wyndham
Roper River
Mission
1906
Rose River
1952
Hopevale 1885-
Lombadina Mission
1910
Kunmunya Mission
(Port George IV)
1908/15
Mornington Is. 1924
Blomfield River 1885-1901
Beagle Bay Mission
1890
Yarrabah 1892

Port Hedland
*GREAT SANDY
DESERT*
**NORTHERN
TERRITORY**
Mount Isa
Townsville

**WESTERN
AUSTRALIA** **A** **U** **S** **T** **R** **A** **L** **I** **A**
QUEENSLAND
Mari Yamba 1884-1901

*ANGLICANS
ROMAN CATHOLICS
PRESBYTERIANS
METHODISTS*
Alice Springs
Hermannsburg
SIMPSON
Tropic of Capricorn

Geraldton
Ernabella
1937
DESERT
SOUTH
*LUTHERANS
ANGLICANS
ROMAN CATHOLICS
PRESBYTERIANS
METHODISTS*
Bundaberg
Fraser Island 1900-05
Brisbane
Gold Coast

30
*GREAT VICTORIA
DESERT*

Mt Margaret
Nepabunna
New Norcia
Kalgoorlie
AUSTRALIA
**NEW
SOUTH
WALES**
Newcastle
Sydney
Perth

METHODISTS
Broken Hill
Darling
LUTHERANS
Koonibba Mission
1901
Murray
Murrumbidgee
Canberra
Albany
Port Lincoln
Adelaide
Point McLeay
VICTORIA
Melbourne

2	**Aboriginal Missions since Australian Federation**

	Aboriginal lands	■	Methodist missions
▪	Roman Catholic missions	■	United Aborigines missions
■	Anglican missions	1908/15	represents separate attempts
■	Presbyterian missions	1900-05	represents duration of mission
■	Lutheran missions	*LUTHERANS*	dominant religions

N

0 ——— 300 miles
0 ——— 450 kms

BASS STRAIT
TASMANIA
Hobart
*TASMAN
SEA*

120
135
150

*Aboriginal elder leading
Bush Mission Choir, Alice
Springs. Since the 1930s the
Anglican Bush Brotherhood and
the Aborigines Friends
Association have worked in Alice
Springs. Aboriginal Evangelical
Fellowship Conventions have
been held in Alice Springs since
1985. Pope John Paul II addressed
a large gathering of Aborigines
there in 1986.*

Catholic missions proliferated between the Wars. On a proportional basis, more Aborigines are Christian than other Australians. Their Christianity ranges from syncretist movements to pentecostalism and revivalism.

Multi-Faith Pacific
Immigration has played a large part in changing the religious character of the Pacific countries. A suburb of Melbourne is the largest Greek city after Salonika, while Serbian and Russian Orthodox churches flourish in the major cities. Australia's large Jewish population, concentrated mainly in Melbourne and Sydney, increased with war refugees. Islam is represented by several communities. Vietnamese refugees were Buddhist as well as Catholic. Fiji's large Hindu and smaller Muslim population has grown phenomenally since the first labourers were imported from India in 1879. In Hawaii numerous waves of immigrants, especially Japanese, have introduced other faiths (*map 3*). There is even an Islamic community in the 'Methodist' Kingdom of Tonga.

While Christianity thrives in the Pacific Islands most of the churches in Australia are in decline, though the Pentecostal movements, Salvation Army and Baptists show growth. Only 20 per cent of Australians claimed to be regular churchgoers in 1998. Both in Australia and Hawaii there are modern indigenous movements which look back to traditional belief systems. These tend to be fuelled by antagonism to traditional Christianity, yet often fused with pseudo-Christian values.

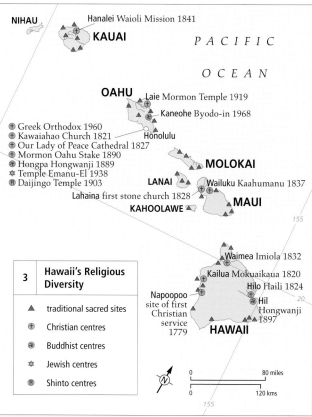

NIHAU
Hanalei Waioli Mission 1841
KAUAI
PACIFIC

OCEAN

OAHU
Laie Mormon Temple 1919
Kaneohe Byodo-in 1968
⊕ Greek Orthodox 1960
⊕ Kawaiahao Church 1821
⊕ Our Lady of Peace Cathedral 1827
⊕ Mormon Oahu Stake 1890
⊕ Hongpa Hongwanji 1889
✡ Temple Emanu-El 1938
⊕ Daijingo Temple 1903
Honolulu

MOLOKAI
LANAI
Wailuku Kaahumanu 1837
Lahaina first stone church 1828
KAHOOLAWE
MAUI

155

Waimea Imiola 1832
Kailua Mokuaikaua 1820
Hilo Haili 1824
Napoopoo
site of first
Christian
service
1779
Hil
Hongwanji
1897
HAWAII

20

| **3** | **Hawaii's Religious
Diversity** |
| --- | --- |

▲	traditional sacred sites
⊕	Christian centres
⊕	Buddhist centres
✡	Jewish centres
⊕	Shinto centres

N

0 ——— 80 miles
0 ——— 120 kms

155

THE ANCIENT NEAR EAST AND EUROPE

IN LOOKING at the religions in this chapter the most obvious connection, geography apart, is that they have almost completely disappeared, and even Zoroastrianism which survives as Parseism is very different from the religion of ancient Persia. From archaeology and their own writings, we know that these religions emerged in highly organized societies. They produced not only great temples, rituals and cults; but also large mythological literatures, the first written theologies, and often tracts on the human condition. Such reflections constitute the earliest written adventures into philosophy, long before the start of formal *philosophia* in ancient Greece.

THOUGH THESE are now dead religions, they asserted themselves over long periods of time, grew, retracted, renewed themselves, and built up religious literary traditions that were as long-lived as Christianity, Buddhism or Islam have been. Egypt, for example, represents a continuous evolution of religious ideas over more that two millennia. Equally, in Mesopotamia the succeeding cultures from Sumer onwards all retained and re-evaluated religious elements from their predecessors. Moreover, they are the precursors of surviving religions. This is very clearly the case with the Parsis, but Jews, Christians and Muslims still read as sacred literature the later variants of tales (e.g. the story of Babel, the story of Noah and the Flood) and prayers (e.g. some of the Psalms) which

were first composed in ancient Mesopotamia. The religion of Babylon may be no more, but tales about it live on with new meanings. In looking at these religions we see the tradition aspect of human religiosity most clearly. Religions conserve their past, carefully collecting and retelling that inheritance until it becomes sacred; all the while re-interpreting the ideas with the addition of new elements so that its past fits new social, ethnic and linguistic situations.

A Shared Social Pattern

One striking common element between these religions is that they arose in similar, stable, economic situations. They come from cities which grew large because of abundant agriculture. In such cities

THE ANCIENT NEAR EAST AND EUROPE

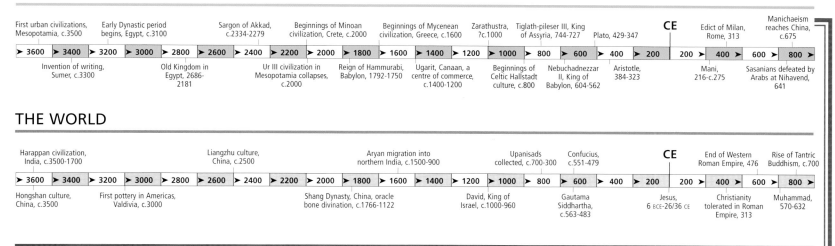

First urban civilizations, Mesopotamia, c.3500 | Early Dynastic period begins, Egypt, c.3100 | Sargon of Akkad, c.2334-2279 | Beginnings of Minoan civilization, Crete, c.2000 | Beginnings of Mycenean civilization, Greece, c.1600 | Zarathustra, ?c.1000 | Tiglath-pileser III, King of Assyria, 744-727 | Plato, 429-347 | **CE** | Edict of Milan, Rome, 313 | Manichaeism reaches China, c.675

> 3600 > 3400 > 3200 > 3000 > 2800 > 2600 > 2400 > 2200 > 2000 > 1800 > 1600 > 1400 > 1200 > 1000 > 800 > 600 > 400 > 200 | 200 > 400 > 600 > 800 >

Invention of writing, Sumer, c.3300 | Old Kingdom in Egypt, 2686-2181 | Ur III civilization in Mesopotamia collapses, c.2000 | Reign of Hammurabi, Babylon, 1792-1750 | Ugarit, Canaan, a centre of commerce, c.1400-1200 | Beginnings of Celtic Hallstadt culture, c.800 | Nebuchadnezzar II, King of Babylon, 604-562 | Aristotle, 384-323 | Mani, 216-c.275 | Sasanians defeated by Arabs at Nihavend, 641

THE WORLD

Harappan civilization, India, c.3500-1700 | Liangzhu culture, China, c.2500 | Aryan migration into northern India, c.1500-900 | Upanisads collected, c.700-300 | Confucius, c.551-479 | **CE** | End of Western Roman Empire, 476 | Rise of Tantric Buddhism, c.700

> 3600 > 3400 > 3200 > 3000 > 2800 > 2600 > 2400 > 2200 > 2000 > 1800 > 1600 > 1400 > 1200 > 1000 > 800 > 600 > 400 > 200 | 200 > 400 > 600 > 800 >

Hongshan culture, China, c.3500 | First pottery in Americas, Valdivia, c.3000 | Shang Dynasty, China, oracle bone divination, c.1766-1122 | David, King of Israel, c.1000-960 | Gautama Siddhartha, c.563-483 | Jesus, 6 BCE-26/36 CE | Christianity tolerated in Roman Empire, 313 | Muhammad, 570-632

---

there arose the specialization that could produce a scribal group, the administrators, and specialists to provide for the cult: everything from sculptors to priests. Nor were they isolated groups, they were in contact with other cities and peoples far away through trade and empire. An idea found in one city could easily travel, mutate, and survive far from its origin. A cult could spread beyond its home, be integrated with other cults, linked to disparate groups and beliefs, and soon it was no longer a particular tribe or city's religious expression, but part of a widespread religion with a pantheon, a sacred deposit of learning and doctrine, and a trained staff of officials. It is significant that in many of these religions there is an original link between the city's storehouses for grain and their temples. Likewise, that the administrative group ('civil service') needed for a city is linked with its priesthoods, and that royal libraries contain the religious texts alongside the accounts. In a similar way, the ruler is the one who organized the productivity of the land, the feeding and defence of the city, and was central to the cult. The cult expressed in its pantheon the agricultural forces by which the city lived, and

central to its activity was the regeneration of the land, fertility, and thanksgiving for successful harvests. Many of the religions in this section present their central concerns as that of proclaiming an ordered cosmos with gods bringing floods and harvests on time, while the king celebrates the annual cycle of the cult on time, and the order, morality and law of the city reflects the order of the universe. It is in the context of this symmetry between social/local and religious/cosmic world views, that we have to locate the connection seen in so many of these religions between the state and the cult, the king and the priest, the history of the city and the history of the gods.

Writing

The most significant difference between the religions examined here and that of earlier societies is the presence of writing. While this is immediately clear in terms of our knowledge of them – we learn about Sumerian religion from what they said about themselves; what is less obvious is the impact of writing on religious development within a society. It allows for the preservation of religious ideas in an inert medium. Ideas held in the mind imperceptibly change with each recollection, a story on stone, skin, papyrus, or a baked clay tablet is frozen. It requires specific skills to compose in writing, skills to read and interpret writing, and it creates a culture where the library becomes as much a part of religion as the temple, and where skills of interpretation and the harmonization of ideas expressed in writing become sacred skills just as much as those who know the memory-impressed rituals of liturgy. In all of these societies, ancient Europe apart, the scribal-cultic group became the bearer of wisdom, the keeper of the religion's memory and integrity, and eventually wrote literature and philosophy. Writing fostered the emergence of traditions that could be both long-living, and capable of exerting influence beyond their original homes. Thus, we could see the religions of this section as the first 'religions of the book.' The exceptions, in ancient Europe, demonstrate that the absence of any one of these elements results in a culture that is all but invisible in time.

Sources and Dating

The information for much of this section is the result of recovering ancient writings from cultures that had in some cases been wholly forgotten (e.g. Sumer, Akkad); in other cases, while the cultures were not forgotten, their writings could no longer be read (e.g. Egypt); while others were only known until recently through their religious enemies (e.g. Canaan). However, what we find preserved is always only a fraction of the religious materials these societies produced. Our knowledge is most imperfect, our understanding of the languages and cultures is subject to major revisions, and statements are provisional as new materials are discovered, deciphered, and edited. Equally, with dating, while we are on fairly steady ground for the last few centuries BCE, the earlier we go the more dates are matters of establishing parallels and approximation. Likewise with the maps, in assessing the range of influences, the extents of particular cultures and empires, indicating trade and other roads, we combine archaeology, with fragmentary records, with the inferences of scholars. These maps represent the consensus of the moment, but each year brings a little more information, and our picture of these religions is therefore volatile.

ANCIENT MESOPOTAMIA: SUMER AND AKKAD

MESOPOTAMIA is the agriculturally productive area watered by the rivers Tigris and Euphrates. In antiquity the region was thickly populated, and prior to 3000 BCE was already an area of many urban cultures. One, however, stands out: that of Uruk (modern Warka in Iraq), the location of the earliest written records, in a language known as 'Sumerian'. The first civilization whose records we possess, Sumer, is the successor to that Warkan culture in the southern part of Mesopotamia (*map 1*). It was a complex urban culture sustained by the social organization that irrigation farming demands. Writing not only allowed the recording of information but brought with it a literate culture which recorded and accumulated fixed traditions; these were transmitted, interpreted and harmonized by a special group, the scribes, at once civil servants and experts in sacred knowledge. It is often said that 'history begins with Sumer', but it is equally true that book-related religion begins there. However, our knowledge of this language is very imperfect, and so all statements about Sumerian religion must be approached with caution.

The city was the central unit in Sumerian religion: its god owned the city and its land, and its inhabitants were his or her servants. The city, in early Sumerian culture, normally had an administrator (*en*) responsible for economic abundance and, in times of threat from other cities, a war-leader (*lugal*). Later these combined in the figure of the king, who was at once a political and sacred figure. He protected the city by building walls, and housed the gods by building temples (ziggurats); his administration ensured the harvest, while as a priestly figure he made a sacred marriage with a representative of the goddess of fertility to bring life to the land (*map 2*).

The Sumerian Pantheon

The gods, whose names and mythology varied from city to city, were, primarily, the environment made divine: sun, moon, wind, food, the harvest. They were invested with human-like attributes, feelings and activities, and their interactions were modelled on social relationships. Enlil, for example, the 'lord wind' who sent moist spring winds for planting, was god of the hoe. He lived in the temple in Nippur, but the city and its land was home to his son, Ninurta, who was 'lord of the plough'.

The temple was the god's home. Originally a great storehouse, it was central to the cult which was two-fold: the daily service performed for the god by the city, which was comparable to the attention paid to a king by his court; and the annual festivals of the gods which brought rebirth to the land, city, animals and people. The new year festival, *Akitu*, of the Sumerians is one of the earliest recorded death and rebirth festivals. The temple brought

The stele of Hammurabi. Found near Susa, this c.2.3m high stele contains Hammurabi's Code. It shows Shamash, the sun-god and presider over justice giving Hammurabi (standing offering respect) the law.

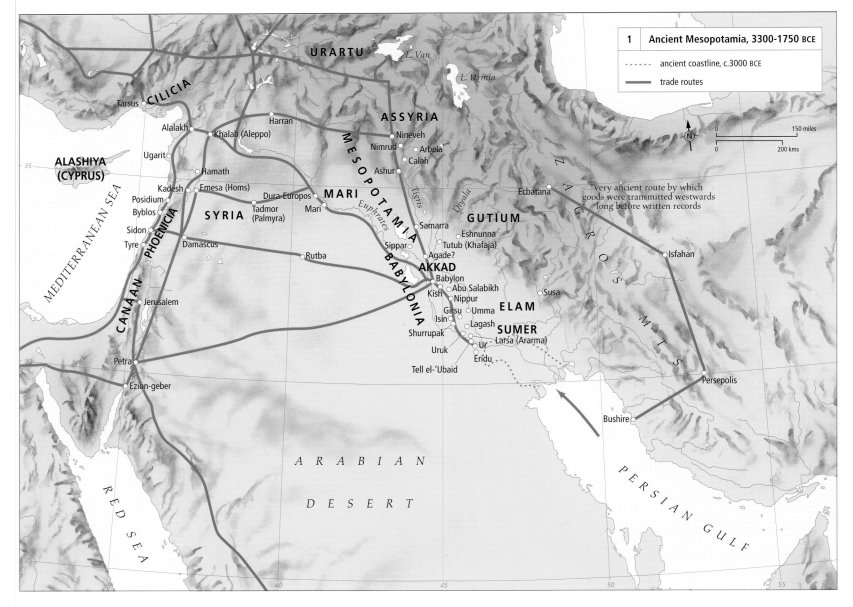

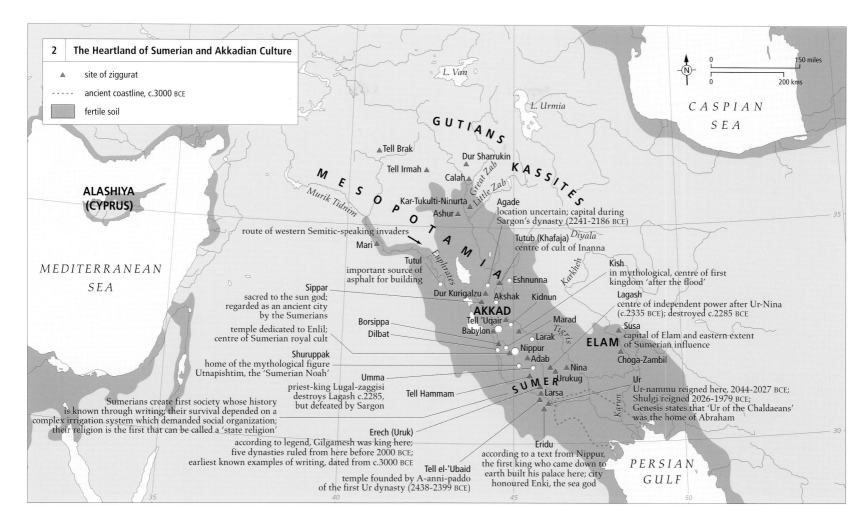

2 | **The Heartland of Sumerian and Akkadian Culture**

▲ site of ziggurat

‑ ‑ ‑ ‑ ‑ ancient coastline, c.3000 BCE

fertile soil

L. Van

L. Urmia

CASPIAN SEA

GUTIANS

KASSITES

MESOPOTAMIA

ALASHIYA (CYPRUS)

▲ Tell Brak

Dur Sharrukin ▲

Tell Irmah ▲

Calah ▲

Kar-Tukulti-Ninurta ▲

Ashur ▲

Agade
location uncertain; capital during
Sargon's dynasty (2241-2186 BCE)

Murik Tidnim

route of western Semitic-speaking invaders

Mari ▲

Tutub (Khafaja) *Diyala*
centre of cult of Inanna

MEDITERRANEAN SEA

Tutul
important source of
asphalt for building

Sippar
sacred to the sun god;
regarded as an ancient city
by the Sumerians

Dur Kurigalzu ▲   Akshak

Eshnunna

Kidnun

Kish
in mythological, centre of first
kingdom 'after the flood'

Lagash
centre of independent power after Ur-Nina
(c.2335 BCE); destroyed c.2285 BCE

temple dedicated to Enlil;
centre of Sumerian royal cult

Borsippa

Dilbat

AKKAD

Tell 'Uqair ▲

Babylon

Marad

Larak

Susa
capital of Elam and eastern extent
of Sumerian influence

ELAM

Shuruppak
home of the mythological figure
Utnapishtim, the 'Sumerian Noah'

Nippur

Adab

Choga-Zambil

Umma

Nina

Sumerians create first society whose history
is known through writing; their survival depended on a
complex irrigation system which demanded social organization;
their religion is the first that can be called a 'state religion'

priest-king Lugal-zaggisi
destroys Lagash c.2285,
but defeated by Sargon

Tell Hammam

SUMER

Urukug

Larsa

Ur
Ur-nammu reigned here, 2044-2027 BCE;
Shulgi reigned 2026-1979 BCE;
Genesis states that 'Ur of the Chaldeans'
was the home of Abraham

Erech (Uruk)
according to legend, Gilgamesh was king here;
five dynasties ruled from here before 2000 BCE;
earliest known examples of writing, dated from c.3000 BCE

Tell el-'Ubaid
temple founded by A-anni-paddo
of the first Ur dynasty (2438-2399 BCE)

Eridu
according to a text from Nippur,
the first king who came down to
earth built his palace here; city
honoured Enki, the sea god

PERSIAN GULF

Euphrates   *Tigris*   *Karkheh*   *Karun*

the god's presence into the city, and to build or restore a
temple required divine approval, for it meant that the
inhabitants could consider themselves living in that
god's shadow. From these cults derive some of the
oldest creation myths, hymns and stories, such as the
account of a great flood, which reappears later in other
Near Eastern religions.

The Akkadian Empire

After a brief attempt by Lugal-zaggisi (c.2285 BCE) to
create a unified empire, power passed to the northern
cities where a Semitic language, Akkadian, was spoken,
and a empire was built up by Sargon. It reached its
zenith, when its power extended as far as the
Mediterranean, from 2371–2230 BCE. Its religion was in
continuity with that of the earlier period, with the same
pantheon and body of sacred myth. From this period
comes the first text with a named author: a hymn by
Enheduanna, Sargon's daughter. The earliest stratum of
the *Epic of Gilgamesh*, which claims to recall the epic
journey of a king of Uruk c.2600 BCE, also comes from

this period. With its encounters with the gods, the
underworld and the secrets of this world, and the trials
of the human condition, it is both a literary masterpiece,
and an outstanding insight into Mesopotamian religion.
Gilgamesh 'two-thirds god, one-third man' is a brutal
king, but an object of special interest to the gods. He can
interact with them in many ways, he can slay monsters,
and learn the future in dreams. Despite discouragement
from many, he embarks on a journey to find Utnapishtim,
the great flood's sole survivor, who tells him about the
deluge and where the tree of life grows. Gilgamesh then
sets out in search of it, but when he locates the tree, it is
stolen by a serpent. Finally, he meets a friend risen from
the underworld and the epic ends in despair as he reveals
its nature: 'to hear of it, sit down and weep'. Probably
originally Sumerian, this story was still being told over a
millennium later in Assyria, c.650 BCE.

After the destruction of the Akkadian empire by the
Gutians, a new Sumerian dynasty arose in Ur (Ur III)
c.2112-2004 BCE, which, in turn, fell to a Semitic-speaking
people from the west, and power shifted to Babylon.

Hammurabi

The greatest of First Dynasty Babylon's kings was
Hammurabi (his reign may have begun in 1792 BCE). He
made Babylon a great religious centre by building and
restoring temples, and he referred to himself as 'restoring
the land after a decline' and as combining and continuing
the cultures of Sumer and Akkad. In order to unify the
traditions of his growing empire he promulgated 282
laws (his 'code'), which present him as the one who has
received the law from Shamash, who offers him sceptre
and ring, the symbols of justice. Hammurabi then offers
justice to his people. The laws were to be written on a
stone column, set up in the city, which would convey his
presence. These laws continued to influence Near Eastern
civilizations for centuries after First Dynasty Babylon was
destroyed by the Hittites (1595 BCE), and remain familiar
through adoption into biblical texts.

*The ziggurat at Ur c.2000 BCE
The word ziggurat, which means
'rising high up', reflects the
desire to place religious things
higher than ordinary life. Unlike
the pyramids, ziggurats are not
tombs but elevated altars and
sanctuaries. It is a building such
as this which underlies the Tower
of Babel story (Gen 11:1-8).*

ANCIENT EGYPT

WHILE MORE IS written about Egyptian religion than about any other non-biblical, ancient faith, it must be noted how little is known; 'Egyptian religion' covers the religious experience of the fertile lower Nile over a period of 3000 years, from c.3100 BCE to Alexander's conquest (332 BCE). During that time there were many different political situations (the classic division into 30 dynasties was produced by an Egyptian priest, Manetho, in c.300 BCE), changes of capital with consequent shifts in cult and theology, as well as the normal growth of ideas. Our picture of Egyptian religion is built up from different times and sites, and further complicated by the fact that material from later periods and from Upper Egypt survives in greater quantity, and much of this material comes from cemeteries, such as the Valley of the Kings, so the emphasis is slanted towards Egyptian beliefs about death and the afterlife. Yet a growing body of texts is emerging which give accounts of the gods and the myths in which they are related to one another. Cultic texts belong to a yearly cycle of festivals – life was dominated by the annual flooding of the Nile which brought fertility to the land – and the daily services of the priests of different gods in their temples. Wisdom texts discuss human-divine interaction and contain ethical reflections on the human condition.

The Sacred Pharaoh

A long-standing element in Egyptian religion was the sacred figure of the king, a divine being representing cosmic order (ma'at). Funerary texts describe his ascent into the sky at death to join with the sun-god in his journeys. In another text the king devours the gods and assumes their attributes. In other texts he is directly related to a pantheon of nine gods. Blessedness in the afterlife is a royal quality and the great royal tombs mark the place of transition between the pharaoh as a god on Earth and a divine being living among the gods.

As the capital moved so did the perception of the king's divinity, but always he was seen as the mediator between divine and human realms. This process reached a high point with Akhenaton (1367–1350 BCE) who moved his capital to El-Amarna mid-way between Thebes and Memphis (map 1). He sought to remove the whole pantheon in favour of a single deity, the solar cult of Aton. For this he has been praised as a 'religious genius', who promoted monotheism. But since he made himself the sole representative and link between Aton and the creation, his actions can also be seen as the complete

The sphinx and pyramid of Cheops at Giza. The pyramids have always been viewed as one of the wonders of the world. These elaborate tombs of prominent rulers are a development of the burial mound and testify to the significance of personal survival into an afterlife in Egyptian belief. Though Mesopotamian ziggurats are older, the pyramids are built of stone rather than brick, so they are the oldest complex human structures which are still relatively intact.

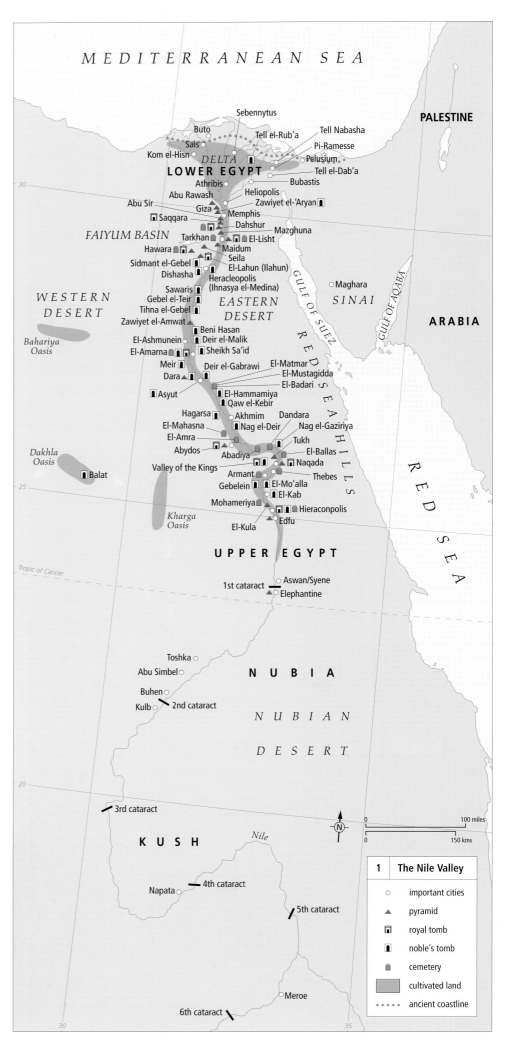

1	The Nile Valley
○	important cities
▲	pyramid
🏛	royal tomb
🏛	noble's tomb
🏛	cemetery
▬	cultivated land
•••••	ancient coastline

deification of his own power. His desire to destroy cults, such as that of Thebes, led to opposition and his almost complete obliteration from the records after his death. Although the king was divine, and the hinge of the whole cult, it was a religious power that was shared with many special cultic groups. A reaction to this concentration of sacred power may lie behind many of the more personal religious texts.

Political Turmoil

During periods of dynastic instability there was a broadening of the range of people for whom the afterlife was a source of order in life. Hymns to the All-Lord Re, who is seen as treating all with equality ('he made all men, great and small; humanity is but his teardrop'), began to appear on the coffins of the nobility. Although Re is perceived as provident for humanity and humans must serve him, they are also charged with moral responsibility. Re is hidden and omniscient, but also just and responsive to prayer. This sense of a personal god marked a major break with the older royal theologies, and prepared the way for the ethical and religious

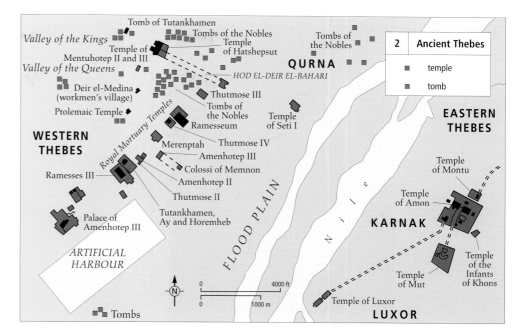

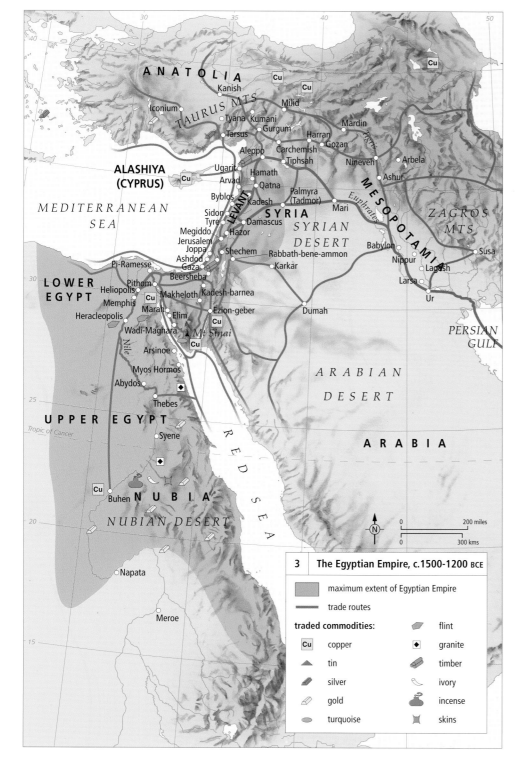

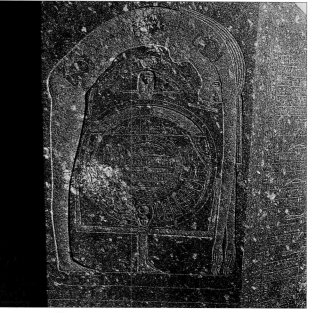

A cosmographical map showing Egypt in the embrace of the goddess Nut on a stone sarcophagus cover from Saqqara (XXX Dynasty, c.350 BCE). Nut is the sky-goddess who is seen here in her characteristic pose, which forms an arch over the Earth. The Egyptians believed that the sun was a child who entered Nut's mouth each evening to pass through her body during the night, and was born from her womb the next morning. Here she is seen surrounding a cosmic map of the Egyptian universe.

writings found in later periods. Several sections of the biblical 'Wisdom Literature', for example, are imports from Egypt; they discuss what constitutes an ethical life and a proper attitude to the sources of the universe: parts of the *Wisdom of Amenemope* are found in Proverbs 22-25. This reminds us that, as a great empire (*map 3*), Egypt exported parts of its religion, as well as importing myths and deities from elsewhere, especially western Asia.

Personal Religion

While pyramids, royal tombs (*map 2*), and their inscriptions dominate our view of Egyptian religion, we also see a theology which is concerned with human self-understanding. People were conceived from Re's mind and uttered by his tongue. Their bodies were fashioned for them and had to be preserved so that they could have an afterlife. Sight, hearing, perception were all gifts from Re and Thoth. Humans have a conscience, a 'soul' (*ba*), of which they become aware and with which they can argue about the purpose of life, and a 'spirit' (*akh*) which is not limited by the body and which can become a 'complete spirit' in the afterlife.

113

ANCIENT PALESTINE

THE EARLIEST religion from this region is known as 'Canaanite', a term which refers to the western Semites in the second millennium BCE, in the area of modern Israel, Jordan, Lebanon and Syria. Until recently, the only source of information about Canaanite religion was biblical condemnations and a few later Greek comments, but our knowledge has been transformed by three excavations, at Ras Shamra (ancient Ugarit), El-Amarna in Egypt and Tell Hariri (ancient Mari). From these it is possible build up a picture of a city culture that lived primarily on trade, exploiting its strategic position at the meeting place of routes from Mesopotamia, the north and Egypt (*map 1*). While it had a distinctive mythology, there is also evidence of exchange in religious ideas with its neighbours and overlords.

The Ugaritic Pantheon

Excavations, begun in 1929, have revealed that Ugarit, near the Syrian coast, was a great trading centre, with a cult area consisting of two large temples (one to Baal, one to Dagan), built over older ruins. A large library provides a closely dated unified source for Ugaritic mythology. It was in this area, in Niqmad II's reign (c.1360 BCE), that the cuneiform script was developed, and the king ordered that the sacred texts should be recorded on clay tablets (*see also* pp. 40-41). They list a typical urban pantheon of up to thirty-four native and imported deities, and are probably recorded in their order of precedence in a great procession. The list begins with three great gods: the first inhabits the sacred mountain, Sapan (Tsafon); the second belongs to the cult of the

Canaanite bronze figurine (235 mm high), covered in gold and silver foil, from Canaan, c.1900 BCE. Such figurines have been found at every site with Canaanite links. They are important evidence for the religion of the general Canaanite population. They are thought to be small representations of temple statues of gods and goddesses, and were possibly votive offerings.

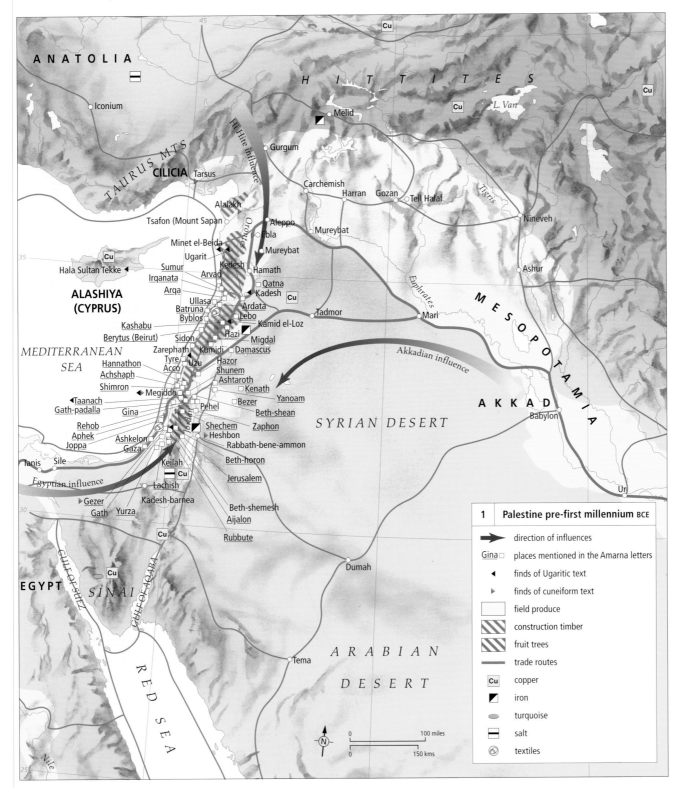

1	Palestine pre-first millennium BCE
→	direction of influences
Gina □	places mentioned in the Amarna letters
◄	finds of Ugaritic text
►	finds of cuneiform text
▢	field produce
▨	construction timber
▨	fruit trees
—	trade routes
Cu	copper
◢	iron
◯	turquoise
⊟	salt
◎	textiles

dead; the third, called a bull, is a source of creation, power, wisdom and virility. Then comes the obscure Dagan, followed by seven Baals (meaning lord). The list continues with lesser male and female deities.

The tablets record many rituals, but all seem to have been carried out for, or by, the king, in the company of an official priesthood. Excavations at the earlier site of Mari have produced a list of Semitic and non-Semitic gods, and it is known that sheep were sacrificed to them in their various temples. In contrast to elsewhere in the Near East, where the divine will is usually discovered by divination, these excavations reveal texts that are oracular in form. The Amarna letters, clay tablets found in the Egyptian archives consisting principally of letters from Palestinian princes to the pharaoh, yield echoes of Canaanite hymns. However, very little is known of the wider religion of the people apart from finds of small ritual items, such as figurines.

A limestone statue of the god El, from Ugarit, thirteenth century BCE. Museum of Latakia, Latakia, Syria. El was the supreme Canaanite god; and, though we lack a creation account, creator of the universe of gods (the 'sons of El' were 70 gods begotten by him), earth and humankind. This statue is of an aged deity ('father of years') with appropriate grey beard, noted as wise, kind and benign. His consort was Athirat, mother of the gods.

The Invasion of the Sea Peoples

Ugarit was destroyed, with other Canaanite cities, by invaders from the northwest, probably Greece, known as the Sea Peoples (1180–1160 BCE), who brought with them new cultural influences and a shift towards sea trade. Yet the influence of Canaanite religion outlasted that destruction. While Hebrew writings use 'Canaan' and Baal-worship as metaphors of evil, Canaan in fact supplied the underlying religion of the Hebrews (for example, texts such as the Psalms). The notion of a clear chasm between Israel and its surroundings ignores how many basic religious notions were from Canaan.

The Phoenicians

The demise of Canaan and the Hittite and Egyptian empires in the region, left a power vacuum, which was filled by the Phoenicians, who were based along the Levantine coast (*map 2*). Phoenician power reached its zenith in the the tenth to ninth centuries BCE, when an alliance was forged between Hiram of Tyre and Solomon

of Israel. Although the Phoenicians were successors of Canaanite culture, many new currents also entered their religion. Through their great trading empire, which stretched across the Mediterranean and into the Atlantic, the Phoenicians absorbed many new religious ideas from Egypt, Greece, Israel and Mesopotamia.

Some themes do, however, recur in Phoenician records: firstly, a number of stories whose central figure is a dying and rising god; secondly, the importance of sacrificial rites; and thirdly, the importance of funeral rites. These ritual activities seem to have taken place in a number of distinct settings. Natural sites, such as mountains or rivers, were sacred to specific deities. In addition, there were also specially built sacred groves, sanctuaries and altars (which correspond to the 'high places' of the Hebrew scriptures). Large temples, constructed around a central courtyard, were used for major public ceremonies.

In the fourth century BCE, Phoenicia disappeared into the Greek empire, and its religion became part of the rich tapestry of Hellenistic religion.

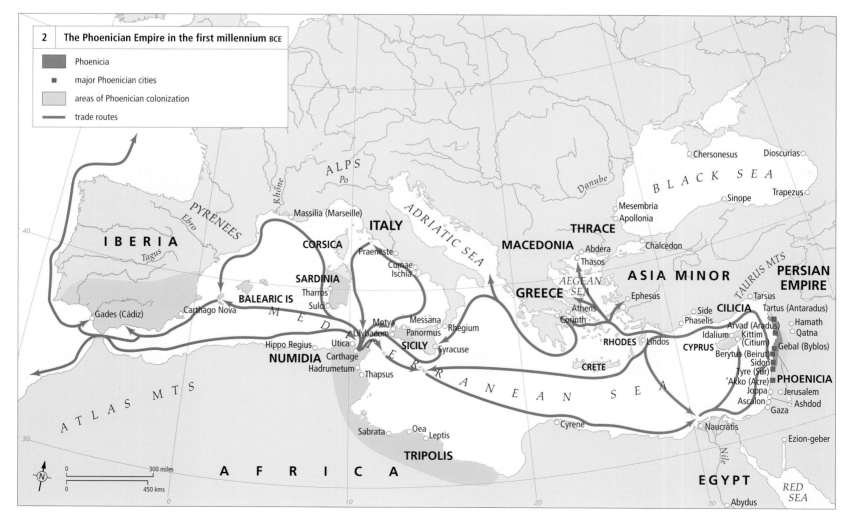

2   **The Phoenician Empire in the first millennium BCE**

- Phoenicia
- ■ major Phoenician cities
- areas of Phoenician colonization
- trade routes

ASSYRIA AND BABYLONIA

BETWEEN 900-600 BCE the dominant Near Eastern power was Assyria. This empire had arisen centuries earlier to the north of the River Tigris, around the cities of Ashur (hence 'Assyria'), Nineveh, Arbela and Calah (*map 1*). Its first great ruler, Ashur-uballit I (1363–1328 BCE), expanded to the west and south, towards Anatolia and Babylon, in the process absorbing much of the earlier Babylonian culture: the cult and rituals of the Babylonian god, Marduk, found a place in Ashur itself beside its native god, Ashur. The Assyrian empire survived declines and revivals, remaining a force in its heartland, but often not far beyond. However, there was a continuity of kings; and the absolute correlation of the date of an eclipse (15 June 763 BCE) visible in Ashur, with the kingly succession lists, provides fixed dates for both Mesopotamia and Egypt.

A major change in Assyrian fortunes came with the reign of Tiglath-pileser III (744–727 BCE), who built the first highly unified empire, transforming Assyria into a power which reached from the Zagros Mountains to Upper Egypt. Assyria's greatest florescence, which began in the mid-eighth century BCE, ended in 612 BCE, when its capital Nineveh fell to a resurgent Babylon.

Assyrian Religion

Records testify that the Assyrian state religion, and its official regulation, were important factors in the unity of the empire – little is known of popular religion. Ashur was 'king of gods', believed to dwell in the city of Ashur. Next came Ishtar, the goddess of battle and love, with temples in Arbela, Nineveh and Ashur, served by a group of women ecstatics. Ninurta, first son of Ashur, god of the hunt and war, lived in Calah. Shamash, the sun god, dispensed justice and, along with Adad, god of storms, presided over divination. Sin, the moon god, lived in Harran and his cult grew in importance in the empire's last years. These divine cults required the maintenance of large temples and priesthoods, and elaborate rituals, such as the daily feeding of the gods; records show the need for extra royal expenditure on these activities.

The king himself was Ashur's earthly representative and chief priest, and the interplay of royal power and religion can be seen in every aspect of Assyrian religion. Marduk, for example, conquered the dragon Tiamet in the *Akitu* (New Year) festival in Ashur; after Sennacherib had destroyed Babylon he made Ashur the victor over Tiamet and central figure in the great ritual. Divination and astrology began as services to the king, revealing the state's, not the individual's, destiny. Nabû, son of Marduk, was god of scribes and of each city's library, in effect the god of the administration.

Babylon

In 626 BCE Nabopolassar of Babylon besieged Nippur, restored to the Elamites the statues of their gods which the Assyrians had taken, and began the revival of Babylonian power (the New Babylonian empire, *map 2*). His successor, Nebuchadnezzar II is famous from the Bible where, in Jer 25-29, he is Yahweh's agent, but is more usually remembered on the basis of the much later Dan 1-4 as Yahweh's enemy. He extended the empire so

A relief carving from the Assyrian king Ashurnasirpal II's palace at Calah (now Nimrud). This mythical being (human body with eagle's head) is called variously a lamassu, *a* shedu, *a* kuribu, *and may be the inspiration of the biblical angels called* cherubim *(see Exodus 25:20).*

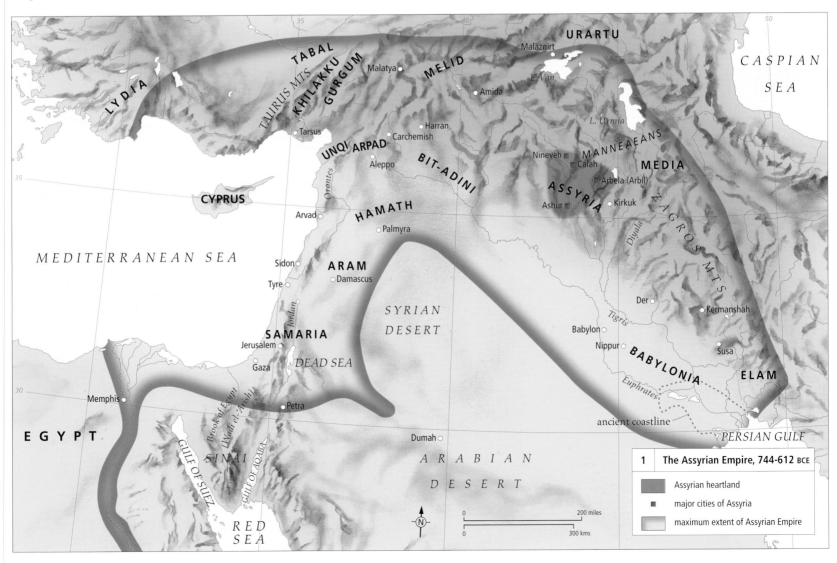

1	The Assyrian Empire, 744-612 BCE

Assyrian heartland

major cities of Assyria

maximum extent of Assyrian Empire

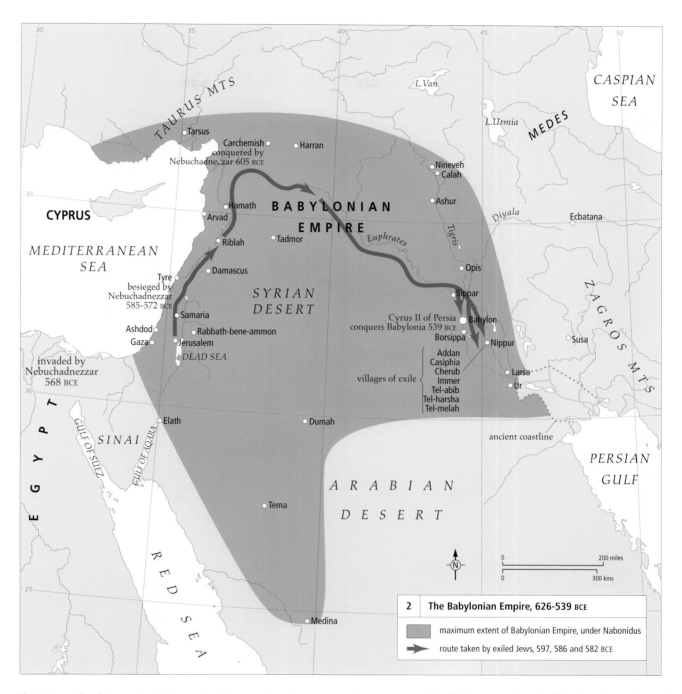

The Babylonian 'world map'
(c.600 BCE) is one of the oldest
maps we possesss. The inner
circle contains Babylon, the
Tigris and Euphrates, some other
cities, and Assyria. This area,
civilization, is surrounded by
the band of the ocean; and
beyond the ocean lie the more
distant regions.

that it matched Assyria at its greatest; he captured Jerusalem (587 BCE), and deported the country's leaders to Babylon. He restored Babylon as the religious centre, rebuilt its ziggurat and the temple of Esagil, shrine to Marduk (restored as paramount deity). Connections between the cult and the state continued. With so much power and wealth linked to particular cult centres, changes in the pantheon could have a political impact. When Nabonidus (555–539 BCE) promoted the cult of Sin,

the moon god, in Ur it caused a rebellion by the priests of Marduk, and led to his self-exile in Tema.

Babylon's extensive pantheon of hundreds of deities, many with temples, priesthoods, texts and festivals, was hierarchically arranged. The king-priest was central, his actions (for example sacred copulation with the chief priestess each new year) brought both success and new life to the kingdom. The gods not only looked down on humanity, but behaved like humans. They lived above in the heavens and below in the underworld, and their fighting created the disk of the earth in the middle. Around and beneath the earth were the great salt waters, and above it rotated the divine heavenly bodies, which looked down upon and influenced all beneath them.

The Legacy
The Babylonian empire lasted until 539 BCE, when it was destroyed by the Persians, under Cyrus the Great. No ancient religion left such an extensive legacy. Hellenistic and Roman religion looked back to the 'Chaldeans' as the discovers of astrology and the secrets of the universe, and viewed them as priest-scientist-magicians. From them we have inherited the seven-day week, the 360° circle and the duodecimal system of time measurement. While in Babylon the Hebrews restructured their traditions, compiled myths countering those of their surroundings and developed a distinctive religious identity, emerging as the Jewish people of the Hebrew scriptures.

117

ANCIENT GREECE AND MAGNA GRAECIA

ANCIENT GREECE, the culture of the city-states in the few centuries before the time of Alexander the Great, has defined the western European view of 'classic' civilization, pervading our understanding of other ancient cultures. From the Renaissance until recently, many of the texts which provide our knowledge of Greek religion were widely studied in schools. Greek mythology has seeped into our own; separating its imaginary world from our very sanitized and rationalized view of the 'classical world' is difficult.

The Aegean

Greek civilization was not a unity based on a single political organism, but a unity forged by trading links and a common language between distinct, and often warring, political entities – the cities. Since the geography of Greece fostered isolation, the key factor in creating the civilization was the sea: it linked cities together, allowed alliances and was the basis of trade and exchange. The Greeks expanded by sea, not to subjugate neighbouring lands, but to establish trading centres and colonies. Greek culture spread through commerce (*map 2*). In the context of religion, different groups shared a body of mythology and then linked their gods, for example by presenting gifts to each other's temples to cement alliances. There was no dominant theology as in unitary states.

When Indo-European tribes arrived in Greece in the second millennium BCE, they combined their beliefs with those of the existing inhabitants, which were far closer in content to those of the Ancient Near East. Both strands survived to produce the basis of later Greek religion, but whether they can be disentangled is disputed.

Examining early texts, such as Homer, and looking at the physical remains of Greek culture, demonstrate that isolating specific cults is very difficult. In almost every case, there are combinations of various cults and strands of mythology. While gods are linked to localities and groups of people, each cult and story also had a wider currency. Through being absorbed in different places and then 'retransmitted', each cult embraces a variety of forms linking it to the rest of the mythology.

Dodona, an ancient sanctuary of Zeus (the paramount god), provides an example. Homer mentions that the site's priests, called *Selloi*, slept on the ground and had unwashed feet. This suggests the cult of an earth goddess, or other chthonic power, with whom its devotees had to keep in constant physical contact. But Homer mentions elsewhere that it was also the site of an oracle (a place where a god is heard to answer questions), which took the form of a spring gushing and the rustling of oak-leaves around the sanctuary. Later, Herodotus (c.450 BCE) mentions priestesses, under a kind of

A plaster and wood plaque showing a sacrifice, from Pitsa near Corinth, c.530 BCE.

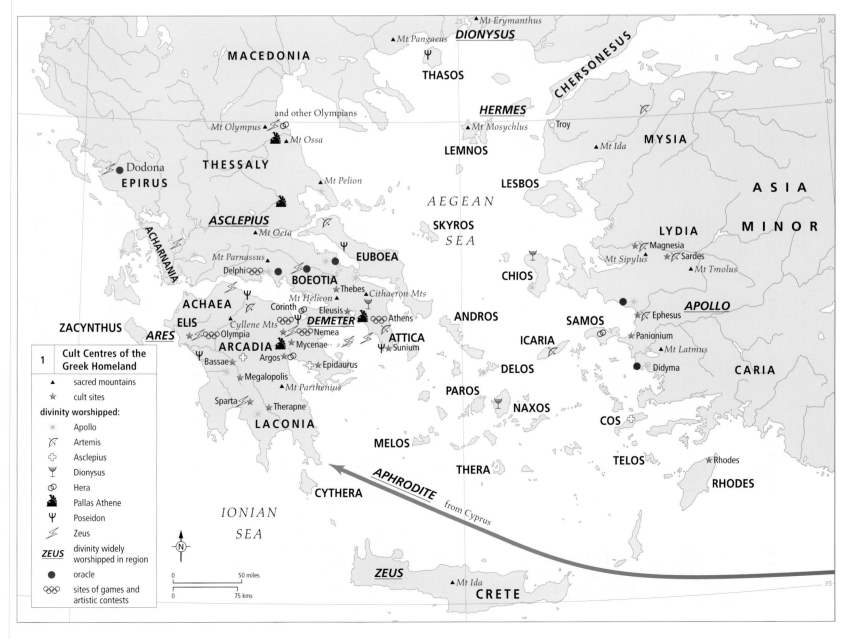

1	Cult Centres of the Greek Homeland
▲	sacred mountains
★	cult sites
divinity worshipped:	
☀	Apollo
⏀	Artemis
✚	Asclepius
ⵑ	Dionysus
☯	Hera
♟	Pallas Athene
Ψ	Poseidon
⚡	Zeus
ZEUS	divinity widely worshipped in region
●	oracle
♒	sites of games and artistic contests

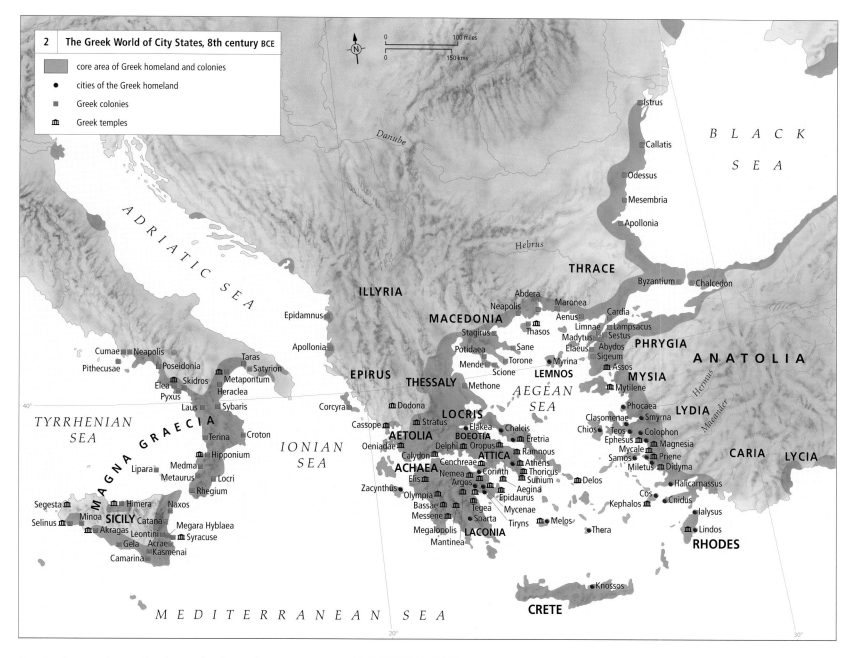

2 The Greek World of City States, 8th century BCE

- core area of Greek homeland and colonies
- • cities of the Greek homeland
- ▪ Greek colonies
- ⛪ Greek temples

inspiration, as the oracle-givers. At about this time it seems that the answers of the oracle were also given through a bronze gong. At Dodona, the consort of Zeus was not Hera, as found elsewhere, but Dione; since this name is a feminine form of Zeus this variant may preserve the myth's oldest strand, perhaps predating its entry into Greece. Zeus himself has a special title here, *Naios* (possibly 'Zeus of the flowing water'), which might indicate that the Zeus cult was grafted on to an earlier earth/water deity or oracle. Dodona, an agglomeration of traditions, became famous throughout Greece.

Such processes of combining and harmonizing traditions produced a vast world of gods, semi-gods, heroes and satyrs, from heavenly divinities (the Olympians) to earth gods (Chthonics). The gods were inter-related, and assigned particular tasks (such as love or war), which could then explain both the cosmos and history. The ideological structure of Greek religion was syncretistic, capable of cultural transformation, and reflected the civil society, with its demarcations of power and function. Mount Olympus, as the assembly of the gods, functioned in a similar way to the assembly governing Athens (*map 1*).

Cult and Culture

Greece is perceived as the home of rational investigation, philosophy and politics, but nevertheless the cult entered every aspect of civil and domestic life. The temple and its *temenos* (sacred precinct) was the centre of city identity, and the bonds within the city were cemented in

ceremonies there. Equally, the alliances between cities and the links that established the Greeks as an ethnic group were forged in the shared mythology and sacred places such as Olympus, and a universal sense of the numinous, demonstrated by the widespread respect for the oracle of Apollo at Delphi which cities consulted in times of crisis.

Altars were widespread in homes, places of business and even on ships. Here, simple liquid offerings were used to invoke the gods' protection for individual events. While the great oracles gave answers to the questions of rulers and states, by the widespread practice of divination (by such means as dice, palmistry and the interpretation of omens and dreams) the ordinary citizens sought to know the future and the outcomes of enterprises, and to allay their indefinite fears.

The temple of Apollo at Delphi. This site belonged originally to a Mother Earth goddess; mythology relates that Apollo slayed the Python who guarded her shrine and then established it as his oracle (uttered in an underground chamber). It became a unifying religious factor in Greek culture; states had their own shrines there where they left thanks-offerings for victories. The site also interwove other cults and strands of religion: it was sacred to Dionysus and his ecstatic worship took place there. It was also the site of the Omphalos stone, believed to be the earth's navel.

ZOROASTRIANISM AND ITS OFFSHOOTS

ZOROASTRIANISM shares with Judaism the distinction of being an ancient Near Eastern religion which is still a living religion today. Named from its founder, Zarathusthra (later called Zoroaster), who is thought to have lived c.1000 BCE, its origins lie not in cities (by contrast with so many ancient Near Eastern religions) but among the pastoralists located on the borders between present-day Afghanistan and Iran (*map 1*). Its influence gradually expanded and it became the main religion of pre-Islamic Persia. Such a long history has generated a large and varied body of sacred writings. Over the course of time, there have been several shifts in doctrine, and numerous groups who have deviated doctrinally (for example, Zurvanism), in some cases generating other semi-independent religions through interaction with other systems – contact with Roman religions produced Mithraism; contact with Christianity, Manichaeism.

The Achaemenid Empire

Persia became a world power with the accession of Cyrus II, the Great (559 BCE). He moved westwards to conquer Babylon and the whole Near East. He is praised in the Bible as 'the Lord's anointed' (Isa 45:1) as he returned the Jews to Palestine and allowed them to rebuild the temple. Under Xerxes I, the Achaemenid empire expanded to the borders of Greece and, despite revolts and reverses, remained a powerful force until its destruction by Alexander the Great (330 BCE). However, Zoroastrianism was more than just the imperial religion, and survived.

Zoroastrian doctrine developed over the centuries; as it related to the religions of conquered lands, and re-absorbed pre-Zarathusthra Persian religions, rituals grew more complex. It is a monotheistic religion which worships a supreme god, Ahura Mazda ('wise lord'). It is distinguished by the radical dualism of two opposing spirits, Spenta Mainyu (good) and Angra Mainyu (evil), which are the twin children of Ahura Mazda. This dualism answers the problem of evil: these spirits are not inherently good or evil, but become so by consistent choice between good and bad actions, between truth and

The tomb of Xerxes I
(486–465 BCE). Famous as the enemy of the Greeks at Thermopylae, in his reign the Achaemenid empire reached its zenith. His predecessors had been tolerant of their conquered lands' religions, but Xerxes desired religious uniformity and he sought to eradicate 'false gods and temples'. While Cyrus allowed the Jews to rebuild their temple, Xerxes removed Marduk's statue from Babylon after a revolt.

lies, light and dark. They offer a prototype to the moral choices faced by humans. Other spirits were added to the belief system, such as good immortal beings who followed the Wise Lord, and demons who inspired humans to evil. This created, in effect, a pantheon with a similarly structured demon-world opposing it.

In Zoroastrianism ritual has a central place: prayer is fundamental, as is meditation before fire, which is the symbol of the religion. Sacrifices date from an early period, but it was not until the late Achaemenid period that statues became part of the religious iconography. Later still, Zoroastrians worshipped in 'houses of fire' (temples which were contrasted with 'houses of idols'). A series of rituals followed the major events of life from initiation to death, and prayer was organized around a cycle of fixed holidays. These rituals no doubt reinforced the religion, helping it to survive conquests to reappear time and again.

It was at the end of the Achaemenid period that Zoroastrianism made its first major impression on religion outside its own territories. Although the empire had been defeated, some elements of its belief system became part of Graeco-Roman syncretism, most notably

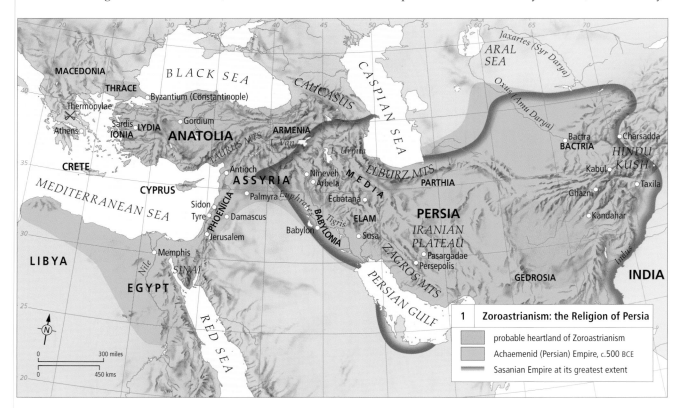

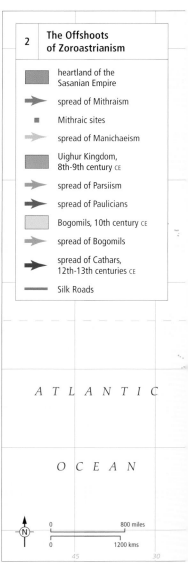

2	The Offshoots of Zoroastrianism
	heartland of the Sasanian Empire
	spread of Mithraism
	Mithraic sites
	spread of Manichaeism
	Uighur Kingdom, 8th-9th century CE
	spread of Parsiism
	spread of Paulicians
	Bogomils, 10th century CE
	spread of Bogomils
	spread of Cathars, 12th-13th centuries CE
	Silk Roads

1	Zoroastrianism: the Religion of Persia
	probable heartland of Zoroastrianism
	Achaemenid (Persian) Empire, c.500 BCE
	Sasanian Empire at its greatest extent

the cult of Mithra. Mithra had been worshipped as one of the major deities in Persia, and became the supreme god in the mystery cult, Mithraism, that spread throughout the Roman empire (*map 2*).

The Sasanian Empire

In the third century CE, a new power arose in Iran, the Sasanians, who built an empire which, for 400 years, challenged the might of both Rome and Constantinople in the East, until it was conquered by the Arabs in the mid-seventh century. The traditional Persian religion underwent a major transformation and formalization to reach its classic form. During the reign of Shapur I (241-272 CE) it became the state religion, fusing popular cults and Achaemenid traditions with Zarathusthra's teaching.

As a formal state religion Zoroastrianism became intolerant of opposition. Shapur's chief priest, Kartir, persecuted Jews, Buddhists, Hindus and Christians, as well as those he considered heretics, most famously Mani (216-c.275). Mani had combined elements of Zoroastrianism with Christianity, producing a religion (Manichaeism) in which he was the final revelation of the supreme god. Kartir executed Mani and sought to expunge his religion, but it had already begun to spread beyond the empire, and survived. In the west it became a heresy and remained a problem among Christians for centuries as it reappeared in various forms among the Bogomils, the Paulicians and the Cathars. In the East it fared much better. Spreading along the Silk Road, its centre became central Asia where, in 762, it became the official religion of the Uighur empire. It also spread into China where it suffered sporadic persecution for centuries, but there was still evidence of its survival in the seventeenth century.

Within Sasanian lands, other developments took place. One group, the Mazdakists, held that the spirits of good and evil were wholly separate in origin. Another group, the Zurvanists, held that they had their origin in infinite time. Both groups had periods of favour and disfavour in later Sasanian times, but neither appear to have lasted long after the Arab conquest.

The Parsis

Today, the largest Zoroastrian communities are in India, where they went following a revolt and repression in the tenth century. The Parsis ('Persians') have evolved a distinct form of the old religion. Their principal centre is Bombay, where contacts with other religions (such as Hinduism) have caused several doctrinal problems, in addition to internal disputes about their traditions. Migration has produced a worldwide diaspora.

The Tower of Silence, *the Parsi burial ground in Bombay, the home of the Parsis since they fled Persia 1,000 years ago. In the nineteenth century they spread from there throughout the East following trading routes within the British Empire; today, as a result of Asian migration, there are now also small communities in Britain, North America, and elsewhere.*

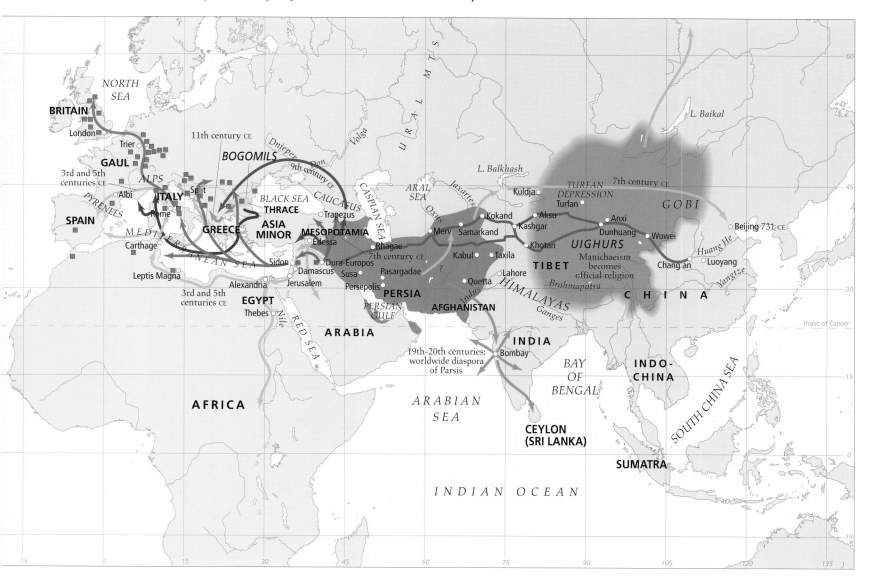

GREECE: HOME OF HELLENISTIC CIVILIZATION

| 2 | The Hellenistic World: the Aftermath of Alexander's Conquests |

— Alexander's Empire

● major cultural centres

successor states, c.270 BCE

Antigonid Empire

independent Greek colonies

Seleucid Empire

Mauryan Empire

Ptolemaic Kingdom

BY THE TIME OF Aristotle's death (322 BCE) two major developments had taken place in Greece which would have profound effects on subsequent religions. First, there was the development of a systematic investigation, philosophy, of human questions, which was separate from religious traditions and mythologies; and second, Greece had risen to be a world power through the conquests of Alexander the Great. His exploits had brought the Greeks into contact with cultures and religions from the Mediterranean to India. The result was Hellenistic religion: a patchwork of religions which borrowed elements of myth, cult, and doctrine from other belief systems. Different pantheons were interrelated pragmatically, for the sake of political unity, and theoretically, as manifestations of the human religious quest.

The Origins of Philosophy
According to ancient tradition, philosophy began with writers from Miletus who pursued questions about the universe's origin in terms of its basic matter, rather than religious cosmological myths (*map 1*). Instead of exploring origins in terms of, for example, the Orphic myth of the cosmic egg, Thales (fl. c.586 BCE) sought the

Earth's origin in terms of an eternally existing element, water, which mutated in various ways to produce our world. While philosophy was separate from religion in its reliance on human enquiry in place of myth, this should not be seen as analogous with the modern distinction between rational enquiry and religious belief. It should be perceived instead as a distinction between subjects and methods, in the way that

A Roman marble bust of Aristotle (384–322 BCE) based on a fourth-century BCE Greek original. While Aristotle's work said little directly about religion, the impact of his thought is still felt today in the theologies of all three Abrahamic religions.

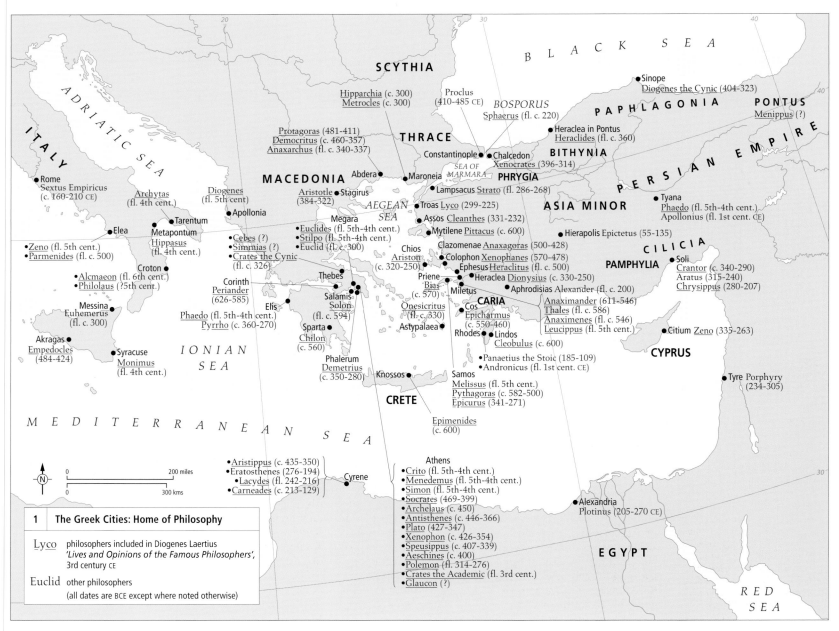

| 1 | The Greek Cities: Home of Philosophy |

Lyco — philosophers included in Diogenes Laertius 'Lives and Opinions of the Famous Philosophers', 3rd century CE

Euclid — other philosophers
(all dates are BCE except where noted otherwise)

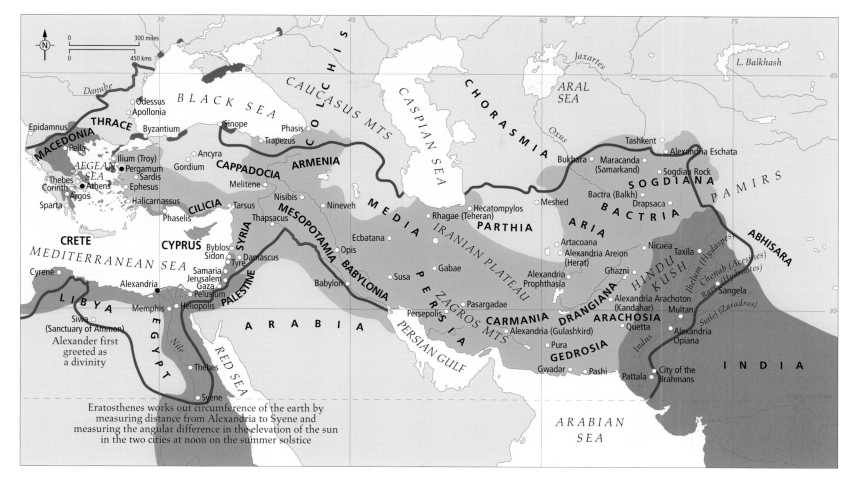

Eratosthenes works out circumference of the earth by measuring distance from Alexandria to Syene and measuring the angular difference in the elevation of the sun in the two cities at noon on the summer solstice

medieval science was distinct from theology, but shared its worldview. The various solutions proposed by Greek philosophy were distinct from myth, but their paradigms for rational investigation were shared with their religion. Moreover, with a few exceptions, most Greeks interested in philosophy also played their part in their cities' cults, reverenced their religious traditions, and continued to study the mythology as a cornerstone of their culture.

Religion and Philosophy

The links between philosophy and religion were often even closer. The followers of Pythagoras (c.582–500 BCE) can be seen as more of a religious cult than as a school. Later thinkers incorporated elements from Asian religions, while philosophy became a religious and mystical quest among the Neoplatonists such as
Plotinus (205–270 CE). Conversely, those who rejected mythology were seen as sceptical of knowledge in general.

An example of how philosophy absorbed elements of eastern religions is astrology. Originally a feature of Babylonian religion, it gradually gained ground as the scientific form of divination. Thus, it became part of a general Stoic theory of the sympathy between all things, a component of medicine, and a popular semi-religious practice in the market-place. It was defended – in a modified form – by Plotinus; yet seen as but another aspect of intellectual credulity by the Roman philosopher, Sextus Empiricus (c.160–210 CE).

Subsequent Greek thought looked back to Athens in the fifth and fourth centuries, and to figures such as Socrates, Plato, and Aristotle, as the golden age of philosophy. As portrayed by Plato, Socrates brought about an intellectual revolution to place moral questions at the centre of inquiry. Plato himself examined questions of human knowledge and the nature of society, and left a school, the Academy, after him. Aristotle produced a vast body of knowledge that would form the basis of formal learning for centuries. Almost down to our day, these thinkers have set the agenda of philosophical questions, and have had a major influence not just on Greek religion, but on Judaism, Christianity, and Islam.

A statue of Artemis of Ephesus (c. 135–75 CE). The cult of Artemis is a paradigm for its syncretism. Before the Greeks arrived, Ephesus was the cult centre of a mother goddess linked to Anatolian cults of the Great Mother. The Greeks identified her with Artemis (daughter of Zeus, virgin huntress, goddess of wild animals and the moon) since she looked after young girls and women in childbirth. Her temple in Ephesus was one of the 'Seven Wonders' of the world and the cult spread widely. She was later identified with the Roman Diana.

Alexander's Legacy

While the Greek adventure eastwards to India has continued to cause amazement, it is very striking how elements from eastern religions came west. In religious terms, Greece received more than it gave. The worldwide empire (*oikoumene*) led to a downgrading of city and local cults in favour of a religion that could be easily carried. This led to the perception of religion as a matter of individual taste, with cults as voluntary associations. Yet it also created a need to find bonds between the various cults to help integrate the many divergent cultures. The unifying link was the cult of the ruler. Alexander himself was first addressed as a divinity – something alien to native Greek culture – at the oracle of the Egyptian god Ammon in Siwa. Ruler cults became basic tests of loyalty, just as, for earlier Greeks, the worship of a city's gods were declarations of loyalty and belonging.

However, it would be wrong to see Hellenistic religion simply as a function of empire. The encounters that occurred between cultures had the effect of causing many societies to re-examine their beliefs, raising questions as to whether there were underlying unities between religions. While Greek became the *lingua franca* of the eastern Mediterranean, the Greeks were not intellectually imperial. The centre of learning shifted from Athens to Alexandria, with Pergamum as a lesser rival (*map 2*). Among the effects of these interfaces of religions was the sense that the world was to be compared to a single city, and that there should be tolerance and diversity between cults.

Among the Stoics, this new cultural reality led to their speculations about a single divine reality underlying all diversity. At a cultic level this new sense of the world's diversity led to a conscious extension of a process that had already begun in the Greek colonies: cults were fused, one culture's deity was seen as having an equivalent elsewhere. Meanwhile, the pressing questions of personal religion – fate, fears for the future, the quest for purpose in life – were seen as the same everywhere and transcending particular cults. It was this religiously diverse world that formed the context for the Jewish Diaspora and rise of Christianity.

ROMAN RELIGION

THE ORIGINAL ROMANS were just one of many cultures in Italy prior to the fifth to fourth centuries BCE: Etruscans in the north; Greeks in Magna Graecia in the south; and, between them, the Latins who gradually came to dominate the central area, and eventually the whole peninsula (*map 1*). Much of our information about their religion comes from sources in early imperial times which praise early Roman religion for its purity, manifested in its lack of statues and 'unseemly' mythology, such as marriages among the gods. But such authors were approving a religious ideal as much as making historical statements. It is clear, however, that most Roman deities were abstractions (the god Fides, for example, represented faithfulness) and that their divinity was defined by action. Their cult was organized around a solar liturgical year, closely linked to the agricultural cycle, and at the ceremonies they were served by teams of priests (*flamines*) who offered sacrifices. Thus food (grain) became the goddess Ceres, with a festival from 12–19 April (*Cerealia*). Similarly, the word for mildew, *robigus*, became a god's name, with processions around the fields to protect them at the *Robigalia* (25 April). The liturgical year also recognized the seasons: the *Diuallia* (21 December) celebrated the winter solstice. The priesthoods of three gods (Jupiter, Mars, Quirinus) were dominant and played a more significant role; the minor gods were seen as their family and their cults were dependent on the greater cults.

Community religion was paralleled in the household by gods such as the Lares and the Penates (perhaps originally the ancestors) who were held as the house's protectors. Sometimes they had a shrine within the home, but it was a more widespread custom to set aside a token part of the meal for them which was then ritually thrown into the fireplace (the *focus*); hence the hearth itself became a household shrine.

The Growth of Roman Power

As Roman power grew in Italy and then spread overseas a major change took place in Roman religion, which now began to interface with those of conquered cultures. As Horace noted: 'Captured Greece led her conqueror captive, and brought the arts to the rural Latins' (*Ep.* 2,1, 156). Greek mythology was adopted *en masse*, and many individual Roman gods were identified with Greek deities. Thus, parallel federations of gods emerged, one Latin, the other Greek, which were held to be simply different names for the same deities (the Latin Jupiter, for instance, was identified with Zeus). The resulting cults reflected both the traditional Roman cult and elements imported from Greece. Other Greek gods became part of the Roman pantheon but had no Roman parallel – the cult of Apollo is the most notable instance of this – while some Roman gods (such as Janus) never found an equivalent.

The Romans promoted public worship, believing that the benevolence of the gods produced the state's well-being. Equally, Roman administrators recognized the importance of ensuring that local cults were assimilated by Rome so that diverse traditions could not produce resentment and rebellion. When cults could not be absorbed into Roman religion, legal formulas were devised to ensure that particular religions (for example, Judaism) were fitted into the imperial framework.

The emergence of a formal empire, and especially the reign of Augustus, produced another development in religion. Now that the empire reached from the Atlantic to the Black Sea (*map 2*) there was an ever greater need to create a unifying culture that could form bonds between these many languages and peoples. The original syncretism of absorbing local cults from Italy and Greece was now extended. Linked pantheons brought local religious identities within Roman structures, but there was also a need for a unifying religion which would extend over the whole empire. This was provided in the

The Pantheon in Rome was built by the emperor Hadrian in c.120 CE. It is a perfect circle with an added portico. The centre of its dome (c.43m diameter) is open to the sky. The pantheon honoured all the gods revered in Rome. In 609 CE it was dedicated as a Christian church, and called Santa Maria Rotonda.

1   The Cultural Homeland of the Roman Empire

0 ——— 100 miles
0 ——— 150 kms

Aquileia
Mediolanum   Brixia   Verona
Ticinum   Patavium
          Placentia   *Po*
     Fidentia   Regium
Veleia   Lepidum
     Parma
          Mutina   Bononia
                Forum Cornelii
          Marzabotto   Ariminum
     Florentia
     Arno
               UMBRIA   A D R I A T I C   S E A
     ETRURIA
          Clusium   Asculum
          Volsinii   PICENUM
     Cosa Vulci Acqua Reate
     Tarquinia Falerii Rossa
               SABINI   FRENTANI
          Caere Veii Alba Fucens
CORSICA   Ostia   Rome
          LATIUM   Norba   SAMNIUM   APULIA
     Tarracina   Capua   Barium
               Cumae   Beneventum
               Neapolis Herculaneum   Brundisium
                    Pompeii
          CAMPANIA   Tarentum   CALABRIA
               Paestum   LUCANIA   Metapontum
                              Heraclea

     T Y R R H E N I A N   Thurii

SARDINIA   S E A   Croton
                         BRUTTIUM

                              Caulonia
                                   Locri
                    Messana   Rhegium
          Segesta   (Zancle)
               Tauromenium
M E D I T E R R A N E A N   Selinus   SICILY   I O N I A N
                    Agrigentum   Megara Hyblaea   S E A
          S E A   Syracuse

This Mithraic temple (Mithraeum) was discovered in the nineteenth century under the church of San Clemente in Rome (map 3). While such sanctuaries have been found throughout the empire, this is one of the best preserved. The Mysteries of Mithras was an offshoot of Zoroastrianism, with elaborate initiation rites and cosmic promises. It arrived in Rome at about the same time as Christianity.

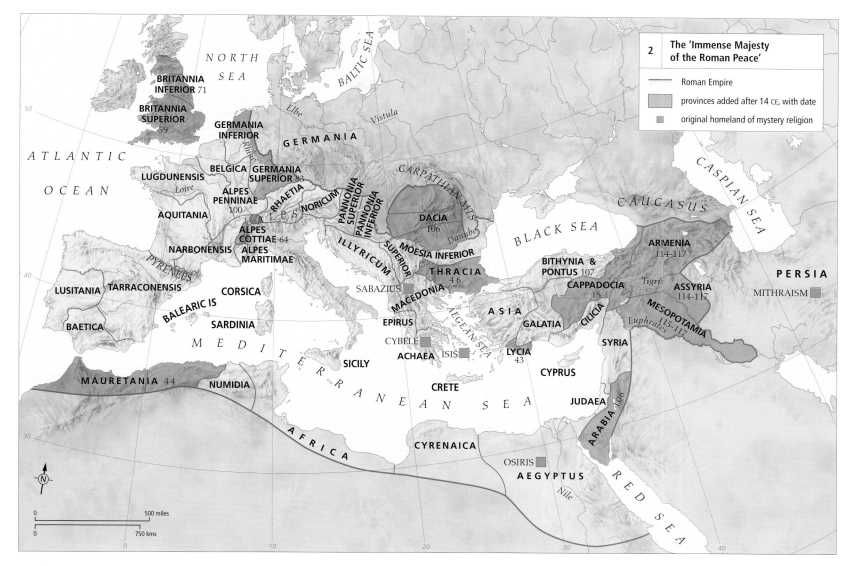

cult of the emperor. Worship of the emperor became both an act of political loyalty and a statement of belief in Rome's religious authority.

Private Religion
While the public cult was the most obvious manifestation of Roman religion, there was a great diversity within Roman religious activity. At the personal level the most obvious point of religious contact between the individual and the society was through the practice of divination, either in traditional forms such as haruspicy (the reading of animals' entrails), or by using 'scientific' means, such as astrology, which by the first century CE was a major part of Roman society. However, the Romans had not only adopted the Greek gods, they had also absorbed much of its religious philosophy. Cicero pursued a personal religious quest with dedication, many other currents of Greek religious thought continued to flourish (for example, Neoplatonism), while the emperor Marcus Aurelius wrote Stoic meditations.

The most striking religious phenomenon of imperial Rome was the spread of the mystery religions. While there is a major problem of definition regarding these, they have certain features in common. They represented individual options rather than official cults, were eastern in origin, offered exotic liturgies and promised their initiates special divine favours. One of the earliest was that of Cybele, brought from Greece in the third century BCE, but it was not until later that these cults really became widespread throughout the empire. Some cults (such as Mithras) can be found from Rome to Britain; while others (for example the Greek cult of Sabazius which spread through the Danubian provinces in the second century CE) were more local. Influences from Judaism and the nascent Christianity also permeated this complex mixture.

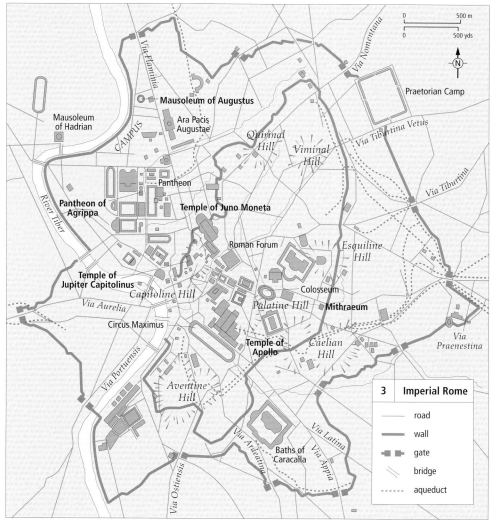

EUROPE PRIOR TO CHRISTENDOM

THE FIRST RELIGIONS of northwestern Europe are prehistoric – we cannot understand them through their own religious writings. In the case of the earliest religions of which archaeological evidence survives (the megalithic tombs of western Europe) there is only the testimony of the spade. The only evidence for later religions is found among people who did not share those beliefs – thus, Roman authors, looking on from outside, describe the beliefs of the peoples who were conquered by Rome, for example the Celts in Gaul. Later, when some Celtic authors did actually write about the beliefs of their people, they did so as Christians looking back on their former paganism. The same is true of the later invaders of the Roman Empire: by the time they write for themselves, they write as Christians.

The only other sources for the content of these pre-Christian beliefs are stories which were later written down, and surviving folklore. However, recent studies have shown that these records have, for the most part, been thoroughly Christianized; the Anglo-Saxon poem *Beowulf*, for example, does not show heroic pre-Christian Germanic religion, but provides a fable in which Christians can view their pagan ancestors as 'saved' in the context of a Christian view of natural religion.

The First European Builders

The distinctive tombs built of large stones ('megalithic') found along the Atlantic coast are the oldest significant buildings on the European continent (*map 1*). Other surviving structures presumably belonging to the same people, for example the stone alignments in Carnac, northwestern France, are only explicable in the context of ritual activity.

The popular notion that the people who built these large structures were 'Celts' is certainly false, as more than a millennium elapsed between them and the arrival of the Celtic peoples. The fact that they built elaborate tombs to house cremated remains, and left valuable grave goods with those remains, indicates that they believed in some sort of personal survival beyond death (at least for those who occupied the stone tombs, who may only represent a particular stratum of society). Some of these sites are aligned with the solstice, indicating some sort of solar liturgical year, probably linked to a notion of agricultural death and revival, with the sun as a major deity. Little more information about their beliefs can be directly inferred from the archaeological evidence.

Celtic Religion

The Celtic people entered Europe some time in the first millennium BCE (*map 2*). Their culture is often identified archaeologically by particular artistic forms (such as 'La Tène' culture). They are mentioned by classical authors, such as Julius Caesar, and some of their languages – Gaelic, Welsh, Breton – still survive. However, their beliefs are refracted by their classical and Christian observers to fit their own religious understandings. The Stoic philosopher, Posidonius (c.135–51 BCE), is the source of much of our information about the druids, the Celtic

The megalithic tomb at New Grange in Ireland. The people who built this, and many of the other great prehistoric structures of northwestern Europe were roughly contemporary with the builders of the pyramids in Egypt. However, we know nothing about their language culture or beliefs, except what can be inferred from these buildings. New Grange contains a burial site whose deep central chamber is so aligned that the sun's rays penetrate its central chamber at the winter solstice, indicating a belief in an afterlife and some sort of regeneration.

1	**Ancient Europe**
	area of megalithic tombs
	megalithic tombs
	maximum extent of Celtic influence
	Celtic religious sites
	other Celtic sites

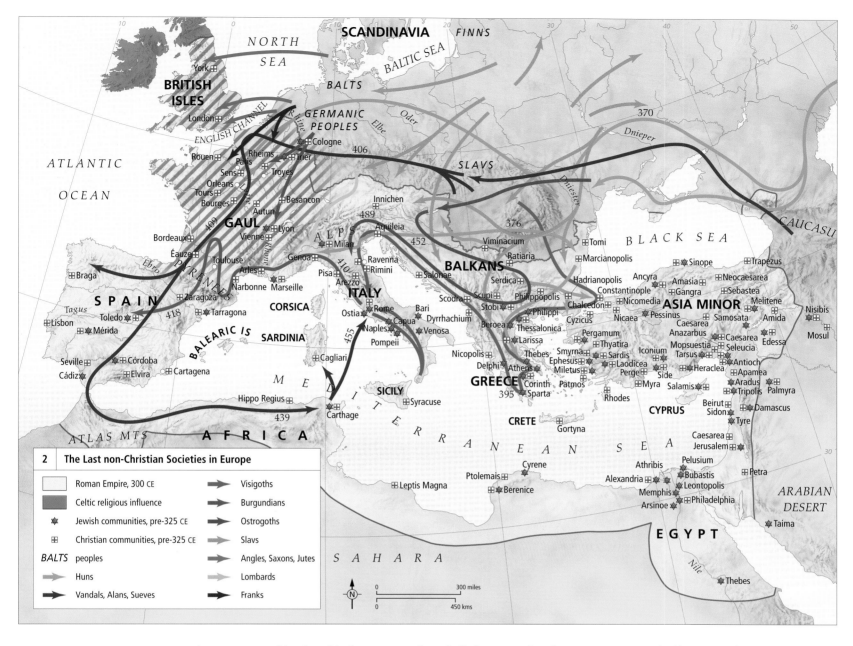

2 The Last non-Christian Societies in Europe

▫ Roman Empire, 300 CE	→ Visigoths
▨ Celtic religious influence	→ Burgundians
✡ Jewish communities, pre-325 CE	→ Ostrogoths
⊞ Christian communities, pre-325 CE	→ Slavs
BALTS peoples	→ Angles, Saxons, Jutes
→ Huns	→ Lombards
→ Vandals, Alans, Sueves	→ Franks

A stone sculpture of a head wearing a torc, found at Mšeckè Zehrovice, represents a Celtic god or hero. Similar artefacts found in other parts of Europe indicate a shared culture with, presumably, shared religious beliefs.

priests, sages and healers. Yet he presents these beliefs as a perfect example of what a Stoic asserts the unsophisticated religion of those living before cities should be. It can be very problematic to separate the actual beliefs of the Celts from the projections of a Stoic theologian. It is not surprising that eighteenth-century seekers after the 'noble savage', or more recent romantics involved in the quest for a pre-systematic religion have been so attracted to the Celts – Posidonius shared some of their aspirations. When a writer such as the seventh-century CE Irishman Muirchú records his own people's beliefs prior to their conversion to Christianity, he categorizes their beliefs in Christian terms in anticipation of their conversion.

Between Empire and Christianity

From the beginning of the fifth century CE there was a series of movements of peoples within western Europe, which led to the resettling of areas of the Western Roman empire by Germanic peoples. These peoples can be divided into groups by forms of language (such as Angles and Goths) and by ethnic groupings (such as Ostrogoths and Visigoths). In addition, other groups, such as the Huns, can be seen as true invaders, in that they had not been settled in eastern Europe for centuries prior to their western incursions.

When they entered imperial territory they absorbed much of the late classical culture, as can be seen by the spread of Romance languages. They also absorbed Christianity, partly directly as a religion and partly as the religious form of the lands they had captured. It was only

after their encounters with Christian religion and imperial culture that their tales of gods and heroes, along with social and religious customs, were written down. The Slavs of eastern Europe did not enter the Romanized and Christianized areas of western Europe, but – like the Germanic peoples – they recorded their religious traditions only in the aftermath of their encounter with European Christianity.

In the case of all these non-Roman, pre-Christian religions the work of piecing together surviving elements produces a picture of a world of gods and heroes. A sky god and a fertility goddess are usually amongst the major deities worshipped. Traces of a liturgical year can be seen in annual practices which are now linked to the Christian year: decorated trees at fixed times; eggs at Easter; bonfires at midsummer; and annual visits to what are now saints' wells, but which were once the shrines of local deities. Overall, the religion is predominantly rural in its imagery, with an emphasis on sacred groves and trees. But this may be because much of the evidence has survived in the countryside, rather than because the adherents of the religion originally belonged to a non-urban society.

However, if these religions are now almost invisible as systems of belief, they have left their mark on the cultures which came after them. Just as Graeco-Roman culture left its imprint on Judaism and Christianity in the period of the Roman Empire, so these cultures had an impact – although, as non-literate cultures, to a lesser extent – on the development of Christianity after the end of the western Empire.

JUDAISM

THE HISTORY of Judaism is the history of a people. A person is Jewish if their mother is Jewish, and Judaism is a family and tribal religion, passed down from one generation to the next. Although it is possible to convert from another religion and become a Jew, the vast majority have inherited the status. Today, there are Jewish communities all over the world, the largest being in the United States and Israel. Despite a wide variety of cultural backgrounds and a diversity of religious practice, the majority of Jews believe that they are the descendants of the patriarch Abraham, his son Isaac and his grandson Jacob whose deeds are described in the Hebrew scriptures. Through their long, often unhappy history, the Jews have seen themselves as God's chosen people, whose mission is to bring knowledge of the one God to the world.

THE JEWISH religion is centred around the Torah ('Law' or 'Teaching'), the book of God's law. Orthodox Jews believe that this was given directly by God to his prophet Moses. Therefore all its 613 commandments must be obeyed in every particular (they cover all areas of life, particularly the ritual and moral). Through the ages much scholarly ingenuity has gone into interpreting and explaining the exact meaning of the commandments and how they should be kept today. The Torah itself consists of the first five books of the Bible: Genesis, Exodus, Leviticus, Numbers and Deuteronomy. A portion from the Torah scroll is read every week in the synagogue, the Jewish house of worship, and the readings are arranged in such a way that the whole is read once

every year. The Torah is the religious Jew's pride and privilege. As the liturgy puts it: 'It is the tree of life to all who cling to it and all conduct is judged by its standards.'

The Early History

The Bible records how Abraham was called to leave his own country and become a wanderer in the wilderness. He was promised that he would be the father of a great nation and that his descendants would be as numerous as the stars of heaven. Although he was elderly at the time and had no children, he obeyed the voice of God and, in time, a son was born to him. Later the tribe went down into Egypt and were enslaved there. It was the prophet Moses (c. thirteenth century BCE)

JUDAISM

Timeline — JUDAISM

Above the line: Era of Patriarchs, ?c.1800-1600 | Era of Judges, c.1200-1000 | Return from Babylon, 538 | Prophets given scriptural status, c.200 | **CE** | Bar Kokhba Revolt, 132-5 | Jerusalem Talmud compiled, 5th century | Karaism founded, c.760 | Era of Crusades, 1095-1291 | Jews expelled from England, 1290 | Foundation of Hasidism, c.1735 | 1st Zionist Conference, 1897 | Holocaust, 1942-5

Scale: 2000 ▸ 1500 ▸ 1000 ▸ 800 ▸ 600 ▸ 400 ▸ 200 ▸ 100 ▸ 200 ▸ 300 ▸ 400 ▸ 500 ▸ 600 ▸ 700 ▸ 800 ▸ 900 ▸ 1000 ▸ 1100 ▸ 1200 ▸ 1300 ▸ 1400 ▸ 1500 ▸ 1600 ▸ 1700 ▸ 1800 ▸ 1900 ▸ 2000

Below the line: Exodus from Egypt, ?c.1250 | Division of kingdom, 930 | Torah given scriptural status, c.450 | Maccabean Revolt, 167-164 | Destruction of the Temple, 70 | Mishnah compiled, c.200 | Babylonian Talmud compiled, 6th century | Jews expelled from France, 1182 | Jews expelled from Spain, 1492 | Reform movement, c.1820 | State of Israel, 1948

THE WORLD

Timeline — THE WORLD

Above the line: Beginnings of Minoan civilization, Crete, c.2000 | Gautama Siddhartha, c.563-483 | **CE** | Mani, 216-c.275 | End of Western Roman Empire, 476 | Text of Qur'an established, c.653 | Christian iconoclasm, 726-842 | End of Buddhism in India, c.1250 | Council of Trent, 1545-63 | Pilgrim fathers to America, 1620 | 2nd Vatican Council, 1961-4

Scale: 2000 ▸ 1500 ▸ 1000 ▸ 800 ▸ 600 ▸ 400 ▸ 200 ▸ 100 ▸ 200 ▸ 300 ▸ 400 ▸ 500 ▸ 600 ▸ 700 ▸ 800 ▸ 900 ▸ 1000 ▸ 1100 ▸ 1200 ▸ 1300 ▸ 1400 ▸ 1500 ▸ 1600 ▸ 1700 ▸ 1800 ▸ 1900 ▸ 2000

Below the line: Zarathustra, c.1000 | Confucius, c.551-479 | Jesus, c.6 BCE-26/36 CE | Christianity tolerated in Roman Empire, 313 | Muhammad, 570-632 | Rise of Tantric Buddhism, c.700 | East and West Christian churches separate, 1054 | Shinran, founder Jodo Shinshu, Japan, 1173-1262 | Fall of Constantinople, to Turks, 1453 | Amritsar founded, 1577 | Mormonism founded, 1830 | 1st Vatican Council, 1870

---

who led them to freedom and to settlement in the Promised Land, what is today the land of Israel. It was during the course of this long journey that God revealed his commandments, not merely the Ten Commandments (Exodus 20), but the whole Torah in all its fullness. Initially, the Israelites rejected the idea of having a king since their only ruler was God. Instead, when they were threatened by enemies local leaders known as judges arose. However, eventually a king became necessary and first Saul, then David and then Solomon ruled over the Israelite people (eleventh–tenth centuries BCE). King Solomon is remembered for building a magnificent temple to God in Jerusalem, which became the centre of all Jewish worship. After his death, however, the kingdom split in two. The ten northern tribes formed the Kingdom of Israel which was destroyed by the Assyrians in 722 BCE. The two southern tribes remained faithful to the house of David and were known as the Kingdom of Judah. This was conquered by the Babylonians: in the terrible year 586, Solomon's Temple was destroyed and the Jews were taken into exile in Babylon.

The Dispersion

This was the start of the great Jewish dispersion. Although the Jews were allowed back to the Promised Land at the end of the sixth century BCE, many chose to remain in Babylon and gradually Jewish communities grew up all around the Mediterranean Sea. The Temple was rebuilt in Jerusalem and the Jews enjoyed a short period of independence before they became part of the Roman Empire. In 70 CE, however, they rebelled against Rome and in consequence the Temple was finally destroyed leaving only the Western Wall, which still stands.

In the dispersion communities, the centre of religious activity was the synagogue. There Jews would come together to hear the Torah and to discuss the law. Over the centuries collections of legal discussions were produced to provide a foundation for later interpretation. The Mishnah (literally 'Repetition' or 'Teaching') was compiled in the second century CE, the Jerusalem Talmud (literally 'Study' or 'Teaching') in the fifth century CE and the Babylonian Talmud in the sixth century CE. These holy books became the main subject of study in the academies throughout the Jewish world. Scholarship and piety were closely intertwined. Every parent hoped that their sons would be learned and that their daughters would marry scholars.

Meanwhile, Christianity, which itself had grown out of Judaism (see pp. 138-39, became the official religion of the West in the fourth century CE while the Islamic empire extended through Asia Minor, North Africa and up into Spain in the seventh In general, the Jews did better under Islam than under Christianity. It suited the empire to have an educated class of Jewish merchants to manage trade. Things were not so happy under Christian rule and the history of medieval European Jewry is a sad catalogue of persecution and expulsion.

The Later Developments of Judaism

By the early nineteenth century, the spirit of liberalism in Western Europe encouraged a new mood of religious tolerance. The Jews gained full citizenship in their countries of residence and many found the old structures of religious orthodoxy inappropriate. The Reform movement, which allowed for interpretation of the Torah, developed in Germany and soon spread to Holland, France, Britain and over the Atlantic Ocean to America. In Eastern Europe regular *pogroms* against Jewish life and property continued and prompted many families also to seek a new life in the New World. Thus, by the end of the nineteenth century, there were both Orthodox and Reform communities in almost every city in the United States.

With the rise of Fascism, Jewry was under threat again and in the terrible period between 1942 and 1945, in Hitler's Europe, six million Jews were systematically murdered. Even before the Second World War, many Jews had come to believe that the only way they could live in total security was to have a land of their own. After the full enormity of the Holocaust was revealed, the State of Israel was created by the United Nations. Many problems still remained. Since 1948 Israel has fought several wars for its own survival and an equitable solution to the rights of the Palestinians is still to be found. Nonetheless, in the last fifty years, Israel has proved a refuge for persecuted communities and a focus of interest to Jews everywhere.

ANCIENT ISRAEL

ACCORDING TO THE Book of Genesis, Abraham was the father of the Jewish people, who was commanded by God to leave his native country (which was Mesopotamia). He was promised that if he was obedient, he and his descendants would be given 'the land of your sojournings, all the land of Canaan, for an everlasting possession' (Genesis 17:8). Abraham had many adventures and, in the course of time, his son Isaac inherited the promise. Isaac had two sons, Esau and Jacob. Genesis records how the younger, Jacob, stole the birthright and blessing from the elder and was forced to flee from his anger. During his journey, at Bethel, he had a dream which renewed the promise to Abraham. Once again God promised that the land would be given to Jacob and his descendants. Several years later, he had another encounter, this time at Penuel, at which he was given the name of Israel; this was said to mean 'You have striven with God and with men and have prevailed' (Genesis 32:28).

The Twelve Tribes

Jacob was the father of twelve sons; Reuben, Simeon, Levi, Judah, Dan, Naphtali, Gad, Asher, Issachar, Zebulun, Joseph and Benjamin. They were believed to be the ancestors of the Twelve Tribes of Israel (*map 1*). Later, when the Israelites were settled in the Promised Land, each tribe held a certain portion of the land. Joseph, who was the eldest son of Jacob's favourite wife, inherited, according to custom, a double portion. As a result, his tribes were named after his two sons, Ephraim and Manasseh.

The tribe of Levi were priests. Later in the history of the Jewish people, they served in the Temple in Jerusalem, ensuring that there was a regular cycle of worship. As a result they were maintained through a system of tithes and did not possess tribal lands.

The Exodus and the Giving of the Law

Jacob and his twelve sons travelled south to Egypt to escape from famine. They settled there, but after several generations, the Egyptian hierarchy turned against them. According to the Book of Exodus, they were enslaved and were compelled to build the grain cities of Pithom and Ramses. But God did not forget his people. Moses, a young Israelite who had been brought up in the Egyptian court, called down a series of disasters on the Egyptian

people. As a result, he was given permission to lead his people to freedom. The story of the Exodus is a pivotal event in Jewish history (*map 2*). It is difficult to establish the precise route from the Biblical text and, in any event, many scholars do not accept that all the tribes of Israel went down to Egypt in the first place. However, Exodus does relate that the Israelites camped at Mount Sinai in the south. There God gave Moses the 613 commandments which have remained the fundamental cornerstone of Jewish life. They govern every aspect of existence and cover everyday details as well as giving an array of ethical and ritual injunctions.

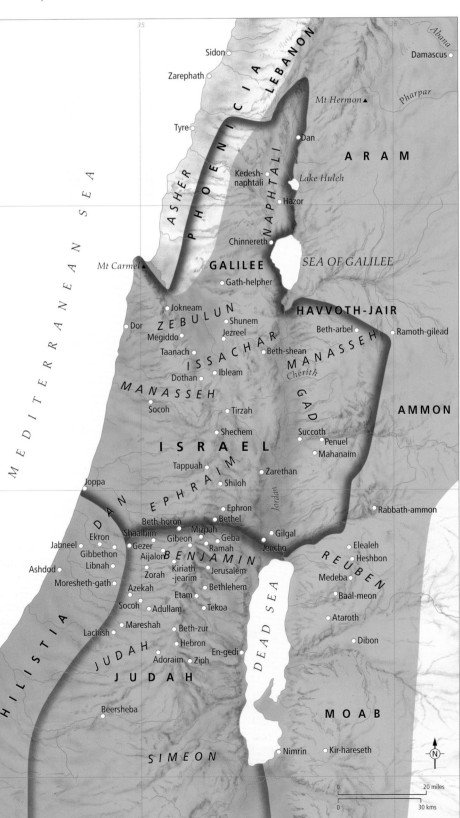

1	**The Kingdoms of Israel and Judah**
DAN	the tribes of Israel
	Kingdom of David and Solomon
	Kingdom of Israel
	Kingdom of Judah

The earliest picture of a Jew. Here, King Jehu of the northern kingdom is shown bowing down before the king of Assyria, offering him gifts. The threat of invasion could only be averted by the payment of regular tribute.

The handing down of the commandments, as portrayed by Rembrandt. The 613 laws are the fundamental principles of Jewish life. The best known are the Ten Commandments, which outline essential duties to both God and neighbour.

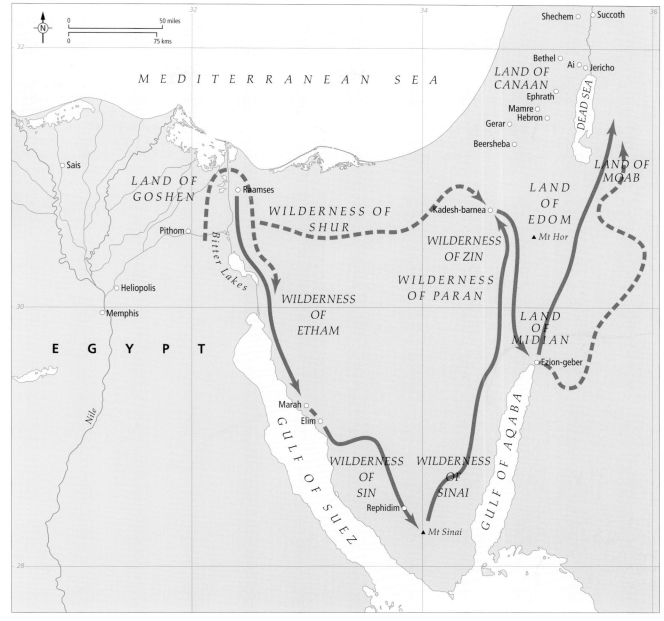

2	The Route of the Exodus

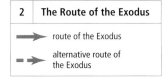

route of the Exodus

alternative route of the Exodus

The Kingdoms of Israel and Judah

The Israelites are said to have spent seventy years wandering in the wilderness. When they finally settled in their tribal lands, initially they believed themselves to be ruled by God alone. Later however, threatened by the surrounding nations, they felt the need for a king. The first king of the Israelites was Saul, a young man of the tribe of Benjamin. He was followed by David and then by David's son Solomon, who built the Temple in Jerusalem. The first three kings were all southerners, from the kingdom of Judah, and as a result the northern tribes became restless. After the death of Solomon, the northern tribes, from the land known as Israel, chose their own king. Although Israel was larger, richer and more powerful than Judah, it was politically less stable.

Meanwhile, the powerful empires of the Egyptians and Assyrians were being established to the east and south of the lands of the Israelites, which were becoming strategically important. For a time the threat of conquest was averted by the regular payment of tribute. In 722 BCE, however, the northern kingdom was overrun by the Assyrians, who settled other peoples in the land. The Israelites intermarried with them and the northern tribes were lost to history. Nonetheless, the idea of twelve tribes remained important. All were included in God's promise to the patriarchs and several groups (such as the Jews of Ethiopia) have claimed to be descendants of one of the 'lost tribes'. As part of their belief in future redemption, traditional Jews still believe that God will again gather together all the descendants of Abraham. All will return to Jerusalem and the tribes will be fully restored.

Exile and Return

Meanwhile, the southern kingdom, still ruled by the dynasty of David, continued its existence, maintaining its religious life in the Jerusalem Temple. Like its northern neighbour, it was in constant danger from surrounding empires and, in 586 BCE, Jerusalem was besieged by the Babylonians. It was a catastrophe; the Temple of Solomon was burnt to the ground and the remaining tribes were taken in a body to exile in Babylon. There they tried to maintain their religious life by meeting together regularly and organizing synagogues and houses of study. Many settled permanently and gradually small colonies of Jews were established all around the Mediterranean Sea. Yet the Promised Land remained home. When the Babylonians were conquered by the Persians in 538 BCE, many Jews seized the chance to return. Their homecoming was discouraging; the land was neglected and the Temple was in ruins. Yet under the leadership of Ezra and Nehemiah, the people were recalled to the law of God. The Temple was rebuilt, admittedly on a less grand scale, and Jewish life returned to the Promised Land.

The next few centuries were to prove equally tempestuous. The Land became part of the empire of Alexander the Great and was quarrelled over by the succeeding Ptolemaic and Seleucid dynasties. For a short period, in the second and first centuries BCE, the Jews enjoyed independence under the Maccabees. But to the west, Rome was stirring. Herod the Great, who restored the Temple to its original magnificence, survived only as an ally of Rome. He died in 4 BCE.

JUDAISM IN THE ROMAN EMPIRE

THE ROMAN EMPIRE in c.1 CE controlled all the territory around the Mediterranean Sea, from Spain in the west to Mesopotamia in the east. Although the Jews had enjoyed a period of independence under the Maccabees, the Promised Land had subsequently come under Roman rule. King Herod was a believing Jew, but he was also an ally of the Romans and was hated by his people. After his death in 4 BCE, his territory was divided between his three sons. Ten years later, however, Herod Archaelus was exiled by the Romans and Judaea was ruled directly by a Procurator. Herod Antipas continued to reign in Galilee in the north, while a third son, Philip, held land to the east of the Sea of Galilee.

Judaism in the Time of Jesus

A great deal is known about Judaism in the first century CE, partly because it was the religion of Jesus, as is recounted in the New Testament, and partly because the Jewish historian Josephus gives a very full picture. In addition, many archaeological sites in Israel have yielded valuable information (*see also* pp. 150-151).

The first King Herod held a considerable kingdom under the Romans. It included Idumaea, Judaea, Samaria and Galilee (*map 2*). By no means all the inhabitants were Jews. Idumaea had been conquered by a Jewish army and the inhabitants had been converted; many Samaritans were descended from Jews who had intermarried with surrounding tribes and they practised

a different form of worship centred round Mount Gerizim near Sebaste. Gentiles as well as Jews lived in Galilee. The centre of Jewish life focused on the Temple in Jerusalem, where the hereditary priests maintained the traditional rituals and sacrifices. Throughout the land there were also synagogues where Jews could come together to read and discuss the law under the guidance of the scribes and

The Qumran Caves. A series of scrolls were discovered in these caves near the Dead Sea. They are thought to have been produced by one of the monastic groups, who dedicated their lives to God, described by the Jewish historian Josephus.

1	The Jewish Diaspora in the Roman Empire
	border of the Roman Empire
	provincial borders
	provinces added after 14 CE, with date
	areas of widespread Jewish settlement
	cities with large Jewish communities
	Jewish settlements

Mosaic from the Beth Alpha synagogue. *This mosaic, representing the Biblical story of Abraham's attempted sacrifice of Isaac, decorated the floor of a first-century synagogue where Jews came together to listen to the scriptures.*

Roman hands and the entire Temple had gone up in flames. All that remained was the mighty Western Wall which stands to this day and is recognized as the most sacred place in the Jewish world. Meanwhile the Zealots fled to the south and took possession of King Herod's old fortress of Masada. The rebels chose to commit suicide rather than submit to capture by the Romans, and Masada has become an inspiration for generations of Jewish freedom fighters.

There was another Jewish revolt in 132 CE led by Simeon bar Kokhba, who was accepted as the long-awaited messiah by the most eminent religious leader of the day, Rabbi Akiva. It was initially successful, but by the end of 135 CE both Simeon and Akiva were dead. Henceforth Jews were forbidden to live in the ruins of the holy city of Jerusalem and a new Roman city, Aeolia Capitolina, was built on the site. From then on, the Jewish leadership pursued a policy of conciliation towards the Romans and concentrated on the development of a religious life separate from the old sacrificial system of the Temple.

The Dispersion

Since the time of the Exile in Babylon, there were groups of Jews living outside the Promised Land. It was the policy of the Christian missionary Paul to preach first to the Jews and then to the gentiles and, in his travels around the Mediterranean Sea, he invariably used the local synagogue as his first base, thus providing evidence of Jewish communities throughout Asia Minor, Thracia, Macedonia, Greece and Italy. Towards the end of his life, he was even planning a trip to Spain, which indicates the extent of Jewish colonization. Other sources refer to communities in North Africa, with a particularly important settlement in the Egyptian city of Alexandria. It was here that the Hebrew scriptures were translated into Greek for the benefit of those Jews who could no longer understand the sacred language. This translation was known as the Septuagint. As the Romans conquered further territory (*map 1*), Jews founded new trading posts and, by the third century, there were settlements north of the Alps in modern-day France and southern Germany. There was no attempt to recreate the sacrifices of the Jerusalem Temple. The major institution of all these colonies was the synagogue, where Jews met together to study, discuss and interpret God's holy law. By the end of the second century, the Jewish people were widely dispersed; they lived as minority groups, regarded as strangers among a variety of different cultures.

2	The Promised Land in the 1st century CE

- Kingdom of Herod
- – – Tetrarchy of Philip
- – – Tetrarchy of Antipas
- • • • Territory of Ethnarch Archelaeus
- ◼ Herod's fortresses
- areas of fighting in the Jewish Revolt, 66–73 CE

pharisees. For some this was not enough. Josephus describes the practices of monastic communities who dedicated their lives to God. Archaeologists have unearthed monastic remains in Qumran near the Dead Sea and the Dead Sea Scrolls were probably produced by such a group.

The Jewish Revolt

There was continual discontent among the Jews, who longed for independence and who were outraged by the Romans' idolatrous ways. Members of the revolutionary party were known as Zealots. They believed that God had given the land to his Chosen People and the presence of the Romans was a sacrilege. In 66 CE, a Roman legion and a group of pro-Roman Jews were killed in a Zealot uprising. The rebels captured land in Galilee, round Caesarea and overthrew the government in Jerusalem. The Roman emperor's son, Titus, was put in charge of the campaign and, with Rome's superior forces, the final outcome was inevitable. In 70 CE, the Romans laid siege to Jerusalem and by the end of September the city was in

MEDIEVAL JUDAISM

URING THE Middle Ages there were Jewish communities located in all major cities around the Mediterranean Sea, from Spain in the west to the furthest extent of Persia in the east. Everywhere the Jews lived as a visible minority, separated by their religion from their neighbours.

The Academies

After the destruction of King Herod's Temple in Jerusalem in 70 CE, Rabbi Johanan ben Zakkai set up an academy, at which scholars met to discuss the meaning of the law. By the mid-second century, there are records of the foundation of several institutions in Palestine. Meanwhile, similar academies existed in Mesopotamia, the most famous being the academies of Sura and Pumbeditha (map 2). By the third century, the interpretation of the law was highly complex and Judah ha Nasi compiled a record which was known as the Mishnah (literally, 'Teaching'). This was divided into six sections and included the laws of agriculture, festivals, marriage, damages, sacrifice and ceremonial purity. The Mishnah became the basis for all future discussions and, by the end of the fourth century, the academies of Palestine collated their debates. A similar exercise was carried out in Babylon and the Babylonian Talmud, as it is called, was compiled in the sixth century. This is a vast work which has remained the chief subject of Jewish

scholarship ever since. Between the sixth and the eleventh centuries, the heads of the two main Babylonian academies were regarded as the most important religious authorities in the Jewish world. They were responsible for interpreting the law, for answering specific questions and for presiding over the central rabbinic court. However, after the ninth century, their influence waned and by the mid-eleventh century, the two academies had merged and other centres had become more important.

Jews in Islamic Lands

In the seventh century, the Prophet Muhammad began to preach against the paganism of his countrymen in Arabia. His message spread astonishingly quickly. By 644 Syria, Egypt, Iraq and Persia had become part of a new Islamic empire and by the start of the eighth century, Islam was established throughout North Africa and soldiers had crossed the Straits of Gibraltar to conquer Spain. In general, the Muslims accepted the Jewish communities. They recognized the Jews, like the Christians, as 'Peoples of the Book'; they were not idolators. Although Jews suffered certain restrictions, such as having to pay an additional poll tax and being compelled to wear distinctive clothing, they were exempt from military service and they enjoyed judicial autonomy and religious toleration. The Muslim leaders even confirmed the authority of the academies. Throughout the Islamic

In Christian Europe, Jews *were commonly demonized and accused of all sorts of nefarious practice, such as stealing the consecrated bread. In this picture, a Jew is appropriating a picture of the Virgin Mary.*

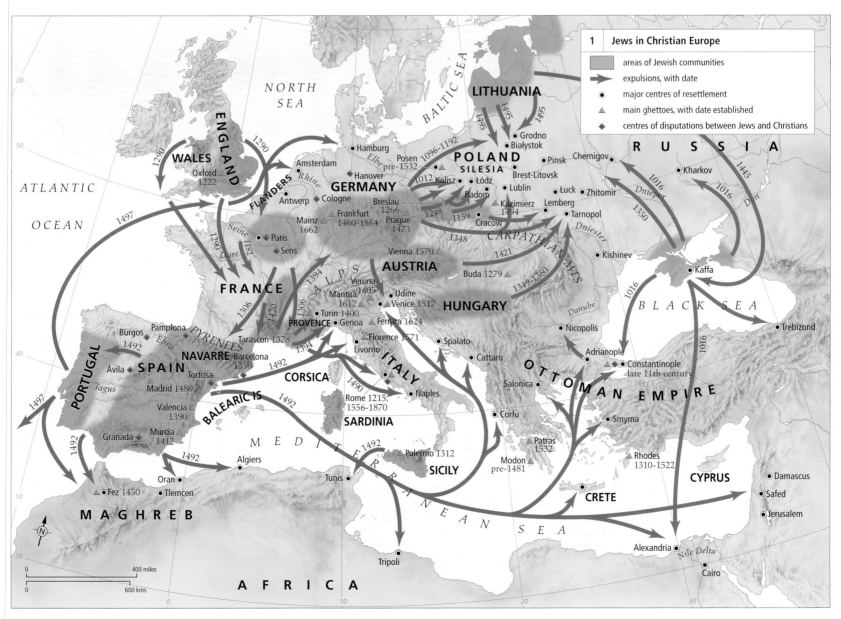

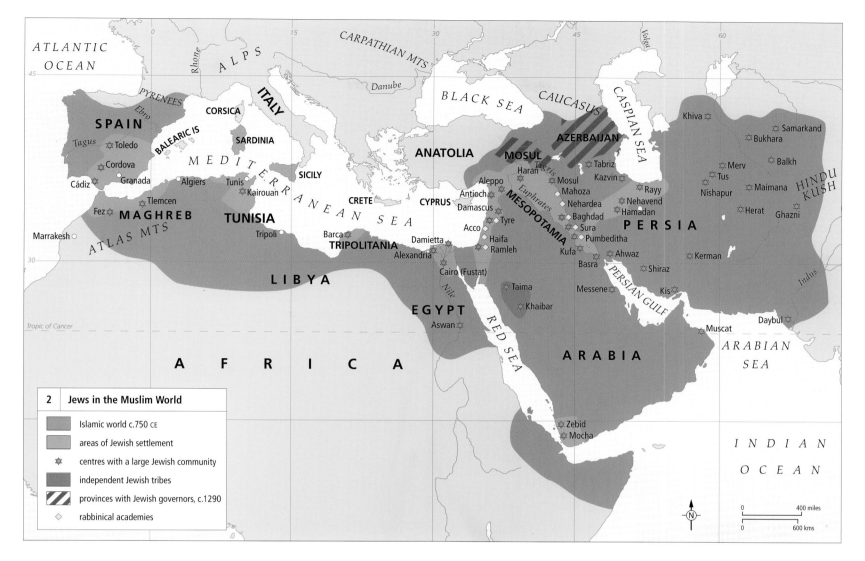

2 Jews in the Muslim World

- Islamic world c.750 CE
- areas of Jewish settlement
- ☆ centres with a large Jewish community
- independent Jewish tribes
- ▨ provinces with Jewish governors, c.1290
- ◇ rabbinical academies

empire there were many important centres of Jewish life and many Jews rose to positions of great importance.

Spain was notable as the scene of a great florescence of Jewish culture. Many Jews held prominent positions: in the tenth century Hasdai Ibn Shaprut was the court physician in Cordova; Samuel haNagid was vizier and army commander of the state of Granada from 1030 to 1056; the work of such poets as Judah haLevi, Moses ibn Ezra and Solomon ibn Gabirol is enshrined in the liturgy even today, and the great philosopher Maimonides (1135–1204) was born in Cordova. While there were pockets of persecution (Maimonides himself had to flee Spain and settle in North Africa), Muslim rule provided a largely stable background against which the Jews could build up their religious life, practise trade and benefit from the free movement of peoples within the Empire.

Christian Europe

The situation was not so positive within Christian Europe (*map 1*). Christianity has traditionally portrayed Jews in a negative light. Even though Jesus himself was a Jew, the Gospels depict him as highly critical of the religious leaders of his day and the Jews have traditionally been blamed for the crucifixion. Although there were many established Jewish communities throughout Europe, their existence was perilous.

After the First Crusade was proclaimed in 1095, Jews were attacked and massacred in several Rhineland towns. As early as 1144, Jews were being accused of using the blood of Christian children in the manufacture of Passover unleavened bread. In most places they were forbidden to own land, and were forced out of trade as a result of the restrictive practices of the Christian guilds. In order to make a living, they often turned to money-lending. Thus, not only were they seen as Christ-killers, they were also considered to be cold-blooded usurers. In 1182 all Jews who lived on the French king's estates were

expelled. In 1290, the entire community was thrown out of England. In the next century, at the time of the Black Death, the Jews were widely accused of poisoning the wells. At formal disputations, held between Christian and Jewish scholars, the Christians were always allowed the last word. All too often these ended with further massacres and expulsions. Then in 1492 the rich and powerful Spanish community was expelled from the Iberian peninsula. In cities where Jews were allowed to remain, they were often only permitted to live in certain parts, the ghetto, where they could be controlled more easily. The notable exception to this catalogue of misery was Poland where the Jews were welcomed and protected from the thirteenth century. Not surprisingly, the Jews settled there in their thousands.

Moses Maimonides *is widely recognized as the greatest Jewish theologian. His philosophical work, the* Guide to the Perplexed, *is studied today and he also produced an important code of Jewish law. This statue was raised in his birthplace, the Spanish city of Cordova.*

JUDAISM IN EARLY MODERN EUROPE

JEWS WHO TRACE their descent from ancestors who lived in mediaeval Christian Europe are known as the Ashkenazim. Ashkenaz is traditionally identified with Germany and the Jews of the early Middle Ages of England, France, the Netherlands, Switzerland and Germany all followed similar customs. After the medieval expulsions, these Jews took their liturgy and way of life to Austria, Prussia, Hungary, Poland and into Russia. On the other hand, Jews who were descended from the communities of Spain, North Africa and the Islamic Empire were known as Sephardim. Once Spain was united under a Christian monarchy and the Jews were driven out in 1492, they settled in other locations within the Islamic Empire. The Sephardim did not use the same prayer book as the Ashkenazim and different religious practices developed. They also spoke a different language; the Ashkenazim used Yiddish while the language of the Sephardim was Ladino (*map 1*).

The Kabbalah
Within Judaism, there is a long tradition of mystical speculation (Kabbalah), which tended to be regarded as

secret knowledge. It was said that mystical ideas should only be imparted to a man who is modest and meek, middle-aged, even-tempered and free from vengeful feelings. Among the Ashkenazim of the Rhineland, mystical texts were studied from the ninth century onwards. Mystical speculation intensified during the eleventh and twelfth centuries, the time of the Crusades and Christian persecution. Several groups of scholars met together and their work, with its emphasis on renouncing one's life for God, provided some consolation during a very difficult period in Jewish history.

Among the Sephardim, important Kabbalistic schools developed in Provence in the twelfth century and later in northern Spain. Through Arabic translations, the mystics were familiar with the work of the classical philosophers and they drew on neo-Platonic ideas to explain the relationship of God with the world. They taught that God was the divine infinite, that the world was created as a result of a series of emanations and that the purpose of contemplation was to ascend these emanations, to be united with the divine. The most famous mystical work was the Zohar, which appeared in Spain at the end of the

A Hasidic Jew prays at the Western Wall in Jerusalem. Hasidim are immediately recognizable by their dress which is hardly different from that of their eighteenth-century forebears. They wear beards and side-curls and their heads are covered at all times.

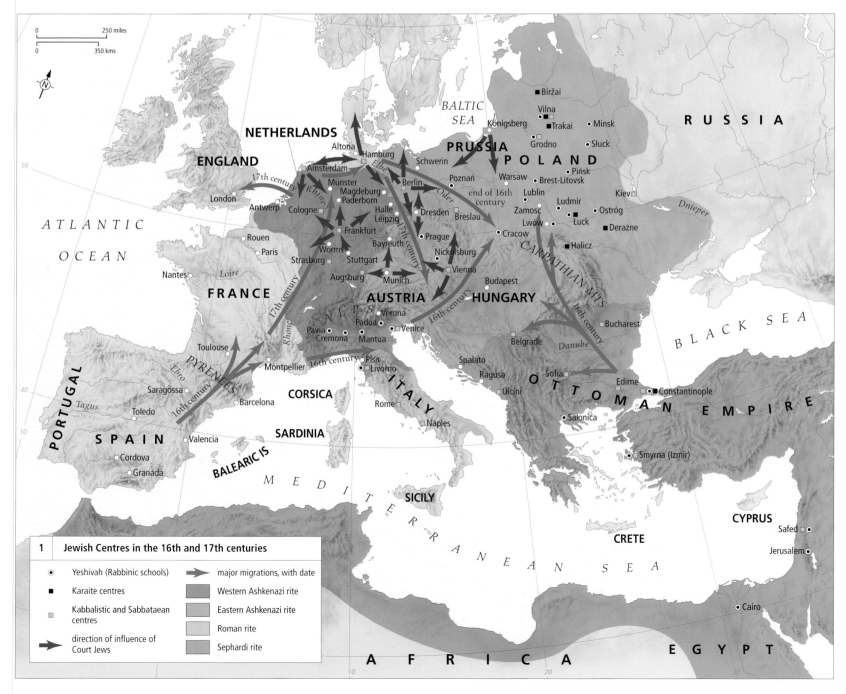

1	Jewish Centres in the 16th and 17th centuries

- ⊙ Yeshivah (Rabbinic schools)
- ■ Karaite centres
- □ Kabbalistic and Sabbataean centres
- → direction of influence of Court Jews
- → major migrations, with date
- Western Ashkenazi rite
- Eastern Ashkenazi rite
- Roman rite
- Sephardi rite

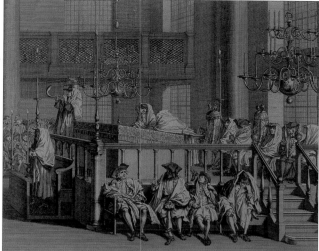

The Jewish New Year is celebrated by the blowing of the ram's horn. This is intended to call the people to repentance. They must purify themselves and put their lives in order before the Day of Atonement which occurs ten days later.

fulfilled, the important thing is to fulfil them whole-heartedly. He and his disciples emphasized the joy of worshipping God and they believed that every aspect of life should be an exercise in devotion. After his death, the movement spread beyond Poland into Lithuania and the Russian Empire *(map 2)*. By the start of the nineteenth century, probably about half of eastern European Jewry were committed to these ideas.

An essential element in Hasidic doctrine is the notion of the Tsaddik ('the righteous one'), the spiritual leader. The Tsaddik is believed to be the channel through which the grace of God flows to the faithful. The mantle of the Baal Shem Tov passed to several of his followers. Soon it became an hereditary position and the various Hasidic groups centred their lives round the court of their particular leader. They regularly visited, they observed his behaviour, they asked his advice and they supported him financially. These communities were decimated by the Holocaust, but even today Hasidic groups survive in the United States and Israel and they are immediately visible by their mode of dress, their pious mode of life and their large families.

Many Jewish leaders, however, were rigorous in their opposition to the new movement. They disapproved of Hasidic enthusiasm, their rejection of painstaking Talmudic scholarship and their establishment of their own schools and synagogues. These traditionalists were described as Mitnagdim ('the opponents'). Their most eminent leader was Elijah ben Solomon Zalman (1720–97), who was known as the Vilna Gaon, the most famous scholar of his day. Vilna is the central city of Lithuania and Lithuanian Jews were renowned for their rabbinic learning. The Vilna Gaon went so far as to pronounce a decree of excommunication against members of Hasidic groups on the grounds that only things acquired by hard labour are worth having. So acrimonious did the conflict become that it was not unknown for Mitnagdim parents to reject their children if they joined a Hasidic group. As a result of this revival of scholarship among the Mitnagdim in Lithuania, a rich Jewish culture grew up which, while rejecting the mystical emotionalism of Hasidism, was characterized by a wry sense of humour at life's absurdities. Many of today's Jewish jokes owe their origin to Lithuanian Jewry and to describe someone as a Litvak is to indicate that they are intellectual and witty.

The enmity between the Hasidim and the Mitnagdim has now largely disappeared. Instead, they have united against the growing secularism and non-observance of the modern Jewish world. Together, the descendants of the Mitnagdim and the Hasidim form a bastion of Orthodoxy in the largely indifferent modern community.

2	The Growth of Hasidism

- growth of Hasidism, 1730-60
- 1760-75
- 1775-1815

thirteenth century. The teachings of this volume later spread into Germany, Italy and the Islamic Empire. It was taken by the expelled Jews of Spain to their new homes and by the sixteenth century it had become part of mainstream Jewish culture. The Kabbalah is less studied today since it is commonly associated with magic and superstition. Nonetheless, there has been a recent revival of interest among non-Jews, particularly among those who are involved in New Age movements.

The Hasidim and the Mitnagdim

During the Middle Ages the Polish government, in contrast to that of most Christian countries, had welcomed Jewish refugees. By the sixteenth century, the community numbered perhaps as many as 150,000 people. In 1648, however, Polish Jewry was devastated by a rebellion against the gentry. Because many Jews were employed by noble families to manage their estates, they were identified with the upper classes and they bore the brunt of the punishment. It has been estimated that perhaps a quarter of the entire Jewish population died in the onslaught. In the aftermath, Jewish life continued to be insecure and the rise of Hasidism ('the movement of the righteous') must be understood against this background. The founder of Hasidism was known as the Baal Shem Tov ('the Master of the Good Name'). He built up a circle of followers in the Carpathian Mountains and taught that true devotion to God was to be valued even above traditional rabbinic scholarship. He taught that it does not matter how many precepts are

THE EMANCIPATION OF EUROPEAN JEWRY

WHILE THE Hasidim and Mitnagdim were fighting their battles in eastern Europe, the political climate had changed in the West. Feudalism had broken down and increasingly it was argued that the government should not interfere with the religious life of the population. In the 1770s the Christian writer, Wilhelm Christian Dohm, produced a pamphlet entitled 'Concerning the Amelioration of the Civil Status of the Jews'. He maintained that Jews could be valuable citizens if all occupations and educational institutions were open to them.

In 1781, the Holy Roman Emperor, Joseph II, issued an Edict of Toleration. In 1789, the revolutionary National Assembly of France declared that no religious opinion should be persecuted. The Emperor Napoleon went so far as to summon an Assembly of Jewish Notables in 1806. These progressive trends were largely suppressed after the Napoleonic wars, but nonetheless the rights of Jews continued to be asserted. By 1871 all restrictions had been removed from the German population and Jews were declared full citizens of the newly unified German Reich. The Scandinavian countries had small Jewish populations, but full emancipation was accomplished in 1848 in Denmark, 1851 in Norway and 1865 in Sweden. Holland was traditionally tolerant and Jewish rights were established early. Great Britain also had a long history of tolerance and, throughout the nineteenth century, the Jewish community enjoyed commercial prosperity and civil respect; nonetheless full equal rights were not granted until 1890. Emancipation was achieved in the Austro-Hungarian empire in 1867 and by 1878 in Serbia and Bulgaria (*map 1*). In eastern Europe, however, Jewish life continued much as it had throughout the previous centuries. It would take the cataclysm of the Revolution and the First World War for the Jews to attain full citizenship in Russia.

Enlightenment and Reform

The roots of the Jewish Enlightenment go back to seventeenth-century Holland where a number of Jewish intellectuals tried to understand their religious tradition in the light of current scientific and philosophical thought. The most famous thinker of the Enlightenment, however, was Moses Mendelssohn (1729–86), a respected and observant member of the Berlin Jewish community. He realized that, if Jews were to be full citizens of the countries in which they lived, they must be comfortable in the modern world. He therefore translated the scriptures into German and he completed a biblical commentary which gave a rational explanation of the law. He encouraged the opening of a Jewish school at which secular as well as religious subjects were taught, and he numbered eminent gentiles among his personal friends. By the 1820s, the centre of the Jewish enlightenment had moved to Vienna where various important journals were published. Among the aspirations of these thinkers was the substitution of Hebrew for Yiddish as the language of the Jews and the creation of a Jewish homeland. These ideas permeated into eastern Europe, even into the Russian Empire where,

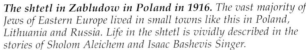

The shtetl in Zabludow in Poland in 1916. The vast majority of Jews of Eastern Europe lived in small towns like this in Poland, Lithuania and Russia. Life in the shtetl is vividly described in the stories of Sholom Aleichem and Isaac Bashevis Singer.

1	The Emancipation of European Jewry, 1789-1918
■	ghettos
◆	major enlightenment centres
▲	other enlightenment centres
→	direction of influence of enlightenment centres
1865	date of emancipation
5,700	Jewish population in the late 19th century

2	The Jews in 19th-century Russia
▼ expulsion of Jews, with date	◇ 10-20,000 Jews
■ cities with 40,000 Jews and over	▲ cities barred to Jewish residents
▫ 30-40,000 Jews	▬ Pale of settlement
◆ 20-30,000 Jews	▨ area of anti-Jewish violence after 1905

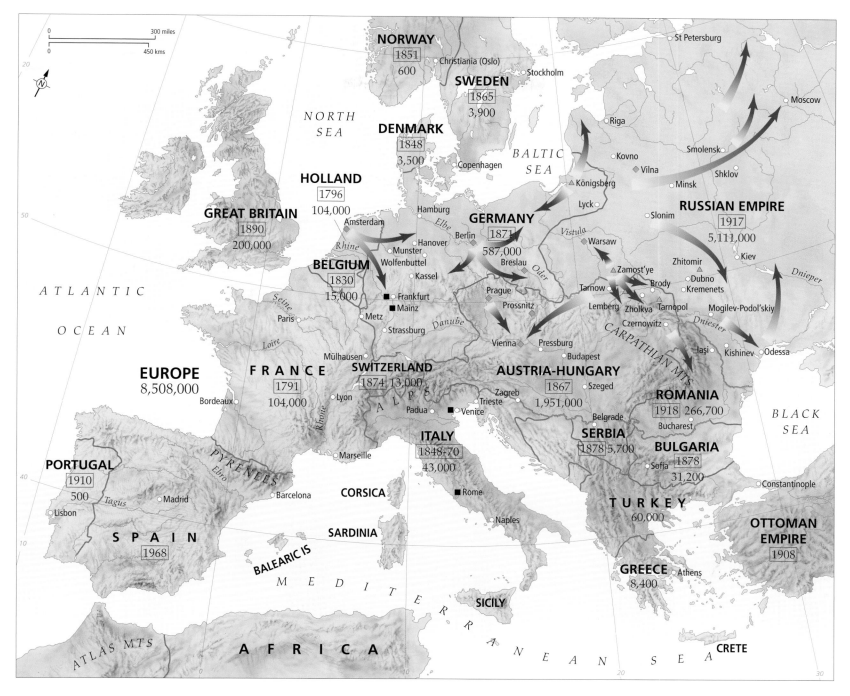

Moses Mendelssohn (left), the most important thinker of the Jewish Enlightenment, with the Lutheran theologian J. C. Lavater and the writer G. E. Lessing. Mendelssohn is thought to be the model used by Lessing in his 'Nathan the Wise.'

in any event, many Jews were beginning to think of emigration to the United States as the only solution to their problems.

Meanwhile, many well-educated western European Jews were becoming increasingly dissatisfied with traditional Orthodox observance. In 1818 a Reform Temple was established in Hamburg. Services included choral singing, a greater sense of decorum, prayers in German as well as Hebrew, and several important changes in the liturgy.

Despite furious Orthodox opposition, the new movement spread. Many German rabbis became involved in a scientific study of Judaism which was an attempt to come to an understanding of the tradition with no religious presuppositions. It was no longer considered an immutable truth that the whole of the law was given directly by God to Moses on Mount Sinai. By the middle of the nineteenth century an Association for Reform Judaism had been founded and a Reform Rabbinical seminary had been set up in Breslau. The Reform West London Synagogue was consecrated in London in 1841, the Berlin Hochschule seminary opened in 1872 and the German Union of Liberal Rabbis was founded in 1899. In addition, German emigrants took the Reform message across the Atlantic Ocean, and the Reform movement was firmly established in the United States by the end of the century.

The Shtetl

Meanwhile, in Lithuania, Poland, Belorussia, the Ukraine and New Russia, Jews continued to live in small towns, known as *shtetlach*, side by side with their gentile neighbours. Such communities were characterized by the values of *Yiddishkeit* (Jewishness) and *Menschlikheit* (humanity). Life centred round the synagogue, where men prayed separately from women, and the home, where the traditional rituals were practised. Marriages were largely arranged and a large family was regarded as a blessing. Sacrifices were made to ensure that sons went to Talmudic academies to become learned in the law and every aspect of life was governed by tradition. The *shtetl* is still regarded with nostalgia and its ways are commemorated in the paintings of Marc Chagall, the stories of Sholem Aleichem and such dramatic productions as 'Yentl' and 'Fiddler on the Roof'.

Yet these communities lived in fear of their neighbours. Towards the end of the nineteenth century, there were constant pogroms during which Jewish property was plundered and many Jews were killed (*map 2*). In general, the civil authorities did little to protect the community, condoning outbreaks of violence to divert attention from the economic and social problems of the Empire. Emigration was seen as the only escape. It is estimated that, between 1881 and 1914, more than two million Ashkenazic Jews left their homes for America.

ZIONISM

THE JEWS HAD never forgotten God's promise to their ancestor Abraham, that they would be the inheritors of the Promised Land. The hope of a return to Palestine had been kept alive throughout the ages. It was expressed in the liturgy, which includes a prayer for the return to Zion; every year the Passover meal ends with the words, 'Next year in Jerusalem!' Traditionally the idea of return was connected with the belief in the coming of the Messiah. The Messiah is God's anointed king. Some time in the future he will gather the scattered tribes of Israel from the four corners of the Earth and will lead them back to Jerusalem. Then all nations will turn to the Jews; recognize the rule of the One True God and paganism will disappear forever.

Theodor Herzl, the Founder of Zionism

The first serious pogrom against the Jews occurred in Russia in 1882. This was a time when emigration to the United States, the new land of opportunity, became a real possibility. Nonetheless, several thousand members of the Jewish community chose instead to settle in Palestine. There they worked as shopkeepers, artisans, farmers and labourers. Many were Marxist by political conviction and were therefore atheists. Nonetheless, they retained an intense sense of Jewish nationalism and encouraged the formation of societies in Russia, Poland and Romania which raised money for the purchase of further land for Jewish settlement (*map 2*).

The real founder of political Zionism, however, was Theodor Herzl (1860–1904). He was a journalist who was born in Budapest and studied in Vienna. Initially he had been an assimilationist, believing that if only the Jews could be absorbed into the majority culture, anti-Semitism would disappear. He was disillusioned by the Dreyfus case in France. Dreyfus was a Jewish army officer who was accused of high treason in 1894. Even when it was discovered that the documents on which his conviction was based were forged, the authorities still insisted he was guilty. The eminent French writer Emile Zola produced his famous polemic *J'Accuse* in his defence, but Dreyfus was only finally vindicated twelve years later. The case convinced Herzl that Jews could never be fully accepted as European citizens. He published his *Der Judenstaat* in which he argued that the

The young journalist
Theodor Herzl was the founder of the international Zionist movement. He was persuaded that the only way Jews could be protected from the effects of anti-Semitism was the creation of a Jewish political state.

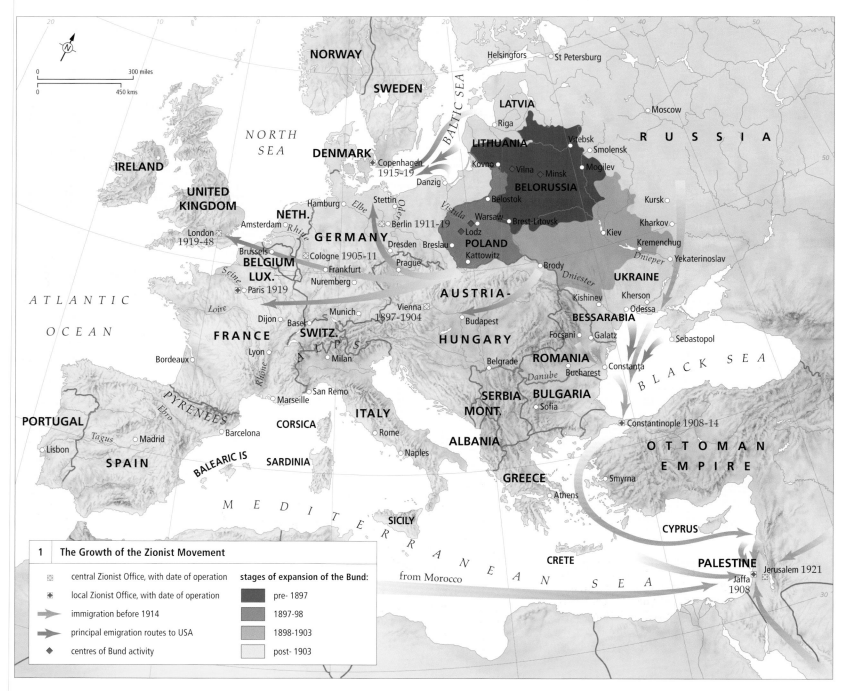

1	The Growth of the Zionist Movement

⊗ central Zionist Office, with date of operation

✤ local Zionist Office, with date of operation

→ immigration before 1914

⇒ principal emigration routes to USA

◆ centres of Bund activity

stages of expansion of the Bund:

pre-1897

1897–98

1898–1903

post-1903

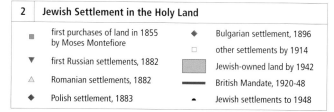

2 | Jewish Settlement in the Holy Land

- ▪ first purchases of land in 1855 by Moses Montefiore
- ▼ first Russian settlements, 1882
- △ Romanian settlements, 1882
- ◆ Polish settlement, 1883
- ◆ Bulgarian settlement, 1896
- ☐ other settlements by 1914
- ▨ Jewish-owned land by 1942
- ▬ British Mandate, 1920-48
- ▴ Jewish settlements to 1948

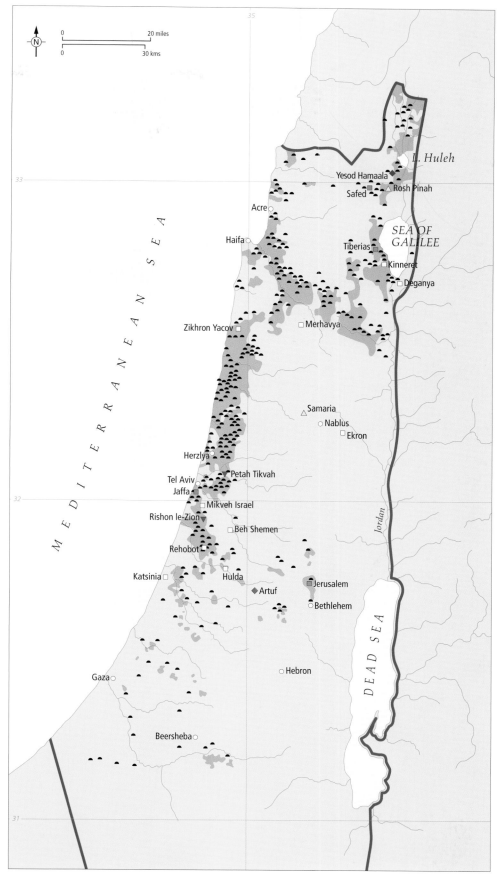

only cure for anti-Semitism was the foundation of a Jewish state in Palestine. He was opposed both by the assimilationists (such as members of the Reform movement), who stressed the importance of complete loyalty to the host country, and by the strictly Orthodox, who believed that it was wrong to anticipate God's messianic plan. Nevertheless, many young Jews were inspired. Herzl convened the First Zionist Congress in Basel in 1897 and spent the rest of his short life building up international support for the project.

Meanwhile, in the same year, the Bund, the General Workers' Union in Lithuania, Poland and Russia, held its first convention. This was a Jewish socialist movement designed to protect Jewish workers against capitalist oppression. Initially, the organization was centred in Lithuania and Belorussia, but it quickly spread to Poland, the Ukraine and beyond. It became an important factor in Jewish public life and did much to revive Yiddish culture. It was essentially an eastern European movement, and the leadership opposed Zionism as reactionary and bourgeois. Yet it consolidated Jewish identity, and many Jewish socialists also joined the Poale Zion, an organization which was determined to promote a socialist programme within the Zionist movement.

The Growth of Zionism

Herzl's movement, the World Zionist Organization, was secular in its focus. In 1901, however, the Mizrachi was formed for the strictly Orthodox who were also in favour of a Jewish national state. A subdivision of the Mizrachi was also formed for the socialists. All these organizations held regular conferences to exchange ideas and to encourage support and raise money for settlement in Palestine. By the start of the twentieth century, a considerable number of Jews had emigrated (*map 1*). The majority lived in the Palestinian cities, but some worked in agricultural colonies. More immigrants arrived after 1904, after further Russian pogroms, and many were determined to earn their living from farming. This was also the period of the great Jewish emigration to the United States. Those who chose to go to Palestine were, for the most part, driven by an internationalist ideology; they were determined to create a Hebrew, rather than a Yiddish, culture because Hebrew was the language of the liturgy for all Jews, while Yiddish was the everyday language only of the eastern Europeans. Children were educated in Hebrew-language schools and the settlers made a point of using Hebrew as their daily language. By the end of the First World War, the Jewish community in Palestine numbered approximately 90,000 people.

The First World War changed the entire European social order. Increasingly, Jews became more vulnerable and were perceived as outsiders. After the Revolution, it is estimated that over 100,000 Jews were murdered in Russia. Because of economic difficulties, emigration to the United States became restricted and the community looked more and more to Palestine. The League of Nations had agreed that the British would administer the region. By 1929 the Palestinian Jewish community numbered about 160,000; by 1939 there were 500,000. When the Jewish settlers organized a National Assembly and an Executive Council, the Palestinian Arab majority felt increasingly threatened. The British responded by restricting Jewish immigration. That was how matters stood on the eve of the Second World War.

By the end of the nineteenth century Zionist conferences were being held throughout Central and Eastern Europe to encourage support for the creation of a Jewish state. Orthodox as well as secular Jews were attracted to the new movement. This shows Herzl and a group of delegates at the Sixth Zionist conference held in Basel in 1903.

JUDAISM IN THE AMERICAS TO 1939

THE EARLY JEWISH SETTLERS in the United States were mainly Sephardim, Jews who originated from Spain, North Africa, the Netherlands and Turkey. They formed small communities not only in the United States, but also in South and Central America. In addition, many Jews, known as Marranos, who had been compelled to convert to Christianity in Spain also made new homes across the Atlantic Ocean. Some, but not all, reverted to the faith of their ancestors once they were away from the oppressions of Europe. Others remained Christian, but continued to retain semi-forgotten Jewish practices such as lighting candles on Friday nights.

Early History of Jews in America

By the early nineteenth century, German Jews were beginning to settle in the United States. The first sign of this development was an attempt in Charleston, South Carolina to introduce new liturgical practices, similar to those of the German Reform Temples. By 1842 there were three German synagogues in the city of New York, the stopping-off place for many new immigrants. In 1845 Temple Emmanuel, the huge Reform temple on Fifth Avenue, was founded, and from its inception it adopted the Reform, rather than the Orthodox, rite.

Several prominent Reform rabbis moved to America and in 1869 the first conference of American rabbis took place in Philadelphia. This resulted in the creation of a permanent rabbinical organization, the Union of American Hebrew Congregations. In 1875, the first American rabbinical seminary, the Hebrew Union College was founded in Cincinnati, Ohio (map 1). Both the college and the rabbinical association provided the essential framework for the growth and development of Reform Judaism in the United States. At the end of the century there was a new flood of Jewish immigration. These migrants were from the villages of eastern Europe, and practised a very different form of Judaism; the easy-going style of their prosperous German co-religionists was totally inappropriate for them.

The Great Emigration

By 1880 the Jewish population of the United States stood at approximately 250,000. Between 1881 and 1914, as a result of pogroms and persecution, about two million eastern European Jews emigrated to the United States.

At the end of the nineteenth century, thousands of eastern European Jews left their villages to seek a new life across the Atlantic Ocean. The vast majority of the Jewish community today is descended from such immigrants.

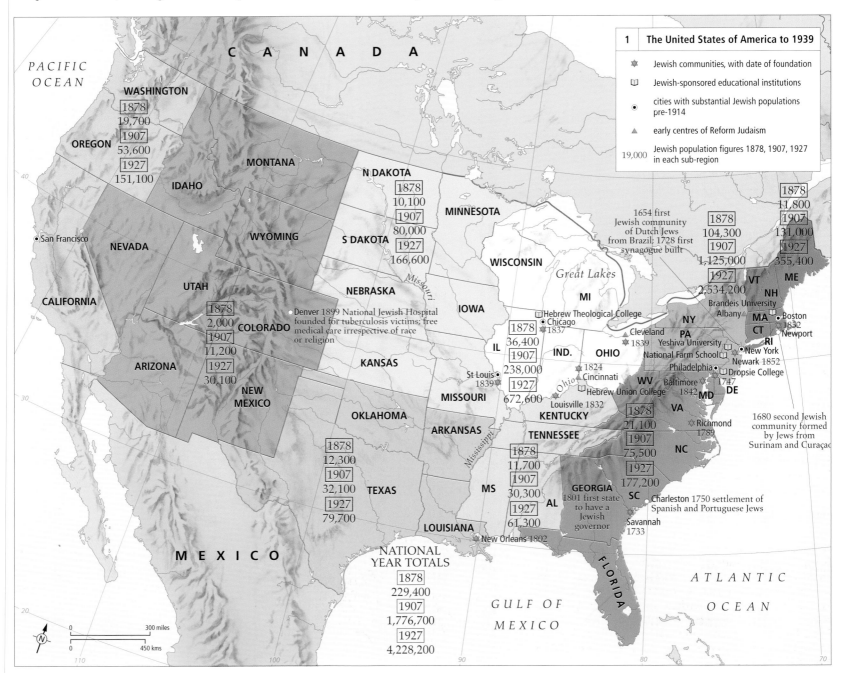

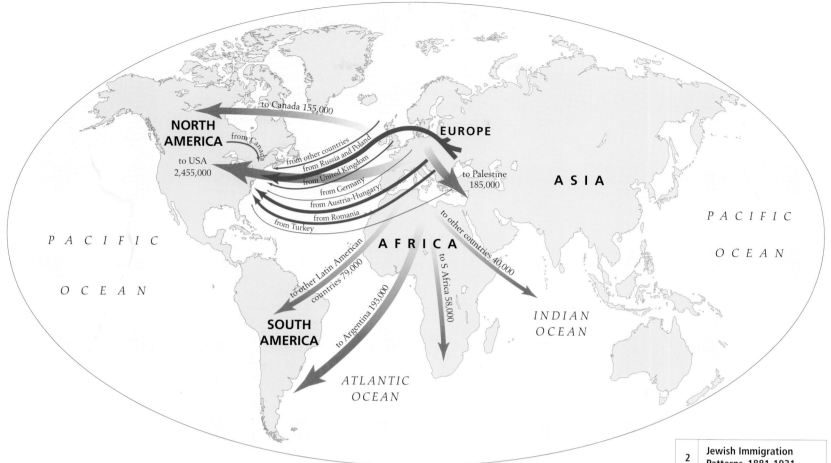

Others settled in western Europe, South Africa, Canada, Palestine and Australia (*map 2*). Everywhere they brought with them their Yiddish institutions and their strict Orthodoxy. They were crowded into the big cities where they worked in sweatshops and on market stalls.

Very often the established German Jews found the new immigrants disconcerting. They were too pious, too unworldly and they spoke English with a foreign accent. Nonetheless, the established communities did feel a sense of responsibility for their co-religionists. The Jewish Theological Seminary in New York was founded to train more traditional rabbis; this was to become the central institution of the Conservative movement. The American Jewish Committee was established to lobby the United States government on Jewish issues abroad while the Anti-Defamation League was organized to combat anti-Semitism at home. A host of Jewish charities was also set up to help the new immigrants, the poor, the disabled, the orphaned, the sick and the aged.

In general, the new arrivals took advantage of the educational and commercial opportunities which were available in the New World. Within a couple of generations, the old distinctions between the prosperous German Jews and the poor Russian immigrants had disappeared. They met at synagogue, in youth groups and on committees. Increasingly there was intermarriage between the two groups. Their children neither knew nor cared about the old distinctions. In a very real sense they had all become Americans.

The American Jewish Experience
It is not true to say that the American Jewish community never experienced anti-Semitism. Until after the Second World War, the prestigious American colleges and medical schools would only take a small quota of Jewish students. 'Gentlemen's agreements' existed to keep Jews from buying houses in particular neighbourhoods and certain private clubs were closed to Jewish candidates. Nonetheless, in general the community prospered. Immigration was considerably restricted in the 1920s and this had an important effect on the community. The old

immigrants had been anxious that their children should be well-educated, should speak English with a mainstream American accent and should integrate themselves into the majority culture. As their children grew up to become middle-class and prosperous, many of them attained influential positions in the spheres of politics, business, science, literature and art. Film-making in Hollywood was virtually a Jewish business.

Today Jews form between 2–3 per cent of the total population of the United States, but their influence extends well beyond their numerical strength. There are no longer any social restrictions and the Jewish community is generally recognized as being one of the most successful groups in the United States.

Religious differences still remain. The strictly Orthodox continue to maintain the traditional Jewish way of life, while the Conservative and the Reform are prepared to make more accommodation with their surroundings. Today, however, the overwhelming concern is assimilation and intermarriage. As Jews become more successful and established, they are all too liable to marry outside the community and the next generation is lost to Judaism.

Many members of the Jewish community have become very prosperous in America. Settling in the suburbs of the big cities, they have built synagogues and other institutions, often in the latest architectural styles.

THE HOLOCAUST

BETWEEN 1941 and 1945 probably about six million Jews were deliberately murdered in concentration camps in Europe. Since 1933, when the Nazis came to power in Germany, the German Jewish community had been persecuted and many had fled abroad. However there was a worldwide economic depression and most countries were unwilling to take in large groups of refugees. As a result too many were compelled to remain behind to be slaughtered. This pivotal event persuaded the newly-created United Nations that the Jews must have a country of their own where there was no bar to immigration. In 1948, the State of Israel, the Jewish State, was created in the historic Promised Land.

The Destruction of the Jews

The Nazis, or National Socialists, under their leader Adolf Hitler, came to power in Germany as a result of successive economic crises and a collective sense of injustice at the provisions of the 1918 European peace. Hitler was convinced that Germany had lost the First World War as a result of the treachery of Jewish socialists,

liberals and pacifists. He also believed that the Bolshevik revolution in Russia was the result of a worldwide Jewish conspiracy. He was determined to expand Germany's empire in the east and to remove all Jewish influence from his new order. Almost immediately after he became German chancellor in 1933, a series of anti-Jewish legislations was enacted. All sexual liaisons between Jews and non-Jews were forbidden, and Jews were compelled to register their property. *Kristallnacht* (1938) brought the systematic destruction of Jewish shops and businesses, and all Jewish communal bodies were put under the direct control of the Nazi police.

Once the German army had invaded Poland in 1939, the full horror of Hitler's plans for the Jews was revealed. Poland had a very large Jewish population and in every conquered town, the Jews were compelled to work as slave labour. This was described as 'destruction through work'. Then, once Hitler had invaded Russia, special troops, known as the *Einsatzgruppen,* were employed. Initially they rounded up the Jewish population, led them out of town, forced them to dig

A famous image of the Warsaw ghetto uprising of 1943. Against impossible odds, the Jews of the city resisted deportation to the death camps. After holding out for several weeks, eventually the whole ghetto was razed to the ground.

After the destruction of the Holocaust, the United Nations accepted the necessity of a Jewish homeland. After consolidating their position against the surrounding nations, David Ben Gurion formally declared the creation of the State of Israel in 1948.

their own graves and then shot them. This method of annihilation was not sufficiently efficient for the German leadership and in 1942, at a secret conference of Nazi leaders, the Final Solution was agreed (*map 1*).

The entire Jewish population was herded into restricted ghettos in the cities. Meanwhile six death camps were built at Chelmno, Auschwitz, Sobibor, Majdanek, Treblinka and Belzek. From the ghettos the Jews were rounded up by soldiers and were transported to the camps by rail in cattle trucks. There was no seating, sanitation or heating and often the journey across Europe lasted several days. Once they arrived the young and fit were selected for slave labour. They survived as long as they could contribute to the economic benefit of the Third Reich. When they were too weak, they joined the old and the infirm and were forced into purpose-built gas chambers where they were exterminated. The death toll was enormous. Auschwitz, the largest camp, could hold 140,000 inmates who were systematically worked to death. Its five crematoria could dispose of a total of 10,000 bodies a day. It has been estimated that about two million people died here between 1942 and 1945.

The Jews were largely powerless, but there was resistance. In Warsaw, the Jewish population was crammed into a ghetto. When the Nazis moved in for the final destruction, they were attacked from all sides with stolen arms and home-made weapons. For several weeks the Jews held out against the German army. When the inevitable end came, many Jews chose to commit suicide rather than fall into enemy hands.

The Creation of the State of Israel

By the end of the Second World War, the Jewish population of Europe was decimated. The old synagogues, houses of learning and Jewish villages had disappeared from eastern Europe for ever. When the full enormity of Nazi crimes was revealed, there was a worldwide shift of opinion towards the Zionist cause. Throughout the Second World War, Palestine had been governed by the British under a mandate from the League of Nations. In attempting to keep a balance between Jews and Arabs, the British tried to prevent illegal Jewish immigration during the war. In response, the Jews increasingly employed terrorist tactics. After the war, exasperated by the whole conflict, the British handed over responsibility to the international community.

In May 1947, the whole question came up for discussion in the United Nations and it was agreed that Palestine should be partitioned into a Jewish and an Arab state (*map 2*). Israel was surrounded by hostile Egyptian, Syrian, Jordanian, Iraqi and Lebanese armies, but nonetheless managed to consolidate its position. On 14 May 1948, the independence of the Jewish State of Israel was declared on the basis of 'national and intrinsic right' as well as by resolution of the United Nations.

This was not to be the end of the story. The War of Independence continued throughout 1948 and war broke out again in 1954, in 1967 and in 1973. There have been ongoing problems with Palestinian refugees, who fled from their homes in Israeli-held territory – many have found no shelter outside hastily constructed refugee camps. Even today peace is problematic and fragile and only time will tell if peaceful coexistence between Israelis and Palestinian Arabs is possible (*see also* pp. 208-209).

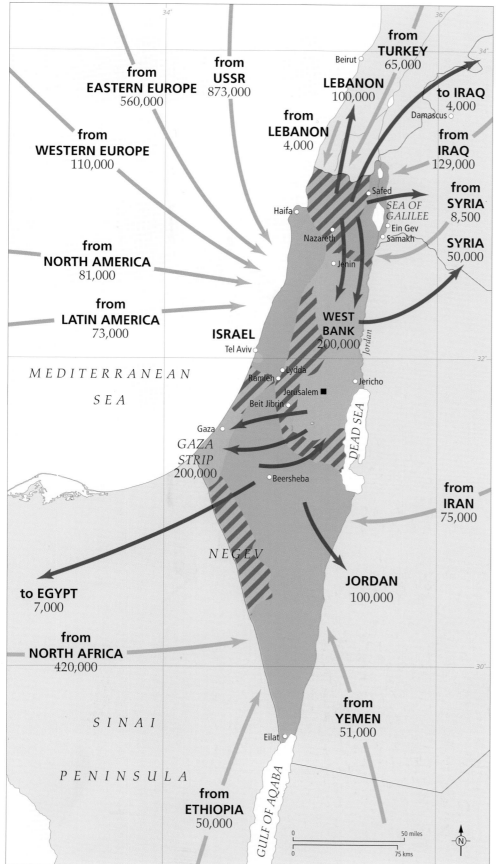

from **TURKEY** 65,000

from **EASTERN EUROPE** 560,000

from **USSR** 873,000

LEBANON 100,000

to IRAQ 4,000

Beirut

from **LEBANON** 4,000

from **IRAQ** 129,000

Damascus

from **WESTERN EUROPE** 110,000

Safed

from **SYRIA** 8,500

SEA OF GALILEE

Haifa

Ein Gev

Nazareth

Samakh

SYRIA 50,000

from **NORTH AMERICA** 81,000

Jenin

from **LATIN AMERICA** 73,000

WEST BANK 200,000

Jordan

ISRAEL

Tel Aviv

M E D I T E R R A N E A N

S E A

Lydda

Ramleh

Jerusalem ■

Jericho

Beit Jibrin

Gaza

DEAD SEA

GAZA STRIP 200,000

Beersheba

from **IRAN** 75,000

N E G E V

to **EGYPT** 7,000

JORDAN 100,000

from **NORTH AFRICA** 420,000

S I N A I

from **YEMEN** 51,000

Eilat

P E N I N S U L A

from **ETHIOPIA** 50,000

GULF OF AQABA

| 0 | | 50 miles |

| 0 | | 75 kms |

N

2	The Creation of the State of Israel
	area under Jewish sovereignty, 1947
	area under Arab sovereignty, 1947
■	under international control
⌗	Israeli territorial gains by the Armistice agreements, 1948-50
→	Arab refugees, 1949-67
→	Jewish migration to Israel, 1948-96

WORLDWIDE JUDAISM IN THE MODERN WORLD

THERE ARE small groups of Jews living in almost every country in the world. There have, however, been many changes in patterns of Jewish settlement since the early twentieth century. Then, the two major centres of Jewish population were Eastern Europe, particularly Poland and Russia, and the United States. The Holocaust destroyed the Jewish civilization of Eastern Europe; Poland, Hungary, Czechoslovakia and the Baltic States were all occupied by the Nazis, who were determined to exterminate the Jews. Very few were able to flee to the United States, South Africa, Australia or Britain. After the Second World War, the large numbers of displaced persons and the horrors of the Holocaust persuaded the international community that a Jewish state was necessary. With the creation of the State of Israel, the entire focus of the Jewish world changed.

A Demographic Survey

The creation of the State of Israel in the historic biblical homeland displaced many Palestinians who became, in effect, stateless persons. The wrath of the surrounding Arab nations was implacable. After the United Nations had partitioned Palestine, a combined Arab army tried to drive out the Jews. Instead the Israelis consolidated their position and extended their territory. Later wars further enlarged the Israeli sphere of influence (*map 2*). By the early 1980s Israeli armies occupied the Sinai peninsula, the Negev Desert and the west bank of the River Jordan, and had invaded Lebanon in pursuit of Palestinian guerrillas. Today, Israel still holds the West Bank, while Jerusalem, instead of being partitioned between Arab and Jew, is the designated capital of the Jewish State.

As a result of these wars, the historic Jewish communities of the Islamic lands found their position impossible. The anger of the Arab nations was turned against their own Jews. Because Israel was created as a refuge for all Jewish people everywhere, the Law of Return stated that any Jew had the right to Israeli citizenship. The Jews of North Africa and the Gulf States felt there was no future for them and they emigrated in their thousands to Israel. Envisioned as a home for displaced eastern European Jews, Israel had quickly

become a sanctuary for Jews from Muslim countries. By the 1960s the population of the land was a mixture of Ashkenazim, eastern European Jews, many of whom were descendants of Holocaust survivors, and Sephardim, Jews from the old Islamic empire.

Other communities were also incorporated. For centuries, the Jews of Yemen had been isolated from their co-religionists, but when civil war broke out, the Israelis organized a mass exodus. The Falashas of Ethiopia, who believed they were descended from King Solomon and the Queen of Sheba, were also threatened by war and famine. Although there was some doubt among the religious establishment as to whether they really were Jews, it was eventually decided that they were descended from the lost tribe of Dan and large numbers were airlifted to safety.

Another threatened group were the Jews of the Soviet Union. Russia has a long tradition of anti-Semitism. The communist government was avowedly atheistic and forbade any practice of the Jewish religion. Instead Jews were regarded as one nationality among many within the empire. During the communist years, small groups of Jews were allowed to emigrate. After the fall of the Soviet

Hasidim praying at the Western Wall in Jerusalem, the surviving part of the outer wall of the Temple. Services have been held there since the Middle Ages and it remains a place of prayer for all Jews.

1	Judaism Today
1,300	Jewish population
⍟	cities with a Jewish population of over 200,000

CANADA 403,000

ATLANTIC OCEAN

see inset

London ⍟
Paris ⍟

TUNISIA 3,800

Chicago ⍟
an Francisco ⍟   **U·S·A**
Los Angeles   Boston
New York ⍟
Philadelphia

5,764,000

⍟ Miami

MEXICO 122,000

PUERTO RICO 2,700

MOROCCO 16,800

ALGERIA 570

COSTA RICA 4,500
PANAMA 3,800
COLOMBIA 10,300
ECUADOR 1,000

VENEZUELA 47,400

other African countries 2,000

other Central American countries 3,200

PERU 9,100

BRAZIL 357,000

PACIFIC OCEAN

CHILE 33,400

URUGUAY 40,900

ARGENTINA 490,000

other South American countries 1,700

NORWAY 820
SWEDEN 16,100
FINLAND 1,200
EST. 2,100

Moscow ⍟

LAT. 13,400

NORTH SEA   **DENMARK** 6,800

BALTIC SEA

LITH. 6,700

500 miles
750 kms

U.K. 302,000
IRELAND 1,700
London ⍟
NETH. 24,900
GER. 96,000
POLAND 6,400
BELARUS 58,300
BEL. 21,300
Paris ⍟
CZ.REP. 7,100
SLOV. 4,800
UKRAINE 220,000
SWITZ. 17,700
AUS. 8,600
HUN. 44,900
FRANCE 591,000
CRO. 2,000
SERBIA 3,500
ROM. 9,900
BUL. 3,900
PORT. 440
SPAIN 13,100
ITALY 33,600
ALB. 2,000
GREECE 5,000
TURKEY 21,600
LEB. 1,900

MEDITERRANEAN SEA

Tel Aviv ⍟ Haifa
Jerusalem ⍟

Empire, this trickle became a flood. The subsequent independence of the Iron Curtain states encouraged the growth of extreme nationalism and Jews were often the victim. As a result, many preferred life in Israel, even though they knew little about the Jewish religion and, as a result of extensive intermarriage in the communist years, the Jewish status of many was in doubt. Today it is not known how many Jews are left in Russia and the old Russian satellite countries. However there are large numbers of new, Russian-speaking Israelis.

Thus the map of worldwide Jewry has been transformed (*map 1*). The United States remains the home of the largest overseas community. There are also successful groups in Australia, South Africa and Canada, countries of the old British commonwealth, and sizeable communities in South America, particularly in Argentina. But the creation of the State of Israel has provided a new home not only for the dispossessed Jews of Nazi-occupied Europe, but also for the ancient communities living in Arab lands and for many lost Jews of Russia. Today more than a third of all Jewish people live in the State of Israel and that proportion is increasing.

The Main Religious Groups

Traditional Judaism teaches that people are Jewish if their mother is Jewish; it has nothing to do with religious belief. Therefore it is possible to find people who accept Jewish identity but who would describe themselves as atheists or even adherents of another religion. Among believers, however, there is a clear divide between those

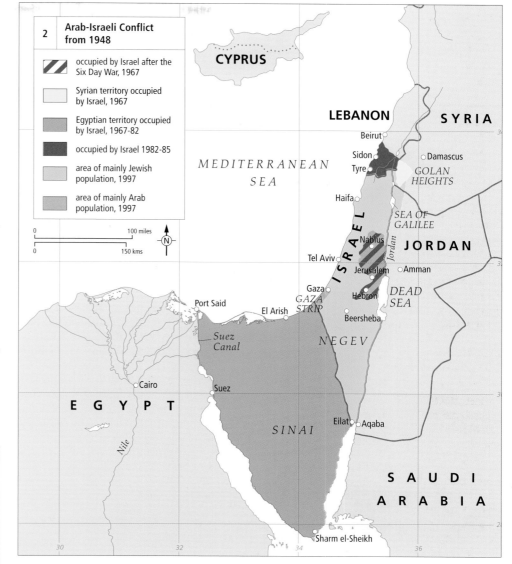

2	Arab-Israeli Conflict from 1948

occupied by Israel after the Six Day War, 1967

Syrian territory occupied by Israel, 1967

Egyptian territory occupied by Israel, 1967-82

occupied by Israel 1982-85

area of mainly Jewish population, 1997

area of mainly Arab population, 1997

who are Orthodox and those who do not keep Jewish law in every particular. The Orthodox, including the Hasidim, continue to believe that the law was given by God to Moses on Mount Sinai and is therefore sacred. In contrast, the non-Orthodox believe that Jewish law grew up in response to particular circumstances and that it can therefore be adapted to the contingencies of modern life. Non-Orthodox groups include the Conservative, Reconstructionist, Reform and Humanist (in America) and the Masorti, the Reform and the Liberal (in Britain). While the religious establishment of Israel is Orthodox, many Israelis are entirely secular in their outlook.

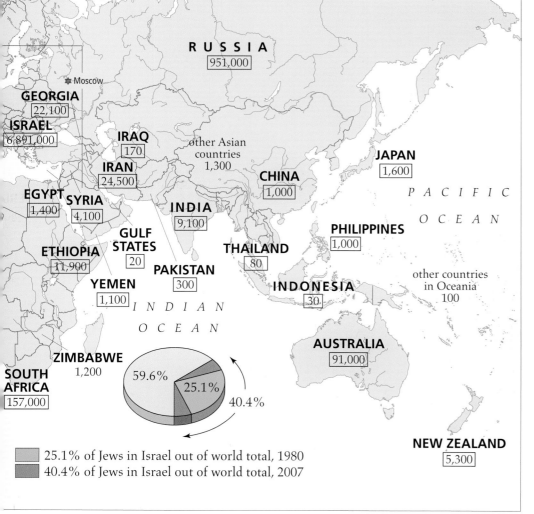

RUSSIA 951,000
Moscow
GEORGIA 22,100
ISRAEL 6,891,000
IRAQ 170
IRAN 24,500
EGYPT 1,400
SYRIA 4,100
INDIA 9,100
GULF STATES 20
ETHIOPIA 11,900
PAKISTAN 300
YEMEN 1,100
other Asian countries 1,300
CHINA 1,000
JAPAN 1,600
PHILIPPINES 1,000
THAILAND 80
INDONESIA 30
other countries in Oceania 100
AUSTRALIA 91,000
ZIMBABWE 1,200
SOUTH AFRICA 157,000
NEW ZEALAND 5,300

59.6% 25.1% 40.4%

☐ 25.1% of Jews in Israel out of world total, 1980
☐ 40.4% of Jews in Israel out of world total, 2007

Ethiopian immigrants to Israel arriving at Tel Aviv airport. The Jewish community of Ethiopia is very ancient. Because the people have been isolated for centuries, they follow very different customs and initially there was some doubt as to their Jewish status.

CHRISTIANITY

ACCORDING to the Gospels, the four books which recount his life and teaching, Jesus Christ was born in Bethlehem in Judaea, most probably in the year 6 BCE. He died by crucifixion when Pontius Pilate was prefect of Judaea, by then part of the Roman province of Syria, sometime between 26 and 36 CE. Central to his teaching is the conviction that the end of the world is imminent, giving way to the reign (or Kingdom) of God. To prepare for this all must repent and live according to an ethic of love. This repentance is described by Jesus in his 'Sermon on the Mount' – his followers must be meek, merciful, peacemakers. The validity of his message is claimed to be demonstrated by the miracle of Jesus' resurrection from the dead. Having been spread by waves of missionary activity, Christianity is now found in all corners of the globe.

ALTHOUGH IT IS difficult to be precise, the Gospels (the word means 'good news') were probably composed between 70 CE and 110 CE. Traditionally they have been attributed to three people who knew Jesus (Mark, Matthew and John) and to one who did not, Luke, a companion of Paul. Paul, a persecutor of Christianity, became after his conversion experience on the road to Damascus its most enthusiastic protagonist. Well before the first of the Gospels had achieved the form in which it has been preserved, he had written a series of letters to Christian communities – 'churches' – he had founded and one, at Rome, which he had not. These letters, and others attributed to Paul by the early Church, as well as a number attributed to other followers of Jesus – Peter, James

and John – and the Book of Revelations (the 'Apocalypse', also said to be by John), constitute the New Testament, the sacred writings of Christianity. Because it sprang from Judaism, Christianity also includes the Jewish canon, or Old Testament, among its sacred books.

Doctrine and the Early Church

The death and resurrection of Christ is presented as the decisive event in history. God had created men and women to love and serve him, but through their sinfulness they had cut themselves off from him. God had therefore sent his son Jesus to offer God's forgiveness for humanity's sins and, by his sacrificial death, to bring about a reconciliation between God and humankind. To avail themselves of

CHRISTIANITY

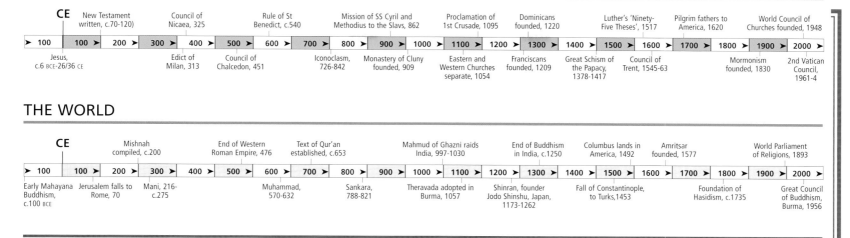

CE		New Testament written, c.70-120)		Council of Nicaea, 325			Rule of St Benedict, c.540			Mission of SS Cyril and Methodius to the Slavs, 862			Proclamation of 1st Crusade, 1095		Dominicans founded, 1220			Luther's 'Ninety-Five Theses', 1517		Pilgrim fathers to America, 1620		World Council of Churches founded, 1948	
➤ 100	100 ➤	200 ➤	300 ➤	400 ➤	500 ➤	600 ➤	700 ➤	800 ➤	900 ➤	1000 ➤	1100 ➤	1200 ➤	1300 ➤	1400 ➤	1500 ➤	1600 ➤	1700 ➤	1800 ➤	1900 ➤	2000 ➤			

Jesus, c.6 BCE-26/36 CE — Edict of Milan, 313 — Council of Chalcedon, 451 — Iconoclasm, 726-842 — Monastery of Cluny founded, 909 — Eastern and Western Churches separate, 1054 — Franciscans founded, 1209 — Great Schism of the Papacy, 1378-1417 — Council of Trent, 1545-63 — Mormonism founded, 1830 — 2nd Vatican Council, 1961-4

THE WORLD

CE		Mishnah compiled, c.200		End of Western Roman Empire, 476		Text of Qur'an established, c.653			Mahmud of Ghazni raids India, 997-1030			End of Buddhism in India, c.1250		Columbus lands in America, 1492		Amritsar founded, 1577		World Parliament of Religions, 1893	
➤ 100	100 ➤	200 ➤	300 ➤	400 ➤	500 ➤	600 ➤	700 ➤	800 ➤	900 ➤	1000 ➤	1100 ➤	1200 ➤	1300 ➤	1400 ➤	1500 ➤	1600 ➤	1700 ➤	1800 ➤	1900 ➤	2000 ➤

Early Mahayana Buddhism, c.100 BCE — Jerusalem falls to Rome, 70 — Mani, 216-c.275 — Muhammad, 570-632 — Sankara, 788-821 — Theravada adopted in Burma, 1057 — Shinran, founder Jodo Shinshu, Japan, 1173-1262 — Fall of Constantinople, to Turks, 1453 — Foundation of Hasidism, c.1735 — Great Council of Buddhism, Burma, 1956

this offer of reconciliation, or redemption, people must accept Jesus as Lord and Saviour (the word 'Christ' means messiah or saviour). They do so by the ritual of baptism, a rite of washing by which converts symbolize putting off their past sinfulness in order to live in accordance with the ethical code which Jesus taught. For Paul and others, conversion meant abandoning the Jewish requirements of circumcision and of abstaining from certain foods, a break with Jewish tradition which occasioned some of the earliest controversies within the Christian communities.

The greatest challenge to the unity of the early church was over the nature of Jesus. The belief had developed – it is arguable whether it is to be found in Jesus' own teaching – that Jesus was God. To safeguard this conviction the doctrine of the Trinity was elaborated, especially in the fourth century. Like Judaism, Christianity insists that there can be only one God, but Christians claim that within this one

God there are three persons, Father, Son (Jesus) and Holy Spirit, all equally God and none subordinate in any way to any other. Next the question arose how Jesus, if he were God, could also be human. In 451, at the Council of Chalcedon, it was agreed that there could be only one person in Christ, but that person existed in two natures, one human, the other divine.

The Spread of Christianity

During the first three centuries Christians had been subject to sporadic persecution. In 313, by what came to be called the Edict of Milan, the Emperor Constantine granted it toleration, and increasingly it became the official religion of the Roman Empire. As the two parts of the Empire, the East based on Constantinople and the West based on Rome, drifted away from each other, so did the churches. Divisions were partly linguistic – the East using mainly Greek but also other languages, and the West Latin – and partly liturgical – great differences developed in the manner of celebrating the Eucharist. There were also questions of jurisdiction, Eastern churches looking to the Patriarch of Constantinople, Western ones to the Bishop of Rome, the Pope. The division was formalized in 1054 when the Patriarch excommunicated the Pope, and the Pope reciprocated.

By this time most of Europe had long been Christian, and Christianity was beginning to make headway into the further reaches of Northern Europe and into what is now Russia, the first through missionaries acknowledging papal authority, the second through those accepting the authority of the patriarch. The formerly Christian lands of North Africa and the Middle East, however, were overrun by the forces of Islam from the seventh century onwards, leaving only isolated pockets of Christians. By the time the next great wave of Christianization came in the sixteenth century with missionary journeys to the Americas, to Africa and to the Far East, Constantinople itself had come under Muslim rule and it was 'Roman Catholic' Christianity which was first taken to these new lands.

The Reformation and Later Christianity

Concerted missionary activity by Protestant churches began only in the late eighteenth century. Protestantism itself had arisen from the sixteenth-century Reformation initiated by Martin Luther and eventually created a division in Western Christianity far more radical than that between Pope and Patriarch. Some later reformers rejected any sacraments as means of obtaining God's grace except baptism and the Lord's Supper, regarding them as the only two unequivocally to be found in the New Testament. They likewise insisted on returning to a church structure as found in the first century, before the office of bishop had developed. All these reformers rejected the authority of the papacy.

In the second half of the twentieth century, though the number of separate churches has vastly increased, especially in Africa and increasingly in both North and South America, the bitterness between groups of Christians which marked the period after the Reformation has largely disappeared. Under the influence of the Ecumenical Movement great effort has been put into restoring the unity which existed before the Reformation, and healing the divisions between Eastern and Western Christendom.

EARLY CHRISTIANITY AND ITS ROOTS IN JUDAISM

JESUS CHRIST ('Christ', meaning 'the anointed one', a title given to him by his followers) was born in 6 BCE and was put to death by crucifixion in 30 CE – though neither date is entirely certain. Like most of those in Palestine he was a Jew. There were several variants of Judaism in his lifetime, but his teaching cannot be identified with any particular strand: his early disciples at first thought themselves to be yet another Jewish sect rather than a separate religion. Jesus's preaching ministry probably lasted three years and, according to the Gospels, mostly took place in Galilee, where he was born and spent most of his life. It was a richly fertile area and lay on trade routes which brought it considerable wealth. The language spoken there – and presumably by Jesus – was Aramaic, though Greek was also regularly used, especially by Hellenized Jews of the cities. It was more cosmopolitan, and consequently more tolerant, than Judaea, a tolerance reflected in Jesus's message. The Judaeans looked somewhat askance on the Galileans, regarding them as tainted by an alien culture. Judaea itself was a much wilder terrain, and depended largely on commerce generated by Jerusalem. The people of Samaria, though claiming that they, too, followed the religion of Moses, used (and continue to use) a different version of the Bible, and had a separate Temple on Mount Gerizim. Jews on pilgrimage to the Jerusalem Temple tried to avoid Samaria, regarding its population as religiously and culturally inferior. Jesus's sympathy for the Samaritans, as shown in the accounts of his life, was therefore remarkable.

The Missionary Journeys of Paul
Jesus's disciples seem largely to have come from Galilee, though there were undoubtedly some sympathizers among the upper classes in Jerusalem. After his death, the first Christians appear to have been limited to a group in Jerusalem. There was clearly a tension among them, dividing those who came from a Hellenistic Jewish background from the more strictly orthodox: Paul, who was born outside Palestine in the city of Tarsus, belonged to the former group. His conversion probably occurred in 34 or 35 CE. We know of his missionary journeys from his surviving letters and the Acts of the Apostles, but there is little agreement over their dates, though they must have taken place during the late forties and fifties. The letters attributed to him are written mainly to Christian communities he established, except for that at Rome, which existed before he went there, probably about 60 CE. There is a possibility that he travelled from Rome to Spain – he wrote that he intended to do so – before returning to die in the city during the persecution instigated by the Emperor Nero in 64 CE. It is now generally agreed that Peter also went to Rome and died in the same persecution, but little is known of Jesus's other followers outside the Gospels and the early chapters of Acts.

The Break between Christianity and Judaism
At the time of Jesus's birth Palestine, which had been annexed to Rome in 63 BCE, was ruled over by Herod the Great, who had been appointed a client king of Judaea in 40 BCE. After his death in 4 BCE his kingdom was divided among his sons, Herod Antipas receiving Galilee and Peraea, Philip the Tetrarch the northern part of Transjordan, and Archelaeus Judaea, Samaria and Idumaea. In 6 CE, however, these last three regions were taken under direct Roman governance of a Procurator, dependent on the province of Syria: Pontius Pilate, the Roman official portrayed in the Gospels as handing Jesus over to death, was appointed Procurator in 26 CE. Direct Roman rule over the whole of Palestine was re-established in 44 CE, bringing heavy taxation and religious insensitivity. The population revolted in 66 CE, but in 70 CE Titus captured Jerusalem and destroyed the Temple, an event generally regarded as marking the definitive break between Judaism and Christianity (*see also* pp.132-133).

The fortress of Masada, ▶
on the western shore of the Dead Sea, was built by Herod the Great as a summer palace. During the Roman occupation it was the site of a small garrison, but was captured by Jewish zealots in 66 CE, at the outbreak of the revolt against Roman rule. On the night of 2 May 73 CE, when it seemed inevitable that the Romans would capture Masada, every one of the almost a thousand who had gathered there, committed suicide rather than fall into Roman hands.

2	The Missionary Journeys of Paul
	Roman Empire
→	Pauls first journey 46-4 8 CE
→	Paul's second journey 49-52 CE
→	Paul's third journey 53-57 CE
→	Paul's fourth journey 59-62 CE
→	Paul's possible journey to Spain 64? CE
⊕	Seven Churches of Asia
⊞	churches of the first century
⊞	churches of the second century

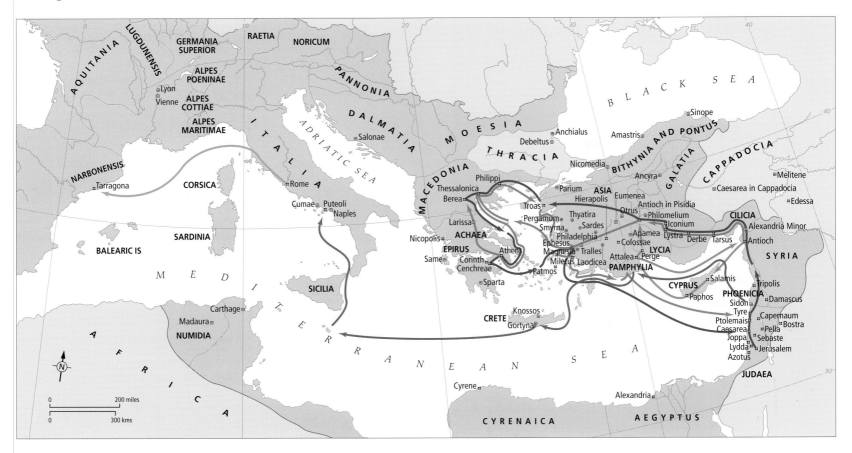

1 Palestine at the Time of Jesus

— Kingdom of Herod the Great c.6 BCE

under Roman administration

tetrarchy of Philip

tetrarchy of Herod Antipas

⊕ places associated with Christ

⊕ places associated with others in the New Testament

— roads

According to Matthew 16,
Jesus Christ appointed Peter, a
fisherman from the Sea of
Galilee, as the rock, or
foundation, on which he was to
build his church. This chapel,
constructed by the Franciscans
in 1933 on the spot where this
event traditionally took place,
stands on the site beside the Sea
of a fourth-century building,
possibly commemorating the
same occasion.

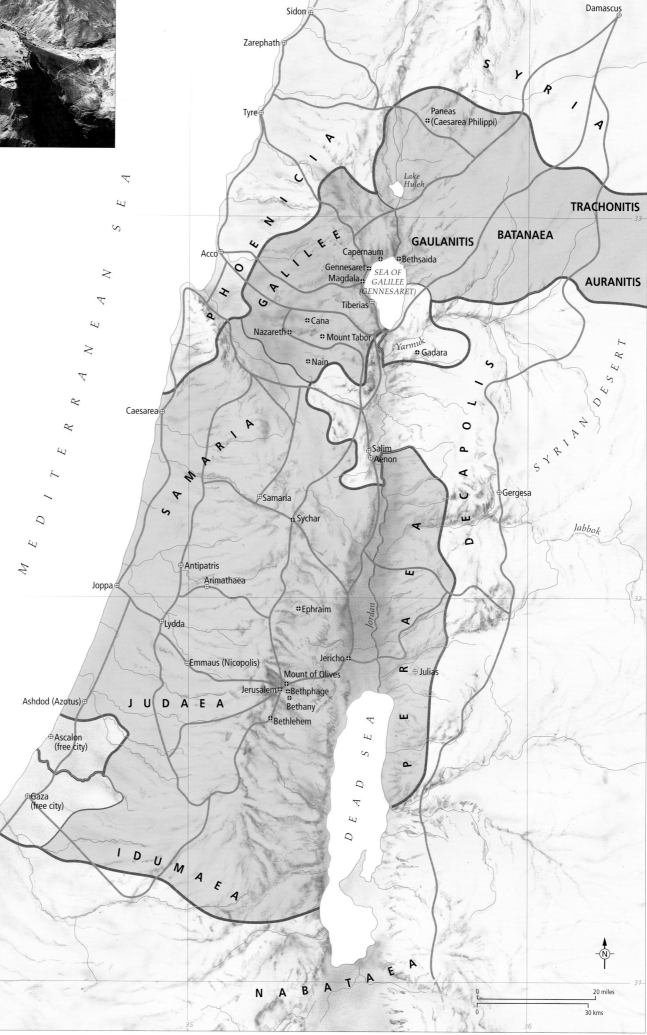

SYRIA

Sidon

Zarephath

Damascus

Tyre

Paneas (Caesarea Philippi)

Lake Huleh

TRACHONITIS

GAULANITIS   BATANAEA

Acco

Capernaum   Bethsaida

Gennesaret   SEA OF GALILEE (GENNESARET)

Magdala

AURANITIS

Tiberias

PHOENICIA

GALILEE

Cana

Nazareth   Mount Tabor

Yarmuk   Gadara

Nain

MEDITERRANEAN SEA

Caesarea

SYRIAN DESERT

DECAPOLIS

Salim
Aenon

SAMARIA

Samaria

Gergesa

Jabbok

Sychar

Antipatris

Arimathaea

Joppa

Ephraim

Jordan

Lydda

PERAEA

Emmaus (Nicopolis)

Jericho

Julias

Mount of Olives

Jerusalem   Bethphage

Ashdod (Azotus)

JUDAEA

Bethany

Bethlehem

Ascalon (free city)

DEAD SEA

Gaza (free city)

IDUMAEA

N

NABATAEA

| 0 | 20 miles |
| 0 | 30 kms |

EARLY CHRISTIAN CHURCHES IN THE ROMAN EMPIRE

A T THE DEATH of Jesus, his followers numbered perhaps no more than a few dozen: by the end of the fourth century the Roman Empire was largely Christian. The major growth in size of the community occurred during the fourth century after the Edict of Milan (313 CE) in which Emperor Constantine declared his toleration of and active support for, Christianity, though he did not himself receive baptism until immediately before his death in May 337 CE. The earliest Christians were Jewish (*see* pp. 150-151) and considered themselves to be something of a Jewish sect: they still went to the Temple to pray. A division was inevitable after the fall of Jerusalem in 70 CE, but by that time important theological differences had emerged, and can be found in the New Testament. The most important was the conviction that the Christians had a mission to include non-Jews among their number. Clearly preaching

to the non-Jews (Gentiles) was what Paul was doing during his missionary journeys, though he took care to speak first in the synagogues. Yet evidence suggests that the first Christian communities outside Palestine were Jewish in origin, and apparently came into existence without any major missionary endeavour. The structure of the first Christian communities mirrored that of Jewish ones. Government was by 'elders', and the office of a permanent presiding or monarchical 'bishop' developed only slowly. These groups met to to celebrate the Eucharist in private houses – in Rome these private houses, it seems likely, became the first churches, named after their former owners. The monarchical episcopate came into being quite late in Rome, probably not until the middle of the second century, but by the middle of the third, under Pope Fabian, the church had become highly structured (*map 2*). By that time the city had seven

The largely twelfth-century basilica of San Clemente stands directly above what may have been one of Rome's very earliest places of Christian worship, dating from the first century.

The columns mark the ruins of the basilica at Hippo Regius (Bone, or Annaba, in Algeria) where Augustine, one of Christianity's greatest thinkers, ruled as bishop from 395 CE. He died in 430 with barbarians besieging his city. Hippo was one of the very large number of bishoprics in North Africa which disappeared with the Arab invasions of the seventh century.

1	Early Christian Churches in the Roman Empire

Roman Empire at abdication of Diocletian, 305 CE

——— boundary of prefectures

——— boundary of diocese

- - - Latin/Greek language division

• churches known through attendance at church councils

○ churches known by other means

ecclesiastical districts, each administered by a deacon and subdeacon, with sundry other assistants. Fabian is also credited with undertaking building works at the Christian cemeteries, the catacombs. The catacombs were not secret places: they were outside the city because that was what Roman law required. They went down deep because, when one level was full, another was burrowed underneath it, so that the oldest burials are in fact the ones nearest to the surface. In these catacombs were certainly interred some of those who died in persecutions, but the number should not be exaggerated. They were for the most part spasmodic and localized, and it was not until the persecution of Emperor Decius (250 CE) that there was a systematic attack on Christianity, which was now clearly strong enough to be regarded as something of a threat to the established order. This was later renewed under Emperor Diocletian in 303 CE.

The Growth of Christian Communities

The presence of Christian communities (*map 1*) is attested by a variety of different sources. Some of these are, indeed, the 'Acts' or deeds of the martyrs, which were often written down and carefully preserved. The existence of 'bishoprics' can be ascertained from the names of the bishops with their sees attached to synodal documents. There are a few succession lists of bishops, and references in early historians of the Church. Some other written sources survive but, outside Rome at least, there is little archaeological evidence for the first three hundred years. From the sources it is difficult to picture the gradual expansion that must have occurred over this period. We know almost nothing about the existence of Christian communities in the Roman province of Africa at the beginning of the third century, yet at the synod of Carthage in 220 CE seventy bishops turned up representing the churches of that region.

A century later there would have been twice as many – if all had agreed to appear. Toleration for Christianity revealed deep

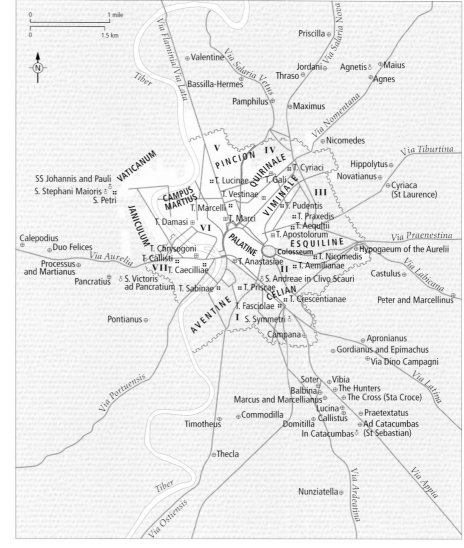

2	Rome c.500 CE	
city walls		churches pre - 311
principal roads		churches post - 311
IV ecclesiastical regions		monasteries
built-up area		catacombs

divisions in Africa. One group, known as the Donatists after their leader, believed that many of the bishops had been traitors during Diocletian's great persecution and so set up their own churches, led by bishops who had remained true. They appealed first to the Bishop of Rome, then to the Emperor. Constantine called a synod to discuss their complaint, which met in Arles and was attended by thirty-three bishops, including three from Britain. It found against the Donatists, but failed to end their schism.

Synods show that, however geographically separate, and possibly even disparate in belief, the churches thought of themselves as closely linked. Christians could, with letters of introduction, move between them. By the Council of Nicaea in 325 CE – called the first ecumenical council because it theoretically represented the whole Church though only a handful of bishops attended from the Western, Latin-speaking, part of the Empire – it is clear that the Church had adapted to its own ecclesiastical purposes the civil reorganization of the Empire into dioceses and provinces undertaken a quarter of a century earlier by Diocletian. At Nicaea certain 'metropolitan' sees were named, in particular Rome and Alexandria, with responsibilities over the bishops of lesser cities. Soon afterwards the 'new Rome', Constantinople, was to be founded, to dispute with Rome for the leadership of Christendom.

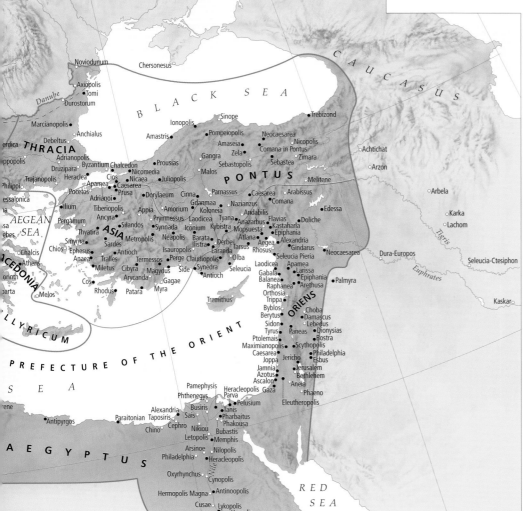

THE SPREAD OF CHRISTIANITY EAST AND WEST

ORTHODOXY, or the formulation of right belief, was achieved in the early Christian church through the gathering of bishops in what have come to be called ecumenical councils – ecumenical in this sense means from the whole inhabited world. The first six councils – from that of Nicaea in 325 CE to the Third Council of Constantinople in 680-81 – were directly concerned with the person of Jesus Christ, and with his relationship to God. The 'Christological' controversies which these councils were called to resolved, proved to be very divisive for the church in the East – far less so for those in the West, which remained much more united.

The Nestorian church (*maps 1* and *2*) took its name from Nestorius. He was Patriarch of Constantinople from 428 until he was deposed by order of the Council of Ephesus in 431 for teaching that there were two distinct 'persons' in Christ, one divine and one human, a view regarded as heretical. Whether he ever taught this is disputed: what was more at issue was a clash between two theological traditions, that of Antioch, represented by Nestorius, and that of Alexandria, for which the most famous spokesman was Cyril, Patriarch of Alexandria from 412 until his death in 444.

In 451 the Council of Chalcedon condemned the belief, which Cyril appeared to teach, that in Christ there was only one nature: the Council insisted there were two natures, one divine and one human, existing – contrary to Nestorianism – in only one person. Those who believed there was only one nature came to be called Monophysites from the Greek meaning 'one nature'; those who upheld the council's definition of there being two natures are referred to as Chalcedonians or Melkites, the latter being a name derived from the Syriac word for king and indicating members of the party favoured by the Byzantine Emperor, as far as belief was concerned.

The Spread of Christianity Eastwards
These divisions reflected the rivalry of the ancient great sees (patriarchates) of the church – those of Antioch, Alexandria and Constantinople, the last named holding to what became the orthodox tradition, the first the Nestorian and the second the Monophysite. The theological views of the Nestorians found a natural home in the school of Edessa, but when the head of that school, Narses (399–c.503), was forced to flee to Nisibis about the year 471, Nestorianism became identified with Persian Christianity. It survived, despite many attempts at reconciliation, as a distinct entity, but because its home was now outside the confines of the Byzantine Empire, it was forced to turn eastwards, towards India and following the Silk Road as far as China. There survives in Chang'an a 'stele' originally set up in 781 to commemorate the arrival of Nestorian missionaries into China a century and a half earlier. In 987, however, a monk reported that the church in China had wholly disappeared, largely perhaps because of a persecution of monks in general – Buddhist as well as Christian – undertaken on the orders of the Chinese Emperor Wu Tsung in 845. At home it survived, though from the mid-seventh century Islam dominated the region and under the Mongols they were dealt with harshly. In the mid-sixteenth century some Nestorians established links with Rome and are now called Chaldean Christians (*see also* pp. 94-95).

Monophysitism followed a parallel development to Nestorianism, and had an alternative hierarchy to those following the Chalcedonian definition. It was established in Syria, particularly by Jacob Baradaeus (c.500-78), whose influence was such that the Syrian church to

which he belonged is often known as Jacobite. Cut off from the Empire like the Nestorians, Jacobite missionaries travelled along caravan routes, especially into northern and central Arabia. Like the Nestorians, they suffered after the arrival of the Mongols and their numbers dropped further after a group united with the papacy in the seventeenth century. Other varieties of Christianity followed a more or less Monophysite creed, particularly the churches of Egypt (the Copts) and the Armenians.

Christianity in the West: The British Isles
The map of the British Isles appears at first glance to indicate a similar division into differing creeds in this part of the Western Church, but this would be misleading. The origins of the 'Celtic' church are obscure,

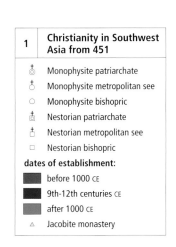

1 Christianity in Southwest Asia from 451

☩ Monophysite patriarchate
☩ Monophysite metropolitan see
○ Monophysite bishopric
☩ Nestorian patriarchate
☩ Nestorian metropolitan see
□ Nestorian bishopric

dates of establishment:
■ before 1000 CE
■ 9th-12th centuries CE
■ after 1000 CE
△ Jacobite monastery

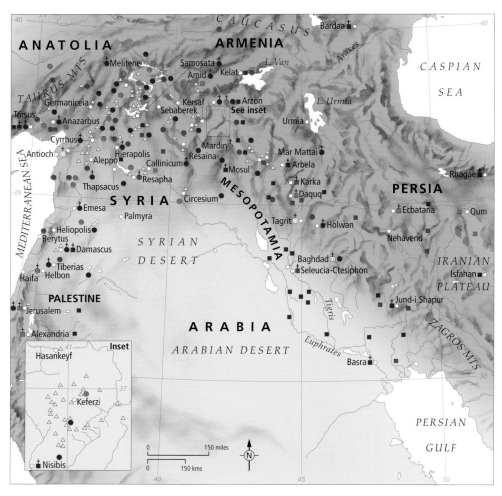

One of the many monasteries carved out of the rocky landscape in central Anatolia. The monasteries were predated by hermitages, going back to the early ninth century. Though some date from the twelfth century, they flourished mainly in the period from c.976 to 1025.

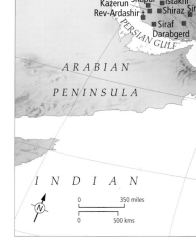

154

but Christianity certainly flourished in Roman Britain and was probably town-based, as elsewhere in the Western Empire. With the decline of the towns in the fifth century, however, church structures changed, and they became more based on monasteries (as they were in Ireland, where large towns did not exist). In the aftermath of the Anglo-Saxon invasions, they were driven into the fringes of the country. In 563 Columba arrived at Iona to found an abbey there and later in the century, under his leadership, Irish monks made their way into Scotland and down the northeast coast of England. They brought their own form of religious customs, which differed from those in most of Europe, as Augustine found when he arrived from Rome as a missionary in 597, the year that Columba died.

For a time the 'Celtic' and 'Roman' varieties of Christianity survived, somewhat uncomfortably, side by side but in 664 King Oswiu of Northumbria, whose own family was divided along these lines and therefore celebrated Easter on different dates, called a council at Whitby. There it was decided that Northumbria should follow Roman practices in disputed matters of ecclesiastical discipline. Some monks who were unhappy with this decision withdrew to Ireland, and Celtic Christianity eventually disappeared in Britain. The debate in the West, however, unlike that in the East, had been over matters of church discipline, not about differences in belief.

Though this 'Psalter of St Swithun' (London, British Library) was produced during Norman times, Swithun himself (d. 862), Bishop of Winchester, is one of the best known of Anglo-Saxon saints if only because of the belief that, if it rains on his feast day (15 July), it will rain for the next forty days.

3 Christianity in the British Isles

○ known sites of Roman-British Christianity
● Celtic bishopric
▲ Celtic monastery
Anglo-Saxon bishopric
▲ Anglo-Saxon monastery

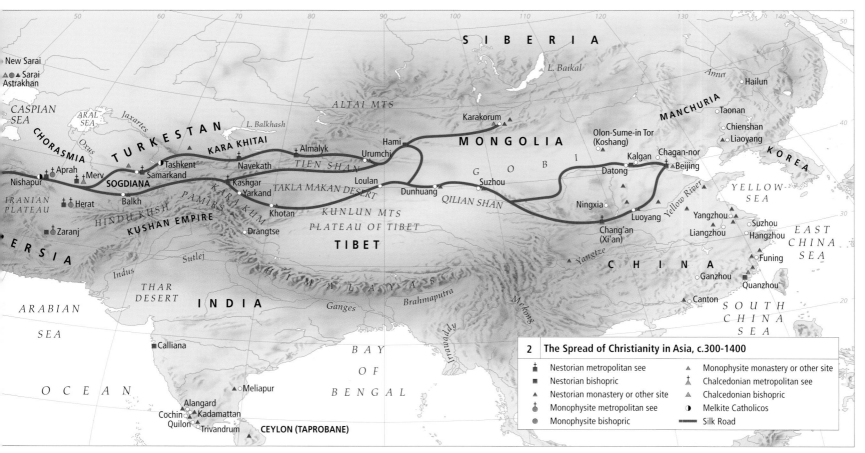

2 The Spread of Christianity in Asia, c.300–1400

Nestorian metropolitan see
■ Nestorian bishopric
▲ Nestorian monastery or other site
● Monophysite metropolitan see
● Monophysite bishopric
▲ Monophysite monastery or other site
Chalcedonian metropolitan see
▲ Chalcedonian bishopric
◖ Melkite Catholicos
▬ Silk Road

CHRISTIAN MISSIONS

THE EARLIEST SPREAD of Christianity into the Roman Empire, apart from the journeys of Paul (*see* pp. 150-151), is difficult to establish. Undoubtedly Christianity reached Egypt very early. The Egyptian (Coptic) Church insists that the original founder of the see of Alexandria was the evangelist St Mark, and certainly Alexandria ranked with Antioch and Rome as one of the leading churches of the first centuries. It was in Egypt that Christian monasticism was founded by St Anthony (251?-356 CE) at the beginning of the fourth century, to be further developed by St Pachomius (c.290-346) from 320 onwards. *Map 2* shows the enormous development of monasticism in the Egyptian desert in the early centuries of Christianity.

Monasticism also played a major part in the Christianization of Europe. *Map 1* shows the main directions of evangelization at different periods. We know little or nothing of the fifth-century St Ninian,

beyond the fact that he founded a monastery at Whithorn (Candida Casa) and preached in southern Scotland. Columba (c.521-97) is better known. After founding several monasteries in his native Ireland he came to Iona in Scotland in 563. He, and even more his immediate followers, preached Christianity in Scotland and one of them, Aidan (d. 651) came to Northumbria in 633 to found the monastery of Lindisfarne. In 597 Augustine (d. c.604), prior of the abbey of St Andrew on Rome's Celian Hill, arrived in Canterbury to preach to the English, sent by Pope Gregory the Great (c.540-604), who had once been abbot of St Andrew's.

Part of the missionary impetus of the Irish monks was the notion that exile for Christ's sake was a form of spiritual discipline. It was this which took Columbanus (c.543-615) into what is now France to found monasteries at Annegrey, Luxeuil and Bobbio. Amandus (d. 675), born near Nantes, was first a monk and then a hermit. He had

A priest of the ancient Ethiopic Church at one of the many churches in Lalibela hewn out of the rock in the twelfth and thirteenth centuries. The Church was under the general supervision of the Coptic patriarch but became self-governing in 1959.

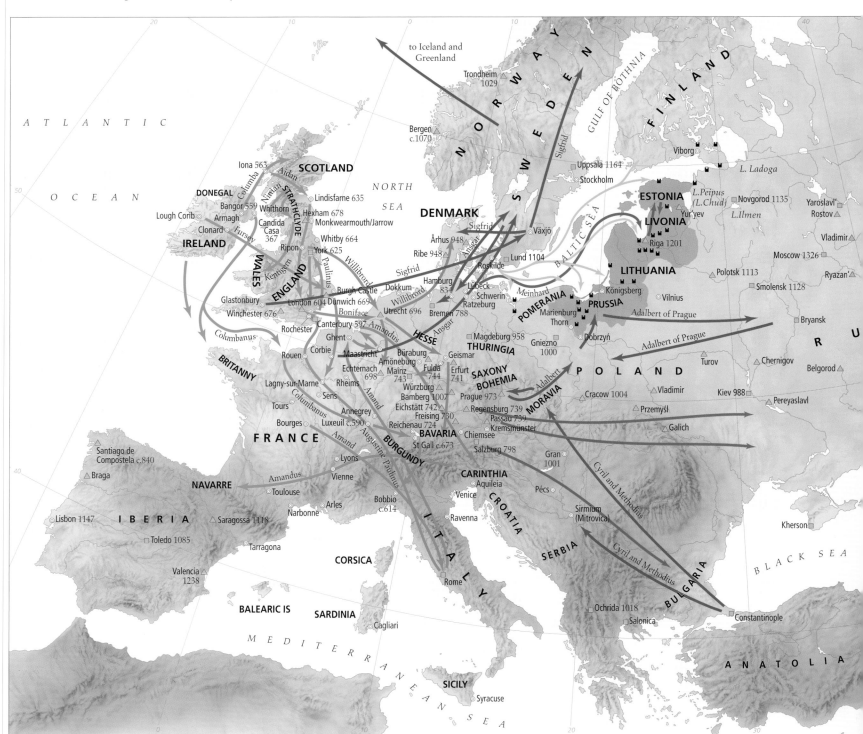

Detail of an icon of the brothers Boris and Gleb, sons of the first Christian prince of Russia, St Vladimir of Kiev (fourteenth century, State Russian Museum, St Petersburg). They were assassinated in 1015, and are venerated as martyrs because they thought it un-Christian to defend themselves by violence.

a varied career as an evangelist, most particularly in Flanders, and as a founder of monasteries. Perhaps the most remarkable of the missionaries of this period, however, was Winfrith, better known as Boniface (c.675-754), the apostle of Germany. He was probably born at Crediton in Devon, and was a monk of the abbey of Nursling near Southampton before embarking on his missionary journeys. He founded several monasteries, including that of Fulda were he was buried after his martyrdom. He was for a time Archbishop of Mainz.

The Spread of Missions East and North

After the evangelization of Western Europe, missionaries turned to the East and to the North. The brothers Cyril (826-69) and Methodius (c.815-85) came from Salonica to Constantinople, and from there set out to evangelize Moravia at the request of the Emperor – there were already German missionaries working in the area, but the local ruler preferred to be aligned with Constantinople. Disputes arose and the brothers went to Rome, where Cyril became a monk, and where he died. Methodius returned to Moravia as Archbishop, and died at Velehrad. Ansgar (801-65), their contemporary, was from Amiens but educated at Corbie, where he became a monk. He went to Denmark under royal protection (the king had become a Christian while in exile), and went on to Sweden. He was appointed Bishop of Hamburg in 832 and in 845 Archbishop over both Hamburg and Bremen. Sigfrid (d. c.1045) also went to Sweden. He was probably English, and certainly from the monastery at Glastonbury. He evangelized remote areas of Sweden before going on to Denmark. He died at Växjö in Sweden, where he was bishop.

Later Missions and the Teutonic Knights

In the later period the pattern of missionary activity changed (*map 1*). There were missions overseen by individual dioceses on the pagan/Christian border. A more unusual means of expanding Christendom, however, was taken when the Teutonic Knights, a religious order of German knights originally dedicated to the care of the sick in the Holy Land, went first to Hungary and then, at the request of Duke Conrad of Masovia, to fight against the pagan Prussians. They crossed the Vistula in 1231, and set about extending their rule – they had been given almost limitless authority in newly-conquered lands – throughout Prussia and into Livonia and Estonia, though with fierce opposition from the pagan Lithuanians. When the Lithuanians eventually accepted Christianity they united with Poland and a combined Lithuanian-Polish army defeated the Knights in 1410 at the battle of Tannenberg.

Missionary Crusades

The Teutonic Knights (the Order still exists, now dedicated to the charitable work for which it was first founded) had originally been crusaders in the Holy

Land. But the concept of 'crusade' and the indulgences attached to it was not necessarily limited to capturing, or defending, the Christian holy places (*see also* pp.162-163). It was transferable to almost any conflict against those believed to be enemies of the Church. The Wend Crusade of 1147, which had the blessing of Bernard of Clairvaux, was intended to win for Christ the pagan Slavs beyond the Elbe, though it also coincided with the economic and military interests of the Saxons. There were several Swedish crusades, the first in 1157, against Finland, and in 1199 one led by Albert of Buxhövden which culminated in the founding of Riga in 1201. Albert also founded the Knights of the Sword to defend and expand the Christian territory – they eventually amalgamated with the Teutonic Knights.

1	**Missionary Activity in Europe**
■	archbishopric/metropolitan see
▲	bishopric
◉	monastery or other religious centre
534	date of foundation

main missionary routes:

→	c.400-750
→	c.750-1000
→	post-1000
Ninian	missionary
→	main routes of Baltic missions/crusades
■	Christian castle
	area controlled by Teutonic Order by 1400

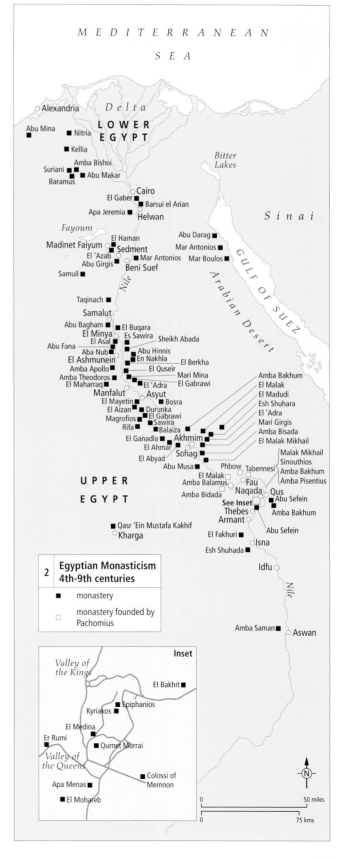

2	**Egyptian Monasticism 4th-9th centuries**
■	monastery
□	monastery founded by Pachomius

THE SPREAD OF THE RELIGIOUS ORDERS

AT LEAST FROM the third century some Christians have embraced a more thoroughgoing understanding of the Gospel by living a communal, celibate existence under the guidance of a spiritual leader. Traditionally, this form of commitment has been expressed by such people taking, explicitly or implicitly, the three 'vows' of poverty, chastity and obedience. They usually do so within structures known as religious orders.

Monastic life is essentially a form of community life where groups of monks (or nuns) live, work and pray together. This form of monasticism is called 'coenobitic' and is contrasted with the 'eremetical' life, a hermit-like existence. The latter is the older form, and began in Egypt with St Anthony (c.251-356) who went out into the desert (the word 'eremetical' comes from the Greek for 'desert') to live a life of asceticism devoted to the worship of God. He attracted disciples in such numbers that eventually he moved to another location ('Anthony's Inner Mountain') once again to seek solitude. The founder of the coenobitic

life is said to be St Pachomius (c.290-346), who likewise went into the Egyptian desert as a disciple of a hermit, but gathered around himself a group of followers to whom he gave a 'rule' by which to live. His first monastery, founded c.320, was at Tabennisi. At his death he was in charge of nine monasteries for men and two for women.

St Pachomius' rule came to be known in the West as well as in the East, and influenced those which followed. One such was that of John Cassian (c.360-c.430). Cassian travelled to Egypt to study monasticism at first hand, and the rule he gave to the two monasteries he founded near Marseilles reflects what he had learned there. But the most significant figure in early monastic history, as far as the West is concerned, is undoubtedly St Benedict (c.480-c.550). He chose first to live as a hermit at Subiaco, east of Rome, but as with St Anthony a group of disciples gathered around him and a monastery was formed there, though Benedict moved from Subiaco to Monte Cassino, between Rome and Naples, two decades before his death.

The Abbey of Cîteaux was inaugurated in 1098 and survived until the French Revolution. It was restored to the Cistercians in 1898 after a gap of 107 years. Part of the discipline of the order required that all monasteries had to be built according to a very similar plan and without excessive ornamentation. Cistercians were distinguished from other monks following the Benedictine rule by wearing white, rather than the more common black, habits.

Early European Religious Orders

- monasteries founded before 900
- religious orders founded 900-1200
- religious orders founded 1200-1550

Map labels:
Iona 563
Derry 546
Bangor c.555
Whithorn c.400
Clonmacnoise 554-58
Durrow c.553
Clonfert 558-64
Melrose c.650
Lindisfarne 635
Monkwearmouth 674
Jarrow 682-85
Hexham c.670
Clonard 549
Whitby 657
Sempringham Gilbertines 1131
Vadstena Bridgettines 1346

NORTH SEA

BRITISH ISLES

Windesheim Congregation of Windesheim 1387
Deventer Brethren of the Common Life c.1379
Clair-Lieu Crosiers 1211
GERMANY
Pavilly 662
Corbie c.657-61
Fécamp c.658
Liège Beguines c.1170
Fulda 744
Wandrille 649
Prémontré Premonstratensians 1120
Jumièges 631
Cefroid Trinitarians 1198
Paris Victorines 1113
Jouarre c.630-34
Echternach 698
Chelles c.656
Savigny
Faremoutiers c.627
Rebais 635
Order of Savigny 1115
Marmoutier c.371
Reichenau 724
Fontevrault
Fleury 651
Luxeuil c.590
Order of Fontevrault 1100
Poitiers 552-69
Ligugé 363
Cluny Cluniacs 910
Besançon Colettines 1410
FRANCE
Cîteaux Cistercians 1098
Brescia Ursulines 1535
Grande Chartreuse Carthusians 1084
Padua Cassinese Congregation 1409
St Ruf
Bobbio 615
Milan Angelicals 1530, Barnabites 1530, Daughters of Mary 1540
Canons Regular of St Augustine 1039
Florence Serrites 1233
Bologna Crutched Friars 1169
Prouille Dominicans 1206
Vallombrosa 1036
Lérins c.410
Camaldoli c.1015
Marseilles c.410
Mount Oliveto
Assisi Franciscans 1209, Poor Clares 1213
Olivetans 1319
Brugliano Observant Friars 1368
CORSICA
Siena
Gesuati 1367
Subiaco 529
Sisters of Visitation of Mary 1367
IBERIA
Tagus
Alcántara
Knights of Alcántara 1197
Barcelona
Knights of St Lazarus c.1100, Mercedarians 1235
Monte Cassino c.529
Monte Morrone Celestine Order 1259
Calatrava
Uclés Knights of Santiago 1171
Knights of Calatrava 1157
SARDINIA
Vivarium c.539
ANATOLIA
Annesi 358
BLACK SEA
AEGEAN SEA
BALEARIC IS
Rome
Canons Regular of the Lateran 1068, Augustinians 1256, Theatines 1524, Jesuits 1540
Paola Minims 1435
GREECE
Ebro
PYRENEES
ALPS
Po
Rhône
Loire
Rhine
Elbe
Danube
SICILY
Tagaste 388
CRETE
CYPRUS
Acre Teutonic Knights 1190
Jerusalem
Knights Hospitaller c.1089
Knights of St Lazarus c.1100
Knights Templar 1119
Bethlehem 385
Mt Carmel
Carmelites c.1190
PALESTINE
SYRIA
MEDITERRANEAN SEA
EGYPT
Antony's Inner Mountain c.300
Antony's Outer Mountain c.271
Tabennisi 315
AFRICA
ATLANTIC OCEAN
N
0 250 miles
0 300 kms

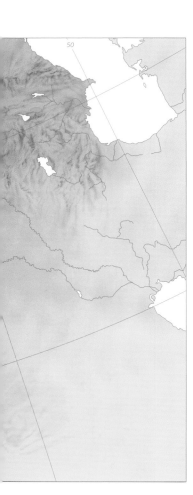

Few of the monasteries on Athos can be dated with certainty. The earliest, the Great Lavra, was founded in 961, and the Dochiarios monastery (above) before 1013, though it did not move to its present site until the end of the eleventh century.

The rule which bears Benedict's name, and which came to dominate monastic life in the West, drew upon many sources, including the rule of St Basil the Great (c.330-c.379), which has become the norm among Eastern monks. Both of these rules envisaged monastic communities, or abbeys, existing independently from each other under the direction of their abbot. Such remains more or less the custom in the East, but in the West monasteries have been brought together in groups now called 'Congregations' which share a common interpretation of the rule of St Benedict and have an abbot general, or president, over the whole Congregation.

The Growth of Religious Orders in the West
This Western model originated with the abbey of Cluny in the tenth century. Cluny, near Mâcon, represented a return to a strict observance of the Benedictine rule together with a concern for the formal recitation of the monastic 'office' (the seven periods of daily prayer said or, more properly, sung in common) and for the solemn performance of other forms of liturgical worship, the mass in particular. The Cluniacs became very powerful and by the end of the eleventh century over a thousand houses subscribed to this form of monasticism (*see map 3*). Inevitably, there was a reaction and in 1098 a monastery was founded at Cîteaux, just south of Dijon, where the (Cistercian) monks strove to return to a more primitive interpretation of the rule, as well as to a simpler form of worship.

In the second half of the eleventh century groups of clerics, many of them already living a form of community life, began to adopt a rule attributed to St Augustine of Hippo (354-430), and so came to be known as Augustinian (or Austin) canons. But canons belonged, like monks, to one locality. At the beginning of the thirteenth century two orders of 'friars' were established, known after their founders as Dominicans and Franciscans. Friars were distinguished from monks because, although they still had a base community and as far as possible said the office in common, they were not tied to one spot, but travelled from town to town preaching: over and above the pursuit of their personal holiness they had an apostolic purpose. The commitment to the office in common, however, proved a limitation on the apostolic effectiveness of these orders. Eventually, others were founded, such as the Society of Jesus (the Jesuits) whose members, although following a common rule, were not obliged to say office together.

Other orders came into being after the Society of Jesus, though most of them were based on the Jesuit model and most, though again not all, were within the Roman Catholic Church. The great flowering of religious orders both within Catholicism and outside it occurred during the nineteenth century, a period which, in particular, saw a phenomenal expansion of religious orders for women.

Religious Orders in the East
In the Eastern churches the pattern was quite different. As with the nineteen houses on Mount Athos, the earliest of which dates from 962, the individual monasteries largely maintained their autonomy: the Ecumenical Patriarch of Constantinople (Istanbul) has little authority over them. The monasteries on Athos represent many of the strands of Orthodoxy: seventeen houses of Greek monks, one Serbian, one Russian and one Bulgarian. There is also a 'skete' – what in the West might be called a priory – especially for Romanian monks. After a long period of decline there are now more than 2,000 monks living on the peninsula (though no women, not even female animals). Religious orders as such have not developed in the Eastern churches, except for those in communion with Rome.

In the Middle Ages monks in the West regularly played a part in the wider church life, and the life of the state. In recent centuries the former has become less true, and the latter has almost entirely died out. In the East the tradition has been different: senior ecclesiastics have been chosen only from among the ranks of the monks, and those in the highest office in the churches have frequently played a significant role in political life.

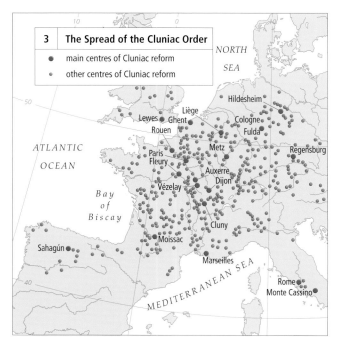

PILGRIMAGE ROUTES

I N 326 CE, when at least seventy years old, the Empress Helena, mother of Constantine, the first Christian Emperor, visited the Holy Land. There she founded basilicas at the Holy Places: on the site of the sepulchre in Jerusalem where Christ had been buried, at the spot on the Mount of Olives from which Christ had ascended into heaven, and in Bethlehem, at the place of Christ's birth. Their construction had been ordered by Constantine a year earlier, and the fact that the precise locations could be identified suggests that they were remembered by Christians. In Rome itself Constantine built a basilica over the alleged grave of St Peter where, we now know, there had long been a memorial. Half a century later Egeria travelled from either Spain or Gaul to the holy places, and recounted in vivid detail the liturgy of the church of Jerusalem, and that in Bethlehem. Pilgrimage, a phenomenon to be found in all the world's major religions, had been born into a Christian dress.

The Growth of Christian Pilgrimage

Pilgrimage to Palestine survived the fall of Jerusalem to Muslim forces in 638, but other shrines developed. Rome was always a major destination, above all because of the bodies of the many martyrs buried there. But relics of these saints found their way to other cities and abbeys throughout Europe, so these, too, attracted pilgrims, as did other shrines of saints, some real, others imaginary (*map 1*). The supposed bones of the Magi, brought from Constantinople to Milan in the fifth century, were taken

on to Germany in the twelfth, and now lie enshrined in Cologne. In England there was the tomb of the murdered Archbishop Thomas Beckett at Canterbury, the destination of Chaucer's travellers. But, Rome apart, chief among European shrines was that of St James, son of Zebedee, who was with Christ at both the Transfiguration and at the Agony in the Garden. According to legend, he journeyed to Spain to preach, though returning to Palestine to be martyred. After his death his body, the legend continues, was taken to Compostela in the far northwest of Spain for burial. He re-appeared to fight alongside Christian Spaniards in the reconquest of their country from Muslims (*see* pp. 162-163), becoming known as Santiago Matamoros, 'St James the Moor-slayer'. The route to Santiago, through the north of Spain, was well marked out. There was even a guidebook produced in the twelfth century, warning would-be pilgrims of danger spots, advising them where they might find lodgings, and describing the cathedral in Santiago, the goal of their journey.

The Route to Santiago de Compostela

The 'Camino de Santiago' is still well marked out, and regularly walked, or cycled over, to this day (*map 2*). Modern pilgrims usually start their journey at, or near, the Spanish border. The routes in the Middle Ages were well-trodden from well within France itself. Not only did religious houses spring up to give travellers shelter, many developed shrines of their own to attract the custom of

The poet John Lydgate (?1370-?1450) together with other pilgrims, leaving Canterbury. A scene from a fifteenth-century manuscript in the British Library, London. Large numbers of pilgrims travelled to the tomb of Thomas Beckett at Canterbury and were the subject of Geoffrey Chaucer's 'Canterbury Tales'.

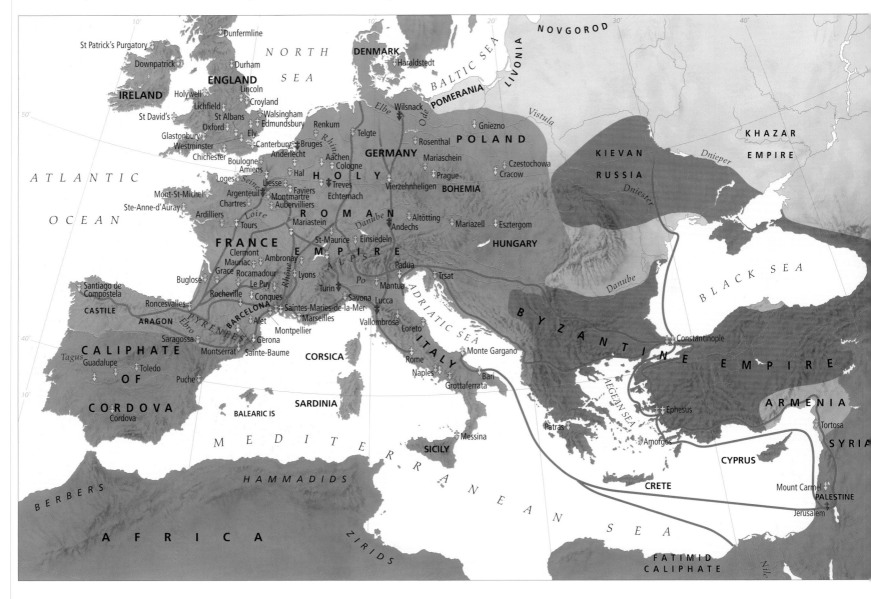

passers-by, none more so, perhaps, than Vézelay which claimed to have the relics of Mary Magdalen. Its monks acknowledged that it was unlikely Magdalen had found her way to Vézelay unaided. Rather, they insisted that she had come to France to do penance, and had died in Provence. But when the town in which she was buried became deserted, her remains were transferred to Vézelay. Towards the end of the thirteenth century, however, the monks of St Maximin, said to have been Magdalen's original resting place, claimed the Vézelay monks had taken the wrong body: the pope of the day, Boniface VIII, endorsed St Maximin's account, and Vézelay, for all its splendour, became almost forgotten thereafter.

The Papacy and the Effects of the Reformation

This story also illustrates papal influence. Pope Boniface himself had instituted – with enormous success – the practice of having a 'Holy (or Jubilee) Year' to attract people to Rome and, incidentally, to fill up the depleted papal coffers. But to whichever major shrine pilgrims travelled they did so under papal protection, and with papal promises of spiritual favours when they arrived. Pilgrims for the duration of their travels became almost a religious order. They were given a blessing as they set out dressed in formal pilgrim's garb of a plain tunic, a purse and a staff with, in the later middle ages, a broad-brimmed hat. On their return journey they commonly wore a badge – palms from the Holy Land or a cockle shell (later a leaden copy of a cockle shell) from Santiago to prove that they had reached their goal.

Even before the Reformation, some churchmen disapproved of the pilgrimages because of the corruption that so often surrounded them, and because of the doubtful authenticity of many of the relics. With the Augsburg Confession of 1530, pilgrimages were condemned as spiritually useless, effectively dissuading Protestants from participation in them.

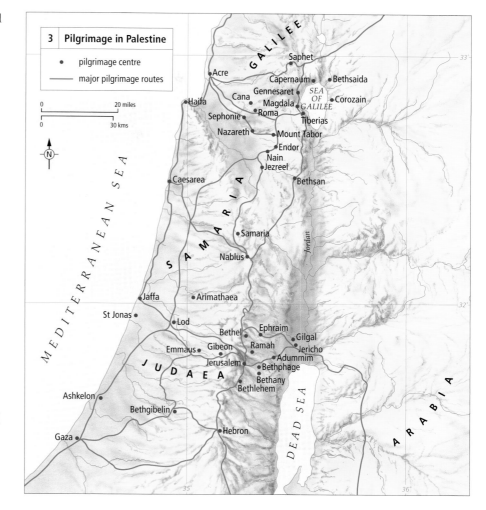

3 Pilgrimage in Palestine

• pilgrimage centre
— major pilgrimage routes

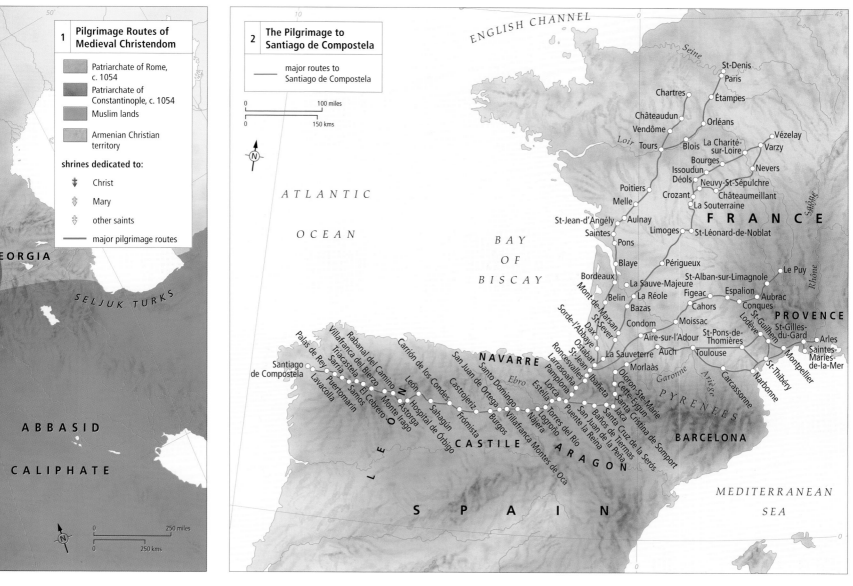

1 Pilgrimage Routes of Medieval Christendom

Patriarchate of Rome, c. 1054
Patriarchate of Constantinople, c. 1054
Muslim lands
Armenian Christian territory

shrines dedicated to:
✝ Christ
✝ Mary
✝ other saints
— major pilgrimage routes

2 The Pilgrimage to Santiago de Compostela

— major routes to Santiago de Compostela

THE CRUSADES

THE PROGRESS of Islam into southeast Europe was generally slow (*see* pp. 200-201). By contrast, the Muslim advance into the Iberian peninsula was swift but its retreat slow and hard-fought. Islam arrived in the spring of 711, with an army, initially, of some 7,000 men. They marched inland without a great deal of opposition until, on 19 July, they were confronted by the Christian king, Roderick of Andalusia, on the River Guadalete. Roderick's claim to his throne was disputed, some of his enemies had already sought support among the Muslims. Two wings of Roderick's army deserted him, and he was heavily defeated, probably dying in the conflict. Muslim forces moved inexorably northwards and into what is now France, which was also weakened by dynastic divisions. Narbonne fell in 719, and in 732 a raiding party sacked Bordeaux and was advancing on Tours when it was defeated by the Frankish ruler Charles Martel. Narbonne was recaptured in 751: thenceforward Muslim territory in Western Europe was confined to the Iberian peninsula.

The Reconquest of the Iberian Peninsula

The reconquest of the Iberian Peninsula ('Reconquista'; *map 3*) took seven centuries. According to tradition it began at Covadonga in the mountains of Asturias where Pelayo, a member of King Roderick's bodyguard, had taken refuge. A party of Arab troops sent to capture him was defeated, perhaps in 718 – the date is uncertain and the entire story comes only from the early tenth century. It is certain, however, that a Christian enclave developed in Asturias, which gradually extended its borders south. At the same time Charlemagne, King of the Franks (768-814) was pushing into eastern Spain – not always successfully, as the romance the *Song of Roland* and the battle of Roncesvalles (778) bear witness. Charlemagne's empire broke up after his death, and the Frankish conquests in Spain became petty kingdoms of their own.

In the reconquest perhaps the most decisive battle was not the last, the capture of Granada, entered by Ferdinand of Aragon and his wife Isabella of Castile on 6 January 1492, but Alfonso VIII of Castile's victory at Las Navas de Tolosa on 16 July 1212. In the campaign which led up to the battle Alfonso had been supported by the Pope, who regarded it as a crusade and called upon all Christian monarchs to cease squabbling until this crusade was over. The Castilian king was indeed joined by some French knights, though the battle itself was fought mainly by Castilian and Aragonese forces. After Las Navas de Tolosa, though the Muslim retreat was slow, it was sure and by 1252 no independent Muslim kingdom was left: Murcia, Niebla and Granada were all at least nominally under Christian suzerainty.

The First Three Crusades, 1095-1192

In contrast, the effort of Christian knights to capture Palestine, seized by Muslims in the eighth century, met with no permanent success. The crusading ideal was born partly out of piety, the desire to go on pilgrimage, and partly out of a need to support the Byzantine Emperor against the onset of the Turkish invasion. Turks had replaced Arabs in control of the Holy Places, and their rule over Christian communities in Palestine was possibly harsher than that of their predecessors. Against this background in 1095, at the end of the Council held at Clermont in France, Pope Urban II urged knights to stop fighting each other and fight Turks instead. He asked them to support Christians oppressed by Turks, and promised the remission of all sins – the origins of the 'crusading indulgence' - should they set out for Jerusalem with the right dispositions.

The First Crusade (*map 1*) was relatively successful: Jerusalem fell in 1099. By that time the crusaders had already set up independent states: the Principality of Antioch, which lasted from 1098 to 1268, and the County

The Crusader assault on Jerusalem in 1099 at the end of the First Crusade. A scene from a fourteenth-century illuminated manuscript of 'Li Romans de Godefroy de Buillon et de Salehadin' in the Bibliothèque Nationale in Paris.

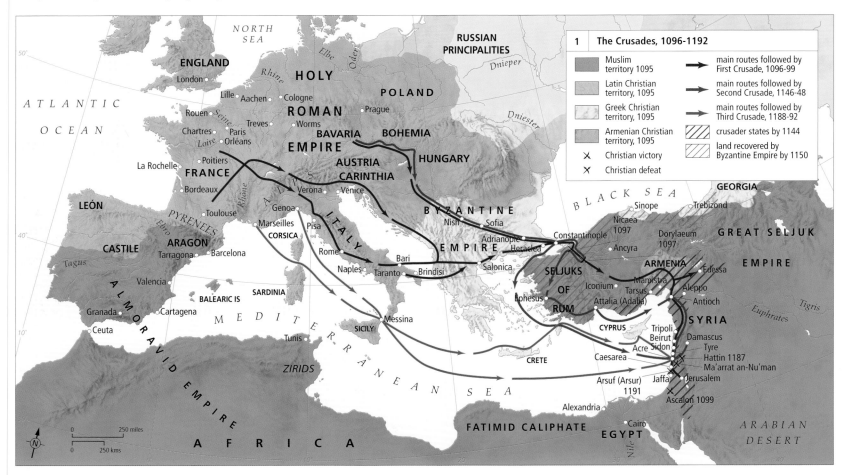

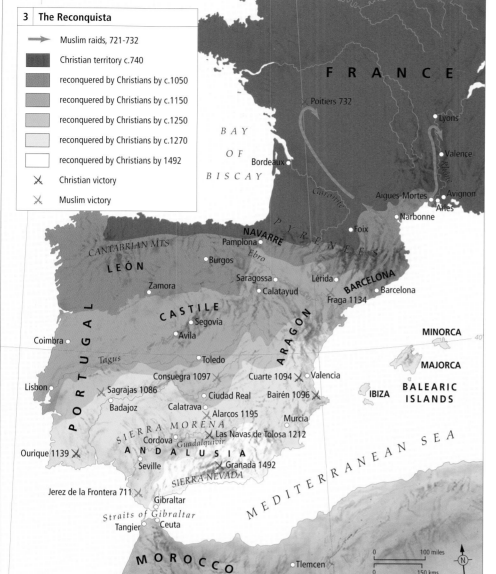

of Edessa (1098-1144). Godfrey of Bouillon took charge of the Kingdom of Jerusalem (1099-1187 and 1229-44). Other parts of Asia Minor taken by the Christian armies were handed back to the Byzantine emperor.

In 1144, however, Edessa was recaptured by the Turks, and a new crusade was launched, though it had little success. It was the capture of Jerusalem by Saladin in 1187 that occasioned the Third Crusade. En route to Jerusalem the English King Richard I occupied Cyprus, and established the Kingdom of Cyprus: this crusader state survived until 1489, though beyond that the crusaders achieved very little.

The Later Crusades

In 1198 Pope Innocent III appealed for another crusade, the Fourth. Venice contracted to ship the army to Egypt but when only a third of the expected numbers arrived in 1202 and the payment could not be raised, they helped the Venetians capture the town of Zara, on the Adriatic coast, from the King of Hungary in return for their passage. They also promised to help restore Alexius IV and his recently deposed father Isaac Angelus to the Byzantine throne. After an assault on Constantinople in 1203, Alexius himself was overthrown in early 1204. The penurious crusaders then sacked the city, many of its valuables – including relics – finding their way to the West. A Latin Empire was established at Constantinople, which lasted until 1261.

Among the later crusades was the crusade of Emperor Frederick II in 1228-9 (*map 2*). In the following year he negotiated a treaty with the Egyptians for the restoration of parts of Palestine, including Jerusalem, to Christian control, in which it remained until 1244. Despite his tenacious commitment to the crusading spirit, the first crusade of King Louis IX of France (1248-50) ended with a humiliating defeat at Damietta in Egypt. He died of disease during a second crusade (1270) against Emir Muhammad I of Tunis.

Though there were other crusades (including a disastrous 'children's crusade' in 1212) in the thirteenth century, they achieved very little apart from hardening Muslim attitudes against Christians.

MYSTICISM AND HERESY

MYSTICISM is a phenomenon which can be found in many, if not all, of the world's major religions. Christian writers of the Middle Ages (*map 1*) mostly understood mysticism as a form of direct experience of God achieved through prayer. Writing in the early sixth century, Dionysius the Pseudo Areopagite (whose exact dates and location are unknown) proposed that Christians can move beyond an intellectual understanding of the 'mysteries' of the faith, expressed in the creeds and the liturgy, to a state in which God acts upon the mind directly. Some later interpreters of Dionysius understood him to mean that there was a special form of knowledge of God; others argued it was a form of experience which lay beyond knowledge. In the High Middle Ages more emphasis was laid on human affection in the desire for greater intimacy with God – a development especially linked with the Cistercian Saint Bernard of Clairvaux (1090-1153). The medieval mystics commonly recounted in their writings their own experience of God, outlining the stages by which others might reach the same end. Many represent 'schools' in

that they reflect the spirituality of their religious order. From the late fourteenth century the Brethren of the Common Life were active in propagating the 'devotio moderna', among lay people as well as members of religious orders. This form of prayer laid great stress on methodical meditation on the person of Christ: its classic exposition is Thomas à Kempis' *Imitation of Christ* – though the book has sometimes been attributed to Gerhard Groote, the founder of the Brethren.

Heresy
While heightened interest in religion led to mysticism, it also prompted criticism of the way Christianity was taught. The dissenting movement (*map 2*) established by the Bohemian Jan Hus (c.1372-1415) had much in common with Lollardy in England, which drew upon the writings of the Englishman John Wyclif (1330-84). Both were reform movements, critical of the moral laxity of the clergy, but both also were sympathetic to the problematic doctrines of predestination (that some people are pre-ordained by God for salvation), and to the notion that the

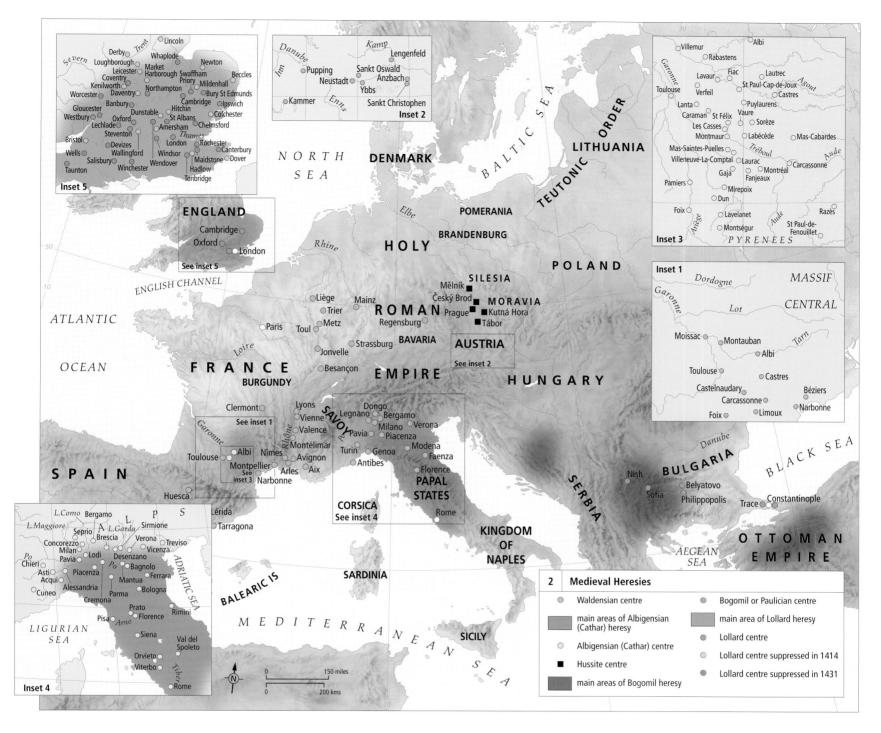

Inset 5

Severn · Trent · Lincoln · Derby · Whaplode · Loughborough · Market Harborough · Leicester · Swaffham Priory · Newton · Beccles · Coventry · Northampton · Mildenhall · Bury St Edmunds · Kenilworth · Daventry · Cambridge · Ipswich · Worcester · Banbury · Hitchin · Colchester · Gloucester · Dunstable · St Albans · Chelmsford · Westbury · Oxford · Amersham · Lechlade · Steventon · London · Rochester · Bristol · Devizes · Windsor · Canterbury · Wells · Wallingford · Maidstone · Dover · Taunton · Salisbury · Winchester · Wendover · Hadlow · Tonbridge · Thames

Inset 2

Danube · Im · Kamp · Lengenfeld · Pupping · Sankt Oswald · Neustadt · Anzbach · Kammer · Enns · Ybbs · Sankt Christopher

Inset 3

Villemur · Albi · Rabastens · Garonne · Lavaur · Fiac · Lautrec · Asout · Toulouse · St Paul-Cap-de-Joux · Lanta · Verfeil · Castres · Caraman · St Félix · Puylaurens · Les Casses · Vaure · Montmaur · Sorèze · Mas-Saintes-Puelles · Labécède · Mas-Cabardès · Villeneuve-La-Comptal · Laurac · Tréboul · Gaja · Montréal · Carcassonne · Pamiers · Fanjeaux · Aude · Mirepoix · Foix · Ariège · Lavelanet · Dun · Razès · Montségur · St Paul-de-Fenouillet · PYRENEES

Inset 1

Dordogne · MASSIF · Garonne · Lot · CENTRAL · Moissac · Montauban · Tarn · Toulouse · Albi · Castelnaudary · Castres · Carcassonne · Béziers · Foix · Limoux · Narbonne

NORTH SEA · DENMARK · BALTIC SEA · TEUTONIC ORDER · LITHUANIA · POMERANIA · BRANDENBURG · HOLY · POLAND · Elbe · SILESIA · Mělník · Český Brod · MORAVIA · Liège · Mainz · ROMAN · Prague · Kutná Hora · Trier · Regensburg · Tábor · Rhine · Toul · Metz · EMPIRE · HUNGARY · Paris · Strassburg · BAVARIA · AUSTRIA · See inset 2 · Loire · Jonvelle · Besançon · FRANCE · BURGUNDY · ENGLAND · Cambridge · Oxford · London · See inset 5 · ENGLISH CHANNEL · ATLANTIC OCEAN · Clermont · See inset 1 · Lyons · SAVOY · Dongo · Bergamo · Vienne · Legnano · Milano · Verona · Valence · Pavia · Piacenza · Turin · Genoa · Modena · Toulouse · Albi · Nîmes · Avignon · Faenza · Montpellier · Arles · Aix · Antibes · Florence · See inset 3 · Narbonne · PAPAL STATES · Huesca · CORSICA · See inset 4 · Rome · SPAIN · Lérida · Tarragona · KINGDOM OF NAPLES · SERBIA · Nish · BULGARIA · BLACK SEA · Sofia · Belyatovo · Philippopolis · Trace · Constantinople · BALEARIC IS · SARDINIA · MEDITERRANEAN SEA · AEGEAN SEA · OTTOMAN EMPIRE · SICILY

Inset 4

L.Como · Bergamo · ALPS · L.Maggiore · Seprio · L.Garda · Sirmione · Concorezzo · Brescia · Verona · Treviso · Milan · Lodi · Vicenza · Chieri · Pavia · Desenzano · ADRIATIC SEA · Po · Asti · Piacenza · Bagnolo · Acqui · Mantua · Ferrara · Cuneo · Alessandria · Bologna · Cremona · Parma · Prato · Florence · Rimini · LIGURIAN SEA · Pisa · Arno · Siena · Val del Spoleto · Orvieto · Viterbo · Tiber · Rome

0 · 150 miles · 0 · 200 kms

2 Medieval Heresies

- ○ Waldensian centre
- main areas of Albigensian (Cathar) heresy
- ○ Albigensian (Cathar) centre
- ■ Hussite centre
- main areas of Bogomil heresy
- ○ Bogomil or Paulician centre
- main area of Lollard heresy
- ○ Lollard centre
- ○ Lollard centre suppressed in 1414
- ○ Lollard centre suppressed in 1431

The savagery of the crusade against the Albigensians at the beginning of the thirteenth century led to the building of strongly defended 'bastide' towns, such as Najac shown here.

Church is the Church of the elect, or chosen ones.

This latter notion was common in the Middle Ages, reflecting a belief that there are two more or less equal creators, one good the other evil, and that material things were the work of the latter. This was the fundamental doctrine of the Paulicians, a sect which emerged in Armenia in the seventh century, and spread within the Byzantine Empire. Taking their name from their tenth-century founder, who was quite possibly influenced by this Paulician doctrine, the Bogomils were strongest in the Balkans ('Bogomil' is the Bulgarian version of the name Theophilus).

The most potent threat to orthodoxy came from the Albigensians ('Cathar' is a general term for this and similar groups, the word 'heretic' being usually applied in the Middle Ages only to Cathars), again adherents of a dualist notion of creation, who were particularly active in Languedoc and northern Italy in the late twelfth and early thirteenth centuries. Attempts to convert them gave rise to the Order of Preachers, the Dominicans, and, when preaching failed, to the establishment of the Inquisition. They were eventually savagely suppressed by Simon de Montfort.

It is less easy to describe Waldensian beliefs because as a group they were fragmented. The founder, Valdo

(d. c.1210), was a layman from Lyons, who underwent a dramatic conversion, leaving his family and giving up his wealth to preach the Gospel. His followers dedicated themselves to preaching, poverty, and works of charity, and ran into trouble over unauthorized preaching. Those who established themselves in northern Italy became more radical, apparently rejecting the validity of the sacraments in the Catholic Church, some adopting views later to be found in the Protestant Reformation.

The Great Schism

A greater threat to the unity of Christendom came from the division of the Western church between opposing Popes during the Great Schism (*map 1*), which followed the election of Pope Urban VI in 1378. It was claimed that he showed signs of insanity when he attempted to make sweeping reforms, and the cardinals then elected Clement VII, who set up court at Avignon. There were thus two 'obediences', one to Rome, the other to Avignon. Though allegiances changed, the rulers of Europe sided with one or the other, usually for political reasons – France naturally associated with Avignon, England with Rome. Spain and Portugal were likewise on opposing sides. The situation was only resolved with the unanimous election of Martin V in 1417.

CHRISTIAN MISSIONS IN THE AMERICAS

I T IS UNLIKELY that there were priests aboard any of the ships that sailed under Christopher Columbus' command in 1492. The following year, when he sailed for the New World with a far larger fleet, a dozen or so clergy accompanied the conquistadors, but they were so motley a group that no serious missionary work was undertaken, and the senior priest returned home in 1494. The first major effort to convert the indigenous inhabitants of the Americas began with the arrival of Franciscans in the Antilles in 1500 (*map 1*).

In 1493 Pope Alexander VI had divided the world in half along a line to the west of the Azores and the Cape Verde Islands. Newly discovered territories to the east of the line were to belong to Portugal, those to the west to Spain. The following year, by the Treaty of Tordesillas, that line was shifted westwards so that Brazil fell under the control of Portugal. Within these territories the respective monarchs were to have responsibility for the conversion of the local inhabitants who, the pope ruled, must be freely, not forcibly, converted to Christianity. This control – the *patronato*, as the Spanish called it, or *padroado* to the Portuguese – determined which missionaries of which nationalities were sent to which territories. Relations between Church and State in the New World were not easy, and held up the establishment of dioceses: the first of these, set up in 1511, were Santo Domingo and Concepción de la Vega on Hispaniola, and San Juan on Puerto Rico. Santa María Antigua del Darién in Panama, established two years later, was the first on the American mainland.

Dominicans arrived a decade after the Franciscans, and although they were not as influential in the conversion of the Americas as were the other religious orders, they included among their number Bartolomé de las Casas (1484-1566), Bishop of Chiapa in what is now Mexico, perhaps the fiercest critic of the colonization policy of the Spanish crown. The conversion of the Americas was, indeed, largely the work of friars, whose vocation even within Europe was essentially itinerant preaching: the Jesuits, though not technically friars, were similar to them at least in this regard.

Later Catholic Missions

In that part of North America which is now Canada a like situation prevailed, except that, in 1534, it had been claimed for France. Missionary activity proper, however, did not begin until 1603 at the urging of Samuel de Champlain (1567-1635), the founder of Quebec. Partly because of the ferocity of the local tribes, partly because control of the territory was disputed by England, the missions took some time to become established. De Champlain attracted from France both Jesuits and Franciscans. They were joined from 1654 onwards by priests of the Society of Saint Sulpice who were not, at least technically, members of a religious order. The travels of such missionaries as the Jesuits Jacques Marquette (1637-75) and Eusebio Kino (1645-1711), or the Franciscan Junipero Serra (1713-84), were as much journeys of discovery as they were of evangelization. Their names have become part of the early history of the Americas.

The Jesuit 'reductions', situated within their Province of Paraguay (the area now falls partly in Paraguay, partly in Argentina and partly in Brazil) were a very different form of missionary activity to that of itinerant preaching. These were Christian townships, founded from 1610 onwards, which afforded places of safety to the indigenous people, the Guaraní, against the depredations

of Spanish and Portuguese settlers. They survived until the suppression of the Jesuits in Spanish and Portuguese dominions towards the end of the eighteenth century and, as townships, some continued on long afterwards.

Non-Catholic Missions in North America

The outreach of non-Roman Catholic missions was rather different. Although the earliest charter granted to an English company to colonize Virginia stressed the need to evangelize the indigenous population, the few clergy who went out there at the beginning of the seventeenth century were ministers, albeit of a Puritan persuasion, of the Church of England. The Pilgrim Fathers, however, arriving at Cape Cod in 1620, were Puritan 'separatists', mainly Congregationalist in Church polity, and it was they who formed the dominant religious tradition in British America for at least a couple of centuries.

Like the English Roman Catholics arriving in Maryland in 1632, or William Penn (1644-1718) establishing Pennsylvania for the Quakers in 1681, the primary purpose of the Pilgrims was not missionary activity but setting up townships where the settlers might freely practise their religion. Some of their ministers evangelized the native inhabitants living in, or near, the areas settled by the English, but their primary duty was to serve their own congregations. Even when the Anglican Society for the Propagation of the Gospel was founded in 1701 to work mainly in the American colonies, its primary objective was to serve the British overseas, and only secondarily to evangelize non-Christians subject to the British Crown.

The missionary journeys of the Roman Catholics were not common, at least in America (it was to be different three centuries later in Africa), among Protestant evangelists. In so far as they did so at all, the Protestants spread their faith outwards from established bases along the east coast (*map 2*). The same was true of the arrival of Dutch settlers in 1626 bringing the (Calvinist) Dutch Reformed Church, and the introduction of Lutheranism by Swedish colonists a dozen years later.

Churches similar to this, founded at Chiu Chiu Calama, northern Chile, in 1611, marked the evangelization of the Americas. A few survive, as do the names of the mission stations themselves, some of them now major cities: Santa Barbara, San Francisco, Los Angeles.

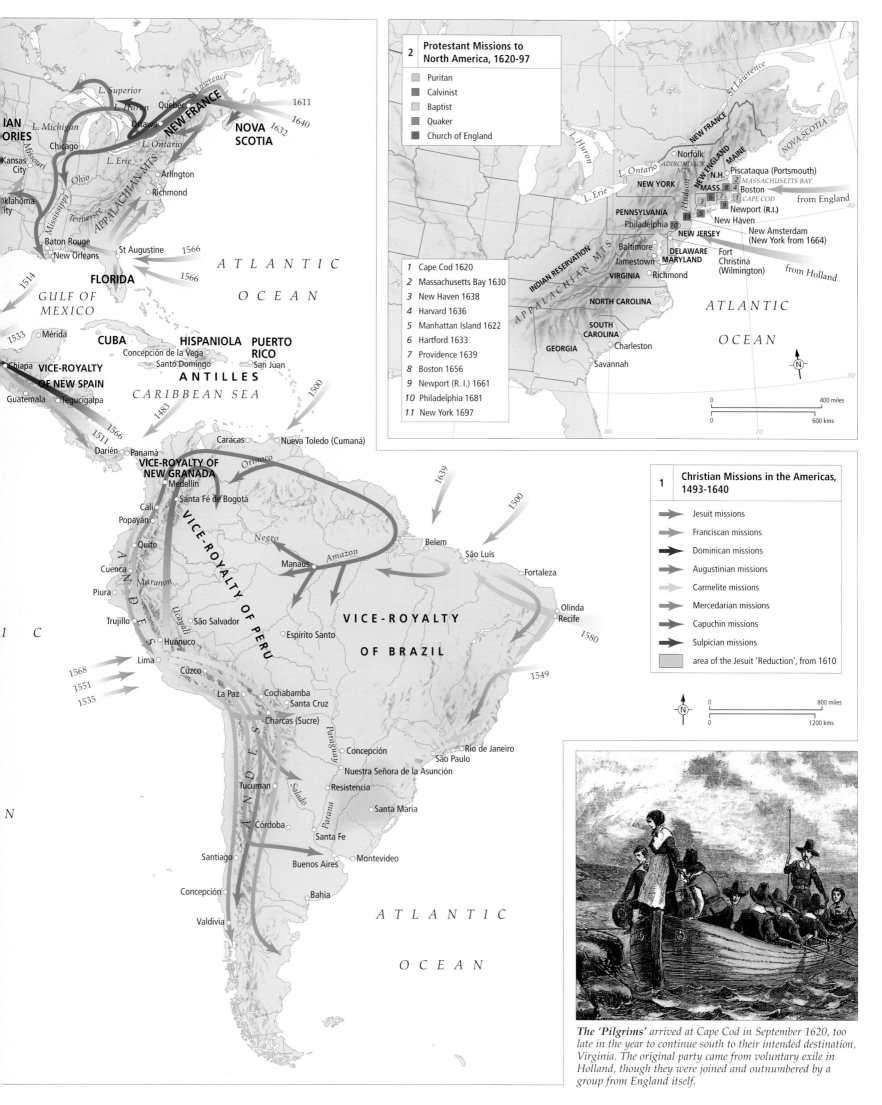

2 — Protestant Missions to North America, 1620-97

- Puritan
- Calvinist
- Baptist
- Quaker
- Church of England

1 Cape Cod 1620
2 Massachusetts Bay 1630
3 New Haven 1638
4 Harvard 1636
5 Manhattan Island 1622
6 Hartford 1633
7 Providence 1639
8 Boston 1656
9 Newport (R. I.) 1661
10 Philadelphia 1681
11 New York 1697

1 — Christian Missions in the Americas, 1493-1640

- Jesuit missions
- Franciscan missions
- Dominican missions
- Augustinian missions
- Carmelite missions
- Mercedarian missions
- Capuchin missions
- Sulpician missions
- area of the Jesuit 'Reduction', from 1610

The 'Pilgrims' arrived at Cape Cod in September 1620, too late in the year to continue south to their intended destination, Virginia. The original party came from voluntary exile in Holland, though they were joined and outnumbered by a group from England itself.

THE REFORMATION AND ITS AFTERMATH

Martin Luther (1483-1546)
by Lucas Cranach. For a time
the reformer was restrained, for
his own safety, in the Wartburg
castle, near Eisenach. While
there he began his translation of
the Bible into German: the New
Testament appeared in
September 1522.

A T THE BEGINNING of the sixteenth century the
Church in Europe was clearly in need of reform.
Earlier reform movements such as the Lollards in
England and the Hussites in Bohemia (*see* pp. 164-165)
had already drawn attention to corruption among
ecclesiastics, but in the end it was a particular incident
that gave rise to what is now called the Reformation.

In 1506 Pope Julius II laid the cornerstone of the new
basilica of St Peter's in Rome. To pay for its construction
he approved the sale of 'indulgences' (a pardon by the
Church for the punishment still due once a sin had been
forgiven). In 1517 the right to sell them was given to
Archbishop Albert of Mainz. Martin Luther (1483-1546),
an Augustinian monk and professor of theology at the
University of Wittenberg, objected to the claims made for
indulgences by Archbishop Albert's chief preacher,
Johann Tetzel. He drew up his 'Ninety-Five Theses'
attacking the abuses of indulgences, and on 31 October
1517 sent them to the Archbishop and other theologians.

The Theses attracted wide attention in Germany,
though the theological status of indulgences was already
a matter of debate. However, Luther had earlier
developed a theory of justification through faith alone
which was more obviously at odds with the received
form of the Catholic faith. In a disputation at Leipzig in
1519 he went on to deny the primacy of the pope and the
infallibility of ecumenical councils. In his *Address to the
Christian Nobility of the German Nation* (1520), he called
upon the German princes to reform the Church. By this
time he identified the papacy with the Antichrist. He was
excommunicated on 3 January 1521, and declared an
'outlaw' in the Empire by the Diet of Worms in May 1522.

Reform in Germany and the Holy Roman Empire

The Reform movement spread quickly in Germany. In
1526 the Diet of Speyer left it to the consciences of the

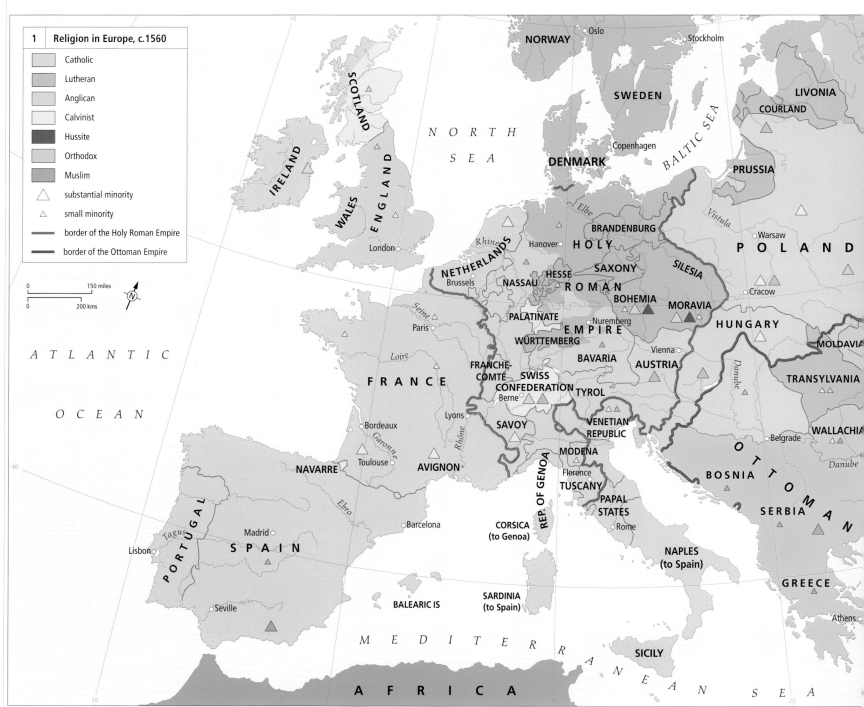

1   **Religion in Europe, c.1560**

- Catholic
- Lutheran
- Anglican
- Calvinist
- Hussite
- Orthodox
- Muslim
- △ substantial minority
- △ small minority
- —— border of the Holy Roman Empire
- —— border of the Ottoman Empire

0   150 miles
0   200 kms

The St Bartholomew's Day Massacre of Huguenots, 23-24 August 1572 (depicted in a contemporary woodcut) is usually blamed on the Queen Mother of France, Catherine de' Medici (1519-89). One of those to die was Gaspard de Coligny, the Protestant, and Catherine's great rival at court.

individual princes what they should do in their own territory, at least until a council of the Church could be called. In 1530 a statement of the Lutheran faith was presented to the Emperor Charles V at Augsburg. This 'Confession of Augsburg' remains the official Lutheran doctrinal profession.

The Emperor was naturally eager that religious unity should be re-established, and urged a reluctant pope to call a council. Pope Paul III agreed in 1536 to do so, though the council did not meet – at Trent – until 1545. The Emperor was also trying to bolster his own authority in Germany, something the Protestant princes resisted, and by now politics and religion were inextricably mixed. At the Peace of Augsburg (1555) it was agreed that the different states of the Empire should be either Catholic or Lutheran, whichever their princes decreed. Variations of Protestantism, such as Calvinism, were ignored (*see* pp. 160-61).

Calvinism and the Reformation in France

Though Jean Calvin (1509-64) was French, he worked mainly in Switzerland, particularly in Geneva where he was visited by the Scottish reformer John Knox (1513-72), who brought Calvin's form of Protestantism to Scotland. Calvin laid even more stress than Luther on the authority of Scripture, and while Luther subjected the Church to the State, Calvin did the opposite. The most distinctive doctrine of Calvinism, however, though not of Calvin himself, is its teaching on predestination, with the concomitant belief that the elect have certain knowledge of their eternal salvation.

In France, Protestantism developed along Calvinist lines – Calvin dedicated his defence of the Reformation, *The Institutes of the Christian Religion*, to the French King Francis I. The Huguenots, as the French Protestants were called (the origin of the name is uncertain), held their first synod at Paris in 1539 and their second at Poitiers in 1561. In between, their numbers had grown considerably and in January 1562,

they were guaranteed a measure of religious toleration. However, as in the Empire, the king wanted religious as well as political unity, and war broke out between Catholics and Protestants. One period of relative peace came to an end on the night of 23-24 August 1572 with the infamous St Bartholomew's Day Massacre of Huguenots in Paris and other large cities. The Protestant Henry IV of Navarre acceded to the throne in 1589, but the wars did not end until after his conversion to Catholicism in 1593.

At Nantes on 13 April 1598 Henry issued an edict which finally gave more or less equal rights to Huguenots, though they were still banned from certain cities, including Paris. They were also given subsidies, and allowed to garrison a number of towns throughout France. Toleration did not last, however. The Edict of Nantes was gradually whittled away to be finally revoked in 1685 by the Edict of Fontainebleau.

The Reformation in England

In England the Reformation was as much a matter of politics as of religion: Henry VIII rejecting papal authority in the matter of his divorce. Henry himself permitted few doctrinal changes. These were to come later and the fundamental formulary of the Church of England, the Thirty-Nine Articles, was only approved in 1563. The Articles are not so much a summary of the faith of the Church of England, as a series of statements rejecting what were regarded as corruptions of Catholic doctrine by the medieval Church, as well as rejecting supposed aberrations by Calvinists and others. The Thirty-Nine Articles are usually taken in conjunction with the Book of Common Prayer, the first version of which appeared in 1549. The version now in common use in England is that of 1662. The term 'Anglican' to describe the Church of England (and, until the end of the seventeenth century, the state Church in the whole of the British Isles) did not emerge until the 1630s.

CHRISTIANITY AND THE OTTOMAN EMPIRE

A saint of the East: the Maronite monk and hermit, Charbel Makhlouf (1828-1898) was born in northern Lebanon, and entered the monastery of Saint Maroun at Annaya in 1851. He was canonized by Pope Paul VI in October 1977.

THE OTTOMAN EMPIRE was a major threat to the hegemony of Christian Europe from the fourteenth to the seventeenth centuries (*see also* pp. 200-201). The origins of the Ottoman dynasty lie in northwestern Anatolia, though it is difficult to say why they suddenly emerged as such a powerful force. One theory proposes that it was because they were strategically well placed to attack the Christian Byzantine Empire, and therefore attracted Muslim fighters who wished to wage holy war against Christianity. They first drove the Byzantines from Anatolia – which they achieved by 1338 – and in 1354 occupied Gallipoli, their first base in Europe, and the one from which they launched their drive into southeastern Europe. In 1389 there occurred the decisive battle of Kosovo. The Serbian King Lazarus, who had been offering sturdy resistance to the Ottoman Turk advance, gathered an army of Albanians, Bosnians, Bulgars, Hungarians, Poles and even Mongols as well as Serbs. Although before the battle the Ottoman sultan, Murad I, was assassinated with a poisoned dagger, the Serbian coalition was decisively defeated, and Lazarus was executed.

The Fall of Constantinople

The greatest shock to Christian Europe came, however, with the fall of Constantinople to the Ottomans in 1453. Many Byzantine scholars fled westward, particularly to Italy, and made a substantial contribution to the Renaissance. Hungary fell after the battle of Mohács, just over one hundred miles south of Buda, when in 1526 the

Hungarian army was annihilated and the king killed. The Turkish army marched on to Vienna, placing the city under siege in 1529 and 1532: it was in part this threat which prevented the Emperor Charles V from giving full attention to the developing Reformation in his German territories. Vienna did not fall, which was something of a success for the Christian armies, but the first notable Christian victory was a sea battle at Lepanto (the Gulf of Corinth) on 7 October 1571. The victorious army was that of the Holy League, a coalition of the Papal States, Genoa, Venice and Spain, originally put together in 1511 by Pope Julius II. At Lepanto the Holy League forces were led by Don John of Austria.

The Decline of the Ottoman Empire

The victory, though hailed as a great triumph by the Christians (the Pope established the Feast of the Holy Rosary on 7 October to mark the event), in effect altered little. The Ottoman Turks were not forced to withdraw from any territory. The turning-point in this Christian–Muslim conflict was the victory over the Turks, once again besieging Vienna, by the Polish King John III Sobieski in 1683, who had already defeated them at Khotin in 1673 in defence of his homeland. The long decline of the Ottoman Empire then began, because of defeats in battle by Austrian and Russian forces, and because of internal weaknesses. (Hungary was recovered by the Habsburgs at the Treaty of Carlowitz in 1699.) Many of the territories within the vast Empire, which stretched into Africa and Asia as much as into Europe,

At the Battle of Lepanto a Christian naval force, commanded by Don John of Austria, of just over 200 galleys defeated a Turkish force of more than 270 galleys. This anonymous painting is in the National Maritime Museum, London.

Map legend:

Christianity and the Rise of the Ottomans

- Ottoman lands, 1326
- Ottoman conquests by 1451
- Ottoman conquests by 1481
- Ottoman conquests by 1520
- Ottoman conquests and areas of loose or temporary control after 1520

Orthodox church:
- major centres of the Orthodox church (patriarchates, autocephalus churches)
- exarchates and metropolitan sees
- archbishopric

Roman Catholic church:
- archbishopric
- bishopric
- destroyed
- ✕ Ottoman victory, with date
- ✕ Ottoman defeat, with date

were effectively self-governing and in time became autonomous: Greece in 1830, Serbia the following year and so on (see *map 2*). In the course of the nineteenth century they became fully independent.

By the mid-nineteenth century the European powers were exerting considerable influence on the Ottomans, partly because of their precarious financial state, and partly on behalf of the large numbers of Christians who lived under Turkish rule: the Armenians in particular had suffered persecution at the hands of the Turks. The final collapse of the Empire was precipitated after the government entered the First World War on the side of Germany.

Varieties of Christianity in the Ottoman Empire

The Christians ruled over by the Turks were not only the Orthodox and Roman Catholics in Europe, but also many Eastern-rite Christians in Asia Minor and North Africa (*see also* pp. 154-157). The communities survived, and *map 3* shows the distribution of their major episcopal sees.

Armenia was the first nation officially to become Christian, with the baptism in 303 CE of King Tiridates III and his court. Shortly afterwards the kingdom disappeared, divided between the Byzantines and the Persians. It has occasionally been re-established for short periods – there is now, of course, an independent Republic of Armenia. Armenian Christians are formally Monophysite, a stance adopted chiefly to distinguish themselves from their Byzantine rulers. The Catholicos of the Armenians has resided at the monastery of Echmiadzin since the fourth century, making Echmiadzin the oldest Christian monastic institution anywhere. Some Armenians united with Rome at the Council of Sis in 1307, and still survive as a separate Church, though 100,000 are thought to have died in massacres by the Turks at the end of the First World War.

The Syrians likewise did not accept the Council of Chalcedon of 451 and adopted a Monophysite understanding of the nature of Christ. An independent hierarchy, under the Patriarch of Antioch, emerged in the course of the sixth century. Again like the Armenians, a separate Church in communion with Rome was established in 1656, though not effectively until towards the end of the eighteenth century. It began at Aleppo, though the seat of the Catholic Patriarch is in Beirut, while that of the Syrian Orthodox Patriarch is now in Damascus. Again like the Armenians, the Syrians underwent considerable persecution in the death throes of the Ottoman Empire.

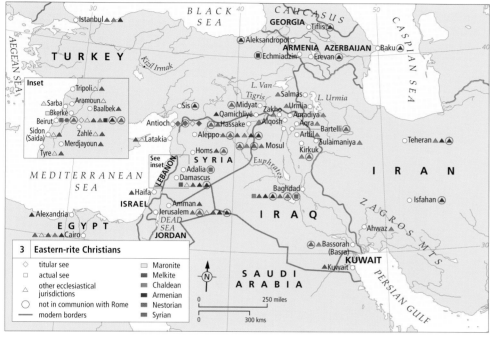

3 Eastern-rite Christians

◇ titular see
□ actual see
△ other ecclesiastical jurisdictions
○ not in communion with Rome
— modern borders
▨ Maronite
▦ Melkite
▨ Chaldean
■ Armenian
▨ Nestorian
▨ Syrian

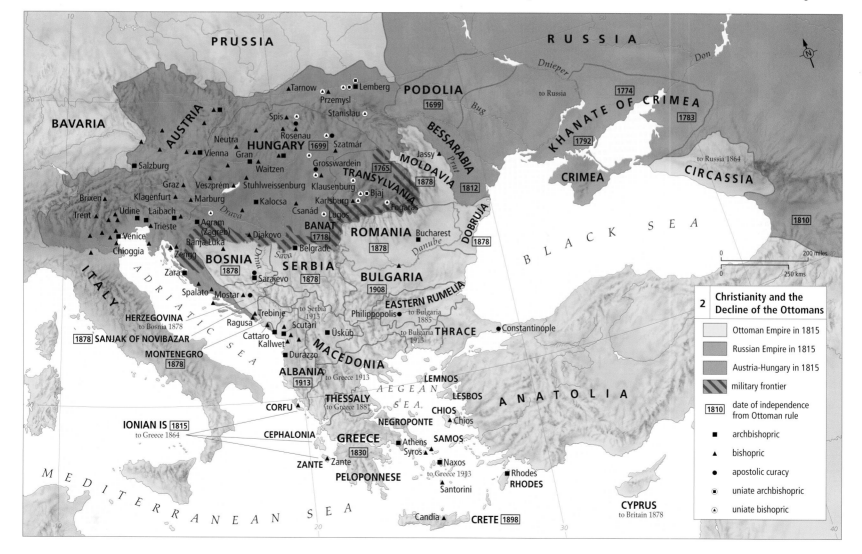

2 Christianity and the Decline of the Ottomans

☐ Ottoman Empire in 1815
▨ Russian Empire in 1815
▨ Austria-Hungary in 1815
▨ military frontier
1810 date of independence from Ottoman rule
■ archbishopric
▲ bishopric
● apostolic curacy
◉ uniate archbishopric
◉ uniate bishopric

POST-REFORMATION CHURCHES

John Wesley had a conversion experience in 1738 which launched him as an itinerant missionary to the poor of Britain and to found Methodism.

I N 1648 THE PEACE OF WESTPHALIA brought to an end the series of wars known as 'The Thirty Years' War', which had been fought for both political and religious motives. The fundamental cause was the decline of the Holy Roman Empire whose ruler had been, since 1440, a member of the House of Habsburg. That the Thirty Years' War was not simply religious is evident from the support for the Protestant King of Sweden, Gustavus Adolphus, by Cardinal Richelieu, effectively the ruler of Catholic France, against the Catholic forces of the Habsburgs. At the Peace, France emerged greatly strengthened, the Empire fatally weakened.

The most important religious outcome of the Peace was the acceptance of the formula *cuius regio, eius religio*, which had first formally been proclaimed a century earlier at the Peace of Augsburg (1555). As the formula neatly phrased it, citizens of a territory were expected to follow the religious creed of the ruler of that territory, though at Augsburg effectively this meant toleration for only Catholicism and Lutheranism: what determined whether someone was a Lutheran was his or her acceptance of the Augsburg Confession of 1530. At Westphalia Calvinists were added to the list of religions that might be tolerated: they were treated as if they had been included in the terms of the Confession. By 1648 some parts of the Empire which had initially adopted Lutheranism had been re-converted to Catholicism, through the efforts especially of the Jesuits.

Many other religious groups emerged in the post-Reformation period, on the whole too small in numbers to be represented on the map. There were various kinds of Anabaptists, for example, whose principle tenet was that they did not believe in infant baptism. Instead they accepted 'believer's baptism', that is to say the baptism of

1 Europe after the Peace of Westphalia, 1648

- Catholic
- Lutheran
- Anglican
- Calvinist
- Hussite
- Orthodox
- Muslim
- △ small minority
- △ substantial minority
- ▬ border of the Holy Roman Empire
- ▬ border of the Ottoman Empire

members of their community only when they had attained adulthood. Of these smaller groups perhaps the best known is the Mennonites, followers of the Dutch reformer Menno Simons (1496-1561), who became very influential in the Netherlands in the seventeenth and eighteenth centuries. Mennonite beliefs were adopted by John Smyth (c.1570-1612) who was ordained in the Church of England but whose radical views led him into exile in Amsterdam. There in 1609 he (re)baptized himself and established in Amsterdam what is acknowledged as the first Baptist congregation. In 1612 a group of Smyth's followers came to London, and from these came various forms of Baptist churches, some of which eventually embraced the Calvinism which Smyth himself had rejected.

England and America

In England Puritans, whose beliefs were influenced more by Calvinism than by the moderate Lutheranism adopted by the official Church of England, diverged into various small communities differing both in doctrine and in practice. Among the more significant were the Presbyterian churches – governed by presbyters, ministers and elders – and Congregationalist ones, in which each community of worshippers is, technically, self-governing. In 1620 these groups with their divergent church polities were exported to North America with the Pilgrim Fathers, so radical Protestantism was established in the New World long before mainstream Anglicanism.

Among the early Anglican missionaries to America were the Wesley brothers, Charles (1707-88) and John (1703-91). Methodism, which John Wesley founded, was at first a movement of spiritual renewal within the Church of England but gradually developed, both in Britain and America, into a separate institution. Nonetheless, both John and Charles are celebrated as saints within the Anglican Communion.

Challenges to Catholicism

Catholicism escaped some of the fissiparous tendencies of seventeenth- and eighteenth-century religion only by containing within itself some major doctrinal differences. The most important doctrinal challenge was that of Jansenism. Named after Cornelius Jansen (1585-1638), its protagonists embraced a deeply pessimistic view of free will which had something in common with Calvinism, and an excessive moral rigorism. It was prevalent particularly in France, northern Italy and the Netherlands (Jansen had been Bishop of Ypres), and was vigorously opposed by the Jesuits.

There even developed within Catholicism a form of *cuius regio, eius religio*, as rulers in, especially, France

(Gallicanism in the seventeenth century), Germany and Austria (Febronianism and Josephinism respectively in the eighteenth century) tried to claim a degree of independence for the Catholicism in their territories from the authority of the papacy.

Map 1 shows an area of Poland, including the Ukraine, as part Catholic, part Orthodox. The factors affecting religion in this region are complex and quite distinct from those in the rest of Europe. In the sixteenth century this region was largely Orthodox, but in 1595 the Metropolitan of Kiev and a number of other bishops by the Union of Brest-Litovsk accepted the authority of Rome. Over time many Ukrainian and – especially – Polish landowners adopted the Latin form of Catholicism, but a separate Church in communion with Rome survived, especially in the Ukraine, performing the liturgy according to the Byzantine, or Eastern, rite.

The Papal States

The Papal States were not greatly affected by the Wars of Religion. The states, ruled by the pope as a temporal sovereign and providing him and his court with a base from which to exercise his spiritual authority, go back to the time of the Emperor Constantine (d. 337) but are here shown at a period of their greatest extent (*map 2*), including the area around Avignon in France. Avignon was seized by the French in 1791, and in the invasion of Italy by the armies of Napoleon, the Papal States disappeared. They were, however, restored to the papacy in 1815 at the Congress of Vienna – with the exception of Avignon. In 1859 several of the provinces of the Papal States placed themselves under the sovereignty of Victor Emmanuel, King of Piedmont, who had effectively taken over the whole of the papal territories with the exception of Rome and its environs early in 1861. Rome was guarded by French troops, but when they were withdrawn in 1870 it, too, became part of the new Kingdom of Italy and the Papal States disappeared. The Vatican City State, the world's smallest sovereign state, was set up in 1929 as an enclave within Rome to serve as a residence for the papacy.

Benedict XII (pope 1334-42) began to build the papal palace at Avignon. His successor, Clement VI (d. 1352) built another one beside it – as well as buying the city as a whole and adding it to the papal states.

IMPERIAL EXPANSION AND COLONIAL MISSIONS

IN DECEMBER 1857, during an address to the University of Cambridge, the great missionary David Livingstone (1813-73) said 'I beg to draw your attention to Africa. I know that in a few years I shall be cut off in that country, which is now open. Do not let it be shut again! I go back to Africa to try to make an open path for commerce and for Christianity'. These words are often taken to epitomize the relationship between missionary activity and colonial trade. But the relationship was not as straightforward as it is sometimes portrayed. Livingstone had been in Africa sixteen years. He was deeply disturbed by the prevalence of the slave trade and believed that the best way to combat it was to improve the condition of Africans by opening their territory up to other forms of commerce (*see also* pp. 228-229).

Catholic Missions

The early missionary activity of the Catholic Church in the Americas is discussed in more detail earlier (*see* pp. 166-167). As missionaries constantly complained, the indigenous peoples of the New World were cruelly exploited by the colonial powers. Rome, however, found itself at a serious disadvantage because monarchs claimed authority to approve the appointment of bishops in their overseas possessions. One way the Vatican proposed to break the control of Spain and Portugal was to establish a special organization in Rome to oversee all the Church's missionary activity: the Congregation for the Propagation of the Faith (*de propaganda fide*) was set up in 1622. Apart from the development of an indigenous priesthood, the general rule that clergy from the colonial powers would serve in the colonial territories continued even when, particularly in the nineteenth century, new religious orders were founded with a specifically missionary vocation.

Reformation Chruches

The churches of the Reformation were rather slower to undertake missionary work, apart, that is, from the Moravian Brethren, who believed their purpose was precisely to evangelize non-Christian peoples. In 1732 they set up a community in the West Indies and, the following year, established one in Greenland. The non-Roman Catholic equivalent of the missionary orders were societies such as the Society for the Propagation of the Gospel founded in 1701. Most of these, however, came into being much later in the eighteenth or in the early nineteenth century: for example, the Methodist Missionary Society (1786), the Baptist equivalent (1792),

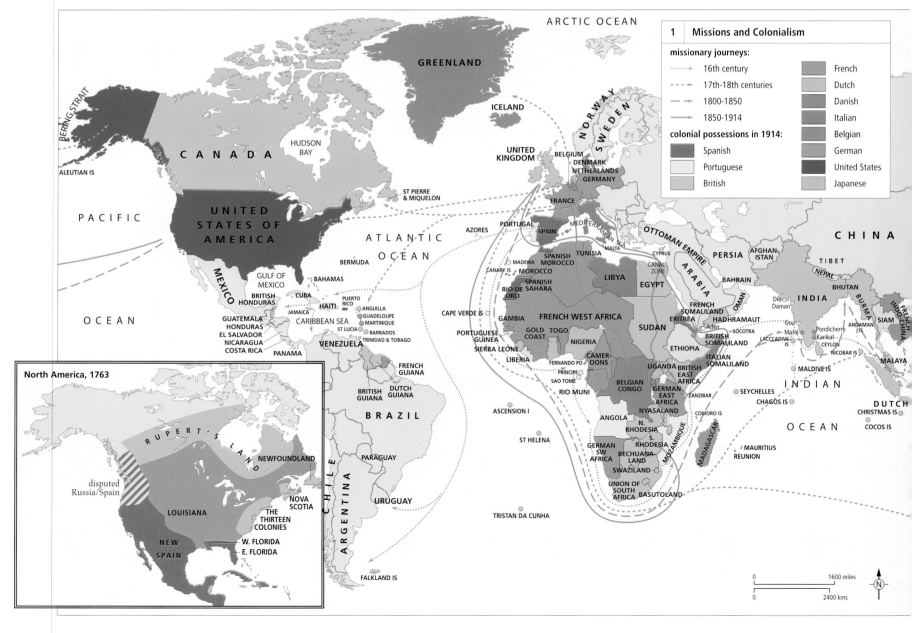

Missionaries at a service of baptism in the Congo, taken from a postcard published in London by the Baptist Missionary Society in 1907. The Belgian government made it increasingly difficult for non-Roman Catholic missionaries to work in the area.

2   **Missions in Africa c.1910**

Roman Catholic missions:

⊙   French

■   Dutch

▲   Belgian

◆   various nationalities

non-Roman Catholic missions:

●   Lutheran

■   Anglican

◆   Congregational

⬡   non-confessional

▽   centre of more than one non-Roman Catholic mission

△   other non-Roman Catholic missions

the Church Missionary Society (1799). This last was originally the Society for Missions in Africa and the East, and the first to send Church of England missionaries to Africa and to Asia. The Universities' Mission to Central Africa was founded as a response to the address by David Livingstone. That, too, was Anglican. The London Missionary Society, which sent its first missionaries to Tahiti in 1796, was a joint venture by Anglicans, Congregationalists, Presbyterians and Wesleyans.

Colonial Power and Missionary Activity

Missions to North America did generally go hand in hand with the expansion of the colonial powers in that region, including efforts by Russian traders to control much of the northwestern seaboard, leaving in their wake Russian Orthodox missions.

In India, however, missionaries were not welcomed by the East India Company. The Company, established in 1600, provided chaplains for their British employees, and had originally intended to spread Christianity among those with whom they did business, requiring chaplains to learn the local language. Very few did, and in the whole of the seventeenth century only one convert to the Church of England is recorded. In the eighteenth century, the Company was so disenchanted

with English clergy that it chose chaplains from Germany, and was disinclined to encourage evangelization, preferring to leave local religious traditions untouched.

The complex situation of missionaries is well illustrated by the story of the Christian Kingdom of the Congo (now the southwest region of the Congo and the adjacent Angola). The king was converted in 1491 after a Portuguese expedition had entered his territory, and the kingdom came under Portuguese influence. Though some indigenous priests were ordained, most evangelization was entrusted to Portuguese missionaries. In an attempt to wrest the Church from Portuguese exploitation, and the country from the slave trade, in 1645 Franciscans from Italy took over responsibility for the region. Missionary activity died away at the end of the eighteenth century, and when it revived there were Protestant missionaries from a number of denominations as well as Catholic ones. In 1885 the Belgian Congo was established: it was annexed to Belgium itself in 1908. By this time, however, there was a clear link between the church and the colonial power. Catholic missionaries, all from Belgium, were granted extensive privileges, which were denied to non-Catholic ones. They were granted equality with Catholics only in 1946.

CHRISTIAN TRADITIONS, SCIENCE AND SECULARISM

I N MODERN TIMES, Christianity has faced a concerted challenge from scientific and secular ideologies. These largely rely on the principle that all truth must be ultimately based on scientifically demonstrable premises, or on what can be directly known through the experience of our senses. One of the earliest exponents of this rationalist position is the French philosopher René Descartes (1596-1650). (Descartes spent much of his time in the Netherlands, and, as for the other figures on *map 1*, is located at the place where he can be said to have exercised most influence). Descartes did not deny the existence of God, indeed he thought he could prove he existed, but he certainly undermined Christian belief in Revelation. The same is true of deism, which developed particularly in England: Lord Herbert of Cherbury (1582-1648) was, if not himself the first deist, then the first to systematize it. The classical exposition of deism, however, is *Christianity not Mysterious* by the

Irishman John Toland (1670-1722). It was while he was at Oxford that, in 1696, he produced his book which argued that neither God, nor Revelation, was beyond human reason. Anthony Collins (1676-1729) in *A Discourse on Freethinking* (1713) went on to insist that only freedom to think for oneself was necessary to discover truth, and that the Bible was an unreliable guide. It was about this time that modern Freemasonry began in England, and its adherents generally held to, and helped propagate, deist ideas. As the title of Collins's book indicates, the line between deism and free thought is a slight one. Deists held on to a notion of God even if, for some of them, God could not or would not intervene in his creation. Free thinkers, on the other hand, expressed a scepticism even about the existence of God, many drawing their inspiration from Michel de Montaigne (1533-92), though Montaigne himself lived and died in submission to the Catholic Church.

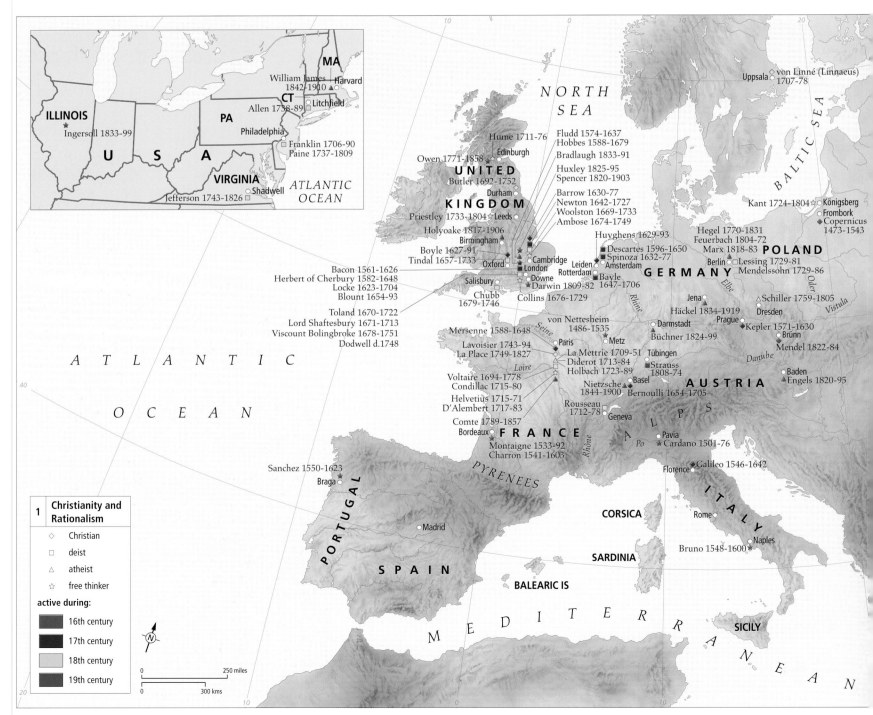

Galileo Galilei in a drawing by Ottavio Mario Leoni. Though most remembered for his clash with the Church over his advocacy of Copernican cosmology, Galileo also developed important laws of motion which prepared the way for Newton's theories.

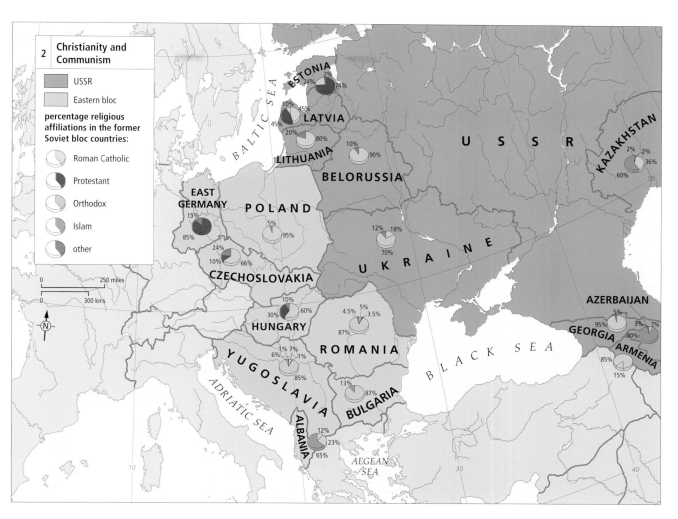

2 Christianity and Communism

USSR

Eastern bloc

percentage religious affiliations in the former Soviet bloc countries:

Roman Catholic

Protestant

Orthodox

Islam

other

Science and Christianity

Those described as atheists denied, either implicitly or explicitly, the existence of God. There are some scientists and philosophers, however, whose researches might have led them away from conventional Christian belief, but who nonetheless held firm to it, and in some instances combatted those who rejected it. One who did not reject his faith, despite much provocation, is Galileo (1564-1642). He was persecuted by the Inquisition for his belief that the world went round the sun rather than vice versa – though his chief crime was to draw attention to the way in which this doctrine, as formulated by the Polish priest Nicolaus Copernicus (1473-1543), apparently contradicted Scripture. The story of Galileo has become something of a *cause célèbre* in the history of conflict between religion and science. Others, such as the botanist Linnaeus (1707-78), the son of a Swedish pastor, or the geneticist Gregor Mendel (1822-84), an Augustinian abbot in Austria, found little difficulty in allying their faith with their scientific researches or, in the case of Mersenne for example, with their philosophy.

Communism and Christianity

The philosophy of Karl Marx (1818-83), however, presented the greatest challenge to Christian belief, not so much because of Marx himself who, though he elaborated an atheist philosophy, was comparatively sympathetic to the role of religion in society. It was Marx's thinking which, at least in theory, underpinned the Communist regime established in Russia following the Revolution of 1917, and the Soviet Union after its creation in 1922. *Map 2* shows the approximate percentages of religious affiliations under Communism (though such statistics should be viewed with caution).

In Russia itself toleration of the Orthodox Church varied according to political need. Christian or Islamic communities in other territories within the USSR suffered persecution. In 1946, for example, Ukrainian Catholics, who followed a rite similar to that of the Orthodox, were forcibly incorporated into Russian

The church at Nova Huta was constructed by Polish workers despite government opposition after the Communist authorities had built a town for 100,000 people without a church. It was consecrated in 1977 by Cardinal Wojtyla (later Pope John Paul II).

Orthodoxy. Attempts to disentangle them since the collapse of the USSR have heightened tension in the newly-independent Ukraine, and soured relations between the papacy and the Moscow patriarchate.

The Eastern Bloc

In countries subject to Communist regimes after the Second World War, those behind 'the Iron Curtain', treatment of Christianity varied. After initial attempts at suppression, the regime in Poland was forced to come to an accommodation with the Roman Catholic Church, whereas in Albania religion was proscribed and all places of worship closed down. In Hungary and Czechoslovakia 'peace movements' were formed among the clergy to foster a compromise between them and the State which, again, drove a wedge between local Christians and the wider Church. Christian groups – Catholics in Poland and Lutherans in East Germany for instance – played an active part in ending the Communist domination of their countries.

CHRISTIANITIES IN SOUTH AMERICA

WHILE CATHOLICISM and Protestantism are the predominant 'world religions' in South America, there is a tremendous diversity of ways in which both have been locally expressed, indigenized, or transformed by native and incoming populations to produce a kaleidoscope of spiritualities (*map 1*). The most spectacular diversity can be found in Brazil, although what is said of Brazil is generally true for the rest of South America.

Catholicism
There is a widely-recognized, although tenuous, distinction in Latin America and Brazil between the 'official' and the 'popular' expressions of Catholicism. 'Official' Catholicism includes pre-Vatican II conservatism which is typically associated with elite families and established wealth; progressive traditions of spiritual renewal such as the Charismatic Revival movement (as in the current popularity of Father Marcello Rossi whose televised masses attract millions of followers); and the post-Vatican II 'peoples' church movement', associated with political and economic reforms, such as the Ecclesiastical Base Communities (CEBS), and other movements that take their inspiration from liberation theology.

'Popular Catholicism' has numerous local expressions, such as devotion to particular patron saints. In Brazil, 'Our Lady of the Blessed Apparition' is officially the patron saint of the country, centred on Rio. 'Godfather' Padre Cicero, a nineteenth-century priest who died after expulsion from the church because he advocated the legitimacy of popular Catholic beliefs of northeast Brazil attracts many followers on yearly pilgrimages to his shrine in Juazeiro, Ceará. Another popular saint of the northeast is 'Our Lady of Sorrows', who expresses suffering and hope for salvation. Saint Benedict is the patron saint of various, predominantly white, towns but also of black mulattoes in general. 'There is not one town, city, profession, or ethnic group' anthropologist Carlos Brandao has written, 'that does not have its patron saint.' Rubber-gatherers of the Amazon forest have sanctified Our Lady into the image of the 'Queen of the Forest'.

Protestant Christianity
The many forms of Protestant Christianity in South America may be grouped into four categories: firstly, Protestant denominations of relatively recent immigrant origin, such as the Lutherans and Episcopalians – by the mid-twentieth century, Lutheranism was the largest Protestant denomination in Brazil brought by German migrants in the nineteenth century, mainly in the south; secondly, long-established Protestant denominations, such as Presbyterian, Methodist and Congregationalist churches; thirdly, other denominations such as Baptists, Adventists and Mormons (*see* pp. 180-181); and finally, Pentecostal and Neopentecostal movements in Brazil, Argentina and Uruguay which have rapidly expanded in recent years (*see* pp. 182-183). It is a commonplace that the Neopentecostal movement has expanded to the detriment of the Catholic majority in Brazil, but it should be remembered that Brazil still has over 120 million Catholics and only 17 million who declare themselves to be Pentecostal or Neopentecostal.

Spiritualism, African and Oriental-derived Religions
Spiritualism was introduced into Brazil in the early twentieth century, based on the French Spiritualist Alain Kardec's doctrine, and largely developed from the 1940s by the prolific medium Chico Xavier, from Minas Gerais. Today, three tendencies characterize the Spiritualist tradition: popular classes seek new syntheses with

African-derived religions, while the middle class are divided between a search for more secular alternatives for the expression of the doctrine (as in parapsychology) or with the New Age and 'neo-esoteric' movements. Today, over two million Brazilians declare themselves to be Spiritualists in Brazil – the third largest religion after Catholicism and Evangelical Protestantism.

Candomblé and Umbanda are the most important African-derived religions in Brazil, and both are widespread but found predominantly in the state of Bahia and the south. Brazil has the second largest population of African descendants in the world. In Colombia, Surinam and the Guyanas, other local, African-derived religions are found, such as the *obeah* (a version of voudoun in the Guyanas).

Candomblé derives from the religions of Yoruba and Bantu-speaking peoples of of West Africa (*see also* pp. 224–225). It developed primarily as a religion of slave resistance and to preserve African traditions, spreading throughout the northeast and south in local variations such as *Xango* (Pernambuco), *Tambor de Mina* (Maranhão), and *Batuque* (Rio Grande do Sul). Both Candomblé and Umbanda rituals are held in *terreiros* or local centres of dance and sacrifice.

Christ the Redeemer, erected on Corcovado mountain in 1931. The statue, with its beckoning arms, embracing the Brazilian city of Rio de Janeiro, has come to symbolize the multitude of variations of Christianity which the nation hosts.

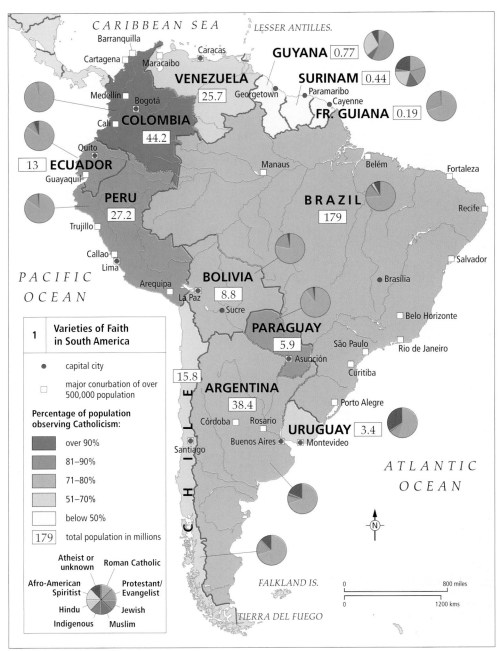

Umbanda emerged at the beginning of the twentieth century in Rio de Janeiro as a synthesis of the old Bantu and *caboclo* (mixed Indian/White) spirits, Candomblé and Kardecist Spiritualism. It spread rapidly throughout Brazil and is considered *par excellence* a 'Brazilian religion' which unites Catholic saints, African and indigenous spirits. In contrast to Umbanda's synthesis of the religiosities of the three main races in Brazil (white, black and Indian), Candomblé for a long time maintained its more genuine African-ness, although recently it has attracted adherents from the non-African middle classes.

Japanese migrants in southern Brazil and Peru introduced new religious movements such as the Soka-gakkai (a form of lay Buddhism), the Messianic Church, and others which maintain strong connections to mother churches in Japan. There is also a large contingent of 'Pure Earth' Buddhists of different ethnic origins found mainly in São Paulo. Other oriental religions include the Bahá'i, Hare Krishna and Sufis, while the immigrant South Asian population of Guyana is largely Hindu.

Indigenous Religious Traditions

Contemporary indigenous religious traditions cannot be easily described. One can speak of geographic areas inhabited by peoples of several different language families who share a common tradition (*map 2*), such as the generalized belief and cult of the *Yurupary*, sacred ancestral flutes and trumpets that are found among many indigenous peoples of the Amazon basin, or the Ture traditions of northeast Brazil, inhabited by indigenous peoples of mixed descent, which involves a cult to the *encantados* (enchanted spirits) the ingestion of psychoactive substances by shamans, and a mixture of indigenous and Afro-Brazilian beliefs. There is also the Kwarup ceremony to commemorate the dead among the indigenous peoples of the upper Xingu in central Brazil. Sometimes it is possible to clearly associate one people with a distinct religious tradition, such as the Guaraní of southern Brazil, Paraguay and Argentina, who share myths and rituals related to an eschatological utopia called the 'Land Without Evil.' From Ecuador to Bolivia, commonalities among indigenous traditions of the highlands include dualism as an underlying cosmological principle, worship of ancient mountain deities and pilgrimages to ancient places of worship. Celestial deities have retained a great deal of importance in the Andes, as has the fertility goddess Pachamama. These deities have often blended with Catholic deities and saints. In the central Andes, the ancient Inca sun cult, Inti Raymi, is celebrated more as a tourist attraction, although millennial beliefs in the return of the Inca king, Inkarri, are widespread as are dances of the conquest, such as the scissors dance among the Hatun Soras of the central Andes. Among Carib-speaking peoples of the border of Brazil and the Guyanas, there is the widespread 'Hallelujah' tradition which began as a prophetic movement in the nineteenth century, combining shamanism with Anglicanism. Today this church is officially recognized, and it is often found in conjunction with a tradition of assault sorcery called *kanaima*. Shamanism is a key feature in nearly all indigenous religious traditions of South America. In numerous cases, shamanism developed into prophetic movements as resistance to the advance of colonialism, although today many native peoples have turned to evangelical Protestantism or Pentecostalism as a way to salvation and shaping new identities in the context of rapid changes.

Ayahuasca, Environmentalism, and the 'Religion-less'

Originally an element of indigenous religions of the Peruvian and Colombian Amazon, the psychoactive (vision-producing) vine called *ayahuasca* (*Banisteriopsis caapi*) was used in ritual dances and shamanism. Peruvian mestizo herbalists, called *vegetalistas*, also knew of the vine's healing powers. In the early twentieth century,

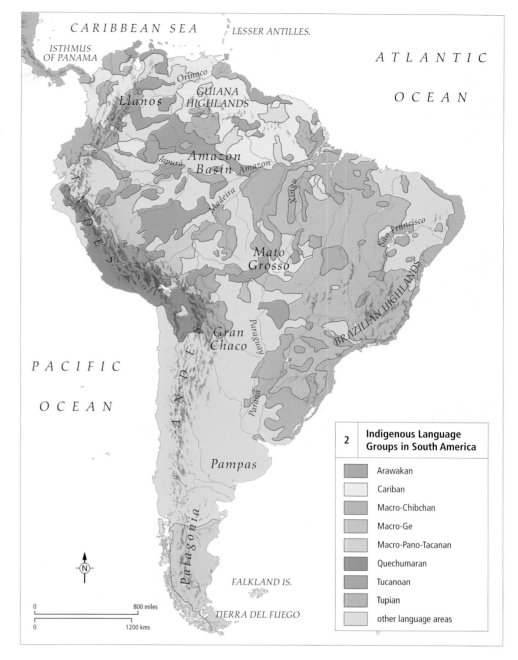

2 Indigenous Language Groups in South America

- Arawakan
- Cariban
- Macro-Chibchan
- Macro-Ge
- Macro-Pano-Tacanan
- Quechumaran
- Tucanoan
- Tupian
- other language areas

during the rubber boom, Afro-Brazilian migrants from the northeast went to the western Amazon and came into contact with these *vegetalistas*, developing a series of prophetic movements, the first being called Santo Daime, the second the 'Little Boat' and the third the *Uniao do Vegetal* (UDV) – all of them originating in Acre state. These movements mixed various traditions – indigenous shamanism, Umbanda, Spiritualism, Tambor de Mina, and popular Catholicism. In the 1960s, the hippies became attracted to the Daime colonies and soon ayahuascan religions found their way to centres such as Rio de Janeiro, São Paulo and Manaus, while tourists often took the religions home – the *ayahuascan* religion coming to be associated with the new spiritual consciousness of younger generations in developed countries, whilst also attracting followers of Eastern religions, psychoanalysts and the New Age generation.

Finally, spiritually-based environmentalist movements such as Deep Ecology and the Gaia Hypothesis have attracted the students of the large cities in southern Brazil, where there has also been an increase in recent years of what some scholars call the 'religion-less' – youth with no religious affiliation.

A ritual dance by natives of the Xingu in western Amazonia displays the use of masks, headdresses and body-paint to invoke local spirits. Increasingly, these indigenous cultures are adapting their traditional iconographies and practices to accommodate tourism and quasi-Christian ideas.

THE MORMONS AND THE CHURCH OF LATTER-DAY SAINTS

THE CHURCH of Jesus Christ of Latter-Day Saints (LDS) was organized in 1830 by Joseph Smith (1805–1844), Junior. Viewed as a prophet by believers, the charismatic Smith claimed to have been given authority by the angel Moroni to restore the primitive Christian church which he claimed had been lost due to apostasy. Smith also 'translated' *The Book of Mormon: Another Testament of Jesus Christ* which believers accept as a book of scripture, from which the term 'Mormon' came to be applied to the church. The new faith grew rapidly, first relocating from Palmyra, New York State, to Ohio, and then to Missouri under the direction of Smith (*map 1*). The abolitionist views of the nascent group led to hostility with settlers from the South, and they were driven from Missouri, establishing an enclave at Nauvoo, Illinois in 1839. Rapid growth of the community to some 12,000 inhabitants, and their resultant dominance of local politics, culminated in mob violence against church members and the murder of Smith in 1845.

The Move West

Brigham Young (1801–1877) directed the exodus of Mormons from Nauvoo in the winter of 1846, establishing a new settlement at Winter Quarters, Nebraska (today's Florence, now a suburb of Omaha) from where they began their odyssey to Wasatch Osasis in the Great Salt Lake Valley in 1847. Until his death in 1877, Young organized the settlement of suitable sites, stretching from Canada to northern Mexico, as Church members from other parts of North America, Europe, and even the Pacific Islands were encouraged to 'gather' with the body of the Church to establish communities across the western United States. Consequently, Salt Lake City and Utah became the focus of the largest concentration of Mormons in the United States. By the end of the nineteenth century, LDS Church membership had increased to 283,000, with over 80 per cent of members concentrated in Utah

1	The Mormon Trail
→	movements of the Mormons

Impressive Mormon temples such as this at Nukualofa, Tonga, dominate many of the Pacific islands, which Mormon missionaries first visited in the nineteenth century.

2	Global Growth of LDS Membership, 1989–2004

Percentage growth of the LDS Church, 1989–2004

- over 150%
- 101–150%
- 51–100%
- 26–50%
- 10–25%
- less than 10%
- ● large LDS temple
- ● small LDS temple
- 🏛 countries with more than 10% population in LDS

and adjacent areas of Idaho, Wyoming, Nevada and Arizona. By 1950, membership had grown to 1,111,000, primarily as a result of a high rate of natural family increase: as late as 1960, baptism of young children of members accounted for 60 per cent of Church increase. The last decades of the twentieth century and the first years of the twenty-first witnessed a dramatic increase in the numbers of new members (*map 2*). By 1997, there were ten million members worldwide: annual growth from natural increase fell below 20 per cent, while over 80 per cent represented converts. There were 13 million members of the LDS Church at the end of 2006 and, while the intermountain states still have the highest concentration of members, a new geography of Church membership emerged.

Recent Growth and Membership

The state of Utah still has the highest proportion of Mormons of any political unit worldwide, with 1,720,000 members – over 70 per cent of the state's inhabitants. Unlike a century earlier, however, this now represents only a fraction of total membership. Conversion surged in the USA in the last few decades, swelling membership to 5,691,000 by the end of 2005 (*map 3*). Growth in California (761,763 members) has given it the second largest number of Mormons in the US, but even more rapid growth in Mexico (980,000), Brazil (897,000), the Philippines (537,000), Chile (535,000), Colombia (417,000), and Peru (402,230) since 1980 put them ahead of any other single state in the United States. Latin American countries combined now have the second largest number of members after the USA.

While current LDS membership is concentrated in North and South America, members are found in the

majority of countries of the world, often reflecting missionary activity that began shortly after the organization of the Church. The Pacific Island states of Tonga (43 per cent Mormon), Samoa (36 per cent Mormon) and American Samoa (24 per cent Mormon) were all the focus of journeys by Mormon missionaries in the late nineteenth century. European countries, although not having as great a concentration of LDS Church members today, were the focus of Mormon missionaries even earlier. Mormon converts from the United Kingdom and Scandinavia were an important part of the Mormon settlement of the West, but membership is only growing slowly in Western Europe today. The Church has expanded into former communist countries of Eastern Europe, the former Soviet Union and Africa more recently, which helps explain the rapid growth rates found in those countries, but total membership remains small compared to membership in countries of the western hemisphere. Although membership in these areas increases, for the foreseeable future the largest increase in total membership will still be in the Americas and the Philippines, where the greatest numbers are currently found. Annual birth rates and convert numbers in these areas also dictate that the greatest change in LDS membership in the last few decades – the emergence of non-US members as the majority of Church membership – will continue to magnify the transformation of the Church of Jesus Christ of Latter-Day Saints from a quintessential nineteenth-century American phenomenon into a global religious organization of the twenty-first century.

Temple Square in Salt Lake City, Utah, forms the inspirational heart of the Church Jesus Christ of Latter-Day Saints. Occupying several city blocks, the towering six-spired granite edifice was completed in 1892, on a site chosen by Brigham Young in 1847. Although the basilica is not open to non-Church members, along with its adjacent domed tabernacle and enormous visitor centres, the complex attracts over 4 million pilgrims and tourists every year.

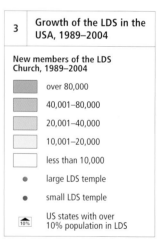

3	Growth of the LDS in the USA, 1989–2004

New members of the LDS Church, 1989–2004

- over 80,000
- 40,001–80,000
- 20,001–40,000
- 10,001–20,000
- less than 10,000
- ● large LDS temple
- ● small LDS temple
- US states with over 10% population in LDS

CHRISTIAN RENEWALISM

CHRISTIAN 'RENEWALISM' is a term that applies to Pentecostal and Charismatic Christian movements. Pentecostalism may be traced to a gathering of post-Resurrection followers of Jesus, upon whom the Holy Spirit descended while they were observing the Jewish holy day of Pentecost. This birth-day of the Church enabled Christians of diverse origins and languages to speak in 'other languages, as the Spirit gave them ability.' Ecstatic 'speaking in tongues', or *glossolalia*, is traced back to this story in *Acts 1-2*. The Charismatic tradition cites its precedents with less precision.

Pentecostalism and the Charismatics

Pentecostalism emphasizes gifts of the Spirit and joyfully expressive congregational worship. Pentecostals founded various denominations once this form of spirituality began to spread, beginning in 1906 with the Azusa Street Revival in Los Angeles, when people spoke in tongues, experienced healing and prophesied. The Assemblies of God and the Church of God in Christ are among the main US Pentecostal denominations that have grown and thrived to the present. There are overlapping links with the Gospel tradition among the African-American chapels of the Caribbean and the South, and also with Appalachian serpent rituals in the east-montaine heartland.

Charismatic Christians are a more diverse range of believers who experience gifts of the Holy Spirit and can belong to any denomination. They may confess to having charismatic experiences, may speak in tongues, and they may claim to be Pentecostalists generically. Many mainstream Christian denominations have parishes in which Charismatic members gather to bear witness to the Spirit's workings in deeply satisfying ways, but generally without the more emphatic ecstatic practices of denominational Pentecostalists.

Pentecostal teachings spread rapidly around the world a century ago: to Norway in 1907 and then throughout Scandinavia; to England at the same time and then to Welsh miners; to Germany (1907) and Italy (1908); to Brazil in 1910; and by the 1920s to Russia, Romania and Bulgaria. Western missionaries were key to Pentecostalism's global spread. India had Pentecostals as early as 1907 (although the movement only grew widely in the 1940s). China received Western Pentecostal missionaries in 1908, Japan in 1913 and Indonesia by the 1920s. South Africa saw strong development of Pentecostalism from 1908, and sub-Saharan Africa by the 1920s, where growth has been strongest.

There have been a great variety of influential leaders and organizations in the development of Pentecostal denominations and movements. Pentecostals have been diverse, independent and entrepreneurial from the beginning. The great television healer Oral Roberts reached millions; he influenced a wealthy businessman to establish the Full Gospel Business Men's Fellowship, which sponsored popular meetings in hotels across America.

Renewalist congregational centres in South America may be enormously impressive or, as here in Florianópolis, Brazil, modestly sited on a commercial block, sandwiched between a motor repair shop and a nightclub.

Renewalism in the Developing World

Pentecostalism appeals greatly to poor, disenfranchised and marginalized people, who then carry it enthusiastically to others, often inspiring hope and confidence in both eternal salvation and worldly success. Since the 1970s, Renewalist movements, beliefs and practices have grown exponentially in the developing world (*map 1*), although here increasingly Charismatics outnumber Pentecostalists.

South America has been one of the most prominent regions for 'liberation theology' (*map 2*). An Argentine theologian once said: 'Liberation theology opted for the poor, and the poor opted for Pentecostalism.' Huge numbers of nominal rural Catholics in Latin America have converted to Pentecostalism (*see also* pp.178-179).

Charismatic and Pentecostal Christians often draw on animistic and spiritist traditions and practices, with which the Renewalist teachings often interact positively. In African societies, multiple spirits are believed to exist and have effects on people, sometimes in negative ways. Jesus exorcized demons and evil spirits, as recorded in the Gospels. Renewalist beliefs and practices are thus seen to be capable of helping African adherents to combat evil spirits in their lives.

Even though Christian Renewalism accounts for one quarter of the world's Christians (c. 500 million out of 2 billion) it is still quite young compared to longer-established and relatively stable mainstream Christian denominations. Although Renewalists generally are sincerely devoted to living moral and upright lives, and to helping others, there have been dark sides as well.

Critical Reaction

One problem has been a widespread neglect of critical discourses and a distrust of Biblical scholars and theologians. Renewalism has also experienced sexual and financial scandals – many leaders have become enormously wealthy – since its beginnings in America. There is a cult of personality that permits its leaders to be regarded as perfect humans who can do no wrong. Traditionally there has been little accountability, but some improvements are being made to oversee independent churches and clergy. Another dark side is an ongoing tendency to overlook dishonest practices of Charismatic leaders. Consequently, in recent years, the Charismatic tradition, most prominently in the USA, has provoked a renewed and politically-charged atheist debate.

Much of the appeal of Renewalist religion lies in the participation in joyous communal worship, frequently demonstrated in spontaneous dance and liberated singing, conditions which foster more transcendent acts such as 'speaking in tongues'.

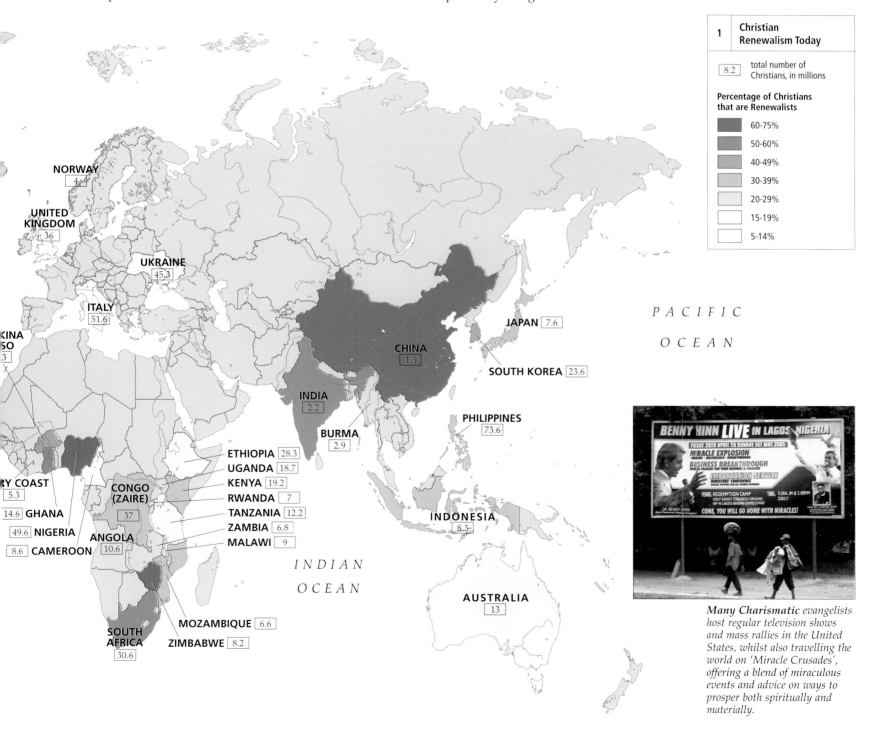

1	Christian Renewalism Today

8.2 = total number of Christians, in millions

Percentage of Christians that are Renewalists

- 60-75%
- 50-60%
- 40-49%
- 30-39%
- 20-29%
- 15-19%
- 5-14%

NORWAY 4
UNITED KINGDOM 36
UKRAINE 45,3
ITALY 51.6
KINA SO 3
JAPAN 7.6
CHINA 1.3
SOUTH KOREA 23.6
INDIA 2.2
BURMA 2.9
PHILIPPINES 73.6
ETHIOPIA 28.3
UGANDA 18.7
KENYA 19.2
RWANDA 7
TANZANIA 12.2
ZAMBIA 6.8
MALAWI 9
RY COAST 5.3
CONGO (ZAIRE) 37
GHANA 14.6
NIGERIA 49.6
CAMEROON 8.6
ANGOLA 10.6
INDONESIA 8.3
AUSTRALIA 13
MOZAMBIQUE 6.6
SOUTH AFRICA 30.6
ZIMBABWE 8.2

PACIFIC OCEAN

INDIAN OCEAN

Many Charismatic evangelists host regular television shows and mass rallies in the United States, whilst also travelling the world on 'Miracle Crusades', offering a blend of miraculous events and advice on ways to prosper both spiritually and materially.

CHRISTIANITY TODAY

A priest of an Eastern rite (Orthodox) Church distributes blessed bread to his congregation after the celebration of the divine liturgy. It is given to all, even those who have not received communion.

THERE ARE various regions of the world where Christianity has flourished, even if it has faded greatly in Western Europe. The demographic centre of gravity has now moved to the South, notably to Subsaharan Africa, Latin America and the Pacific.

North America
Following its renewed vigour in the nineteenth century, the American scene remains vibrant. New movements, such as Mormonism and Christian Science, have given a distinctively American complexion to the tradition to which they lay claim. Modern Christianity in America has characteristics which make it different from that in Europe. Certain forms of Protestantism are much stronger there: Unitarianism (especially in New England), Baptism (in the South), Methodism (in the East and among African Americans), Congregationalism and new religions ultimately springing from the Protestant milieu. These forms are intermingled within the whole of the population. Canada has a more conservative bent, and while in the USA Catholicism was not so much concentrated (save in Louisiana and Maryland), in Canada there is an overwhelmingly Catholic province, Quebec. Especially in the last decades of the twentieth century, however, the great influence of Mexican, Cuban and other Latinos has given Catholicism an Hispanic aspect, especially in the southwest and Florida. Eastern Orthodoxy is weaker in numbers, save perhaps in New York, with a growing Russian community. In California Korean and Chinese evangelicals are prominent. Many Americans blend various beliefs with Christian themes into the New Age, which tends to be individualistic.

Though the US constitution lays down a separation between Church and State, politics is considerably influenced by Christian forces. Questions of abortion and homosexuality, for instance, have led to an alliance of conservative views among Catholics and some right-wing Protestant organizations. On the other hand, liberal Christian denominations have been forward in recognizing women pastors and have become sharper on ethical issues than on doctrinal ones. The churches also played a powerful role in the civil rights struggle in the 1960s.

Eastern Europe and Elsewhere
The collapse of the Soviet Union and the freeing of satellite states in Eastern Europe and elsewhere, together with a partial breakup of the Soviet empire, has led to a revival of Christianity (together with Judaism, Islam and other religions; *map 1*). The Pope with his visits to Poland involved backing the Solidarity Movement and played a vital role in the demise of the Soviet Union. Russian President, Boris Yeltsin, with his sometimes heroic and sometimes wavering leadership helped restore Orthodoxy to its prominent position in the new Russia. In Poland and elsewhere in Eastern Europe Catholicism is resurgent and new religions have also been active in the region.

In Central and South America, there are new religions often blending African themes and Christianity; Liberal Theology; and new evangelical and pentecostal missions, primarily from the North. Catholicism has undergone a transformation through the work of activist priests

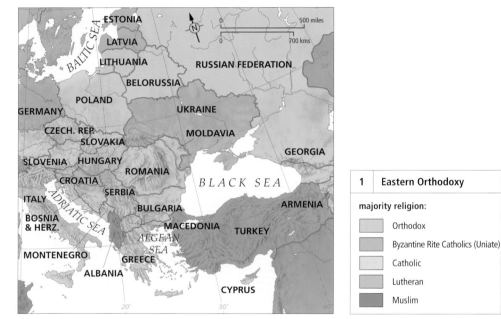

1	Eastern Orthodoxy
majority religion:	
	Orthodox
	Byzantine Rite Catholics (Uniate)
	Catholic
	Lutheran
	Muslim

ASIA

COUNTRY: *% of population by denomination*	COUNTRY: *% of population by denomination*
Afghanistan ....OR **4.5**	Macao...RC **10**
Armenia.......................................OR **78**/RC **4.6**	Malaysia...........................Less then 8% Christian
Azerbaijan......................Less then 5% Christian	Maldives ....(100% Muslim)
Bangladesh .... Less than 1% Christian	Mongolia.........................Less than 2% Christian
Bhutan.............................Less than 1% Christian	Nepal................................Less than 3% Christian
Brunei................................PR **1.8**/RC **2**/IND **2.5**	North Korea ....Less than 1% Christian
Burma................................Less than 6% Christian	Oman................................Less than 5% Christian
Cambodia ....Less than 1% Christian	Pakistan...........................Less than 3% Christian
China ....Less than 1% Christian	Palestine..............................IND **4.5**/RC **2**/OR **2**
....(mostly Renewalist)	Philippines...................REN **44**/PR **5**/RC **82**
Cyprus..OR **87.5**	Qatar ....RC **6**/AN **1.3**/IND **1.7**
East Timor ....RC **95**	Saudi Arabia ....RC **3**
Georgia ....Georgian Orthodox 58	Singapore ....12.3% Christian
Hong Kong ....RC **8**/PR **8**	South Korea...................IND **16**/PR **19**/RC **8**
India ....Less than 3% Christian	Sri Lanka ....9.4% Christian
Indonesia...RC **3**/PR **6**	Syria ....OR **5**/RC **2**
Iran ....Less than 1% Christian	Taiwan................................RC **1.3**/PR **2**/IND **2**
Iraq ....RC **1.2**/OR **0.6**	Tajikistan........................Less than 3% Christian
Israel......................2% Christian (mainly RC/OR)	Thailand.......................Less than 2.2% Christian
Japan..............................Less than 5% Christian	Turkey ....Less than 1% Christian
Jordan.............................Less than 5% Christian	Turkmenistan ....Less than 3% Christian
Kazakhstan..........................OR **8.6**/RC **3**/IND **4**	United Arab Emirates..........IND **2**/RC **5**/PR **1.5**
Kuwait................................5% Christian (RC **2.5**)	Uzbekistan ....Less than 2% Christian
Kyrgyzstan...OR **7.7**	Vietnam...RC **6.7**/PR **1.5**
Laos ....Less than 1% Christian	Yemen..............................Less than 1% Christian
Lebanon ....30% (mostly Maronites/RC)	

EUROPE

COUNTRY: *% of population by denomination*	COUNTRY: *% of population by denomination*
Albania...OR **16**/RC **17**	Lithuania ....RC **85**/OR **3**
Andorra ....RC **99**	Luxembourg..RC **94**
Austria ....OR **2**/RC **76**/PR **5**	Macedonia ....RC **3.5**/OR **60**
Belgium..RC **81**	Malta ....RC **95**
Belarus....................Russian Orthodox 48/ RC 13	Moldavia ....IND **15**/Russian OR **45**/PR **2**
Bosnia-Herzegovina ....Serbian Orthodox 31/	Monaco ....RC **90**
....RC **15**	Montenegro ....OR **74**/RC **3.5**
Bulgaria ....IND **7**/OR **71.6**	Netherlands ....RC **35**/PR **27**
Channel Islands..................AN **44**/RC **15**/PR **7**	Norway ....Lutheran Church of Norway 86
Croatia........................RC **48**/Serbian Orthodox 6	Poland ....RC **92**/OR **3**
Czech Republic ....RC **40**/PR **3**	Portugal ....RC **91**
Denmark ....PR **88**	Romania ....Romanian OR **86**/RC **14.5**
Estonia......................Luth.60/OR **13**/BP **2**	Russian Fed. ....Russian OR **52**/
Finland ....Lutheran 90/OR **2**	..............................Less than 7% other Christian
France ....RC **82**/PR **3**	San Marino..............RC **90**/United Meth **10**/PB **7**
Germany ....Lutheran 34/RC 34	Serbia ....Serbian OR **65**/RC **4**
Gibraltar ....RC **85**/AN **8**	(former Yugoslavia)
Greece ....OR **93**	Slovakia ....RC **68**/PR **11**
Hungary ....PR **25**/RC **63**	Slovenia ....RC **83.6**
Iceland ....Luth. National Ch. 90/Luth. 7	Spain...RC **96**
Ireland..RC **85**/AN **3.6**	Sweden.................Lutheran Church of Sweden 87
Isle of Man ....AN **42**/RC **9**/PR **14**	Switzerland.............RC **44**/Fed. Of Prot. Chs **41**
Italy ....RC **97**	Ukraine ....Russian OR **84**/RC **11**
Latvia ....Luth. 24/RC 21/Russian OR 24	United Kingdom ....AN **45**/RC **10**/PR **8.6**
Liechtenstein.....................................RC **74**/PR **8**	Vatican City ....RC **100**

espousing Liberal Theology, combining left-wing views and the Biblical message (a type of activism often opposed by the Vatican). Nevertheless, Protestantism appeals strongly because of its experiential vibrancy and conservative, though often individualist, ethics.

In Africa, especially Western and Southern, the formation of many African Independent Churches, often blending indigenous, classical African themes and those of the Bible, adds a new dimension to Christianity. It is often, especially in South Africa, beginning to eclipse the mainstream tradition. Christianity was successful in the Philippines and Korea (though in the rest of Asia, its successes are much more modest) – Catholicism in the former and Protestantism in the latter. There is some re-emergence of religion in China, Vietnam and other communist countries, where Renewalist churches haved been successful.

Christian Persecution

The secular communist states which arose in the twentieth century were among the most significant political entities to persecute Christians in recent years, actively suppressing worship and closing churches. Today, despite the rapid decline of communist states since the 1980s (see pp. 20), Christians continue to suffer legal and social limitations in a number of countries, and sometimes face sectarian violence (map 2). North Korea is probably the most extreme, but many Muslim countries are making Christians feel increasingly uncomfortable. In Sudan, the power-holding Muslims of the north have been conducting a covert campaign of ethnic cleansing against the Christian population of the Darfur region in the south. Ironically, the Christian community in Israel has also dwindled alarmingly by almost one third in the last decade.

KEY TO MAIN ABBREVIATIONS
AAC = African Apostolic Church
AI = African Indigenous
AN = Anglican (Church of England)
BP = Baptist
BRT = Brethren
CJC = Church of Jesus Christ
EC = Evangelical Church
EP = Evangelical Protestants
JW = Jehovah's Witnesses
ME = Methodists
OR = Orthodox
PB = Presbyterian
PE = Pentecostal
PR = Protestant
RC = Roman Catholic
SDA = Seventh Day Adventists
UCC = United Church of Canada

AFRICA

COUNTRY: *% of population by denomination*	COUNTRY: *% of population by denomination*
Algeria ....Less than 1% Christian	Libya ....Less than 3% Christian
Angola.............................RC 62/PR 15	Madagascar ....RC 25/PR and AI 16
Benin............................PR 4/RC 21	Malawi ....RC 25/PR 39
Botswana ....IND 31/PR 11/RC 14	Mali ....Less than 2% Christian
Burkina Faso........................RC 9/PR 7	Mauritania ....Less than 1% Christian
Burundi ....AN 8/PR 12/RC 58	Mauritius ....RC 27/PR 10
Cameroon...........RC 26.5 PR 21/Cam. EC 7	Morocco ....Less than 1% Christian
Cape Verde ....RC 97	Mozambique ....Christian 38
C.A.R.................RC 25/PR 25/AI 35	Namibia ....Lutheran 50/RC 18/PR 10
Chad ....RC 7/PR 10/Evang. Ch. of Chad 8	Niger ....Less than 1% Christian
Comoros ....RC 0.5	Nigeria ....RC 12/PR 12/AN 18
Congo (Republic of)...................Christian 38	Rwanda ....RC 51/PR 21/AN 8/Adventist 11
Congo.........RC 51/PR 20/Kimbanguist 10	Sao Tome ....PR 4/IND 10/RC 75
(Dem. Rep. of, formerly Zaire)	Senegal ....RC 5
Djibouti ....Less than 1% Christian	Seychelles.........................RC 90/AN 7
Egypt.............................Coptic OR 14	Sierra Leone ....RC 4/PR 7
Equatorial Guinea..................RC 86/PR 7	Somalia ....Less than 1% Christian
Eritrea ....Coptic OR 46	South Africa ....PR 31/Dutch Reformed 16/
Ethiopia..................Ethiopian OR 37/PR 14	..................ME 11/AI 9/RC 9/AN 8
Gabon..................55-75% Christian (mostly RC)	Sudan ....RC 11/PR 3/AN 8
Gambia ....Less than 10% Christian	Swaziland ....PR 15/AI 22/RC 6/AN 4/IND 13
Ghana.............RC 10/PB 12/ME 12/AI 10/IND 19	Tanzania ....Christian (PR, RC, AI) 30
Guinea ....Less than 5% Christian	Togo ....RC 24/PR 10
Guinea-Bissau ....RC 12	Tunisia ....Less than 1% Christian
Ivory Coast ....RC 15/PR 5	Uganda ....RC 42/AN 40
Kenya ....AN 10/RC 33/PR 21/IND 15/AI 10	Western Sahara ....RC 20
Lesotho................RC 38/AN 10/Les. EC 25/AI 6	Zambia ....RC 33/PR 30
Liberia ....AI 13/Liberian BP 6/Un. Meth. 6/	Zimbabwe..............AI 15/RC 14/PR 8/AAC 7/
..................PR 9/RC 5	.................AN 4/ME 4/Salvation Army 4

AUSTRALASIA & OCEANIA

COUNTRY: *% of population by denomination*
Australia ....AN 22/RC 30/
...................Uniting Church 10/OR 3
Fiji ....Christian 52%
French Polynesia.................RC 43/PR 26/
...................Evang. Ch. of Polynesia 25
Kiribati ....RC 53/PR 45
Marshall Islands................United Church of
..............Christ 45/Other PR 40/RC 8
Micronesia ....RC 63/PR 40
Nauru ....PR 51/RC 26
New Zealand .....AN 22/PB 23/RC 13/ME 7
Palau ....RC 45/PR 30
Papua New Guinea ....RC 22/PR 34
Samoa ....Congregationalist 51/RC 22/
..............................Other PR 23
Solomon Islands ....Ch. of Melanesia 22/
..............RC 11/SDA 9/AN 38/PR 5
Tonga............................Free Wesleyans 41/
...........RC 16/Indig. Churches 23/PR 6/
..............................Mormon 14
Tuvalu................PR (Congregationalist) 97
Vanuatu....................PB 37/AN 15/RC 15/
...........Indig.Churches 8/SDA 6/ other PR 2

NORTH & CENTRAL AMERICA

COUNTRY: *% of population by denomination*
Anguilla ....PR 50/AN 32/RC 4
Antigua and Barbados ....AN 34/RC 12/
..............................PR 31
Bahamas......AN 9/RC 4/Pent 8/PR 54/ME 9
Barbados......AN 29/ME 9/PE 8/RC 4/PR 15
Belize ....RC 57/AN 4.5/PR 17
Bermuda ....AN 38/RC 16/ME 7/PR 23
Canada....RC 42/UCC 18/AN 3/PR 15/OR 3
Cayman Islands ....PB 37/Ch. of God 25/
.................Pilgrim Holiness Ch. 12/RC 25
Costa Rica ....PR 8/RC 91
Cuba ....RC 39/PR 2
Dominica ....PR 16/RC 80
Dominican Republic.................PR 4/RC 87
El Salvador.........................PR 8/RC 92
Grenada ....RC 53/AN 14/SDA 3/PR 33
Greenland ....Lutheran 70
Guatemala.................PR 12/RC 85/EP 10
Haiti ....RC 80/PR 18
Honduras.........................PR 7/RC 86
Jamaica...............AN 4/BP 18/SDA 18/RC 5/
..............................United Church 9
Martinique ....PR 6/RC 93
Mexico ....RC 94/Evangel. PR 5
Nicaragua...........................RC 85/PR 12
Panama ....RC 78/PR 12
Puerto Rico ....PR 13/RC 75
St Kitts and Nevis........RC 13/AN 25/PR 58
St Lucia ....AN 13/RC 75/PR 13
St Vincent & Grenadines.........RC 9/AN 17/
..............................PR 30
Trinidad & Tobago................RC 31/AN 12/
..............................PB 4/PR 8
United States.............PR 50/IND 20/ RC 26

SOUTH AMERICA

COUNTRY: *% of population by denomination*
Argentina...................RC 91/PR 6
Bolivia ....RC 88/PR 6
Brazil ....RC (nominal) 74/PR 15
...............(huge Renewalist population also)
Chile ....RC 80/PR 5
Colombia.............................RC 95
Ecuador ....RC 95
Falkland Islands ....RC 12/PR 65
French Guiana...................PR 4/RC 80
Guyana...............AN 9/RC 10/PR 20
Paraguay...................PR 3.6/RC 90
Peru...............................RC 96
Surinam ....RC 23/ PR 25
Uruguay...................RC 78/PR 3
Venezuela.............................RC 95

2 Christian Persecution Today

- extreme persecution
- oppressive legislation
- social and legal limitations
- social limitations
- ▲ inter-communal violence

4mm gap from box rule

ISLAM

ISLAM, which means in Arabic 'submission' (to God), presents itself as the continuation of the Semitic monotheistic message which had been partially codified in the Bible. Its prophet, Muhammad (c.570-632 CE), considered to be fully human, was chosen as the passive vessel of divine revelation; and, being illiterate, he memorized such revelation and then transmitted it to others. Within only a few decades of Muhammad's death, Islam had rapidly spread eastwards to Central Asia and westwards as far as Spain. Islam is now the majority religion of such areas as Indonesia, Central Asia, the Middle East and North Africa and, worldwide, is the faith of about one billion people. It is one of the most dynamic, multifaceted, and yet still much misrepresented, of the universal religious traditions.

BORN INTO a well-respected but not influential clan of Mecca, Muhammad was underprivileged by the standards of his own society. Orphaned at an early age, he had no legal rights or financial backing; he succeeded thanks to the protection firstly of his grandfather and then later of his well-respected uncle, Abu Talib. While working in the caravan trade, he married his employer Khadijah, a wealthy widow. At the age of forty he had the first of a series of divine revelations. Like his Biblical antecedents, Muhammad was at first afraid of his awesome experiences and doubted their origin, but he found support in his wife who became his first supporter. The divine revelations consisted of the dictation of verses which Muhammad was required to memorize. Islamic tradition insists on his illiteracy, so making him untouched by any interpolation in the transmission of revelation.

The revealed message was primarily an attack on the polytheistic practices and lack of ethical standards of the Meccan society of his time, which was accused of individualism and selfish short-term gain to the detriment of its weakest members: the poor, the orphans, women. This message was revolutionary enough to worry the comfortable tribes representing the Meccan establishment. The deaths of Abu Talib and Khadija, together with the adverse conditions in Mecca, prompted Muhammad to emigrate to the more receptive environment of Medina. The Hijra, 'emigration', was to become the first crucial event in Muslim history and its date, 622 CE, was taken as

600	700	800	900	1000	1100	1200	1300	1400	1500	1600	1700	1800	1900	2000

Above the line:
Muhammad (570-632); Death of Husayn, 680; Dome of the Rock, Jerusalem, 692; Death of al-Bukhari, 870; Greater occultation of 12th Shi'i Imam, 941; Death of al-Ghazali, 1111; Delhi sultanates, 1206-90; Shi'ism as state religion in Safavid Persia, 1501-1629; Fulani wars and Muslim dynasties in West Africa, 1680-1776; Mahdist state in Sudan, 1885-98; Islamic Republic in Iran, 1979

Below the line:
Hejira, 622; Official recension of Qur'an, c.653; Lesser occultation of 12th Shi'i Imam, 874; Death of mystic al-Hallaj, 935; Fatimid Dynasty, 909-1171; Death of mystic Ibn al-Arabi, 1240; Ottomans take Constantinople, 1453; Ottoman siege of Vienna, 1529; Al-Wahhab's campaign for renewal in Arabia, 1740; Ataturk's revolution in Turkey, 1919-23

THE WORLD

600	700	800	900	1000	1100	1200	1300	1400	1500	1600	1700	1800	1900	2000

Above the line:
Prince Shotoku, patron of Buddhism in Japan, 574-620; Rise of Tantric Buddhism, c.700; Angkor founded as capital of Khmer Empire, 802; East and West Christian churches separate, 1054; Shinran, founder Jodo Shinshu, Japan, 1173-1262; Columbus lands in America, 1492; Council of Trent, 1545-63; Foundation of Hasidism, c.1735; Mormonism founded, 1830; 2nd Vatican Council, 1961-4

Below the line:
Buddhism in Tibet, c.640; Sankara, 788-821; Monastery of Cluny founded, 909; Death of Ramanuja, 1137; End of Buddhism in India, c.1250; Jews expelled from Spain, 1492; Amritsar founded, 1577; Methodism founded, 1730; 1st Zionist Conference, 1897

---

the starting point of the Muslim calendar. In Medina Muhammad led, as prophet, statesman and strategist, the newly established Muslim community (*ummah*), which, unlike the pre-Islamic societies, was to be based on faith rather than tribal bonds. There Muhammad laid the foundations for community rules, including those regulating relations with Jews and Christians.

The Message of Revelation and the Qur'an

The divine revelations lasted for twenty-two years until Muhammad's death (632 CE). Muslim tradition tells us of the effort on the part of Muhammad and his companions to commit to memory and to check against human error the exact wording of each revelation. Accordingly, the revealed text of the Qur'an (Koran; Arabic for 'recitation') is for Muslims the *verbatim* utterance of God as dictated to Muhammad and then recorded by his companions.

The main emphasis of these revelations is on the concept of *tawhid*, the oneness of a God who has no partners, no sons and 'who begets not and neither is He begotten' (Qur'an 112.3). It is the same God who spoke to the Biblical prophets but, because of human corruption and misinterpretation of that original message, a new and final prophet was needed to rectify and reform the human understanding of such revelation. All Biblical prophets are acknowledged in the Qu'ran, from Adam and Abraham to Jesus (a fully human prophet) ending with Muhammad, the 'Seal of the Prophets', who comes to complete the religion for humankind.

In order to achieve salvation in God the believer is to submit to and obey God's will. The right path to be followed is epitomized by the Five Pillars of Islam, which summarize the belief and practices of the Muslim community. They are: *shahada* or witness to faith expressed in the formula: 'There is no god but Allah (God) and Muhammad is God's messenger'; ritual prayer (*salat*) to be ritually performed five times a day; alms-giving (*zakat*) for the poor and needy; fasting (*sawm*) during the holy month of Ramadan when the Qur'an is believed to have been first revealed, and pilgrimage to Mecca (*hajj*) to be carried out at least once in a Muslim's lifetime. (The focus of *salat* and *hajj* is the Ka'bah (*see* picture), a black cube-shaped shrine which houses the Black Stone.) These pillars are not mentioned as 'pillars' in the Qur'an; however, because they are referred to in several of its verses, they have become legitimized. Details on their ritual requirements and performance are provided in the *hadiths*, which are short reports of what the prophet Muhammad and his closest companions are supposed to have said and done on specific occasions. Both Western and Muslim scholars are still debating the authenticity and reliability of the *hadiths*, most of which undoubtedly reflect customs, opinions and legal issues of the early generations of Muslims rather than those of Muhammad's time.

Later Development of Islam

The theological, legal, philosophical and mystical doctrines of Islam later developed outside the Arabian peninsula, mainly in areas like Syria and Iraq, where 'Islamic identity' was formed through a merging of Arab culture with the refined Near East cultures which had been assimilated through conquest and conversion.

By the middle of the seventh century, Islam had spread to North Africa as far as Tripoli (647) and to Central Asia as far as Balkh (652). Under the Umayyad and Abbasid caliphates, Islam expanded further into parts of China, the whole of North Africa and Spain. By the sixteenth century it had reached west Africa and the African eastern coast, eastern Europe, and most of India and Indonesia. As a result of its historical and territorial development, Islam flourished in a variety of cultural and artistic forms. Variety was also expressed on the doctrinal level through specific emphasis on spiritual experience as in the case of Sufism, or through particular political and social interpretations as in the cases of Kharijism and Shiism.

From being the religion of a group of settled Arab nomads and semi-nomads, Islam has become a world-wide faith, most of whose believers are non-Arabs, yet regard Arabic as their ritual language. Its appeal in the West is due to its ethical and spiritual message as well as its unifying ritual practices, both of which have been able to accommodate variety and change without losing their identity.

PRE-ISLAMIC ARABIA

THE HISTORY OF the Arabian peninsula immediately prior to the rise of Islam (which is referred to by Islamic sources as *Jahilyah*, or 'age of ignorance') is known only in broad terms, through literary and archaeological sources. By the seventh century CE two 'superpowers' dominated the area: the Christian Byzantine empire, with Constantinople as its capital, and the Zoroastrian Sasanian empire with Ctesiphon as its main centre. These empires had been locked in conflict with one another since the middle of the sixth century, alternately seizing and losing control of important centres such as Antioch, Jerusalem and even of their respective capital cities. They used their influence to limit the power of other states by supporting different religious traditions. The Sasanian empire, for example, backed first Judaism and later Nestorian Christianity in the Yemen, while the Byzantine rulers made an alliance with the Monophysite Christians of Abyssinia. The Yemen, strategically located along the east-west trade routes, was no longer a major exporter of frankincense and was affected by the decline of the Himyari kingdom in the southwest of Arabia, whose capital, Zafar, together with its Jewish king, fell to the Abyssinians in 525 CE.

Within the Arabian peninsula the major powers exercised further influence by creating two tributary buffer-states: one was formed by the Monophysite Ghassanid tribes, backed by the Byzantines, while the Sasanians backed the state of the Nestorian Lakhmids, with its capital at Hira (*map 1*).

Society and Economy in the Arabian Peninsula

The peninsula covers a wide, scarcely populated area, one-third of the size of the USA. There are no large rivers or permanent lakes, the centre is dominated by sandy

A Himyaritic inscription with camel: Himyaritic was a language belonging to the south Semitic group. The camel (here a dromedary) was domesticated as early as the fourteenth century BCE and was used by the Arabs mainly for transport across the desert, for raids in regions unsuitable for horses and for agricultural work. Camel's milk was its most precious product, its wool was used for clothing, its pelt and bones were used as shelter and its dried dung was used for fuel.

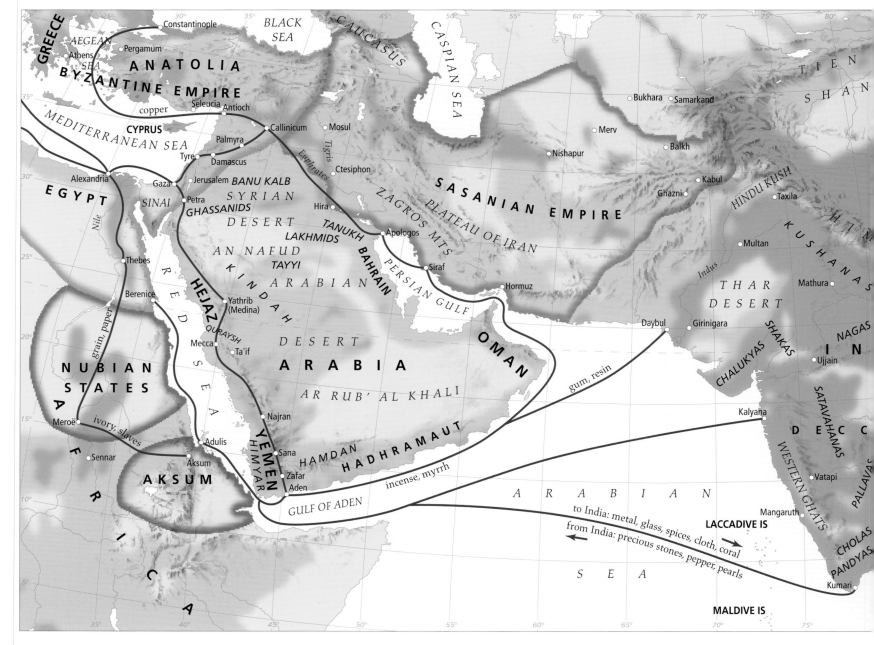

Terraced fields in the Mahwit area, Yemen. *The Yemen, called by the Romans Arabia Felix, is a fertile agricultural area with diversified vegetation. Terracing is used on sloping terrains to maximize harvest and control irrigation.*

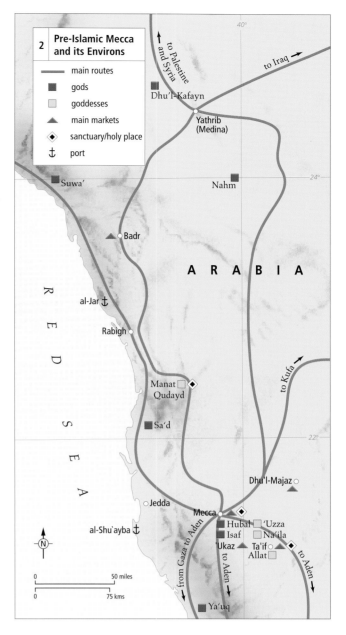

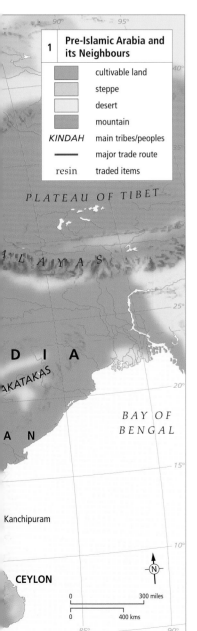

desert, mountains fringe the Red Sea, and only the south is fertile. Cultivation was therefore limited to the Yemen and to some oases. Nevertheless, there were exchanges between the nomadic and semi-nomadic tribes of the north and the more sedentary tribes of the south, as well as an interdependence between pastoral and agricultural economies. The common feature of all the areas of the peninsula was the structure of its societies: large tribes, smaller clans and extended families, with evidence of both matrilineal and patrilineal descent.

Along with pastoralism and agriculture, trade provided the other main revenue of the area. It is likely that cities strategically situated along the trade route from Aden to the Mediterranean and the Fertile Crescent enjoyed a thriving economy. Mecca, in particular, has been singled out as deriving much of its wealth from international trade by Islamic histories, which naturally tend to re-interpret the importance of the area in the context of religious considerations. However, new revelations about changes in international and local markets have called this prominence into question.

Religion in the Arabian Peninsula

Religion was linked to the social structure of the peninsula. Archaeological discoveries in the Yemen confirm the existence in the south of a polytheistic, temple-based religion, with priests performing animal sacrifices (especially of camels and sheep), and with offerings of incense and perfumes. A variety of gods and goddesses were revered as protectors by individual tribes, while many minor deities and spirits (*jinn*) were linked to clans and individual families. Some of the main gods and goddesses worshipped in the south resembled those of other Near Eastern religions, especially astral deities such as Athtar. Gods and goddesses such as Suwa', Ya'uq and the couple Isaf-Na'ila, worshipped in the Hejaz, were in fact of South Arabian origin. This is hardly surprising given the mobility of southern tribes, some of which had become an integral part of the northwestern Hejazi society.

In the Hejaz, religion was also polytheistic and tribal. The Qur'an, in its condemnation of polytheistic practices, mentions several deities (derogatively called *asnam*, 'idols') which were worshipped by individual tribes in the area. 'Uzza, for example, was the goddess of the powerful Quraysh tribe (which had controlled Mecca since the fifth century) and, along with two other goddesses, Manat and Allat, she is referred to in the

Qur'an (53.19-22) in what later Muslim commentators call the 'Satanic verses'.

These tribal deities were represented in the form of stones (Allat), trees ('Uzza) and also by sculptures (Hubal). Some of them were associated with a sacred place, even though the number of permanent, stone-built sanctuaries appears to have been limited. The sanctuary in Mecca was a main place of pilgrimage; it contained a sacred meteorite, the 'Black Stone', and was reported to 'house' more than 300 deities (*map 2*)

The Foundations of Islam

By the seventh century, three major developments formed the background to the revelations of Islam. Politically, the Near East was becoming more and more unsettled while, within the peninsula itself, local Arab tribes were increasingly being manipulated by foreign powers. Culturally, the development of a common poetic language began to unify tribes which were otherwise politically disjointed. Finally, a significant religious transition had been developing since the fourth or fifth century; forms of henotheism or even monotheism were starting to appear in the south as well as in the Hejaz, where the warrior god Hubal was worshipped in Mecca on an inter-tribal level. This shift may have been the outcome of an independent development of local beliefs, or it might be related to the proximity of other monotheistic religions – the presence of Judaism in the Yemen and in other areas such as Yathrib and, to a lesser extent, Christianity in the northern states and isolated pockets such as Najran.

ARABIA AT THE TIME OF MUHAMMAD

O UR KNOWLEDGE of the life of the prophet Muhammad is based primarily on Islamic sources written at least a century after his death, mainly eighth- and ninth-century texts such as the *Sirah* (the biography of the Prophet) and Quranic commentaries. Muhammad ('the praised one') was born around 570 CE into the Hashim clan of the wealthy Quraysh tribe at Mecca. His father 'Abd Allah died before he was born and his mother Aminah died during his infancy. As an orphan, he was only able to be a part of the tribal society thanks to the tutelage of his grandfather and later the protection of his well-respected uncle Abu Talib.

According to tradition, he worked in the caravan trade and, aged twenty-five, married his employer Khadijah, a rich widow a few years his senior. They had several children but only four daughters survived their infancy. At the age of forty, during one of his periods of meditation and retreat in a cave near Mecca, Muhammad had a vision about his call to prophethood: 'Recite in the name of your Lord who created, created man from a clot of blood' (Qur. 96.1-2). At first frightened, he found comfort and encouragement in his wife Khadijah who, according to tradition, became the first Muslim 'convert'. The revelations continued, mostly in the form of a voice dictating verses which Muhammad memorized. The message, at first powerful and apocalyptic, insisted on a return to morality and on accountability for one's own actions, as well as on the belief in one creator and just god, Allah ('the God').

The response of Meccan society and, in particular, of the Quraysh tribe to such a message was hostile. Twelve years after his first revelation, Muhammad had only about seventy devoted supporters coming mostly (like Muhammad himself) from the less powerful clans of the Quraysh tribe, but also from the poor, the slaves, the tribeless and the younger members of rich families.

The Hijra and the Later Life of Muhammad

Muhammad and his supporters were constantly persecuted in Mecca, and the situation worsened when the backing and protection of the Hashim clan was withdrawn in 619 with the death of its leader, Abu Talib. Muhammad's wife Khadijah also died around this time; their marriage had been monogamous but, after her death, Muhammad married several times, mostly for political reasons. After searching for possible places to live and spread the message, Muhammad opted for Yathrib, an oasis cultivated mainly with date palms, 200 km north of Mecca. Because of its agricultural basis, Yathrib did not exclusively depend on Meccan-related trade and, because of the presence of Jewish tribes there, might have proven a fertile ground for Muhammad's monotheistic message.

In 622, Muhammad sent his companions ahead, and left Mecca at night from the south, reaching Yathrib along a tortuous route. The Hijra or 'emigration' to Yathrib, later renamed Medina ('the city [of the prophet]'), marks the beginning of a more active phase of preaching. An unsuccessful preacher in his own city, Muhammad now became a respected military commander, as well as being a recognized political and religious leader among several tribes. Medina did indeed prove a more receptive ground for the Prophet's message, although it was not accepted by the Jewish tribes (*map 1*). As the Muslim community began to define its identity, the direction of prayer (*qiblah*) was changed from Jerusalem to Mecca and the obligatory pilgrimage (*hajj*) was to be performed in Mecca. This points to Muhammad's final aim of returning to Mecca,

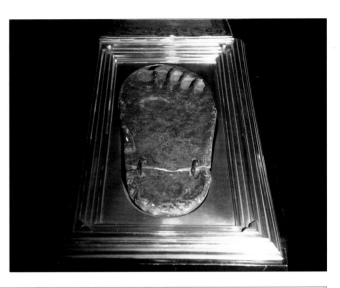

The Prophet's footprint, Topkapi Museum, Istanbul. Popular piety expresses its veneration of the Prophet through the belief that relics associated with him transmit a special blessing power (barakah) to those who touch them. Several such relics are found throughout the Muslim world and include the Prophet's coat, his hairs and beard and his footprint (qadam rasul).

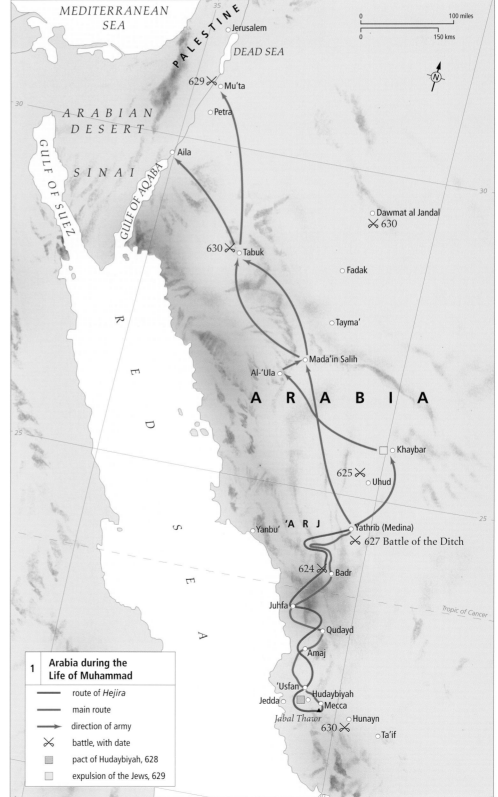

1 **Arabia during the Life of Muhammad**

— route of *Hejira*
— main route
→ direction of army
✕ battle, with date
▪ pact of Hudaybiyah, 628
▫ expulsion of the Jews, 629

Pilgrims during the hajj. *Early* descriptions of the Prophet Muhammad emphasize the beauty of his thick beard. In emulation of him, many pious Muslim men grow a beard. The symbolism of hair is present during the hajj rituals when both men and women pilgrims trim a few of their hairs to mark the beginning and the end of the hajj proper.

the place where Allah had first revealed his message to him. After a series of battles and raids on Meccan caravans, the treaty of Hudaybiyah (628) allowed Muhammad and his supporters to enter Mecca and perform the *hajj* there (*map 2*). His involvement in warfare has been criticized by Christian commentators, but there are several militant Biblical antecedents, such as Moses. In Muhammad's social and historical context, raids were commonly used as a source of revenue and a strategic tool to undermine Meccan trade.

At Mecca in 630, Muhammad 'purified from the idols' the Ka'bah, devoted it to the worship of Allah and excluded non-Muslims from entering the city. On the last year of his life, the prophet performed the so-called 'Farewell pilgrimage' delivering a touching address to all Muslims which emphasized the unity of their community based on the concept of brotherhood in faith. Following a brief illness, Muhammad died, attended by his favourite wife 'Aishah, in his home at Medina in 632.

The *Ummah* and the *Hajj*

The new community of faith (*ummah*) that Muhammad had built was gradually defined, shaped and organized. Its constituent elements, however, were already present during the Medinan period of revelation: a form of welfare system for the needy (*zakat*), dietary laws, norms of family law emphasizing the nuclear rather than tribal unit and, above all, a set of religious duties enjoined by Allah. One of these duties, the *hajj* had been inherited from the 'pagan' past and then re-interpreted in an Islamic manner: the association of the Ka'bah and the Meccan shrine with Abraham (Ibrahim) and Ishmael epitomizes the place of Islam within the monotheistic tradition. Moreover, the ritual actions during the *hajj*, seen as the exact re-enactment of Muhammad's last pilgrimage, constantly reaffirm – to this day – the status and prophetic authority of the Seal of all monotheistic prophets (*map 3*).

To perform the *hajj*, for today's Muslims, is a religious duty, but also a way to reinforce faith through the affirmation and display of the unity, the identity and the sacred history of the Muslim community.

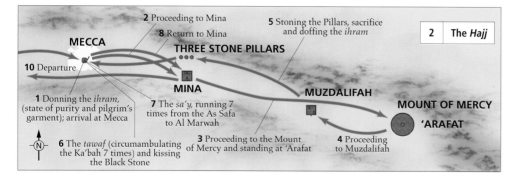

2 | The *Hajj*

MECCA
2 Proceeding to Mina
8 Return to Mina
10 Departure
1 Donning the *ihram*, (state of purity and pilgrim's garment); arrival at Mecca
6 The *tawaf* (circumambulating the Ka'bah 7 times) and kissing the Black Stone
THREE STONE PILLARS
MINA
7 The *sa'y*, running 7 times from the As Safa to Al Marwah
5 Stoning the Pillars, sacrifice and doffing the *ihram*
MUZDALIFAH
3 Proceeding to the Mount of Mercy and standing at 'Arafat
4 Proceeding to Muzdalifah
MOUNT OF MERCY 'ARAFAT

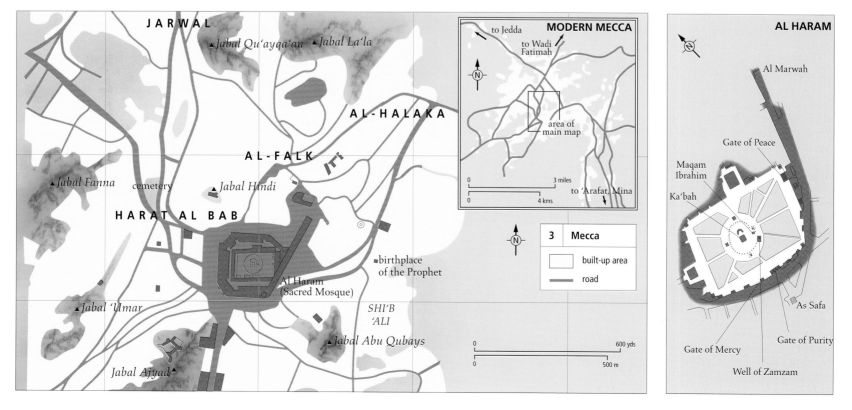

JARWAL
Jabal Qu'ayqa'an
Jabal La'la
AL-HALAKA
AL-FALK
Jabal Fanna
cemetery
Jabal Hindi
HARAT AL BAB
Jabal 'Umar
Al Haram (Sacred Mosque)
birthplace of the Prophet
SHI'B 'ALI
Jabal Abu Qubays
Jabal Ajyad

MODERN MECCA
to Jedda
to Wadi Fatimah
area of main map
to 'Arafat, Mina
0   3 miles
0   4 kms

3 | Mecca
built-up area
road

0   600 yds
0   500 m

AL HARAM
Al Marwah
Gate of Peace
Maqam Ibrahim
Ka'bah
As Safa
Gate of Mercy
Gate of Purity
Well of Zamzam

THE SPREAD OF ISLAM

WITH THE DEATH of Muhammad, the Muslim community found itself without a leader. While as the 'seal of the prophets' he could have no successor, as a political guide Muhammad was succeeded by the so-called *al Khulafa' al Rashidun*, the four 'rightly-guided caliphs' who were chosen from his most loyal companions. It was during the leadership of these caliphs (632–56), and particularly under the second caliph and great statesman 'Umar ibn al Khattab (634–44), that the conquest of territories outside Arabia began. Influenced by the political systems of these conquered areas, the leadership became hereditary, and the Umayyad dynasty (661–750) emerged out of the aristocracy of the Quraysh. While the Rashidun caliphs were based at Mecca and Medina, the Umayyads moved the seat of power to Damascus. Their successors, the 'Abbasids (750–1258), who were less Arab-centred, built a new capital, Baghdad, in a fertile area on the main routes between Iraq, Iran and Syria.

The History of the Conquests
The Arab conquests started as sporadic tribal raids. A proper army was probably not organized before 634, but once formed, it made expeditions eastwards towards the Sasanian empire and northwards to Palestine and Syria against the Byzantine empire (*map 1*). Under the leadership of commanders such as 'Amr ibn al 'As and Khalid ibn al Walid, the army defeated the Byzantines at Yarmuk (636), and the newly organized Muslim navy destroyed the Christian fleet at the Battle of the Masts (655). Constantinople was sporadically besieged during this period, though never captured. On the oriental front, the Sasanian army suffered a crushing defeat at the battle of al Qadisiyah (637), and Ctesiphon was taken soon afterwards; this caused the disintegration of the Sasanian empire. 'Amr ibn al 'As then moved westwards towards Egypt in 639, and by 646 Heliopolis and Alexandria had fallen. The city of Fustat was founded in 643, and northeast Africa was occupied. From Alexandria, naval expeditions were launched against Cyprus and Sicily and under the Umayyad dynasty the Muslims emerged as a major seapower. The eighth century saw further expansions eastwards as far as the river Indus and the Sind region and westwards through northern Africa to Spain and France where the over-stretched army was stopped at the battle of Poitiers by Charles Martel.

The surprising speed at which the conquests took place can be attributed to the weakness of countries debilitated by long external conflicts (the Sasanian empire) or by the fragility of internal structure (Spain). There was also discontent with despotic leadership and heavy taxation among the local population, especially in Syria and Spain.

Army and Society
The expanding Muslim army was at first only composed of Arab tribal groups, mostly infantry and some cavalry forces. Gradually it transformed itself by recruiting locally during its campaigns. The role played by the *mawali* ('converted non-Arab clients'), such as Berber warriors in the western campaign to Spain and, eastwards, Persians and Turks, is well-known. The Umayyad armies relied on elite Syrian corps and increased the role of the cavalry and especially of units in armour, though the infantry was predominant. The first Abbasid armies, on the other hand, relied mostly on Khurasani elite forces and, by the early ninth century, the cavalry became clearly dominant. From the eleventh century onwards the horse-back archery techniques of Central Asian and Turkish origin began to play a major role in Muslim warfare.

Muslim commanders left the social structure of the conquered territories almost intact by appointing local Muslim governors and relying on local administrative and financial systems. The populations were not converted *en masse* but in time the frequency of conversions increased. The reasons for embracing Islam ranged from a desire to come closer to the new masters and share their privileges, to an acknowledgment of, or belief in, the tolerant and syncretistic nature of the new faith. Tolerance, however, could only be granted to the *Ahl al Kitab* ('the people of the Book') that is, those people whom the Qur'an cites as having received revealed scripture: Jews, Christians and the 'Sabians'. These could not, in principle, be forcibly converted (as could polytheists and disbelievers), and were guaranteed protection and religious autonomy against the payment of a special tax.

Islam in Spain
By the end of the first Muslim campaign into Spain (711-13) all but the northwest corner of the Iberian peninsula came under Arab rule (*map 2*). When the Umayyad dynasty collapsed in Damascus at the hand of the 'Abbasids, one of its few surviving princes, 'Abd al Rahman I, moved to the far west and seized Cordova in 755, founding the Umayyad dynasty of Spain which was to last for over 300 years. The achievements of this period

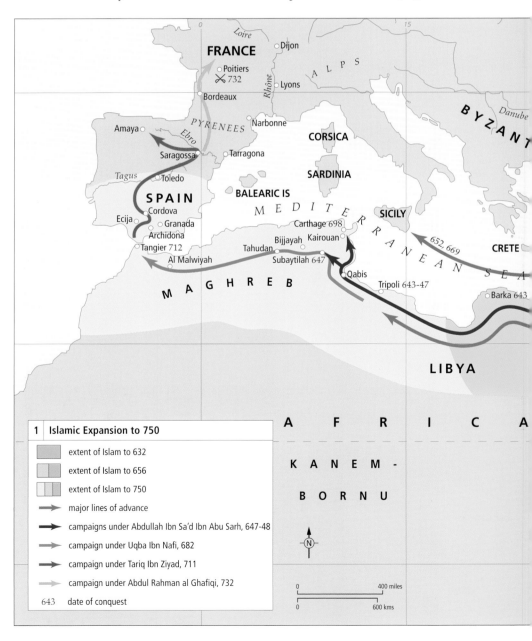

Alhambra Palace, Granada, fourteenth century. Abstraction, one of the characteristics of Islamic art, is achieved through the transfiguration of materials: mass and weight are disguised by arches, decorative patterns and landscaping.

1	**Islamic Expansion to 750**
	extent of Islam to 632
	extent of Islam to 656
	extent of Islam to 750
→	major lines of advance
→	campaigns under Abdullah Ibn Sa'd Ibn Abu Sarh, 647-48
→	campaign under Uqba Ibn Nafi, 682
→	campaign under Tariq Ibn Ziyad, 711
→	campaign under Abdul Rahman al Ghafiqi, 732
643	date of conquest

are embodied in the building in 788 of the Great Mosque of Cordova, which became a vibrant centre of learning. In time, however, the central authority of the state declined and, by the early eleventh century, Spain had broken up into a multiplicity of small kingdoms. The Christian states of the north captured Toledo in 1085 and this marks, to some extent, the first step towards the Crusades of the Middle Ages (*see* pp. 162-163).

Islamic Spain then came under the rule of Berber dynasties such as the Almoravids (1056–1147) and the Almohads (1130–1269), who held the entire political power of the western lands of Islam. The coalition of Christian states eventually reduced the presence of Islam to a strip of country in the southeast around Granada where, for a further 250 years, the Nasrid dynasty ruled. The Alhambra ('the red' castle) at Granada, the architectural masterpiece of Western Islam, belongs to this last period of Muslim rule. In 1492, Granada surrendered to the Christians and, within a few years, all Muslims (and Jews) were expelled from Spain. Islamic Spain had played an important role as the intellectual Muslim centre in the West, through which Far and Near Eastern as well as Greek and Arabic technical, scientific and philosophical knowledge reached medieval Europe.

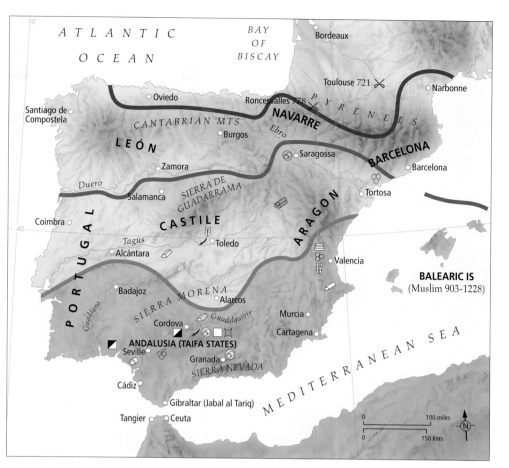

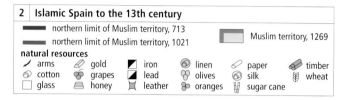

2 | **Islamic Spain to the 13th century**

- northern limit of Muslim territory, 713
- northern limit of Muslim territory, 1021
- Muslim territory, 1269

natural resources
arms · gold · iron · linen · paper · timber
cotton · grapes · lead · olives · silk · wheat
glass · honey · leather · oranges · sugar cane

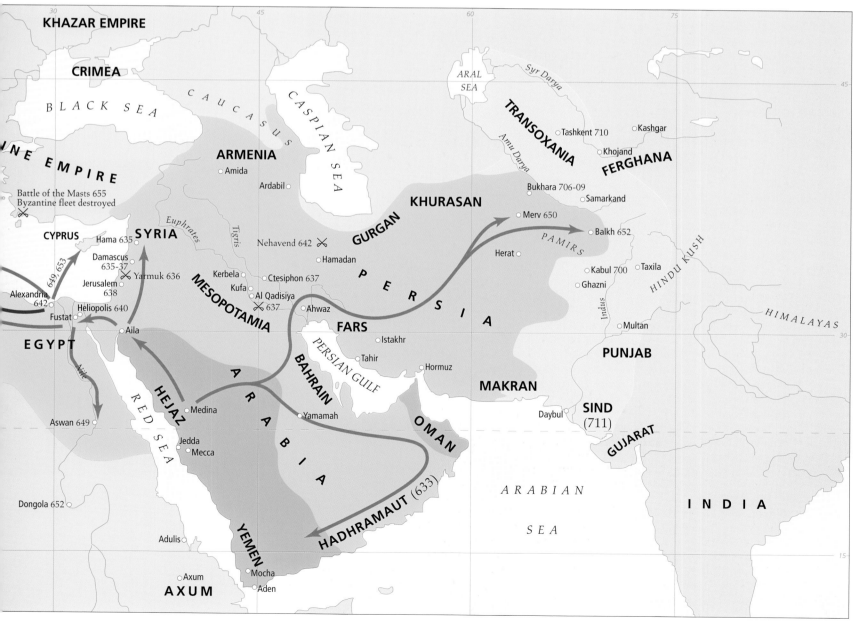

THE HISTORY OF THE SHI'A

THERE ARE TWO main traditions within Islam: the Shi'a and the Sunna. The origins of the Shi'a ('party of 'Ali') have traditionally been associated with a group of supporters of 'Ali ibn Abi Talib. They claimed that he was entitled to be Muhammad's immediate successor on the basis of his appointment by Muhammad, of his blood links to the prophet (he was Muhammad's cousin) and his marriage to the prophet's daughter Fatima. 'Ali, however, only became the political guide of the Muslim community after the death of the third caliph. 'Ali's caliphate (656–61) was marred by dissent and civil war which culminated in his death at the hands of one of his opponents. This political instability led to the emergence of a new force which eventually gave rise to the Umayyad dynasty.

The issue of who should lead the Muslim community and the nature of such leadership has divided Islam. The Shi'a emphasis on the figure of 'Ali and his descendants, the imams (guides), is expressed both doctrinally ('Ali is included in the *shahadah*) and ritually (there are special festivals to commemorate the birth and death of the imams and associated shrines are places of pilgrimage). Shi'a eschatology, their martyrdom-related vision of history and some aspects of family law also differ from mainstream Islam.

Shi'i Groups and Dynasties

Mainstream Muslims, known as Sunnis ('followers of the *sunna* [custom]'), differentiate between political authority, represented by the caliphs, and spiritual authority represented by the religious scholars ('*ulama*'). Shi'is, instead, believe that spiritual and political authority, both embodied in the prophet, were transmitted first to 'Ali and then through him and his wife Fatima to the imams . The Shi'is disagree over which line of descent to follow and from this, various groups originate, broadly: the Zaydis, the Twelvers and the Seveners (*map 1*).

The Zaydis (following the line of imam Zayd ibn 'Ali, d. 740) are seen as the most 'moderate' of all Shi'i groups; they believe that the imam can be any pious Muslim descendant of 'Ali. They founded two states, one south of the Caspian Sea (864–1126), another in the northern mountains of Yemen where, despite internal feuds and external invasions, they succeeded in holding power until the Republican coup in 1962. Today's Zaydis are still an important social and religious force in Yemen.

The Twelvers, the largest group, acknowledge a line of twelve imams, from 'Ali through his sons Hasan (d. 669) and Husayn (d. 680) to the last, Muhammad al Muntazar, who they believe went into occultation (withdrew from the world) in 874. This 'hidden' imam eventually cut off all links with the community in 941, thereby initiating the 'greater occultation' and – it is believed – will reappear at the end of time to fill the earth with justice. Since the 'greater occultation', religious authority has been exercised on behalf of the 'hidden' imam by religious scholars. During the ninth and tenth centuries, several dynasties professed Twelver Shi'ism, upholding Shi'ism also as a political means to oppose the Sunni 'Abbasid power. In 1501 the Safavid king Isma'il proclaimed Twelver Shi'ism the state religion in the predominantly Sunni region of Persia. Gradually, Persia converted to Shi'ism.

The third main Shi'i group is that of the Seveners (or Isma'ilis) whose line of seven imams ended in 760 with the alleged occultation of Isma'il (or Muhammad ibn Ismai'il). Belonging to this group are the Qarmatians, who ruled from a principality around al Ahsa'. In 930 they entered Mecca taking the Black Stone to their capital, only to return it in 951. Later, their power was reduced to that of a local dynasty which lasted until the

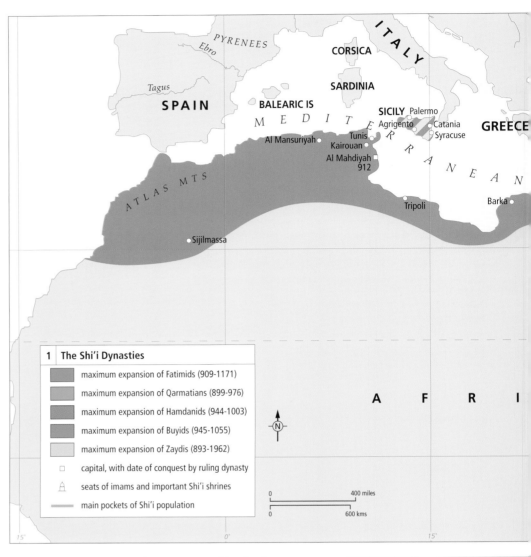

1 The Shi'i Dynasties

- maximum expansion of Fatimids (909-1171)
- maximum expansion of Qarmatians (899-976)
- maximum expansion of Hamdanids (944-1003)
- maximum expansion of Buyids (945-1055)
- maximum expansion of Zaydis (893-1962)
- □ capital, with date of conquest by ruling dynasty
- ⚑ seats of imams and important Shi'i shrines
- main pockets of Shi'i population

fourteenth century. Another group within the Seveners claimed that the line of imams had continued secretly until the emergence in 909 of the imam al Mahdi. He was the founder of the Fatimid dynasty (909–1171) which, first from Mahdiyyah and later from Cairo, controlled a vast territory, from the Mediterranean to the Yemen. Fatimid imams had both religious and political authority, they were considered infallible but still human. However, the Druzes, an offshoot branch, considered one of the Fatimid imams to be a manifestation of the divine. Since the Fatimids, the line of imams has reputedly continued to this day with the forty-ninth imam, the Aga Khan Karim, being acknowledged as the religious leader of the Isma'ili communities scattered throughout the world.

The Shi'is Today

Shi'is constitute around 10 per cent of the overall Muslim population and are especially concentrated in the Middle East and parts of Central Asia (*map 2*). The Western media has clearly associated some groups with local conflicts: the Druzes in the Lebanese civil war, the Shi'is among the *mujahidin* in Afghanistan, the Shi'i Azeris in the Nagorno-Karabakh conflict with Christian Armenians, and the Shi'is of Iraq in revolt first against Saddam Hussein's regime, and, after the Western coalition invasion in 2003, being one of the factions in the civil war. But by far the best-known political and social event associated with Shi'ism is the Iranian Islamic Revolution of February 1979 under the leadership of the cleric Ayatollah ('sign of God') Khomeini (1902–89). This has given Shi'ism in general an image of militancy and intolerance, thereby ignoring its history of persecution and its deeply spiritual nature.

A procession in Karachi.
During the religious festival of Muharram, Shi'is re-live and mourn the murder of their third Imam Husayn (the younger son of 'Ali), 'the prince of martyrs'. He was brutally killed by the Umayyad army at Karbala' on 10 Muharram 680. His martyrdom had a profound impact on the Shi'i community.

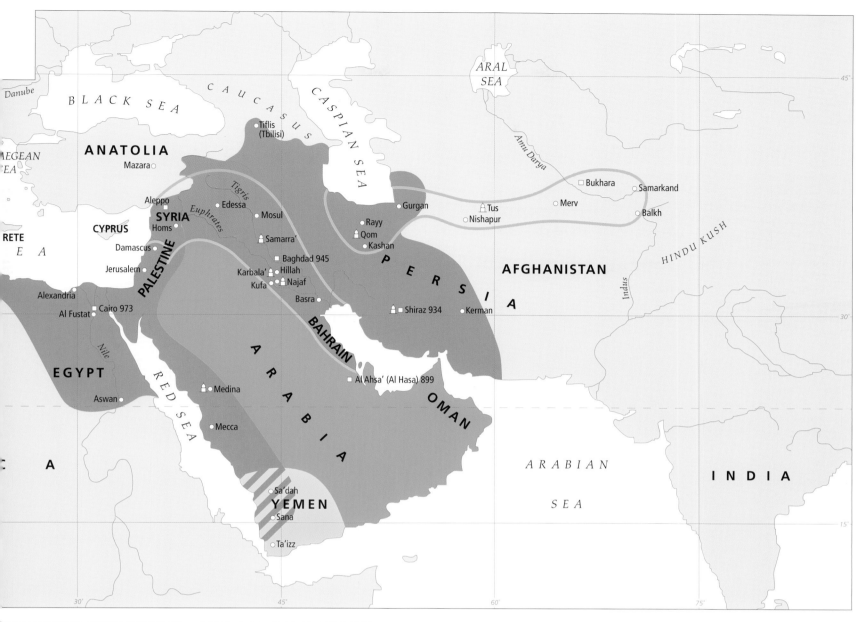

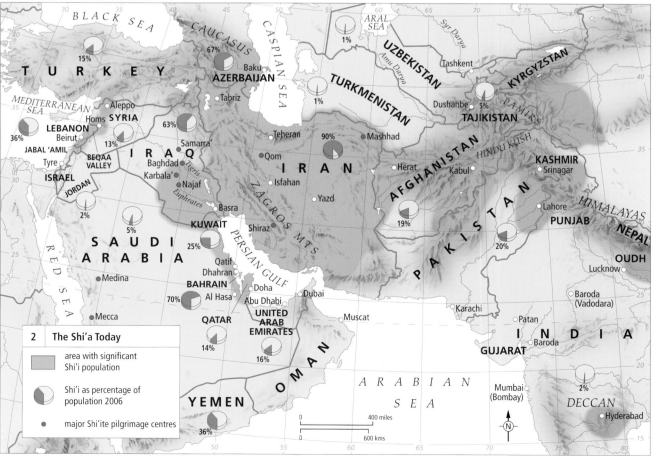

2 The Shi'a Today

area with significant Shi'i population

Shi'i as percentage of population 2006

● major Shi'ite pilgrimage centres

0   400 miles
0   600 kms

THE RISE AND SPREAD OF SUFISM

SUFISM REFERS to the inner and spiritual dimension of Islam. The term 'sufi' itself originated from the Arabic term *suf* ('wool'), because of the coarse woollen garment worn by Muslim ascetics. Theologically, Sufism emphasizes the personal and intense relations between a merciful and caring God and a believer in the process of spiritual ascent. The believer expresses this relationship through practices such as meditation, dance and *dhikr* (the constant remembrance of God's name) which can be recited individually or in groups.

In its association with the cult of pious holy men or women (*awliya'*, 'saints') who are believed to have miraculous powers, Sufism can be the expression of popular religiosity yet also serve as the elitist expression of a highly sophisticated individual quest. Among its most famous figures are the theologian Abu Hamid al-Ghazali (d. 1111), the sophisticated theoretician Ibn al-'Arabi (d. 1240) as well as the popular Persian poet Jalal al-din Rumi (d. 1273) who inspired the Mawlawiyah order, known in the West as the 'Whirling Dervishes'.

Sufi Orders

During the twelfth and thirteenth centuries, Sufi orders, or *tariqas* ('way/path'), started to play a significant role as major social organizations within Muslim society, as a result of the theologically-based acceptance of Sufism within mainstream Islam. The two principal rituals of these orders were daily devotional exercises, such as meditation and retreat, and regular group meetings including *dhikr*, the recitation of prayers and songs. As *tariqas* formalized, a period of apprenticeship became customary before followers could become full members of the order. *Tariqas* were open to celibates as well as married men (like the Qadiriyah and Bekhtashiyah), and, occasionally, to women. Their hierarchical organization placed a *shaykh* (or founder) at the top, and was based on a master–disciple relationship. The majority of orders developed around their founder, whose teachings or writings became the core of their doctrine. For example, the Qadiriyah, the most widespread Sufi order, derived from 'Abd al-Qadir al-Jilani (d. 1166). The reputation of the *shaykhs* of the *tariqas* travelled along the main trade routes where followers organized meeting places and founded shrines (*mazar*) in honour of the founders or famous holy men or women. In this way Sufism reached areas and sections of society previously untouched by mainstream Islam (*map 1*).

Three main areas of tradition have been identified in Sufi orders. The Mesopotamian tradition, centred in Baghdad, is seen as closer to mainstream Islam than other

The mausoleum of Rukn al-din Rukn-i 'Alam (d. 1335), an eminent Suhrawardi shaykh of Multan (now in Pakistan), is considered a masterpiece of early Muslim architecture, and its three-floored structure and wooden and cut-brick decorative design became the model for several other buildings in the area.

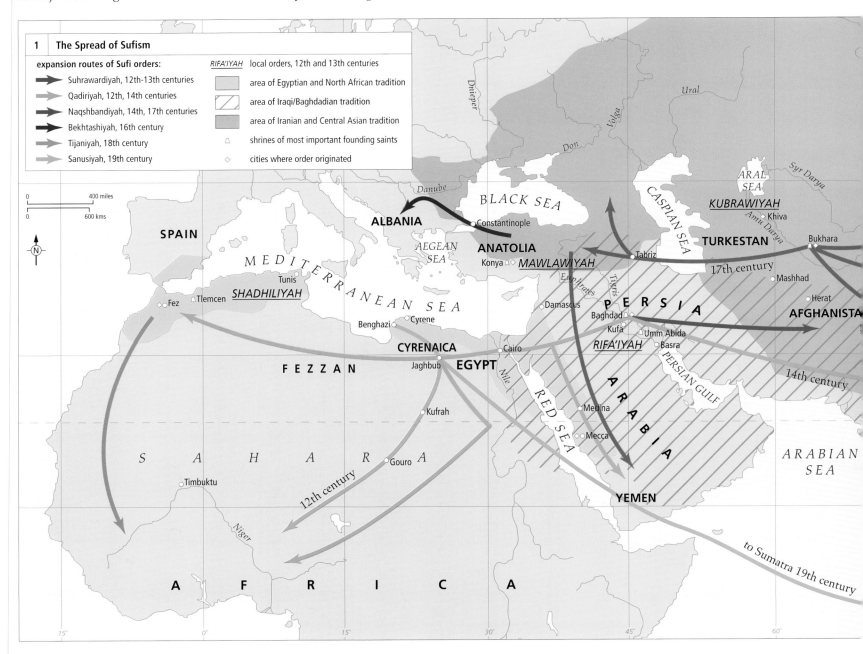

| 1 | The Spread of Sufism |

expansion routes of Sufi orders:

→ Suhrawardiyah, 12th-13th centuries
→ Qadiriyah, 12th, 14th centuries
→ Naqshbandiyah, 14th, 17th centuries
→ Bekhtashiyah, 16th century
→ Tijaniyah, 18th century
→ Sanusiyah, 19th century

RIFA'IYAH local orders, 12th and 13th centuries

area of Egyptian and North African tradition
area of Iraqi/Baghdadian tradition
area of Iranian and Central Asian tradition

⌂ shrines of most important founding saints
◇ cities where order originated

A Mughal miniature of 'A female Sufi visiting a female hermit', eighteenth century. By stressing spiritual achievement and playing down social constructs, Sufism has been, since its early times, relatively open to women. Apart from famous female Sufis such as Rabi'a of Basra (d. 838), and the existence of 'convents' for women as early as the twelfth century, there have been numerous women 'saints'.

traditions. Adverse political circumstances meant that the Egyptian and North African tradition developed slowly and did not extend beyond its original confines. The third tradition spread from Central Asia and Iran to Turkey and India; it exhibits greater divergent and antinomian tendencies and, in some cases (Bekhtashiyah and Ni'matullahiyah), is linked to the Shi'a.

The different orders emphasized many different paths to spiritual achievement. The Chishtiyah, with its vow of poverty, was an ascetic order, while the members of the Shadiliyah earned their own living. The Sanusiyah and the Qadiriyah, both politically active orders, were instrumental in organizing anti-colonial movements. The members of the more ecstatic Mawlawiyah used dance and music to achieve spiritual ascent.

Later Sufism and Sufism in the West

The last two centuries have witnessed dramatic shifts in attitudes towards Sufism. Sufi popular devotional practices, such as saint veneration, have been condemned as un-Islamic by several Islamic reformers and revivalists. Islamic modernists have also attacked Sufi orders for their alleged resistance to change and progress, and in 1925 they were outlawed in Turkey by Atatürk. Yet significant political events like Western colonialism and Soviet Communism have revealed the major role played by Sufi orders in forming ethnic or national identity in areas such as Afghanistan, the Caucasus and the former Russian Turkestan (map 2). In Algeria and Libya Sufi leaders fought against French and Italian occupation.

Because of their inter-regional network system, Sufi orders have been instrumental in missionary activities among non-Muslims, especially in Africa and, more recently, in the West. Sufi teachings have reached the West through a vast number of popular as well as intellectual texts by classical and contemporary Sufis like Javad Nurbakhsh or writers like Idries Shah (1924–96). Well-known personalities have also played an influential but limited role in the diffusion of Sufi beliefs: in certain European intellectual circles, scholars and thinkers such as Titus Burckhardt, René Guénon or Martin Lings are known to have become Sufis. In America the Chishti master and musician Inayat Khan (1882–1927) has inspired several young seekers of a deeper spirituality.

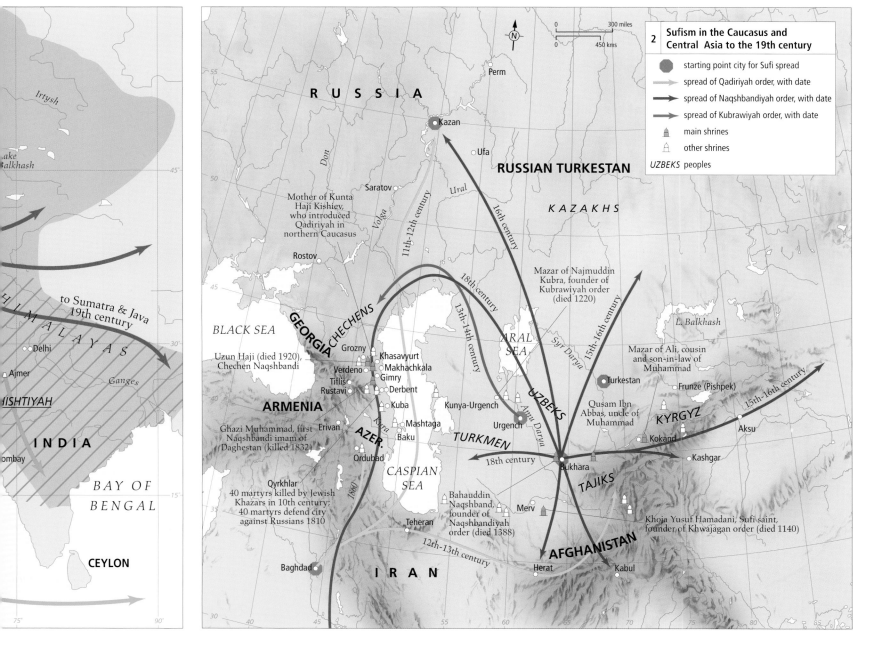

THE SPREAD OF ISLAM IN SOUTH AND SOUTHEAST ASIA

WITH NEARLY 550 million Muslims altogether, South and Southeast Asia encompass the largest Muslim population in the world. Characterized by linguistic and ethnic variety, the majority of Muslims in the area is Sunni, but significant Shi'i communities can be found in Kashmir, Sind and Pakistan (*see also* pp. 60-61).

There are two constants associated with Islam in the region: the role of trade and the missionary activities of Sufi orders. The symbiosis with other world religions such as Hinduism and Sikhism in India, Buddhism in Thailand or Christianity in the Philippines, at times erupts into direct confrontation. At a popular level, there is more than one instance of religious syncretism, where ritual practices such as pilgrimages to holy places are shared across the official religious divide.

Islam in South Asia

Islam entered India via two main routes: from the south, where Arab traders' colonies along the southwest coast of India are recorded since pre-Islamic times , and from the north, where Islam arrived through military conquest by land from Central Asia. In the north, Sind was a crucial outpost for the diffusion of Islam, which spread from there to Punjab and Gujarat. But it was from the eleventh century onwards that Muslim penetration became more substantial. When a new Turkish dynasty under its ruler Mahmud started to expand from Ghazni, a number of Hindu rulers from Delhi, Kalinjar, Ajmer and other cities formed a confederacy to oppose him, only to be defeated at the battle of Waihind in 1008. Mahmud, attracted by the wealth of the Hindu rajas, carried out several campaigns, culminating in the capture of Somnath, but only annexed Punjab. After the Ghaznavids, other dynasties succeeded in expanding Islam into new areas: by 1212, the Ghurids controlled most of the former Ghaznavid territories and had expanded as far east as Bengal. After a few decades, the Khaljis defended this territory against repeated Mongol raids and, under the great sultan 'Ala' al-din, extended it to the extreme south. The Turco-Indian Tughluqids expanded to the south and east (*map 1*) but the vast empire began to disintegrate with the rise of independent Muslim principalities.

The subcontinent was reunified during the seventeenth century, under the Mughal emperors. However, by the 1770s the Mughal empire (1526–1858) had shrunk to a small province around Dehli. Its legacy re-emerged in 1947 when, upon the British withdrawal from India, the newly-created Muslim state of Pakistan re-affirmed its links with Persia and the Middle East.

The religious stand of the majority of Muslim rulers of India has been that of tolerance, mass conversion of Hindus being an impossibility. Even though Islam was often strongly supported by the state, the rapid growth of Muslim population was mainly due to the missionary activity of Sufi orders, particularly the Chishtiyah, Suhrawardiyah, Qadiriyah and Naqshbandiyah.

Islam in Southeast Asia

Islam in Southeast Asia is also linked to trade, which had been controlled by the Arabs from the twelfth to fifteenth centuries (*map 2*), when the Portuguese entered the international maritime commercial arena. From the fourteenth century onwards, local rulers converted to Islam, and within two centuries almost the entire region was Islamized. By the mid-fifteenth century Malacca had become the chief trading-centre for Southeast Asia as well as the main centre for the spread of Islam (*map 3*), which came to be identified with the state and with its main language: Malay. The mass conversion in this area was the result of many factors: the missionary activities of Sufi orders; political opportunism and obedience to the

The Taj Mahal, a mausoleum built, just ouside Agra, by the Mughal emperor Shah Jahan for his wife Mumtaz (d. 1631). It is famous for its immaculate white marble, proportions and rich ornamentation.

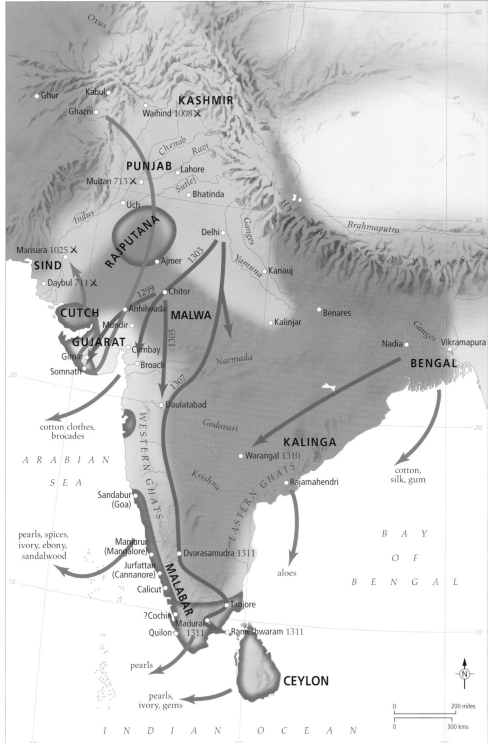

1	**Islam in South Asia**

	Umayyads' eastern limit, 713-50		area conquered by Mahmud 1004-22
	Abbasids' eastern limit, to 871		independent territories
	Ghurids' new territories, 1150-1215	→	campaign of Sultan Mahmud 1024-25
	new territories conquered by Khaljis (1290-1320) and early Tughluqids (1320-35)	→	raids and conquests under Khalji Sultan 'Ala'al-din 1296-1316
		cotton →	traded commodities

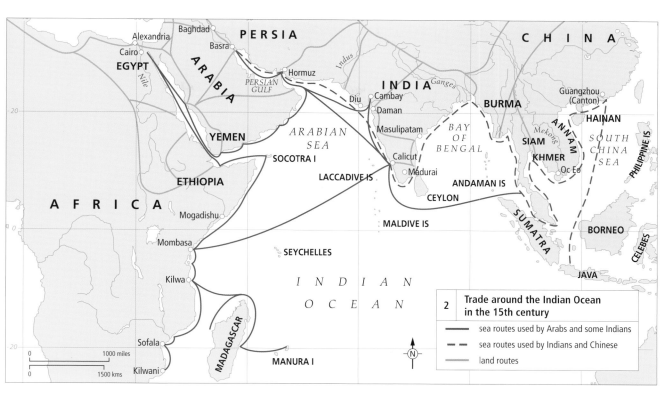

Islam in Pakistan (97% Muslim) is manifested by different doctrinal interpretations and related ritual practices. One of the main Sunni traditions is the Barelwi movement, originat-ing in the 1880s in north India, which emphasizes the role of Sufi 'saints' as guides and intercessors for the believers. As a result, their tombs are visited and the anniversaries of their death ('urs) celebrated. The Wahhabis strongly reject these practices as being un-Islamic and leading eventually to a form of polytheism.

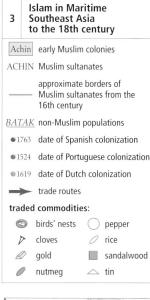

Muslim sultans; old and repeated contacts with Muslim traders; and, after the arrival of Christian missionaries with the Portuguese, a revival of Islamic proselytism. With its strong emphasis on mysticism and speculative theology, Islam is characterized by intermingling with local custom, especially in both family and civil law.

The Impact and Legacy of Western Colonialism

The imposition of British rule in India profoundly affected the religious development of the subcontinent. Despite their initial policy of tolerance, the British began to suppress some religious practices, favoured English as the language of administration, increased the influence of the Hindu and Sikh communities and, gradually, made Muslim religious law redundant. The Muslim responses to change were either moderate modernism, outright rejection of Western values, or the creation of a modern Muslim political identity. This latter position led to the formation of West and East Pakistan in 1947, as a nation for the Muslims of India. The issue of national or religious identity was not really solved and, eventually, the national element prevailed in East Pakistan which became the independent state of Bangladesh in 1971.

Control of trade as well as exploitation of natural resources motivated European colonial interests in Southeast Asia. The effects of the colonial presence are felt in the polarization of disputes between states and within states, but, above all, in a secularization of society. By and large the modern states emerging after independence were defined along European lines, with little or no place for religion. The conflict of identity still exists between a secular and an Islamic Southeast Asia, between the reality of a largely secular (although nominally Islamic) state, a Muslim communal religious movement and the commitment of some groups to the achievement of the ideal Islamic state.

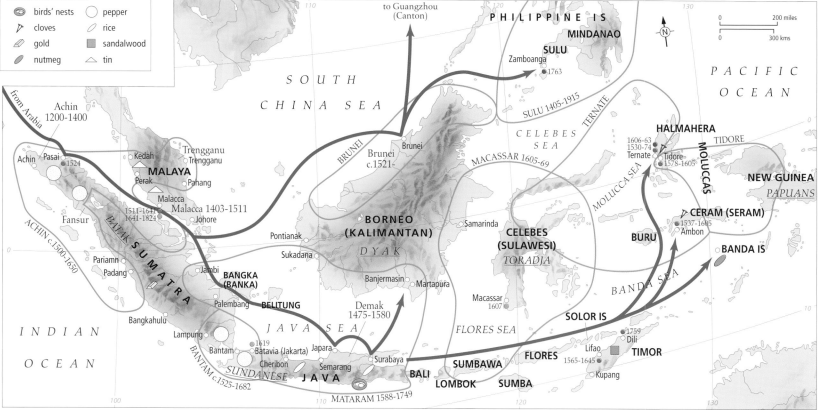

THE OTTOMAN EMPIRE

FROM OBSCURE BEGINNINGS at the end of the thirteenth century under a minor Turkish leader in northwest Anatolia called Osman I (hence the name of the dynasty: Osmanli, Ottoman), the Ottoman dynasty expanded from their base around Bursa, and came to control vast territories stretching from eastern Morocco to western Persia. Under Sultan Selim I (r. 1512–20), the annexation of Egypt and parts of Persia, which were major commercial and intellectual centres of Islam, marked a significant step in the history of the empire. Under Süleyman (r. 1520–66) the empire expanded further into Europe with the conquest of Hungary in 1526. Three years later Ottoman forces besieged the Habsburg capital, Vienna. Even though, because of the approaching winter, the siege was lifted after three weeks, it resulted in the continued presence of Ottoman armed forces in the heart of Europe. A powerful navy was also created to oppose the Habsburg power and, under the leadership of the governor of Algeria, the Mediterranean came under Ottoman control (*map 1*).

Under Süleyman the Ottoman administration achieved its classic form, dividing society into two main classes: a very small, basically Muslim ruling elite and a larger class of Muslim and non-Muslim subjects. Members of the elite were either from old Turkoman families, or 'slaves' recruited from Christian subjects through the *devshirme* (levy) recruitment system. This levy, introduced on a regular basis around the mid-fifteenth century, selected young men, carefully trained them for military or administrative service, educated them in Arabic, Persian and Ottoman Turkish, and converted them to Islam. By the sixteenth century, they came to dominate key administrative and military positions. Some non-Muslims were also included in the Ottoman elite: from Greek Orthodox high clergy and wealthy Christian Balkan and Greek families to rich Jewish traders and bankers who had emigrated from Spain as a result of the 1492 expulsions (*see also* pp. 170-171).

Religion in the Empire

Muslim subjects were organized into several schools of law and Sufi orders, and, under a complex educational system, the state supported and controlled religious instruction. Sufi organizations were particularly important because of their role at a local, rural and popular level: they inspired warriors in battle, safeguarded travellers and pilgrims in hospices (*tekke*), and transmitted and kept alive literary and religious culture.

Two Sufi orders were particularly influential: the Bekhtashis who, during the sixteenth century, were brought under state control by becoming the regular 'chaplains' of the Janissari (infantry) corps; and the Mevlevis, who played a principal part in the ceremonial investiture of the sultan. But state control of religious knowledge and Sufi orders eventually led to a loss of autonomy for religious organizations, which came to be identified with the Ottoman regime and its interests.

Non-Muslim subjects were organized according to

The siege of Vienna of September to October 1529. On one side of the picture the bastions of the city are visible, and, on the other side of the Danube, the Turkish artillery and camps. In the foreground, Süleyman holds a council of war after which he will decide to lift the siege because of the approach of winter.

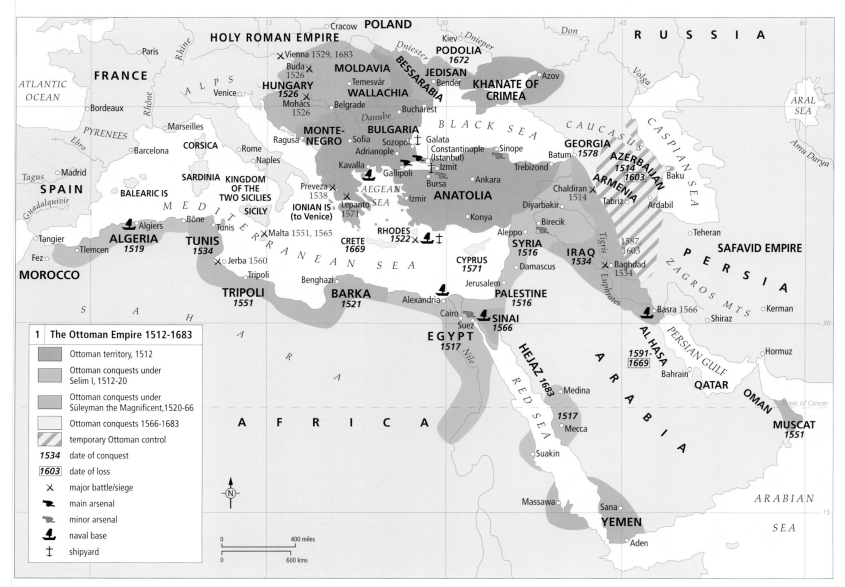

1	The Ottoman Empire 1512-1683
	Ottoman territory, 1512
	Ottoman conquests under Selim I, 1512-20
	Ottoman conquests under Süleyman the Magnificent,1520-66
	Ottoman conquests 1566-1683
	temporary Ottoman control
1534	date of conquest
1603	date of loss
✕	major battle/siege
	main arsenal
	minor arsenal
	naval base
✝	shipyard

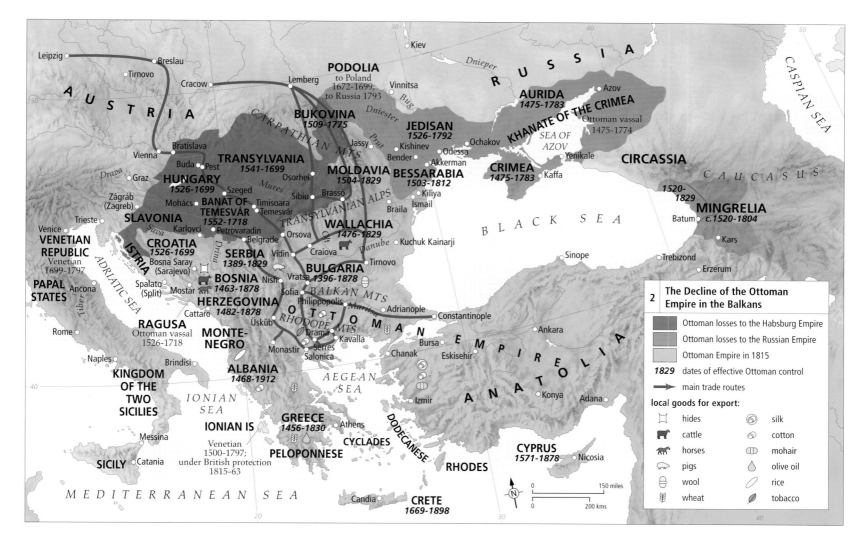

2	**The Decline of the Ottoman Empire in the Balkans**	

Ottoman losses to the Habsburg Empire

Ottoman losses to the Russian Empire

Ottoman Empire in 1815

1829 dates of effective Ottoman control

→ main trade routes

local goods for export:

⊔	hides	◉	silk
🐂	cattle	◎	cotton
🐎	horses	⫴	mohair
🐖	pigs	△	olive oil
⊖	wool	⬭	rice
▦	wheat	🍃	tobacco

0   150 miles

0   200 kms

religious denomination and granted internal and localized self-government status under their own leaders, subject to payment of a poll-tax. The religious leaders were usually appointed by the Muslim government and were responsible for relations with the authorities but also for community disputes and local taxation. In official documents the main *millet* ('religious community') are identified as Greek Orthodox, Armenian, and, later, Roman Catholic and Jewish.

Before the Turkish migrations of the thirteenth century, the vast majority of the population in Anatolia was Christian; by the end of the fifteenth century, 90 per cent had become Muslim. This was due to widespread Muslim immigration, but, above all, to the conversion of Christians to Islam. Such a successful rate of conversion can be traced back to the weakening of both the Byzantine state and the Greek Orthodox church. The consequent demoralization of the Christian population, and the breakdown of Anatolian society enhanced the appeal of Sufi missionaries. They presented Islam in terms of religious syncretism, and emphasized mutual beliefs as well as the high status of Jesus in Islam.

Detail of the **tughra** *of* **Sultan** *Süleyman, known in the West as 'the magnificent' and by Turks as 'the lawgiver'. The* tughra *was a validating signature of the sultan, designed by skilled calligraphers, and was put on all the official documents coming from the Imperial Chancellery. This* tughra *reads: 'Sultan Süleyman, the son of Selim, ever-victorious'.*

Islam in the Balkans

By contrast to Anatolia, after the Ottoman conquest of the Balkans during the fourteenth century, the majority of the population remained Christian. A census of 1520–30 reveals that 81 per cent of the overall Balkan population was Christian, with a high percentage of Muslims (45 per cent) concentrated in Bosnia. In a second wave of Islamization during the seventeenth century, Albania, Montenegro, Macedonia and Crete witnessed a high percentage of conversions. At present, Islam is a majority religion in Albania, Bosnia and the Kosovo region of Serbia. Along with indigenous peoples who converted to Islam, Muslims in this area can also be traced back to Turkish-speaking settlers and Muslims from other regions of the Ottoman empire who arrived in the wake of the conquests. The majority of Muslims is Sunni of the Hanafi school, with some Shi'is (Alevis) in Bulgaria. The influence of the Sufi orders is also important, especially the Bekhtashiyah, a syncretistic egalitarian *tariqa* with strong Shi'i features.

Decline of the Empire

By the 1792 Treaty of Jassy, the empire lost all its territories north of the Black Sea to Russia. In the west, after the second siege of Vienna in 1683 and the Ottoman retreat from an Austro-German-Polish army, the empire pulled back to its 1512 frontiers while, in other areas, many local rulers had become virtually independent (*map 2*). From the mid-nineteenth century the disintegration extended to parts of the Arabian peninsula and Egypt; Algeria was lost to the French and the Balkan provinces were fighting for their autonomy. By the end of World War One, as a result of the colonial expansion of Western powers, the Ottoman empire had lost its Arab provinces of Lebanon, Syria, Palestine, Iraq and the Yemen. In 1922 the Ottoman sultanate was abolished and the Turkish republic founded; two years later the last Ottoman caliph was deposed.

ISLAM IN AFRICA

Mud-built mosque of the Delta region, Mali. Mud-bricks are one of the traditional building materials in Africa; they are laid with layers of mud mortar to bind them together. Projecting from the walls are bundles of palm sticks which serve as decoration and a form of scaffolding for maintenance.

THE RELIGIOUS SITUATION of Africa today is diverse and fluid, reflecting a rich variety of historical developments. Islam and Christianity have co-existed with, and partly assimilated indigenous religions, where the emphasis is on harmony and unity within the clan and the family as well as with the dead and the spirits. While there are Christians of many denominations, the overwhelming majority of Muslims are Sunnis of the Malikite legal school. Exceptions to this can be found in scattered areas of North and East Africa where the Ibadiyah tradition is still present, among Sufi *tariqas* and in areas of Asian Muslim immigration such as East Africa. Estimates of the number of African Muslims range from 250 to over 400 million – confrontations between Christian and Muslim missionaries make information about religions in Africa unreliable.

The Spread of Islam in Africa

The Muslim penetration of Africa has traditionally been associated with conquest, trade, migration and missionary activities (*map 1; see also* pp. 226-227), occurring in four main phases. The first dates to the seventh to eighth centuries, with the military conquests of Egypt and much of North Africa; Islamization of the area slowly followed the military presence, with the conversion of much of the Berber population.

During the second phase (eleventh to fourteenth centuries), Islam spread across the Sahara into West Africa and up the Nile into the Sudan, travelling along the expanded trade routes which connected West to North Africa. From an area between Morocco and Senegal new Berber converts, later known as the Almoravids, conquered Morocco, crossed to Spain,

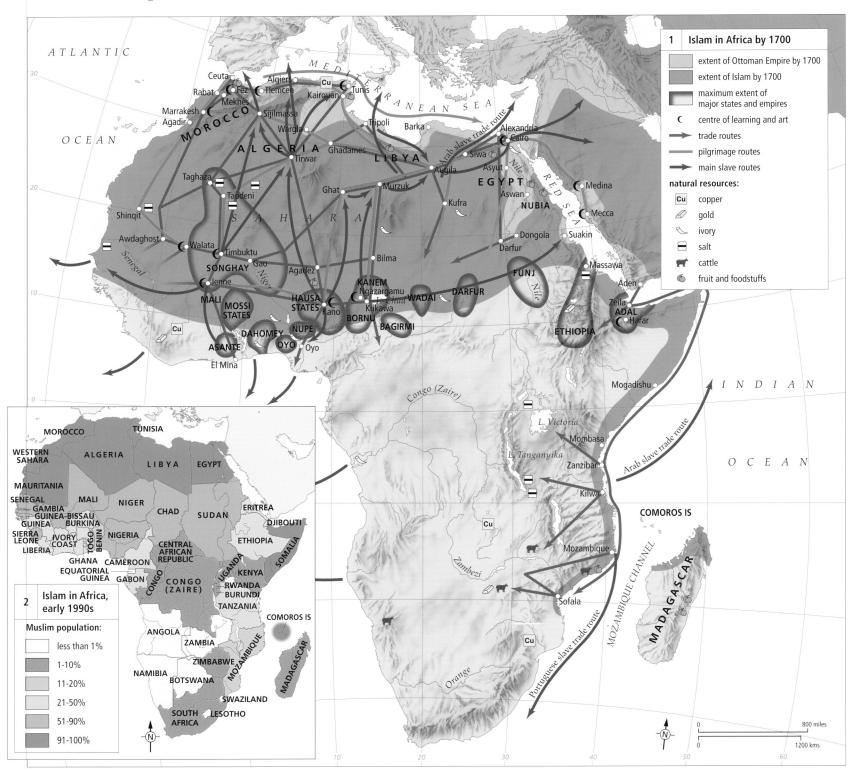

1 Islam in Africa by 1700

- extent of Ottoman Empire by 1700
- extent of Islam by 1700
- maximum extent of major states and empires
- ☾ centre of learning and art
- → trade routes
- — pilgrimage routes
- ➤ main slave routes

natural resources:
- Cu copper
- gold
- ivory
- salt
- cattle
- fruit and foodstuffs

2 Islam in Africa, early 1990s

Muslim population:
- less than 1%
- 1-10%
- 11-20%
- 21-50%
- 51-90%
- 91-100%

fought the Christian rulers, and ruled there for nearly a century (1056–1147). In East Africa, Islam travelled down the coast with seafaring Arabs, some of whom settled there and built up coastal cities, such as Sofala and Kilwa, which were major gold-trade ports.

During the third phase (sixteenth to eighteenth centuries), the influence of Muslim scholars and Sufis, along with Muslim traders, was instrumental in the formation of states ruled by Muslim princes, such as the Muslim sultanate of Funj, or the kingdom of Kanem-Bornu, which became a great trading and military power in the late sixteenth century, famous for the devotion of its rulers and the authority of its 'ulama'. The greatest state of Saharan Africa was the Songhay empire, Muslim since 1493, which controlled the trans-Saharan gold trade until its power diminished in the early seventeenth century. During this period, Malays and Javanese emigrated from the Dutch East Indies to South Africa, especially the Cape Town region – the first settlement of Muslims in South Africa.

Islamic Revival and the Colonial Period

The fourth phase of Islamic expansion into Africa began in the eighteenth century and was characterized by the influence of Sufi orders, especially the Qadiriyah and the Tijaniyah, as well as Islamic revival and activism,

A Sufi shrine at the Nefta oasis, Tunisia. The part of the shrine surmounted by a dome usually indicates the tomb of a Sufi saint. After the mosque, shrines represent the other main focus of Muslim piety, and their visitation (ziyarah) is especially undertaken by women. Of all the Muslim schools, the Hanbalis (and hence the Wahhabis of Saudi Arabia) are the only ones to forbid women from ziyarah.

upheld by militant Sufi leaders who declared a *jihad*, seized political authority and aimed to establish 'pure' Islamic governments. The best-known example is the Sokoto state in Hausaland, established in 1804 by Uthman Dan Fodio, while the Mahdist state of Eastern Sudan (1882–96) was the result of a religious-political movement of Islamic renewal fighting against colonists.

The symbolic start of the colonial era was Napoleon's invasion of Egypt in 1798. French expansion across North and West Africa had a great impact on both cultural and political developments in the area. The British held the other main share of power, absorbing the sultanate of Sokoto in the West, and controlling a large area of Eastern Africa (*map 3*). In some countries Sufi orders played a major role in resisting foreign domination. In Libya, for example, a vast network of Sanusi lodges stretched as far west as Timbuktu. The Sanusiyah, with its role in the development of trans-Saharan trade, its organized structure and its local tribal links, served to spread Islam and to organize anti-colonial resistance.

Contemporary Islam

In the last few decades there has been a revival of Islam in Africa (*map 2*). In some instances it was a response to secularism, whether imposed from above, as in Nimeiri's Sudan in 1983, or arising from a popular level as in Nigeria. Islamic missionary activities, often using local missionaries, are flourishing. The close relation of Islam with some African beliefs, for example the belief in good and bad spirits, which is associated with the Muslim belief in *jinn*s, is another reason for Islam's expansion.

Recent immigration waves from South and Southeast Asia to East Africa and, as a result of Ugandan ruler Idi Amin's (1971–9) persecution of Asians, to South Africa, have added to the variety of Islam in the continent. Among them are Sunnis of the Shafi'i legal school, Shi'is and Pakistani Ahmadis.

ISLAMIC MODERNISM AND ISLAMIC REVIVAL

ISLAMIC MODERNISM and revival are two of the many intellectual responses, operating within an Islamic framework, to Western colonial influence and to the eighteenth-century political decline of Muslim powers. Islamic modernists, while acknowledging with varying degrees of criticism or emulation, the technological, scientific and legal achievements of the West, aimed to overcome a perceived impasse in the development of Islamic societies. Islamic revivalists objected to Western colonial exploitation of Muslim countries and the imposition of Western secular values. They aimed to reassert 'original' Islamic values.

Islamic Modernism

Islamic modernist ideas promoted a re-interpretation of Islam which would fit in with the modern world. They were formulated during the last decades of the nineteenth century and implied an acknowledgement that the Muslim world had lost its position in the world. For many modernists the reason for this loss rested in the lack, in Muslim countries, of a modern and dynamic understanding of science. Ironically, they claimed, Islamic medieval knowledge with its transmission of classical science to the West was instrumental in the development of modern European science and technology.

Countries such as Egypt, Turkey, Persia, Indonesia and India were influenced by Islamic modernist ideas

(*map 1*). In Egypt, scholars such as al-Tahtawi (d. 1873) and Muhammad 'Abduh (d. 1905) re-discovered the role of Islamic philosophical principles, and affirmed that revealed knowledge and individually-sought rational knowledge could co-exist. Thus, they sanctioned the study of Western science as acceptable to Islamic education. In Turkey during the 1860s, the Young Ottomans movement discussed constitutional and political principles along western lines. Jamal al-din al-Afghani (d. 1897), while condemning European colonial aggression and opposing its political domination of Muslim countries, called for the need to acquire the tools of modern science to combat the West. In India, where in 1857 the British had abolished the Muslim Mughal dynasty, the emphasis was again on reforms in the educational field. Indonesia, under Dutch rule, was also active in implementing modern curricula combining religion with modern sciences.

The Reforms of Atatürk and Reza Shah

The legacy of the debates among modernist scholars, combined with Western-inspired nationalistic ideas, re-emerged in the reforms brought about in Turkey by Mustafa Kemal 'Atatürk' (the 'father of the Turks') (d.1938) and in Persia by Reza Shah Pahlavi (d. 1944). Unlike the modernists before them, both Atatürk and Reza Shah created secular modern nation-states. Although they were not necessarily anti-Islamic in their

A schoolgirl in Turkey. Over the 1923–38 period Atatürk's reforms positively affected women. Education played a major and lasting role: in 1924 primary education was made compulsory and free for all children and in 1926 the state system became co-educational (vocational schools excepted).

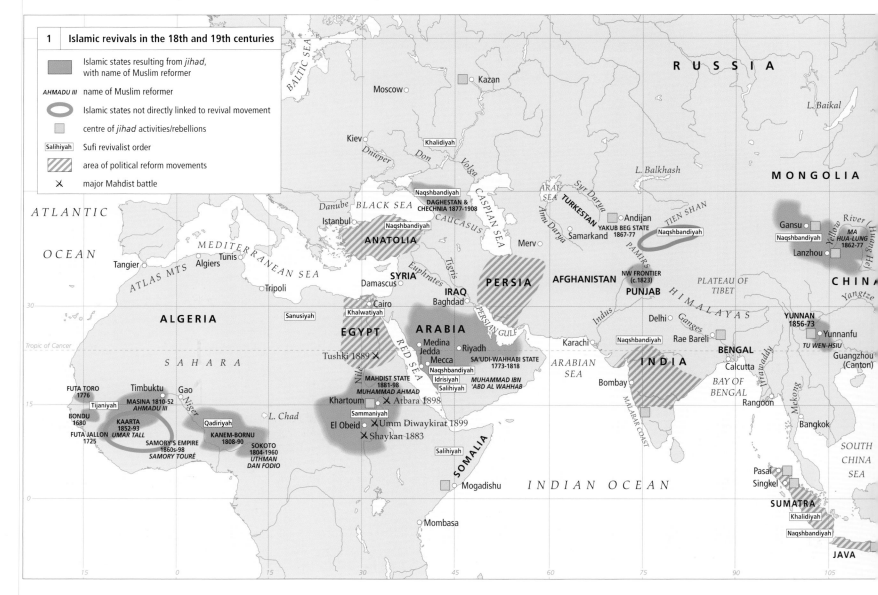

1 Islamic revivals in the 18th and 19th centuries

- Islamic states resulting from *jihad*, with name of Muslim reformer
- *AHMADU III* name of Muslim reformer
- Islamic states not directly linked to revival movement
- centre of *jihad* activities/rebellions
- Salihiyah Sufi revivalist order
- area of political reform movements
- ✕ major Mahdist battle

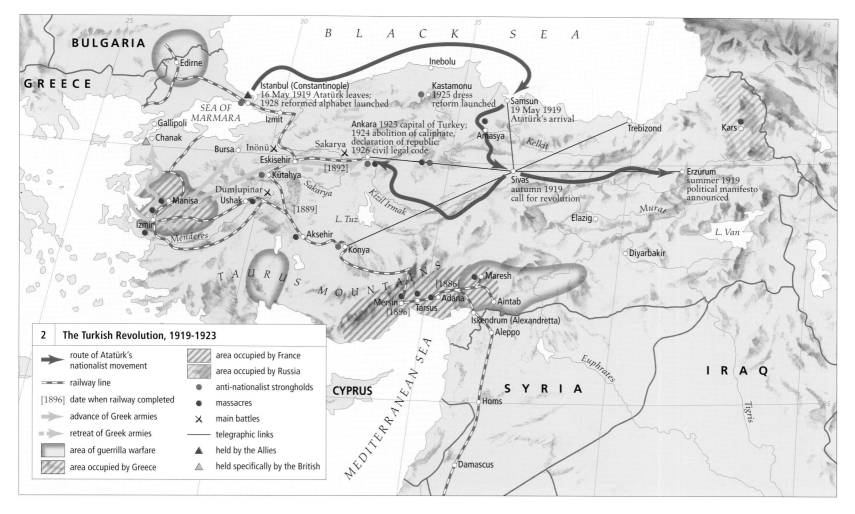

2   The Turkish Revolution, 1919-1923

→ route of Atatürk's nationalist movement

━━ railway line

[1896] date when railway completed

⇒ advance of Greek armies

⇢ retreat of Greek armies

▨ area of guerrilla warfare

▨ area occupied by Greece

▨ area occupied by France

▨ area occupied by Russia

● anti-nationalist strongholds

● massacres

✕ main battles

━━ telegraphic links

▲ held by the Allies

△ held specifically by the British

programmes, and despite the very different political outcomes, both Atatürk and Reza Shah faced stern opposition from the *'ulama'* classes. In Turkey (*map 2*), political reforms led to the declaration of the Turkish republic and the nationalization of railways, ports and utilities. Economic reforms promoted industrialization. It was in the cultural field, however, that the reforms had their most far-reaching consequences. Organized institutions of Islam such as the sultanate and the caliphate were abolished, Sufi orders were declared illegal in 1925 and the *'ulama'* were placed under the authority of a state-controlled office of religious affairs. The Arabic script was replaced by Latin characters. In family law, a Swiss-modelled legal code replaced the *shari'a*: in 1924 polygamy was abolished, divorce was no longer a male prerogative but became subject to court ruling. Gender equality was constitutionally guaranteed in education, employment and in the right to vote (1934).

In Persia similar modernizing reforms affected the military, the administration, the economy and

Iranian women at Persepolis. *Modernist legislation introduced Western-style dress for men and women, and the wearing of the veil for women was prohibited in Turkey in 1935 and in Iran in 1936. In response to such reforms, Muslim revival movements re-claimed their Islamic roots, rejecting 'alien' Western customs. Since 1983 in the Islamic Republic of Iran the veil is compulsory for all women.*

education while constitutionally the country was declared a monarchy in 1925. However, no equivalent political reforms were introduced. As in Turkey, the secularization of education and state control of religious funds aimed to reduce the influence of the *'ulama'*.

Islamic Revival

Islamic revival (*ihya'*) refers to the support for an increased influence of Islamic values on the modern world as a response to Western and secular trends. Accordingly, a return to Islam in its purest form is seen as the solution for the ills of Islamic societies and modern society as a whole. One expression of *ihya'* was the Salafiyah movement, especially in its Wahhabi form. Muhammad Ibn 'Abd al-Wahhab (d. 1791) was concerned about the survival of religion and sought to rectify the dangerous innovations that had been introduced into Islam. By emphasizing the concept of *tawhid* (the unity and oneness of God), he rejected all forms of mediation between Allah and the believer. In particular, he aimed to eliminate Sufi ideas and practices, such as the veneration of holy persons and the *ziyarah* to their tombs, as well as condemning excessive veneration of the prophet Muhammad. Wahhabi ideology shaped the religious character of the first Sa'udi-Wahhabi state, which was crushed by Egyptian forces in 1818. The second Sa'udi state, which was proclaimed the Kingdom of Saudi Arabia in 1932, continues to be shaped and informed by Wahhabi ideology.

Other formulations stemming from the Salafiyah include *jihad* movements such as the Mahdiyah of Sudan and activist Sufi orders like the Sanusiyah of North Africa, both of them revival movements spurred by the struggle against Western control

A twentieth-century development of revivalist ideas is the so-called 'Islamic fundamentalism', or radical Islamism. Fundamentalism in fact originated in the 1920s among conservative Protestant circles in America, and is the militant statement of the infallibility of Scripture and of ethical absolutism.

MODERN ISLAM: CENTRAL ASIA AND CHINA

THE LANDS from the Black Sea through the Caspian Sea to China have been linked since medieval times by trade routes: the fur route along the River Volga and the Silk Road to China. Islam expanded along these routes, occasionally through conquest but predominantly through trade and Sufi missionary activity. Initially, Islam in the region was characterized by slow conversion and adaptation to local customs. In modern times the common link between Muslims in this area has been political, as most countries were under Soviet or Chinese communist rule. Since 1991, with the breakdown of the Soviet Union, there has been a revival of religious activities and new Muslim countries have emerged as independent states within the newly formed C.I.S.

Islam and Russian Imperialism

Between the seventh and the ninth centuries Islam spread to Central Asia and the Caucasus through conquest. It later expanded by peaceful means through commerce, and by the twelfth century stretched from the Urals to the areas now known as Kazakhstan and Kyrgyzstan and modern Xinjiang. By the sixteenth century Islam extended as far as the Russian steppes, to the north of the Black and Caspian Seas. Russian imperial expansion, from the fourteenth to the nineteenth centuries, led to the incorporation of Muslim territories. With the exception of Catherine the Great (r. 1762–96), Russian leaders denied Muslims religious rights. Sufi-inspired *jihad* movements, like that of the famous Naqshbandi imam Shamil (r. 1834–59) and Uzun Haji (d. 1920), were organized against the Russians in the northern Caucasus (*see also* p. 198-197).

With the Bolshevik revolution of 1917 and the ensuing anti-religious policy, overt religious rituals and practices were greatly reduced, mosques destroyed and legal and educational Muslim institutions outlawed. Anti-religious campaigns intensified during the 1950s and 1960s. Meanwhile, diplomatic links had been established between the Soviet Union and Islamic countries, especially in the Arab Middle East, reflecting international cold-war politics. However, pro-Russian sentiments among Islamic countries suffered a heavy blow when the Soviets invaded Afghanistan.

Gorbachev's *glasnost* policy marked the beginning of Muslim political revival. The Soviet census of 1989 identified 41 Muslim ethnic groups out of a total of about 56 million Muslims (*map 2*). By 1991, the Muslim states of Kazakhstan, Uzbekistan, Tajikistan, Kyrgyzstan, Turkmenistan and Azerbaijan had emerged as independent republics which later joined the newly-formed Commonwealth of Independent States (C.I.S.).

Most Muslims of southern Russia, Central Asia and the Caucasus are Sunnis following the Hanafi school of law, while most Daghestanis, Chechno-Ingush and some Kurds follow the Shafi'i school. There are Shi'i Muslims among the Tajiks, the Uzbeks, the Baluchis, the Azeris and the Tats. There are also Isma'ilis, especially in the Pamirs in Central Asia, and some Baha'is in southern Russia, Azerbaijan and Turkmenistan. Sufi orders are particularly important in Central Asia and the northern Caucasus.

The Case of Afghanistan

Afghanistan, strategically located half way between India and Central Asia, had long been a focus of conflict between the British and the Russians. When the Soviet Union backed coups that changed Afghanistan from a monarchy to a communist republic, several Muslim resistance movements grew to oppose the communist regime. In December 1979 the Soviet army entered Afghanistan but was never able to control it because of resourceful and well-trained guerrilla groups, known as Mujahidin ('jihad'-warriors'). Almost ten years later, Soviet troops withdrew from Afghanistan and internal disputes among differing Afghan groups contributed to marked instability. In 1992 the Mujahidin captured Kabul, but between 1994 and 2002 the Taliban ('students') movement, aiming to unite the country on the basis of their interpretation of an Islamic state based on 'original Islam', took control of the country until 2002 when their regime fell as a result of the Western coalition war in Afghanistan.

Islam in China

According to the Chinese National Census, there were over 26 million Muslims in China. However, because the census was based on nationality rather than religion, the exact number of Muslims is still unknown. The two most representative ethnic groups are the Hui, who speak Sino-Tibetan languages like Tibetan and Mongolian, and the Uighur who speak a Turkic language (*map 1*).

The first Muslim settlers in China were merchants who arrived as early as the seventh century. Those coming by sea settled in the southeastern coastal region around modern-day Guangzhou (Canton). Those coming via the Silk Road reached Xinjiang; some headed to modern-day Xi'an (Chang'an), often stopping at Lanzhou. These early settlers were from various ethnic backgrounds: Arabs, Persians and Mongols. Further migrations to several parts of China took place under the Mongol Yüan dynasty (1279–1368), during which Muslims were successfully engaged in trade, especially with Central Asia, and employed in the administration. The establishment of the first Muslim community in Yunnan province can be traced back to this time. The Ming dynasty (1368–1644) was generally tolerant towards Muslims and encouraged assimilation – Chinese converts to Islam are known as Hui. Sufism entered China as a major force late in the seventeenth century, arriving from Central Asia along the main trade routes.

A pavilion of the Great Mosque of Xi'an. The Great Mosque dates back to the early Ming dynasty and the complex, occupying an area of 12,000 square metres, is made of several halls and Chinese-style courtyard buildings

MEDITERRANEAN SEA
ROMANIA
BULGARIA
GREECE

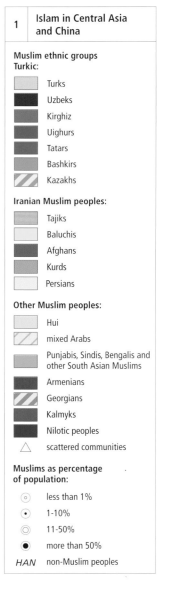

1   **Islam in Central Asia and China**

Muslim ethnic groups
Turkic:

Turks

Uzbeks

Kirghiz

Uighurs

Tatars

Bashkirs

Kazakhs

Iranian Muslim peoples:

Tajiks

Baluchis

Afghans

Kurds

Persians

Other Muslim peoples:

Hui

mixed Arabs

Punjabis, Sindis, Bengalis and other South Asian Muslims

Armenians

Georgians

Kalmyks

Nilotic peoples

△   scattered communities

Muslims as percentage of population:

⊙   less than 1%

⊙   1-10%

◎   11-50%

●   more than 50%

HAN   non-Muslim peoples

When the Qing dynasty (1644–1911) expanded into Central Asia, discontent with their policies led Muslims to rebel, assert their identity and denounce any compromises with local religions. Two major nineteenth-century Muslim rebellions in Yunnan and the northwest were violently crushed by the Qing. The Muslims of the northwest were only granted autonomy (1911–49) after the fall of the dynasty, and in 1955 the Uighur Autonomous Region was created.

The policy of the People's Republic towards Muslims has alternated between tolerance and radicalism; during the 1966–76 Cultural Revolution Muslims in Yunnan were persecuted by anti-ethnic and anti-religious policies. Recently, more moderate policies have benefited Muslim communities which, however, remain divided along ethnic lines. Islamic militancy, especially in the northwest, has prompted an increased Chinese military presence. This region is also becoming commercially and strategically important for China for its mineral resources and trade links with Central Asia, the Middle East and the West.

Students at Mir-i Arab madrasa, Bukhara. Madrasas are teaching colleges for Islamic sciences. During the tenth century Bukhara, on the Silk Road, became one of the greatest centres of learning of the Islamic world, renowned for its 100 madrasas. Most were destroyed by the Mongol invasions of the thirteenth century. The Mir-i Arab madrasa, built in 1535, is the only functioning religious college that remains.

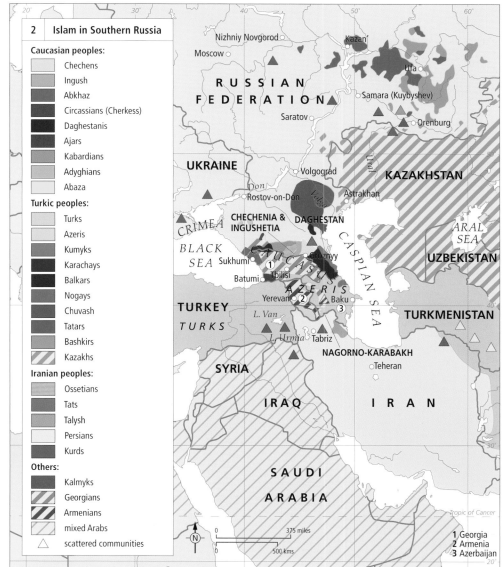

2 Islam in Southern Russia

Caucasian peoples: Chechens, Ingush, Abkhaz, Circassians (Cherkess), Daghestanis, Ajars, Kabardians, Adyghians, Abaza

Turkic peoples: Turks, Azeris, Kumyks, Karachays, Balkars, Nogays, Chuvash, Tatars, Bashkirs, Kazakhs

Iranian peoples: Ossetians, Tats, Talysh, Persians, Kurds

Others: Kalmyks, Georgians, Armenians, mixed Arabs

△ scattered communities

1 Georgia 2 Armenia 3 Azerbaijan

207

ISRAEL AND THE ARABS

IN 1947, the General Assembly of the United Nations voted to set up an Arab and a Jewish state in Palestine (then under British mandate) and establish their respective borders. While Jews accepted the Partition Plan, Arabs rejected it and attacked Jewish settlements in Palestine. The greater part of Palestine became the independent state of Israel on 14 May 1948, but was invaded the day after by a coalition of Arab armies. By 1949 armistice agreements were signed between Israel and Egypt, Lebanon, Syria and Transjordan. The western area of old Palestine was amalgamated with Transjordan (to be renamed Jordan in

1950 with the annexation of the West Bank), the Gaza Strip was occupied by Egypt. The Arab countries refused to recognize the existence of the state of Israel.

In 1956, Egyptian President Jamal Abd al Nasir (Nasser) seriously disrupted Israel's sea trade by blockading the Suez Canal and the Gulf of Aqaba. In October 1956 Israeli forces, secretly backed by France and Britain, occupied Sinai and the Gaza Strip and defeated the Egyptian army. However, as a result of international pressure, Israel withdrew from Sinai and a UN peace-keeping force was stationed in Gaza and took position along the Israeli–Sinai border.

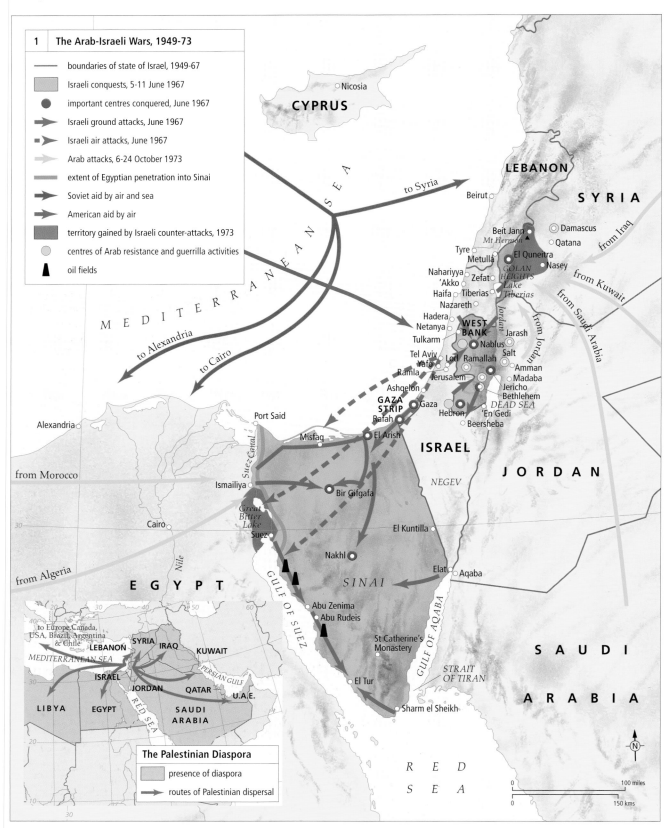

1	The Arab-Israeli Wars, 1949-73

	boundaries of state of Israel, 1949-67
	Israeli conquests, 5-11 June 1967
●	important centres conquered, June 1967
→	Israeli ground attacks, June 1967
▸	Israeli air attacks, June 1967
→	Arab attacks, 6-24 October 1973
	extent of Egyptian penetration into Sinai
→	Soviet aid by air and sea
→	American aid by air
	territory gained by Israeli counter-attacks, 1973
○	centres of Arab resistance and guerrilla activities
▲	oil fields

The Palestinian Diaspora

| | presence of diaspora |
| → | routes of Palestinian dispersal |

The Dome of the Rock, built in 691, is believed to be the site from which the prophet Muhammad ascended to heaven (mi 'raj) during the Night Journey (isra') (Qur. 17.1). Its importance as one of the oldest extant Muslim buildings is linked to the assertion of Islamic identity by the early Muslim community over Christianity (as the polemical tone of some of its Arabic inscriptions reveal) and Judaism.

The Israeli West Bank Barrier was begun in 2002 as a security measure to inhibit the movement of Palestinians into Israeli territory. Over 800 miles in length, and constructed of dense fences in rural areas and 25-foot concrete blocks in urban areas, it follows the 1949 Armistice line (or Green Line). A similar barrier was built around the Gaza Strip in the 1990s.

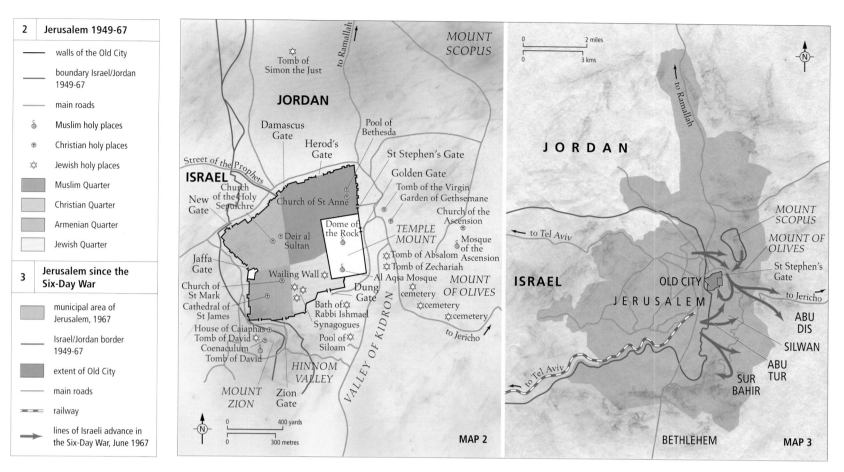

2 Jerusalem 1949-67

— walls of the Old City

— boundary Israel/Jordan 1949-67

— main roads

◔ Muslim holy places

◉ Christian holy places

✡ Jewish holy places

▨ Muslim Quarter

▨ Christian Quarter

▨ Armenian Quarter

▨ Jewish Quarter

3 Jerusalem since the Six-Day War

▨ municipal area of Jerusalem, 1967

— Israel/Jordan border 1949-67

▨ extent of Old City

— main roads

⊢⊣ railway

➔ lines of Israeli advance in the Six-Day War, June 1967

MAP 2

MAP 3

On 13 September 1993 the Washington Agreement was signed between Israel's Prime Minister Yitzhak Rabin and PLO chairman Yasser Arafat. The PLO renounced the use of terrorist acts and committed itself to a peaceful solution of the conflict. Israel, on its part, recognized the PLO as the representative of Palestinians, and agreed to a proposal of a five-year interim period of Palestinian self-rule in the West Bank and Gaza Strip. Arafat's death in 2004 led to a state of renewed uncertainty as a struggle for control of the Palestinian administration developed between Arafat's al-Fatah party and the more extreme Hamas faction.

Arab-Israeli Conflict

By 31 May 1967 Egypt, supported by Syria, Iraq, Jordan and Saudi Arabia, deployed troops across Sinai and declared the Strait of Tiran closed to Israeli shipping. This, combined with Syrian attempts to divert the headwaters of the River Jordan, Israel's main water source, led Israel to a pre-emptive strike. On 5 June, Israel destroyed Egyptian air-bases in Sinai and beyond, attacked the Golan Heights, captured the area and entered El Quneitra. The Jordanian West Bank was occupied and the Old City of Jerusalem annexed as Israel's capital (*maps 1 and 3*). The Six-Day War (5–11 June) destabilized Egypt, paving the way for future agreements between Egypt and Israel. Another result of the 1967 war was the increasingly active role of the Palestinian Liberation Organization (PLO).

After Nasser's death (1970) and Anwar Sadat's succession, the conflict resumed. On 6 October 1973, the Jewish Day of Atonement (Yom Kippur), Egypt and Syria attacked the Golan Heights and Sinai. Despite initial Arab victories, Israeli counter-attacks resulted in further territorial expansion. Negotiations eventually brought an end to the war and in 1977 Sadat made the first visit by an Arab head of state to Israel. The Camp David Accords marked an end to over thirty years of conflict. Sinai was returned to Egypt in 1982. Israel's invasion of southern Lebanon in 1978, to counter Palestinian guerrilla activity,

opened a new front. Despite partial withdrawal in 1985, a nine-mile buffer zone is still held by Israeli troops.

Jewish settlements continue to be built on the land occupied by Israel in 1967. This, coupled with Israeli discrimination against the Palestinians, culminated in December 1987 in the *intifada* (uprising). PLO support for Iraq during the 1990 Gulf War alienated the Arab Gulf states, and eroded its credibility, nevertheless further Israeli-Palestinian agreements were signed (the Declaration of Principles in 1993 and the Wye Accords in 1998) as progress towards a complex solution.

Of an estimated population of five million Palestinians, more than two million have fled from Israel to adjacent Arab lands since 1948 (*map 1, inset*). In addition, more than one million migrated to other Arab countries and to the USA and South America.

The Religious Dimension

The formation of the state of Israel and the 1948, 1956 and 1967 wars were seen as humiliations for Muslims worldwide. Two pan-Islamic organizations, supported by Saudi Arabia, were established to assert international Muslim solidarity: the World Muslim League (est. 1962) and the Organization of the Islamic Conference (1969, 1971). The latter was a direct response to the 1967 Arab defeat, Israel's annexation of east Jerusalem and an arsonist attack against the al-Aqsa mosque. However, these pan-Islamic organizations were at times seen as serving political and national (Saudi) interests. In fact, as the active role played by Christian Palestinians in the *intifada* suggests, the fight for recognition and liberation can be perceived as national rather than purely religious.

One of the issues where religion and politics cannot be separated is the dispute over Jerusalem. For Muslims, the city is the third holy place, after Mecca and Medina. The first Muslims prayed towards Jerusalem before the *qiblah* (direction of prayer) was changed towards Mecca, and Muhammad was believed to have ascended to heaven from Jerusalem. Moreover, its centrality in Judaism and Christianity was inherited by Islam with its acknowledgement of the monotheistic message of the Biblical prophets (*map 2*). To this day, the status and control of the city are major issues of contention.

THE SPREAD OF ISLAM IN THE MODERN WORLD

THE HISTORICAL presence of Islam in Europe can be traced back to the rule of Muslim empires: the Umayyads in Spain, the Fatimids in Sicily and the Ottomans in eastern Europe. The population of Muslim Spain and Sicily remained essentially Christian, but the number of converts to Islam in eastern Europe was considerable; the two largest homogeneous Muslim communities in eastern Europe, the Albanian and the Bosnian, date back to the fifteenth century. Eastern European Muslims are mostly Sunni, of the Hanafite legal school, with some Shi'is (Alevis) in Bulgaria (map 2).

Five centuries of Ottoman rule over Albania resulted in a majority Muslim population (c.70 per cent) at the time of independence in 1912. A communist ban (1967–85) on all religious activities affected the three main religious communities: Muslim, Greek Orthodox and Catholic. However, a religious revival during the 1990s opened the country up to missionaries of other denominations.

About two million, mainly Muslim, ethnic Albanians used to live in the Kosovo province of modern-day Yugoslavia (Serbia and Montenegro). After General Tito's death in 1980 the fragile ethnic and national balance of the country collapsed. Serbian nationalism revived under Yugoslavian president Slobodan Milosevic who, in 1989, removed Kosovo's autonomy. Continued displacement of ethnic Albanians by the Serbs came to the world's attention in 1998 and NATO intervened. The diaspora of ethnic Albanians from the province exceeded half a million, and there were unknown numbers of casualties.

Islam in Europe

Unlike eastern Europe, the presence of Muslims in western Europe mainly results from modern economic and political migration from Muslim countries. Waves of immigration often reflect historical links, as in the case of migration from former colonies (from the Maghreb to

A Halal butcher's shop in south London. Halal ('that which is allowed') denotes, in Islamic legal terms, the dietary rules of permissible food and drink. Halal meat is from permitted animals which have been ritually slaughtered, that is killed in one stroke to allow the blood to pour out of the main artery. Ritual slaughtering is allowed in several European countries, such as Denmark and Britain, but to date it is not permitted in Sweden or Switzerland.

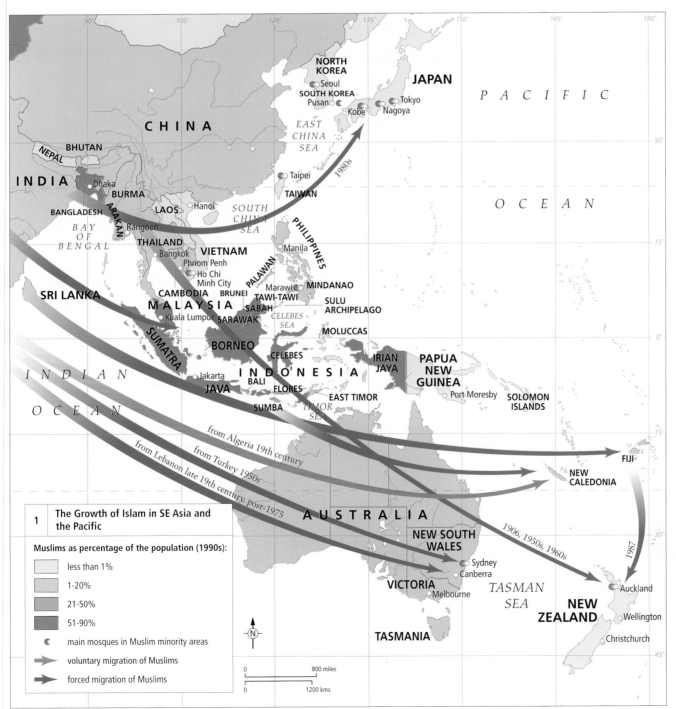

1 | **The Growth of Islam in SE Asia and the Pacific**

Muslims as percentage of the population (1990s):

- less than 1%
- 1-20%
- 21-50%
- 51-90%
- ☾ main mosques in Muslim minority areas
- → voluntary migration of Muslims
- → forced migration of Muslims

0 — 800 miles
0 — 1200 kms

Protests against the American-led invasion of Iraq in 2003 caused widespread demonstrations, not just from the Muslim community, throughout Europe and the United States.

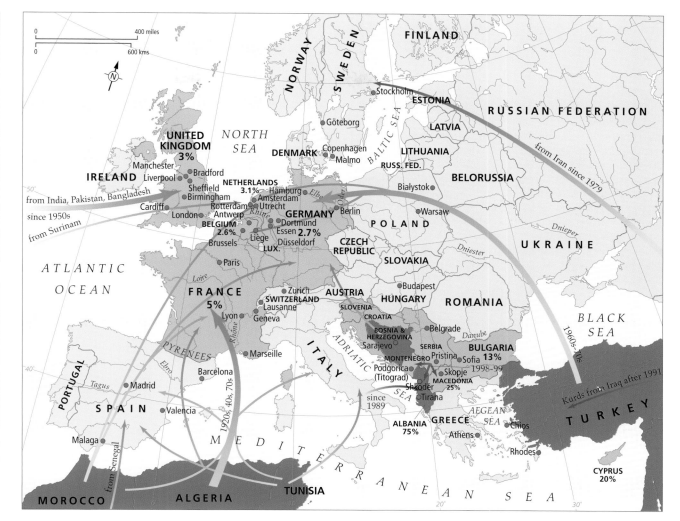

2 | Islam in Europe Today

Muslims as percentage of population:

- less than 2%
- 2% and over (with percentage given when known)
- more than 50%
- • cities with significant Muslim population
- → voluntary migration (less than 750,000)
- ⇒ voluntary migration (more than 750,000)
- → forced migration
- → some repatriation

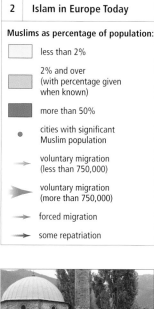

Sarajevo ('the plain of the palace'), the capital of Bosnia, was reported in 1991 to have a population of over 500,000, fifty per cent of which was Muslim. Famous for its buildings, as well as its economic and cultural activities, the city flourished under the Ottomans, especially during the sixteenth century. In 1984, it hosted the Winter Olympics and became a major tourist resort. Following the breakdown of the Yugoslavian Federation, Bosnia declared its independence in 1992 but suffered greatly under the Serbian siege which was only lifted after the Dayton Peace Accords of 1995. More than two million Bosnians have been displaced by the war.

The introduction of legislation to ban the wearing of the hijab (veil) in French schools in 2004 was seen by the Muslim community as a direct infringment of personal liberty and of the right to observe religious tradition. In fact France was not alone, with the Netherlands, Belgium and Norway introducing similar bans.

France, from Commonwealth countries to the UK). The favourable economic and political circumstances of host countries also play a relevant part, as in the case of Turkish migration to Germany. Several factors have an impact on the flow of Muslim migrants; political circumstances; national legislation; the displacement of communities as a result of the Balkan war. Official figures are not always reliable, as shown by the case of illegal immigrants, such as France's 'sans papier'.

European attitudes to Islam in general were severely undermined following Islamic *jihadist* attacks by al-Qaida on the West, notably the 9/11 outrages in America in 2001, which were followed by bomb attacks in Madrid (2004) and London (2005) and a rash of security alerts. Nevertheless, these events did much to foster renewed efforts to establish closer relations between Muslim and Christian communities in Europe.

The religious configuration of Muslims in western Europe reflects the varieties of Islam in the originating countries. While most immigrants are Sunni Muslims, the role of traditions such as Sufi brotherhoods should not be underestimated, especially for the North African immigrants to France. Popular or reformist movements, such as the Barelwis and Deobandis among Indo-Pakistani immigrants to Britain, are also significant.

Islam in Contemporary Southeast Asia

Indonesia and Malaysia are the most important countries in Muslim Southeast Asia (*map 1*). Indonesia, though not constitutionally an Islamic state, has the world's largest Muslim population (about 160 million in 1985, c.87 per cent of the total). It is overwhelmingly Sunni, following the Shafi'i school of law. In Malaysia Islam (c.58 per cent of the total in 1990) is the official religion, co-existing with traditional Chinese religions as well as Hinduism and Christianity. Independent Indonesia and Malaysia have built largely secular states on European models, but the political and cultural role of Islam has been consistently increasing.

In the Philippines and Thailand, less than five per cent of the total population is Muslim. Islam is a minority religion which is trying to resist state control. In the Philippines, the community was marginalized by a process of de-islamization, provoking the emergence of radical groups like the Moro National Liberation Front which used armed struggle and guerrilla techniques to achieve recognition of independence for the Muslim population, concentrated mainly in the south. Autonomy was eventually granted to the Muslim region in Mindanao in 1987 and limited executive powers were transferred to the regional government in 1990. Thailand, although predominantly Buddhist, also has a concentration of Muslims in the south, near the border with Malaysia. Some Islamic separatist movements, allegedly backed by Iran, are active in the southern provinces.

Minority Islam in the Pacific

Although the first Muslim migrations to the Pacific region date back to the late nineteenth century, it is not until the 1950s that Muslim communities can be identified. In Australia, Muslims are estimated at c.1.4 per cent of the total population (1993). The vast majority of Muslims in Australia comes from Turkey and the Lebanon, along with others from the former Yugoslavia. Students from neighbouring Muslim countries, especially Malaysia, form an increasingly important presence. New Zealand's small Muslim community is mainly from Southeast Asia, and there was a particularly important immigration wave after the 1987 *coups d'état* in Fiji. The mosque in Christchurch is said to be the furthest from Mecca in the world. Both Fiji and New Caledonia have sizeable Muslim communities. Fiji's Muslims can be traced back to the late nineteenth century when French authorities deported anti-colonial leaders from the Maghreb, particularly Algeria, to the penal colony of Fiji.

The small Muslim community of Japan, in part allegedly of Turkish origin, increased during the twentieth century by immigration from South Asia.

VARIETIES OF ISLAM TODAY

THE ARABIC term *umma* (community of believers) indicates the unity of all Muslims beyond ethnic, linguistic, cultural and national boundaries. During the Prophet's time, the first Muslim *umma* was almost exclusively composed of Arabs. Historical developments such as conquest and conversion led to the incorporation of Persians, Berbers, Turks and other peoples (*map 3*)

Muslim unity found in its ritual language, Arabic, its most vivid expression. By the late seventh century Arabic had become the administrative language of the Muslim empire. Varieties of spoken Arabic emerged as a result of ethno-linguistic influences and historical developments. The Arabic dialects of North Africa, for instance, were influenced by the Berber languages and, more recently, by decades of French colonialism and French education.

Despite the influence of Arabic, some vernacular languages of the Muslim empire survived (*map 2*): during the ninth century Persian re-emerged as a literary language, while Turkish became the official language of the Ottoman empire. The impact of Arabic remained in lexical and stylistic borrowings as well as in the adoption of its script, which is used not only for Ottoman Turkish (up until 1928), modern Persian and Urdu, but also for Malay and, until recently, for Bahasa Indonesian.

Ethnicity and Religious Minorities

Ethnicity plays an important role in the expression of religious allegiance to Islam (*map 1*). Among the majority Sunni population of northern Africa, for example, some Berber groups in Algeria and Libya affirm their ethnic identity by adhering to the Ibadiyah, a moderate Khariji group. New trends within, or stemming from, Islam have been discouraged, sometimes persecuted, as in the case of the Baha'is, who originated in Iran during the nineteenth century and were forced to migrate or to conceal their faith. Today, the largest Baha'i community lives in India. Muslim religious minorities are also occasionally able to assume political power; the 'Alawis of Syria, for example, while representing probably no more than 10 per cent of the total population, became influential during the

French mandate and, in 1971, an 'Alawi military leader, Hafez al-Assad (1930–2000) became Syria's president, and was succeeded by his son, Bashar.

Islam in the Americas

The presence of an estimated 6 to 7 million Muslims in the Americas (*map 4*) is due to distinct waves of Muslim migration as well as local conversions. It is commonly accepted that the first Muslim migrations to the Americas date to the late fifteenth century, when Moriscos, expelled from Spain by the Reconquista, reached South America. From the seventeenth century, black Africans, captured and bought as slaves in West Africa, arrived in America. With the abolition of slavery in the mid-nineteenth century, Asian immigrants arrived as indentured labourers from the Indian subcontinent and Java.

More recent migrations to North America pre-dated the First World War and consisted of mainly Arabs from Greater Syria, followed by Muslims from eastern and southern Europe. After the Second World War, more

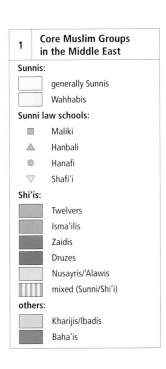

1 Core Muslim Groups in the Middle East

Sunnis:
- generally Sunnis
- Wahhabis

Sunni law schools:
- ▪ Maliki
- ▲ Hanbali
- ● Hanafi
- ▽ Shafi'i

Shi'is:
- Twelvers
- Isma'ilis
- Zaidis
- Druzes
- Nusayris/'Alawis
- mixed (Sunni/Shi'i)

others:
- Kharijis/Ibadis
- Baha'is

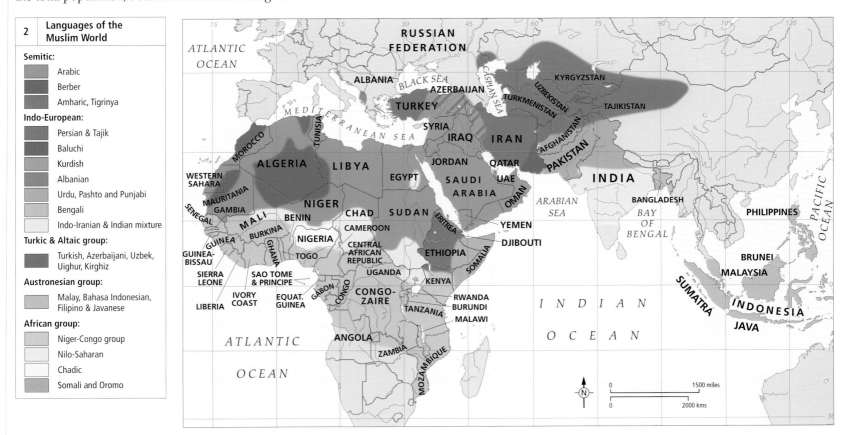

2 Languages of the Muslim World

Semitic:
- Arabic
- Berber
- Amharic, Tigrinya

Indo-European:
- Persian & Tajik
- Baluchi
- Kurdish
- Albanian
- Urdu, Pashto and Punjabi
- Bengali
- Indo-Iranian & Indian mixture

Turkic & Altaic group:
- Turkish, Azerbaijani, Uzbek, Uighur, Kirghiz

Austronesian group:
- Malay, Bahasa Indonesian, Filipino & Javanese

African group:
- Niger-Congo group
- Nilo-Saharan
- Chadic
- Somali and Oromo

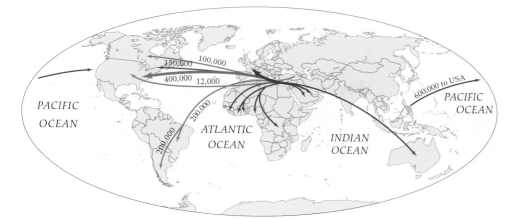

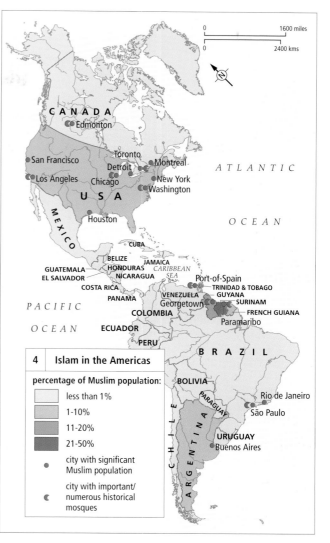

5	Some Inter-continental Migrations of Muslims

major Lebanese migrations (since 1945)

Palestinian migrations (since 1948)

Kurdish migrations (since 1945)

Philippine migrations (since 1945)

other migrations of Lebanese Muslims

numbers refer to total numbers by country of origin, with varying percentages of Muslims

The annual hajj brings together pilgrims from across the Muslim world, Indonesians, Africans, Pakistanis, Chinese and many from believers from the Western hemisphere as well.

3	Ethnicity and Culture

Arab

Berber (including Tuareg)

Nubian and Nilotic

Amhara and Tigray

Somalis

Malay

mixed Afghan and Brahui

Tatar, Bashkir, Kazakh, Uzbek

Uighur

Persian, Bakhtiari

Kurd

Baluchi

Afghan, Hazara & Nuristani

Bengali

Indian & mixed Indian

Fulani, Yoruba and others

Slav

mixed Caucasian, Turk & Turcoman

Tamil

Javanese and others

Sundanese

Minangkabau

Muslims emigrated from the Middle East and some from South Asia. American immigration laws were liberalized in 1965, and Muslims arrived from the Arab countries, as well as Turkey, Iran, Afghanistan and Pakistan.

The immigrants of the early years of this century were scattered geographically. Without the benefit of organized community support, they expressed religious identity in general terms. More recent immigrants, however, enjoy the support of Islamic organizations and networks and tend to resist assimilation.

The Nation of Islam, a black 'nationalist' and messianic movement, was founded in Detroit in 1930 by Farad Muhammad. It emphasized black liberation through self-development and elaborated a mythology in which the white race was the creation of evil forces. Its message appealed to the unemployed youths of inner-city black ghettos. Since 1978, Louis Farrakhan has been the leader of a minority group of the Nation of Islam which has continued the policy of black separation. The majority branch, (the 'American Muslim Mission'), has been successful in aligning with Sunni Islam. Here, a universalistic doctrine has opened its affiliation to all Muslims, irrespective of race.

Some Muslim Diasporas

Most Muslim diaspora communities have spread as a result of conflict, as with the Palestinians, or persecution, as with the Kurds. Mostly Muslim, the Kurds originally lived in an area bordering Iran, Iraq, Turkey, Syria and Armenia. Many have since migrated to Germany,

Sweden and the USA. The Lebanese diaspora (*map 5*), at first mainly of Christians, was economic in nature. After the Second World War, more Sunnis and Shi'is migrated to France, the Americas, West Africa and Australia. The 1975–89 Lebanese civil war has increased the number of Lebanese abroad: the Lebanese diaspora worldwide is now estimated at 2.5 million.

AFRICA

THE MAPPING of indigenous religious practice in Africa is problematic. Most African languages in the past did not include a word which can convincingly be translated as 'religion', and it can therefore be argued that separate and distinct indigenous 'religions' as such did not exist. Furthermore, relatively few of those concepts and practices which one might describe as 'religious' seem to be confined to a single ethnic community or language group; many more transcend language and ethnic differences and exhibit a regional significance.

Religious Concepts

In the absence of local definitions in Africa, the 'religious' can be defined as those relationships between living persons and the spiritual entities and invisible forces which they believe affect their lives. A schematic representation of these relationships is presented in the table below, which illustrates that interaction between human beings and spiritual entities is mediated through religious experts (priests, mediums, etc.) usually in specially prepared ritual spaces or sacred places, such as shrines or altars.

The specific characteristics of spiritual entities and forces and the nature and scope of their influence on living beings varies considerably, but most societies posit the existence of a creator deity, often referred to as the God of the Sky. Paradoxically, this god (usually gendered as male, but sometimes as female) is conceptualized as the 'god of everyone', although individuals have relatively little, if any, direct ritual relationship with him or her. Most religious activity is directed towards other categories of spiritual entities who directly affect the lives of individuals and communities.

Different spiritual entities interact with different groups within the living community. Thus, ancestors are generally concerned with the welfare of their own descendants, who in return are required to maintain proper ritual relationships with them. Deities and other spirits may be concerned with the productivity of the land or the welfare of broader-based social communities, such as villages or chiefdoms, and are served by specially trained religious experts. Persons might also maintain ritual relationships with individual spirits. African religion is therefore characterized by a rich diversity of spiritual entities and ritual activities, of which only a few representative examples can be explored here.

Religious Practice

Unlike Christianity and Islam, African religion is concerned, not with attaining eternal salvation in an afterlife, but with sustaining the welfare of the living community. Because of its primary emphasis on sustaining life, much of African religious practice is addressed to ensuring good fortune and to assuaging misfortune; the theme of

First Kushite state in Kerma, 3500		Second Kushite state in Napata, 750		Rome defeats Carthage and occupies North Africa, 146	**CE**	Rise of Axum; Ezana converts to Christianity, 400	Arabs conquer North Africa, 501	King of Kanem converts to Christianity, 1051	Kongo King converts to Christianity, 1056	Usman dan Fodio's *jihad* in Hausaland, 1804	Emergence of prophetic Christian movements, 1920s
►	to 1,000	►	1,000	► 500		500 ►	1000		1500	►	2000 ►
	Capital of Kushite state moves from Napata to Meroë, c.500			Bantu languages spread east and south from present-day Nigeria-Cameroon, 200		Nigerian Nok culture in existence, 500	Development of trans-Saharan trade, 800	Islam expands in the Sahel,1055	Dutch settlers in Cape of Good Hope, 1652	Mahdist state in Sudan, 1885	African states achieve independence 1960s-70s

THE WORLD

First urban civilizations, Mesopotamia, c.3500		Upanisads collected, c.700-300		Gautama Siddhartha, c.563-483	**CE**	Mani, 216-c.275	End of Western Roman Empire, 476	Text of Quran established, c.653	First Crusade, 1095	Columbus lands in America, 1492	2nd Vatican Council, 1961-4
►	to 1,000	►	1,000	► 500		500 ►	1000		1500	►	2000 ►
	Aryan migration, India, c.1500-900	Zarathustra, c.1000		Confucius, c.551-479	Aristotle, 384-323	Jesus, c.6 BCE-26/36 CE	Christianity tolerated in Roman Empire, 313	Muhammad, 570-632	East and West Christian churches separate, 1054	Fall of Constantinople to Turks,1453	Council of Trent, 1545-63	1st Zionist Conference, 1897

social and personal healing therefore informs most religious thought in Africa. Many creation myths posit a deistic view of a productive and bountiful world created in perfect harmony which can only be maintained through proper religious practice. Many of life's misfortunes, from the failure of rains and the resulting poor harvests to the high incidence of infant mortality, are understood in religious terms to have been caused by human failures in maintaining appropriate ritual relationships with spiritual entities.

Although individuals can personally entreat certain spiritual entities to support and protect them, most religious activities are mediated by religious experts who have received specialized training, often in the form of lengthy initiations, to prepare them to interact with spiritual entities and forces. Much of this kind of expert religious knowledge is secret because it is believed that association with spiritual entities and powers is potentially dangerous and must therefore be carefully controlled.

Individuals do not normally become religious experts by personal choice, but because they have been selected for this service, either by members of the relevant social group or by the spiritual entities themselves. For example, ritual relations with ancestors are often maintained by the eldest male of the lineage or household head who has been trained and prepared for this role by virtue of his birth. Similarly, individuals might be selected by community elders to train for the priesthood of one or more communal deities. By contrast, a calling from spiritual entities to serve them often manifests itself as a kind of 'illness' in which an individual begins to manifest symptoms of unusual or abnormal social behaviour. When such symptoms are diagnosed by religious experts as a religious calling, the individual is expected to undergo the appropriate religious initiations into the priesthood of the deities or spirits concerned.

Ritual relationships with spiritual entities can take several forms: invocations or prayers which are offered as entreaties for the well-being of communities or individuals; exchanges such as sacrifices and gifts which are offered in appreciation or anticipation of well-being; and medium-ship, when spiritual entities communicate directly with the living community through specially prepared religious experts.

Religious Change

The adoption of Christianity and Islam introduced its converts to many fundamental changes in religious concept and practice, for example, the promise of eternal life in paradise, as well as the concomitant notion of personal sin, new forms of religious worship to a monotheistic God in church and mosque, and so forth. However, Africans often adapted the principles of Christianity and Islam to conform with indigenous understandings of religion. For example, leaders of independent Christian churches often reinterpreted Biblical themes of healing in the light of local concept and practice, and medium-ship took on new prophetic forms as well as becoming focused on possession by the Holy Spirit. Similarly, the perceived efficacy of Muslim healing practices was a major reason for Islam's expanding influence, and many African Muslims tempered the severe monotheism of orthodox Islam with continued relationships with other spiritual entities, such as *jinn* and other spirits.

Similarly, the millions of Africans who were transported to the countries of the western hemisphere as slaves managed to combine and adapt their religious practices to their needs in this new hostile environment. Candomblé and Tambor da Mina in Brazil, Voudoun in Haiti, and Santería in Cuba are examples of new religious forms which are amalgamations of religious practice from many different parts of western Africa but which nonetheless have retained most of the characteristics of African religious concept and practice described above.

THE VISIBLE WORLD OF MANIFEST REALITY	RELIGIOUS PERSONS AND SACRED PLACES	THE INVISIBLE REALM OF SPIRITUAL ENTITIES AND FORCES WHICH SUSTAIN THE VISIBLE WORLD
❑ **Human society**	**Religious experts:** ❑ priests ❑ mediums ❑ prophets	
	Sacred places: ❑ sacred groves ❑ shrines ❑ altars	**Spiritual entities** ❑ God above or the god of everyone ❑ deities ❑ ancestors ❑ spirits

EARLY RELIGION IN NORTHEAST AFRICA

THE THIRD MILLENNIUM BCE saw the emergence of the first known Kushite kingdom around the town of Kerma in Upper Nubia. Little is known of this kingdom, the remains of which were only discovered at the turn of the century. Archaeological digs have shown, however, that the Kushites shared with their Egyptian contemporaries a belief in an afterlife in which the social status of individuals was perpetuated. The kings of Kush were elected by the gods, who entrusted them with the well-being of this world and gave them a share of their own divinity to help fulfil their mission.

In the sixteenth century BCE, Kerma was destroyed by the Thebans. For the following seven centuries, Nubia fell under the political, economic and cultic control of the flourishing New Kingdom. Successive pharaohs established temple-towns along the Nile and imposed their religion, especially the political cult of Amun of Thebes, upon the Kushites.

The Rise of Meroë

In the course of the eighth century BCE, a second Kushite kingdom emerged around the town of Napata. The

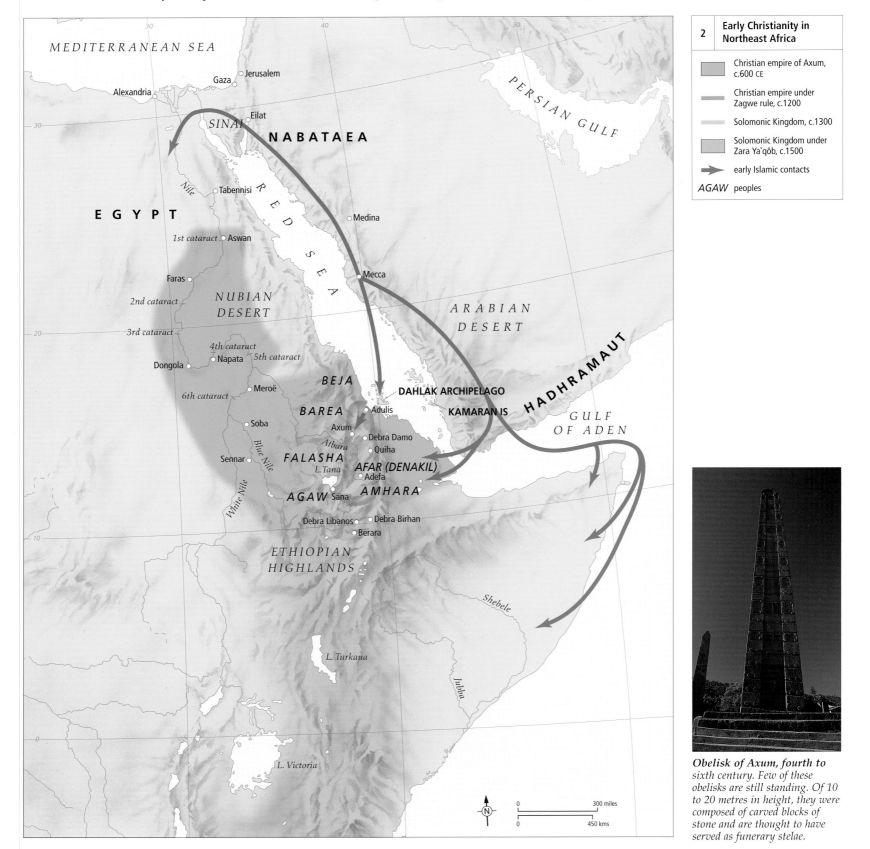

2	Early Christianity in Northeast Africa
	Christian empire of Axum, c.600 CE
	Christian empire under Zagwe rule, c.1200
	Solomonic Kingdom, c.1300
	Solomonic Kingdom under Zara Yaʿqôb, c.1500
→	early Islamic contacts
AGAW	peoples

Obelisk of Axum, fourth to sixth century. Few of these obelisks are still standing. Of 10 to 20 metres in height, they were composed of carved blocks of stone and are thought to have served as funerary stelae.

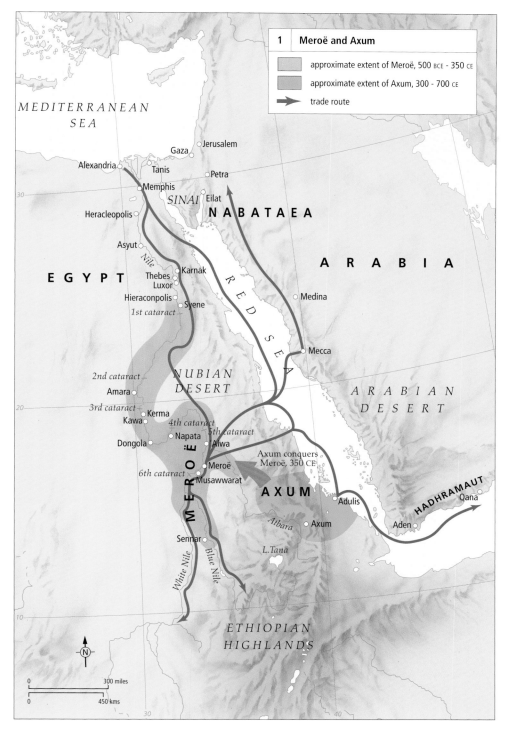

St George of Lalibela. This cruciform church was carved into the rock below ground level in the twelfth century during King Lalibela's campaign to further spread the Christian message amongst his peoples. It still serves as a pilgrimage centre.

part of southern Arabia and conquered Meroë in the fourth century CE, converted to Christianity through the intervention of two young prisoners who had been given clerical functions in his court. One of these, Frumentus, became the first 'Abba, or bishop, of Axum. After they converted to Christianity, the kings of Axum came to be considered the elect of God on Earth. As such, they enjoyed considerable influence over the church's worldly administration. Their rule also was legitimized by this divine sanction.

Championed by the royal family, Christianity spread rapidly in Axum. During the fifth century CE, nine saints toured the country destroying shrines and temples and replacing them with churches and sanctuaries. One of these, Debra Damo, which replaced a temple dedicated to a serpent god, is still standing today.

Closely associated with the ruling family, the decline of Axum in the following centuries led also to the stagnation of the Christian Church. It is only during the twelfth century, under the Zagwe dynasty, that Christianity recovered some sway over the Ethiopian population (*map 2*). King Lalibela's reign especially was marked by a renewal of religious fervour. He ordered the construction of several churches, destined to serve as pilgrimage centres for those Ethiopian Christians who could not make the trip to Jerusalem.

The Kingdom of Solomon

In 1270, a member of the Solomonite dynasty conquered the throne. The rise of this dynasty brought to an end Kushite domination over Upper and Lower Nubia. The Solomonites, who ruled Ethiopia until Haile Selassie was ousted by a military coup in 1974, were Semitic and imposed their Semitic tongue, Amharic, upon Ethiopia. They also imposed their peculiar reading of Ethiopian history. The *Kubra Nagast* or 'Glory of the Kings', a volume composed in the thirteenth century to legitimize their claim to the throne, explains the rise of Christianity in Ethiopia with reference to Solomon and Sheba's encounter. The *Kubra Nagast* holds that a son, Menelik, was born of this encounter. After meeting his father in Jerusalem, Menelik is said to have returned to Ethiopia with all the first-borns of Israel and the Ark of the Covenant, a chest containing the Tables of Jewish law. To this day, a *tabot*, or shard of wood symbolizing this Ark is carefully preserved in the inner sanctum of every Ethiopian church.

kings of Napata occupied much of Upper Egypt until 654 BCE. The Kushite kings championed the cult of Amun, suggesting that the New Kingdom had imposed both its pantheon and its theology upon the Kushites.

However, after the capital was moved from Napata to Meroë in the sixth century BCE (*map 1*), indigenous customs and gods unknown in the Egyptian pantheon gained a new lease of life. Excavations have shown that the Kushites resumed the practice of human and animal sacrifice during funerary rites. Apedemek, a lion god of war unknown to the Egyptians, gained pride of place in the Meroitic pantheon. Even Amun took on a distinctly Meroitic guise, and was increasingly associated with warfare. During the Meroitic period indigenous elements meshed with a theology inherited from Egypt. In Meroë, these cults disappeared only after the region was conquered by the Christian Axumites in the fourth century CE.

Christianity in Ethiopia

Prior to the introduction of Christianity, the Ethiopian population venerated gods drawn from several pantheons, including those of Persia, Greece and southern Arabia. King Ezana of Axum, who ruled over

THE SANCTIFICATION OF POLITICAL OFFICE

THE INSTALLATION of the rulers of many African polities into political office was accompanied by a series of rituals which imbued them with special religious powers. This sanctification of political office was based on the idea that the welfare and prosperity of the state, chiefdom, or even empire was intimately associated with the personal health and welfare of the ruler.

Life-Giving Powers

The rituals which accompanied the elevation of an individual to high political office in such societies in effect transformed an 'ordinary' human being into a potent, even dangerous, personage. Invested with exceptional religious powers, the body of such a ruler was often treated with numerous precautions. Accordingly, sacred rulers were submitted to various ritual prohibitions: many were not allowed to leave their palaces, they could receive their courtiers only from behind screens and curtains, their subjects could not set eyes upon them, they only ever spoke through spokesmen, they ate alone, and their bare feet were never to touch the ground. Their bodies were washed and their hair cut according to intricate cosmological calendars. Sacrifices were made to them and their bodies were adorned with countless amulets and charms which would sustain or feed their life-giving powers.

Because the welfare of the polity and the ruler were so closely inter-connected, some sanctified rulers were not allowed to die a natural death. Even a failure in the health of such a ruler might be interpreted as a sign of impending social or political crisis. Consequently, some sacred rulers were at times required to commit suicide or were put to death when they fell ill or before they became too aged. This was believed to maintain the continuity of the religious forces which sustained the general well-being of the polity.

Rites of Passage

The association of political with spiritual power existed throughout much of Africa, in many different social and political contexts, although concepts and practices varied in detail. In some areas, rulers were thought to be invested with a vital force which infused all creation, variously termed *ase* (Yoruba), *bulopwe* (Luba) or *kra* (Ghana). Various myths account for how the founding ancestors of different societies gained access to this force and made it available to the world of the living through certain of their descendants who themselves became sanctified rulers. However, in most societies, these

Painting depicting the ninth-century burial chamber of a king of Igbo Ukwu. The king was buried seated, in full regalia. He is shown here wearing his beaded crown and carrying the staff that symbolized his office. Around him are scattered further objects associated with his office.

religious powers were not simply inherited but were transmitted to a newly selected ruler in the context of an often lengthy series of rituals.

These rituals of investiture follow the pattern of most transformative rites of passage in which the individual 'dies' to his or her existing social roles and status and is 'reborn' as a new person. Although such rituals vary in complexity, all consist of three phases. First the newly selected candidate is removed from ordinary life and stripped of all physical and social relationships with it. The second stage is a more or less prolonged period of seclusion under the supervision of special religious experts. They bring about the candidate's religious transformation into a sanctified ruler whose very person is placed into contact with the spiritual entities and forces which guarantee the continued welfare of the polity. The new ruler's body becomes the medium of the spiritual forces which will sustain the polity. The third stage of the ritual process is the 'rebirth' of the sacred office in the person of a newly sanctified ruler who is invested with the symbols of office and who is often carried to the palace, throne or stool.

These kinds of rituals were prevalent throughout Africa. For example, in Ife, Oyo and Benin (*map 2*), the institution of sanctified kingship originated with Oduduwa, an *orisa* (deity) who descended from the sky as the agent of Olorun (god of the sky) first to create the earth and then as the first 'divine' king of the Yoruba. Only descendants of Oduduwa can don the beaded crown that symbolizes divine kingship. In Oyo, the newly appointed king is captured by his courtiers, stripped of his ordinary clothing, dressed anew in white robes, isolated for a period of three months and only then presented to the people for his enthroning.

Perpetual Kinship

In Luba and in much of central Africa, a similar ritual is enacted. In addition, a mechanism known as perpetual kinship serves to further separate the king from his subjects: new kings do not only inherit the wealth and office of their predecessors, they also take on their name and their kin relations. In this way, two distant cousins descended from brothers will literally become brothers. The kin relations established by mythical ancestors are thus perpetuated through the agency of sanctified political office.

Sanctified political offices were prominent in all the kingdoms and empires illustrated on the maps and are examples of relatively powerful and extensive polities. However, the sanctification of political office was common on all levels of political life, even in the smallest polities. All available evidence suggests that successful political leadership in Africa was consistently attributed to the effective use of religious knowledge and powers.

1	Sacred Kingship

approximate extent of kingdoms, with dates:

	pre-800
	9th–13th centuries
	14th–15th centuries
	16th–19th centuries
FANG	language groups

The asantehene *ruler of the Asante Confederation, founded in the eighteenth century. The power and authority of the Confederation was symbolized by the Golden Stool which descended from the sky, and which is here placed on its own throne next to the* asantehene.

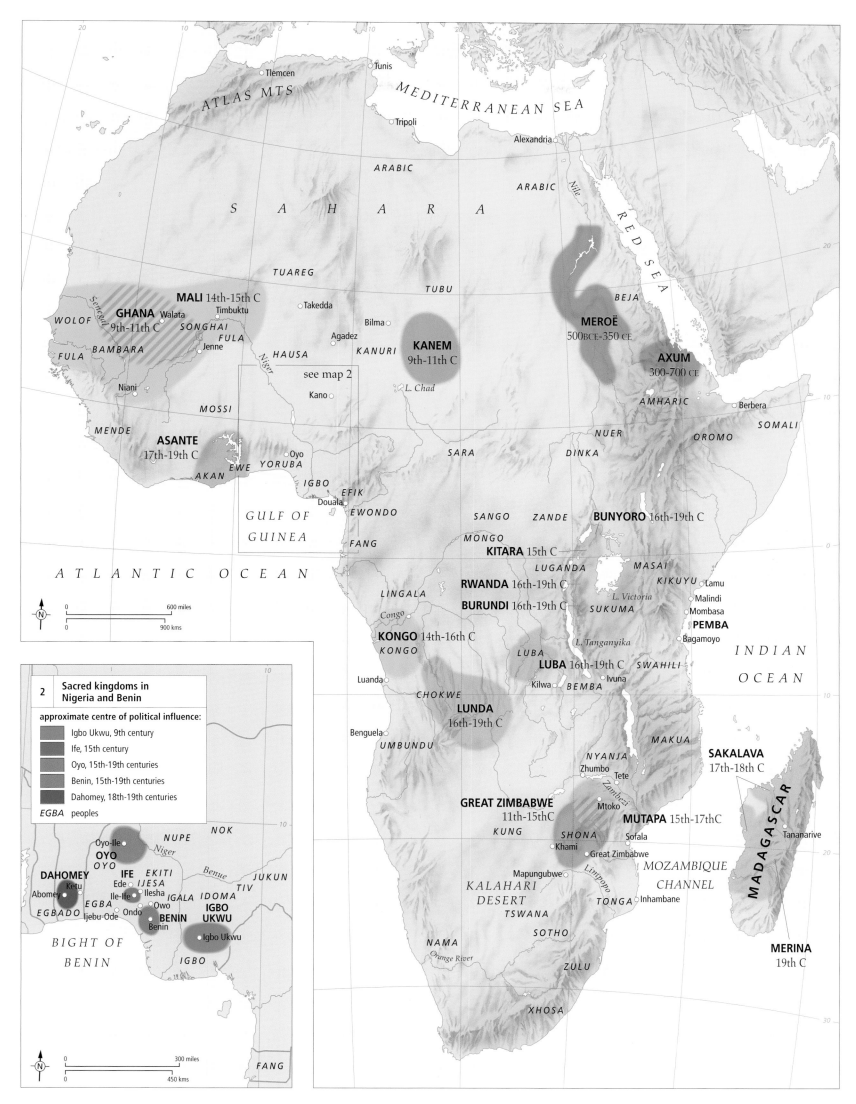

ATLAS MTS

MEDITERRANEAN SEA

Tlemcen

Tunis

Tripoli

Alexandria

ARABIC

ARABIC

S A H A R A

RED SEA

TUAREG

TUBU

BEJA

MEROË
500BCE-350 CE

MALI 14th-15th C

GHANA
9th-11th C

Walata

Timbuktu

Takedda

Bilma

Agadez

KANEM
9th-11th C

AXUM
300-700 CE

WOLOF

SONGHAI

FULA

KANURI

Jenne

Niger

HAUSA

see map 2

L. Chad

AMHARIC

Berbera

BAMBARA

FULA

Niani

Kano

SOMALI

MENDE

MOSSI

NUER

OROMO

ASANTE
17th-19th C

Oyo

YORUBA

SARA

DINKA

AKAN

EWE

IGBO

EFIK

Douala

EWONDO

BUNYORO 16th-19th C

GULF OF
GUINEA

FANG

MONGO

SANGO

ZANDE

KITARA 15th C

LUGANDA

MASAI

ATLANTIC OCEAN

LINGALA

RWANDA 16th-19th C

KIKUYU

Lamu

BURUNDI 16th-19th C

SUKUMA

Malindi

L. Victoria

Mombasa

N

600 miles

900 kms

Congo

KONGO 14th-16th C

KONGO

LUBA

PEMBA

Bagamoyo

L. Tanganyika

INDIAN
OCEAN

2 Sacred kingdoms in
Nigeria and Benin

approximate centre of political influence:

Igbo Ukwu, 9th century

Ife, 15th century

Oyo, 15th-19th centuries

Benin, 15th-19th centuries

Dahomey, 18th-19th centuries

EGBA peoples

Luanda

CHOKWE

LUBA 16th-19th C

SWAHILI

Kilwa

Ivuna

BEMBA

LUNDA
16th-19th C

SAKALAVA
17th-18th C

UMBUNDU

MAKUA

Benguela

NYANJA

Zhumbo

Tete

Zambezi

GREAT ZIMBABWE
11th-15thC

Mtoko

MUTAPA 15th-17thC

Tananarive

NOK

SHONA

Sofala

NUPE

Oyo-Ile

Niger

OYO

OYO

Benue

JUKUN

KUNG

Khami

Great Zimbabwe

MOZAMBIQUE
CHANNEL

MADAGASCAR

DAHOMEY

IFE

EKITI

Ede

IJESA

TIV

Mapungubwe

Abomey

Ketu

Ile-Ife

Ilesha

IGALA

IDOMA

KALAHARI
DESERT

Limpopo

TONGA

Inhambane

Owo

EGBA

EGBADO

Ijebu-Ode

Ondo

BENIN

Benin

IGBO
UKWU

TSWANA

Igbo Ukwu

NAMA

SOTHO

BIGHT OF
BENIN

IGBO

Orange River

ZULU

MERINA
19th C

N

300 miles

450 kms

FANG

XHOSA

HEALING CULTS

HEALING CULTS, also known as 'cults of affliction', are religious associations which respond to 'illnesses' that are believed to be the result of intervention by spiritual entities in the lives of living persons. One defining characteristic of these cults is that the healing process includes a religious initiation which enables the patient to maintain an appropriate ritual relationship with the spirit who has afflicted him or her. Spirit-caused 'illnesses' or afflictions can therefore be likened to a religious calling.

The Healing Process

Such healing cults share a number of common features. Each is devoted to the treatment of afflictions caused by specific spirits or collectives of spirits who can be recognized, in part, by the symptoms from which the patient suffers. These afflictions are generally thought to be caused by a spirit coming near to, or sometimes possessing, the patient. However, the healing process is not intended to exorcize the spirits but to empower the patient to sustain close proximity to them and to use this relationship for the benefit of others.

When a spirit-caused affliction is suspected, a patient will consult a diviner or other religious expert to determine which spirit or spirits is responsible and which healing association should be approached in order to effect a 'cure'. The healing process proceeds through two stages: the treatment of the physiological symptoms to return the patient to 'normal' health is followed by a series of initiations and rituals which transform the patient into an adept of the healing cult. Adepts may subsequently continue their religious training and themselves become healers. This process therefore transforms a sufferer into a healer, and it has been said that the most characteristic feature of these healing cults is their transformation of misfortune and adversity into power and wholeness.

Zar/Bori

Zar originated in Ethiopia, and is thought by some to have derived from Kushitic religious practice. It spread to the Sudan in the 1820s, to Egypt in the 1850s, and to the Gulf states towards the end of the nineteenth century (*map 1*); the practice is known among Somali-speakers as *sar*. The origins of *bori* are obscure, although the practice was recorded among Hausa-speakers as early as the fifteenth century. The spirit fields associated with *zar* and *bori* tend to be represented as spirit communities which

reflect the social categories of the living community as well as their changing socio-political circumstances. *Bori* pantheons include Muslims and non-Muslims, chiefs and commoners and different ethnic categories. *Zar* pantheons in Sudan can include Sufis (Darawish), Ethiopians (Habashi), Europeans (Khawajat), servants and slaves.

Zar/bori healing cults are generally found in Muslim societies; *zar/bori* spirits primarily (but not exclusively) afflict women and can justifiably be described as a women's religious practice, thus illustrating one of the ways in which gender is asssociated with religious practice in Africa. One of the most common symptoms of affliction by *zar* spirits is female fertility problems. Some scholars have argued that Islamization tended to marginalize the religious status of women, who in effect continued to maintain their ritual relationships with pre-Islamic spiritual entities in a manner which evolved into *zar/bori* practice.

Zar/bori adepts become the mediums of the spirits which initially afflicted them, usually through possession; that is, the spirits enter the bodies of their mediums, through whom they speak and interact with the living community. Mediums who are possessed in this manner in effect serve their spirits by giving over their bodies to them for the benefit of others. When in a state of possession, the medium becomes completely passive and is therefore not responsible for anything said or done.

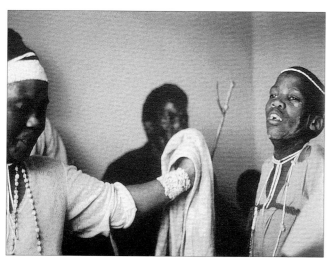

Two novices participating *in one of the many ritual sessions which constitute their lengthy initiation. Here they are presenting their 'new' selves through the medium of a call and response song-dance performance. (Cape Town, South Africa)*

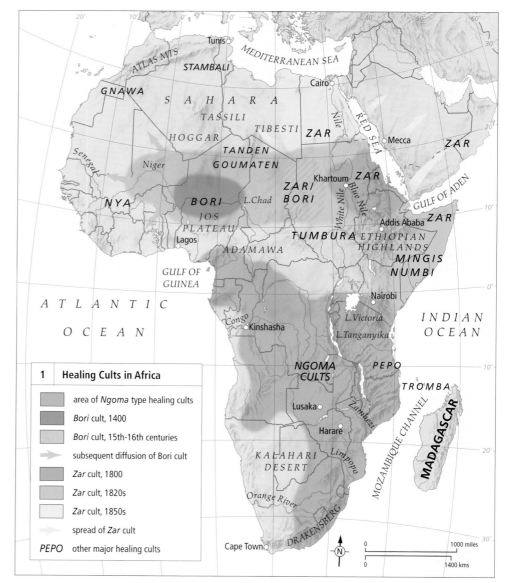

1	**Healing Cults in Africa**
	area of *Ngoma* type healing cults
	Bori cult, 1400
	Bori cult, 15th-16th centuries
→	subsequent diffusion of Bori cult
	Zar cult, 1800
	Zar cult, 1820s
	Zar cult, 1850s
→	spread of *Zar* cult
PEPO	other major healing cults

A young woman possessed by a bori *new witch spirit, a category of spirits particularly concerned with human fertility and reproduction. Both her physical posture and facial expression indicate that she has been 'mounted' by a spirit. (Niger)*

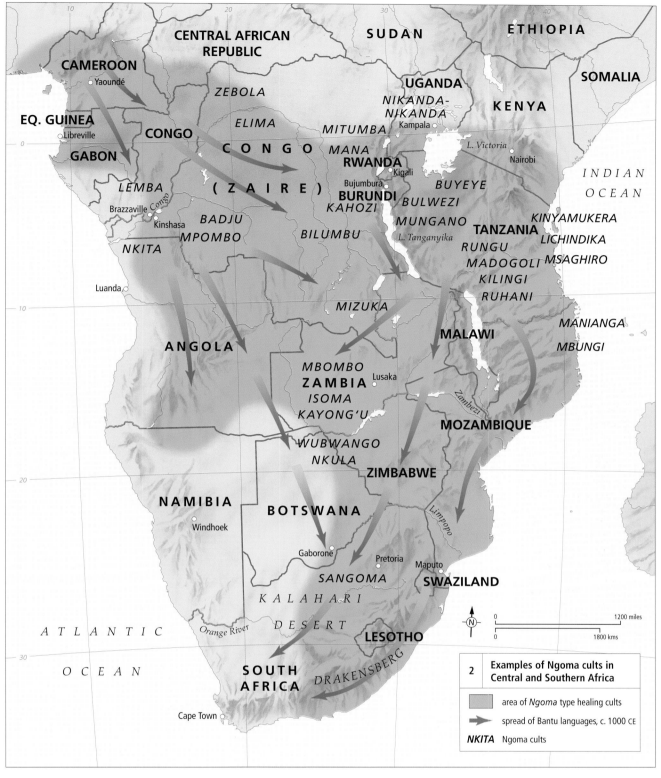

2 Examples of Ngoma cults in Central and Southern Africa

- area of *Ngoma* type healing cults
- → spread of Bantu languages, c. 1000 CE
- *NKITA* Ngoma cults

Ngoma

Ngoma-type healing cults are to be found among the Bantu-speaking peoples of central and southern Africa (*map 2*). It has been argued on the basis of linguistic evidence that these cults may have originated as early as the first millennium CE. Only a few of the literally hundreds of different kinds of *ngoma* cults are indicated on the adjacent map, and they perform numerous different functions. For example, the *isangoma* among Zulu speakers is primarily a female cult of diviners. Women are 'called' into the cult by their ancestors, with whom they learn to maintain a proper ritual relationship through a lengthy initiation.

The *lemba* cult in the lower Congo was a powerful association of male priests who controlled the markets and long-distance trade in the region for several centuries. Characteristically of *ngoma* healing cults, *lemba* was the name of the healing cult as well as the affliction which it healed. *Lemba* was also the name of the powerful 'sanctified medicine' controlled by the *lemba*

priests which enabled them both to heal those afflicted by *lemba* illness and to exact punishments from those persons who contravened the *lemba* taboos.

Possession is not so common among *ngoma* adepts and priests as in *zar/bori*, but they are in close contact with the spirits with whom they are ritually associated and are often thought to be able to control them. The ancestor spirits are said to hover over *isangoma* diviners, from where they can assist in divination seances.

Music and dance are integral to much *zar/bori* and *ngoma* ritual practice. Music is one of the most important mediums through which living persons can communicate with spiritual entities. Each *zar/bori* spirit has its own musical phrases or signatures which, when played, summon them to participate in ritual activities by possessing their adepts, who often dance in order to prepare themselves to receive their spirits. The word *ngoma* actually means drum, as well as music and dance; the *ngoma* drum, or other musical instruments, are also used to summon spirits in most healing rituals.

REGIONAL CULTS

REGIONAL CULTS share many features with healing cults. However, whereas healing cults tend to address the suffering of individuals, regional cults are concerned above all with ecological and societal ills such as droughts, floods and epidemics. The spirits to whom these cults are devoted are thought to ensure the fertility of the land and its inhabitants. These same spirits also have the power to cause misfortune in retaliation for breaches in ritual prescriptions or the mismanagement of the land.

The communities created through, and by, these cults are thus cemented by pragmatic considerations as well as by a moral code. They can extend across ecological zones and they attract adepts from different national and ethnic backgrounds. Regional cults are cults of the middle-range: their appeal is neither universal nor strictly local. In this respect, they challenge the common assumption that religion in Africa is ethnically specific.

The leading figures in the regional cults are mediums who, as in the healing cults, have been called to the service of the spirits by a persistent illness, which is treated by initiation into the cult. These mediums enjoy a peculiar position: since it is through them that the spirits communicate with the living community and voice their discontent, the mediums' declarations carry a degree of social, moral and political critique.

Regional cults are found in many parts of the African continent. In north and west Africa, they can be expressed in a Muslim idiom through forms of saint worship. However, these cults have been most significant in southern Africa (*map 1*). The Mbona cult of southern Malawi illustrates many of the characteristics of the regional cults.

The Mbona Cult

A popular myth holds that the Mbona cult emerged in the fourteenth to sixteenth centuries when the Mang'anja conquered the lower Shire valley. King Lundu of the Mang'anja was threatened in his office by Mbona, a popular rain-maker. He ordered that Mbona be arrested, executed and his head severed from his body and presented to the people. In retaliation, Mbona possessed a villager through whom he ordered the king to bury his head, to erect a shrine over the site, and to devote a woman to the shrine. Lundu complied with these demands and since that day, Mbona has guaranteed adequate rainfall to the lower Shire valley.

This myth establishes the paramount power of King Lundu rather than the Mbona cult. Mbona is thought to have been the medium of a cult which already existed before the arrival of the Mang'anja in the lower Shire. As this myth makes clear, it is upon the authority of Mbona that Lundu, a foreigner, erected the shrine, was entrusted with its upkeep and through it with the well-being of the region as a whole. By consecrating Mbona, Lundu re-established the cult as a specifically Mang'anja institution. The cult legitimized Lundu's paramount position, anchoring the Mang'anja in the lower Shire valley.

Mbona in Regional Politics

In later years, the Mang'anja conquered the Makua-Longwe, who were given minor functions in the cult. They were thereby integrated into the lower Shire ritual complex while political control remained firmly in the hands of Mang'anja chiefs. By contrast, in the 1850s, the Sena people who attacked the Mang'anja on several occasions were never allowed to participate in the cult.

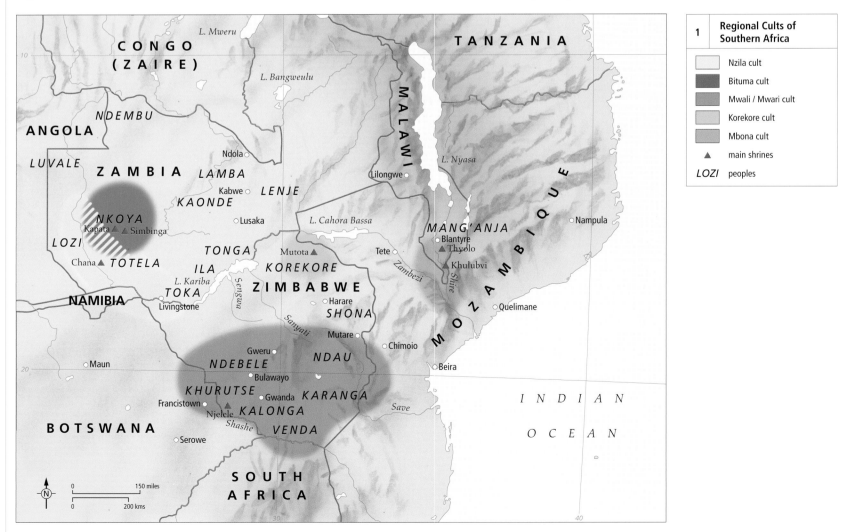

1 Regional Cults of Southern Africa

- Nzila cult
- Bituma cult
- Mwali / Mwari cult
- Korekore cult
- Mbona cult
- ▲ main shrines
- *LOZI* peoples

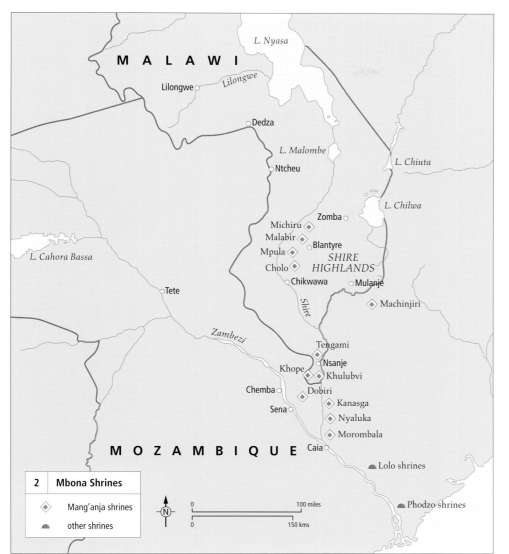

Thus, through the Mbona cult, the Mang'anja were able, at different historical junctures, to assert their control over the lower Shire valley, to integrate and control the Makua-Longwe people and to halt the Sena invasion. Today, if the Mang'anja make up only half of the population of the lower Shire, they still control most of the Mbona shrines.

Mbona's Formal Organization

The cult's formal organization, its main rituals and the cyclical nature of cultic activities are all summarized in the chart (*below*). The cult is organized spatially into three concentric circles. The chiefs residing in each of these circles have different ritual functions and their services are called upon at different intervals. Approximately every five years, for instance, the shrine in Khulubvi, made of such perishable materials as grass, reeds, wood and bamboo, has to be rebuilt. This ritual is ordered by the principals (the two or three chiefs residing closest to the shrine) and requires the participation of all the chiefs in the second circle.

The Exercise and Restraint of Political Power

The call for such an important ritual is also a way of making a statement about the social and moral well-being of the inhabitants of the lower Shire valley. If the shrine is in need of rebuilding, then it must have been neglected. If the cult officials have neglected the shrine, they have also exposed the cult's adepts to Mbona's anger. The order to rebuild the shrine is therefore a complex process; it both diagnoses a crisis and assigns responsibility for it to the chiefs.

These chiefs, however, may not accept this diagnosis. They may be reluctant to recognize any wrong-doing on their part, or refuse to lend their support to the principals who order the ritual. As a result the decision to rebuild the shrine often gives rise to interminable negotiations. If these negotiations last longer than is customary, Mbona may visit his medium.

If people are suffering from a real crisis, such as poor rains, the medium may accuse the chiefs of negligence and those incriminated will have to pay reparations and may even be stripped of their offices. If no sense of crisis prevails amongst Mbona adepts, or if the indicted chief is especially popular, the medium may be accused of faking possession. In such cases, the medium risks being discredited and ultimately replaced.

The Mbona cult has therefore to be seen both as a means of legitimizing the chiefs' position and as a powerful check upon these chiefs' authority. This power is in the hands of the medium who, if he or she is not to be discredited, has to speak for the people.

Clearly, regional cults are as important politically as they are in religious terms. Like the sanctification of political office, they illustrate the close relationship between political and religious powers in Africa.

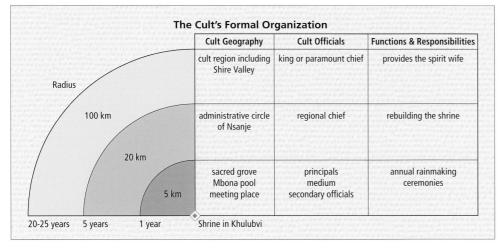

The Cult's Formal Organization

Cult Geography	Cult Officials	Functions & Responsibilities
cult region including Shire Valley	king or paramount chief	provides the spirit wife
administrative circle of Nsanje	regional chief	rebuilding the shrine
sacred grove Mbona pool meeting place	principals medium secondary officials	annual rainmaking ceremonies

Radius — 100 km — 20 km — 5 km — Shrine in Khulubvi
20–25 years — 5 years — 1 year

The Mbona ritual cycle spans 25 to 30 years. During this period several different rituals are performed at varying intervals, each of which requires the participation of specific classes of chiefs. Through this process, the Mbona cult serves to integrate the Mang'anja chiefdoms into an extended network and to bolster the authority of the chiefs.

Worshippers at Mbona's shrine, Malawi. *The shrine is made of perishable materials and must never be repaired but only completely rebuilt, which happens approximately every five years. Its gradual decay and rejuvenation is therefore expressive of the Mbona cult's relationship to the ecological and social welfare of the region.*

AFRICAN RELIGIONS IN THE WESTERN HEMISPHERE

THE ATLANTIC slave trade extended over several centuries and resulted in the transportation of millions of Africans to North and South America as well as to the islands of the Caribbean. Intensive slave trading began as early as the seventeenth century and imports of slaves to Brazil continued until the 1880s when slavery there was finally abolished (*map 1*).

The Reformulation of Religious Practice

The survival of African religious practice in conditions of slavery and post-slavery emancipation depended very much on local social and demographic factors. Although many African cultural survivals can be found among African-American communities in the United States, for example, very few African religious institutions were reconstituted there, probably due to the relatively small numbers of slaves imported into this region. By contrast, identifiable forms of African religious practice were reconstructed in Cuba, Haiti (formerly Santo Domingo) and parts of Brazil where much larger numbers of slaves were imported. However, African religious concepts and practices were reformulated to conform to the new social conditions in which displaced African communities now found themselves.

Religious practice in each new community varied according to its own particular population mix. In Jamaica, for example, there is a mixture of Akan (for example, *obeah*) with BaKongo concepts and practices (for example, *kumina*). Santería in Cuba is a mixture of largely Yoruba and Roman Catholic religious practice. Voudoun in Haiti, on the other hand, has been influenced by the religion of the Fon-speaking peoples of Benin (formerly Dahomey) and their neighbours; the word 'Voudoun' is derived from a Fon word for deity, *vodun*.

The reformulation of African religious practice can be illustrated by a comparison between the religion of the Yoruba-speaking peoples of southwestern Nigeria and the Afro-Brazilian religion of Candomblé.

Yoruba Religion

Religious practice among the Yoruba-speaking peoples of southwestern Nigeria was complex, rich and varied. Religious activities focused on relationships with a vast array of spiritual entities. These included the male Olorun (Lord of the Sky), literally hundreds of *orisha* deities, lineage ancestors and various earth and nature

spirits. In some areas there were cults which served Onile, goddess of the earth.

Most accounts of Yoruba religion justifiably focus on the *orisha* deities, given their prevalence in public religious activities. Concepts of *orisha* deities and relationships with them were highly complex. Some *orisha*, such as Oduduwa (the mythical creator of the earth and progenitor of the Yoruba people) and Obatala (moulder of human beings), were dispatched from the

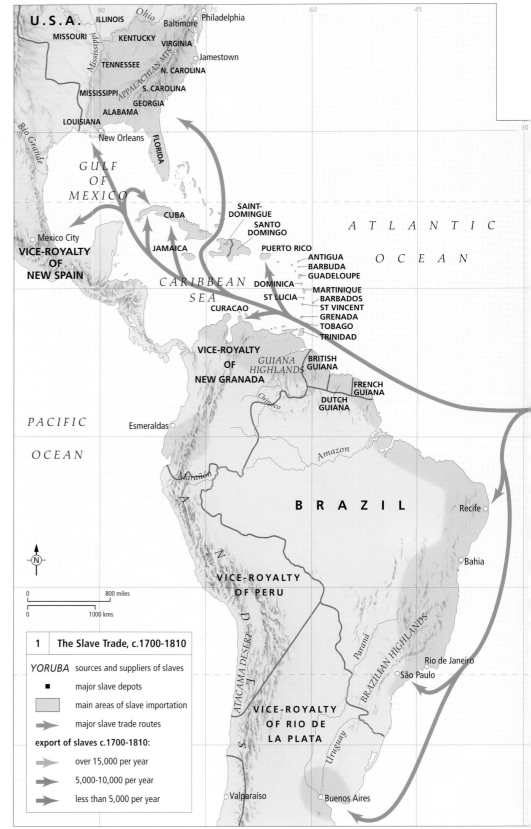

3	Plan of a Candomblé *terreiro* in Brazil
IYA	shrines of deities (orixá)

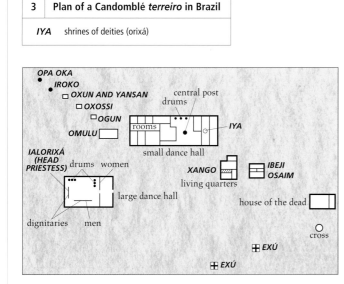

1	The Slave Trade, c.1700-1810

YORUBA sources and suppliers of slaves

■ major slave depots

main areas of slave importation

→ major slave trade routes

export of slaves c.1700-1810:

→ over 15,000 per year

→ 5,000-10,000 per year

→ less than 5,000 per year

Shango greeting his devotees through one of his initiated mediums who holds two sacred Shango staffs (oshé).

A statue of St Jérome whose association with the orisha Shango is indicated by the oshé *symbol surmounting his head (Bahia, Brazil).*

sky by Olorun to complete their tasks of creation. Shango, by contrast, was an early king of Oyo (*map 2*), who was deified following his unnatural death by a bolt of lightning. Shango is usually described as the god of thunder and lightning, but he is also an ancestor of the Oyo kings (*alafin*). Indeed, all Yoruba are seen to be descendants of one or another orisha, with whom they have a ritual relationship.

Orisha Deities

Orisha are associated with all kinds of phenomena. Ogun is the deity of iron and of war; Oko is the deity of farming; Ifa (also Orunmila) is the *orisha* of divination; Eshu is a trickster deity who must be appeased to guarantee harmonious social relationships, from maintaining peace in the marketplace to ensuring the successful performance of religious rituals. These are only some of the most important of the *orisha*; there are many more. Even the most important deities tend to proliferate in a multitude of forms, so that Shango, Obatala, and Ogun, for example, can appear in many different manifestations.

All Yoruba in the past had a religious relationship with one or more *orisha*, both as a result of their birth, and also because they were called to the service of the

orisha (usually in the form of an affliction or illness), or because they were directed to do so by the findings of Ifa divination.

The basic perception of the *orisha* is of a deity who should protect and care for the interests of his or her devotees. They can be approached individually with such requests, but ritual relationships are also maintained to ensure their support for their descendant lineages, or the towns and villages which they protect. Many ritual performances are designed to bring the *orisha* into the living community by encouraging them to 'mount' their mediums.

Candomblé in Brazil

Candomblé in Brazil is an amalgamation of many African and local Brazilian elements, including Roman Catholicism, but it has retained a strong focus on ritual relationship with the *orisha*, known in Portuguese as *orixá*.

One of the major contrasts between the Old and New World relationship to *orishas* can be illustrated by comparing the distribution of *orisha* shrines in Oyo and in a Candomblé *terreiro*, or religious compound (*map 3*). In Oyo, the various shrines and temples are maintained by separate priestly orders, each devoted to a single *orisha*. By contrast, the priests and priestesses of the *terreiro* maintain relationships with all the *orixá* located there. Similarly, whereas rituals and ceremonies are performed for each *orisha* separately in Oyo, ritual performances in the *terreiro* address all the *orixá*, who 'mount' their mediums during the same ceremony. The *terreiro* therefore developed as a kind of microcosm of Yoruba religious practice.

Despite these changes, much has also survived. The music, songs and dances associated with each *orisha* which are performed on ritual occasions and which call him or her to mount their mediums, as well as much of the associated mythical lore and symbolism of the *orisha*, have survived, often in a recognizable form, in Candomblé practice.

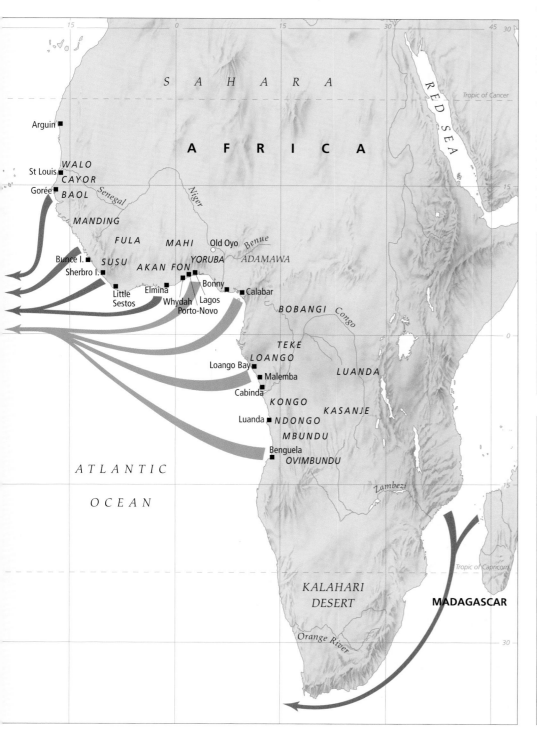

2	Temples and Religious Shrines in Oyo
▬	central temples
●	secondary temples
▲	domestic shrines
• • • •	links in hierarchy of cult organization
——	ward boundaries
——	boundary of royal section of Oyo
IYAJI	ward heads

ISLAM AND THE SPREAD OF THE SUFI ORDERS

ISLAM SPREAD to North Africa during the seventh century. The trade routes that spanned the Sahara and descended along the East African coast contributed to the diffusion of the faith in sub-Saharan Africa. (*map 1; see also* pp. 202-203) By the tenth century, Muslims were playing a prominent role in many African polities. The capital of the empire of Ghana, for instance, was divided into two sections, one organized around a mosque for the Muslims in the king's employ, and another for the king and his court. Muslims acted as accountants, treasurers, councillors and advisors and, in many cases, were sought after for the divine protection and remedies they could procure for the king and his entourage.

Variations in Muslim Practice
In these early years, the spread of Islam in sub-Saharan Africa was largely peaceful. Muslims tended to establish themselves slightly apart in the villages and towns where they settled, built mosques, and opened Qur'anic schools. Their success in trade, their mastery of the written word of the Qur'an, to which many ascribed miraculous powers, as well as the perceived efficacy of the Muslim healing arts, attracted a growing number of non-Muslims. In this way, Islam gained new converts throughout the sub-Saharan region.

From the early nineteenth century and into the period of European colonization, however, parts of Muslim Africa were wracked by successive *jihads,* or religious

The central mosque in Jenné, Mali, reconstructed in the early twentieth century in the classical Sudanese style. Jenné's weekly market is held in the open square in front of the mosque.

wars. These campaigns were waged in the name of Islam against both non-Muslims and Muslims who were deemed lax in their practice of the faith. They show the extent to which Islam had become implanted in African culture. At the same time, they contributed to the further diffusion of Islam; the Muslim polities that were established as a result of the conflict have had a lasting influence in Africa.

In North Africa, as in much of sub-Saharan Africa, the strict monotheism of Islam has been tempered by popular beliefs in the pervasive influence of various spirits (*jinn*), the intercessory powers of deceased saints and holy men and the healing skills of Muslim clerics.

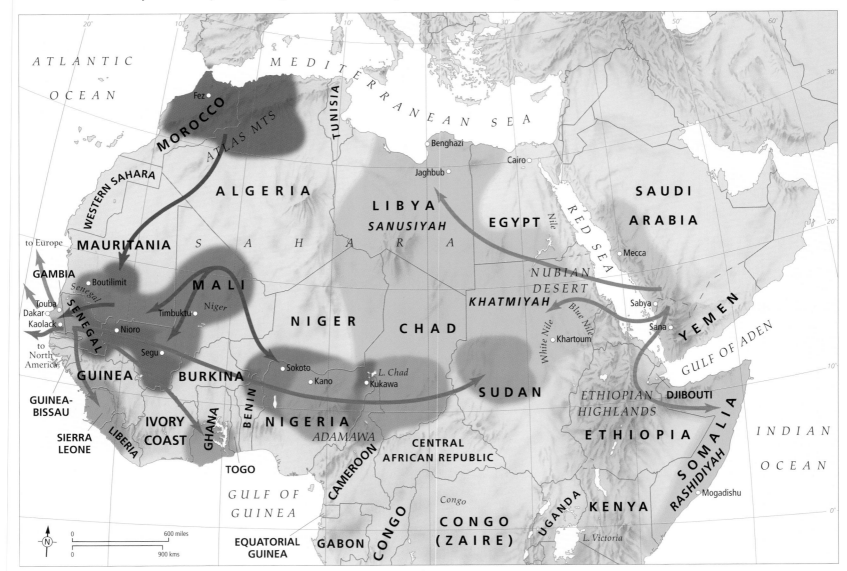

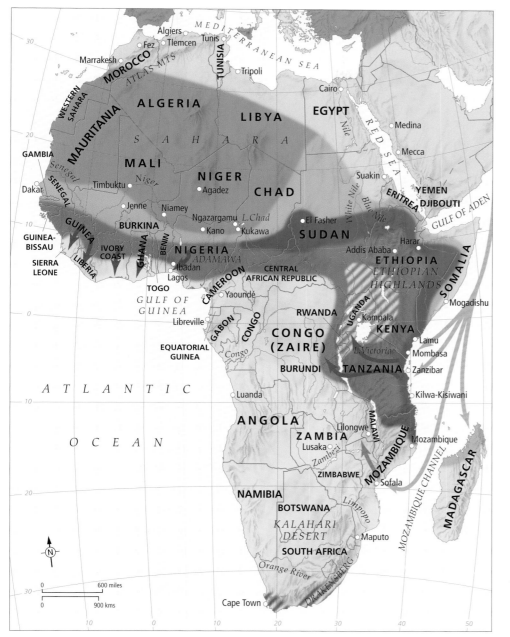

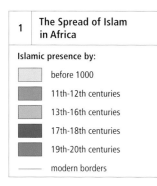

Several orders have taken root in Africa (*map 2*). The Qadiriyah, which derives its name from 'Abd al-Qadir al-Jilani, a Sufi of twelfth-century Baghdad, is one of the most widespread Sufi orders in the Muslim world, and it was present in Africa from an early period. Among its most important adherents were Sidi al-Mukhtar al-Kunti (d. 1811), who was responsible for reinvigorating the order in West Africa, and Shaikh Usman dan Fodio (d. 1817), leader of the nineteenth-century *jihad* in northern Nigeria. The Muridiyah order of Senegal, founded by Amadu Bamba (d. 1927), is a branch of the Qadiriyah. The Qadiriyah also became influential in East Africa during the late nineteenth and early twentieth centuries, where it was spread by Shaikh Uways b. Muhammad al-Barawi (d. 1909).

The Tijaniyah was founded in the Maghreb by Ahmad al-Tijani (d. 1815), and was spread extensively in West Africa during the nineteenth century, primarily through the influence of al-Hajj 'Umar al-Futi (d. 1864), also leader of a major *jihad* in West Africa. Two of the more important sub-branches of the Tijaniyah order which appeared in the twentieth century are the Hamalliyah, founded by Shaikh Ahmad Hamallah (d. 1943), and the Niassiyah or Ibrahimiyah, founded in Senegal by Shaikh Ibrahim Niass (d. 1975). The Ibrahimiyah is based in Kaolack in Senegal, but has attracted large numbers of adherents in Ghana, Nigeria and Sudan, and has recently begun to spread to the United States among African-American Muslims.

Ahmad Ibn Idris (d. 1837) did not himself claim to found a brotherhood, although several of his followers were responsible for establishing Sufi orders which became some of the most influential in nineteenth- and twentieth-century Africa. Muhammad al-Sanusi (d. 1859) was the founder of the Sanusiyah order which came to prevail in Libya and the central Sudan. Muhammad 'Uthman al-Mirghani (d. 1852) was the founder of the Mirghaniyah or Khatmiyah order in the Sudan. From the teachings of Ibrahim al-Rashid (d. 1874), another student of Ibn Idris, there emerged three Sufi orders which would become influential in northeastern Africa and beyond. The most prominent of these, the Rashidiyah, is well represented in Somalia.

Islam, like Christianity, is a religion of conversion, but it was spread in Africa by Africans and was never associated with nineteenth-century colonialism. Unlike Christianity, Islam accepts polygamy, and conversion follows upon the ritualized recitation of a profession of faith rather than upon a lengthy process of education and training. Islamic religious culture also shares many epistemological and practical features with non-Muslim African religious practice.

Both Muslims and non-Muslims have looked to these religious experts and intermediaries to resolve the problems of everyday life, to heal illnesses, to bring adequate rains and to provide blessings for themselves and their families.

The Sufi Orders

The most widespread institutional expression of these intercessory powers is to be found in the Sufi orders. A Sufi order is a religious rule which prescribes a set of prayers or litanies to be recited and a set of spiritual exercises to be pursued, as well as dispensing various disciplinary injunctions which define the relationship between the acolyte, or disciple, and his or her spiritual guide. Such orders provide a context and method for spiritual development which is transmitted from guide to initiate.

The litanies and special prayers of these different orders are often referred to as secrets. They are believed to be imbued with spiritual power which is activated through their repeated recitation. This power is believed to derive from the fact that Sufi prayers have been transmitted in dreams or visions to the founders of the various Sufi orders by the Prophet Muhammad himself or by an earlier deceased Sufi. The Sufi orders are therefore associated with, and named after, their founders, whose personal religious experience became the basis of their spiritual rule and discipline. By affiliating with a specific order the initiate benefits from the *baraka*, or spiritual blessings, of the founder.

The Murid mosque in Touba, Senegal. *Touba, founded by Amadou Bamba, is considered a holy site by the Murids and hosts the annual Magal, a pilgrimage and religious ceremony which attracts tens of thousands of adherents each year. During the last century, Touba became a major urban centre, reflecting the economic success of many Murids.*

227

EUROPEAN CHRISTIAN MISSIONS

CHRISTIANITY was firmly established in North Africa in Roman times. During the seventh century however, it all but disappeared following the Arab invasions and the spread of Islam. Sizeable Christian minorities only survived in Egypt and Ethiopia.

Christianity was introduced to sub-Saharan Africa at a much later date and in two successive waves. The first, extending from the late fifteenth to the mid-seventeenth centuries, was the work of Portuguese priests and traders. Portuguese rulers were keen to contain the spread of Islam by converting to Christianity the peoples who resided south of the Sahara. To this end, the Vatican granted the Portuguese full control over the Church overseas. As a result, the spread of Christianity in Africa was also a means for successive Portuguese kings to extend their control over large tracts of Africa (*map 1; see also* pp. 174-175).

Portuguese Missionaries

The outlook of many European Catholics in the fifteenth and sixteenth centuries was not as far removed from that of their African counterparts as is often believed. In both settings, misfortune could be attributed to a wide range of spiritual entities. Communication with, and propitiation of, these entities followed similar procedures, and these rituals were overseen by ritual specialists who, in both cases, were 'called' to the task. Religion was embedded in the social and political makeup of both African and Medieval European society. The rulers enjoyed divine sanction in both societies. It was therefore to the rulers of different African kingdoms that the Catholic missionaries directed their attention.

Delegations were sent to the courts of Benin, Warri, Kongo and Mutapa. These missionary endeavours however were always confused with Portugal's commercial and political interests. In Kongo, for instance, the king converted to Catholicism in the late fifteenth century and made a sustained effort to spread the faith amongst his subjects. But the provision of teaching aids and the envoy of priests was conditional upon his delivering vast numbers of slaves, captured in the African interior, to Portuguese traders. The rulers of Benin refused categorically to provide Portuguese traders with slaves and treated Portuguese embassies with marked distrust. The king of Warri did convert and was willing to pay his due in slaves. However, the kingdom was so small as to be insignificant and had no access to the sea. In Mutapa, the kings converted, recognizing the dominant position of Portugal in the region, but Christianity never spread beyond the royal family.

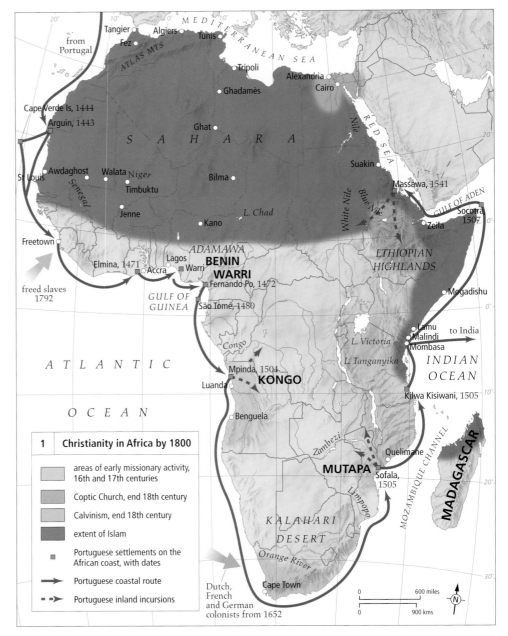

1 | Christianity in Africa by 1800

- areas of early missionary activity, 16th and 17th centuries
- Coptic Church, end 18th century
- Calvinism, end 18th century
- extent of Islam
- Portuguese settlements on the African coast, with dates
- → Portuguese coastal route
- --▶ Portuguese inland incursions

German missionaries in East Africa c. 1890, *negotiating with local inhabitants through an interpreter about the possible establishment of a mission station.*

Renewed Missionary Activity

With the collapse of the Portuguese empire in the seventeenth century, Portugal's monopoly on all missionary activity in Africa ended. That, and the social and political disruption caused by the slave trade, led to the steady decline of Christianity in Africa. By 1700, there were only a few African Christians to show for several centuries of missionary activity. Some converts lived in the trading posts established along the coast and a small number of converts, with little or no links with the Vatican, maintained the Catholic faith in the Kongo.

Kings also featured prominently in Africa's second encounter with Christianity in the nineteenth century (*map 2*). Missionaries established close relationships with several African kings, believing that converting them would inevitably lead to the conversion of their subjects. Experience subsequently taught the missionaries, however, that the kings were too involved in the religious activities of their societies to forsake their ritual functions. Kings, therefore, came to be regarded as the principal obstacle to the spread of Christianity in Africa.

There were other stumbling blocks. Polygamy was often an important means of cementing or forging new political relations. The missionaries nonetheless required that all converts abandon the practice. More generally, these latter-day missionaries found it difficult to understand the importance of ancestors, spirits and gods in the makeup of African societies.

The Impact of Technology and Medicine
The missionaries of the nineteenth and twentieth centuries sought to purvey new technologies as well as new religion. This is especially true of Protestant missionaries who were keen to exemplify their work ethic, and impressed many of their converts with their farming skills and printing presses. Missionaries were often called upon to cure a variety of ailments. To the missionaries, the success of their drugs proved simply the superiority of science over 'magic'. To their patients, however, it showed that the Christian God had superior powers. African attitudes to scientific medicine were rather more religious than those of the missionaries.

The African Response
The responses of Africans to the missionaries' efforts were determined largely by their own understandings of religion and its role in every day life. Christianity did introduce some concepts and practices alien to African religion. In the coastal societies most exposed to the slave trade and in the towns that burgeoned throughout Africa during the colonial period, the preaching of eschatological themes gained an enthusiastic audience. Notions of sin and evil took on new contours and personal responsibility for misfortune was invoked with ever-increasing regularity.

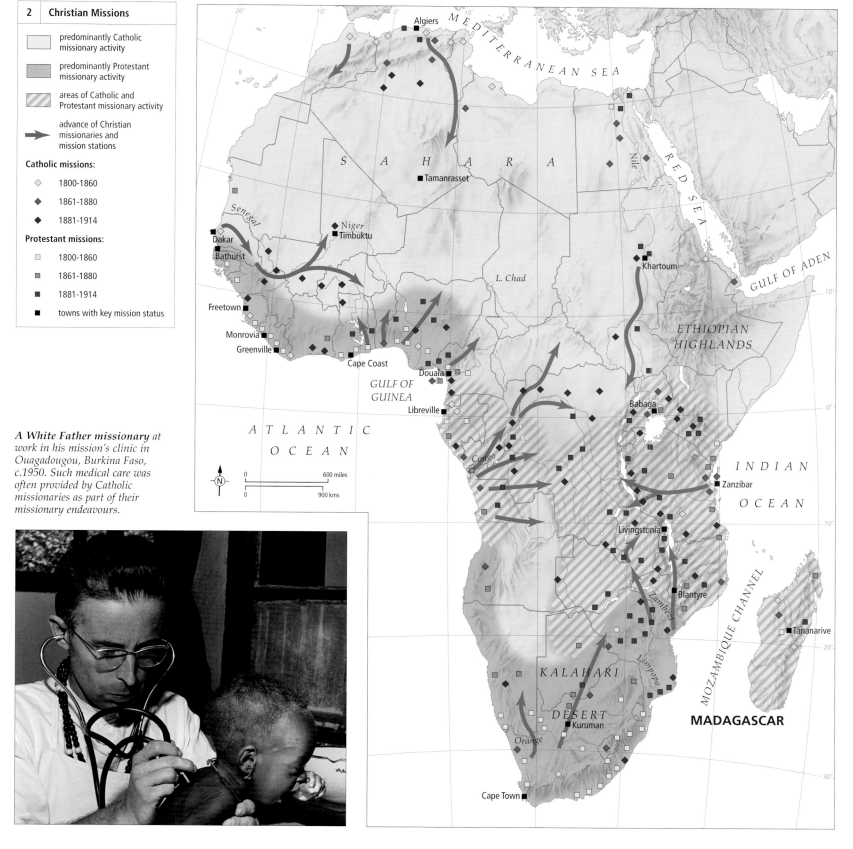

2 | Christian Missions

predominantly Catholic missionary activity

predominantly Protestant missionary activity

areas of Catholic and Protestant missionary activity

advance of Christian missionaries and mission stations

Catholic missions:
◇ 1800-1860
◆ 1861-1880
◆ 1881-1914

Protestant missions:
□ 1800-1860
▣ 1861-1880
■ 1881-1914
■ towns with key mission status

A White Father missionary at work in his mission's clinic in Ouagadougou, Burkina Faso, c.1950. Such medical care was often provided by Catholic missionaries as part of their missionary endeavours.

INDEPENDENT CHRISTIANITY IN AFRICA

THE FIRST INDEPENDENT Christian churches were established in the late nineteenth century in South Africa and, to a lesser extent, in Nigeria (*map 1*). They were founded by African converts who were frustrated by the racial discrimination they suffered at the hands of European missionaries – despite their training, they were forbidden from advancing in their churches' hierarchy. These 'Ethiopian' churches differed little from mainstream missions in doctrine, liturgy and ritual. The use of the term 'Ethiopian' served mainly to express their trust in the possibility of creating an authentic African Christian church.

By contrast, the Zionist churches that emerged in southern Africa at the turn of the century shared many features with African religious practice (*map 5*). Religious healing, speaking in tongues and baptism all achieved pride of place in the Zionist movement. Most Zionist churches, however, had identifiable missionary origins. The founder of the Zion Christian Church (ZCC) in the Northern Transvaal, for instance, was inspired by Pentecostalist missionaries working in South Africa.

The Prophetic Movements

During the 1920s there was a blossoming of prophetic movements throughout much of the continent. In these churches too, religious healing, dreams and visions were of primary importance. They developed outside the missions' purview and, initially, attracted only individuals on the margins of colonial society. The Church of Nazareth, the EJCSK, Church of Jesus Christ

on Earth (*map 4*), the Harrist churches (*map 2*) and the Aladura movement (*map 3*) all formed around prophetic figures, such as Isaiah Shembe, Simon Kimbangu, William Wade Harris and Joseph Babalola. These churches differed from both Ethiopian and Zionist Churches in the reverence, even veneration, their adepts showed towards the founding prophets. Both Shembe and Kimbangu were regarded as Messiahs. Harris, meanwhile, presented himself as the last prophet of

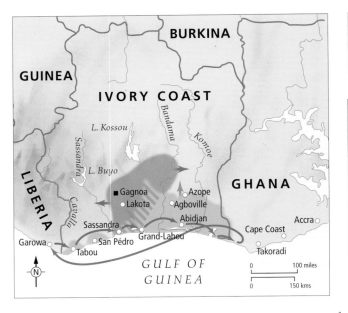

1	Independent Christianity
	approximate extent of independent Christianity

2	Harrism in Ivory Coast
■	sacred site
→	Harris's route
	distribution of Harrist churches
	extent of Deima
—	modern border

5	Two Zionist Churches of South Africa
■	sacred city/site
	distribution of Zionist Christian Church
	distribution of Church of Nazareth
▨	former homelands
—	provincial boundaries
—	modern borders

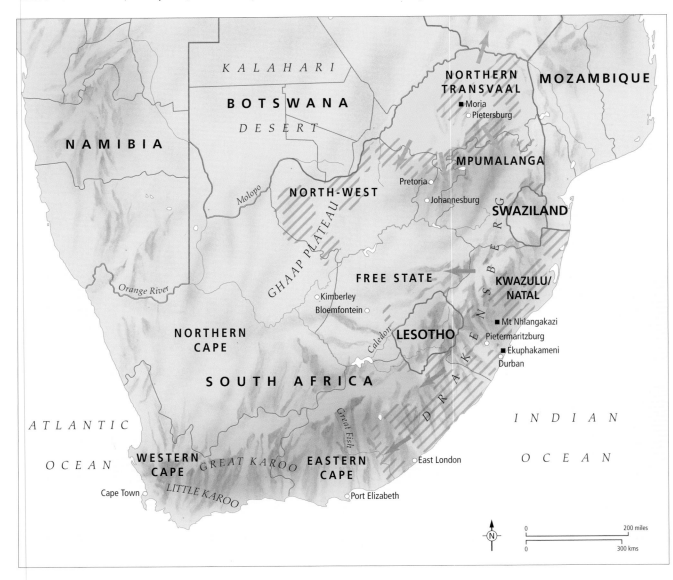

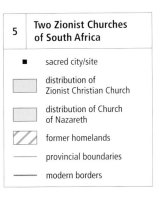

A member of the ZCC in official dress. Both male and female ZCC members can be identified by the star shaped badges on their caps. Members have also to foresake alcohol and tobacco.

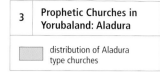

3 Prophetic Churches in Yorubaland: Aladura

distribution of Aladura type churches

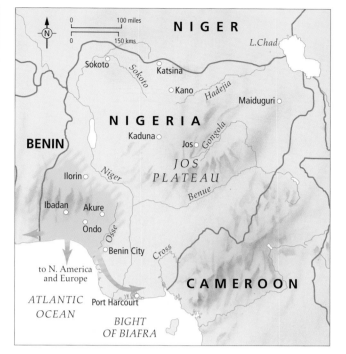

Prophet Harris in his customary dress, preparing to baptise the three women by his side. The ritual quality of this act is attested by the number of onlookers such ceremonies attract.

God. All the prophets claimed to enjoy a privileged relationship with God, and could tap His powers to cure their societies of the ills brought about by slavery and colonialism. Shembe and Kimbangu all but replaced Christ in their Church's hymnal.

Charismatic Leaders

The new social and environmental conditions brought about by colonialism provide a context for the emergence of these prophetic figures. Under these new circumstances, compounded in West Africa by the outbreak of an influenza epidemic in the second decade of the twentieth century, people had to confront problems not addressed by existing religious practice, and the prophetic movements filled this vacuum. The authority of the prophets was charismatic – they were able to crystallize the hopes and aspirations of their

people. The prophets healed people through the laying on of hands, protected them from evil through lavish use of baptismal water and waged energetic campaigns against perceived sources of evil. Both Kimbangu and Harris urged their followers to burn the icons of African religious practice, disempowering the witches whom they held responsible for these new ills.

Unlike the missions, which also urged people to abandon African religious practices, these prophetic figures offered them an alternative source of spiritual power. All had previous missionary training and had mastered the key symbols of Christianity. Harris for instance, toured the Ivory Coast wearing a white robe and carrying a Bible, a cross, a gourd rattle and a bowl of water he used to baptize new converts, who were given a cross and a Bible for protection against evil.

Oppression and Revival

Most of these prophetic figures, with their large and difficult to control followings, were viewed with utmost suspicion by the colonial authorities. Many colonial officials believed that these religious activities were, in fact, proto-political movements intended to undermine colonial rule, and consequently were ruthless in their treatment of the religious leaders. Kimbangu, for instance, was jailed within six months of having performed his first miraculous healing. He died in his cell in Elizabethville (present day Lubumbashi) some thirty years later in 1951. Harris was expelled from Ivory Coast by the French authorities.

Paradoxically, the removal of these prophets from their audiences may have actually institutionalized their charisma. After Kimbangu was jailed, his relatives organized his followers into a church that has become the third largest in the Democratic Republic of Congo (formerly Zaire). Harris meanwhile nominated twelve apostles whose task it was to organize his followers and ensure that they followed his teachings. The Deima church, founded by priestess Bague Honoyo, was an offshoot of Harris' ministry, It also achieved official status in Ivory Coast and is estimated to have 400,000 adherents including the deceased President Houphouët-Boigny.

Recent years have seen a veritable explosion in the number of such churches in Africa (*see also* pp. 182–183). In the Democratic Republic of Congo (Zaire) alone, one scholar has counted several hundred. They vary considerably in size and nature. Some enjoy large followings, have achieved official recognition and have been integrated into international ecumenical organizations (EJCSK, ZCC). Others count only a few dozen members and bring into play concepts and practices that are not universally recognized as Christian. All these churches are united in their thorough re-appropriation of the Christian message, its symbols and rituals by Africans in an effort to address problems peculiar to the continent.

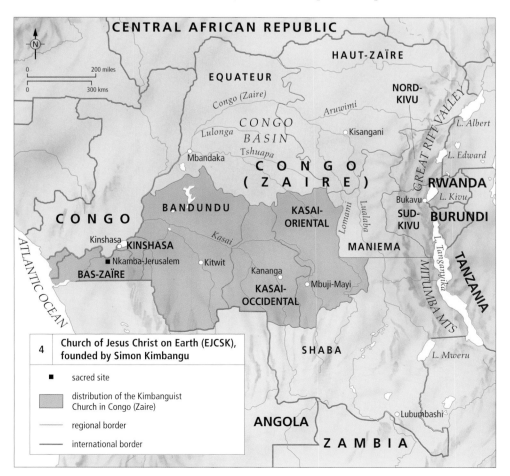

4 Church of Jesus Christ on Earth (EJCSK), founded by Simon Kimbangu

■ sacred site

distribution of the Kimbanguist Church in Congo (Zaire)

regional border

international border

INDIGENOUS RELIGIONS

THE FIRST IMPORTANT POINT to discuss with regard to 'indigenous religions' is that the term 'indigenous' is interpretive, as are such related terms as 'traditional', 'primitive', 'non-literate' or 'oral'. Historically, people who have not seen themselves as members of these groups have used all of these terms to categorize others and to draw distinctions between themselves and these groups. In many cases such classification has taken place in a colonial context. What makes the term 'indigenous' different from the others is that in recent history members of many such groups have used the term to self-identify. Such individuals now publicly assert their identities (for example through legally registered land claims that cite pre-colonial ownership of homeland territories), actively produce scholarship and question both the conclusions and labels once associated with them.

The afterlife is very often thought of in quite literal terms. In this bark painting, from Arnhem Land, Australia, people and animals are seen as progressing, in physical form, to the next world.

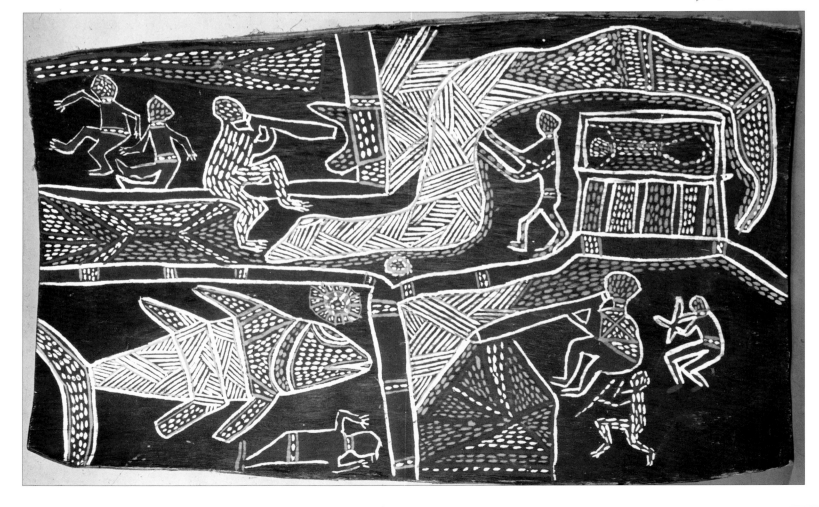

FURTHER, WHILE an outsider perspective might delineate specific activities, narratives or beliefs as 'ritual', 'religious' or 'sacred', such distinctions do not convey the manner in which such cultural elements are seamlessly integrated into the daily lives of many of these communities. This is borne out by the fact that many cultures around the world do not have a discrete term for 'religion'. What is more, many contemporary scholars of religion agree that 'religion' is a cultural construction, itself a reflection of European Enlightenment philosophies and Christian theological discourse and that, historically, assumptions about what 'religion' should be have been employed in colonial contexts to distinguish the 'observer' from the 'observed' as much as to highlight cultural similarities.

Beliefs

A variety of beliefs that range from abstract conceptions of a force or entity, to a focus on one particular god or being, to a universe full of a variety of gods or beings characterize different indigenous religions. For example, many religions of tropical Africa conceptualize a Supreme Being who created the universe but who remains remote from human affairs, while other gods mediate relationships with humans. The Yoruba of Nigeria believe that *Olodumare* is this Being, and there are *orishas* who, though distinct and multiple (they are said to number between four hundred and one and six hundred and one), all are in fact aspects of *Olodumare*. As facets of *Olodumare*, they animate various forces and elements of the universe. Chief among the orishas is *Orish-nla*, who sculpted human beings. Some of the *orishas* once were human, and some were not. Most religions of Micronesia likewise believe a large number of beings inhabit the cosmos, and there is a category of such beings that inhabit the sky. The people of the Chuukic Islands call these beings or spirits *énú*. However, according to scholars, a Supreme Being is typically not part of the conceptual universe for these religions.

Narratives

Throughout the world, certain members of societies interpret narratives or myths in a variety of ways: some interpret them metaphorically, others think of them as historically accurate, while still others consider them to be untrue. This is the case as well with members of indigenous religions. In general, narratives suggest answers to such questions as: where do we come from? why we are in our present situation? what does the future hold for us? They also suggest how certain features of the world or of particular communities came to be (such as features of the landscape, or modes of subsistence) and also how individuals might respond to challenges faced. In this way they can provide a connection or continuum for people between past, present and future. The Maori of Aotearoa in New Zealand relate a narrative about *Tane Mahuta* (God of the Forest) who journeyed to the highest reaches of a multi-level heaven to retrieve *wananga*, three baskets of knowledge which he then offered to the people. This knowledge concerned the nature of aspects of the universe, potentially both positive and negative, as well as details about prayers and ritual. Such information requires responsibility as well as reverence. The quality of being associated with the *atuas*, gods or spirits, bestows what is called *tapu* upon an entity. *Tapu* is said to be a state of being of something which is said to have *mana*. Depending on the *atua* this can be beneficial or not. These words are difficult to translate accurately, some individuals translate *tapu* as 'sacred'. There are Maori who

This nineteenth century Navajo rug depicts diyin dine'e, or yei (Holy People). *A rainbow yei encircles the picture; this motif expresses the idea that the yei protect the other figures in the scene. The other two figures, also yei, likely are First Man and First Woman. The central figure is a corn stalk rising out of a Navajo wedding basket. Navajo people use corn pollen as a blessing agent.*

believe that a Supreme God, *Io*, created the world and gave the baskets to *Tane Mahuta*, while others see this as a nineteenth-century innovation borne from contact with Christian missionaries and the Hebrew Bible text. Another type of narrative is told by means of the *whakapapa* (recital of genealogy), in which individuals use carved wooden sticks or staves to link communities with their past as they look toward the future.

Ritual Practices

There is great variety not only among the rituals of indigenous groups, but also in terms of the modes of activity employed, including, among other forms, dancing, singing, theatrical performances and athletic contests. Rites of passage, rituals that commemorate important life events, are performed for both men and women in a number of different societies. Rites of passage that celebrate a woman's menarche are widespread. *Ndé* ('The People') of New Mexico, also known as the Mescalero Apache, celebrate '*Isánáklésh Gotal* (ceremony or 'singing' for '*Isánáklésh*). This public ritual, which takes place over a period of four days, is this group's major communal celebration. Not all young women are required to participate in the public ceremony, however, and individuals may choose to mark this life-cycle event in private. Participation in the public event is a great undertaking for the families of the young women involved, as they are responsible for feeding the gathering, giving gifts, and securing the services of ritual specialists. In the ceremony, the individual transforms into '*Isánáklésh* (White Painted Woman), an important other-than-human person, for the duration of the ceremony. According to a narrative, '*Isánáklésh* once was cared for by the People and thus continues to aid them; during the ceremony she offers her blessings to the gathering. Through this ritual the individual women, aided by a *nade 'klehen*, a female sponsor and mentor, and a male *gutaal* ('singer') are educated about their future roles in society as well as other cultural information.

INDIGENOUS RELIGIONS TODAY

THE EXPLORATION of indigenous religions can take one into the world's most geographically remote regions, but it can also take one to the door of a neighbour. In the most inaccessible areas – upper Amazonia, inner New Guinea, and Borneo, the hinterland of island Malaysia — the stereotype is that indigenous religions have remained largely impervious to outside forces, and are to be found in their most traditional forms. However, obviously all religions change, and do not remain static. In general, members of indigenous religions, like those of other religions, can combine an interest in preserving aspects of what might be called 'traditional' religion with ongoing interaction with ever-changing circumstances. While particular members of indigenous religions may reject elements of other religious systems, others have been interested to combine elements. Some indigenous religions have thus

retained what members understand to be traditional features, while other religions have to different extents combined with, absorbed elements from, or been absorbed into, other religious systems. All in all, indigenous religions continue to illustrate a considerable diversity of belief and practise, as well as innovative tendencies.

Considered together, indigenous religions worldwide have hundreds of millions of adherents today, while individual communities vary in size. What distinguishes them is that most are centred on a particular place of importance, imbued with religious or spiritual significance, with which they have retained historical and social ties. However, this place can be anywhere on Earth.

The Ainu of Hokkaido ▶
innorthern Japan, of which there are an estimated 150,000, believe that there are kamuy *('gods') in all objects and other aspects of the universe. Certain gods come to aid humans in the form of animals and other objects, and there are a variety of religious ceremonies to send their spirits back to their abode. Offerings of food, wine, and willow sticks are made to these* kamuy *in return for their assistance.*

1	A Global View of Indigenous Religions
AINU	indigenous groups
FORE	most isolated indigenous groups
	areas where indigenous beliefs are widely held
	areas where indigenous beliefs are found in smaller localities

Elaborate ritual dancing involving costume and body painting is widespread among sub-Saharan African indigenous groups. The Dogon people of the sahel are particularly noted for the complexity of their masks and headgear.

It is also important to stress that a condition of diaspora, or separation from their homeland, is a circumstance for many individuals and communities who self-identify as indigenous. Diaspora and the colonial actions that in many cases devastated or scattered communities are thus shared experiences among many communities.

Isolation and Identity

Whereas in the past scholars have cited the characteristic of relative isolation as fundamental to indigenous religions in terms of maintenance of traditions, in the present-day world such distinctions are less significant than ever. Even a relatively simplified world map of indigenous groups (*map 1*) reveals an abundance and broad distribution of distinct cultures. Colonial incursions and communications technology have made the concept of 'isolation' less tenable with regard to entire societies and cultures; and it is the case that in every country throughout the world there are individuals and groups who are relatively more isolated and those who are less so. Furthermore, as noted above, someone who practises an 'indigenous' religion may be as

close as a neighbour's door. What continues to distinguish certain of these communities is their desire to preserve a unique identity (and a geographical distance from other communities can aid in that goal) but the notion that there are 'pre-modern' peoples who have not come into contact with the modern world is outmoded. That is not to say that there may be groups of people existing who have not had a great amount of contact with other groups, but the notion that they are somehow frozen in a previous time period is untenable by current scholarly standards.

Today, differences between these religious systems as well as other religious systems associated with societies who do not consider themselves 'indigenous' continue to present interpretive challenges, as what aspects of culture are considered to be 'religious' can vary. However, it has become expedient at present for a variety of reasons, not the least of which is political, for certain groups to stress the similarities. It is certainly accurate to say that there are differences as well as certain similarities among particular indigenous communities with regard to narratives, beliefs, and rituals.

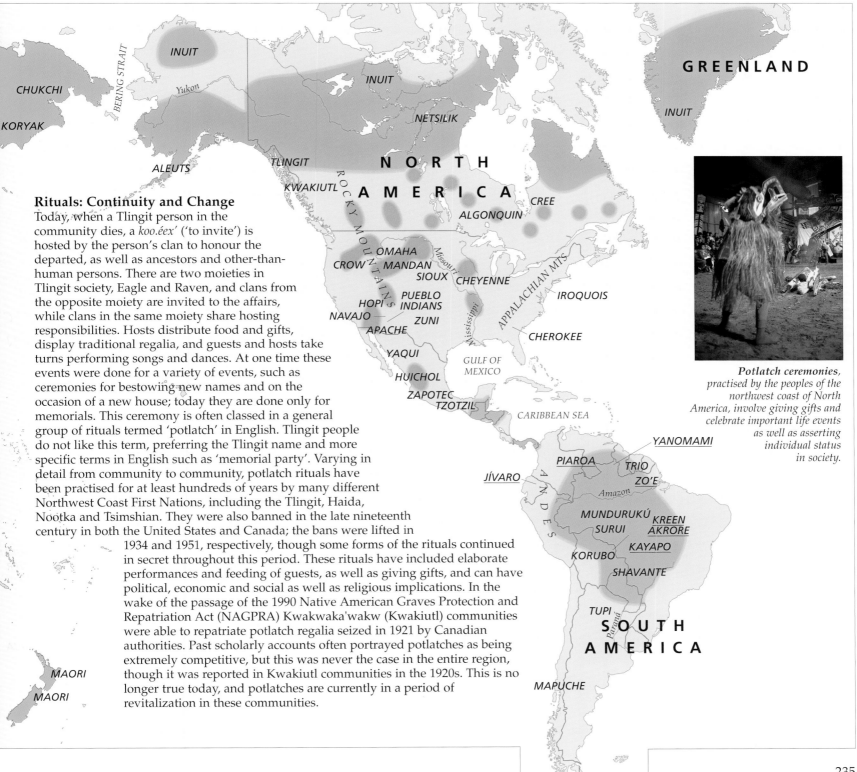

Rituals: Continuity and Change

Today, when a Tlingit person in the community dies, a *koo.éex'* ('to invite') is hosted by the person's clan to honour the departed, as well as ancestors and other-than-human persons. There are two moieties in Tlingit society, Eagle and Raven, and clans from the opposite moiety are invited to the affairs, while clans in the same moiety share hosting responsibilities. Hosts distribute food and gifts, display traditional regalia, and guests and hosts take turns performing songs and dances. At one time these events were done for a variety of events, such as ceremonies for bestowing new names and on the occasion of a new house; today they are done only for memorials. This ceremony is often classed in a general group of rituals termed 'potlatch' in English. Tlingit people do not like this term, preferring the Tlingit name and more specific terms in English such as 'memorial party'. Varying in detail from community to community, potlatch rituals have been practised for at least hundreds of years by many different Northwest Coast First Nations, including the Tlingit, Haida, Nootka and Tsimshian. They were also banned in the late nineteenth century in both the United States and Canada; the bans were lifted in 1934 and 1951, respectively, though some forms of the rituals continued in secret throughout this period. These rituals have included elaborate performances and feeding of guests, as well as giving gifts, and can have political, economic and social as well as religious implications. In the wake of the passage of the 1990 Native American Graves Protection and Repatriation Act (NAGPRA) Kwakwaka'wakw (Kwakiutl) communities were able to repatriate potlatch regalia seized in 1921 by Canadian authorities. Past scholarly accounts often portrayed potlatches as being extremely competitive, but this was never the case in the entire region, though it was reported in Kwakiutl communities in the 1920s. This is no longer true today, and potlatches are currently in a period of revitalization in these communities.

Potlatch ceremonies, practised by the peoples of the northwest coast of North America, involve giving gifts and celebrate important life events as well as asserting individual status in society.

NATIVE NORTH AMERICAN RELIGIONS

CONTRARY TO POPULAR OPINION, there is no one single 'religion' of the many indigenous communities or First Nations on the North American continent. It is estimated that at the time of contact with Europeans there were approximately 500 autonomous nations in North America (*map 1*). Today, the Navajo Nation and the Cherokee Nation of Oklahoma both count several hundred thousand members, and there are many other communities that range in size from this number to some that are comprised of less than a thousand. These communities are diverse, and differences are cultural, social, linguistic and political, as well as religious.

Today, certain communities are located in places that they consider to be ancestral, others in places to which they have migrated, and some in places to which they were forced or coerced to migrate, particularly reservations (*map 2*). In addition, many First Nations people live elsewhere. As is the case with religious systems throughout the world, communities and individuals maintain, change and adapt aspects of their religious systems to the circumstances that face them. Moreover, as is the case in many societies in which Christianity has been introduced, there are a range of responses to it, including for some people acceptance of elements of both religious systems. In what follows, only the most superficial review of selected key elements from two particular religious systems can be addressed.

The Lakota

The Lakota religious system is associated with people once commonly known as 'Sioux', (a pejorative Algonquian term meaning 'lesser adder') who at the time of contact with Europeans lived in the Dakotas and Minnesota. As is the case with many other groups, these people have a complex social structure with many interlocking levels of kinship, which the term 'tribe' really does not explain adequately. A concept of *Wakan Tanka*, conventionally translated as 'power of the universe' or 'great Mystery', denotes an essential power or force that is timeless, ethically charged and multi-faceted. Lakota converts to Christianity often have stated that *Wakan Tanka* is synonymous with 'God'. By means of ritual interactions, in times of need individuals strive to interact humbly with beings in the universe whom they understand as kin; thus the Lakota statement *Mitakuye oyas'in* ('all my relations', 'I am related to all that is') reflects this core belief. Such interactions can be either on an individual basis or in communal activity and in both cases they are often, but not always, mediated by religious specialists known as *wica_a wakan* ('man sacred') and *winyan wakan* ('woman sacred').

An example of the former type is the *hanbleceya* ('crying for a vision/dream') upon which an individual will embark to receive guidance and abilities for the benefit of the community. An example of the latter type is the *Wiwanyang Wacipi* ('gaze-at-the-sun-dance'). Often misunderstood by outsiders, and even banned on United States reservations a century ago, this communal event today is typically three to four days in length, and involves a range of ceremonial activities including singing, dancing, fasting and the piercing of flesh. It is the latter activity which has caused such consternation among some non-Lakota individuals. This action typically is understood as a physical expression of the ethic of sacrifice as well as of extreme humility; it can, however, be done for individual benefit. Lakota people will undergo this trial as a result of a vow made during the previous year either on behalf of themselves or other individuals, such as a sick family member, or for the future well-being of the entire community.

The Navajo

The Diné or Dineh ('The People') are the group popularly known as Navajo ('cultivated fields' a modified Tewa word, short for the Spanish *Apaches de Navajo*). Many individuals today continue to reside in *Dinéh Bikéyah* ('Navajoland') bounded by the Four Sacred Mountains: San Francisco Peaks, Hesperus Peak, Blanca Peak, and Mt Taylor. Residence in this traditional homeland is considered particularly relevant as armed conflict in the nineteenth century with the US Army resulted in a forced march known as the Long Walk and internment in New Mexico for four years. Refusal to emigrate elsewhere finally resulted in the Navajo Nation being allowed to return to their land, albeit with its borders greatly reduced.

The nature of the Diné religious system is such that, as with Buddhism, scholars often characterize it as a philosophy as much as a religious system. A core concept of the system is *hózhó* ('beauty', 'harmony' or 'balance'), which revolves around maintaining or restoring such a condition in individuals' lives. Religious specialists called *hataalii* ('chanters') officiate at ceremonies in which chanting and prayer effect such desired results of 'healing', understood broadly to incorporate physical,

1	**Native North American Cultural Areas**
	Arctic
	Subarctic
	Northwest Coast
	Plateau
	Great Plains
	Northeast
	Great Basin
	California
	Southwest
	Southeast
	Mesoamerica
	Circum-Caribbean
CREE	indigenous groups

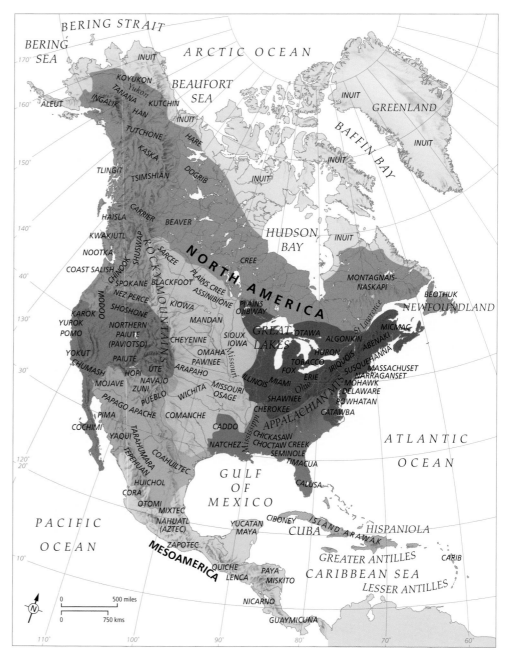

mental and spiritual issues. Such ceremonies, or 'chantways', invoke relationships with the *diyin dine'é* (Holy People); in certain ceremonies the *diyin dine'é* come into the presence of a gathering by means of *'iikááh* ('places where the gods come and go') and complicated designs – 'drypaintings' – are drawn on the floor with crushed minerals and other substances, not only sand. In such situations the 'once-sung-over' (the subject of the ceremony) becomes for that time the focus of the *diyin dine'é*; a physical identification with the individual, and

thus the universe, is effected at that time, and *hóchó'* ('ugly conditions', 'disharmony' or 'imbalance'; the opposite of *hózhó*) is removed from that individual. After the ceremony is over the painting is destroyed. This acknowledges the fact that the Holy People should not be unnecessarily detained or summoned after the ceremony is completed, as well as to diffuse any evidence of lingering *hóchó'*. That the painting is destroyed also indicates that it is a religious tool, and not an art object, as has often been assumed by non-Navajo observers.

A graphic representation of the Lakota Sun Dance created by Black Chicken at the end of the nineteenth century, a time of particular tension between many of the Native American peoples and the European settlers. Performance of the Sun Dance, a central Lakota ritual, was banned in reservations by the US authorites.

2	**Native North American groups today**
▨	Federal reservations
△	State reservations
▲	Native North American groups without reservation
▨	Nunavut

This Blackfoot shaman is dressed in the pelt of a bear, festooned with fragments from many other species. His garments are one of the means he uses to obtain the power to make contact with dangerous spirits.

INDIGENOUS RELIGIONS IN THE ARCTIC AND AUSTRALIA

A T EITHER END OF THE PACIFIC are two rich domains of indigenous peoples living in extreme conditions who, in their relative remoteness, have developed very contrasting belief systems.

Arctic Religions

The numerous culturally-diverse peoples who live in the tundra (land with permafrost) and taiga (land with coniferous forests) regions surrounding the North Pole represent several language families. Formerly grouped as 'Eskimos', today there are communities in Greenland, Alaska and Canada who self-identify as Inuit in addition to their own names for themselves. Other groups such as the Yup'ik of southern Alaska and Siberia consider themselves distinct in terms of identity. In addition, the vast Arctic littoral is home to numerous other societies (*map 1*).

Due to climatic similarities, and to some extent in modes of subsistence, there are comparable features in their religious systems. Historically, most groups conducted a round of festivals that focused on relationships between people and their neighbours, between different communities, with animals crucial for survival, or with community members and relatives who had died. Such festivals served social, economic, and political functions as well as redistributing food and wealth, easing tension between villages and increasing the prestige of local individuals; ceremonies during the sunless winter months also maintained a positive frame of mind.

Historically, such communities have relied to a large extent on hunting land or sea animals for subsistence, and religious systems reflect this; several groups conduct communal rituals in which animals critical for

subsistence, or beings who oversee these animals, are propitiated. Often these ceremonies include dancing, singing, and in some cases dramatic performances. These performances include the use of masks, which variously represent animals or other beings. Like humans, animals and other beings are understood to have 'souls' or 'persons', and thus must be treated as one would other humans. Most groups also had religious specialists with the ability, by means of a differentiated state of consciousness, to travel to the realms of those animals or beings 'other-than-human persons' with impact on the community in order to communicate and negotiate with them. For example, among the Inuit, *angakkut* travelled to the bottom of the sea to interact with *Sedna*, female overseer of animals. In the *Nakaciuq*, or Bladder Festival, Yup'ik *angalkut* returned the bladders of seals to the water, thus also returning the seals' *yuit* ('persons' or 'souls') to their home, to ensure that the seals returned to sustain the community. Such specialization requires initiation, and much of the activity of such individuals is done in private, sometimes within the confines of a tent in which the individual is physically bound to accentuate the fact that they indeed have the power to transcend normal boundaries of human movement and interaction.

At present many groups no longer observe these ceremonies, due to over half a century of suppression by Christian missionaries and assimilation. Certain communities of northern Alaskan Inupiaq have revived the 'Messenger Feast', and the Yup'ik version of the ceremony, *Kevgiq*. Continuation and revival of activities such as dancing are evident in these festivals, as well as in events such as the World Eskimo and Indian Olympics. Individual hunters continue to perform rituals with regard to game animals across Alaska and

A carved Yup'ik mask used in ceremonies to make contact with the animal-like spirits which are believed to control the balance of nature. Like most Arctic peoples, the Yup'ik are reliant upon hunting and fishing for subsistence.

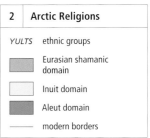

2	Arctic Religions
YULTS	ethnic groups
	Eurasian shamanic domain
	Inuit domain
	Aleut domain
—	modern borders

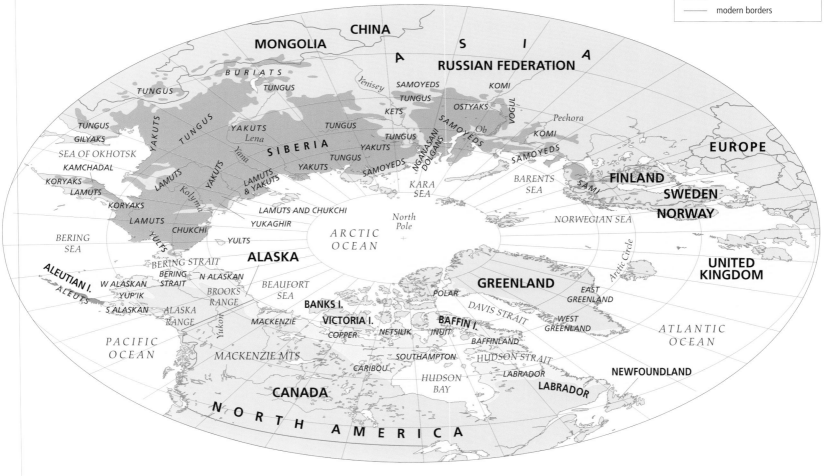

religious specialists continue to practise, though such information is often private.

Australian Aboriginal Religions

The hundreds of distinct indigenous communities with different languages who, for an estimated 50,000 years or longer, have lived on the Australian continent and the adjacent islands of Tasmania and the Torres Strait are termed 'Indigenous Australian'; of course, they all have their own names for themselves (*map 2*). As with other indigenous religions of a similarly circumscribed geographical area, while there may be certain similar general features in their religious systems, these are marked by distinctive particularities in individual communities.

Perhaps the most well-known yet misunderstood concept is what is termed in English the 'Dreaming' or 'Dreamtime'. These terms are misleading, suggesting a lack of reality, or a fixed previous historical epoch. Encompassing aspects of both 'myth' and 'ritual', as well as a deep connection to 'place', these are complex concepts that incorporate the persons and actions of the historical ancestors of a particular people, the narratives about those ancestors, the present-day physical features of the landscape and the contemporary individuals'

continuing interaction with both those ancestors and the land during ritual occasions as well as in daily life. It is the notion of time that is often difficult for people from different religious systems to understand: termed 'the everywhen' by the anthropologist W.E.H. Stanner, it allows for interaction between ancestors and their relatives.

It is the ongoing responsibility of successive generations to aid in the continuation of all that the 'Dreaming' entails by the performance of activities that include singing, dancing, storytelling, travelling along particular routes and the creation of specific designs. This educates oneself and others, and knowledge is maintained and transmitted. Men and women have different responsibilities depending on the individual society, and within the society clans and other social groupings also divide the responsibilities or 'business'.

British colonization, starting in the late eighteenth century, means that today there is an abiding political aspect to the relationship between Indigenous Australians and their homelands. Since the late 1960s, repatriation efforts and ongoing efforts to secure their homelands, along with efforts to redress social inequalities, have added another layer to the 'business' that Indigenous Australians conduct.

This sacred woman, depicted on a bark painting from western Arnhem Land, lived during the time of the Dreaming; the time of magic and wonder. Her re-creation enables contemporary aboriginal women to use her power in love magic.

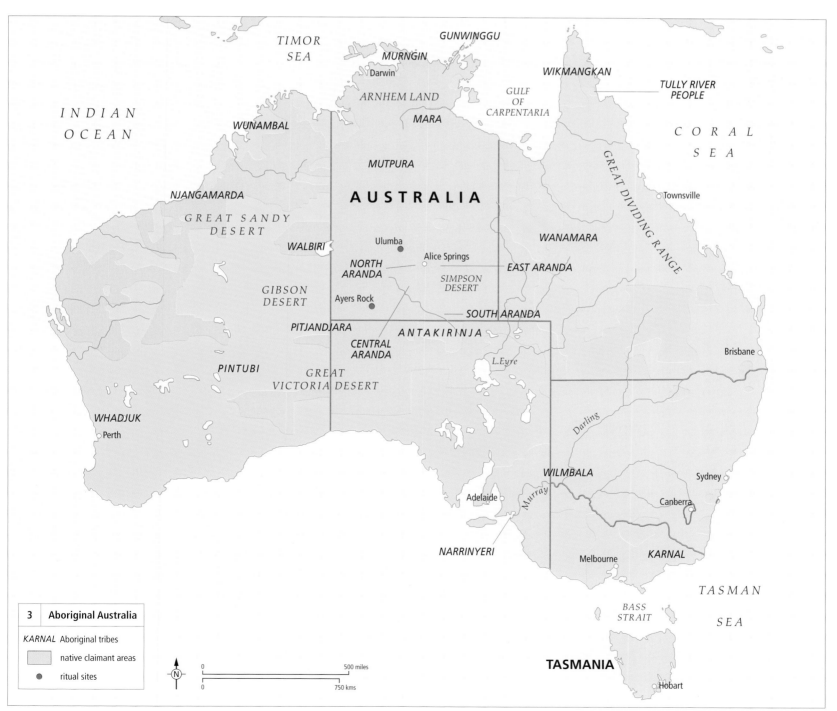

GLOSSARY

Abraham First of the three patriarchs of the Jews (Abraham, his son Isaac, and Isaac's son Jacob). He journeyed from Ur in Mesopotamia to Canaan (Palestine), the land promised by God to his descendants.

Adad Assyrian god of storms who presides over divination.

adat Customary law or tradition, which supplements the *shari'a* in Muslim countries in East Asia.

adhan Islamic call to prayer, broadcast from mosques five times a day.

Adi Granth The sacred book of the Sikhs written in the fifteenth century by Kabir.

advaita In Hinduism, a position of philosophical monism or 'non-dualism', arguing the identity between the soul and the absolute, championed by Shankaracharya in the eighth century.

Adventism Belief in the imminent second coming of Jesus Christ.

African Independent Churches (also known as African Indigenous Churches) African-based Christian faith groups which range from variations of Western denominations to syncretistic tribal groups, combining selective elements of Christianity with local existing traditions.

agamas A set of revered Sanskrit texts, which expand on the liturgical, theological and philosophical teachings of the different Hindu theistic orders.

Agami Jawi Islamic tradition in Indonesia which contains some Hindu elements.

Agni The sacred Hindu fire god.

Agnosticism The belief that nothing can be known of the existence of God, or of anything beyond the purely material.

agraharam In India, a liturgical community of Brahmin householders.

ahisma The fundamental Jain religious tenet of non-injury to any living being.

Ahl al-kitab The People of the Book, i.e. Christians, Jews and 'Sabians'. They are protected within a Muslim state as long as they recognize the political authority of the Muslim ruler and they pay the required taxes.

Ahura Mazda Literally 'wise lord'; the supreme god in Zoroastrianism; *see also* Zoroastrianism and Angra Mainyu.

aitu Samoan term for a spirit, also used of gods (*atua*) in some Polynesian islands.

akh In Egyptian religion, the human soul as immortal spirit.

Akitu The new year festival in Mesopotamian religion which renews the cosmos.

Alafin The title given to the kings of Oyo, Nigeria.

'Ali The cousin and son-in-law of Muhammad (d. 661). He became fourth caliph in 656, but his accession led to civil war and he was murdered. His descendants, the Shi'a, claim to be direct heirs to the Prophet Muhammad.

Allah The one God in Islam.

Al-Ashari (874–936) Famous Islamic theologian, founder of the most influential school of theology in Islam.

Albigensianism (Albigenses) An heretical Manichaeist Christian movement particularly prevalent in southern France in the twelfth and early thirteenth centuries, taking its name from the town of Albi. Adherents were sometimes known by the more generic term Cathars, which was also applied to earlier heresies.

al-khulafa' al-rashidun The 'rightly guided' four caliphs (632–661), successors of Muhammad in political leadership.

Ama In Hinduism, the Vaisnava god who forms the divine agent and main character in the Ramayana, the Hindu epic about Prince Rama, defender of good.

Amaterasu O-mikami The Sun-goddess and progenetrix of the Japanese Imperial family.

Amesha Spenta In Zoroastrianism, any of the six divine beings (three male, three female) created by Ahura Mazda to help govern creation.

Amida The Buddha of infinite light, revered by Pure Land Buddhists as the intermediary between humanity and Supreme Reality.

Amish A very conservative Christian group, which broke away from the larger Anabaptist movement in the Alsace region in France during the late seventeenth century. Most Amish now live in self-imposed isolation in the northeast USA and Canada.

Amitabha A celestial Buddha, described in the scriptures of the Mahayana school of Buddhism.

Ammon Egyptian god, represented as a ram with curled horns, who has a famous oracle at the Siwa oasis in the Libyan desert.

Amun The invisible double of the Sun-god in the Egyptian pantheon, championed by the Thebans during the Middle Kingdom.

Anabaptist Religious movements that demanded a removal from all worldly affairs, and promoted adult baptism. They represented the radical wing of the Protestant Reformation in the sixteenth century.

Analects An account of the dialogues between Confucius and his students.

anatman The Buddhist belief that there is no permanent human soul.

ancestor worship The widespread belief, especially in Africa, that rituals must be performed to influence deceased kinspeople.

angel An divine servant of God in Christian, Zoroastrian, Jewish and Islamic traditions.

anekantwad In Jain belief, the principle of open-mindedness.

Angra Mainyu In Zoroastrianism, the evil spirit who, beneath Ahura Mazda, opposes the good spirit known as Spenta Mainyu.

animism The belief that spirits reside in all living things.

Annunciation In Christian belief, the appearance of the Angel Gabriel to the Virgin Mary, to tell her that she would bear Jesus, the Son of God, conceived by the Holy Spirit.

Apedemek Lion-god of war in the Kushite pantheon.

aparigraha The Jain principle of non-acquisitiveness.

apocalypse The dramatic end of the present age, in both Christian and Jewish traditions.

Apollo A major god in Greek religion, linked with sun and light, he slew the Python at Delphi.

apostle One of the twelve closest followers of Jesus. They are named in the Gospels as having been especially chosen by him.

Aranyaka Any of several Sanskrit religious and philosophical treatises, closely connected with either the Brahmanas or Upanisads, and intended to be read by hermits in the quiet of the forest. This contrasts with the Grhyasutras, which are treatises relating to domestic life.

arhant A 'worthy one', who has followed the Buddha's Eightfold Path to liberation and arrived at nirvana.

Arius (c.250–356) Originator of the doctrine that became known as the 'Arian heresy'. He believed that the Son of God was not consubstantial or coeternal with the Father. His teachings divided the Christian Church for many centuries.

Ark of the Covenant In Judaism, the shrine containing God's Ten Commandments to Moses.

Artemis An Anatolian earth mother goddess who was incorporated into Greek religion.

artha A Sanskrit term relating to the idea of material prosperity. In Hinduism it is one of the four goals of human life, known as *Purusharthas*.

arya-satya According to the Buddha, the Four Noble Truths of human life: there is suffering (*duhkha*); every suffering has a cause (*duhkha-samudaya*); it is possible to overcome this suffering (*duhkha dirodha*); there is a way to overcome suffering (*duhkha-nirodha-marga*). Without fully comprehending these realities there is no way to achieve peace or happiness in life.

Asantehene Kings of Asante, Ghana.

ase Vital force or power in Yoruba.

Ash'ariya The most influential school of theology in Islam.

Ashkenazi(m) Jews whose ancestors were settled in Christian Europe.

ashram *see asrama*

ashtangika-marga Noble Eightfold Path: the Buddhist route to salvation.

Ashur The 'king of gods' in Assyria.

asnam *(sanam)* 'Idols': how Muslim sources termed the pre-Islamic gods and goddesses.

asrama (ashram) In Hinduism, a 'refuge', referring either to a 'station' or 'place' in life, or a compound of forest-dwelling seers and sages.

asuras The race of supernatural beings that oppose the gods of Hinduism.

Atharva In Hinduism, an additional Veda (or knowledge) of injurious and remedial rites connected with the sacrifice.

atheism The belief that God does not exist.

Athirat In Canaanite religion, the consort of El and mother of the gods.

atman The Hindu concept of the soul.

Augustine of Hippo, St (354–430) The leading thinker of the early Christian Church. He converted in 386 and became Bishop of Hippo in North Africa. His greatest work was *The City of God*.

avatara Literally 'crossing over'; an incarnation of divinity, usually the Hindu god Visnu.

avidya Ignorance of the true world or self; in Hindu belief this is the main cause of bondage to the cycle of life and death.

Avignon During a period of schism in the Catholic Church, seven popes reigned from Avignon in southern France between 1309 and 1376. They were succeeded by two antipopes.

awliya' **(pl. of wali, qv)** Literally 'the friends' of Allah, pious holy men and women, Muslim 'saints'.

ayatollah Literally, 'a sign of Allah', a high-ranking member of the Twelve Shi'ite Muslim clergy of Iran.

ba In Egyptian religion, the human soul as conscience.

Ba'al/ba'al Literally 'my lord'/'master'; a designation used of many deities in Canaanite religion, but when used as a single name it refers to the storm god, Hadad, who rules the weather and so fertility.

Babel *see* Tower of Babel.

Baha'i Faith founded in 1844 CE by Baha'ullah (Glory of God) in Iran. It has spread across the world. Its roots are based in Islam. With the exception of its beliefs about homosexuality, it promotes peace and democracy with equal rights to all, regardless of gender, race or nationality.

baptism The sacrament by which people are initiated into Christianity through ritual washing. In the early Church the convert was immersed; many churches now symbolically pour water over the head.

Baptists Members of a Christian Protestant movement that dates from the sixteenth century. Many follow the practice of baptism by total immersion. They are now represented by many churches and groups around the world.

barakah Grace/blessing power, found in persons, places and objects. In Islamic mysticism, the spiritual wisdom transmitted by a master to his pupil.

Benedictine A follower of the Rule of St Benedict (c.480–547), who established a monastery on Monte Cassino, near Naples, Italy. The Benedictine rule became the foundation of Christian monastic organization.

betel chewing Chewing betel nut with lime is a method of relieving tension in many South Asian and Pacific cultures; betel was used to manipulate or propitiate spirits, and is often chewed at ceremonies and gatherings.

Bhagavad-gita 'The Song of the Lord', a short dialogue within the Mahabharata (with the Ramayana, one of the two Sanskrit epics of ancient India) between Krsna and Arjuna.

bhakti In Hinduism, complete devotion to one aspect of the deity.

Bible The sacred book of Christians. It is in two parts: the Old Testament is identical with the sacred book of the Jews, though there is some divergence among Christian Churches about what is to be included; and the New Testament, containing the four Gospels – the accounts, attributed to Matthew, Mark, Luke and John, of the life of Christ – letters attributed to early followers of Jesus, and an apocalyptic book, the Book of Revelation.

bikkhu A Buddhist monk or nun who renounces worldliness.

bishopric The seat of a bishop, though often taken as equivalent to a diocese or see, the area over which a bishop, the leading Christian minister or priest, has jurisdiction.

Bodhi Tree The tree, at Buddh Gaya in northern India, under which the Buddha was believed to have achieved enlightenment.

bodhisattva A being who is inspired by great compassion to dedicate their spiritual life over many incarnations to becoming a Buddha for the benefit of all beings.

Bogomils A Gnostic dualistic sect found in the Balkans in the early Middle Ages, and which survived there well into the fifteenth century.

Bon The indigenous religion of Tibet.

Bori Healing cult first recorded among the Hausa in the fifteenth century, West Africa.

Brahma Hindu creator of the universe. With Visnu and Siva he forms one of the leading trinity of Hindu gods.

Brahman In Hinduism, the eternal Reality that supports the known universe.

Brahmanas Explanatory manuals, which provided a commentary on the Vedas, explaining Vedic rituals. They are thought to have been composed between 900 and 500 BCE.

Brahmin The highest of the four castes that make up the Hindu social order; traditionally priests of Hinduism.

Buddha (*see also* Siddhartha Gautama) One who has achieved perfect enlightenment. The historical Buddha was Siddhartha Gautama (also known as Shakyamuni) but the existence of other celestial Buddhas is posited by some Buddhist schools.

Buddhism Major religion of South and Southeast Asia founded by Siddhartha Gautama (c.563–c.483 BCE), who was born the son of a Hindu nobleman, but abandoned his earthly status to seek spiritual enlightenment. Buddhism maintains that it is possible to obtain release from the sorrow that is inherent in life by releasing oneself from desire and self-delusion.

Buddhacarita 'Acts of the Buddha', biographies of the Buddha, probably composed in the second century CE. They are believed to have been written by monk poets at the court of the great Buddhist emperor Kaniska.

bulopwe Vital force or power in Luba, Central Africa.

bund An Eastern European Jewish socialist organization.

burka (*burkha*) Garment worn in public by Muslim women covering the head and entire body.

caliphate The office of the caliphs, understood by Sunnis as the successors to the Prophet Muhammad.

caliphs Leaders of the Muslim community after Muhammad's death.

Calvin, Jean (1509–64) Theologian and leader of the Protestant Reformation in France and Switzerland. He established the first Presbyterian government in Geneva. His *Institutes of the Christian Religion* (1536) set out his main principles: biblical authority should overrule Church tradition; the state should support the Church; the sacraments, though desirable, are not essential to true religion.

Calvinism The theological system of the French reformer Jean Calvin, in which pre-destination and justification by faith are important elements.

Canaanite Designation given by scholars to the culture and religion of the Levant in the second millennium BCE.

Candomblé Afro-Brazilian religion.

Cao Dai A syncretic Vietnamese religion which contains elements of Confucianism, Daoism, Buddhism and Christianity.

cardinals Bishops in the Roman Catholic church who advise the Pope. They meet as a group to elect a new pope when needed.

cargo cult/movement A generalized term used to cover religious or social movements that appeared in Melanesia to explain and appropriate Western knowledge, often with millennial or syncretist features. Cargo was seen as wealth that had been sent by God or spirits and misappropriated by Europeans.

Carvaka An Indian philosophical school of thought that holds nothing to exist except the visible, material world.

caste A social distinction in the Hindu world based on heredity or occupation.

catacombs Underground galleries which served as burial places for the early Christians.

catechism From the Greek *katecheo*, 'to sound aloud'. A summary or exposition of religious doctrine, used to educate a person in the fundamentals of Christianity. It is often organized in a question and answer format.

Cathars A general medieval term for Christian heretical movements; *see also* Albigensianism

Catholic A term derived from the Greek *katholikos* meaning 'universal', and first used of the Church by Ignatius of Antioch (d. c.107) to indicate the unity of the wider Christian community, beyond the local church. After the division of the church into East and West in 1054, the latter used the term of itself, while the former preferred the term 'Orthodox'. After the Reformation it was used by those in communion with Rome ('Roman Catholics').

CCM *see* Counter Cult Movement

Celestial Masters Orthodox Daoist sect, founded by Zhang Daoling in 142 CE.

Cerealia Annual Roman festival, 12–19 April, of Ceres.

Ceres Roman goddess of grain.

Ch'an (Chan) Buddhism A form of Chinese Buddhism which eschews good works and scriptural study but instead claims the practice of meditation alone can lead to a sudden awakening to enlightenment. Certain forms of Ch'an were introduced in Japan, Korea and Vietnam.

Cheng-I The school of Daoism which claims to be the continuation of the earlier Celestial Masters tradition.

Chalcedonians Those who accept the definition of the Council of Chalcedon (451) that in Christ there is one person, but two natures – the one divine, the other human.

Chaldean The name given to Middle East (Arab) Christians, especially those in Iraq, who are in communion with Rome.

Charismatics Christian groups, present within various denominations, that emphasize the Holy Spirit.

cherubim Angelic beings frequently mentioned in the Hebrew scriptures as agents of Yahweh.

chi Literally 'breath' or animating force; in eastern traditions, the vital energy in the universe and our bodies.

chi-kung A Daoist system of gathering inner energies in order to achieve spiritual fulfilment.

Christ From the Greek *Khristos*, meaning 'The anointed one', and used as the translation for the Hebrew term *Messiah* or 'Deliverer'; as such, applied to Jesus by the Gospels; *see also* Jesus of Nazareth.

Christianity One of the world's great monotheistic religions, which emerged in Palestine in the first century CE, and was based on the teachings of Jesus of Nazareth. In the central traditions of Christianity the single God is held to be a trinity: the Father, the Son (who became incarnate in Jesus of Nazareth) and the Holy Spirit.

Christian Science Religion founded by Mary Baker Eddy in the 1870s, which teaches that physical illness can be overcome by purely spiritual means.

Christological controversy The debate about the figure of Jesus, both his relationship to God and whether and how he was both divine and human.

chung Loyalty, a Confucian virtue.

chun-tzu The 'gentleman', someone who follows the teachings of the Confucian school.

chthonics In Greek religion, these are the earth and underworld deities; *see also* Olympians.

Chuang-tzu Writings attributed to the eponymous Confucian sage.

Church of England Protestant church founded by King Henry VIII in 1534. Under the Act of Supremacy, the English monarch became the head of the church in England, rather than the Pope. Also known as the Anglican Church.

Church of Jesus Christ of Latter-Day Saints (Mormons) A millenarian religion founded by Joseph Smith in 1830, on the basis of revelations in *The Book of Mormon*.

Cistercians Roman Catholic order following a strict form of monasticism based on the rule observed at the monastery of Cîteaux, founded in France in 1098.

Cluniac Relating to the monastery of Cluny, founded in 910 in Burgundy, France, which wielded a considerable influence over the Christian Church for the next two centuries.

Confucius (K'ung-fu-tzu, Kongzi) A Chinese philosopher (551–479 BCE), accountant and administrator, whose writings and teachings codified the Chinese political and social system until the twentieth century. He identified the inherent good in proper conduct, ethics, education, respect and ritual observance and his values were elevated to the status of a religion.

Confucianism The religion, culture, system of education and government based on the teachings of Confucius.

Congregationalism A form of democratic Church government, which stresses the independence of each congregation and the right of members to have their say in its governance.

Copts Members of the ancient Egyptian Christian Church with its headquarters in Alexandria. The Church did not accept the Chalcedonian definition. In 1741, a small section of Copts united with Rome. Today, its three to four million followers still use the Coptic language, derived from ancient Egyptian, for their version of the Greek liturgy.

Counter Cult Movement (CCM) A group made up mainly of Fundamentalist and other Evangelical Protestant organizations, which opposes and criticizes new religious movements (NRMs) because of their unorthodox and/or novel theological beliefs.

Counter-Reformation The move, in the sixteenth and seventeenth centuries, to renew and reinvigorate the Catholic Church in the face of the sixteenth-century Protestant Reformation.

crusade A Christian form of 'Holy War', understood primarily of the expeditions to recover the Holy Land from Muslim rule. The first was launched by Pope Urban II in 1095. The term has also been applied to other military expeditions approved by the papacy, especially for the conquest of non-Christian peoples.

cult Any religion that focusses on the worship of a particular person or deity. Also, often a rigorously disciplined and exclusivist, smaller religious movement.

culture hero In indigenous religions, the figure, found in many myths, who is seen as having played a key role in the creation of social life.

Cybele The central figure in a Greek mystery cult which spread in Rome.

Dagan (Dagon) Canaanite/Philistine deity of storms; linked with the Mesopotamian En-lil.

daimoku The name of the Lotus Sutra, which is repeated in Nichiren Buddhism as a mantra.

Dalai Lama Literally 'Ocean of Wisdom,' the Buddhist spiritual and temporal leader of the Tibetan people.

Daoism (Taoism) Major Chinese religion, believed to have been founded by Lao-Tszu (Laozi), based on the concept of Dao ('the way'), living selflessly, in harmony with nature, and revering the example of the ancestors.

Daodejing (Tao-te ching) Writings attributed to the Daoist sage Lao-Tszu (Laozi).

Daojia (Tao-chia) Philosophical Daoism.

Daojiao (Tao-chiao) Religious Daoism.

daoshi A Daoist master.

darshan Visual contact with the divine, mediated through Hindu images or gurus.

Deism A system of belief in God which emerged in the seventeenth century. It took various forms, but generally rejected any notion of divine revelation contained in the Scriptures, and frequently denied that God, once he had created the universe, had any further interest in its well-being.

Delphi In Greek religion, an oracular shrine of Apollo which was consulted by all the city states.

dervish In Muslim tradition, a Sufi mystic.

devas Literally 'the shining ones'; the gods of Hinduism.

devshirme Levy system during the Ottoman empire.

Dewi Sri Balinese rice goddess.

dhimmi protected status given to peoples of the book under Islamic suzerainty.

dharma The underlying principle of reality, seen as the content of the Buddha's enlightenment and his subsequent teachings, which is intended to lead other beings to the same experience.

dhikr Remembrance of Allah's name, Sufi ritual.

Diamond Vehicle *see* Vajrayana

Diaspora the movement of peoples, and specifically religious groups, away from their cultural/religious homeland into host cultures as a result of exile, war or social and economic pressures; *see also* Dispersion

Dione The consort of Zeus at the Greek oracle of Dodona.

Dionysus In Greek religion, a suffering god who dies and comes back to life; god of vegetation and wine who inspires music.

Diophysitism The belief that Christ had two natures: both divine and human. This concept was asserted at the church council at Chalcedon in 451 CE and is contained in the Chalcedonian Creed. *See also* Monophysitism.

Dispersion (Diaspora) The scattering of the Jews outside the Land of Israel.

Divali (Diwali) Hindu winter festival celebrating the end of the monsoon, associated with Lakshmi, the goddess of property.

Divallia Early Roman festival for the winter solstice.

Dodona An important oracle site in northwest Greece.

Dominicans An order of friars founded by St Dominic in 1215, particularly to preach against the Albigensians – the formal title is 'Friars Preachers'.

Donatists A schismatic group which arose at the beginning of the fourth century within the North African Church in the aftermath of the persecution of the Emperor Diocletian.

dream-time/the dreaming The Australian aboriginal belief in a time when gods-cum-animals-cum-humans were constructing the world.

druid Literally 'wizard'; the name applied generically to the obscure group that were the Celtic pre-Christian religious leaders.

dualism The concept that the spritual and material occupy two separate realms.

Dukduk Tolai secret society of masked spirit dancers, New Britain.

duhkha In Buddhist teaching, an inescapable fact of human life; suffering, frustration, lack of harmony with the environment. *See also arya-satya*.

Durga In Hinduism, the Great Goddess as destroyer of evil.

Eastern Orthodox Church Following the definitive schism in the Roman Catholic Church in 1074 the Church permanently separated into the Eastern Greek-speaking Orthodox Church centred on Constantinople, and the western Latin-speaking Church, centred on Rome. Today, it embraces all those Churches that are in communion with the Patriarch of Constantinople.

Ecology and Religion Religious perspectives on how organisms interact with their environment, particularly in order to sustain it responsibly.

ecumenism The movement to achieve understanding and tolerance between different branches of Christianity, or between different faiths.

Eclectic Movement A renaissance movement founded in eastern Tibet during the eighteenth century which aims to overcome sectarianism by its eclectic approach to doctrine and practice.

Eid The Islamic festival after Ramadam, celebrating the end of the month's fasting.

Eight Immortals Legendary figures who became gods in Daoism and Chinese popular religion.

El The supreme Canaanite god.

en Element in the names of kings and gods in Mesopotamia; originally as city administrator.

Enlightenment The total comprehension of reality and its workings together with liberation from the cycle of rebirth achieved by Buddhas. Also, the period in post-Renaissance eighteenth century Europe which saw the development of secular and empirical science, philosophy, political science, economics, humanism and rationalism.

Enlil Sumerian 'lord wind'; the god who sent moisture in spring and so fertility.

Epic of Gilgamesh Long Mesopotamian poem in 12 parts which is known today in its first millennium BCE form.

Esagil The great temple of Marduk at Babylon.

eschatology Beliefs about the end of the world and humanity.

Eshu *Orisha* (spirit) of change, uncertainty and communication, also referred to as a 'trickster' (Yoruba).

Essene Member of a Jewish sect founded between the second century BCE and the second century CE. It was characterized by a severe asceticism, a communal life of rigorous withdrawal, and a mystic belief in immortality. The Dead Sea Scrolls, found in Qumran between 1947 and 1956, probably belonged to an Essene community.

Esoteric Buddhism Refers to the 'hidden' doctrines, which must be revealed by a master, as opposed to 'open' doctrines, which can be found in texts and *sutras*.

Eucharist The central act of worship of the Christian Church. The word is derived from Greek, and means thanksgiving: it is most properly applied to the main prayer of the act of worship, during which bread and wine are 'consecrated'. Through this consecration the bread and wine are thought to become the body and blood of Christ – churches are divided on how this might be so – which are then distributed to worshippers in the act called '(Holy) Communion'.

Evangelism Proclaiming of the Christian gospel; preaching and prosleytizing.

Exodus Name of the second book of the Bible; the liberation of the Jews from slavery in Egypt.

exorcism Rituals performed to cast out evil spirits which have come to dwell within the person.

Fa-hsiang The Chinese term for Yogachara Buddhism (Mind-Only School).

Falasha Member of the Ethiopian Jewish community.

Falun Gong 'Law of the Wheel', a religious sect that emerged in China in 1992, when Li Hongzhi, known as 'the master', set up a study centre in Beijing. Combining a mixture of Buddhist and Daoist beliefs, its adherents follow a philosophy and regime of exercises that are believed to lead to spiritual enlightenment and improve health. The sect was banned in China in 1999.

Fatima Youngest daughter of Muhammad, wife of 'Ali, and founder of the Fatimid dynasty.

fatwa A learned legal opinion delivered by a Muslim jurisconsult, known as a *mufti*.

feng shui The Daoist practice of observing natural flows of energy in order to determine the most auspicious position for a building and its contents.

fiqh ('understanding'), a thorough comprehension of the **legal** responsibilities of Islam.

flamines (sing. *flamen*); the teams of priests that were responsible for particular cults in Roman religion.

focus Literally 'the hearth'; and hence a place of domestic sacrifice in Roman religion.

Franciscans An order of friars founded by St Francis in 1209 and marked from the beginning by a commitment to absolute poverty.

frashokereti In Zoroastrianism, the final resurrection into eternal life.

Friends, Society of *see* Quakers

fundamentalism An adherence to historical forms of a religion, with no concession to modernity or change. In some cases, religious tenets are rigidly, or even violently, upheld.

Gelugpa One of the four principal schools of Tibetan Buddhism, and the school to which the Dalai Lama belongs.

Gentiles A Jewish term meaning non-Jews, and used as such in the New Testament. Much later it came to be applied to 'foreigners' and non-Christians.

ghetto Area in a city where all Jews are compelled to live, from the Jewish Quarter in Venice.

Gilgamesh King of Uruk, and hero of the Babylonian epic poem, who goes to find the survivor of the Great Flood. *See also* Epic of Gilgamesh.

glossolalia Ecstatic speaking in tongues, a feature of Pentecostalism.

Gnosticism A mystical understanding of spiritual knowledge, characterized by the belief that matter is evil, and that emancipation comes through *gnosis*, knowledge; the name derives from a Christian heretic cult of the first to third centuries.

Gospels *see* Bible

Great Schism A term sometimes used of the events of 1054 which divided the Eastern (Orthodox) Churches led by the Patriarch of Constantinople from the Church of the West led by the Pope, and sometimes of 1378–1417, during which time there were usually two but sometimes three people competing for the title of Pope, each backed by some of the nations of Europe.

Gregory I, St (c.540–604) Pope and one of the Fathers of the Christian Church. He reorganized the church administration, reformed the liturgy, initiated missionary activity, and asserted the influence of Rome.

Gregory VII, St (c.1020–1085) A great reforming Pope of the Middle Ages, who criticized various abuses within the Church.

Grhyasutras Hindu Sanskrit treatises relating to domestic life.

gurdwara The Sikh place of worship.

guru An enlightened religious teacher, who is able to lead individuals out of the cycle of birth and death.

Guru Granth Sahib The Sikh sacred scripture.

Guru Nanak *see* Nanak

hadith In Islam, a traditional report of the pronouncements or actions of the Prophet Muhammad.

hafiz Someone who has committed the Qur'an to memory.

hajj Ritual pilgrimage to Mecca during the month of Dhu'l- Hijjah (8-13), the fifth pillar of Islam. Expected of every Muslim, health and means permitting, at least once during their lifetime.

halal In Islam, permissible/lawful food and drink, **as well as behaviour,** according to *shari'a*.

Hare Krishna *see* ISKCON

haruspicy Form of divination, popular in Roman religion, by the inspection of an animal's entrails by one skilled (an haruspex) in reading such 'signs'.

Hasid Member of a Jewish ultra-Orthodox, semi-mystical group.

Heavenly Masters Sect School of Daoism founded by Chang Ling in the first or second century CE.

Hera In Greek religion, the queen of heaven and the usual consort of Zeus.

heresy The formal denial of one of the doctrines of the Christian faith, leading to a separation from the Catholic Church.

hermeneutics A study of methods used to interpret the Bible.

Hermeticism An occult or esoteric tradition, named after Hermes Trismegistus, a second-century CE writer on magic and alchemy.

heyoka In Native American spiritual traditions, 'contrary' wisdom and the person who embodies it.

High Place(s) Term used in the Hebrew Scriptures for the sanctuaries of Canaanite/Phoenicians gods.

hijab In Islam, the veiling of women to preserve modesty.

hijra (*hejirah, hegira*) Muhammad's 'emigration' from Mecca to Yathrib (Medina) in September 622, later (c. 637) to become the first year of the Muslim era.

hijri A year in the Muslim lunar calendar since the *hijra*. The Islamic *hijri* calendar contains 12 months that are based on the motion of the moon. This calendar is consistently shorter by approximately eleven days than a solar year, and therefore it recedes with respect to the Christian calendar. The *hijri* calendar is based on the Qur'an, and its proper observance is a sacred duty for Muslims.

hilal The crescent moon; the point from which the lunar cycle of the Muslim calendar is calculated.

Hinayana Literally the 'Lesser Way', a negative term for the limited aspirations of the early monastic form of Buddhism, which focussed largely upon individual liberation from the cycle of birth and death.

Hinduism The dominant religion in India, which has no single founder, but has evolved over the last 4000 years. It involves the belief in destiny (*karma*) and cycles of reincarnation (*samsara*). It is all-embracing, with many cults and ritual practices, and ranges from monotheism to polytheism, but is united in its emphasis on mystical contemplation and self-denial as the route to spiritual enlightenment. Its most sacred scriptures are the Vedas.

Holocaust The destruction of European Jewry under the Nazis, 1942–45.

Holy Trinity The belief, common in many branches of Christianity, that within God there are three aspects: God the Father, the Son and the Holy Spirit.

hon Vietnamese word for spirits.

Horus The son of two archetypal Egyptian deities, the goddess Isis and the god Osiris, who was in ancient times believed to be incarnated in the living Pharaoh, whereas the actual Pharaoh, after death, became identified with Osiris in a pleasant afterlife. Horus is symbolized by a falcon.

hsiao Filial devotion, a Confucian virtue.

hsin The Confucian virtues of honesty and faithfulness.

Huang-Lao Eclectic form of Daoism followed by the Han court, until the adoption of Confucianism in 136 BCE.

Hua-yen School of Chinese Buddhism based on the Avatamsaka (or 'Flower Adornment') Sutra.

Huguenots French followers of the Swiss religious reformer Jean Calvin. Many Huguenots fled the country when the Edict of Nantes (1598), intended to safeguard the co-existence of Catholics and Huguenots, was revoked by Louis XIV in 1685.

Humanism, Secular A non-theistic philosophy that promotes man as the measure of all things. It had its roots in the Renaissance and the rationalism of the eighteenth century Enlightenment and in the free thought movement of the nineteenth century.

Humanistic In Judaism, an American non-Orthodox religious movement.

Hussites Followers of the Bohemian reformer Jan Hus (c.1372–1415), who was executed for heresy at the Council of Constance. Hus rejected the prevailing doctrine of the Eucharist, and was highly critical of the moral laxity of the clergy.

icon A sacred image, revered in the Eastern Orthodox Christian Church.

iconoclasm The practice of banning, and sometimes destroying, religious images, imposed in Byzantium in the eighth and ninth centuries. Icon-veneration was finally restored in 843, and is still celebrated at the Feast of Orthodoxy in the Eastern Church.

Ifa A complex system of divination in West Africa; also the *orisha* (spirit) of divination, Yoruba.

Ignatius of Loyola (1491–1556) The founder of the Jesuit order, which was devoted to converting the infidel and counteracting the Protestant Reformation. He was canonized in 1622.

ihya' Islamic revival.

Ijtihad Independent Muslim legal reasoning, done by a *mujtahid*.

incarnation Physical embodiment of the divine.

imam The leader of Muslim congregational prayer; in Shi'ism also the religious and political leader of the community.

indulgences In the Roman Catholic Church, the remission of the 'penalty' incurred by a sinner, even though the sin itself has been forgiven. The granting of an indulgence is now reserved to the papacy.

Innocent III (r. 1198–1216) Pope who presided over the apogee of papal power in the Middle Ages at the time of the Latin conquest of Constantinople in the Fourth Crusade.

infidel The Muslim and Christian term for a non-believer.

Inquisition Established by Pope Gregory IX in 1233 as a supreme Church court to repress heresy following the Albigensian Crusade; those found guilty were handed over to the secular authorities for punishment.

intifada Palestinian uprising against Israeli occupation/domination.

Isangoma A predominantly female association of diviners; Zulu, South Africa.

Ishtar Assyria's second deity after Ashur; goddess of love and battle.

Isis A principal goddess in ancient Egypt, the wife and sister of the god Osiris, who together had a son, the god Horus (qv). Later worshipped throughout the Mediterranean Basin and known as "Mother of God" and "Queen of Heaven."

ISKCON International Society of Krishna Consciousness (Hare Krishna), a devotional movement that brought Hinduism to the West in the 1960s.

Islam The religion of the Muslims, founded by the Prophet Muhammad (c.570–632). It teaches that there is only one god, Allah, whose words were dictated to Muhammad, and recorded in the sacred book of Islam, the Qur'an.

Ismailis Branch of the Shi'a division of Islam, which split from the other groups because of a dispute over the succession of the sixth imam, and gradually developed its own theological doctrines. Ismailis still exist in Pakistan, India, Iran, Syria and Yemen.

Israel Name given by God to the patriarch Jacob; name of the kingdom of the ten northern tribes; name of the modern Jewish state.

Israelite Descendant of the patriarch Jacob.

ithihad see *mujtahid*

Izanami and Izanagi In Japanese mythology, the *kami* (gods) who created Japan and the Japanese.

Jacobite A name derived from Jacob Baradaeus (c.500–78), and used by the Monophysite Syrian Orthodox Church. As bishop of Edessa, he was the prime mover in the establishment of that Church's hierarchy.

Jahiliyah The 'age of ignorance', the way Muslim sources termed the pre-Islamic era.

Jainism Sect of Hindu dissenters, dating to the seventh century BCE. Characterized by a respect for all living things, the sect believes that liberation from the transmigration of souls can be achieved through discipline, self-denial and abstinence.

janapada Hindu realm.

Jansenism A name derived from the Flemish Catholic reformer Cornelius Otto Jansen (1585–1638), Bishop of Ypres, from whose book *Augustinus*, the main tenets of Jansenism were derived. It taught an extreme moral rigour, attacking in particular the moral teaching of the Jesuits, and was deeply pessimistic about human freedom under God.

Janus A major Roman god, a guardian deity; he had no Greek equivalent.

Jap Ji The morning prayer of the Sikhs, written by Guru Nanak.

Jataka A popular tale that relates to one of the former lives of the Buddha.

Jehovah's Witnesses Founded in 1881, a millenarian group in the Adventist tradition. It is engaged in worldwide missionary activity.

jen/ren The Confucian virtue of humaneness and benevolence.

Jesuits The Society of Jesus is a religious order, founded formally in 1540 by St Ignatius of Loyola. Members of the Society (Jesuits) have been engaged particularly in education and in missionary work.

Jesus of Nazareth (c. 4 BCE–29 CE) The inspiration of the Christian religion, believed by his followers to be the Son of God. He was born in Roman-occupied Palestine, and was crucified as a troublemaker by the Romans. His followers believe he was resurrected and ascended to heaven. The story of his life, teachings and miracles is recounted in the New Testament, which forms part of the Christian Bible; *see also* Christ

Jesus People A movement that combines evangelical Christianity with a counter-cultural 'hippy' lifestyle.

jihad Struggle/effort; refers to individual effort for spiritual achievement and material effort to affirm and expand Islam, hence the common misleading translation to 'holy war'.

jina In Jainism, an individual who has achieved full enlightenment.

jinja A Shinto shrine.

jinn (*djinn*) Spirits, made of fire or air; some are good and converted to Islam, others are evil. The singular, *jinni*, is the basis for the English word 'genie.'

jiva In Jainism, the eternal soul or life force possessed by all living beings.

Jodo Shinshu A Japanese form of Pure Land Buddhism founded in the Kamakura period (1192–1333) by Shinran.

Judah Name of the kingdom of the two southern tribes of Israel.

Judaism The religion of the Jewish people, based on the belief that there is one God, and developed by the ancient Hebrews.

Judge An early biblical leader.

Jupiter The chief Roman god, a sky deity who was later equated with the Greek god Zeus.

Ka'bah Cube-shaped shrine in Mecca, containing the Black Stone, a meteorite believed to be the symbol of allegiance between Allah and humankind.

Kabbalah Jewish mystical tradition.

Kabir (1440–1517) Indian mystic and poet and founder of the Sikh faith, which he saw as a fusion of the best elements of Hinduism and Islam. He was succeeded by his disciple Nanak. Much of his thinking is recorded in the Adi Granth, the sacred book of the Sikhs.

Kali In Hinduism, the destroying and transforming mother of the world.

kachh Underclothes worn by Sikhs, and designed to remind them of sexual continence and moral restraint.

kama Pleasure or love, one of the four goals of human life in post-Vedic Hinduism.

kami Shinto gods, immanent in nature and the spirits of the ancestors.

kamidana A household shrine for the Shinto gods, *kami*.

kanga A comb worn in the hair by Sikhs.

kara In the Sikh religion, a bangle worn on the right wrist, to symbolize the wheel of life.

karadji New South Wales Aboriginal term for a spirit man or shaman, also called *wingirin* (Queensland) and *kuldukke* (Victoria.)

Karaites Adherents of a Jewish heretical sect founded in the eighth century CE, known for their rejection of rabbinical authority, and their efforts to live according to the sole authority of the Hebrew Bible.

karma In Buddhist and Hindu thought, the sum of a person's actions in a previous existence, and how they bear on his or her fate in future existences.

Kava ceremonial In Polynesia, the elaborate ritual preparation and presentation of the kava (piper methysticum) drink to persons according to their place in the social hierarchy.

kavya Ornate Sanskrit poetry, written by Indian court poets in the early centuries CE.

Kenoticism In the Russian Orthodox Church, an ascetic monastic tradition, combined with service in the world.

kensho In Zen Buddhism, the moment of sudden enlightenment.

kesh In Sikhism, long hair held in place by the *kanga* and a turban.

kevala In Jainism, the supremely perfected state.

kirpan In Sikhism, the sword (or a symbolic representation of a sword), signifying the wearer's willingness to fight for his beliefs.

kirtan In Sikhism, the devotional singing of hymns.

koan A story, dialogue, question, or statement in Zen Buddhism, generally inaccessible to rational understanding but comprehensible through intuition. *Koans* originate in the sayings and deeds of sages and legendary figures.

Kojiki 'Record of Ancient Matters' An eighth-century document tracing the mythical origins of Japan.

Kokka Shinto 'State' Shinto, which became a national religion of Japan after the Meiji Restoration of 1868.

kosher Foods that fulfil the requirements of Jewish law.

kra Vital force or power, Akan, Ghana.

Krsna (Krishna) God who forms the divine agent in the Mahabharata and is widely worshipped in Hinduism as the avatar of Visnu.

kshatiryas The second of the four traditional divisions of Hindu society: warriors and rulers.

Kubra Nagast 'Glory of the Kings', a volume celebrating the rise of the Solomonite dynasty in Ethiopia.

Kufic script Named after the town of Kufa in Iraq, which was one of the main Islamic cultural centres in the early period. This script was often used for the calligraphy of Qur'ans. It replaced most of the earlier scripts and reached its perfection in the eighth century CE.

kufr 'Covering, hiding, ingratitude', which came to mean 'unbelief.' This Arabic root is used in the Qur'an also as *kafir*, 'infidel,' *one* who does not believe in the dominion or authority of Allah.

kuldukke see *karadji*

kuribu see *lamassu*

La Tène Archaeological designation for the material culture found in Celtic lands in the early first millennium CE.

Ladino Language of Sephardic Jews.

lama A Tibetan Buddhist monk.

Lamaism A form of Buddhism that developed in Tibet in the mid-eighth century. It is based on the Mahayana tradition, and incorporates elements of Tantrism and Shintoism. In 1641 the Dalai Lama was appointed by the Mongols to rule Tibet. The last Dalai Lama was exiled to India in 1959. Lamaism now has widespread support in Tibet.

lamassu A variously named mythical being (human body with eagle's head) referred to in Assyrian texts and frequently depicted on their monuments. In Akkadian, referred to as kuribu, possibly the origin of the word cherub.

Lao-tszu (Laozi, 'The Old Master') Probably mythical sixth-century BCE Chinese philosopher and sage, the inspiration of Daoism, who revered self-sufficiency, restraint, and a sense of respect for nature and ancestors. Also the name of an early Daoist text; *see also* Daoism

Lapita Pottery and people named from an archaeological site in New Caledonia.

Lares With the Penates these were the Roman gods of the household/family.

Lateran Councils Four Church Councils, held at the Lateran Palace in Rome, in 1123, 1139, 1179 and 1215.

lemba A *ngoma*-type healing cult (using drumming, dancing and singing), Lower Congo, Africa.

Lent In Christianity, the 40 days from Ash Wednesday to Good Friday, representing the 40 days that Jesus spent in the wilderness. A time of fasting, prayer and contemplation.

Leo I, 'The Great' (d. 461) He became Pope in 440, and defined Catholic doctrine. He condemned the Monophysites at the Council of Chalcedon (451), and asserted the primacy of the see of Rome against Constantinople.

li In Confucianism, ceremonies, proper conduct and rituals.

Liberal In Judaism, a British, non-Orthodox religious movement.

liberation theology The interpretation of religious faith, frequently within Christianity, from the perspective of the poor, oppressed and victimized

Lin-chi The Chinese form of Rinzai Zen Buddhism.

liturgy A term derived from Greek meaning 'the work of the people'. In a Christian context it is used as a general term for formal religious services.

Lollards A religious reforming order which emerged in Europe in the fourteenth and fifteenth centuries. It attacked the corruption of the Church and asserted the right of the individual to interpret the Bible. It achieved notable popularity in England, under the leadership of John Wyclif.

lotu Post-mission term for belief system or religion in western Polynesia, usually Christianity.

Lotus Sutra Important Mahayana scripture that gave rise to various Japanese Buddhist sects.

lugal Element in the names of kings and gods in Mesopotamia; originally a Sumerian war leader.

Luther, Martin (1483–1546) German reformer whose questions about practices and beliefs within the Catholic Church led to the Protestant Reformation. He first became a controversial figure when he nailed his 95 Theses to the church door in Wittenberg, attacking the sale of indulgences – the forgiving of sins by the Pope and clergy in exchange for remuneration.

Lutheranism A theological system derived from the German reformer Martin Luther, which forms the basis for the creeds of several Churches. It generally stresses Luther's fundamental conviction of justification by faith alone.

ma'at The state of cosmic, political order, justice and well-being in Egyptian religion.

Madhyamika One of the two main schools of Mahayana Buddhism, founded in the second century CE by the Indian philosopher Nagarjuna, which teaches that all mundane phenomena are intrinsically devoid of actual existence and that all theories designed to describe reality are ultimately valueless.

madrasa Teaching college of Islamic doctrines and disciplines, often with boarding facilities for students.

Mahabharata A major Sanskrit epic of ancient India, the story of the contest for succession between the families of the Kauravas and Pandavas, the latter supported by lord Krsna, an avatar of Visnu. It is the longest epic poem in the world, and a major text of Hinduism.

mahajanapada Great realm, located in the north and northwest of the Indian subcontinent; sixteen are mentioned in sources at the time of the Buddha.

Mahavira (c.540–468 BCE) Brought up near Patna, northern India, Mahavira renounced his family and became an ascetic who sought enlightenment. He was the foremost preceptor of the Jain religion.

Mahayana Literally the 'Great Way', the Buddhist movement which emerged during the first century BCE, emphasizing the cultivation of compassion and insight for the benefit of all beings.

mahdi In Islam, the concept of a Messianic figure, who will one day bring faith, justice and prosperity to the earth.

Mamaia Tahitian 'visionary heresy' from word meaning 'rotten fruit'.

mana In Polynesia, a sacred force or quality that could be inherited or achieved; essential for sacred chiefs and political leaders and sometimes enshrined in ritual objects.

mandala In Tibetan Buddhism, a symbolic depiction of the universe, which acts as a mystic guide in meditation and religious rituals.

mantra A short repeated formula that is spoken or chanted as an aid to meditation in all Indian religions.

Manichaeism A dualist religion founded by in Persia by Manes (c.216–c.275) which combined elements of Zoroastrianism, Buddhism and Christianity. Noted for its Gnostic elements, it was regarded at the time as a Christian heresy, it has influenced many other sects, both Christian and otherwise.

Marcion (c.100–160) Founder of a religious sect that challenged Christian doctrine. He preached the existence of two gods: the Old Testament creator (the God of Law) and the God of Love, revealed in the teachings of Jesus, who would overthrow the first. The *Instrumentum* was his own version of the New Testament. After his death, the Marcionite sect continued to survive, remaining active in Syria into the tenth century.

Marduk Chief Babylonian deity in whose honour the Akitu (new year festival) was held; his annual victory over Tiamet (the primordial mother goddess) restores the universe.

Marranos Spanish Jews who were forcibly converted to Christianity.

Mars In Roman religion he was originally a god of vegetation; he became a major state god responsible for war.

Masorti A British non-Orthodox Jewish movement analogous to the American Conservative movement.

Mass The Roman Catholic term for the Christian Eucharist.

Matsuri A Shinto festival.

mawali Non-Arab converts to Islam.

maya Illusion. In Hindu thought, one of the primary causes of bondage to the cycle of life and death.

Mazakism A sect in Zoroastrianism, which held that the spirits of good and evil had no common origin.

mazar An Islamic shrine, usually the tomb of a holy person.

Mbona Regional rain-making, Malawi. Also the name of the ancestral spirit to whom the cult is devoted.

megalithic Literally 'big stones'; archaeological designation for the earliest European culture whose structures, usually ritual centres or burial monuments, have survived.

Melkites Originally those Christians of Syria and Egypt who accepted the definition of Chalcedon and were therefore of the Constantinopolitan, or imperial, party. Some Melkites are in communion with Rome, and the term is more commonly used for them.

Mencius (c.371–c.289 BCE) A Chinese philosopher who followed the teachings of Confucius, and travelled widely throughout China propagating Confucian thought. He believed that humanity was fundamentally good, but required proper conditions for moral growth.

Mennonites Members of independent church congregations inspired by the teaching of the Dutch priest Menno Simons (1496–1561). Common to all congregations is a belief in 'believer's baptism' (i.e., the baptism of adult committed members).

Mesopotamia Literally 'the [land] between the rivers'; the once fertile area, mainly in modern Iraq, irrigated by the Tigris and Euphrates.

Messiah A future anointed King who will establish God's rule on earth.

metta The concept of loving kindness in Buddhist thought.

Methodism An evangelical movement, originally founded by John Wesley (1703–91) as a revivalist movement within the Church of England but which had, by the end of the eighteenth century, effectively become a separate Church with supporters in both North America and England.

mihrab Niche in the wall of a mosque, often elaborately decorated, indicating the direction of prayer (towards Mecca).

mikva In Jewish tradition, a deep bath for ritual cleansing.

millennial The belief in the coming of a future, utopian age.

millet Ottoman Turkish term for a religious community, nation, usually referring to Christian and Jewish communities.

minyan The gathering of ten adult males required for Jewish communal worship.

mi'raj Muhammad's heavenly ascent from Jerusalem.

Mishnah Collection of Jewish oral law compiled by Judah ha Nasi, which served as the basis for the Talmud.

Mithra/ Mithras A major Persian deity, the god of justice and law, whose worship was central in an offshoot cult of Zoroastrianism that became popular in Rome in imperial times. Worship of Mithras, the divine saviour, was the most widespread of the mystery religions.

Mithraeum A specially-constructed sanctuary for the rituals of Mithraic religion.

Mitnagdim Orthodox eastern European Jews who were opposed to Hasidism.

mitzvah In Judaism, a divine commandment, or the sacred deed that follows the fulfilling of a commandment.

Mizrachi An Eastern European Orthodox Zionist movement.

mofa In Buddhism, the final period in the current cosmic epoch, in which people are no longer able to achieve enlightenment.

Mohism Form of Confucianism which emphasized universal love.

moksha In Hinduism, the liberation of the soul from the cycle of suffering and worldly illusion.

Monism Life seen as a unified whole, without a separate 'spiritual' realm.

Monophysitism The belief that there was only one single nature, partly human and partly divine, in the person of Jesus Christ. This doctrine was condemned by the Council of Chalcedon (451). Although they are Orthodox in tradition, the Coptic, Syrian and Armenian Churches retain some terminology that is derived from Monophysitism.

Montanism A heretical Christian tradition founded in Phrygia in the second century CE. The group was mystical and ecstatic, believing in prophecy and the power of the spirit.

Moonies *see* Unification Church

Mormons *see* Church of Jesus Christ of Latter-Day Saints

Moses Israelite prophet and lawgiver, who lived some time between the fifteenth and thirteenth centuries BCE.

Mount Olympus Cult centre of the Ancient Greeks.

muhajirun Those who accompanied Muhammad on his migration (*hijra*) from Mecca to Medina.

Muhammad (c.570–632) The original prophet of Islam, believed by Muslims to have received a divine revelation from God, which is manifested in the Qur'an , the holy text of Islam. Born in Mecca, Muhammad and his followers were forced to move to Medina in 622, and this migration (the *hijra*) marks the beginning of the Muslim calendar. He went on to conquer Mecca in 630, destroying the pagan idols and uniting much of Arabia.

Muharram The first Muslim month; the first ten days are a period of mourning for Shi'is who re-enact the murder of their third imam Husayn, killed at Kerbela in 680.

Mujahidin Literally '*jihad* warriors', resistance fighters and guerrilla groups in Afghanistan aiming to reassert Islamic law and principles.

muni A Jain monk.

mujtahid A learned Muslim scholar, who has the right to engage in independent legal reasoning (ijtihad).

mystery religions Ritualistic cults of Near Eastern origin in the later Roman empire which promised special knowledge and experience to their initiates as a preliminary to salvation.

mysticism The immediate experience of God achieved, it is claimed, by the exceptionally devout (the mystics) usually after long periods of spiritual training and prayer.

myth Stories concerning gods and superhuman beings, often serving to explain the origins and characteristics of society, culture and nature.

Mu'tazila One of the most influential theological schools, with a strong rationalist bias, in the history of Islam.

nabi The Islamic Arabic term for prophet, whether Jewish, Christian or Muslim.

Nabû In Mesopotamian religion, the son of Marduk, god of scribes and libraries.

Naios The specific title of Zeus at the Dodona oracle.

Nam The holy name of God, as repeated by the Sikhs.

namaz Islamic ritual prayer, *see salat*

Nanak (1469–1539) Follower of Kabir and one of the founding gurus of the Sikh faith, which combines both Hindu and Muslim beliefs. His teaching, which found a large following in the Punjab, advocates intense meditation on the divine name; many of his hymns still survive.

nats Tibeto-Burman word for spirits.

Neo-Confucianism Renewal of Confucianism resulting from a critique of Buddhism in the twelfth century.

Neopagan A person who follows a religion which is reconstructed from, or based upon, an ancient Pagan religion.

Neopentecostalism Modernist and fundamentalist form of Pentecostalism which prospers among the poor in the developing nations of South America and Africa, often offering ways to spiritual and material enrichment.

Neoplatonism A philosophical movement in the later Roman empire, which stressed the religious nature of the universe, and which was influential in the development of Christianity.

Nestorianism The doctrine that in Christ the human and divine natures were quite separate. Nestorianism derives its name from Nestorius, Patriarch of Constantinople from 428, but exiled into the Egyptian desert for his views in 436.

New Testament *see* Bible

ngoma Generic term for a type of healing cult found throughout central and southern Africa; the term ngoma can also mean drum, music and dance.

Nicene Creed Promulgated at the Council of Nicaea in 325, it affirmed the consubstantiality of Christ the Son and God the Father.

Nichiren Buddhism Based on the teachings of the thirteenth-century Japanese monk, Nichiren (1222–1282), it is notable for its focus on the Lotus Sutra, and its belief that people possess an innate Buddha nature, and are therefore capable of attaining enlightenment.

Nien-fo The Chinese practice of calling on the name of the Buddha.

Nihonshoki/Nihongi 'History of Japan' eighth-century CE document tracing the mythical origins of Japan.

Ninurta In Assyrian religion, Ashur's firstborn and god of hunting and warfare.

nirvana The eternal and blissful state of enlightenment achieved by one, usually a Buddha, who has become liberated from the cycle of birth and death.

Noah In the Hebrew Flood story (Genesis 6-9), he is the just man who builds an Ark to escape the destruction of humanity with his wife, three sons and their wives, and breeding stock of the world's animals.

norito A hymn or chant used in Shinto ceremonies.

Nut Egyptian goddess of the sky who embraces the earth.

Obatala *Orisha* (spirit), moulder of human beings (Yoruba).

Occultism A secret, esoteric tradition.

Oduduwa *Orisha* (spirit) who spread earth upon the primordial waters and descended from the sky to become the first 'divine' king of Ile Ife (Yoruba).

Ogun *Orisha* (spirit) of iron and war (Yoruba).

Oko *Orisha* (spirit) of farming (Yoruba).

Old Testament *see* Bible

Olorun God of the Sky (Yoruba).

Olympians In contrast to the *chthonics*, these are the sky-gods in Greek religion whose abode is on Mount Olympus.

om The sacred symbol and sound representing the ultimate; the most scared of Hindu words.

Omphalos Literally 'the navel'; in Greek religion a sacred stone in the sanctuary at Delphi which marked the centre of the universe.

Onile Goddess of the earth (Yoruba).

Opus Dei An organization of the Catholic Church, founded in Spain in 1928 by the Roman Catholic priest Josemaría Escrivá and given final approval in 1950 by Pope Pius XII. It emphasizes the Catholic belief that ordinary life may be a path to sanctity. The great majority of its approximately 85,000 members are lay people.

Origen (c.185–254) A scholar and theologian who was deeply influential in the emergence of the early Greek Christian Church.

orisha Generic term designating Yoruba spiritual entities (orixá in Brazilian Portuguese).

Orphism Early Greek mystery cult, dedicated to Orpheaus, which focused on the individual as a moral being.

Osiris *See* Horus, Isis.

Orthodox In Judaism, faithful to the literal meaning of the Torah.

orthodoxy A term meaning 'right thinking', relating in general to adherence to the established traditions of a religion. In Christianity, it is contrasted with heresy. As applied to the 'Orthodox Church' it includes those Churches that are in communion with the Patriarch of Constantinople.

pa Polynesian palisade or Maori fortification.

Pali Canon Buddhist scriptures of the Theravada School.

pantheism The belief that God is identifiable with the forces of nature; worship that admits, and tolerates, all gods.

papacy The office or position of the Pope as head of the Roman Catholic Church.

Parsis Literally 'the Persians'; the modern Zoroastrians.

Passover In Judaism, the spring festival celebrating the Exodus.

Patriarchs Abraham, Isaac and Jacob, biblical ancestors of the Jews.

patriarch In Christianity, a title given to the head of the five main sees or bishoprics, Alexandria, Antioch, Constantinople, Jerusalem and Rome. In more recent times the title has been extended to the heads of a number of Orthodox Churches, e.g. the Patriarch of Moscow (a title dating from 1589) governs the Russian Orthodox Church.

patu In Polynesia, a paddle-shaped hand club made from wood or greenstone.

Paul, St (martyred between 62 and 68 CE) Jewish Pharisee, who was converted to Christianity on the road to Damascus, and became the leading missionary and theologian of the early Christian Church. His letters to communities in Greece and Asia Minor are fundamental documents of the Christian faith.

Paulicians A sect founded in Armenia in the mid-seventh century: the origins of the name are uncertain. They believed that matter was evil, and therefore denied the reality of Christ's body. In the ninth century, after persecution, some fled to Bulgaria after which they disappear from history.

Pelagianism A concept proposed by the British monk Pelagious (c. 356–c. 418) who denied the existence of original sin inherited from Adam. He taught that humans are born morally neutral. They can fall into habits of sin but can overcome sin through mental effort, and can therefore choose God by the exercise of their free will and rational thought. His beliefs were strongly opposed by St Augustine of Hippo and declared heretical by successive Church Councils.

Penates *see* Lares

Pentateuch The five books of Moses at the beginning of the Old Testament: Genesis, Exodus, Leviticus, Numbers and Deuteronomy, known among the Jews as the Torah.

Pentecost Christian holy day when the Holy Spirit descended amongst the disciples of Jesus after his death and resurrrection. His followers found that they were able to communicate in other languages, the origin of 'speaking in tongues'.

Pentecostalism Recent Christian churches that emphasize the workings of the Holy Spirit, focussing on prophesy, charismatic experiences, divine healing and speaking in tongues.

Perfect Truth Sect A monastic school of Daoism which developed in the Yuan dynasty (1279–1368).

Peter, St (died c. 64 CE) The foremost of Jesus' disciples, recognized by the Roman Catholic Church as the first Pope.

Pharaoh The title for the ruler, a divine king, in ancient Egypt.

Pharisee Interpreter of Judaic law in the first centuries BCE/CE.

phi Thai word for spirits.

Pietism A religious reawakening in the Lutheran and Reformed churches in Germany and the Anglican church in England during the seventeenth and eighteenth centuries. Pietism stresses the importance of Bible study, and at the same time emphasizes the role of devotional piety.

Pillars of Islam Five duties that are the foundation of a devout Muslim life: faith or belief in the oneness of God and the finality of the prophethood of Muhammad; daily prayers; concern for and almsgiving to the needy; self-purification through fasting; and the pilgrimage to Mecca for those who are able.

Plymouth Brethren A Christian evangelical movement that began in Plymouth, England c.1830. The movement rejected what it perceived as the abandonment of fundamental truths of Christianity by the established Church, and emphasized meeting together without reference to denominational difference.

Poale Zion A socialist Zionist movement.

pogrom A violent outburst against the Jews in Eastern Europe.

pope From the Greek *pappa* meaning father, it was a term regularly applied to bishops in the early Church, but from the sixth century onwards was restricted in the West to the bishop of Rome.

potlatch Rituals found in (traditional) northwest America; spiritual purity is restored by way of the destruction of valued possessions.

pralu'n Khmer (Cambodian) word for spirits.

prana In Indian thought, the invisible life force.

prasad In Hindu tradition, blessed food.

predestination A doctrine that certain people are determined by God to be saved or redeemed, usually with the corollary that some are not. It is a central tenet of Calvinism.

Presbyterian A member of a Church that is governed in the main by elected elders (the Greek term 'presbyter' used in the New Testament means 'elder'). The doctrinal stance of Presbyterian Churches is generally Calvinism.

Promised Land The land promised to the patriarch Abraham.

Protestant A rather broad term in contemporary usage to describe all those Churches which are opposed to the rituals and doctrines of Roman Catholicism. When first coined in 1529, however, it tended to signify the more moderate Lutheran, as distinct from the radical or 'reformed' Calvinist, tendency in theology.

Proverbs A book of the Hebrew scriptures that presents a collection of worldly wisdom along with some spiritual advice, and which preserves many excerpts from Egyptian wisdom writings.

Psalms A book of the Hebrew scriptures made up of 150 prayers and hymns, many of which reflect the liturgy and poetic style of Israel's Ancient Near Eastern neighbours.

puja In Hindusim, the act of honouring an icon of god.

Pulotu Mirror-image world in Western Polynesia and people with this belief.

Puranas In Hinduism, a series of comsological histories, recording the early history of humanity, written from theistic perspectives. These sacred texts relate to the expansion of the Aryan tribes in northern India, and their formation into small states in the first millennium BCE.

Pure Land Any one of the realms elsewhere in the universe set up by celestial Buddhas that are endowed by them with all the conditions conducive to the rapid attainment of enlightenment. Beings from our world may be reborn in such Pure Lands through recollecting the name of the specific Buddha associated with such realms.

Purgatory In some Christian thought, a place of temporary suffering and expiation, where sinners are spiritually cleansed after death.

Puritans An imprecise term for those of a radical Protestant stance within the Church of England for a century or so from 1570 onwards. A common theme was opposition to bishops, which led some to Presbyterianism and others into Congregationalism.

purusha In Hindu thought, the cosmic spirit, the soul of the universe.

Purusharthas In Hinduism, the canonical four aims of human life: righteousness and morality (*dharma*); material wealth (*artha*); pleasure and love (*kama*) and liberation from the cycle of reincarnation (*moksha*).

pyramid In Egyptian religion, a massive stone-built royal tomb.

Python In Greek religion the serpent/dragon who guarded Delphi until slain by Apollo.

qadi An Islamic judge.

qiblah The Muslim direction of prayer, originally to Jerusalem, then (since 2 H.) to Mecca.

Qingdu Chinese Pure Land Buddhism.

Quakers More correctly, the (Religious) Society of Friends, which was founded in the mid-seventeenth century – the term 'Quaker' as applied to them dates from 1650 and refers to the 'spiritual tremblings' they experienced at their meetings. Quakers reject the notion of ordained ministers, preferring to commit themselves to their inner experience of God.

Quirinus A local deity of the area near Rome who later became one of the three main state gods; *see also* Jupiter, Mars

Qur'an (Koran) 'The Recitation,' that is, the Islamic scripture, believed to have been revealed orally by God, through the angel Gabriel, to the Prophet Muhammad. It consists of 114 chapters (*suras*), and serves as a basis of Islamic law and social morality as well as a devotional text.

rabbi An official Jewish teacher.

Ramadan The ninth month of the Islamic lunar calendar, during which Muslims observe strict fasting.

Ramayana The Sanskrit epic, dating to between 500 and 100 BCE, which is the story of Rama's rescue of his wife Sita from the demon Ravana. Not just a love story, it contains the teachings of ancient Hindu sages, as well as philosophical and theological speculations.

Rastafarianism A religion that developed in Jamaica in the 1930s, which venerates the former Emperor of Ethiopia, Haile Selassie and promotes black nationalism.

Re In Egypt, god of the sun and of creation and one of the most important in the pantheon.

Reconstructionist An American non-Orthodox Jewish religious movement.

Reform In Judaism, a non-Orthodox religious movement.

Reformation A religious revolution in the Roman Catholic Church, led in the sixteenth century by Martin Luther and John Calvin. It was to lead eventually to the foundation of Protestantism in much of northern Europe.

reincarnation Upon death, the migration of the soul into a new body.

religious orders The collective name for those organizations, mainly within Roman Catholicism, in which men or women live according to a particular rule of life (cf. for example, Benedictine, Jesuits, and particularly monasticism).

Renewalism A general term for recent Pentecostal, Neopentecostal and Charismatic Christian churches.

Rig Veda Possibly the world's oldest scripture, the religious foundation of Hinduism. It consists of a collection of sacred hymns tracing the religious development of the Aryan settlers in northern India.

Rinzai A form of Zen Buddhism founded in the Kamakura Period (1192–1333) by the Japanese monk Eisai.

rites of passage Rituals, found in all indigenous religions, marking the transition from one state of being (e.g. youth) to another (e.g. adulthood).

Rk (*Rig*) In Hinduism, the knowledge or Veda related to hymns sung at the sacrifice.

Robigalia Annual Roman agricultural festival held on 25 April.

Roman Catholic Church The largest and most powerful branch of the Christian Church, governed by the Pope in Rome. The popes claim an unbroken line of apostolic succession from St Peter, one of Jesus Christ's twelve disciples.

Rosicrucianism Relating to several international organizations that teach esotericism and mystical lore.

Sabbath In both Judaism and Christianity, the day of the week that is set aside for rest and worship.

Sabazius Greek mystery cult which spread in the Danubian provinces of the Roman empire in the second century CE.

sacrament A formal, ritual act by which a Christian associates him or herself with the redemption brought by Christ.

sadhu In Hinduism, an ascetic holy man.

sahaba (companions) The first converts to Islam, to whom Muhammad recited the Qur'an.

Sah-ch'ing The 'Three Pure Ones', the highest Daoist deities.

Saigu Shinto priestesses; the office was filled by the Japanese imperial princesses.

saints Men and women within Christianity who have been recognized by the Church as worthy of veneration because of the holiness of their lives or, in the case of martyrs, because they died for their faith.

Saiva, Saivism Relating to one of several Hindu religious orders holding Siva as the lord of the Universe.

sajda Bowing down, or prostration, during Islamic prayers.

sakti The creative, female aspect of Deity in Hinduism.

salat The five daily ritual prayers towards Mecca; the second pillar of Islam. *See namaz*

Sama Knowledge or Veda related to the melodies sung at the Hindu sacrifice.

Samhita Literally 'collection', here referring to the collections of the Vedic hymns and formulas.

samsara In Hinduism and Buddhism, the cycle of births and realms, as well as the movement through them, which constitute the world.

sanam see asnam

sangat A Sikh conregation, in which all are considered equal.

Sangha The Buddhist monastic community.

Sankara see Shankaracharya

San-lun 'Three treatise school' of Buddhism, based on the Indian Madhyamaka tradition. The name derives from the three principal texts: the Treatise of the Middle Way; the Treatise on the Twelve Gates; The One-Hundred-Verse Treatise.

Sanskrit The language of classic Hindu scriptures.

Santería Afro-Cuban religion.

sastra In Hinduism, a term meaning 'science' or treatise.

Satnamis Members of one of a group of Hindu sects in India. The oldest of these sects, founded by Girbhan in the sixteenth century, was an attempt to bring together Hinduism and Islam.

satori In Zen Buddhism, the moment of enlightenment.

satyrs In Greek mythology, the attendants of Dionysus, connected with woods and hills, and so with the general notion of fertility.

sawm Fasting throughout the day during the month of Ramadan; the fourth pillar of Islam.

Scientology Founded by L. Ron Hubbard in 1954, a religious movement that focusses on self-improvement and self-knowledge.

Second Coming The prophesied return of Jesus Christ to Earth.

secular A mode of thought or government without regard to religious or spiritual matters.

see see bishopric

Selloi The early Greek priests at the oracle of Dodona.

senzo kuyo The offering of memorial services to ancestors; an enduring feature of Japanese religious tradition.

Sephardi(m) The Jews of Iberia, and after the expulsion of 1492–97, their descendants.

Septuagint The first Greek translation of the Hebrew Bible.

Shabd The Sikh term for a name of God, recited in sacred hymns.

shahadah Testimony of faith ('there is no god but Allah (the God) and Muhammad is God's messenger'); the first pillar of Islam.

Shakti The Goddess. In Hindu belief, the female principle or power of the universe.

Shakyamuni see Siddhartha Gautama

shaman In indigenous religions, a man or woman who has undergone spiritual ordeals and is able to travel to and communicate directly with the spirit world.

shamanism The experience of travelling to other worlds to obtain beneficial wisdom and power.

Shamash In Mesopotamian religions, the sun god who dispenses justice.

Shango *Orisha* (spirit) associated with thunder and lightening; an early alafin of Oyo who was killed by lightning, subsequently deified and is therefore the ancestor of all subsequent alafin.

Shang-ti/Shangdi 'Lord on High'; sometimes synonymous with 'Heaven' in Confucianism.

Shankaracharya (Sankara, c.788–820) Brahmin philosopher, famous for his interpretation of the *Vedanta*, and the originator of the Monist (Advaita) system of Hindu thought. He argued that the visible world is illusory; reality lies beyond the five senses.

shari'a The holy law of Islam based on the Qur'an and *hadith*.

Shastra A Sanskrit word, used to denote knowledge in a general sense, or relating to a treatise or text written as an explanation or commentary on religious matters.

shaykh A spiritual guide/sufi master in Muslim tradition.

Shi'ite The largest minority group of Muslims, who follow Muhammad's son-in-law 'Ali. The Shi'ites separated from the Sunni majority as a result of a dispute over the status of 'Ali as the successor to the Prophet Muhammad. From shi`a, "party, partisan group," supporting Ali.

Shingon School A major school of Japanese Buddhism, established by the monk Kukai in the ninth century. 'Shingon' means 'true word' or 'mantra'.

Shinto The way of the gods: the indigenous religion of Japan. It is characterized by ancestor worship, devotion to the gods of natural forces, and reverence for the deity of the Emperor.

shtetl An eastern European town with a largely Jewish population.

shudra The fourth and lowest division of traditional Hindu society; the servant class.

Siddhartha Gautama (Shakyamuni, c.563–c.483 BCE) A spiritual teacher from ancient India and the historical founder of Buddhism. Born in Nepal, the son of a nobleman, he abandoned his affluent home at the age of 29 and led an ascetic life, begging for alms. He embarked on a spiritual quest, culminating – according to tradition, after 49 days meditating – in a moment of enlightenment, while seated under a tree at Bodh Gaya. He spent the next 40 years teaching, and gaining disciples and followers.

Sikhism A monotheistic religion that began in Punjab, northern India, in the sixteenth century CE. Founded by Guru Nanak (1469–1539), who preached a devotion to God that was neither Muslim nor Hindu. Sikhs emerged as a militant force in the eighteenth and nineteenth centuries, under the leadership of Ranjit Singh, and were defeated by the British in the Anglo-Sikh Wars.

Sikhs Followers of the Sikh religion. Originally characterized by the five K symbols: *Kesha* (uncut hair); *Kanga* (a small comb); *Kara* (an iron bangle); *Kirpan* (a small dagger); *Kacha* (a type of underwear).

Sin The Assyrian moon god.

Siovili Samoan cult named for a religious innovator named Joe Gimlet.

Sirah The traditional biography of Muhammad.

Siva (Shiva) A Hindu deity, associated with powers of creation and destruction, understood by many to be the supreme being.

Smartism A denomination of the Hindu tradition, generally referring to followers of the Advaita Vedanta philosophy, the monistic school of thought.

smriti/smarta 'That which is remembered', a term denoting the mass of post-Vedic literature which sought to reinterpret and rework the Vedas, particularly that school (*smarta*) which reworked the public sacrifice around a domestic cult of householders.

Soka Gakkai A Japanese New Religious movement, based on Nichiren Buddhism, and with an international membership.

Songni-hak Korean Neo-confucianism.

Soto A form of Zen Buddhism founded in the Kamakura period (1192–1333) by the Japanese monk, Dogen.

Spenta Mainyu see Angra Mainyu

spiritualism A movement that dates to the mid-nineteenth century, and is based on the belief that the spirits of the dead can be contacted by the living.

spirit possession The experience of being taken over by external religious agents, whether for good or for bad.

sruti 'That which is heard', the post-Vedic term referring to the entirety of Vedic literature as 'revealed', and opposed to *smriti*.

Stoicism A Hellenistic philosophical movement which saw all reality as interconnected; humans had to accept that they too were enmeshed in this universe.

stupa A Buddhist monument. Some stupas are thought to contain relics of the Buddha.

Sufi A mystical sect of Islam.

sunna The way of the Prophet Muhammad; eyewitness accounts of everything he said, did, caused or allowed to happen.

Sunni The majority sect in Islam, followers of the *sunna*.

supreme being Found in many indigenous religions, supreme beings rule over other religious agencies.

sura Individual chapters within the Qu'ran.

sutra The discourses of the Buddha – short aphoristic saying or collection of such sayings on a topic.

synagogue A meeting house for Jewish prayer.

syncretism A form of religion in which different traditions coalesce.

synod A council of church officials who seek agreement on matters of doctrine and organization.

Synoptic Gospels Relating to three similar books within the New Testament: Matthew, Mark and Luke.

Tabot A shard of wood kept in every Ethiopian Orthodox Church that symbolizes the Ark of the Covenant.

t'ai-chi-ch'uan A set of exercises designed to cultivate and preserve *chi* (Daoist).

Taiping Rebellion Christian-influenced rebellion against the Qing dynasty in China (1851–64).

Taliban Literally 'students' (of religious schools), a movement and politico-military force in Afghanistan, which aims to unite the country and make it an Islamic state. They officially claim not to be affiliated with any Mujahidin group.

Talmud Compilations of Jewish oral law, made in Palestine and Babylon in the 6th century CE, consisting of the Mishnah and the Gemarra, an explanation of the Mishnah.

Tambor de Mina An Afro-Brazilian religion.

tamrasasanam 'Order on copper', copper-plate inscription usually recording a Hindu king's donation to a group of liturgical specialists of the *smarta* tradition.

Tantra The rapid path to enlightenment that makes use of esoteric forms of meditation that enable the practitioner to achieve identity with various aspects of enlightenment embodied as Buddhas and other deities. Now practised mainly by Tibetan Buddhists and the Shingon School in Japan.

Tantras In Hinduism, the liturgical texts of theistic orders.

Taoism see Daoism

tariqah Sufi brotherhood/order.

taulaaitu Samoan term for a shaman or 'spirit anchor'.

tawhid The concept of divine unity, central to Islamic belief.

tekke Sufi hospice for pilgrims and travellers during the Ottoman empire.

temenos Literally 'the [area] cut off'; in Greek religion, the sacred precincts of a temple.

Temple, The Structure in Jerusalem where regular sacrifice was performed.

Ten Commandments According to Biblical tradition this set of religious and moral imperatives was handed by God to Moses on Mount Sinai in the form of two stone tablets. The Ten Commandments, or Decalogue, are listed in Exodus 20.

Tendai The Japanese form of Chinese T'ien-t'ai Buddhism, an eclectic form of Mahayana based on the teachings of the Lotus Sutra.

Tenrikyo Japanese Shinto-based New Religious movement, founded by Nakayama Miki in 1838.

Theosophy A religious movement, started in 1875, that combines Hindu, Buddhist and esoteric beliefs.

Theravada The form of Buddhism widely practised in Sri Lanka and other Southeast Asian countries. Sometimes erroneously called Hinayana. It teaches that enlightenment should come through the aspirant's experience, reasoning and investigation, rather than blind faith.

Thien Vietnamese form of Ch'an (Zen) Buddhism.

Thoth Egyptian god of learning and of judgement after death, the representative of Re on earth.

Tiamet The great dragon of chaos and the depths in Babylonian religion who is conquered by Marduk.

t'ien-chih The Will of Heaven in Confucianism.

T'ien t'ai An eclectic form of Mahayana Buddhism based on the teachings of the Lotus Sutra.

Tirthamkaras The enlightened teachers of Jainism.

tohunga Maori expert or priestly practitioner similar to the Hawaiian *kahuna*.

Toponymy Place names of specific regions.

Torah Hebrew name for the Law of Moses, both written and oral; the first five books of the Bible; *see also* Pentateuch.

Tower of Babel Hebrew story in Genesis 11 about a tower, clearly based on a ziggurat, built to reach heaven which leads to divine punishment.

transubstantiation The belief, in some branches of Christianity, that at the Eucharist the bread and wine are mystically transformed into the body and blood of Christ.

Trent, Council of Nineteenth ecumenical council of the Roman Catholic Church (1545–63), which played a vital role in revitalizing the Church after the Reformation, and spearheading the reforms of the Counter-Reformation.

trickster In indigenous religions, mythological agents who deploy their wiles to help themselves and assist in the development of social and cultural life.

Trinity (Holy Trinity) The belief, central to mainstream Christianity, that God exists in three distinct persons (Father, Son and Holy Spirit), while remaining one single undifferentiated being.

Tripitaka The Buddhist scriptures, divided into three parts: the Vinaya (rules of conduct), the Sutras (discourses of the Buddha), and the Abhidarma (philosophical analysis).

Triple Gem The three pillars of Buddhism: Buddha, Dharma, Sangha.

trliaksana 'Three Marks of Existence'; the Buddhist analysis of the nature of being.

Tsaddik Hereditary leader of an Hasidic group.

Tsao-tung The Chinese form of Soto Zen Buddhism.

Tu'i Tonga Sacred ruler in Tonga.

tughra Official signature of the Ottoman sultan.

Twelver Shi'ites An important Shi'ite sect, who believe that twelve imams were the legitimate descendants of Muhammad. Today, they are the largest group of Shi'ite Muslims.

Twelve Tribes Biblical tribes descended from the twelve sons of Jacob.

ulama The influential leaders in traditional Muslim society, for example Islamic religious scholars.

ummah In Islam, the worldwide community of faith/of the faithful.

umra A pilgrimage to the Ka'bah in Mecca, which is carried out at any time of the year, except that of the *hajj*.

Unification Church Religious movement founded by Rev. Sun Myung Moon in Korea, in 1954; popularly known as the 'Moonies'.

Unitarians Members of a Protestant Christian denomination, characterized by a belief in one God as opposed to the Trinity. The movement emerged in Poland and Transylvania in the sixteenth and seventeenth centuries, and gained a wide following in England and North America.

Upanisads Hindu sacred texts, literally 'sitting near', a term referring to the philosophical and metaphysical speculations of the Hindu Vedas.

'urs Anniversary of saint's death, especially practised in Pakistan.

Utnapistim The survivor of the flood in the Mesopotamian religious epic who reveals his knowledge to Gilgamesh.

vaishya The third of the four divisions of Hindu society; farmers and tradespeople.

Vaisnava, Vaisnavism Relating to one of several religious orders holding Visnu as the lord of the Universe.

Vajrayana 'Diamond Vehicle' Buddhism, a form of esoteric practice that developed in northern India from the sixth to seventh centuries. It is now the form of Buddhism found primarily in Tibet and Mongolia.

Vatican Council The first Vatican Council of the Roman Catholic Church was held in 1869–1879. Its most famous achievement was to declare that proclamations by the Pope on faith and morals are infallible. The second Vatican Council was held in 1962–65, and introduced many liberalizing reforms.

Veda In Hindu philosophy, term denoting either the entirety of the knowledge relating to the Vedic sacrifice, or more specifically the Samhita (collections of hymns, mantras and chants). There are four Samhitas: the Rk (or Rig), Yajur, Sama and Atharva.

Vedas Collection of ancient Hindu verses and hymns, dating from 1800 BCE onwards, possibly the oldest surviving sacred scriptures in the world.

Vedanta A Hindu philosophy based on the Upanisads. It argues the existence of an Absolute Soul in all things; salvation exists in the union of the individual and the Absolute Soul.

Vinaya The compilation of texts governing all aspects of Buddhist monastic life.

virgin birth The belief, found in traditional Melanesia and northern aboriginal Australia, that women can conceive without the assistance of men. Also, the Christian belief that Jesus of Nazareth was similarly conceived.

Visnu (Vishnu) Hindu god, the object of exclusive worship by the Vaisnavas, a major Hindu sect. Traditionally, Visnu has manifested as nine incarnations (including the Buddha); the tenth is yet to be revealed.

visistadvaita The philosophy of 'qualified non-dualism', maintaining a simultaneous identity and difference between the soul and absolute, propounded by the Vaisnava philosopher Ramanuja in the twelfth century.

vodun Generic term designating spiritual entities in Fon language, Benin.

Voudoun (Voodoo) Afro-Haitian religion, derived from the Fon *vodun*.

Wahhabism A strictly orthodox Siunni Muslim sect, based in Saudi Arabia, which rejects the corruption of the modern world, and urges a return to the Muslim society which existed during the time of the Prophet Muhammad.

Waldensians A group founded in the late twelfth century, possibly by one Valdes, a merchant of Lyons, which embraced voluntary poverty and carried out works of charity. The group spread throughout Europe, but was particularly concentrated in the valleys of the southwest Alps. It is only there that they have survived as a separate, now Protestant, Church.

Walî An Islamic term for a 'friend of God' or 'saint'.

Warkan The name given by archaeologists to the Mesopotamian material culture which immediately preceded the Sumerian.

Western Wall The surviving wall of the Temple in Jerusalem. It is the holiest location in Judaism that is available for public prayer.

White Lotus Society Buddhist movement popular from the twelfth to nineteenth centuries.

wingirin see karadji

Wisdom Literature Name given by scholars to several Jewish writings from the first millennium BCE, some of which various groups of Jews and Christians consider sacred, and which share many characteristics with philosophical reflections of their neighbours.

Wisdom of Amenemope An Egyptian wisdom text which promotes a practical worldly wisdom and from which excerpts were adopted into the Jewish Book of Proverbs.

Wu-ching The Five Classic texts in Confucianism.

wudu In Islam, the ritual washing that precedes prayer.

Wyclif, John (c.1330–1384) English religious reformer, and leader of the Lollards. Critical of the power and wealth of the Church, he looked to the Bible as the sole source of religious authority, instituting the first English translation of the Bible.

Yahweh The never pronounced name of the single, creator god of Hebrew religion.

Yajur In Hinduism, the knowledge, or Veda, related to the physical manipulations of the sacrifice.

Yakushi The medicine Buddha (Japanese form).

Yatra Pilgrimage to one of the holiest sites in India.

Yiddish The language of Ashkenazi Jews.

yin and yang The complementary opposites of traditional Chinese thought.

yoga Hindu technique of meditation and asceticism, found in several Eastern traditions.

Yogachara One of the two main schools of Mahayana Buddhism which developed a complex psychological analysis of experience, sometimes called subjective realism, and proposed that only consciousness was true, and all objects in the world external to the mind, false.

yogin One who practises the tantric form of Buddhism.

yuga In Hindu philosophy, an epoch or era within a cycle of four ages.

zakat Alms-giving, for the poor and the disadvantaged; the third pillar of Islam.

zar/sar Healing cult which spread from Ethiopia to neighbouring regions in northeast Africa, such as Sudan and Somalia, and which may have originated in Kushitic religious practice.

Zaidis (Zaydis) A Shi'ite sect, largely restricted to Yemen.

zazen Sitting meditation, the main practice of Soto Zen Buddhism.

Zealot Member of an anti-Roman guerrilla group in the first century CE.

Zen Buddhism Form of Buddhism developed and practised in China, Korea and Japan. Enlightenment is sought through extreme austerity, meditation and monasticism.

Zeus The supreme god in Greek religion, a sky-deity who dispenses good and evil fortune. Later identified with Jupiter in ancient Roman religion.

ziggurat In ancient Mesopotamia, large stepped edifices upon which there was a sanctuary and altar.

Zionism Movement working for the creation of a Jewish State.

ziyara In Islam, a local pilgrimage, usually involving the visitation of holy persons' tombs.

Zurvanism A sect in Zoroastrianism which held that the spirits of good and evil had a common origin in infinite time.

Zoroastrianism A monotheistic religion founded by Zoroaster (c. 628–551 BCE). Based on the polytheistic folk myths of India, Zoroastrianism revered a single wise god, Ahura Mazda, who was opposed to a malignant deity, Angra Mainyu. It was the religion of Sasanid Persia before the Arab conquests in the seventh century CE.

Zwingli, Ulrich (1484–1531) Swiss religious reformer who established the Protestant Reformation in Zurich.

BIBLIOGRAPHY

GENERAL

E. Badone and S.R. Roseman, *Intersecting Journeys: The Anthropology of Pilgrimage and Tourism*, Urbana, IL, 2004.

G. Barraclough, ed., *The Times Atlas of World History*, London, 1978, 1984, 1989, 1993.

G Barraclough, R.Overy, eds, *The Times History of the World*, 1999.

D. Barrett, ed., *World Christian Encyclopedia: A Comparative Study of Churches and Religions in the Modern World, AD 1900-2000*, Nairobi, 1982 (with periodic supplements). 2nd ed., Oxford, 2001.

E. Bernbaum, *Sacred Mountains of the World*, San Francisco, 1990.

J. Black, ed., *The DK Atlas of World History*, London, 1999, 2005

J. Bowker, ed., *The Oxford Dictionary of World Religions*, Oxford, 1997.

P .B. Clarke, ed., *The World's Religions: Understanding the Living Faiths*, London, Sydney, Cape Town, 1993.

S. Coleman and J. Elsner, *Pilgrimage Past and Present in the World Religions*, Cambridge, MA, 1995.

E. Cousins, ed., *The Classics of Western Spirituality*, 70 vols, New York, Ramsey, Toronto, 1975-

E. Cousins, ed., *World Spirituality: An Encyclopedic History of the Religious Quest*, 25 vols, New York, 1980-

M. Eliade, ed., *The Encyclopedia of Religions*, 16 vols, London & New York, 1987. 2nd ed., L. Jones,ed, Detroit, 2005.

J.L. Esposito, ed., *World Religions Today*, New York, 2002.

I.A. al Faruqi and D.E. Sopher, *Historical Atlas of the Religions of the World*, New York, 1974.

R. Foltz, *Spirituality in the Land of the Noble: How Iran Shaped the World's Religions*, Oxford, 2004.

W. Foy, ed., *Man's Religious Quest*, London, Crook Helm, New York, 1978.

R. Goring and F. Whaling, eds., *The Larousse Dictionary of Beliefs and Religions*, Edinburgh, 1994.

N. Grove, ed., *Atlas of World History*, Washington D.C., 1997.

I. Harris, S. Mews, P. Morris, J. Shepherd, eds., *Contemporary Religions: A World Guide*, Harlow, 1992.

J. R. Hinnells, ed., *A New Dictionary of Religions*, Oxford, London, 1995.

J. R. Hinnells, ed., *A New Handbook of Living Religions*, London, 1997.

H. Kung, ed., *Yes to a Global Ethic*, London, 1996.

T. Ling, *A History of Religion: East and West*, New York, 1970.

W.H. McNeill, *A World History*, New York, London & Toronto, 1967.

T. Masuzawa, *The Invention of World Religions, or, How European Universalism was Preserved in the Language of Pluralism*, Chicago, 2005.

D.S. Noss and J.B. Noss, *A History of the World's Religions*, New York, 1990.

M. Pye, ed., *Macmillan Dictionary of Religions*, London, 1993.

E. J. Sharpe, *Comparative Religion: A History*, London & New York, 1976. 2nd. ed. LaSalle IL, 1986.

N. Smart, *The World's Religions*, Cambridge, 1998.

H. Smith, *The Religions of Man*, New York, 1978.

W.C. Smith, *The Meaning and End of Religion: A New Approach to the Religious Traditions of Mankind*, New York, 1978.

F. Streng et al., *Ways of Being Religious: Readings for a New Approach to Religion*, Englewood Cliffs N.J, 1973.

S. Sutherland and P.B. Clarke, *The Study of Religion: Traditional and New Religions*, London, 1992.

W.H. Swatos and L. Tomasi, eds., *From Medieval Pilgrimage to Religious Tourism: The Social and Cultural Economics of Piety*, Westport, CT, 2002.

B.R. Taylor, ed., *The Encyclopedia of Religion and Nature*, 2 vols, London, 2005.

J. Waardenburg, *Classical Approaches to the Study of Religion*, New York, Berlin, 1995.

R.C. Zaehner, ed., *A Concise Encyclopedia of Living Faiths*, London, 1988.

THE HINDU WORLD

A. Ahmad, *Studies in Islamic Culture in the Indian Enviornment*, Oxford, 1964.

B. and R. Allchin, *The Rise of Civilization in India and Pakistan*, Cambridge, 1982.

A.L. Basham, ed., *The Origins and Development of Classical Hinduism*, annotated by Kenneth Zysk, Delhi, 1989.

A.L. Basham, *The Wonder that Was India*. London, 1956.

T. Basu, et. al., *Khaki Shorts and Saffron Flags*, Hyderabad, 1993.

Bhagavad-Gita trans. R.C. Zaehner, London, 1969.

S.M. Bhardwaj, *Hindu Places of Pilgrimage in India*, Berkeley, 1973.

M. Biardeau, *Hinduism: The Anthropology of a Civilisation*, Delhi, 1989.

E. Bumiller, *May You be the Mother of a Hundred Sons: a Journey among Women of India*, New York, 1990.

T. Chand, T*he Influence of Islam on Indian Culture*, Allahabad, 1946.

C. Chapple and M.E. Tucker, eds., *Hinduism and Ecology: The Intersection of Earth, Sky, and Water*, Cambridge, MA, 2000.

F.W. Clothey, *Ritualizing on the Boundaries: Continuity and innovation in the Tamil Diaspora*, Columbia, SC, 2006.

G. Coedes, *The Indianized States of Southeast Asia*, Honolulu, 1968.

H. Coward, J.R. Hinnels, and R.B. Williams, eds., *The South Asian Religious Diaspora in Britain, Canada, and the United States*, Albany, NY, 2000.

C.J. Fuller, *The Camphor Flame: Popular Hinduism and Society in India*, Princeton, 1992.

K. Illiah, *Why I am not a Hindu: A Sudra Critique of Hindutva*, Delhi, 1996.

R. Inden, 'The Temple and the Hindu Chain of Being', *Purusartha*, 8 (1985), pp. 53-73.

H. Kulke and D. Rothermund, *A History of India*, New York.

D. S. Lopez, Jr., ed., *Religions of India in Practice*, Princeton, 1995.

P.J. Marshall, ed., *The British Discovery of Hinduism in the 18th Century*, Cambridge, 1970.

G. Michell, *The Penguin Guide to the Monuments of India*, London: 1990.

Poems of Love and War, trans. A.K. Ramanujan, New York, 1985.

M. Ramstedt, ed., *Hinduism in Modern Indonesia: A Minority Religion Between Local, National, and Global Interests*, London, 2004.

L. Renou, *Vedic India*, trans. P. Spratt, Varanasi, 1971.

R.S. Sharma, *Looking for the Aryans*, Delhi, 1995.

R.S. Sharma, *Material Culture and Social Formations in Ancient India*, Delhi, 1983.

R. Thapar, *Ancient Indian Social History: Some Interpretations*, Hyderabad, 1978.

R. Thapar, *Early India: from the Origins to AD 1300*, Berkeley, CA, 2002.

The Laws of Manu, trans. W. Doniger, Harmondsworth, 1991.

Upanisads, trans. P. Olivelle, Oxford, 1996.

Visnupurana, trans. H.H. Wilson, 2 vols, Calcutta, 1961.

R.B. Williams, ed., *A Sacred Thread: Modern Transmission of Hindu Traditions in India and Abroad*, Chambersburg, PA, 1992.

A. Wink, Al Hind: *The Making of the Indo-Islamic World*, Volume 1: Early medieval India and the Expansion of Islam, Leiden, 1990.

BUDDHISM

M. Aung-Thwin, *Pagan: The Origins of Modern Burma*, 1985.

J.F. Avedon, *Tibet Today: Current Conditions & Prospects*, 1988.

M. Batchelor, *Women in Korean Zen: Lives and Practices*, Syracuse, 2006.

S. Batchelor, *The Jewel in the Lotus: A Guide to the Buddhist Traditions of Tibet*, London, 1987.

H. Bechert, *The World of Buddhism*, 1984.

S. Beyer, *The Cult of Tara. Magic and Ritual in Tibet*, 1973.

M. Brauen, *The Mandala*, London, 1997. Buddhist Society. *Buddhist Directory*, 1997.

J.I. Cabezon, ed., *Tibetan Literature*, 1996.

L. Chandra, *Buddhist Iconography*, 1987.

K. Crosby and A. Skilton, *The Bodhicaryavatara*, Oxford, 1996.

S.M. Darlington, 'The Ordination of a Tree: The Buddhist Ecology Movement in Thailand', *Ethnology*, vol. 37, no. 1 (Winter, 1998)

W.T. de Bary, ed., *Sources of Indian Tradition*, New York, 1958.

S. Dutt, *Buddhism in East Asia*, New Delhi, 1966.

S. Dutt, *Buddhist Monks and Monasteries of India*, 1962.

S. Heine and C.S. Prebish, eds., *Buddhism in the Modern World*, New York, 2003.

R. Lester, *Theravada Buddhism in Southeast Asia*, 1972.

L. Lhalungpa, *Life of Milarepa*, 1996.

D. Lopez, Jr., *The Story of Buddhism: A Concise Guide to its History and Teachings*, New York, 2002.

H.A. van Oort, *The Iconography of Chinese Buddhism*, 1986.

W. Rahula, *The History of Buddhism in Ceylon*, 1966.

H. Saddhatissa, *Buddhist Ethics*, 1997.

R.H. Seager, *Buddhism in America*, New York, 2000.

W.D. Shakabpa, *Tibet: A Political History*, 1967.

S. Sivaraksa, *Conflict, Culture, Change: Engaged Buddhism in a Globalizing World*, Somerville, MA, 2005.

D. Snellgrove, *The Image of the Buddha*, 1978.

D. Snellgrove, *Indo-Tibetan Buddhism*, 1987.

D.T. Suzuki, *An Introduction to Zen Buddhism*, New York, 1991.

D. Swearer, *The Buddhist World of Southeast Asia*, Albany, NY, 1996.

K. Vaidya, *Buddhist Traditions and Culture of the Katmandu Valley*, Shajha Prakashan, 1986.

K.E. Wells, *Thai Buddhism*, Bangkok, 1975.

R. Whitfield, *The Art of Central Asia*, 3 vols, London, 1982-5.

P. Williams, *Mahayana Buddhism: The Doctrinal Foundations*, New York, 1989.

L. Yeshe, *Introduction to Tantra*, London, 1987.

E. Zürcher, *The Buddhist Conquest of China*, Leiden, 1959.

EAST ASIAN TRADITIONS

B.J. An et al, *Korean Cultural Heritage*: vol 2, *Thought and Religion*, 1996.

J. H. Berthrong et al, *Confucianism: An Introduction*, Oxford, 2000.

C. Blunden and M. Elvin, *Cultural Atlas of China*, Oxford, 1983.

J. Ching, *Chinese Religions*, London, 1993.

M. Collcutt, M. Jansen, I. Kumakura, *Cultural Atlas of Japan*, Oxford, 1988.

R. Cribb, *Historical Atlas of Indonesia*, London, 1998.

W.T. de Bary, ed., *Sources of Chinese Tradition*, New York, 1960.

J. Esposito, *Islam in Asia: Religion, Politics, and Society*, New York, 1987.

I.R. Al Faruqui and D. Sopher, *Historical Atlas of the Religions of the World*, London, 1974.

Fung Yu-lan, *A Short History of Chinese Philosophy*, New York, 1958.

P.M.J. Geelan, *The Times Atlas of China*, London, 1974.

D. Hall et al, *Atlas of South East Asia*, London & New York.

F. Hardy, ed., *The Religions of Asia*, London, 1988.

I. Harris et al, *Contemporary Religions: A World Guide*, Harlow, 1992.

J. Kitagawa, *Religion in Japanese History*, New York, 1996.

D.C. Lau, trans., *The Tao Te Ching*, Harmondsworth, 1963.

D.C. Lau, trans., *Mencius*, Harmondsworth, 1970.

D.C. Lau, trans., *Confucius: The Analects*, Harmondsworth, 1979.

P. H. Lee, ed., *Sourcebook of Korean Civilization*, Vol. 2, New York, 1996.

J. Legge, *The Travels of Fa-hien or Record of Buddhistic Kingdoms*, Oxford, 1886.

D.S. Lopez, Jr., ed., *Religions of China in Practice*, Princeton, 1996.

J. Miller, *Daoism: A Short Introduction, Oxford, 2003.*

S. Ono, Shinto: *The Kami Way*, Tokyo, 1962.

W. Oxtoby, *World Religions: Eastern Traditions*, Toronto, 1996.

M. Palmer, *Taoism*, 1991.

I. Reader, *Religion in Contemporary Japan*, London, 1991.

E.O. Reischauer, *Ennin's Travels in T'ang China*, New York, 1995.

F. Robinson, *Atlas of the Islamic World Since 1500*, New York & Oxford, 1982.

J.E. Schwartzberg, *A Historical Atlas of South Asia*, Oxford & New York.

B. Silvers, *The Taoist Manual: An Illustrated Guide Applying Taoism to Daily Life*, Nederland, CO, 2005.

B.L. Smith, ed., *Religion and the Legitimation of Power in Thailand, Laos and Burma*, Chambersburg, 1978.

D. Steinburg, *The Philippines: A Singular and a Plural Place*, Boulder, 1982.

F. Stockwell, *Religion in China Today*, Beijing, 1993.

G. J. Tanabe, Jr., ed., *Religions of Japan in Practice*, Princeton, 1999.

R.L. Taylor, *The Illustrated Encyclopedia of Confucianism*, 2 vols., New York, 2005.

Tsunoda, Ryusaku, ed., *Sources of Japanese Tradition*, New York, 1958.

R. Ulack, *Atlas of South East Asia*, New York, 1989.

Yao Xinzhong, *An Introduction to Confucianism*, Cambridge, 2000.

THE PACIFIC

J. Barker, ed., *Christianity in Oceania, Ethnographic Perspectives*, Lanham, Maryland, 1990.

E. Best, *Maori Religion and Mythology*, 2 vols, Wellington 1976, 1982.

R. Border, *Church and State in Australia 1788-1872. A Constitutional Study of The Church of England in Australia*, London, 1962.

J.A. Boutilier, D. T. Hughes and S. W. Tiffany, eds., *Mission, Church and Sect in Oceania*, 1978.

K.O.L. Burridge, *New Heaven, New Earth: A Study of Millenarian Movements*, Oxford, 1969.

M. Charlesworth, H. Morphy, D. Bell and K. Maddock, *Religion in Aboriginal Australia. An Anthology*, Brisbane, 1984.

R. Firth, *Rank and Religion in Tikopia*, London, 1970.

C.W. Forman, *The Island Churches of the South Pacific: Emergence in the Twentieth Century*, New York, 1982.

J. Garrett, *To Live Among the Stars: Christian Origins in Oceania*, Suva, 1982.

J. Garrett, *Footsteps in the Sea: Christianity in Oceania to World War II*, Suva, 1992.

J. Garrett, *Where Nets Were Cast: Christianity in Oceania Since World War II*, Suva, 1997.

J. Garrett, *The History of Christianity in Oceania*, 3 vols, Suva, 1982-97

N. Gunson, *Messengers of Grace. Evangelical Missionaries in the South Seas 1797-1860*, Melbourne & New York, 1978.

E.S. Craighill Handy, *Polynesian Religion*, Honolulu, 1927.

J. Harris, *One Blood. 200 Years of Aboriginal Encounter with Christianity: A Story of Hope*, Sutherland, New South Wales, 1990.

P. Hayward, *Christianity in Australia and the traditions which have shaped it*, Concord West, New South Wales, 1998.

J. McLeod Henderson, *Ratana. The Man, the Church, the Political Movement*, Wellington, 2nd ed., 1972.

M. Hogan, *The Sectarian Strand. Religion in Australian History*, Melbourne, 1987.

P. Lawrence and M. J. Meggitt, eds., *Gods Ghosts and Men in Melanesia. Some Religions of Australia New Guinea and the New Hebrides*, Melbourne, 1965.

H. Mol, *Religion in Australia: A Sociological Investigation*, Melbourne, 1971.

H. Mol, *The Faith of Australians*, North Sydney, New South Wales, 1985.

D. Munro and A. Thornley, eds., *The Covenant Makers. Islander Missionaries in the Pacific*, Suva, 1996.

P. O'Farrell, *The Catholic Church and Community in Australia. A History*, Melbourne, 1977.

J. Siikala, *Cult and Conflict in Tropical Polynesia. A Study of Traditional Religion, Christianity and Nativistic Movements*, Helsinki, 1982.

W.E.H. Stanner, *On Aboriginal Religion. Oceania Monograph II*, Sydney, 1963.

T. Swain and D.B. Rose, eds., *Aboriginal Australians and Christian Missions. Ethnographic and Historical Studies*, Bedford Park, South Australia, 1988.

T. Swain, *A Place for Strangers. Towards a History of Australian Aboriginal Being*, Cambridge, 1993.

R. Thompson, *Religion in Australia: A History*, Melbourne, 1994.

G.W. Trompf, ed., *The Gospel is Not Western: Black Theologies from the Southwest Pacific*, Maryknoll, New York, 1987.

G.W. Trompf, *Melanesian Religion*, Cambridge, 1991.

D. Wetherell, *Charles Abel and the Kwato Mission of Papua New Guinea 1891-1975*, Melbourne, 1996.

E.A. Worms and Helmut Petri, *Australian Aboriginal Religions*, Kensington, New South Wales, 1998.

P. Worsley, *The Trumpet Shall Sound. A Study of 'Cargo' Cults in Melanesia*, 2nd ed., London, 1968.

THE ANCIENT NEAR EAST AND EUROPE

J. Barnes, *The Presocratic Philosophers*, London, 1979.

M.A. Beek, translated by D.R. Walsh, H.H. Rowley, ed., *Atlas of Mesopotamia: A Survey of the History and Civilisation of Mesopotamia from the Stone Age to the Fall of Babylon*, London, 1962.

J. Black and A. Green, *Gods, Demons and Symbols of Ancient Mesopotamia: An Illustrated Dictionary*, London, 1992.

P. Grimal, *Dictionary of Classical Mythology*, Oxford, 1985.

W.K.C. Guthrie, *A History of Greek Mythology*, 6 vols, Cambridge, 1962-81.

T. Jacobsen, *The Treasures of Darkness: A History of Mesopotamian Religion*, New Haven & London, 1976.

C. Kerényi, *The Heroes of the Greeks*, London, 1959.

G.S. Kirk, J.E. Raven and M. Schofield, *The Presocratic Philosophers: A Critical History with a Selection of Texts* (2nd edition), Cambridge, 1983.

G. Leick, *A Dictionary of Ancient Near Eastern Mythology*, London, 1991.

E. Lipinski, ed., *Dictionnaire de la civilisation Phénicienne et Punique*, Turnhout, 1992.

R. Morkot, *The Penguin Historical Atlas of Ancient Greece*, Harmondsworth, 1996.

T. O'Loughlin, *St Patrick: The Man and his Writings*, London, 1999.

S. Piggott, *The Druids*, London, 1968.

B. Raftery, *Pagan Celtic Ireland: The Enigma of the Irish Iron Age*, London, 1994.

M. Ring, *Beginning with the Pre-Socratics*, Palo Alto C.A., London, 1987.

H.W.F. Saggs, *The Encounter with the Divine in Mesopotamia and Israel*, London, 1978.
R. Simek, *Dictionary of Northern Mythology*, (English translation, Angela Hall) Woodbridge & Cambridge, 1993.
D.R. Welsh, ed., *Babylon*, London, 1982.

JUDAISM
S. Averini, *The Making of Modern Zionism*, 1981.
E. Barnavie, ed., *A Historical Atlas of the Jewish People from the Time of the Patriarchs to the Present*, New York, 1992.
J. Baskin, ed., *Jewish Women in Historical Perspective*, 2nd ed., Detroit, 1998.
H.H. Ben-Sasson, *A History of the Jewish People*, 1976.
D. Biale, ed., *Cultures of the Jews*, New York, 2002.
A. Cohen, *Everyman's Talmud*, 1949.
D. Cohn-Sherbok, *A Concise Encyclopaedia of Judaism*, Oxford, 1998.
L. Dawidowicz, *The War against the Jews*, Harmondsworth, 1975.
N. De Lange, *Judaism*, Oxford, 1986.
Encylopaedia Judaica, 17 vols, Jerusalem, 1972.
E. Fackenheim, *What is Judaism?*, 1987.
R.S. Feuerlicht, *The Fate of the Jews*, 1983.
M. Gilbert, *The Holocaust*, London, 1986.
M. Gilbert, *Israel*, London, 1998.
R. Gordis, *Conservative Judaism*, New York, 1970.
M. Grant, *The History of Ancient Israel*, London, 1984.
I. Greenberg, *On the Third Era in Jewish History*, New York, 1980.
D. Hartman, *A Living Covenant*, New York, 1985.
W.B. Helmreich, *The World of the Yeshiva*, New Haven & London, 1982.
A. Hertzberg, ed., *The Zionist Idea: A Historical Analysis and Reader*, New York, 1972.
D. Hillel, *The Natural History of the Bible: An Environmental exploration of the Hebrew Scriptures*, New York, 2006.
L. Jacobs, *The Jewish Religion*, Oxford, 1995.
P. Johnson, *A History of the Jews*, London, 1987.
M. Kaplan, *Judaism as a Civilization*, New York & London, 1957.
H. Kung, *Judaism*, London, 1989.
Z. Kurzweil, *The Modern Impulse of Traditional Judaism*, New York, 1985.
R. Mahler, ed., *Jewish Emancipation: A Series of Documents*, New York, 1941.
J. Marcus, *The Jew in the Mediaeval World*, Cincinnati, 1938.
M. Meyer, *Response to Modernity: A History of the Reform Movement*, Oxford, 1988.
C.G. Montefiore and H. Loewe, *A Rabbinic Anthology*, London, 1974.
J. Parkes, *The Jew in the Mediaeval Community*, London, 1976.
J. Plaskow, *Standing Again at Sinai: Judaism from a Feminist Perspective*, New York, 1990.
H. Rabinowicz, *Hasidism*, London, 1988.
R. Rubenstein and J.K. Roth, *Approaches to Auschwitz*, London, 1987.
H.M. Sachar, *The Course of Modern Jewish History*, New York, 1977.
S. Sandmel, *Judaism and Christian Beginnings*, Oxford, 1978.
A. Segal, *Rebecca's Children: Judaism and Christianity in the Roman World*, Cambridge, MA, 1986.
E. Umansky, and D. Ashton, eds., *Four Centuries of Jewish Women's Spirituality: A Sourcebook*, Boston, 1992.
D. Vital, *The Future of the Jews*, Cambridge, MA, & London, 1990.
R.J.Z. Werblowsky and G. Wigoder, ed., *The Oxford Dictionary of the Jewish Religion*, Oxford, 1997.

CHRISTIANITY
D. Barrett, ed., *World Christian Encyclopedia*, Oxford & New York, 1982, 1999, 2001.
H.S. Bettenson, ed., *Documents of the Christian Church*, 3rd ed., London, 1999.
C.C. Black, ed., *Atlas of the Renaissance*, London, 1994.
S.K. Brown, D.Q. Cannon, R.H. Jackson, eds., *Historical Atlas of Mormonism*, New York, 1994.
H. Chadwick and G.R. Evans, eds., *Atlas of the Christian Church*, London, 1987.
P. Chauna, ed., *The Reformation*, Gloucester, 1989.
D. Chidester, *Christianity: A Global History*, San Francisco, 2000.
T. Cornell and J. Matthews, eds., *Atlas of the Roman World*, Oxford, 1982.
F.L. Cross, and E.A. Livingstone, eds., *The Oxford Dictionary of the Christian Church*, 3rd ed, Oxford, 2005.
A. Freitag, ed., Atlas *du Monde Chrétien*, Paris, 1959.
W. H. C. Frend, *The Rise of Christianity*, London, 1984.
E.S. Gaustad and P.L. Barlow, *New Historical Atlas of Religion in America*, New York, 2000.
Y. Y. Haddad and J.L. Esposito, eds., *Daughters of Abraham: Feminist Thought in Judaism, Christianity, and Islam*, Gainesville, FL, 2001.
R.T. Handy, *A History of the Churches in the United States and Canada*, Oxford, 1976.
D. T. Hessel and R.R. Ruether, eds., *Christianity and Ecology: Seeking the Well-Being of Earth and Humans*, Cambridge, MA, 2000.
E. von Ivanka, J. Tyciak and P. Wiertz, *Handbuch der Ostkirchenkunde*, Düsseldorf, 1971.
H. Jedin, ed., *History of the Church*, 10 vols., London, 1980-81.
H. Jedin, K.S. Latourette, and J. Martin, eds., *Atlas d'Histoire de l'Église*, Tournai, Brepols, 1990.
K. S. Latourette, *A History of Christianity*, 2 vols, New York & London, 1976.
J. Leighly, 'Biblical Place-Names in the United States', *Names*, vol. 27, no. 1 (March 1979)
C. Lindberg, *The European Reformations*, Oxford, 1996.
C.H. Lippy, R. Choquette and S. Poole, *Christianity Comes to the Americas*, New York, 1992.
A. Mackay, and D. Ditchburn, eds., *Atlas of Medieval Europe*, London, 1997.
D. Martin, *Pentecostalism: The World their Parish*, Oxford, 2002.
W. Melczer, *The Pilgrim's Guide to Santiago de Compostela*, New York, 1993.
F. van der Meer and C. Mohrmann, eds., *Atlas of the Early Christian World*, London, 1966.
G. Mollat, *The Popes at Avignon*, London, 1963.
S. Neill, revised by O. Chadwick, *A History of the Christian Missions*, London, 1986.
R.E. Olson, 'Pentecostalism's Dark Side', *Christian Century*, March 7, 2006.
J. Pelikan, *Jesus through the Centuries: His Place in the History of Culture*, New Haven, CT, 1985.
J. Pelikan, *Mary Through the Centuries: Her Place in the History of Culture*, New Haven, CT, 1996.
PEW Forum, 'Spirit and Power: A 10-Country Survey of Pentecostals', The PEW Forum on Religions and Public Life (Oct. 2006), pewforum.org/surveys/pentecostal/
PEW Forum, 'The New Face of Global Christianity: The Emergence of Progressive Pentecostalism', The PEW Forum on Religions and Public Life (April, 2006), pewforum.org/events
J.B. Pritchard, ed., *The Times Atlas of the Bible*, London, 1987.
R. Ricard, *The Spiritual Conquest of Mexico*, Berkeley, 1966.
J. Riley-Smith, ed., *The Times Atlas of the Crusades*, London, 1991.
J. Sumption, *Pilgrimage: An Image of Medieval Religion*, London, 1975.
W. Urban: *The Baltic Crusade*, DeKalb, 1979.

ISLAM
L. Ahmed, *Women and Gender in Islam: Historical Roots of a Modern Debate*, New Haven, CT, 1992.
S. Akiner, *Islamic Peoples of the Soviet Union*, London, 1986.
D. Aqsha, *Islam in Indonesia: a Survey of Events and Developments from 1988 to 1993*, Jakarta, 1995.
A. Benningsen, and S.E. Wimbush, *Mystics and Commissars (Sufism in the Soviet Union)*, Berkeley and Los Angeles, 1985.
C.E. Bosworth et al, eds., *The Encyclopaedia of Islam*, 2nd ed, Leiden, 1960-77.
R. Boustani and P. Fargues, *The Atlas of the Arab World: Geopolitics and Society*, New York, 1991.
W. Brice, ed., *An Historical Atlas of Islam*, Leiden, 1981.
C.Broadhurst, 'The New Islamic Environmemntalism in Indonesia', *Jakarta Post*, May 15, 2006.
M. Cook, *Muhammad*, Oxford, 1983.
P. Crone, *Meccan Trade and the Rise of Islam*, Princeton, 1987.
R.H. Davison, *Turkey: A Short History*, Huntingdon, 1998.
F.M. Denny, *An Introduction to Islam*, 3rd ed., Upper Saddle River, NJ, 2006.
J.J. Donohue and J.L. Esposito, eds., *Islam in Transition: Muslim Perspectives*, 2nd ed., New York/Oxford, 2007.
A.A. Engineer, ed., *Islam in South and South East Asia*, Delhi, 1985.
F. Esack, *The Qur'an: A User's Guide*, Oxford, 2005.
J.L. Esposito, *Unholy War: Terror in the Name of Islam*, Oxford, 2002.
J.L. Esposito, *Islam and Politics*, Syracuse, New York, 1991.
J. Esposito, ed., *The Oxford Encyclopedia of the Modern Islamic World*, 4 vols, New York & Oxford, 1995.
R. Foltz, *Animals in Islamic Traditions and Muslim Cultures*, Oxford, 2006.
R. Foltz, F.M. Denny, and A. Baharuddin, eds., *Islam and Ecology: A Bestowed Trust*, Cambridge, MA, 2003.
G.S.P. Freeman-Grenville, *Historical Atlas of the Middle East*, New York & London, 1993, 2002
H.A.R. Gibb, et al eds., *The Encyclopaedia of Islam*, 1st ed. Leiden, Brill, 1913-36.
Y. Haddad, ed., *The Muslims of America*, New York, 1991.
Y.Y. Haddad, J. I. Smith, and J.L. Esposito, eds., *Religion and Immigration: Christian, Jewish, and Muslim Experiences in the United States*, Walnut Creek, CA, 2003.
H. Halm, *Shi'ism*, Edinburgh, 1991.
H.M. al-Kalbi (d. 819), *Kitab al-asnam*, Paris, 1969.
H. Kennedy, ed., *An Historical Atlas of Islam / Atlas historique de l-Islam*, Leiden, 2002.
G. Kepel, *Allah in the West*, Cambridge, 1997.
R. Israeli, *Muslims in China: a Study in Cultural Confrontation*, London, 1980.
B. Jelavich, *History of the Balkans: vol. 1 18th-19th Centuries and vol 2: Twentieth Century*, Cambridge, 1983.
M. Leavitt, *Hamas: Politics, Charity, and Terrorism in the Service of jihad*, New Haven, 2006.
M. Lee, *The Nation of Islam*, Syracuse, 1996.
L. Lemarchande, *Atlas geopolitique du Moyen-Orient et du Monde Arabe: le croissant des crises*, Paris, 1994.
J.D. McAuliffe, ed., *Encyclopaedia of the Qur'an*, 5 vols., Leiden, 2001-2006.
M. Momen, *An Introduction to Shi'i Islam*, New Haven & London, 1985.
H. Mu'nis, H., *Atlas ta'rikh al-islam, al-Qahira: al-zahra' li'l-I'lam al-'arabi*, 1987.
J. Nielsen, *Muslims in Western Europe*, Edinburgh, 1992.
M. Nisan, *Minorities in the Middle East: A History of Struggle and Self-Expression*, Jefferson, North Carolina, 1991.
M.M. Pickthall, *The Meaning of the Glorious Koran* [transl. of the Arabic Qur'an], New York.
A.L Popovic, *L'Islam balkanique: les musulmanes du sud-est europeen dans la periode post-ottoman*, Berlin, 1986.
M.I. Qureshi, *World Muslim Minorities*, Islamabad, 1993.
A. Rippin, *Muslims: their Religious Beliefs and Practices*, 2 vols, London, 1990-93.
F. Robinson, *Atlas of the Islamic World since 1500*, New York & Oxford, 1989.
M. Ruthven, with A. Nanji, *Historical Atlas of Islam*, Cambridge, MA, 2004.
O. Safi, ed., *Progressive Muslims: On Justice, Gender and Pluralism*, Oxford, 2003.
A. Schimmel, *Islamic Names*, Edinburgh, 1989.
A. Schimmel, *Mystical Dimensions of Islam*, Chapel Hill, NC, 1975.
F. Shaikh, Islam and Islamic Groups: A Worldwide Reference Guide, Harlow, 1992.
B. Tibi, *Islam Between Culture and Politics*, 2nd ed., Basingstoke, UK, 2005.
S. Trimingham, The Sufi Orders in Islam, Oxford, 1998.
R. V. Weekes, ed., *Muslim Peoples: A World Ethnographic Survey*, 2nd ed., 2 vols., Westport, CT, 1984.

AFRICA
J.F.A. Ajayi and I. Espie, *A Thousand Years of West African History*, Ibadan, 1965.
J.O. Awolalu, *Yoruba Beliefs and Sacrificial Rites*, London, 1979.
S.T. Barnes, ed., *Africa's Ogun. Old World and New*, Bloomington & Indianapolis, 1989.
R. Bastide, *The African Religions of Brazil*, London, 1971.
G. Brandon, *Santeria from Africa to the New World*, Bloomingtom, 1993.
L. Brenner, *West African Sufi: The Religious Heritage and Spiritual Search of Cerno Bokar Saalif Taal*, London, 1984.
M. Brown, *A History of Madagascar*, London, 1995.
P. B. Clarke, *West Africa and Christianity*, London, 1986.
D. Cruise O'Brien, *The Mourides of Senegal: The Political and Economic Organisation of an Islamic Brotherhood*, Oxford, 1971.
D. Cruise O'Brien and C. Coulon, *Charisma and Brotherhood in African Islam*, Oxford, 1988.
M. Deren, *Divine Horsemen, The Living Gods of Haiti*, London & New York.
S.M. Friedson, *Dance Prophets : Musical Experience in Tumbuka Healing*, Chicago, 1996.
J. Girard, Deima, *Prophètes Paysans de l'Environnement Noir*, Grenoble, 1974.
R. Gray, *Black Christians and White Missionaries*, New Haven & London, 1990.
A. Hastings, *The Church in Africa 1450-1950*, Oxford, 1994.
M. Hiskett, *The Course of Islam in West Africa*, Edinburgh, 1994.
E. Isichei, *A History of Christianity in Africa from Antiquity to the Present*, London, 1995.
J.M. Janzen, *Ngoma: Discourses of Healing in Central and Southern Africa*, Berkeley, 1992.
J.M. Janzen, *The Quest for Therapy in Lower Zaire*, Berkeley, 1978.
T. Kendall, *Kerma and the Kingdom of Kush 2500-1500 bc*, Washington, 1996.
M. Lambek, *Knowledge and Practice in Mayotte: Local Discourses of Islam, Sorcery and Spirit Possession*, Toronto, 1993.
R. Law, *The Oyo Empire c. 1600-1836: a West African Imperialism in the Era of the Atlantic Slave Trade*, Oxford, 1977.
R. Lemarchand, ed., *African Kingships in Perspective: Political Change and Modernization in Monarchical Settings*, London, 1977.
N. Levtzion, *Ancient Ghana and Mali*, London, 1973.
I.M. Lewis et al, *Women's Medicine: the Zar-Bori Cult in Africa and Beyond*, Edinburgh, 1991.
B.G. Martin, *Muslim Brotherhoods in Nineteenth Century Africa*, London, 1976.
M.L. Martin, *Kimbangu: An African Prophet and his Church*, Oxford, 1975.
J. Mercier, *Art that Heals: The Image as Medicine in Ethiopia*, Prestel, 1997.
E.L.R. Meyerovitz, *The Divine Kingship in Ghana and Ancient Egypt*, London, 1960.
R.S. O'Fahey, *Enigmatic Saint: Ahmad Ibn Idris and the Idrisi Tradition*, Evanston, Illinois, 1990.
R. Oliver, *The Middle Ages of African History*, London, 1967.
J.D.Y. Peel, *Aladura, a Religious Movement among the Yoruba*, London, 1968.
R. Pouwels, *Horn and Crescent. Cultural Change and Traditional Islam on the East African Coast, 800-1900*, Cambridge, 1987.
L. Sanneh, *West African Christianity: The Religious Impact*, London, 1983.
M. Schoffeleers, *Religion and the Dramatisation of Life: Spirit Beliefs and Rituals in Southern and Central Malawi*, Blantyre & Bonn, 1997.
M. Schoffeleers, *Rivers of Blood: The Genesis of a Martyr Cult in Southern Malawi, c. a.d. 1600*, Madison, 1992.
D.A. Shank, *Prophet Harris: the Black Elijah of West Africa*, Leiden, 1994.
B.G.M. Sundkler, *Bantu Prophets in South Africa*, London, 1948.
S. Tcherkézoff, *Dual Classification Reconsidered: Nyamwezi Sacred Kingship and Other Examples*, Paris, London, 1987.
L. Török, *The Kingdom of Kush: Handbook of the Napatan-Meroitic Civilization*, Leiden, 1997.
H.W. Turner, *History of an African Independent Church*, Oxford, 1967.
V. Turner, *The Drums of Affliction: A Study of Religious Process among the Ndembu of Zambia*, Oxford, 1968.
J. Vansina, *Kingdoms of the Savanna*, Madison, 1996.
D.A. Welsby, *The Kingdom of Kush: the Napatan and Meroitic Empires*, London, 1996.
S.S. Walker, *The Religious Revolution in the Ivory Coast: the Prophet Harris and the Harrist Church Chapel Hill*, North Carolina, 1983.
R. Werbner, ed., *Regional Cults*, London, New York & San Francisco.

INDIGENOUS RELIGIONS
J. Beattie, *Other Cultures*, London, 1966.
J. Campbell, *The Way of the Animal Powers: Historical Atlas of World Mythology*, vol 1, London, 1984.
J. Campbell, *The Way of the Seeded Earth: Historical Atlas of World Mythology*, vol 2, New York, 1989.
E.E. Evans-Pritchard, *Nuer Religion*, London, 1956.
M. Griaule, *Conversations with Ogotemmeli: An Introduction to Dogon Religious Ideas*, London, 1972.
J. Grim, *The Shaman: Patterns of Religious Healing among the Ojibway Indians*, Norman, OK, 1983.
B. Hayden, *Shamans, Sorcerers and Saints: A Prehistory of Religion*, Washington, DC, 2004.
N. Holm, *Religious Ecstasy*, Stockholm, 1982.
L. Kendall, *The Life and Times of a Korean Shaman*, Honolulu, 1988.
I. Lewis, *Ecstatic Religion*, London and New York, 1989.
J.W. Martin, *The Land Looks After Us: A History of Native American Religion*, New York, 2001.
R. Pelton, *The Trickster in West African Religion: A Study of Mythic Irony and Sacred Delight*, Berkeley, CA, 1989.
W. Stanner, *White Man God No Dreaming*, Canberra, 1979.
P. Vitebsky, *The Shaman*, London, 1995.
C. Waldman, *Atlas of the North American Indian*, New York and Oxford, 1985, 2000.
P. Worsley, *The Trumpet Shall Sound: A Study of 'Cargo' Cults in Melanesia*, New York, 1968.

INDEX

PICTURE ACKNOWLEDGEMENTS

Every effort has been made by the publishers to trace the copyright holders and we apologize in advance for any unintentional omissions. We would be pleased to insert the appropriate acknowledgement in any subsequent edition of this publication.

ACSAA, University of Michigan: 57

AKG London: 139, 229

Alamy: Painet Inc. 25 top, Smoke Dog 22 *bottom*, 40, ISP Photography 42 *top*, Masa Uemura 235 top

Ancient Art & Architecture Collection, London:158

Andes Press Agency, London: 166

The Art Archive: Bibliothèque Municipale, Troyes 41

Associated Press, London: 211 *top*

Bibliothèque Nationale, Paris: 74

Bridgeman Art Library, London: 29, 32, 33, 35, 37 *top*, 38 left, 53 *top*, 62, 80-81, 84, 100, 101, 103, 105 right, 115, 118, 122, 123, 131, 148-149, 157, 160, 162, 168, 169, 170, 172, 177, 232, 237

British Library, London: 56, 155, 197

British Museum, London: 48, 54, 116, 117, 130

Ann and Bury Peerless: 38 right

Christine Osborne Pictures/MEP: 12-13, 15, 31, 44-45, 77, 94, 106, 107, 111, 128-129, 132, 136, 143, 156, 184, 188, 189, 190, 191, 192, 194-195, 196, 198, 199, 201, 202, 203, 204, 205, 207, 208 *top*, 216, 217, 226

Church of the Latter Day Saints: William Floyd Holdman © 1986 IRI 180

C&K Archive: 30

C. Coles & B. Mack, eds: Hausa Women in the Twentieth Century, University of Wisconsin Press, Madison, (1991): 221

Corbis UK Ltd: 19, 25 *bottom*, 183 *bottom*, 208 *bottom*, 209, 210 *top*, 211 *bottom*, Smithsonian Institution 237 *top*

E.T. Archive, London: 228

Getty Images: Dorling Kindersley/Toby Sinclair 23; Stone/Hans Strand 42 bottom; Photographer's Choice/Tim Thompson 178; Newsmakers/Michael Smith 181; Jacob Silberberg 183 top; 210 bottom; AFP/Mohammed Abed 213; The Image Bank/ Eric Meola 234

G. M. Haliburton: The Prophet Harris, Longman, London, (1971): 231

G.H.R. Heritage: 182

Huntington Archive, Ohio State University: 51

The Hutchison Library, London: 14, 20, 34, 49, 60, 64, 65, 69, 74-75, 83, 86, 87, 88, 90, 92, 93, 95 *top*, 95 *bottom*, 98-99, 105 left, 112, 119, 126, 146, 147, 154, 173, 206, 224, 225, 230, 217 right

J. M. Janzen: Ngoma: Discourses of Healing in Central and Southern Africa, University of California Press, Los Angeles, (1992): 220

Images Colour Library, London: 21, 46-47, 58, 66-67, 72, 73, 77 *bottom*, 79 *top*, 79 *bottom*, 165

Image Bank, London: 84, 85

Images of India Picture Agency, London: 53 *bottom*

Impact Photos, London: 15

Institut Amatller d'Art Hispanic, Madrid: 134, 135

Louvre, Paris © RMN: 110

Madhuvanti Ghose: 55

Mary Evans Picture Library: 137, 167, 175

McQuitty International Collection: 50, 63, 68, 71

Metropolitan Museum of Art, New York: 113

Michael Walsh: 171

Musée Guimet, Paris: 59

Narodni Muzeum, Prague: 127

Polska Agencia Informacyjna: 177

Popperfoto/Reuters: 89

Rene David, Galerie Walu, Zürich: 218 *bottom*

Rex Features: Michael Friedel 179

Robert Harding Picture Library, London: 37 *bottom*, 120, 121, 186-187, 227

J. M. Schoffeleers: Rivers of Blood: The Genesis of a Martyr Cult in Southern Malawi, c. a.d. 1600, University of Wisconsin Press, Madison, 1992: 223

Sisse Brimberg/NGS Image Co.: 28

Sonia Halliday: 200

Still Pictures: Andia /Boëlle 22 top; Ron Giling 24

T. Shaw: Unearthing Igbo Ukwu: Archeological Discoveries in Eastern Nigeria, Oxford Univerity Press, Ibadan, 1977: 218 *top*

Tibetan Monastic Institute at Rikon, Switerland: Peter Grieder 18

Tibet Images, London: 70

P. Verger: Orisha: les Dieux yorouba en Afrique et au nouveau monde, A.M. Métailié, Paris, 1982: 224, 225

Werner Forman Archive, London: 26-27, 102, 114, 124 *top*, 124 *bottom*, 159, 238

Wiener Library, London: 138, 140, 141, 142, 144, 145; Schindler Collection, New York 233, 238

Zev Radovan, Jerusalem: 133